Deanna Swaney

Despite an erstwhile career in computer programming, Deanna has managed intermittent forays away from encroaching yuppiedom and, at the first opportunity, made a break for South America where she wrote the first edition of this book. Subsequent projects led through an erratic circuit of island paradises – Arctic and tropical – and resulted in three more travel survival kits: *Tonga, Samoa,* and *Iceland, Greenland & the Faroe Islands.*

Accustomed to wild company back home in Alaska, Deanna found furry faunal diversity in Africa while researching her next book, *Zimbabwe, Botswana and Namibia – a travel survival kit.* Deanna was also a co-author of Lonely Planet's 2nd edition of *Brazil – a travel survival kit.* She's currently in search of large, extinct birds and yet more island paradises in the Indian Ocean.

Robert Strauss

In the early '70s Robert Strauss took the overland route to Nepal and then studied, taught and edited in England, Germany, Portugal and Hong Kong. For Lonely Planet he has worked on travel survival kits to *China, Tibet, Japan,* and *Brazil.* For Bradt Publications he wrote the *Trans-Siberian Rail Guide.* He has contributed photos and articles to other books, magazines and newspapers in the USA, Australia and Asia. Robert, who was last seen spitting at llamas in Devon, is currently researching menus and wine lists in Portugal.

From the Authors

For their hospitality, friendship and help during our travels in Bolivia, we're grateful to Tico Tudela, Leo & Negro in Rurrenabaque; Omar Claure, Abel Castillo, Zelso Montenegro, and Pieter & Margarita in Samaipata; Eduardo Garnica in Potosí; Sigrid Frönius in Coroico; Mavis Randall in Tarija; Albert & Aileen Randall in Tupiza; Padre Larry Dugas; Guy & Jane in Santa Cruz; and Huáscar Muñoz Pacheco in La Paz. For their companionship and insights, we also raise a glass to fellow travellers Toot Ostveen, Mark & Heather, Daniel & Melinda, Suzanne & Leif, Bryan Cummings, and Kelly Zajechowski. The expert and much appreciated mountaineering information in the Facts for the Visitor chapter is courtesy of Todd Miner at the University of Alaska, Anchorage.

It seems Bolivia has inspired numerous travellers with its wacky and wonderful ways and we received an amazing number of entertaining and informative letters in response to the first edition of this book. We'd especially like to acknowledge the following readers, parts of whose letters were extracted for use in the text: Katie & Greg Cumberford (your address was missing from the letter or we'd have replied personally), Daniel & Melinda Harvey (USA) for enlightenment on buying a charango, Mike Stambovsky (USA), TB Burgess (UK), Ms Alex Rossi (UK), Peter A Thompson & Sandy A Edelsward, (C), Paul L Younger, (Bolivia), Dan Golopentia (USA) and Brent Maupin (USA).

Other readers who provided useful information include Jacqueline Marovac (USA), Jill Buckingham (NZ), Mark & Heather (C), Per Gregarsen & Tine Graversen (DK), Jan King & Tom Harriman (USA), Michèle Rouleau (C), Susan McCallum & Peter Hedlin (AUS), Gregory William Frux (USA), Markus Miller & Heike Drexel (D), Annalena Hedman (S), Ruth & Claudell Baker (USA), John Feihl (C), Paul Pichler (A), Rochelle Rhea Brand (USA), Nancy Epanchin (USA), Brent Maupin (USA), Sigrid Frönius (Bolivia), Pieter & Margarita (Bolivia), Giancarlo & Anna Perlo (I), Mark Selzer (C), Dave Lynch & Gail Strachan (UK), Mario Morpurgo (I) and Danny Schechter (USA).

Finally, we'd like to pass along our love and appreciation to Earl Swaney, Joyce Strauss, Dave Dault, Keith & Holly Hawkings and Keith & Sarah Jenkins for their considerable various and sundry contributions and support.

A – Austria, AUS – Australia, C – Canada, D – Germany, DK – Denmark, I – Italy, S – Sweden, UK – United Kingdom, USA – United States of America

From the Publisher

This edition of *Bolivia – a travel survival kit* was edited by Michelle Coxall. Matthew King was responsible for design, mapping and illustrations, with help from Greg Herriman and Jane Hart. Additional illustrations were provided by Trudi Canavan, Ann Jeffree, Margaret Jung and Valerie Tellini.

Thanks to Rob Rachowiecki for permission to reproduce material from *Peru – a travel survival kit*. Special thanks to Jeff Williams for checking the trekking maps in the Cordilleras & Yungas chapter and to Krzysztof Dydynski for help with queries. Thanks also to Dan Levin for computer assistance.

Warning & Request

Things change – prices go up, schedules change, good places go bad and bad places go bankrupt – nothing stays the same. So if you find things better or worse, recently opened or long since closed, please write and tell us and help make the next edition better.

Your letters will be used to help update future editions and, where possible, important changes will also be included in a Stop Press section in reprints.

We greatly appreciate all information that is sent to us by travellers. Back at Lonely Planet we employ a hard-working readers' letters team to sort through the many letters we receive. The best ones will be rewarded with a free copy of the next edition or another Lonely Planet guide if you prefer. We give away lots of books, but, unfortunately, not every letter/postcard receives one.

To all those readers who wrote to us about the first edition of this guide – thank you! Your names are listed on page 402.

Contents

Bolivia

a travel survival kit

Deanna Swaney
Robert Strauss

Bolivia – a travel survival kit

2nd edition

Published by
   Lonely Planet Publications
   Head Office: PO Box 617, Hawthorn, Vic 3122, Australia
   Branches: PO Box 2001A, Berkeley, CA 94702, USA and London, UK

Printed by
   Singapore National Printers Ltd, Singapore

Photographs by
   Krzysztof Dydynski (KD)
   Ward Hulbert (WH)
   Todd Miner (TM)
   Robert Strauss (RS)
   Deanna Swaney (DS)
   Jeff Williams (JW)

   Front cover: Local market in La Paz (KD)
   Back cover: Morning on the Río Tuichi (RS)

First Published
   December 1988

This Edition
   December 1992

Although the authors and publisher have tried to make the information as accurate as possible, they accept no responsibility for any loss, injury or inconvenience sustained by any person using this book.

National Library of Australia Cataloguing in Publication Data

   Swaney, Deanna
   Bolivia: a travel survival kit

   2nd ed.
   Includes index.
   ISBN 0 86442 160 5.

   1. Bolivia – Guidebooks. I. Strauss, Robert. II. Title. (Series:
   Lonely Planet travel survival kit).

918.40452

Map Legend

BOUNDARIES

▬ ▬ · ▬ · ▬ · ▬	.... International Boundary
▬ ▬ · ▬ · ▬ ·	.... Internal Boundary
+·+·+·+·+·+·+·	.... National Park or Reserve
▬ ▬ ▬ ▬ ▬ ▬	.... The Equator
··	.... The Tropics

SYMBOLS

◉	NEW DELHI	.... National Capital
●	BOMBAY	.... Provincial or State Capital
●	Pune	.... Major Town
•	Borsi	.... Minor Town
■		.... Places to Stay
▼		.... Places to Eat
⬟		.... Post Office
✈		.... Airport
i		.... Tourist Information
⊖		.... Bus Station or Terminal
66		.... Highway Route Number
⚲ † ‡		...... Mosque, Church, Cathedral
∴		.... Temple or Ruin
✚		.... Hospital
※		.... Lookout
⚐		.... Camping Area
⌐		.... Picnic Area
⌂		.... Hut or Chalet
▲		.... Mountain or Hill
		.... Railway Station
		.... Road Bridge
		.... Railway Bridge
		.... Road Tunnel
		.... Railway Tunnel
		.... Escarpment or Cliff
		.... Pass
		.... Ancient or Historic Wall

ROUTES

▬▬▬▬▬▬	.... Major Road or Highway
▬ ▬ ▬ ▬ ▬ ▬	.... Unsealed Major Road
▬▬▬▬▬▬	.... Sealed Road
▬ ▬ ▬ ▬ ▬	..... Unsealed Road or Track
▬▬▬▬▬	.... City Street
+++++++++	.... Railway
●━━●━━●	.... Subway
····················	.... Walking Track
▬ ▬ ▬ ▬ ▬	.... Ferry Route
+++++++++	...... Cable Car or Chair Lift

HYDROGRAPHIC FEATURES

	.... River or Creek
	.... Intermittent Stream
	.... Lake, Intermittent Lake
	.... Coast Line
	.... Spring
	.... Waterfall
	.... Swamp
	.... Salt Lake or Reef
	.... Glacier

OTHER FEATURES

	Park, Garden or National Park
	.... Built Up Area
	... Market or Pedestrian Mall
	.... Plaza or Town Square
	.... Cemetery

Note: not all symbols displayed above appear in this book

Introduction

Bolivia is the poorest, highest and most isolated of the Latin American republics. With 65% of the population belonging to the Quechua, Aymará and a score of other indigenous groups, it is the most 'Indian' nation in South America. It is also the one least affected by outside customs and values. Foreign visitors have only recently discovered the country's attractions and exceptional value for money.

Despite its ample measure of historical strife, Bolivia is currently a relatively safe country for visitors. The problems with theft, guerrilla factions and violence that plague some of its neighbours aren't as prevalent in Bolivia.

Although the country has suffered a good deal of bad press, its most serious problems aren't immediately obvious. Its reputation for frequent political shuffling and scuffling, and the increasing international consumption of its most popular export conjure up all sorts of negative images: American DEA raids on ramshackle jungle laboratories where cocaine is made; a country of drug barons living in opulent mansions and driving Mercedes; and revolution-torn landscapes littered with the corpses of the innocent masses.

While cocaine does account for over 60% of Bolivia's foreign exchange revenue, few of Bolivia's 6.5 million inhabitants benefit from the very tightly organised system of production and trade, and most citizens are involved in more down-to-earth economic activities such as mining, herding and agriculture. The political situation has also improved greatly, and although the Bolivian presidency still isn't the most secure of positions, for the past decade the country has enjoyed a stable – albeit slightly highly strung – version of civilian democracy.

For the traveller, Bolivia provides a sampling of everything South America has to offer – with the exception, perhaps, of a palm-fringed seacoast (or any seacoast at all,

for that matter!). The country's natural attractions range from the peaks of the Andean Cordillera to the stark beauty and startling colours of the lakes and windswept deserts of the Altiplano; from the jungle-choked waterways of the Amazon and Paraná basins to the thorny scrublands of the Chaco.

Sites of great historical interest include the ancient ceremonial site of Tiahuanaco; Potosí, where legendary mines dating back to the 14th century are still worked under tortuous conditions; the ornate Jesuit churches of the eastern lowlands; and vestiges of Inca culture set against the dramatic backdrop of Lake Titicaca. The architecture of Bolivia's colonial cities is best preserved in the churches, narrow streets and museums

of La Paz, Sucre, and Potosí. Dinosaur trackers and fossil fiends will enjoy the dinosaur footprints at Torotoro south of Cochabamba or the many fossil sites around Tarija.

There are also ample opportunities for hiking, trekking and wildlife viewing – the Bolivian Amazon is highly recommended for excursions into the rainforest – and several national parks have recently been established with facilities for visitors.

Bolivian music, played on native instruments at *peñas* and festivals such as Oruro's La Diablada, is in itself a compelling reason to visit.

In every corner of this little known and underrated country, travellers will discover a wealth of distinctive cultures, natural beauty and the sort of unforgettable experiences and characters that still match the classic expectations of visitors to South America.

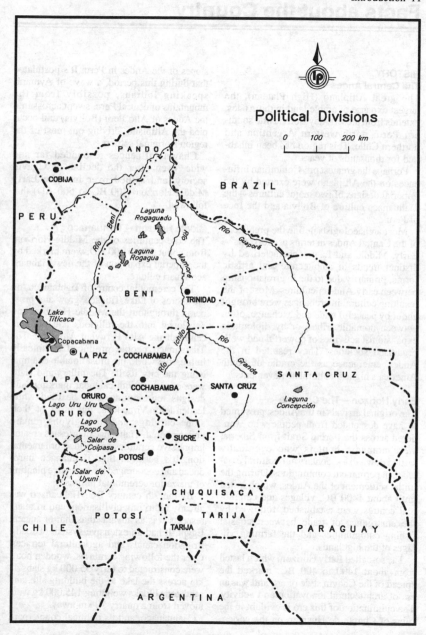

Political Divisions

0   100   200 km

Facts about the Country

HISTORY
The Central Andes

The great Altiplano (High Plateau), the largest expanse of arable land in the Andes, extends from present-day Bolivia into southern Peru, north-western Argentina and northern Chile. This region has been inhabited for thousands of years.

Perhaps the greatest pre-Columbian influences on the Altiplano were exerted by the imperial designs of two major cultures – the Tiahuanaco culture of Bolivia and the Inca of Peru.

Most archaeologists define the prehistory of the Central Andes in terms of 'horizons' – Early, Middle and Late – characterised by distinct trends in architecture and artistic forms, primarily due to the interrelationship between early Andean cultures. Most of the resulting cultural interchanges were brought about by peaceful trade and exchange, often between nomadic tribes, or by diplomatic expansionist activities of powerful and well-organised societies. They resulted in the Andes' emergence as the cradle of South America's highest cultural achievements.

Early Horizon – The Chavíns

The original arrivals in the Andes, presumed to have descended from people who wandered across the Bering Strait from Siberia, were nomadic hunters who eventually settled down to a sedentary agricultural existence in permanent communities. During the initial settlement of the Andes, which lasted until about 1400 BC, villages and ceremonial centres were established, followed by the emergence of trade between coastal fishing communities and the farming villages of the highlands.

The so-called Early Horizon, which lasted from about 1400 to 400 BC, marked the spread of the Chavín style of art, and was an era of architectural innovation and activity. The culmination of this era is evident in the ruins of Chavín de Huantar, on the eastern slopes of the Andes in Peru. It's postulated that during this period, a wave of Aymará-speaking Indians, possibly from the mountains of central Peru, swept across into the Andes of Alto Peru (Bolivia) and occupied the Altiplano, driving out most of the region's original settlers.

Chavín influences resounded far and wide, even after the decline of Chavín society, and spilled over into the Early Middle Horizon (400 BC to 500 AD) that followed.

Middle Horizon – Tiahuanaco

The core centuries of the Middle Horizon, from about 500 to 900 AD, were marked by the imperial expansion of the new Tiahuanaco-Huari culture.

The ceremonial centre of Tiahuanaco, on the shores of Lake Titicaca, grew and prospered throughout the Middle Horizon, and developed into the religious and political centre of the Alto Peruvian Altiplano. The Tiahuanaco people produced technically impressive work, the most notable example being the city itself. The pillars and slabs were engraved with calendar markings and designs representing their bearded white leader/deity Viracocha, but most of their stone carvings and hieroglyphs remain undeciphered. Tiahuanacan artesans created impressive ceramics and gilded ornamentation. It's believed that Tiahuanaco introduced and encouraged the extensive planting of maize for ceremonial purposes.

By the 7th century BC, Tiahuanaco was already a thriving civilisation, and in many respects was as advanced as that of ancient Egypt. It had an extensive system of roads, irrigation canals and agricultural terraces. Over the following centuries, wooden boats were constructed to ferry 55,000 kg slabs 48 km across the lake to the building site, and sandstone blocks weighing 145,000 kg were moved from a quarry 10 km away.

Tiahuanaco, and its political counterpart,

Huari, in the Ayacucho valley (which now falls within Peru's borders), developed into well-organised, prosperous and ambitious societies. Though the relationship between these two widely separated towns is not really clear, the architecture and iconography in the changing art forms of the Middle Horizon suggest close cultural ties. While they may have been dual capitals of the same state, many theories favour the idea that Tiahuanaco was the real power centre. Its art and architecture were more refined than Huari's, and it's possible that Tiahuanaco served as the ceremonial and political centre, while Huari functioned as a strategic military outpost in the north. Whatever the relationship, the Tiahuanaco-Huari culture extended its influence as far north as Ecuador, expanding, trading and imposing its artistic values and construction methods on the conquered regions.

Although the Tiahuanaco site had been inhabited since about 1500 BC and remained occupied until 1200 AD, its period of power lasted only from the 6th century BC to the 9th century AD (Huari had been abandoned before 800 AD). During the Late Middle Horizon, Tiahuanaco's power was waning, and its civilisation declining. One theory speculates that Tiahuanaco was uprooted by a drop in the Lake Titicaca water level, which left the lakeside settlement far from shore. Another postulates that it was attacked and its population massacred by the warlike Kollas (sometimes spelt Collas; also known as Aymará) from the west. When the Spanish arrived, they learned of an Inca legend about a battle between the Kollas and 'bearded White men' on an island in Lake Titicaca. These men were presumably Tiahuanacans, of whom only a few were able to escape. Some researchers believe the displaced survivors migrated southward, and developed into the Chipaya tribe of the western Oruro Department.

Today, collections of Tiahuanaco relics may be found in museums throughout the country, and what remains of Tiahuanaco lies on the plain between La Paz and the southern shore of Lake Titicaca. For further informa-tion, refer to the Around La Paz section in the La Paz chapter.

Late Horizon – The Inca

The Inca, the last of South America's indigenous conquerors, arrived shortly after the fall of Tiahuanaco. They pushed their Tahuatinsuyo (The Four Corners) Empire from its seat of power in Cuzco (Peru) east into present-day Bolivia, south to the northern reaches of modern Argentina and Chile, and northward through present-day Ecuador and southern Colombia. The Late Horizon, from 1476 to 1534 AD, marked the zenith of Inca civilisation. For all its widespread power and influence, however, the Inca political state thrived for less than a century before falling to the might of the invading Spanish.

Although the Inca had inhabited the Cuzco region from the 12th century, they were little more than a minor chiefdom. Inca legend recounts tales of bearded White men coming to them from the shores of Lake Titicaca and bringing civilisation to the Inca before pushing off to sea. It wasn't until about 1440 that the Inca became serious about extending their political boundaries beyond the immediate neighbourhood. In the space of just over 50 years, they managed to establish a highly unified state that took in most of the central Andes.

While their origins are the stuff of myths and legends (see the History section in the Lake Titicaca chapter), their achievements certainly were not. Renowned for their great stone cities and their skill in working with gold and silver, the Incas also set up a hierarchy of governmental and agricultural overseers, a viable social welfare scheme, and a complex road network and communication system that defied the difficult terrain of their far-flung empire.

The Inca Manco Capac, first in the line of Inca emperors, and his sister/wife Mama Ocllo (also known as Mama Huaca), convinced their people they were children of the Sun God. Their progeny were the first of the Inca nobles, and to keep the line pure and increasing, they adopted a structured system of marriage. Consequently, each subsequent Inca ruler, the Sapa Inca, was considered a direct descendant of the Sun God. Nobles were permitted an unlimited number of wives and their children were considered legitimate Inca nobles.

While the traditional history of the Inca is certainly romantic, there are naturally more down-to-earth theories regarding their origins, including that of the 17th-century Spanish chronicler Fernando Montesinos, who believed the Inca had descended from a lineage of Tiahuanaco wise men. There were indeed many similarities between Tiahuanaco and Inca architecture. When the Inca arrived to conquer the shores of Lake Titicaca, the Kollas who inhabited the region around Tiahuanaco regarded the site as taboo.

The Inca government could be described as an imperialist socialist dictatorship with the Sapa Inca as reigning monarch, head of the noble family and the extended Inca clan, and unquestionable ruler of the entire state. The state technically owned all property within its vast and expanding realm, and taxes were usually collected in the form of labour. The government organised a system of mutual aid in which relief supplies were collected from prosperous areas and distributed in other areas which might be suffering from natural disasters or local misfortune.

This system of benevolent rule was largely due to the influence of the eighth Inca, Viracocha (not to be confused with the Tiahuanaco leader/deity, Viracocha), who believed that the mandate from the Sun God was not just to conquer, plunder and enslave, but to organise defeated tribes and absorb them into the realm of the benevolent Sun God. When the Incas arrived in Kollasuyo (present-day Bolivia), they assimilated local tribes – as they had done elsewhere – by imposing taxation, religion and their own Quechua language (the *lingua franca* of the empire) upon the region's inhabitants.

The Kollas living around the Tiahuanaco site were among the most recalcitrant additions to the empire. Although they were absorbed by the Inca and their religion was supplanted, they were permitted to keep their language and social traditions.

By the late 1520s, internal rivalries had begun to take their toll on the Inca Empire; in a brief civil war over the division of lands, Atahuallpa, the true Inca emperor's half-brother, had imprisoned the emperor and assumed the throne himself.

The Spanish Conquest

The arrival of the Spanish in 1531 dealt the ultimate blow. Within a year, Francisco Pizarro, Diego de Almagro and their bands of merry conquistadores had pushed inland toward Cuzco in search of land, wealth and adventure. When they arrived in the capital, Atahuallpa was still the incumbent emperor, but he was not considered the true heir of the Sun God. The Spanish were aided by the Inca belief that the bearded White men had been sent by the great Viracocha Inca as revenge for Atahuallpa's breach of established protocol. In fear, Atahuallpa ordered the murder of the real king, which not only ended the bloodline of the Inca dynasty, but brought shame on the family and dissolved the psychological power grip held by the Inca hierarchy.

The Spanish were naturally unconcerned about the death of the true emperor, but they did turn the resulting guilt to their own advantage. Atahuallpa's shame at having killed the divine descendant of the Sun God, combined with the Inca nobility's initial trust in the Spanish 'gods', made the conquistadores' task easy. Within two years, the government had been conquered, the empire had been dissolved, and the invaders had divided Inca lands and booty between the two leaders of the Spanish forces.

Alto Peru, which would later become Bolivia, fell for a brief period into the possession of Diego de Almagro, who was assassinated in 1538 and didn't have the chance to make the most of his prize. Three years later, Pizzaro himself suffered the same fate at the hands of mutinous subordinates. It was during this period that the Spanish got down to exploring and settling their newly conquered land. In 1538, the town of La

Plata was founded as the Spanish capital of the Charcas region.

The Legacy of Potosí

By the time the wandering Indian Diego Huallpa revealed his earth-shattering discovery of silver at Potosí in 1544, Spanish conquerors had already firmly implanted their language, religion and customs upon the remnants of Atahuallpa's empire. Spanish Potosí, or the 'Villa Imperial de Carlos V', was founded in 1545 when the riches of Cerro Rico (Rich Hill) were already on their way to the Spanish treasuries. Potosí, with 160,000 residents, became the largest city in the western hemisphere.

The Potosí mine became the world's most prolific. The silver extracted from it underwrote the Spanish economy, particularly the extravagance of its monarchy, for at least two centuries, and spawned a legendary maritime crime wave on the Caribbean Sea.

Atrocious conditions in the gold and silver mines of Potosí guaranteed a short life span for the local Indian conscripts, who were herded into work gangs, as well as for the millions of African slaves brought to the mines. Those not actually worked to death or killed in accidents succumbed to pulmonary silicosis within just a few years. Africans who survived migrated to the more amenable climes of the Yungas north-east of La Paz, and developed into an Aymará-speaking minority.

The Spanish soldiers, administrators, settlers, adventurers and miners who poured into the region developed into a powerful land-owning aristocracy. The indigenous peoples became tenant farmers, subservient to the Spanish lords, and were required to supply their conquerors with food and labour, in exchange for subsistence-sized plots of land. Coca, once the exclusive privilege of Inca nobles, was introduced among the general populace to keep people working without complaint.

The Cities

In 1548, the city of La Paz was founded by Captain Alonzo de Mendoza as an administrative and strategic staging post for the huge shipments of silver en route from Potosí to the Peruvian ports on the Pacific. Santa Cruz de la Sierra was founded in 1561 by the Spanish who had migrated from Paraguay.

Increased agricultural productivity and the growing prosperity of the Spanish landowners also promoted the growth of farming townships. The city of Cochabamba was founded in 1574 and soon became the granary of Alto Peru, while the foundation of Tarija in the same year created a defence post against incursions by the independent Indians of the region.

It was the discovery of silver that elevated the village of Oruro to the status of a town in 1606. In the 18th century it was producing nearly 50% of Alto Peru's silver, and later, its prosperity (and that of Potosí) was revived by reworking the mines for tin.

Independence

In May of 1809, the first independence movement in Spanish America had gained momentum and was under way in Chuquisaca (Sucre). Other cities quickly followed the example, and the powder keg exploded. During the first quarter of the 19th century, the soldier and liberator General Simón Bolivar succeeded in liberating Venezuela

General Simón Bolivar

and Colombia from Spanish domination. In 1822 he dispatched Mariscal (Major-General) Antonio José de Sucre to Ecuador to defeat the Royalists at the battle of Pichincha. In 1824, after years of guerrilla action against the Spanish and the victories of Bolivar and Sucre in the battles of Junín (6 August) and Ayacucho (9 December), Peru won its independence.

At this point, Sucre incited a declaration of independence for Alto Peru, and exactly one year later, the new Republic of Bolivia was born (for further information, see under History in the Sucre chapter). Bolivar and Sucre became Bolivia's first and second presidents. After a brief attempt on the part of Andres Santa Cruz, the third president, to form a confederation with Peru, things began to go awry. One military junta after another usurped power from its predecessor, setting a pattern of political strife that would haunt the nation for the next 162 years.

Few of the 189 governments to date have remained in power long enough to have had much intentional effect, and some were more than a little eccentric. The cruel and ignorant General Mariano Melgarejo, who ruled from 1865 to 1871, drunkenly set off with his army on an overland march to the aid of France at the outset of the Franco-Prussian War. History has it that he was sobered up by a sudden downpour and the project was abandoned (to the immense relief of the Prussians, of course). Melgarejo was also responsible for the murder of a penitent conspirator; seizure of Indian lands; the senseless cession of territory to Brazil; and the squandering of the nation's reserves on his own personal projects.

Shrinking Territory

Bolivia's misfortunes during its earlier years were not limited to internal strife. At the time of independence, its boundaries encompassed well over two million sq km, but by the time its neighbours had finished paring away at its territory, only half the original land area remained.

The first and most significant loss occurred in the War of the Pacific, which was

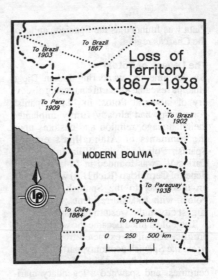

Loss of Territory 1867–1938

fought with Chile between 1879 and 1884. In the end, Chile wound up with 850 km of coastline from Peru and Bolivia. The loss was most severe for Bolivia, which had been robbed of its port of Antofagasta, the copper and nitrate-rich sands of the Atacama Desert, and, most significantly, the country's only outlet to the sea. Although Chile did attempt to recompense the loss by building a railroad from La Paz to the coast and allowing Bolivia free port privileges in Antofagasta, Bolivians have never forgotten the devastating *enclaustromiento* which left them without a seacoast. Even today, the government uses the issue as a rallying cry whenever it wants to unite the people behind a common cause.

During the years that followed, Peru, Brazil and Argentina each had their turn hacking away at Bolivia's borders. The next major loss was in 1903 during the rubber boom. Both Brazil and Bolivia had been ransacking the forests of the remote Acre territory, which stretched from Bolivia's present Amazonian borders to about halfway up Peru's eastern border. The area was so rich in rubber trees that Brazil engineered a dispute over sovereignty and sent in its army.

Brazil convinced Acre to secede from the Bolivian republic, and then promptly annexed it.

Brazil attempted to compensate Bolivia's loss with a new railway, this one intended to open up the remote northern reaches of the country and provide an outlet to the Amazon Basin by circumventing the rapids that rendered the Río Mamoré unnavigable below Guayaramerín. The Madeira to Mamoré line (nicknamed Mad María), however, never reached Bolivian soil. Construction ended at Guajará-Mirim on the Brazilian bank of the Mamoré, and is now used only infrequently as a tourist novelty.

The boundaries between Bolivia and Paraguay had never been formally defined, and in 1932, a border dispute with Paraguay for control of the Chaco erupted into full-scale warfare. This time, the conflict was caused partly by rival foreign oil companies which had their eye on concessions, should their prospecting activities reveal huge deposits of oil in the Chaco. In a bid to secure favourable franchises, a quarrel was engineered, with Standard Oil supporting Bolivia, and Shell siding with Paraguay.

Paraguay, badly beaten after taking on Argentina, Uruguay and Brazil in the War of the Triple Alliance, needed an outlet to avenge its loss. Victory in this respect would also guarantee a prosperous economic future – if the oil companies' theories regarding the prevalence of oil proved correct. Bolivia fell victim to Paraguayan pride, and within three years, had lost another 225,000 sq km, 65,000 young men and a dubious outlet to the sea via the Río Paraguaí. (It was not until 1938 that Bolivia formally ceded to Paraguay all land taken over and occupied by Paraguay during the 1932-35 war.) The anticipated reserves of oil were never discovered, but several fields in the area that remained Bolivian territory now keep the country self-sufficient in oil production.

MODERN PROBLEMS

During the 20th century, Bolivian farming and mining interests were controlled by tin barons and wealthy landowners, while the peasantry was relegated to a non-feudal system of peonage known as *pongaje*. The beating Bolivia took in the Chaco War paved the way for the creation of reformist associations, civil unrest among the *cholas* (see the Population & People section in this chapter for details about these people), and a series of coups by ostensibly reform-minded military leaders.

The most significant development was the formation of the the the Movimiento Nacionalista Revolucionario (MNR), a political party which united the masses behind the common cause of popular reform. It sparked labour unrest and friction between peasant miners and absentee tin bosses. The miners' complaints against outrageous working conditions, pitifully low compensation and the export of profits to Europe raised the political consciousness of all Bolivian workers. The MNR, under the leadership of Victor Paz Estenssoro, prevailed in the general elections of 1951, but a last minute military coup prevented it actually taking power. The coup provoked a popular armed revolt by the miners which became known as the April Revolution of 1952, and after

Victor Paz Estenssoro

heavy fighting, the military was defeated and Victor Paz's MNR took the helm for the first time. He nationalised the mines, evicted the tin barons, put an end to pongaje and set up the Corporación Minera de Bolivia (COMIBOL), the state entity in charge of mining interests.

The revolutionaries were also concerned with agrarian and educational reform, and universal suffrage, and pressed ahead with a diverse programme of reforms, which included redistribution of land amongst share-cropping peasants and the restructuring of the educational system to include primary education in the villages. To open up the long-isolated and underrepresented Oriente lowlands, a road was constructed between Cochabamba and Santa Cruz.

All these social and economic reforms were aimed at ensuring political participation of all sectors of the population. In the end, the miners and peasants felt they were being represented, and the relatively popular government of the MNR lasted an incredible 12 years under various presidents. Victor Paz himself served three nonconsecutive terms of varying lengths.

Even with US support, however, the MNR was unable to substantially raise the standard of living or increase food production, and its effectiveness and popularity ground to a standstill. As dissent increased within his ranks, Victor Paz was forced to become more and more autocratic. In 1964, his government, weakened by internal quarrels, was overthrown by a military junta headed by General René Barrientos Ortuño.

This fresh round of military rule was strongly opposed, and General Barrientos lashed back at his detractors. In 1967, the Marxist folk hero Ché Guevara, who had been training guerrillas in southern Bolivia, was executed by a US-backed military delegation working with the Bolivian Armed Forces. It was thought the Argentine-born soldier/politician was heading a Cuban-style peasant revolt in the south-east. In the same year, military forces massacred miners who had gathered at Catavi to form an anti-government front.

Following the death of General Barrientos in a 1969 helicopter accident, military governments rolled in and out of La Paz like tumbleweeds, and the familiar pattern of coups replaced one military officer with another. Right wing coalition leader, General Hugo Banzer Suárez, took over in 1971 and served a turbulent term until 1978 when he mandated a return to democratic process and scheduled general elections. Although he lost the elections, the results were ignored on the grounds that serious tampering had occurred. Soon after, however, Banzer was forced to step down when his opponent General Juan Pereda Asbún spontaneously assumed power for a short time.

His successor, Juan Pereda, had the top job snatched from him by General David Perdilla, who at least had the support of the democratic opposition. He announced elections in 1979, but they failed, and National Congress appointed Guevara Arze as interim president. His government was overthrown, however, in a bloody coup of 1979 and replaced by Colonel Alberto Natusch Busch, who stepped down after only two weeks in office due to widespread lack of support.

At this stage, the country enjoyed a brief respite from military mania under the National Congress-appointed Lidia Gueiler Tejada, Bolivia's first woman president. Elections were held and it became apparent that Congress would select Hernán Siles Zuazo and his UDP party, but the process was interrupted by a military coup led by General Luis García Meza Tejada under the direction of cocaine traffickers and resident Nazi activist, Klaus Barbie, the Butcher of Lyons. During this hideous regime came a rash of torture, arrests and disappearances, as well as an incredible increase in cocaine production and trafficking.

In 1981, García Meza, who lost control of the military and had to step down, was replaced by General Celso Torrelio Villa. At this stage, the populace, who had had enough of military scuffling, called for democratic rule, but the Torrelio government resisted. In 1982, an attempted coup by García Meza led to the appointment of General Guido Vildoso

Calderón to oversee a peaceful return to democratic rule. When the military regime ended, power was assumed by Dr Hernán Siles Zuazo, the civilian left-wing leader of the Communist-supported Movimiento de la Izquierda Revolucionaria (MIR). His term was beleaguered with labour disputes, ruthless government spending and monetary devaluation. The result was a staggering inflation rate that at one point reached 35,000% annually! When Siles Zuazo gave up after three years and called general elections, Victor Paz Estenssoro returned to politics to become president for the third time. He immediately set about stabilising the shattered economy by ousting labour unions; removing government restrictions on internal trade; slashing the government deficit; imposing a wage freeze; eliminating price subsidies; laying off workers at inefficient government-owned companies; allowing the peso to float against the US dollar; and deploying armed forces to keep the peace.

Inflation was curtailed within weeks, but spiralling unemployment, especially in the poor mining areas of the Altiplano, threatened the stability of the government. Throughout his term, however, Victor Paz remained committed to programmes which would return the government mines to private cooperatives and develop the largely uninhabited lowland regions of the north and east. To encourage the settlement of the Amazon region, he promoted the building of roads (with Japanese aid) through the wilderness, opening up vast Indian reserves and pristine rainforest to logging interests.

The 1989 presidential elections, free from threat of military intervention, were characterised primarily by apathy. The three candidates were Hugo Banzer Suárez of the Acción Democrática Nacionalista (ADN), MNR's Gonzalo Sánchez de Lozada and MIR's Jaime Paz Zamora. Banzer and Sánchez placed ahead of Paz Zamora, but no candidate received a majority, so it was left to National Congress to select one. Longtime enemies Banzer and Paz Zamora joined forces and managed to prevail over Sánchez, with the Congressional selection of Paz Zamora as the new president.

The Drug War

In 1989, one-third of the Bolivian work force was dependent on the illicit production and trafficking of cocaine. Far and away the most lucrative of Bolivia's economic mainstays, it was generating an annual income of US$1.5 billion, of which just under half remained in the country. Most of the miners laid off during Victor Paz's austerity measures turned to cocaine as a source of income. Ensuing corruption, acts of terrorism and social problems threatened government control over the country, which in the international perspective had by now become synonymous with cocaine production.

US threats to cease foreign aid unless efforts were made to stop cocaine production forced Victor Paz to comply with their proposed coca eradication programme. Instead of eliminating the trade, however, the US eradication directive brought about the organisation of increasingly powerful and vociferous peasant unions and interest groups. This, combined with lax enforcement, corruption and skyrocketing potential profits, actually resulted in an increase in cocaine production. The Bolivian government refused to chemically destroy coca fields, and instead urged coca farmers to replace their crops with other cash-producing commodities such as coffee, bananas, spices and cacao.

Peasants were offered US$2000 each by the government to destroy their coca plantations and plant alternative crops. In early 1990, a drop in the price of coca paste brought about a temporary lull in production, and some farmers sold out to the government's proposed crop substitution programme. Many, however, simply collected the money and moved further north to replant.

All Bolivian drug enforcement police and military units were paid by the US government, and as early as 1987, the USA had been sending Drug Enforcement Agency (DEA) squadrons into the Beni and Chapare regions to assist in the programme. In May 1990, Paz Zamora appealed for a major increase in US aid to augment the weakened Bolivian economy. In response, US President George Bush sent US$78 million in aid and stepped up US 'Operation Support Justice' activities in northern Bolivia. In June 1991, Bolivian police and DEA agents staged a daylight helicopter raid on Santa Ana del Yacuma, north of Trinidad, and seized 15 cocaine labs, nine estates, numerous private aircraft and 110 kg of cocaine base; however, no traffickers were captured, having been given sufficient warning to escape. Several later surrendered under Bolivia's lenient 'repentance law'.

The US forces' greatest fear is that peasant resistance will fuel leftist insurgencies and guerrilla groups, while the millions pumped into Bolivia for drug enforcement operations will only fatten corrupt military and government officials. Meanwhile, some US military personnel in Bolivia claim that the ultimate winners will be the drug cartels; at least 85% of Bolivian antinarcotic trainees, many of whom have family members involved in cocaine production and trafficking, are on one-year stints. It's presumed that once they're free of active duty, many will simply use their expertise in US military operations to secure work as highly paid informants and security guards for cocaine producers and traffickers. Even so, the US 1992 budget for South American antinarcotic operations was US$1.2 billion.

As this book was going to press, Bolivia's Senate voted to expel US troops participating in antinarcotic activities.

GEOGRAPHY
Bolivia currently encompasses 1,098,000 sq km. It is 3½ times the size of the British Isles, slightly smaller than Alaska, and just less than half the size of Western Australia. It's bordered on the west by Chile and Peru, on the north and east by Brazil, and on the south by Argentina and Paraguay. The country is shaped roughly like an equilateral triangle. From east to west it measures 1300 km at its widest point and 1500 km from north to south.

Much of Bolivia's appeal for the visitor lies in its awesome geography. Physically, the land is divided into five basic and diverse regions: the high Altiplano, the highland valleys, the Yungas, the Gran Chaco and the

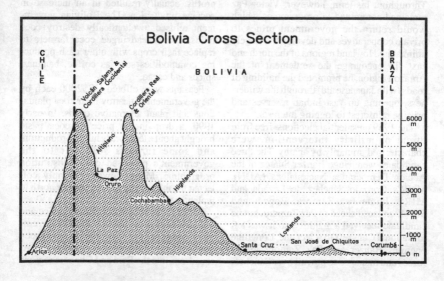

Bolivia Cross Section

forested lowlands of the Amazon and Paraná basins.

Altiplano

The Altiplano, whose name means 'high plain', is the most densely populated region of the country, although it is by no means crowded. This great plateau runs from the Peruvian border north of Lake Titicaca southward to the Argentine border, and spills over into neighbouring Peru, Chile and Argentina.

Despite its name, the Altiplano is anything but flat. Basin altitudes range from 3500 to 4000 metres, but the snow-capped peaks of the Cordillera Real and the many isolated volcanic summits of the Cordillera Occidental reach much higher. Nevado Sajama, a volcano near the Chilean border and disputably Bolivia's highest peak, rises to an elevation of 6542 metres. The average elevation of peaks in the Cordillera Real near La Paz is 5500 metres.

The Altiplano is a rather haunting place – a cold, windy and practically treeless land where horizons and distant mountains seem to melt into the sky, and mirages cause phantom lakes to appear and disappear. Above it all, building clouds or trailing wisps of windblown snow, the great white-capped giants loom like sentinels over the chameleon-like landscape. The entire impression is one of grave solitude.

Bolivia's 'great lakes' are also found on the Altiplano. Lake Titicaca, the most important and beautiful, is the second largest in South America, after Venezuela's Lake Maracaibo. Lakes Uru Uru and Poopó, south of Oruro, are little more than immense puddles just a few metres deep.

South of the lakes, where the land becomes drier and less populated, are the remnants of two other lakes, the Salar de Uyuni and the Salar de Coipasa. These two salt deserts and the surrounding plains form eerie white expanses of salt deposited by leeching from the surrounding peaks.

Highland Valleys

The highland valleys south and east of the Altiplano boast the most hospitable living conditions in the country, with near optimum climatic conditions and fertile soils. This is the Cordillera Central, an area of scrambled hills and valleys, fertile basins and intense agriculture. With a reversed Mediterranean climate – rain falls in summer instead of winter – the land supports olives, nuts, wheat, maize and grapes, and wine is produced in the city of Tarija. The cities of Cochabamba, Sucre, Potosí and Tarija support most of the population. Due to its exposed and lofty location, only Potosí suffers from an unfavourable climate.

Yungas

North and east of Cochabamba and La Paz, where the Andes fall away into the Amazon Basin, are the Yungas – the transition zone between dry highlands and humid lowlands. Above the steaming, forested depths rise the near-vertical slopes of the Cordillera Real and the Cordillera Quimsa Cruz, which halt Altiplano-bound clouds, causing them to deposit bounteous rainfall on the Yungas. Vegetation is abundant and tropical fruits, coffee, sugar, coca, cacao, vegetables and tobacco grow with minimal tending.

Chaco

In the south-eastern corner of Bolivia, along the Paraguayan and Argentine borders, lies the flat, nearly impenetrable, scrubland of the Chaco. Because the region is almost entirely uninhabited, native flora and fauna thrive, and the Chaco provides a refuge for such rare animal species as the jaguar and peccary, which have been largely displaced in other parts of the country. The only settlement of any size is Villamontes, on the rail line, which prides itself on being the hottest spot in Bolivia. Temperatures frequently reach the mid-40s and thick red dust (or if it's raining, sticky mud) covers everything.

Lowlands

Encompassing about 60% of Bolivia's total land area, the lowlands of the north and east are hot, flat and sparsely populated. Recently, efforts have been made to develop

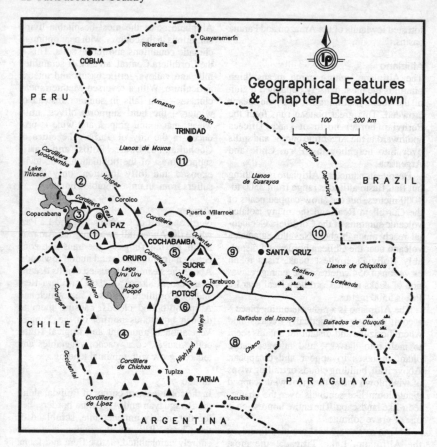

Geographical Features & Chapter Breakdown

1	La Paz	7	Sucre
2	Cordilleras & Yungas	8	South Central Bolivia & The Chaco
3	Lake Titicaca	9	Santa Cruz
4	Southern Altiplano	10	Eastern Lowlands
5	Cochabamba	11	Amazon Basin
6	Potosí		

the forestry, agricultural and mineral potential of the region.

Two great river systems drain this vast area. The Acre, Madre de Dios, Abunã, Beni, Mamoré, Ichilo, Ibare, Grande, Paraguá and a score of other rivers flow northward toward Brazil into Amazon tributaries. The Río Paraguaí flows southward into the Paraná Basin and eventually to the Atlantic via the Río de la Plata.

The only breaks in the flat green monotony of the south-western Beni and northern Santa Cruz departments are the natural monoliths and ranges of low hills which rise from the Llanos de Moxos, Guarayos and Chiquitos.

CLIMATE

Bolivia has as wide a range of climatic patterns as it has of elevation and topography, but the overall temperatures are probably cooler than most people expect. Even in the humid forest regions of the north, frosts and subzero temperatures are not unheard of during a *surazo*, a cold wind blowing from Patagonia and the Argentine pampa.

Although most of Bolivia lies as near the equator as Tahiti or Hawaii, its elevation and unprotected expanses contribute to variable weather conditions. The two poles of climatic misery in Bolivia are Puerto Suárez for its stifling, humid heat, and Uyuni for its near-Arctic cold and icy winds. But there are no absolutes in the Bolivian climate; there are times when you can sunbathe in Uyuni and freeze stiff in Puerto Suárez!

The summer rainy period lasts from November to March. In La Paz, mists swirl through the streets and the city is literally wrapped in the clouds; rain falls daily and cold air currents sweep down the canyon from the Altiplano. On the Altiplano above La Paz, the lakes swell to devour the landscape, and livestock stand in knee-deep puddles. Of the major cities, only Potosí normally has snow, but it isn't uncommon in Oruro and La Paz.

In the flooding of 1985-86, Lake Titicaca rose several metres and flooded roads, homes and villages, and in Bolivia and neighbouring Peru, an estimated 200,000 people lost their homes and crops. In the jungle areas to the north, violent electrical storms and tropical downpours can be expected during the summer. This area was particularly affected in 1985-86, with many

Monthly Temperatures & Precipitation

Average Maximum & Minimum Temperatures (°C)

	Jan	Feb	Mar	Apr	May	Jun	Jul	Aug	Sep	Oct	Nov	Dec
La Paz	18	18	18	19	17	17	17	17	18	19	19	19
	6	6	6	5	3	2	1	2	3	5	6	6
Cochabamba*	20	20	19	19	18	17	18	19	19	21	21	20
Sucre	24	23	24	24	23	22	21	23	23	24	23	22
	11	11	10	10	6	5	5	6	7	8	9	10
Santa Cruz	31	31	30	28	25	23	24	28	29	30	31	31
	21	21	20	19	16	15	15	16	19	20	20	21
Villazón *	14	14	14	13	6	2	2	6	9	10	14	14
Trinidad *	27	27	27	27	27	27	26	26	27	28	28	28

* No average minimum temperature figures available for these places

Average Monthly Precipitation (mm)

	Jan	Feb	Mar	Apr	May	Jun	Jul	Aug	Sep	Oct	Nov	Dec
La Paz	138	87	80	32	2	2	2	3	25	50	51	88
Oruro	158	138	80	9	3	0	3	5	15	25	25	42
Cochabamba	121	137	133	23	7	2	0	0	0	10	130	137
Potosí	180	119	100	9	5	2	2	2	5	12	12	81
Sucre	151	137	118	37	2	3	9	19	44	48	98	117
Tarija	115	75	64	34	2	2	11	14	18	40	108	129
Santa Cruz	84	159	40	48	50	81	43	118	120	324	125	119
Trinidad	260	140	140	23	9	29	16	49	50	130	165	169
Cobija	257	290	346	130	129	42	0	0	146	412	400	307

deaths attributed to the swollen rivers and flood-related disease. Such disasters may be repeated at any time.

During the winter, the climate is drier and more pleasant. Throughout the country, nighttime temperatures drop dramatically, and on the high Altiplano, the sun has only to pass behind a cloud for a significant temperature difference to be noticed. Subzero temperatures are frequent, especially at night, and precipitation is not uncommon, but is of shorter duration than in the rainy season.

In Cochabamba, Sucre and Tarija, winter is the time of clear, beautiful skies and optimum temperatures, and there is hardly a healthier or more ideal climate on earth. The lowlands experience hot sunny days and an occasional 10-minute shower to cool things off and settle the dust. Due to their steep elevation, the Yungas may experience rain on any day of the year. For more details about Bolivian climatic patterns, refer to the table on the previous page.

FLORA & FAUNA

Due to its relatively sparse population, lack of extensive development and diverse geography, Bolivia is one of the best places on the continent for viewing South American wildlife. You'll need to venture beyond the cities, but that doesn't necessarily mean slogging through snow, swamp and rainforest to catch a glimpse of it. Quite a lot of Bolivia's animal life may be observed from the windows or decks of the country's buses, trains and boats.

The Altiplano

Although they're hardly 'wild', having been domesticated for centuries in the Andean highlands, you're bound to see plenty of llamas and alpacas on the Altiplano. Despite their cute and cuddly appearance, however, they have a nasty reputation for biting and spitting, so beware when observing at close range. These ill-tempered cameloid domesticates, cousins of the equally ill-tempered dromedaries and bactrians of Africa and Asia, also have other cousins in the New

Blue Macaw

World. Guanacos are quite rare in Bolivia, but the delicate little vicuñas are occasionally seen along the railway line between Uyuni and the Chilean border, as well as throughout the remote south-western part of the country.

Vicuñas are unfortunately on the decline. Their incredibly soft and fuzzy little hides fetch a bundle on the illicit market, and thus far, Bolivia has been lax about saving their skins. Although a few skittish vicuñas remain in south-western Bolivia, the best place to see them is just across the Chilean border in Parque Nacional Lauca, where they survive in their thousands, and are zealously protected. Other wild inhabitants of the Altiplano include Andean wolves, foxes, and deer (also known as *huemules*), but again, your chances of seeing them are much better in Parque Nacional Lauca.

The Southern Altiplano is also the exclusive habitat of the James flamingo; just look for any shallow lake and it will probably be full of them. Also relatively common is the versatile *ñandu* or rhea (the South American ostrich) which is found from the Altiplano to the Beni, the Chaco and the Santa Cruz lowlands. Then there's the *viscacha*, a cute, long-tailed rabbit, which spends most of its time huddled under rocks. Viscachas are very docile but become easily alarmed and don't normally allow strangers to approach too closely.

If you're very lucky, you might see a condor or two in the highland regions. Highly revered by the Incas, these rare New World vultures are the world's heaviest birds of prey. They have a wingspan of over three metres and have been known to effortlessly drag a carcass weighing 20 kg.

The Highland Valleys

At lower elevations, the temperate hills and valleys of the highlands support vegetation similar to that found in Spain or California, including date palms and cactus; there are few forests, and most of the trees are eucalyptus which were transplanted there to counter soil erosion.

Unfortunately, this well-populated region is nearly devoid of wildlife. The puma, native throughout the Americas, is a reclusive creature and there's little chance of seeing one without actively searching for it. It was considered sacred by many of the tribes conquered by the Incas, and the Inca capital at Cuzco was laid out in the shape of this feline deity. Even today, many Bolivians believe that lunar eclipses are caused by hungry pumas nibbling at the moon, which

is also a deity. On such occasions, the people stage noisy celebrations in hopes of frightening it away.

The Chaco

The level terrain of the Chaco is covered by a tangled thicket of small thorny trees and cactus. The jaguar, tapir and *javelí* (peccary), which occupy the nearly inaccessible expanses of the Chaco in relatively healthy numbers, are quite elusive. Slightly more common but still threatened with extinction is the giant anteater, which exists in far eastern Bolivia near the Pantanal.

The Amazon Basin

In the more humid regions, the land is comprised largely of swampland, low jungle scrub and rainforest. There is an incredible variety of lizards, parrots, monkeys, snakes, butterflies, fish and bugs (by the zillions!). River travellers in the Amazon Basin are almost certain to spot capybaras (large amphibious rodents), turtles, alligators, pink dolphins and occasionally giant river otters. It's not unusual to see anacondas in the rivers of the Beni, and overland travellers frequently see armadillos, *jochis* (agoutis – agile, long-legged rodents), rheas and sloths.

Many of the more common animals wind up in the stewpot. Locals roast turtles in the shell and eat their eggs. Jochi and armadillo are considered staples in some areas, and a great many of the latter are also turned into *charangos*, a Bolivian ukulele-type instrument.

Rarer still, but present in national parks and remote regions of the Beni and Pando departments, are the jaguar, peccary, tapir, giant anteater and spectacled bear, but unless you're really looking for them, chances are they'll elude you.

Amazon Notes

While the insects will demand a great deal of your time – shooing, squashing, slapping and cursing – the birds constitute the most pleasant common encounter in the rainforest. Due to the dense vegetation, they're rarely seen, but their cries are distinct, and although you may not match the sounds to a mental image, they will become familiar after awhile. Some of them appear to have been designed by a Japanese electronics firm: there's one that sounds like a travel alarm clock, another like an auto burglar alarm and yet another like a doorbell. Then there's the toho, which sounds unmistakably like a cash till ringing up a purchase. Another does raucous cat whistles. One seems to be practising on a penny whistle but never quite gets the tune right and constantly has to start over again. One night bird has a hauntingly eerie cry that sounds like a howling wolf.

Because we couldn't begin to describe – much less scientifically identify – the incredible varieties of bird, insect, reptile and plant life of the Amazon rainforests, we've compiled a short list of some of the stranger items we encountered. The names used were those given when we enquired of local people, and are in a variety of languages; we ask botany and biology experts to excuse our lack of scientific identification:

ajo-ajo – a tree whose sap has a strong smell of garlic. It's used as a very effective insect repellent.

arbol vaca – literally, 'cow tree'. It's similar in appearance to the deadly poisonous *soliman* (see this list), but its smooth white sap looks and tastes like cream. It's only good when freshly extracted.

Big Mac – there's a seed of a particular liana which, when germinating, opens up to look exactly like a McDonald's hamburger: it's just the right size, and is complete with burger, mustard, ketchup and pickle, all encased in a golden brown bun!

buna – a giant ant over one cm long. Its bite causes 24 hours of excruciating pain throughout at least half the body.

cascavel – rattlesnake

gusano de chancho – this hideous mass of worms is one of the rainforest's most bizarre items. The worms in the rear of the mass are constantly crawling up and over those in front, thereby causing the advance of the whole mass.

jejene – pesky, biting yellow flies that leave huge welts.

leafcutter ant – these social insects are the role model for the *comercio de hormigas*, the contrabandists' 'ant trade' along the Argentine border. The ants construct 'highways' through the forest and spend their time in a steady stream of traffic transporting huge chunks of cut leaves from their source to a specially excavated hole hundreds of metres away.

mariwí – pesky, biting black flies similar to gnats, sandflies and no-see-ums found in other parts of the world. The only proven effective repellent is Avon Skin-So-Soft, but it's not available in Bolivia, so bring a supply from home.

pitón – a small forest seed. Peel off the husk and suck on it for a slightly sweet and refreshing taste similar to cranberry sauce.

pucarara – a dangerous poisonous snake common to the rainforest.

red ants – social ants which can amass in millions and attack forest camps. Local wisdom maintains that the only way to get rid of them is to distract them with grapefruit rinds and quickly relocate your camp while the ants are busy munching.

soliman – a large tree with a highly toxic sap similar to curare. The Indians use it to tip poison darts and arrows, and they also put it in pools to kill fish.

tabano – pesky, biting black horseflies, with half opaque and half transparent wings.

uña de gato – the cat's claw liana. This wonderful plant, when cut with a machete, delivers a stream of clear, sweet water. ■

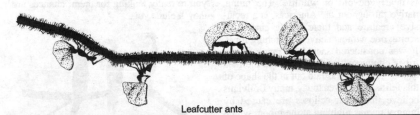

Leafcutter ants

National Parks & Reserves

There are a number of national parks and reserves in Bolivia, which are home to a myriad of animal and bird species. Some of these parks have only recently become accessible to visitors. Following is a brief outline of parks and reserves included in this guide. More comprehensive information can be found in relevant chapters.

Parque Nacional Amboró
Amboró, which was expanded and classified as a national park in 1990, is home to the rare spectacled bear, jaguars, capybaras, peccaries and an astonishing variety of birdlife. For more information, see the Santa Cruz chapter.

Reserva Biosférica del Beni
The 334,200-hectare Beni Biosphere Reserve, in conjunction with the adjacent Reserva Forestal Chimane, has at least 500 species of tropical birds and more than 100 species of mammals. See the Amazon Basin chapter for more details.

Parque Nacional Isiboro-Sécure
Unfortunately, due to a 1905 policy to colonise this area, the Indian population has been either displaced or exterminated, and most of the wildlife has vanished, except in the more remote areas. As this park is positioned along a major cocaine-producing route, extreme caution is required if you plan to visit this area. More details can be found in the Amazon Basin chapter.

Parque Nacional Noel Kempff Mercado
This park is named in honour of the distinguished Bolivian biologist who was murdered by renegades in 1986. It contains some of the most inspiring natural scenery in Bolivia. See the Amazon Basin chapter for details.

Reserva de Vida Salvaje Ríos Blanco Y Negro
This 1.4 million-hectare wildlife reserve contains vast tracts of undisturbed rainforest. Wildlife includes giant anteaters, peccaries and tapirs, and there are over 300 bird species. Further details can be found in the Amazon Basin chapter.

Parque Nacional Sajama
This national park, which abuts the Chilean border, contains Volcán Sajama (6542 metres), disputably Bolivia's highest peak. See the Southern Altiplano chapter for access details.

Parque Nacional Torotoro
Palaeontologists will be interested in the Cretaceous-period biped and quadruped dinosaur tracks which can be found in the enormous rock formations near the town of Torotoro. This park is difficult to reach unless you have private transport. The Asociación Experimental Torotoro sometimes offers escorted tours to the park. See the Cochabamba chapter for more details.

Parque Nacional Tunari
This park contains Lagunas de Huarahuara, small lakes containing trout. Picnic areas and wild campsites are available. See the Cochabamba chapter for details.

Parque Nacional Ulla-Ulla
Excellent hiking is possible in this park, which was established in 1972 as a vicuña reserve. It contains 2500 vicuñas and is home to a large population of condors. See the Cordilleras & Yungas chapter for further details.

ECOLOGY & ENVIRONMENT

The early 1990s have seen a dramatic surge in international and domestic interest in ecological issues and environmental attitudes in the Amazon region. This was clearly demonstrated by the choice of Brazil as the venue for ECO-92, a mega environmental and ecological bash organised by the United Nations to thrash out appropriate priorities for the environment and economic development.

Little explored and relatively ignored, Bolivia's lowlands have only recently begun to figure in the consciousness of the Bolivian government. With the current push toward the securing of undeniable sovereignty of the lowland regions, and the potential fortunes to be made in minerals, agricultural opportunities and forest products, conservation isn't as convenient as it once was. With so many economic advantages, there's unfortunately little incentive to consider long-term effects.

Although environmental problems have not yet reached apocalyptic proportions, change is coming rapidly, and it is not being accompanied by the sort of careful thought required to maintain a sound ecological balance. Bolivia fortunately lacks the population pressures of Brazil, but it is nevertheless promoting indiscriminate development of its lowlands. With government encouragement, settlers are leaving the highlands to clear lowland forest and build homesteads. Despite increasing criticism at home and abroad, this movement continues, and unless some intelligent controls are instituted soon, Bolivia will be heading down the path toward exhaustion of its forest and wildlife resources.

The Fate of the Amazon

Although books, magazines, TV shows and myriad international causes seem to be debating ecological issues, and the words 'fate of the Amazon' have begun to seem trite, it is appropriate to consider the issue a planetary concern. The Amazon, a very large, complex and fragile ecosystem – containing one-tenth of the earth's total number of plant and animal species and draining one-fifth of the world's fresh water – is endangered. Without change, the rainforests will be cleared for more ranches and industries; the land will be stripped for mines; and the rivers will be dammed for electricity. Already jaguars, caimans, anteaters, armadillos, dolphins, monkeys and a host of other wildlife and plant species are threatened with extinction. As in the past, Indians will die with their forests, and the invaluable, irreplaceable Amazon may be lost forever.

The construction of roads is a prerequisite for exploiting the Amazon. The new roads have created a swathe of development across the former Beni wilderness from La Paz to Guayaramerín and Yucumo to Trinidad. The Riberalta-Cobija road is currently spreading the frenzy into the Pando Department. These roads are the direct result of 'humanitarian aid' and earth-moving equipment donated by Japanese interests (Japan, along with the USA, has a seemingly insatiable appetite for forest products!), but similar projects throughout the Amazon have been encouraged and financed with collaboration from the World Bank, the IMF, US and other international banks, and a variety of private corporations, politicians, and military figures. The inevitable conclusion is that new highway projects such as these will follow established patterns of development and open up the region for further decimation. According to calculations based on Landsat photos, the damming of rivers, and the burning and clearing of the forests between 1970 and 1989, destroyed about 400,000 sq km, or around 10%, of the Amazon forest.

In late 1988, Chico Mendes, a rubber tapper and opponent of rainforest destruction, was assassinated in the town of Xapurí, Acre, Brazil, by a local landowner. This sparked an international reaction which eventually pressured the World Bank and the IMF to declare that they would no longer fund rainforest destruction.

Economic Development of the Amazon

Most biologists doubt that the Amazon can support large-scale agriculture. The lushness

of the rainforest is deceptive: apart from volcanic lands and flood plains which can support continuous growth, the forest topsoil is thin and infertile, and most of it is acidic and contains insufficient calcium, phosphorus and potassium for crops to be grown effectively.

Small-scale slash-and-burn, a traditional agricultural technique adopted by nomadic Indians, supported small populations on such fragile lands as those of the Amazon Basin, without ecological compromises. Indians would fell a five or 10-acre plot of land and burn off remaining material. The resulting ash would support a few years of crops: squash, corn, manioc, plantains and beans. After a few seasons, however, the nutrients would be spent and the Indians would move on. Clearings were small and few, and once the land was no longer productive, it was left fallow long enough for the forest to recover.

In contrast, modern agricultural emphasis in the region has been placed on cattle ranching, which does not give the land a rest once it has been spent. Ranchers clear enormous tracts of land – some larger than European nations – which are never left fallow, so once any nutrients or topsoil are gone, the land is permanently wasted.

Effects of Development

The Indian tribes in the Amazon have borne the brunt of the destruction, which has systematically wiped out their lands and their forest habitat. New roads have attracted settlers and opportunists into the last refuges of tribes who, as a consequence, have been virtually wiped out by new diseases, pollution, over-hunting and violent confrontations.

Mineral prospectors stream into the Alto Beni region to work the streams and rivers, and unfortunately, their principal technique involves the use of mercury to extract gold from ore. Large quantities of highly poisonous mercury are washed into the water which becomes a major health hazard for local inhabitants and remaining wildlife.

Since the failure of its early 1950's attempt at agrarian reform on the Altiplano, the Bolivian government has officially encouraged immigration and development in the lowland regions of the country. The 1950's programme entailed allotting each farmer with a plot of land known as a *minifundio*. These private plots made obsolete the communal *ayllu* system of shared responsibility and production which had been in practice since Inca days. However, the minifundio parcels were too small to sustain life on the

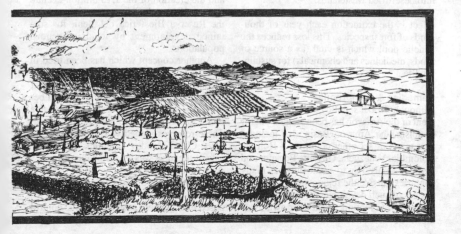

harsh Altiplano, and in the end, farmers were forced to somehow wrest a living from the land or relocate. Although it has meant a complete change in lifestyle, the recent government promises of 50 free hectares per farmer in the verdant and productive Beni region has been too inviting for many to pass up.

One of the most dramatic and disturbing sights in the forest is the burning of immense tracts to clear the area for agriculture or cattle ranching. According to meteorologists, the smoke cloud, primarily from the burning of the Brazilian forests, has already reached Africa and Antarctica. Scientists generally agree that the torching of the forest on such a massive scale contributes to the greenhouse effect, but opinions differ regarding the scale of damage involved.

Although the theory that the Amazon forests are the prime source of the world's oxygen is no longer given much credence by the scientific community, researchers are becoming increasingly concerned by regional and global climatic changes brought on by massive deforestation and smoke from the clearing process. The water cycle which depends on transpiration from the forest canopy has been interrupted, resulting in diminished rainfall in surrounding areas, and deforested zones are being baked by the sun into desertified wastelands.

Perhaps the most devastating long-term effect is the extinction each year of thousands of forest species. This loss reduces the genetic pool which is vital (as a source of foods, medicines and chemicals) for sustaining life.

Remedies & Compromise

Although Brazil's policy toward development of the Amazon has been singled out for criticism, the Amazon Basin also includes vast tracts of six other countries – Bolivia, Colombia, Venezuela, Guyana, Ecuador and Peru. It's only fair to point out that many countries outside the region were once supporters of such development, and have only recently been reminded that their own treatment of the environment was hardly exemplary. The general consensus for the '90s, however, is that a series of different approaches must be developed to halt and remedy the destruction. The following are a few of the ways now being tried:

Debt-for-nature swaps are international agreements whereby a portion of a country's external debt is cancelled in exchange for local funding of conservation initiatives. Negotiation of such swaps requires that the sovereignty of recipient countries is kept intact, and that inflationary effects on their economies are avoided.

Bolivia already has quite a few parks and reserves on the books, but boundaries are loosely defined, and in many, conservation enforcement is either a low priority or nonexistent. In August 1987, the US-based organisation Conservation International kicked off the idea by making Bolivia an offer: it agreed to pay US$650,000 of Bolivia's foreign debt (which totals US$4 billion!) in exchange for permanent official protection of the 334,200-hectare Reserva Biosférica del Beni near San Borja. Bolivia retains management of the land, but wildlife is theoretically protected, and haphazard development is curtailed.

Conservation International has also succeeded in setting aside the 351,000-hectare Parque Regional Yacuma in the central Beni, and the creation of the 1.15 million-hectare Reserva Forestal Chimane, which adjoins the Reserva Biosférica del Beni, for sustained development by local indigenous populations.

Another concept which has been tried in Brazil involves creation of extractive reserves for the sustainable harvesting of brazil nuts, rubber, and other non-timber products. The idea is to use the forest as a renewable resource, without destroying it. These reserves gained worldwide attention when Chico Mendes, an enthusiastic advocate of the idea, was assassinated in Brazil's Acre state.

Alternatives are also being suggested to stop wasteful clear-felling of timber. Proposed management schemes include control over the size of parcels being logged and the manner in which they're logged so that forest land will continue to be a sustainable resource. In many cases, huge tracts of forest are flattened and laid waste in order to extract a few commercially valuable tree species. When land is cleared exclusively for cattle ranching, however, timber is often simply burnt and squandered. We encountered teams from US universities in Bolivia examining different methods of controlling the types of timber cut, of utilising 'waste' species and of thwarting exploitation of local workers who don't recognise the true value of forest products (or the scope of commercial profits) on the international market.

Many foreign environmental groups – as well as businesses hoping to purchase a 'green identity' – are contributing funds directed at the Amazon's environmental needs. Much of the action promised by South American governments, however, appears only on paper. Funds donated and appropriated to maintain and manage wilderness parks have a habit of losing their way somewhere en route. Many of the country's environmental protection units, therefore, suffer from lack of funds, staff, and equipment, resulting in an inability to act or even to survive. If any success is to be achieved, such schemes must be underpinned with finance and enforcement, monies contributed to 'save the Amazon' must be carefully accounted and watched, and parks and reserves will have to be stringently policed by reliable, well-informed, and committed 'green rangers'.

Environmental Movements

Preservation of the rainforest and carefully managed development must be achieved through the combined efforts of concerned individuals and groups both within Bolivia and abroad. Bolivia requires capable people and organisations to educate the public and enlist its support in reducing consumption of tropical forest products; to pressure US and other international banks to stop financing wasteful or destructive development projects; and to persuade its own and other governments responsible for the Amazonian rainforests to adopt more rational uses for the region.

Ecotourism provides a financial incentive for countries such as Bolivia to preserve rather than exploit their environment. For information about ways you can help reduce the impact of tourism on the fragile ecosystem, read the Minimum Impact Camping section under Accommodation in the Facts for the Visitor chapter.

It is important that the organisations which proclaim an interest in environmental issues prove they are not just jumping onto the green-painted bandwagon, but are actively making progress toward preservation of the environment. One example of active involvement is the growing pressure exerted by consumers, who can change economic trends on a global scale by simply changing purchasing patterns. For further details, contact any of the following environmental and ecological organisations:

Australia
Friends of the Earth, 222 Brunswick St, Fitzroy, 3065 (☎ (03) 419-8700)
Greenpeace Australia Ltd, 3/389 Lonsdale St, Melbourne, 3000 (☎ (03) 670-1633)
Bolivia
Fundación Amigos de la Naturaleza (FAN), Casilla 1615, Avenida Irala 421, Santa Cruz, Bolivia (☎ 333806)
Conservación Internacional, Señor Guillermo Rioja Ballivián, Casilla 5633, Avenida Villazón #1958-10A, La Paz, Bolivia (☎ 341230)
Instituto de Ecología, Casilla 10077, Calle 27, Cotacota, La Paz, Bolivia (☎ 792582, international fax: (591-2) 391176)
UK
Friends of the Earth, 26/28 Underwood St, London N17JU
Survival International, 310 Edgeware Rd, London W2 1DY (☎ (071) 723-5535)
USA
The Rainforest Action Network (RAN), 301 Broadway, Suite A, San Francisco, CA 94133, (☎ (415) 398-4404)
Conservation International, 1015 18th St, NW, Suite 1000, Washington, DC 20036 (☎ (202) 429-5660)
Cultural Survival, 11 Divinity Ave, Cambridge, MA 03128
The Nature Conservancy, 1815 N Lynn St, Arlington, VA 22209 (☎ (703) 841-5300)

Survival International USA, 2121 Decatur Place, NW, Washington, DC 20006

Friends of the Earth, 218 D St, SE, Washington, DC 20003 (☎ (202) 544-2600)

Greenpeace, 1436 U St, NW, Washington, DC 20009 (☎ (202) 462-8817)

Earthwatch, 680 Mt Auburn St, Box 403, Watertown, MA 02272 (☎ (617) 926-8200)

The Chico Mendes Fund, Environmental Defense Fund, 257 Park Ave South, New York, NY 10010

Rainforest Alliance, 270 Lafayette St, Suite 512, New York, NY 10012

The Rainforest Foundation Inc, 1776 Broadway, 14th floor, New York, NY 10019

GOVERNMENT

In theory, Bolivia is a republic, much like the USA, with legislative, executive and judicial branches of government. The first two convene in La Paz, the de facto capital, and the Supreme Court sits in Sucre, the legal capital.

The president is elected to a four-year term by popular vote and cannot hold more than one consecutive term. Once elected, the president appoints a cabinet of 15 members and also selects departmental and local government officers.

The Legislature consists of a Senate and a Chamber of Deputies which convenes in legislative session for 90 days per year. Each department (there are nine of them) sends three elected senators for terms of six years, with one-third elected every two years. The Chamber of Deputies has 102 members who are elected to four-year terms.

The fact that Bolivia has had nearly as many leaders as years of independence and has been ruled by military juntas for much of its existence may seem to mock the democratic processes outlined in its constitution. In truth, however, the late 1980s and early 1990s have seen peaceful and democratic transitions of government. Politically, the country is currently one of the most stable in Latin America.

ECONOMY

With the decline of the world tin market in 1985 and the ensuing labour strife between miners' unions, cooperatives and the state, the days of the supremacy of tin as Bolivia's mainstay export are over for the time being. In 1987, mining accounted for only 36% of Bolivia's export income and 2% of its labour force. In the far south-west there are rich deposits of sulphur, antimony, bismuth and lead/zinc. The legendary silver mines of Potosí are being reworked for tin and other lesser minerals, and Oruro's mines are winding down to a near standstill. The nation is currently looking toward the Oriente, the humid lowlands, where significant deposits of natural gas, iron manganese and petroleum have been discovered and have supplanted ores as the primary mineral exports of the country.

Agriculturally, Bolivia remains a subsistence country, and most of the food produced, with only a few notable exceptions, remains within its borders. A small amount of Yungas coffee is exported and a moderate quantity of sugar, grown in Tarija and Santa Cruz departments, goes to Argentina. Timber extraction, also quite lucrative, is the largest source of legal export income.

And then, of course, there's coca... In 1986 alone, Bolivia's star export brought between US$600 million and US$1 billion into the country – more than all legal exports combined. Coca production and refining currently account for about 350,000 jobs and it's clear that as long as there's a strong market and profit potential, one way or another, Bolivia will continue to produce. Currently there are at least 54,000 hectares of coca under cultivation in the Chapare region alone, and in 1986, they yielded 100,000 kg of cocaine, all of which was exported. Most of the Yungas coca is used primarily for domestic consumption in the form of tea and leaves for chewing.

Bolivia is hoping to boost its weak economy by promoting tourism, but the country's internationally perceived synonymity with drug trafficking, and the general confusion of Bolivia with such violent countries as Peru and Colombia, tends to put off the sort of big-money tourism the government hopes to attract.

A	B
C	D
E	F

A: (DS) D: (DS)
B: (RS) E: (RS)
C: (RS) F: (RS)

A	B
C	D
E	F

A: (RS) D: (RS)
B: (RS) E: (RS)
C: (DS) F: (RS)

POPULATION & PEOPLE

Modern Bolivians are a rugged and strong-spirited people. Many of the dispersed communities of Aymará-speaking Indians, whose kingdoms were once centred on the Altiplano, fought historic battles against the cultural dominance and oppression of the expanding Inca Empire. In pre-Hispanic Bolivia, they flourished as one of the most influential cultures in the Andes. Furthermore, the first resistance to Spanish rule in South America was in Bolivia, with mestizo revolts in 1661 and 1780, and was continued during the Indian insurrections that lasted from 1776-80. The characteristic bowler hats and voluminous skirts worn by the cholas were imposed on them in the 18th century by the Spanish king, and the customary centre-parting of the hair was the result of a decree by the Viceroy Toledo.

Bolivia has a population of about 6.6 million, 70% of whom live on the bleak Altiplano in the west. Most of these people are concentrated in the northern end of this region in the environs of La Paz, Lake Titicaca and Oruro.

Between 50 and 60% of the population is of pure Indian stock and most of these people speak either Quechua or Aymará as a first language. About 35% are *mestizo*, people of Spanish American and American Indian parentage or descent. They are locally known as *campesinas* (female) or *campesinos* (male) or *cholas/os* (female/male), although this latter term also refers to anyone, even pure-blooded Indian, who has migrated to the city but continues to wear ethnic dress. About 1% of the population is of African heritage, mostly descended from the slaves conscripted to work in the mines of Potosí.

The remainder of the people are of European extraction, and have a wide variety of origins. Some are descendants of the early conquerors, but there are also colonies of Platt-Deutsch-speaking Mennonites from Canada, missionaries of a number of foreign churches and escaped Nazi war criminals. A small Asian minority, consisting mostly of Indians, Japanese and Chinese, has taken root, primarily in Santa Cruz Department.

Bolivia is currently the second poorest country in South America (after Guyana) and the third in the western hemisphere (Haiti is the poorest) with a gross national product that reflects annual earnings of only US$640 per inhabitant. Fortunately, this is not as severe as it sounds because a good many rural Bolivians operate outside the currency system and enjoy relatively comfortable subsistence lifestyles.

The state of health care, particularly in rural areas, is also quite poor. It's estimated that a shocking 10% of infants born in Bolivia can be expected to die in their first year. Similarly, the average life expectancy in the country is only about 55 years compared with 70 to 75 years in most developed nations.

EDUCATION

Although school attendance is theoretically compulsory for children aged seven to 14, schools in many rural areas are either poor or nonexistent. Overall, only 87% of primary school-aged children are enrolled in classes. As a result, Bolivia's official literacy rate of 75% is one of the lowest in Latin America.

ARTS & CULTURE

Music

Although the musical traditions of the Andes have evolved from a series of pre-Inca, Inca, Spanish, Amazonian and even African influences, each region of Bolivia has developed distinctive musical traditions, dances and instruments. The strains of the Andean music from the cold and bleak Altiplano are suitably haunting and mournful, while those of warmer Tarija, with its complement of bizarre musical instruments, take on more vibrant and colourful tones.

Although the original Andean music was exclusively instrumental, recent trends toward popularisation of the magnificent melodies has inspired the addition of appropriately tragic, bittersweet or morose lyrics.

In the far eastern and northern lowland regions of Bolivia, Jesuit influences upon Chiquitano, Moxos and Guaraní musical talent left a unique legacy which is still in evidence and remains particularly strong in the musical traditions of neighbouring Paraguay. In addition to economic ventures, the Jesuits promoted education and culture among the tribes. Extremely able artists and musicians, the Indians handcrafted musical instruments – the renowned violins and harps featured in Chaco music today – and learned and performed Italian baroque music, including opera! In the remotest of settings, they gave concerts, dances, and theatre performances which could have competed on a European scale.

Musical Instruments Although the martial honking of tinny and poorly practised brass bands seems an integral part of most South American celebrations, the Andean musical traditions employ a variety of instruments which date back to pre-colonial days.

Only the popular ukelele-like *charango*, based on the Spanish *vihuela* and *bandurria*, early forms of the guitar and mandolin, has European roots. By the early 17th century, Andean Indians had blended and adapted the Spanish designs into one which would better reproduce their pentatonic scale: a 10-stringed instrument with llama-gut strings arranged in five pairs and a *quirquincho* (armadillo carapace) soundbox. Modern charangos are scarcely different from the earliest models, but due to the paucity and fragile nature of quirquinchos – as well as efforts to improve sound quality – wood is nowadays the material of choice for charango soundboxes. Another stringed instrument, the *violín chapaco* originated in Tarija and is a variation on the European violin. Between Easter and the Fiesta de San Roque (held in early September) it is the favoured instrument.

Prior to the advent of the charango, melody lines were carried exclusively by woodwind instruments. Best recognised are the *quena* and the *zampoña* (pan flute) which feature in the majority of traditional musical performances. Quenas are simple reed flutes played by blowing into a notch at one end. The more complex zampoñas are played by forcing air across the open ends of reeds

Zampoña

lashed together in order of their size, often in double rows. Both quenas and zampoñas come in a variety of sizes and tonal ranges. Although the quena was originally intended for solo interpretation of musical pieces known as *yaravíes*, the two flutes are now played as part of a musical ensemble. The *bajón*, an enormous pan flute with separate mouthpieces in each reed, accompanies festivities in the Moxos communities of the Beni lowlands. While being played, it must be rested on the ground or carried by two people.

Other prominent wind instruments include the *tarka* and the *sikuri*, the lead instrument in the breathy *tarkeadas* and *sikureadas* of the rural Altiplano, and the *pinquillo*, a Carnival flute which comes in various pitches.

Woodwinds unique to the Tarija area are the *erke*, the *caña* and the *camacheña*. The erke, also known as the *phututu*, is made from a cow's horn and is played exclusively between New Year's and Carnival. From San Roque in early September to the end of the year, the camacheña, a type of flute, is used. The caña, a three-metre-long cane pole with a cow's horn on the end, is similar in appearance and tone to an alphorn. It's featured year round in Tarija.

Percussion also figures in most festivals and other folk musical performances as a backdrop for the typically lilting strains of the woodwind melodies. In highland areas, the most popular drum is the largish *huankara*. The *caja*, a tambourine-like drum played with one hand, is used exclusively in Tarija.

For guidelines on purchasing native instruments, refer to the Things to Buy section in the La Paz chapter.

Artists & Recordings Although there is a wealth of yet-to-be-discovered musical talent in Bolivia, key players are influencing musical trends and tastes worldwide with their recordings and even occasional performances abroad.

In Bolivia, folk music shows for locals and tourists are called *peñas* and operate in most larger cities. Many visitors, especially those who've attended peñas or fiestas, are taken with the music and set out in search of recordings to take home. Compact disks haven't yet made their debut in Bolivia, so unless you have space to carry bulky and fragile record albums in your luggage, you'll have to resort to cassette tapes. Unfortunately, original recordings are hard to come by and those sold in music shops and markets are typically low quality bootlegged copies which are prone to rapid self-destruction. They are cheap, however – around B12 each – but copy them onto a better tape before giving them much play time.

Major artists you may want to look for include charango masters Ernesto Cavour, Celestino Campos and Mauro Nuñez. Look especially for the recording *Charangos Famosos*, a selection of well-known charango pieces.

The Bolivian group that's been the most successful abroad is Los Kjarkas. They've recorded at least a dozen albums and their superb *Canto a la Mujer de Mi Pueblo* is unsurpassed. The track entitled *Llorando se Fue* by the late Bolivian composer Ulisses Hermosa and his brother Gonzalo, was recorded by the French group Kaoma in 1989 and became a worldwide hit as *The Lambada*. In June 1990, the Hermosa brothers finally received official recognition for their authorship of the song.

Other groups worth noting are Savia Andina, known for their protest songs, Chullpa Ñan, Rumillajta, Los Quipus, Grupo Cultural Wara, Los Masis and Yanapakuna.

In the USA, tapes of Bolivian music are available through the South American Explorers Club (see under Useful Organisations in the Facts for the Visitor chapter).

Dance

The pre-Hispanic dances of the Altiplano were celebrations of war, fertility, hunting prowess, marriage or work. After the Spanish arrived, traditional European dances and those of the African slaves brought to work in the mines were introduced and massaged into the hybrid dances that characterise Bolivian festivities today.

If Bolivia has a national dance, it is the *cueca*, danced by handkerchief-waving couples to three-four time. It is derived from the Chilean cueca which in turn is a Creole adaptation of the Spanish fandango. Its liberally interpreted choreography is danced primarily during fiestas by whirling couples, called *pandillas*. The dance is intended to convey a story of courtship, love, loss of love and reconciliation. A favourite part of the dance comes at the shouting of *Aro, aro, aro*, which indicates that it's time for the couple to stop dancing for a moment and celebrate with a glass of spirits each. Another very popular dance is the *huayño*, which originated on the Altiplano.

The *auqui-auqui*, or 'old man' dance, parodies high-born colonial gentlemen by portraying them ludicrously with a top hat, gnarled cane and an exaggerated elderly posture.

Another tradition is the *tinku*; although it resembles a kind of disorganised dance, it is actually a ritual fight which takes place primarily in northern Potosí Department during festivals. Tinkus normally begin innocently enough, but near the end of the celebrations, they often erupt into drunken – and unfortunately rather violent – mayhem.

In the south around Tarija, where musical traditions depart dramatically from those of the rest of Bolivia, the festival dance is known as the *chapaqueada*. It is normally associated with religious celebrations, especially San Roque, and is performed to the strains of Tarija's host of unusual musical instruments. Also popular in Tarija is *la rueda* (the wheel) which is danced at all fiestas throughout the year.

In San Ignacio de Moxos and around the Beni lowlands, festivities are highlighted by the dancing of the *machetero*, a commemorative folkloric dance accompanied by drums, violins and bajones. Dancers carry wooden machetes and wear elaborate crowns of brilliant macaw feathers, wooden masks, and costumes made of cotton, bark and feathers.

Other popular dances in the northern lowlands include the *carnaval* and the *taquirari Beniano*, both adapted from the Altiplano, and the *chovena*, indigenous to northeastern Bolivia.

Some of the most unusual and colourful dances are those performed at festivals on the high Altiplano, particularly during Carnival, especially *La Diablada* (The Dance of the Devils) fiesta at Oruro, which draws a large number of both foreign and Bolivian visitors.

The most famous and recognisable of the Diablada dances is *la morenada*, which is a re-enactment of the dance of the Black slaves brought to the courts of Viceroy Felipe III. The costumes consist of hooped skirts and shoulder mantles, and dark-faced masks adorned with plumes. Another dance with African origins is *los negritos*. Performers beat on drums and the rhythm is reminiscent of the music of the Caribbean.

The *los llameros* dancers represent Andean llama herders, the *waca takoris* satire Spanish bullfighters and the *waca tintis* represent the *picadores*, also of bullfighting fame. The *los Incas* commemorates the original contact between the Incan and Southern European cultures; and the *las tobas* is performed in honour of those Indian groups of the tropical lowlands which were conquered by the Inca and forcefully absorbed into the empire.

Weaving

Spinning and weaving methods have changed little in Bolivia for 3000 years. In rural areas, girls learn to weave before they reach puberty, and women spend nearly all their spare time spinning with a drop spindle or weaving on heddle looms. Prior to Spanish colonisation, llama and alpaca wool were the materials of choice, but sheep's wool has now emerged as the most readily available and least expensive medium.

Bolivian textiles come in diverse patterns and the majority display a degree of skill that results from millennia of experience. The beautiful and practical creations are true works of art, and motivated visitors who avoid such overtouristed haunts as Tarabuco and Calle Sagárnaga in La Paz may find real quality for good prices.

Regional differences are manifest in weaving style, motif and use. Weavings from Tarabuco, near Sucre, are made into the colourful costumes (men wear a *chuspa*, or coca pouch, and a trademark red poncho) and zoomorphic patterns seen around the popular and touristy Sunday market in Tarabuco.

Most famous and celebrated of Bolivian weavings are the red and black zoomorphic designs from Potolo, north-west of Sucre. Patterns range from faithful representations of animals to creative and mythical combinations of animal forms: horses figure prominently, as do avian aberrations. The patterns are not necessarily symmetrical, and the relative size of figures represented often does not conform to reality – it is not unusual for a gigantic horse to be depicted standing next to a tiny house. Potolo pieces are prized by weavings buffs and command relatively high prices.

Zoomorphic patterns are also prominent in the wild Charazani country north of Lake Titicaca and in several areas in the vicinity of La Paz, including Lique and Calamarka. Some extremely fine weavings originate in

Sica Sica, one of the many dusty and non-descript villages between La Paz and Oruro, and in Calcha, south-east of Potosí near the boundary of Chuquisaca, expert spinning and extremely tight weave – over 150 threads per inch – combine into some of Bolivia's best clothing textiles.

Those interested in Bolivian textiles may want to look at the books *A Travellers' Guide to Eldorado and the Inca Empire* by weavings expert Lynn Meisch, or the hard-to-find *Weaving Traditions of Highland Bolivia* by Laurie Adelson and Bruce Takami, published by the Los Angeles Craft & Folk Art Museum. Another excellent booklet on Bolivian textile arts is *Bolivian Indian Textiles* by Tamara E Wasserman & Jonathon S Hill, available through the South American Explorers Club (see under Useful Organisations in the Facts for the Visitor chapter).

Architecture
The pre-Columbian architecture of Bolivia is represented primarily by the largely ruined walls and structures of Tiahuanaco and the numerous Inca remains scattered about the country. Restoration of these sites has been based on architectural interpretation by archaeologists without revealing much about their artistic values. The only examples of the classic polygonal cut stones which dominate many Peruvian Inca sites are on Isla del Sol and Isla de la Luna in Lake Titicaca.

Surviving colonial architecture, the vast majority of which is religious, is divided into four major overlapping periods: renaissance (1550-1650), baroque (1630-1770), mestizo (1690-1790), which was actually a variation on baroque, and the modern period (post-1790). Around 1790, the beginnings of the modern period were marked by a brief experimentation with the neoclassical style, which was then followed by a return to the neogothic.

Some Andean renaissance churches indicate Moorish *mudéjar* influences. Renaissance churches are simple in design. They were constructed primarily of adobe with courtyards, aisle-less naves and massive buttresses. One of the best examples may be seen at the village of Tiahuanaco. The three classic examples of mudéjar renaissance design are found at San Miguel and San Francisco in Sucre, and at Copacabana on the shores of Lake Titicaca.

Baroque churches were constructed in the form of a cross with an elaborate dome and walls made of either stone or reinforced adobe. The best examples of pure baroque are the churches of the Compañía in Oruro, San Agustín in Potosí and Santa Bárbara in Sucre.

Late in the baroque period, mestizo elements in the form of whimsical decorative carvings were introduced and applied with what appears to be wild abandon. Prominent themes included densely packed tropical flora and fauna, Inca deities and designs, and bizarre masks, sirens and gargoyles. The interesting results are best seen at the churches of San Francisco in La Paz, San Lorenzo, Santa Teresa and the Compañía in Potosí, and at the rural churches of Sica Sica and Guaqui in La Paz Department.

Neoclassical design, which dominated between 1790 and the early 20th century, is observed in the church of San Felipe Neri in Sucre, and the cathedrals in Potosí and La Paz.

Paralleling the mainstream church construction in the mid-18th century, the Jesuits in the Beni and Santa Cruz lowlands were designing churches showing evidence of Bavarian Rococo and Gothic influences. Their most unusual effort, however, was the bizarre mission church at San José de Chiquitos, the design of which is unique in Latin America. Its European origins aren't clear, but it bears superficial similarities to churches in Poland and Belgium.

Chola Dress
The distinctive ensemble of the Aymará and Quechua women's dress, both colourful and utilitarian, has become a representative image of Bolivia. The most noticeable characteristic of the traditional Aymará dress is the ubiquitous dark green, black or brown bowler hat that would seem more at home on

Chola Dress

a London street than in the former Spanish colonies. You'd be hard pressed to find a chola or campesina without one.

The women normally braid their hair into two long plaits which are joined by a tuft of black wool known as a *pocacha*. The short *pollera* skirts they wear are constructed of several horizontal bands tucked under each other. This garment tends to make most of the women appear overweight, especially when several of them are combined with multiple layers of petticoats.

On top, the outfit consists of a factory-made blouse, a woollen *chompa* (pullover/jumper), a short vest-like jacket, and a cotton apron, or some combination of these. Usually, the women will add a woollen shawl known as a *llijlla* or *phullu*.

Slung across the back and tied around the neck is the *ahuayo*, a rectangle of manufactured or handwoven cloth decorated with brilliantly coloured horizontal bands. It is used as a carryall and is filled with everything from coca or groceries to babies.

The Quechua of the highland valleys wear equally colourful but not so universally recognised attire. The hat, called a *montera*, is a flat-topped affair made of straw or finely woven white wool. It's often taller and broader than the bowlers worn by the Aymará. The felt montera of Tarabuco, patterned after the Spanish conquistadores' helmets, is the most striking.

RELIGION

Roughly 95% of Bolivia's population professes Roman Catholicism and follows it to varying degrees. The absence of Roman Catholic clergy in rural areas has led to the emergence of a hybrid Christian/folk religion in which the Inca and Aymará belief systems blend with Christianity into an interesting conglomeration of doctrines, rites and superstitions.

The most obvious aspect of native religion is the belief in various gods and animistic characters. A diverse array of beneficent and malevolent characters seem to have their fingers in everything, and expect constant appeasement by their devotees. If a person has a problem with a particular god then the *yatiri*, or witch doctor, will often be able to help. To find out what dangers lie ahead in life, a visit to the *thaliri*, or fortune-teller, is in order. This will give the yatiri an idea of what he's supposed to prevent from happening and which god he can bribe to prevent it. There is, however, a particularly insidious night phantom called *Kharisiri* who preys on sleeping humans, and once a person is on his bad side, not even the best yatiri can help.

Ekeko, which means 'dwarf' in Aymará, is the normally pleasant little household god of abundance. He is responsible for matchmaking, finding homes for the homeless and ensuring success for business people – a good friend to have. The Alasitas festival in La Paz is dedicated to Ekeko and there's even a monument in his honour at the end of Calle Comercio in La Paz.

The evil *Happiñuñoz* are dreaded, however. These personifications of beautiful women seduce men, cause them to lose their powers of reason and then abscond with their souls. The inevitable result is death for their poor victims.

The most important of all the deities is *Pachamama*, the earth mother. She shares herself with human beings, helps bring forth abundant crops and distributes riches to those who venerate her. She seems to have quite an appetite for such things as coca, alcohol and the blood of animals, particularly llamas. If the earth needs to be disturbed for any reason, such as ploughing, construction or mining, an apology must be offered to her.

In the mines of Oruro and Potosí, a number of superstitions and beliefs have developed and persisted over the years. Luck, the miners assume, is procured by avoidance of certain 'unlucky' practices, and by propitiation of *El Tío*, the sovereign ruler of hell and owner of the minerals. Women, for instance, may not enter certain mines, and whilst underground, miners may not whistle or eat toasted *haba* beans, or season llama meat with salt. Breaking any of these taboos, they believe, would surely bring bad luck and low mineral production.

LANGUAGE

The official language of Bolivia is Spanish, but only 60 to 70% of the people actually speak it, and then often only as a second language. The remainder speak Quechua, the language of the Inca, or Aymará, the pre-Inca language of the Altiplano. A host of other minor indigenous tongues are used in limited areas throughout the country.

Most travellers in South America either arrive with at least a basic knowledge of Spanish or very quickly acquire a workable vocabulary of say 300 to 500 words. English in Bolivia won't get you very far, but fortunately it's not difficult to learn the basics of Spanish. With a short course or self-teaching programme, you may not be able to carry on a philosophical or political discussion, but you will be able to communicate, and will gain a basis on which to improve your Spanish language skills.

For those who haven't studied Spanish, the following is a brief rundown of basic grammar and pronunciation, and common words and phrases. For a more comprehensive reference, track down Lonely Planet's *Latin American Spanish Phrasebook*.

Pronunciation

Vowel pronunciation in Bolivian Spanish is easy and consistent. In the following vowel list the nearest equivalent English vowel is highlighted:

a is similar to 'f**a**ther'
e is similar to 'm**e**t';
at the end of a word, as in 'gr**e**y'
i is similar to 'mar**i**ne'
o is similar to '**o**ld'
u is similar to 'p**oo**l'
y is the same as **i**

Spanish consonants are more or less the same as their English counterparts, but there are a few variations:

c is only soft before *i* or *e* (ie like an 's')
d is a cross between English 'd' and 'th'
g is only soft before *i* or *e* (ie like German 'ch', something like an English 'h' only with more friction)
h is never (under any circumstances) pronounced
j is pronounced like English 'h', only with more friction
ll is pronounced more or less like the 'll y' in 'will you' but **ll** often sounds more like a simple English 'y'
ñ is the equivalent of the 'ny' in 'canyon'
gu are used to get the hard consonant sound (ie like English 'g' and 'k' in 'get' and 'kit') in front of *e* or *i*. In this case, the **u** is silent unless it is altered with an

umlaut. In front of *a* or *o* the **u** is pronounced like an English 'w'

qu is the same as **gu**

rr is a rolled or trilled 'r'

r is a slap of the tongue against the palate and sounds like a very quickly spoken 'd' or 't' as in 'ladder' or 'matter'. At the beginning of a word, some Bolivians pronounce it 'zh'

v is a cross between English 'v' and 'b'

x is pronounced as in 'taxi'

z is pronounced as 's'

Emphasis in Spanish is placed on the second last syllable unless an accent mark is employed to alter it. Accents also serve to break up vowel sounds in a diphthong.

Grammar

Articles, adjectives and demonstrative pronouns must agree with the noun in both gender and number. Nouns ending in *a* are generally feminine and the corresponding articles are *la* (singular) and *las* (plural). Those ending in *o* are usually masculine and require the articles *el* (singular) and *los* (plural).

There are, however, hundreds of exceptions to these guidelines which can only be memorised or deduced by the referent of the word. Plurals are formed by adding *s* to words ending in a vowel and *es* to those ending in a consonant.

In addition to using all the familiar English tenses, Spanish also uses the imperfect tense and two subjunctive tenses (past and present). Tenses are formed either by adding a myriad of endings to the root verb or preceding the participle form by some variation of the verb *haber* (to have/to exist).

There are verb endings for first, second and third person singular and plural. Second person singular and plural are divided into formal and familiar modes. If that's not enough, there are three types of verbs – those ending in 'ar', 'er' and 'ir' – which are all conjugated differently. There are also a whole slough of stem-changing rules and irregularities which must be memorised.

Greeting & Civilities

good morning
buén día or *buenos días*

good afternoon (or good evening)
buenas tardes

yes
sí

no
no

hello
hola

See you later.
Hasta luego.

How are you?
¿Que tal? or *¿Como estás?* (familiar) or *¿Como está?* (formal)

please
por favor

thank you
gracias

It's a pleasure.
Con mucho gusto.

Some Useful Phrases

Do you speak Spanish?
¿Habla usted castellano?

Where do you come from?
¿De donde es usted?

What is your country?
¿Cual es su país?

Where are you staying?
¿Donde estás alojado? (familiar)

What is your profession?
¿Cuál es su profesión?

What is the time?
¿Que hora tiene?

Don't you have smaller change?
¿No tiene sencillo?

Do you understand? (familiar)
¿Me entiende?

Where can I change money/travellers' cheques?
¿Donde se cambia monedas/cheques de viajeros?

Where is the...?
¿Donde está el/la...?

Where is the toilet?
¿Donde está los servicios? or *el baño?* (nb: 'servicios' can often be identified by the initials: SS.HH)

How much is this?
There are fortunately several variations on this well-worn phrase:
¿A como?, ¿Por cuanto sale esto?, ¿Cuanto cuesta esto?, ¿Cuanto vale esto?
too expensive
muy caro
cheaper
más barato
I'll take it.
Lo llevo.
I would like a...
Quisiera un/a...
What's the weather like?
¿Que tiempo hace?
Buy from me!
¡Comprame!
to the right
a la derecha
to the left
a la izquierda
Continue straight ahead.
Siga derecho.
I don't understand.
No entiendo.
more or less
más o menos
when?
¿cuando?
how?
¿como?
How's that again?
¿Como?
where?
¿donde?
What time does the next plane/bus/train leave for...?
¿A que hora sale el próximo avión/omnibús/trén para...?
where from?
¿de donde?
around there
para allá
around here
por aquí
It's hot/cold.
Hace calor/frío.

Around Town
airport
aeropuerto
bank
banco
block
cuadra
bus terminal
terminal terrestre
church
templo, catedral, iglesia
city
ciudád
embassy
embajada
exchange house
casa de cambio
police
policía
post office
correo
railway station
estación de ferrocarril
town square
plaza

Directions
downhill
para abajo
uphill
para arriba
here
aquí
there
allí

People
son/daughter
hijo/a
husband/wife
marido/esposa
Indian/subsistence farmer
campesina (female) or *campesino* (male) (or *chola/o* (female/male) – if they live in the city – but never *indio*)
mother/father
madre/padre
people
la gente

Weather

rain
  lluvia
snow
  nieve
wind
  viento

Time & Dates

What time is it?
  ¿Que hora es? or *¿Que horas son?*
It is one o'clock.
  Es la una.
It is two o'clock.
  Son las dos.
midnight
  medianoche
noon
  mediodía
in the afternoon
  de la tarde
in the morning
  de la mañana
at night
  de la noche
half past two
  dos y media
quarter past two
  dos y cuarto
two twenty-five
  dos con veinticinco minutos
twenty to two
  veinte para las dos

Sunday	*domingo*
Monday	*lunes*
Tuesday	*martes*
Wednesday	*miércoles*
Thursday	*jueves*
Friday	*viernes*
Saturday	*sábado*

spring	*primavera*
summer	*verano*
autumn	*otoño*
winter	*invierno*

today	*hoy*
tomorrow	*mañana*
yesterday	*ayer*

Numbers

1	*uno*
2	*dos*
3	*tres*
4	*cuatro*
5	*cinco*
6	*seis*
7	*siete*
8	*ocho*
9	*nueve*
10	*diéz*
11	*once*
12	*doce*
13	*trece*
14	*catorce*
15	*quince*
16	*dieciseis*
17	*diecisiete*
18	*dieciocho*
19	*diecinueve*
20	*veinte*
21	*veintiuno*
30	*treinta*
40	*cuarenta*
50	*cincuenta*
60	*sesenta*
70	*setenta*
80	*ochenta*
90	*noventa*
100	*cién (to)*
101	*ciento uno*
200	*doscientos*
201	*doscientos uno*
300	*trescientos*
400	*quatrocientos*
500	*quinientos*
600	*seiscientos*
700	*setecientos*
800	*ochocientos*
900	*novecientos*
1000	*mil*
100,000	*cien mil*
one million	*un millón*

Aymará & Quechua

For your interest, we have included a list of Quechua and Aymará words and phrases. The grammar and pronunciation of these languages are quite difficult for native English speakers. If you're serious about learning them, or will be spending a lot of time in remote areas, you should look around in La Paz for a good course.

Dictionaries and phrasebooks are available through Los Amigos del Libro and larger bookstores in La Paz, but a fairly sound knowledge of Spanish will be needed to use them. Lonely Planet's *Quechua Phrasebook* is primarily for travellers to Peru, but will also be of use in the Bolivian highlands. It provides useful phrases and vocabulary in the Cuzco dialect.

Pronunciation of the following words and phrases will be similar to the way they would be pronounced in Spanish. Some consonants need to be delivered explosively but you'll have to listen to get the hang of it. An apostrophe is a glottal stop (the 'sound' in the middle of 'oh-oh!').

Aymará & Quechua: Some Useful Words & Phrases

English	Aymará	Quechua
be	*ucanquir*	*kaskai*
cheap	*pisitaqui*	*pisillapa'g*
condor	*malku*	*cóndor*
distant	*haya*	*caru*
downhill	*aynacha*	*uray*
father	*auqui*	*tata*
food	*manka*	*mikíuy*
friend	*kgochu*	*kgochu*
give	*churaña*	*koi*
go (travel)	*saraña*	*purina*
grandfather	*achachila*	*awicho- machu*
grandmother	*hacha-mama*	*paya*
hello!	*laphi!*	*raphi!*
house	*uta*	*huasi*
I	*Haya*	*Ñoka*
learn	*yatiña*	*yachaska*
llama	*yama-karhua*	*karhua*
lodging	*korpa*	*pascana*
man	*chacha*	*k'gari*
miner	*koyiri*	*koya'g*
moon	*pha'gsi*	*kiya*
mother	*taica*	*mama*
near	*maka*	*kailla*
no	*janiwa*	*mana*
river	*jawira*	*mayu*
ruins	*champir*	*champir*
snowy peak	*kollu*	*riti-orko*
sun	*yinti*	*inti*
teacher	*yatichiri*	*yachachi'g*
thirst	*phara*	*chchaqui*
to work	*irnakaña*	*lank'ana*
trail	*tapu*	*chakiñan*
very near	*hakítaqui*	*kaillitalla*
water	*uma*	*yacu*
when?	*cunapacha?*	*haiká'g?*
woman	*warmi*	*warmi*

yes	*jisa*	*ari*
you	*huma*	*khan*
young	*wuayna*	*huayna*

Where is...?	*Kaukasa...?*	*Maypi...?*
to the left	*chchekaru*	*lokeman*
to the right	*cupiru*	*pañaman*
How do you say...?	*Cun sañasa uca'ha...?*	*Imainata nincha chaita...?*
It is called...	*Ucan sutipa'h...*	*Chaipa'g sutin'ha...*
Please repeat.	*Uastata sita.*	*Ua'manta niway.*
It's a pleasure.	*Take chuima'hampi.*	*Tucuy sokoywan.*
What does that mean?	*Cuna sañasa muniucha'ha?*	*Imata'nita munanchai'ja?*
I don't know.	*Janiwa yatkti.*	*Mana yachanichu.*
I am hungry.	*Mankatawa hiu'ta.*	*Yarkaimanta wañusianiña.*
How much?	*K'gauka?*	*Maik'ata'g?*

Numbers

	Aymará	Quechua
1	*maya*	*u'*
2	*paya*	*iskai*
3	*quimsa*	*quinsa*
4	*pusi*	*tahua*
5	*pesca*	*phiska*
6	*zo'hta*	*so'gta*
7	*pakalko*	*khanchis*
8	*quimsakalko*	*pusa'g*
9	*yatunca*	*iskon*
10	*tunca*	*chunca*
11	*tuncamayani*	*chunca u'niyo'g*
12	*tuncapayani*	*chunca iskai'niyo'g*
13	*tuncaquimsani*	*chunca quinsa'niyo'g*
14	*tuncapusini*	*chunca tahua'yo'g*
15	*tuncapescani*	*chunca phiska'niyo'g*
16	*tunca zo'htani*	*chunca so'gta'niyo'g*
17	*tuncapakalkoni*	*chunca khanchisniyo'g*
18	*tunca quimsalalkoni*	*chunca pusa'gniyo'g*
19	*tunca yatuncani*	*chunca iskoniyo'g*
20	*pa tunka*	*iskai chunca*
21	*pa tunk mayani*	*iskai chunca u'niyo'g*
30	*quimsa tunca*	*quinsa chunca*
40	*pusi tunca*	*tahua chunca*
50	*pesca tunca*	*phiska chunca*
60	*zo'hta tunca*	*so'gta chunca*
70	*pakalka tunca*	*khanchi chunca*
80	*quimsakalko tunca*	*pusa'g chunca*
90	*yatunk tunca*	*iskon chunca*
100	*pataca*	*pacha'g*
101	*pataca mayani*	*pach'u'niyo'g*
200	*papataca*	*iskaipacha'*
201	papataca mayani	*iskaipacha'u'niyo'g*

300	*quimsapataca*	*quinsapacha'*
400	*pusipataca*	*tahuapacha'*
500	*pescapataca*	*phiskapacha'*
600	*zo'htapataca*	*so'gtapacha'*
700	*pakalkapataca*	*khanchispacha'*
800	*quimsakalkopataca*	*pusa'pacha'*
900	*yatuncapataca*	*iskonpacha'*
1000	*waranka*	*huaranca*
100,000	*pataca waranka*	*pacha'g-huaranca*
one million	*mapacha'*	*hunu*

Contemporary Craft Design

Facts for the Visitor

VISAS & EMBASSIES

Visa requirements for Bolivia change with astonishing frequency. Currently, citizens of the UK, Scandinavian countries (including Finland and Iceland), Argentina, Austria, Ecuador, Israel, Switzerland, Uruguay and the EC countries (except France, the Benelux countries and Portugal) do not require visas for stays of up to 90 days. Citizens of the USA, France, Belgium, Netherlands, Luxembourg, Portugal and most other non-Communist and non-Middle Eastern countries are granted stays of 30 days without a visa. At the present time, Canadians, Australians, New Zealanders, South Africans, Brazilians, Chileans and Bangladeshis require visas issued by Bolivian consulates either in their home countries or in neighbouring South American countries.

In addition to a visa, citizens of many Middle Eastern, Asian and Communist countries (including South Korea, Malaysia, Singapore, Thailand and Pakistan) officially require 'personal permission' by cable from the Bolivian Ministry of Foreign Affairs before a visa will be issued. Further information is available from Bolivian consulates and embassies.

Officially, everyone entering Bolivia requires proof of onward transport and sufficient funds for the intended length of stay, but in practice, officials rarely scrutinise these items.

Minors under 18 must be accompanied by their parents. Those travelling with only one parent may be required to produce a notarised letter from the parent not accompanying them to Bolivia, which grants permission to travel and guarantees financial responsibility. An official-looking statement that the missing parent is deceased should obviate this requirement.

Those travelling on business are required to obtain a visa. To apply, you'll need a passport, letter of intent and a financial guarantee from your employer. A business visa costs US$50 and is valid for a visit of 90 days.

Officially, your passport must be valid for one year beyond your date of entry into the country. Most border immigration officials will give only 30-day entrance stamps but lengths of stay may be extended at immigration offices in major cities. The fee at the time of writing was US$70, but travellers have reported that the fee is flexible, and in Sucre, extensions have been granted free of charge.

Diplomatic, official, student and missionary visas are officially issued free of charge. Permanent residence and work visas are also available through consulates abroad, but be prepared for a complex stream of paperwork and expenditure.

Bolivian Embassies & Consulates

Bolivian diplomatic representation can be found in the following countries:

Australia/New Zealand
  Bolivian Consulate, Suite 517, 5th floor, Pennys Bldg, 210 Queen St (GPO Box 53), Brisbane, 4000 (☎ (07) 221-1606)
Canada
  Bolivian Embassy, 17 Metcalfe St, Suite 608, Ottawa, Ontario K1P 426
France
  Consulate General of Bolivia, 12 Ave du Président Kennedy, 75016 Paris
UK
  Embassy of Bolivia, 106 Eaton Square, London SW1W 9AD (☎ (071) 235-4255)
USA
  Consulate General of Bolivia, 211 E 43rd St, Room 802, New York, NY 10017
  Bolivian Embassy, 3014 Massachusetts Ave, NW, Washington, DC 20008
  Consulate of Bolivia, 870 Market St, San Francisco, CA

Foreign Embassies in Bolivia

Many foreign embassies and consulates are located in La Paz. See the La Paz chapter for a comprehensive list.

Visas for Adjoining Countries Visas for Chile, Peru, Brazil, Paraguay, Argentina and other South American countries may be obtained at consulates in most large Bolivian cities and in many smaller towns near frontiers. For details and addresses, see individual city and town listings.

DOCUMENTS

Anyone entering Bolivia from an area where yellow fever is prevalent, which is usually interpreted as Sub-Saharan Africa, some parts of Central America, the Caribbean and the Guianas, must carry a certificate of yellow fever vaccination. Officially, a yellow fever certificate is also required for travel in Santa Cruz Department, although visitors to this area are rarely asked to produce one. Travellers planning to enter Brazil from Bolivia are also supposed to carry a yellow fever certificate, but Brazilian border checks are sporadic.

Personal documents (passports, visas, *cédulas* (identification cards), etc) must be carried at all times to avoid fines during police checks and several lost hours while paperwork is shuffled at the police station. This is strictly enforced in lowland regions – especially Santa Cruz – where drug trafficking is rife.

MONEY

Bolivia's unit of currency is the boliviano, divided into 100 centavos. 'Every Bolivian is a millionaire', one Paceño (a resident of La Paz) told me before six zeros were lopped off the massively inflated peso denomination on 1 January 1987. Currently, Bolivia enjoys South America's lowest inflation rate, which at the time of writing was running at about 15%.

Currency

Bolivianos come in two, five, 10, 20, 50, 100 and 200 denomination notes, two, five, 10, 20 and 50 centavos, and one boliviano coins. Bolivian currency is practically worthless outside Bolivia, so don't change more than you'll need.

Exchange Rates

Exchange rates as at August 1992 were as follows:

US$1	=	B4.02
UK£1	=	B7.72
A$1	=	B2.89
NZ$1	=	B2.17
C$1	=	B3.38
DM1	=	B2.74
FFr1	=	B.809
SwFr1	=	B3.04
Y100	=	B3.19
BraCz1000	=	B.913
Arg$1	=	B3.95
Per Int 1	=	B3.04
Chil$100	=	B.40

Changing Money

The black market in currency was abolished in late 1985 and since the boliviano now floats more or less according to its actual value, a parallel market remains unnecessary.

Although currencies of neighbouring countries may be exchanged in border areas, the US dollar is the only foreign currency accepted throughout Bolivia. American Express seem to be the most popular travellers' cheques, but other brands shouldn't cause any problems.

As a rule, Bolivian banks do not exchange money, but in La Paz, Cochabamba, Santa Cruz and Sucre you'll find *casas de cambio* (exchange houses) that will change notes and travellers' cheques. If you're travelling further afield, don't count on being able to exchange travellers' cheques; carry enough cash to get you back to one of these cities.

Often, good rates for cash US dollars will be found at travel agencies, jewellery and appliance stores, bookshops, pharmacies and any business that carries on trade with the USA. Since they must wait at least 20 business days to receive cash for travellers' cheques, however, these businesses probably won't exchange them unless they're particularly short of foreign exchange. Those that do change travellers' cheques will nor-

mally offer 5 to 10% less than for cash. In La Paz and Cochabamba, several merchants and casas de cambio exchange travellers' cheques for cash US dollars, but they take a 1 to 3% commission.

If you'd like to purchase travellers' cheques in Bolivia, try Citibank at 16 de Julio 1434 in La Paz. For up to US$1000 in cheques, they charge US$10 commission. American Express (Magri Turismo) in La Paz sells cheques for 1% commission, payable in cash or with an American Express card.

Casas de Cambio usually open around 9 am and close at 6 pm, with a two to three hour lunch break beginning at noon. Hotels and restaurants rarely accept travellers' cheques. Street changers provide more or less round-the-clock exchange services, but they offer only slightly higher rates than everyone else.

I found street money changers easy to deal with. There is an established way of changing money: first, tell them how much you want to change. They will then tell you the rate, which will always be slightly higher than in hotels and casas de cambio. If you agree, they count out the money in their hand. You then tell them that you don't want anything larger than B10 notes (authors' note: you can accept larger notes but change for anything larger than B10 or B20 notes may be hard to come by) and they re-count. They give you the money and then you count it out yourself. Then, and only then, do you produce the dollar notes from your pocket, which you count out in front of them. They then count the dollars and both of you put your respective lots of money away. This routine is acceptable to both and reduces the risks in dealing on the street. This should be done only in daylight as it is so easy to mix up the values of the notes.

T B Burgess, UK

Credit Cards

Major cards, such as VISA, MasterCard and American Express, may be used in larger cities at first-rate hotels, restaurants and tour agencies.

With travellers' cheques expensive and sometimes difficult to change, there's a good case for carrying a VISA card. VISA cash withdrawals of up to US$300 per day are available in 20 minutes with no commission and a minimum of hassle from the Banco de Santa Cruz in La Paz, Sucre, Cochabamba and Santa Cruz. Banco Mercantil offers similar services without commission, as does Banco Nacional de Bolivia. Banco de La Paz charges 1.75% commission on cash draws.

Notes & Change

Boliviano notes with tiny pieces missing, repaired with opaque tape, sewed with thread or even reconstructed from several other notes, are quite common and in many places, especially La Paz and Oruro, vendors and consumers engage in a battle of wits over these notes. Vendors employ sneaky methods of giving them as change, particularly to foreigners and inattentive Bolivians, so it's wise to check your change and return any mangled bills, or you'll have to devise an equally sneaky method of getting another vendor to accept them.

Change is also a problem: nobody has it. If the amount due you is small, you may receive your change in boiled sweets or other token items, but just *try* to use a B10 or larger note to buy a B2 bottle of soda! Vendors become flustered at the sight of high denomination notes and have to go begging change from other vendors, which no one wants to part with. The vendor invariably returns defeated and reports that there is no change. You've derailed the system and if you've already consumed the product you're purchasing, settle in for a wait while the vendor combs the city in search of change.

Costs

Overall, prices for food, services, hotels and transportation are slightly higher than in other Andean Republics, but lower than in Brazil, Argentina and Uruguay. When converted to US dollars, prices for most items, including lodging, are actually lower than they were in the late 1980s.

Thanks to Bolivia's whopping import duty on consumer goods produced outside the country, automobiles, electronics and camera equipment, and film and books from outside cost at least twice what they would in Europe or North America. For example, a paperback novel costs US$10 to US$12, a box of corn flakes up to US$8, and non-black market electronics equipment is astronomical.

Another practice you may run across, especially in cities, is 'gringo pricing', a deliberate overcharging of foreigners. An attitude somewhere between acceptance and paranoia is advised. If you want to avoid an unpleasant scene, agree on food, accommodation and transport prices before the goods or services are consumed.

Tipping

Except in four and five-star hotels and exclusive restaurants or clubs, tipping is uncommon. Most formal restaurants will add a service charge of 10% to your bill anyway, so further tipping is unnecessary. As a rule, bus and taxi drivers are not tipped.

Bargaining

In Bolivia, as in most of Latin America, few prices are fixed. Almost everything is negotiable, not only for *artesanía* (local handicrafts), but also for food, transport and even lodging. Expect to pay 80 to 85% of what is initially quoted. Bolivians expect to haggle over prices and so-called 'gringo pricing' is caused by foreigners who pay the first price named, perhaps due to guilty feelings about the amount of cash they have on hand relative to the local economy.

Bolivians don't usually understand this sort of thinking and imagine it is the result of ignorance. So don't worry about shortchanging the merchants; they have a price below which they will not sell and it's your job to discover what that price is. Furthermore, tourists who voluntarily pay higher than market value actually cause increases in the market price and thereby put some items out of reach for locals, who generally have considerably less disposable cash.

WHEN TO GO

Bolivia is in the southern hemisphere, so

winter lasts from May to October and summer from November to April. The most important thing to remember is that the weather is generally wet in the summer and dry in the winter!

On the Altiplano, dress as you would in Scotland or southern New Zealand in the respective season. In the highland valleys, the climate is similar to that of Madrid, Los Angeles or Perth, but a little cooler and with the seasons reversed; that is, summer in those cities corresponds to winter in Cochabamba or Sucre and vice versa. The humid lowlands experience a climate similar to that of Miami or Darwin and the wet season can be utterly miserable with mud, heat, bugs and relentless tropical downpours.

WHAT TO BRING

For those travellers who always manage to wind up with too many haphazardly packed kgs, the following guidelines may help you with your preparations:

Bags

The type of luggage you should carry will depend largely upon your style of travel. If you prefer prearranged tours and finer hotels, and consistently use taxis around town, traditional but strong suitcases or shoulder bags will work fine.

If you're planning to travel more casually, an internal frame backpack or a pack that zips into a suitcase would be more suitable because you will probably be carrying it for longer distances. The most important factors to consider are comfort, strength, weight and manageability. A flimsy, bulky or awkward piece of luggage will quickly become a nightmare of repairs, back pains and bodily contortions.

Essentials

As always, the most important advice is to travel light: only take along that which is indispensable. Unfortunately, everyone has a different idea about what indispensable means and when it comes to travelling light, we're not the best authorities. With what we considered only the bare essentials, our packs weighed nearly 30 kg each! We aren't sure how they got that way, but there were times when we wished they'd be stolen. To help you try to avoid this and related emotions, the following is a checklist of items which are either difficult to obtain in Bolivia or will probably be used often enough to justify their weight throughout the duration of your trip.

- First-aid kit (refer to Health section for specifics)
- Malaria tablets
- Travel alarm clock
- Small torch and extra batteries
- Water bottle – aluminium is better than plastic because it doesn't flavour the water or allow light to pass through and stimulate the growth of bacteria
- Water purification tablets – iodine-based if possible since non-iodine tablets don't kill amoebas
- Swiss Army-type pocketknife with bottle opener, corkscrew, scissors, can opener, etc
- Spare glasses or contact lenses and a copy of optical prescription
- Towel
- Flip-flops (thongs) – for dealing with dodgy Bolivian plumbing
- Clothesline – two or three metres of cord is useful for all sorts of things
- Sewing kit
- Writing implements – few South American pens will function on airmail paper
- Spanish/English dictionary and possibly Quechua and Latin American Spanish phrasebooks (Lonely Planet publishes phrasebooks with handy words and phrases in both these languages)
- Contraceptives
- Tampons – napkins are available everywhere, but tampons are scarce and are quite expensive
- Any prescription medications you normally take

Amazon Basin Essentials

If you're doing a jungle trip in the lowlands, the following items should be included in your checklist: two sets of clothing, one for slogging through the forests, rivers and mud and an extra set to keep dry and wear in camp; extra shoes, also to keep dry; plastic bags for wet gear, shoes and other items which should never get wet; binoculars; camera and telephoto lens; gaiters; strong torch for night walks and animal spotting; *strong* insect repellent; sleeping bag; towel; swimming costume; long-sleeved shirt for cool and/or bug-infested evenings; sunscreen; hat; and a large plastic bag for rubbish.

Clothing

Without going completely overboard and carrying your entire wardrobe around in your pack, you do need to be reasonably prepared for the extremes of Bolivia's climate. The minimum we'd recommend for the cold is a warm jacket suitable for freezing temperatures, several pairs of warm wool or polypropylene socks, a fuzzy pullover, a pair of wool gloves and a hat with ear coverings (the last three items may be purchased in Bolivia for good prices). Thermal underwear will be welcome at night and some Gore-Tex rain gear will come in handy if you're visiting during the wet season or hiking in the mountains.

If you'll be travelling in the lowlands, two sleeveless shirts, a pair of thongs or sandals and shorts will be about all you'll need. For women who don't want to attract a lot of annoying attention, however, the shorts should be replaced by a light skirt or dress. There is still a prejudice against women wearing shorts in Bolivia, especially in the Andes and highland valleys, but men will encounter no social restrictions regarding dress.

In addition, you'll need two pairs of trousers – one to wash and one to wear; a long-sleeve, lightweight shirt to wear under itchy woollen or alpaca sweaters; underwear and socks; swimming gear – there are lots of waterfalls and hot springs; one pair of sneakers or comfortable walking shoes; and perhaps even a nicer set of clothing for evenings out or other occasions.

If you don't want to carry a pack full of clothing in preparation for all the variables in climate, it's not difficult to find fairly inexpensive clothing in major Bolivian cities. The average Bolivian is smaller than the average foreigner, however, and those who wear extreme sizes may run into difficulties. Even in tourist shops, larger shoe and clothing sizes, as well as children's pullovers and gloves, are hard to come by.

Books

You may want to carry any novels or guidebooks you'll be needing; English language books and guides are scarce and expensive in Bolivia. To keep weight down, many travellers just rip out (no, we won't be offended) or photocopy sections of guidebooks covering the areas they plan to visit.

For long plane and boat rides, you may want to carry a thick paperback. When you're finished, it can be easily traded with other travellers, and those who've resorted to reading *Condorito* comic books will probably bless you. If you're carrying an address book, be sure it's not the only copy in existence. This would be a devastating item to lose!

Photos

Lastly, think about bringing some photos of your friends and family. Bolivians are always anxious to share their family album with visitors and will want to see yours, too. Some postcards of your city or country would also be helpful in describing your home to locals and fellow travellers alike.

TOURIST OFFICES

Although Bolivia's appeal should not be underestimated, much of its attraction lies in the fact that it has been largely ignored by large-scale tourism. Although this seems to be changing, the Bolivian tourist industry is still in its formative stages, and the government hasn't committed its resources to developing and touting the country's numerous natural and cultural attractions.

The cities of La Paz, Oruro, Cochabamba, Sucre, Tarija, Potosí, Santa Cruz and Trinidad all have offices of the Dirección Nacional de Turismo (Dinatur), the successor to the Instituto Boliviano de Turismo (IBT), whose name still appears on many offices and publications. These offices range in quality from helpful to worthless, but most will at least provide street plans of their respective city and can answer simple questions about local transport and attractions. The offices in La Paz, Santa Cruz and Cochabamba are especially worth visiting.

In this book, tourist office locations are marked on city maps where applicable, but they do tend to move around. Opening hours are officially 9 am to noon and 2 to 6 pm, but as with many Bolivian government operations, the functioning is left largely to the whims of employees, so actual hours of operation will vary.

USEFUL ORGANISATIONS

One of the most useful resources for visitors to South America is the South American Explorers Club, 126 Indian Creek Rd, Ithaca, NY 14850, USA. This organisation provides services, information and support to travellers, scientific researchers, mountaineers and explorers; sells a wide range of books, guides and maps for South America; and publishes a quarterly journal and a mail order catalogue. The club maintains clubhouses in the following South American countries: Ecuador (☎ 566076) at Toledo 1254, Apartado 21-431, Eloy Alfaro, Quito; and Peru (☎ 314480) at República de Portugal 146, Casilla 3714, Lima 100. Considering the massive package of benefits offered, membership is quite a bargain.

Disabled travellers in the USA might like to contact the Society for the Advancement of Travel for the Handicapped (☎ (718) 858-5483), 26 Court St, Brooklyn, New York, NY 11242. In the UK, a useful contact is the Royal Association for Disability & Rehabilitation (☎ (071) 242-3882), 25 Mortimer St, London W1N 8AB.

For information about Bolivia's nascent youth hostel organisation, Asociación Boliviana de Albergues Juveniles, contact Valmar Tours (☎ 361076), Edificio Alborada, Piso 1, Oficina 105, Juan de la Riva 1406, La Paz.

BUSINESS HOURS & HOLIDAYS

Even restaurants which serve breakfast don't normally roll up their aluminium doors until 9 or 9.30 am, so don't bother wandering the streets in search of a caffeine fix any earlier than that. Shops, travel agencies and financial institutions will likewise open around 9 or 10 am. If you want to eat or shop before

those hours, you'll have to go to the street markets where dribbles of activity begin as early as 6 am.

At noon, cities virtually close down, with the exception of markets and restaurants serving lunch-hour crowds. The afternoon resurrection begins at around 2 pm but some businesses remain closed until as late as 4 pm, and then remain open until at least 8 or 9 pm. Many bars and restaurants close at 10 pm, although some serve until midnight.

On Saturdays, shops, services and even some eateries close down at noon but street markets remain open until mid-afternoon at least, and often into the evening. On Sundays, nearly everything remains dead until evening.

Post offices are open from 9 am (8.30 am for some services) to noon and 2.30 to 7 pm. Banks generally open from 9 to 11.30 am and 2.30 to 5 pm.

Public Holidays

Bolivian Public holidays include: New Year's Day (1 January); Carnival (February/March); Semana Santa (Easter Week: March/April); Labour Day (1 May); Corpus Christi (May); Independence Days (5-7 August); Columbus Day (12 October); All-Souls' Day or Día de los Muertos (2 November); and Christmas (25 December).

In addition, each department has its own holiday: La Paz (16 July); Tarija (15 April); Cochabamba (14 September); Santa Cruz (24 September); Pando (24 September); Beni (18 November); Oruro (22 February); Chuquisaca (25 May).

CULTURAL EVENTS

Bolivian fiestas are invariably of religious or political origin, normally commemorating a Christian or Indian saint or god, or a political event such as a battle or revolution. They typically include lots of folk music, dancing, processions, food, alcohol, ritual and general unrestrained behaviour. Water balloons (tourists are especially vulnerable!), fireworks and brass bands figure prominently.

Fiestas can be lots of fun and anyone who wants to experience Bolivian culture will want to attend at least one. Bolivian towns stage fiestas whenever an excuse arises, so you'll probably be able to catch two or three during even a short visit to the country.

The following is a partial list of the major Bolivian festivals, but the dates given are subject to change, so check before going too far out of your way to attend one.

6 January
Día de Reyes; the Día de Reyes or 'Kings' Day' is celebrated as the day the three wise kings visited the baby Jesus after his birth. The largest celebrations are in Reyes (Beni); Sucre; Tarija; and rural villages in Oruro, Cochabamba and Potosí departments.

24 January
Alasitas Fair, or Festival of Abundance; this dates from Inca times and is dedicated to Ekeko, the little household god of abundance. It's celebrated in La Paz.

February (first week)
Fiesta de la Virgen de Candelaria; this week-long festival is held in honour of the Virgin of Candelaria in Aiquile (Cochabamba); Samaipata (Santa Cruz); Angostura (Tarija) and Challa-pampa (Oruro). The biggest celebration, however, is at Copacabana in La Paz Department.

February-March (week before Lent)
Carnival; celebrations are held nationwide, but the most spectacular event is *La Diablada*, which is staged in Oruro.

March (date varies)
Fiesta de la Uva; this Tarija festival is dedicated to grapes and wine and the spirits derived from them.

March (2nd Sunday)
Phujllay; the name of this festival held in Tarabuco (Sucre) means 'play' in Quechua. Phujllay (pronounced 'POOKH-yai') commemorates the Battle of Lumbati, and is one of Bolivia's major festivals.

March-April
Semana Santa; Holy Week activities take place nationwide in either March or April. One of the most impressive is the Good Friday fiesta in Copacabana, when hundreds of pilgrims walk from La Paz to Copacabana.

15 & 16 April
Efemérides de Tarija & Rodeo Chapaco; Tarija's town anniversary celebrations commemorating the battle of La Tablada culminate in a rodeo recalling the city's gaucho and Argentine connections.

3 May
Fiesta de la Cruz; this fiesta commemorates the cross on which Christ was crucified. In Tarija, it's celebrated with 15 days of music, parades, and alcohol consumption. The fiesta is also held in Vallegrande (Santa Cruz), Cochabamba and Copacabana (La Paz).

25 May
Efemérides de Sucre; celebrates Sucre's 'first cry of independence in Latin America' in 1809.

27 May
Día de la Madre; Mothers' Day celebrations are held nationwide. In Cochabamba, the festivities are known as *Heroínas de la Coronilla* in honour of the women and children who defended their cities and homes in the battle of 1812.

May-June
Festividad de Nuestro Señor Jesús del Gran Poder; this animated festival, one of Bolivia's largest, is held in either May or June. It's dedicated to the 'great power of Jesus Christ', and is held in La Paz.

June (date varies)
Santísima Trinidad; the festival of the Holy Trinity takes place in Trinidad with music, dancing and a bullfight.

24 June
San Juan Batista; the festival of San Juan is held nationwide, but the largest bash takes place in Santa Cruz.

25 July
Fiesta de Santiago; the festival of Santiago is celebrated in Sipe-Sipe and Tarata (Cochabamba), Quime (La Paz) and Yamparaez (Chuquisaca) as well as other small municipalities around the country.

31 July
Fiesta del Santo Patrono de Moxos; this local festival in the unique Indian community of San Ignacio de Moxos is unique and highly worthwhile.

6 August
Independence Day Fiesta; excessive raging nationwide! The largest celebration, the *Virgen de Copacabana*, is held at Copacabana.

15-18 August
Virgen de Urcupiña; this festival, the largest held in Cochabamba Department, is staged at Quillacollo. A related celebration, the *Virgen de Chaguaya*, is held in Chaguaya (Tarija).

September (1st Sunday)
Fiesta de San Roque; although San Roque's feast day is 16 August, the wild Tarija celebration begins a couple of weeks later. Participants wear brightly coloured clothing, feathers and belts. San Roque is the patron saint of dogs, so canine revellers take part, too. The unique Chapaco music figures prominently.

8 September
Virgen de Guadalupe; festivals in honour of the

Virgin of Guadalupe are held at Viacha (La Paz), Sucre and Guadalupe (Santa Cruz).

14 September
Exaltación de la Santa Cruz; the largest festivities are held in Cochabamba which also celebrates its departmental anniversary on this day. Other sites include Sorata (La Paz), Potosí and Oruro.

October (1st week)
Virgen del Rosario; this celebration is held on different days in different locations, including Warnes (Santa Cruz), Tarata, Morochata and Quillacollo (Cochabamba), Tarabuco (Chuquisaca), and Viacha (La Paz) and Potosí.

1 & 2 November
Fiesta de Todos los Santos; cemetery visits and decoration of graves nationwide.

25 December
Christmas; naturally, Christmas is celebrated throughout Bolivia, but some of the most unique and colourful festivities take place in San Ignacio de Moxos (Beni) and Sucre.

POST & TELECOMMUNICATIONS

All major and minor cities have both ENTEL (Empresa Nacional de Telecomunicaciones) and post offices (Correos de Bolivia).

Post

Postcards *(postales)* to the rest of the Americas cost B.80. To Europe, they cost B1 and to anywhere else in the world they're B1.20. Airmail letters up to 10 grams cost B1 to the Americas, B1.20 to Europe and B1.40 to Australia and the rest of the world. Up to 20 grams, they're B1.40, B1.60 and B1.70 respectively. Express mail service to all overseas destinations costs US$20 for the first 500 grams and US$4 for each additional kg.

For B1 extra, any piece of mail to anywhere may be certified. Special precautions are taken to ensure that these items aren't lost or pilfered and even locals reckon it's worth the price. To destinations within Bolivia, Express Mail (Expreso) is available for an additional B1. It's best not to mail anything from small town post offices; sacks of mail have been known to lie around for months awaiting vehicles to carry them to larger postal centres.

Parcels Parcels (*encomiendas*) are a bit more tricky to send. Firstly, the unwrapped parcel must be taken to the customs office (*aduana*) for inspection. You'll have to wrap and seal the parcel in the presence of a customs official, so carry along a box, paper, tape, string and the address. Once the parcel is ready to mail, the customs official stamps it and it's ready for the post office.

There is sometimes a customs agent working in the post office, but in some cities, such as Oruro, the customs office is across town. The most straightforward procedures exist at the new main post office in La Paz, where onsite inspectors check the parcel, oversee the wrapping and point you toward the proper window for posting. It couldn't be easier.

A one-kg airmail parcel costs US$15 to any foreign destination in the Americas or Europe. Certification is recommended and costs an additional B1.

Sometimes, you'll have to present the parcel to a *revisor* who determines whether or not you've paid enough, which you usually haven't. As soon as the postal clerk and the revisor agree that the parcel bears sufficient postage, it will be accepted.

The chances of arrival of any posted parcel increase inversely in proportion to its value and the number of 'inspections' to which it is subjected. In other words, although Bolivia's postal system is relatively reliable, don't post anything you can't risk losing.

Receiving Mail General delivery services in Bolivia are called *poste restante*, also known as *lista de correos*. Letters should include the name of the addressee followed by 'Poste Restante, Correo Central' and the name of the city and country. As many towns in different departments have the same name, if the letter is destined for a small town or village, it's wise to include the department name, as well. There's a San Ignacio in both Beni and Santa Cruz departments, for example, and a Santa Ana in Beni and La Paz. Poste Restante letters will be delivered to the city's main post office and will be held

for 90 days, more or less, before being returned to the sender. Recipients must present a passport when collecting post.

Names in Bolivia, as is the case in all Spanish-speaking countries, are constructed of any number of given and acquired names followed by the father's family name and the mother's maiden name. The *apellido*, or surname, is therefore not the 'last' name used. This can lead to confusion in receiving mail filed or listed alphabetically.

For instance, a letter to the president of Bolivia, Jaime Paz Zamora, would be filed under 'P' for 'Paz'. Similarly, a letter addressed to Mary Ann Smith may well wind up in the 'A' pigeonhole. Given the way things tend to work, however, Mary would be wise to check under 'M' and 'S', as well. Even capitalising and underlining the surname doesn't always alleviate the confusion, but it may help.

In addition to poste restante, mail may also be received at an American Express agency or representative office. You will have to show your passport and some proof that you're an American Express customer – a few travellers' cheques or an American Express card will suffice. In La Paz, the representative is Magri Turismo Limitada (☎ 341201) at Avenida 16 de Julio 149, Piso 5 Edificio Avenida, La Paz, Bolivia. Limited English is spoken in this office.

Some, but not all, consulates and embassies will receive and hold mail for citizens of their home country, so check beforehand. The Netherlands, Norway, Germany, Canada, the USA, France and Austria currently provide this service. Australia and New Zealand are represented in Bolivia by the UK Consulate, which will not receive mail.

Receiving Parcels If you're having anything shipped to you in Bolivia, it's helpful to declare the lowest possible value at the point of origin. When you go to pick up the package, you'll find yourself in a quagmire of muddled red tape and owing an import duty of up to 100% of the item's declared value.

Telephones

Local Telephone Calls Don't waste your time searching for public telephone boxes on the streets: we've seen only two or three in the entire country. Local calls can be made from ENTEL offices and cost just a few centavos. Old peso coins are sold as *fichas*, or tokens, and are used in public pay telephones.

Alternatively, small street kiosks are often equipped with telephones which may be used for brief local calls. These will cost from B.50 to B1. Hotels and restaurants sometimes allow the public to use their telephones; expect to pay around B.50 for a local call.

International Calls Bolivia's country code is 591. From private telephones, normal or reverse charge international calls can be made by phoning the International Operator (☎ 356700, La Paz) and providing the country code, area or city code and the phone number desired. The code to access an international line is 00. To reverse the charges, explain that the call is *por cobrar*. ENTEL offices will not accept reverse charge calls.

To make an international call from an ENTEL office, secure a call request form and fill out the pertinent information detailing the city, country, person and number you wish to call. You must leave your passport or a deposit at the desk while the call is being made. ENTEL will then make the connection and announce your name when it's ready for you to talk. A three-minute telephone call to North America will cost around US$6 station-to-station and US$8 person-to-person. To Europe and the rest of the world, you'll pay at least 30% more.

Long-distance calls to locations within Bolivia are inexpensive and can be made from ENTEL offices in less than 10 minutes. International calls no longer need to be routed through La Paz, so delays are less prevalent than just a couple of years ago. In smaller towns, waits may be longer.

Fax

ENTEL offices in most major Bolivian cities have a fax desk, and although the service is slow and still has some rough edges, it works remarkably better than one would expect. Fax charges to Europe are B14.70 per minute; to the USA, B11.30 per minute; to Canada, B13.50 per minute; and to Australia or New Zealand, B19.70 per minute.

Faxes may be received at public fax numbers in most cities. If the document includes the name, address and telephone number of the recipient's hotel, ENTEL will deliver the fax free of charge! In this book, public fax numbers are included under Post and Telecommunications in the Information section for the respective city.

TIME

Bolivian time is four hours behind Greenwich Mean Time. When it's noon in La Paz, it's 4 pm in London, 11 am in New York, 8 am in San Francisco, 4 am the following day in Auckland and 2 am the following day in Sydney and Melbourne.

Those impressive-looking world clocks in the La Paz ENTEL office should probably be ignored; they're not very convincing when they claim that it's simultaneously 12.15 pm in La Paz and 7.40 am in New York!

ELECTRICITY

Bolivia uses a standard current of 220 volts at 50 cycles except in La Paz and a few selected locations in Potosí which use 110 volts at 50 cycles. Ask before you plug in.

In some small towns like Copacabana and Camiri, demand for power exceeds the power stations' ability to supply it, so power outages are frequent and, in some places, are even scheduled during hours of high usage. In some cities, the water and power are routinely turned off between midnight and 5 am, so if you're a night owl, have a torch on hand.

WEIGHTS & MEASURES

Like the rest of South America, Bolivia uses the metric system. For converting between metric and imperial units, refer to the table at the back of this book.

BOOKS & MAPS

English, German and some French-language books are available from Los Amigos del Libro, which has outlets in La Paz and Cochabamba. They tend to be quite pricey, but have a good selection of popular paperbacks, guidebooks, dictionaries and histories, as well as glossy coffee-table books dealing with the anthropology, archaeology and scenery of Bolivia.

The bookshop at El Alto Airport in La Paz also sells guides and souvenir books, but at staggering prices which are not negotiable. Some bookshops have a shelf or a box of used English-language paperbacks stashed away in a corner. Even if you don't find them displayed, it's worth asking. *Newsweek* and *Time* are available at kiosks and bookshops in La Paz and other large cities like Santa Cruz and Cochabamba.

If you read Spanish, classic literature and popular novels are also available at Los Amigos del Libro and similar shops. The majority of *librerías* (bookshops) and street sellers, however, mainly sell pulpy local publications, comics and school texts.

If you'd like to read more about Bolivia and related topics, the following list may help:

Fiction

At Play in the Fields of the Lord, Peter Mathiessen; a fictional work by the man who has become well known to world-roaming travellers. It's a strong and well-written tale of missionaries in the Amazon rainforests.

One Hundred Years of Solitude, Gabriél Garcia Marquez (Picador, 1978); the Nobel Prize-winning author's classic tale of South American life.

The Bridge of San Luis Rey, Thornton Wilder (Grosset & Dunlap, 1927); this fiction classic takes place in Peru, but deals with characters and ideals of the Andes.

The Lost World, Sir Arthur Conan Doyle (Buccaneer Books, 1977, originally published 1912); rollicking science-fiction tale of a prehistoric world in the rainforested mountains of South America. It was inspired by tales from Colonel Fawcett's survey of the north-eastern Bolivian plateaux in the first decade of the 20th century.

History

Ché Guevara, Daniel James (Stein & Day, 1969); quite interesting, slightly right-leaning biography of the folk hero, with emphasis upon his activities and ultimate demise in Bolivia.

The Incredible Incas & Their Timeless Land, Loren McIntyre (National Geographic Society Press, 1975); easily digested account of Inca history and description of Inca lands in modern times by one of the last South American explorers. Typical informal 'Geographic' style and lots of colour photos and illustrations.

Kingdom of the Sun God – A History of the Andes & Their People, Ian Cameron; this illustrated history of the Andes covers pre-Inca, Inca, Colonial and modern developments in western South America.

Tales of Potosí, Bartolomé Arzáns de Orsua y Vela (Brown University Press, 1975); an anthology of stories about the city whose history reads more like fiction than fact. It offers a very good insight into colonial life in Bolivia.

Miners of Red Mountain, P Bakewell; this work is about the treasures and tragedies of Potosí's silver boom days. Although the book is now out of print, it should be available in libraries.

The History of Coca 'The Divine Plant of the Incas', W Golden Mortimer, MD (And/OR Press, 1974); everything you've ever wanted to know about the Andean wonder drug – and more. Originally published in 1901.

The Conquest of the Incas, John Hemming (Harcourt, Brace, Jovanovich, 1970); this book is the definitive work on the Spanish takeover of the well-established Inca Empire. A good companion book is John Hemming's and Edward Ranney's *Monuments of the Incas* with illustrations and explanations of major Inca sites.

Royal Commentaries of the Incas, Garsilaso de la Vega, 1539; this 16th-century work includes the history, growth and influence of the Inca Empire, as well as a first-hand account of its decline and demise.

Travelogue & Personal Narrative

In Quest of the Unicorn Bird by Oliver Greenfield (HB Michael Joseph, UK 1992); this simply written but appealing narrative traces the 19-year-old author's journey through Bolivia in search of the blue-horned curassow.

Exploration Fawcett by Colonel Percy Harrison Fawcett (Century, 1988); quirky travels of the unconventional explorer, including details of his term as a surveyor for the Bolivian government.

Wildlife of the Andes (formerly *Land Above the Clouds)*, Tony Morrison (None-such Press, 1988); a study of the land and wildlife of the Andes.

The Old Patagonia Express, Paul Theroux (Pocket Books, 1980); the tale of a train journey from Boston to Patagonia. Theroux takes a rather poor attitude toward budget travellers and doesn't really seem to enjoy his trip, but it's an interesting story.

The Incredible Voyage, Tristan Jones (Sheed Andrews & McNeel, Inc., 1977); includes narrative about several months' sailing and exploring on Lake Titicaca.

Sons of the Moon – A Journey in the Andes, Henry Shukman (Charles Scribner & Sons, 1989); this well-written account of a fairly ordinary journey from north-western Argentina, across the Bolivian Altiplano and on to Cuzco, Peru, includes superb observations of Altiplano cultures.

Passage through El Dorado, Jonathon Kandell (William Morrow & Company, 1984); this book describes a journalist's journey through the boom-and-bust country of the Amazon Basin. Interesting and well written, it flows along on an optimistic current that, with the benefit of hindsight, now seems sadly inappropriate for many areas, particularly Rondônia, Brazil. We do, however, dispute Kandell's assessment of the relatively small and beautiful Río Mamoré as a vast, uninteresting, 'main-stream Amazon' sort of waterway. Are we talking about the same river?

Journey along the Spine of the Andes, Christopher Portway (Oxford Illustrated Press, 1984); this book describes the author's travels in the Andes from Bolivia to Colombia.

The Cloud Forest, Peter Mathiessen (Collins Harill, 1960); while it's not all about Bolivia, this account of Mathiessen's 30,000-km journey across the South American wilderness from the Amazon to Terra del Fuego, is well word a read. The author is extraordinarily proficient at describing the environment.

The Saddest Pleasure: A Journey on Two Rivers, Moritz Thomsen (Graywolf Press, 1990); a highly recommended and competently written book – skip the sickly introduction – about the author's experiences in South America, including journeys around the Amazon region.

Let Me Speak, Domitila Barrios de Chungara; this is a Bolivian's compelling and touching account of life in the Siglo XX mine. It was originally published in Spanish as *Si Me Permite Hablar*.

We Eat the Mines and the Mines Eat Us, June Nash (Columbia University Press, 1979); an anthropologist's study of life and death in the Bolivian tin mines. Recommended.

Highways of the Sun – A Search for the Royal Roads of the Incas, Victor W von Hagen (Plata Press, 1975); this interesting treatise about a 1950's expedition along ancient Inca roads will prove fascinating for ruins buffs and those interested in pre-Columbian paving.

Lizzie – A Victorian Lady's Amazon Adventure, Tony Morrison, Ann Brown & Anne Rose (BBC Books, 1985); this tale, compiled partly from her letters, chronicles the journey of a Victorian lady, Lizzie Hessel, to the settlement of Colonia Orton in the Bolivian Amazon during the rubber boom. The book has been made into the BBC film production *Letters from Lizzie*.

Brazilian Adventure, Peter Fleming (Penguin, 1957); this is the story of the author's early 1930's expedition across the Mato Grosso and down to the Amazon to track down the missing explorer, Colonel Fawcett. All right, it's not about Bolivia, but this humorously well-written work is one of the best travel books around and Fleming's descriptions and impressions of the Brazilian Amazon are equally applicable to the Bolivian rainforests.

Ecology & the Amazon Region

Amazonia (1991); Loren McIntyre, the renowned explorer and photographer, records on film the gradual demise of the Amazon region and its original inhabitants. To learn more about McIntyre's many journeys in search of the source of the Amazon and his extraordinary psychic experiences with indigenous tribes, pick up a copy of *Amazon Beaming* (1991) by Petru Popescu.

Henry Walter Bates, Naturalist of the Amazons, George Woodcock (Faber & Faber, 1969); you may still be able to find secondhand copies of this fascinating account of Bates' many years spent in pursuit of plantlife during the mid-19th century.

Wizard of the Upper Amazon – the Story of Manuel Córdova-Ríos (Houghton Mifflin, 1975) and the sequel *Río Tigre and Beyond* by F Bruce Lamb; those interested in *yagé*, the hallucinogenic drug used by certain tribes of the upper Amazon, will find either of these worthwhile reading.

The Fate of the Forest: Developers, Destroyers, and Defenders of the Amazon, Susanna Hecht and Alexander Cockburn (Verso, 1989); this is one of the best analyses of the complex web of destruction of the Amazon, and it provides ideas on ways to mend the damage.

Tropical Rainforest: A World Survey of Our Most Valuable and Endangered Habitat with a Blueprint for its Survival, Arnold Newman; this is a massive analysis of rainforest destruction and possible alternatives for sound forest management.

People of the Tropical Rainforest (University of California Press & Smithsonian Institute, 1988); this is a compilation of writings about the rainforest by experts on the subject. Augusta Dwyer also delivers a fierce indictment of corruption and mismanagement in the Amazon in *Into the Amazon: The Struggle for the Amazon*.

The Rainforest Book, Scott Lewis (Living Planet, 1990); a concise analysis of rainforest problems and remedies. It's packed with examples which link consumer behaviour with rainforest development, and has lists of organisations to contact, and advice on individual involvement. A similar publication compiled by the Seattle Audubon Society and the Puget Consumers Co-operative is the booklet entitled *Rainforests Forever: Consumer Choices to Help Preserve Tropical Rainforests* (1990).

Emperor of the Amazon (Avon Bard, 1980) & *Mad Maria* (Avon Bard, 1985); Márcio Souza is a modern satirist based in Manaus, Brazil. His biting humour captures some of the greater horrors of the Amazon region and the absurdity of personal and governmental endeavours to conquer the rainforest. Both this and his other work, *Mad Maria*, which deals with the aborted Madeira-Mamoré railway to Guayaramerín and Riberalta, should be of interest to anyone travelling around Bolivia's northern frontiers.

Flora & Fauna Guides

Rainforests – A Guide to Tourist and Research Facilities at Selected Tropical Forest Sites in Central and South America, James L Castner; this book is full of information and is well worth reading if you want to do some research or even just visit the rainforest.

In Search of the Flowers of the Amazon Forest, Margaret Mee; this beautifully illustrated book is highly recommended for anyone (not just botanists) interested in the Amazon.

Neotropical Rainforest Mammals: A Field Guide, Louise Emmons & François Feer; this book provides colour illustrations to identify mammals of the rainforest. For a reference work (as opposed to a field guide) consult the *World of Wildlife: Animals of South America* (Orbis Publishing, 1975) by F R de la Fuente.

Birders in the Amazon region of Bolivia often use field guides for other South American countries – many species overlap. Amateur interests should be satisfied with titles such as *South American Birds: A Photographic Aid to Identification* (1987) by John S Dunning; *A Guide to the Birds of Colombia*, Stephen L Hilty & William L Brown, or *A Guide to the Birds of Venezuela*, Rodolphe Meyer de Schauensee and William Phelps.

For more definitive tomes, you could start with *A Guide to the Birds of South America*, Rodolphe Meyer de Schauensee (Academy of Natural Science, Philadelphia). The high-priced reference work, *The Birds of South America*, R S Ridgley & G Tudor (University of Texas Press, 1989), comes in several volumes; amateurs will find it extremely detailed and technical.

Last, but not least, for some fascinating oddities you should dip into *Ecology of Tropical Rainforests: An introduction for Eco-tourists* (Free University Amsterdam, 1990) by Piet van Ipenburg and Rob Boschhuizen. This booklet is packed with intriguing and bizarre scientific minutiae about sloths, bats, the strangling fig, and more extraordinary details of rainforest ecology. Available in the UK from J Forrest, 64 Belsize Park, London NW3 4EH; or in the USA from M Doolittle, 32 Amy Rd, Falls Village, CT 06031. All proceeds from sales of this booklet go to the Tambopata Reserve Society which is funding research in the Reserva Tambopata in the rainforests of south-eastern Peru.

Coffee-Table Books

Exploring South America, Loren McIntyre; this wonderful coffee-table book, the best of its kind, is a compilation of photos from McIntyre's nearly 60 years in South America.

Lungo i Sentieri Incantati, Antonio Paolillo (Centro Studi Ricerche Liqabue di Venezia, 1987); even if you can't read the Italian text in this coffee-table study of Bolivia, the photos are lovely.

Language

University of Chicago Spanish-English/ English-Spanish Dictionary (Pocket Books 1972); emphasises Latin American usage and pronunciation.

Quechua phrasebook (Lonely Planet, 1989); this phrasebook gives useful phrases and words in the Cuzco dialect of this Inca language, which is also spoken in the Bolivian highlands.

Latin American Spanish phrasebook (Lonely Planet, 1991); a handy language guide for travellers to almost every country in Latin America.

Travel Guides

South America on a shoestring, Geoff Crowther (Lonely Planet, 1990); regularly updated general guide for those travelling on a budget throughout South America. Lots of maps and plenty of info in a well-organised format. If you're travelling overland, see also Lonely Planet's *Mexico – a travel survival kit* and *Central America on a shoestring*.

Along the Gringo Trail, Jack Epstein (And/Or Press 1977); an outdated but humorous budget guide which covers the 'Gringo Trail', the well-worn route from the US/Mexico border to Tierra del Fuego. Emphasis is on '60s ideals.

A Traveller's Guide to El Dorado & the Inca Empire, Lynn Meisch (Penguin Books, 3rd printing, 1980); a thoroughly entertaining and informative book providing background information about Colombia, Peru, Ecuador and Bolivia. It's highly recommended!

Adventuring in the Andes, Charles Frazier (Sierra Club Books, 1985); sparse coverage of off-the-beaten-track travel in Bolivia, Ecuador and Peru, with most of the space devoted to Peru. Bolivia is given a mere 18 pages.

Backpacking & Trekking in Peru & Bolivia, Hilary Bradt (Bradt Publications, 1989); this rundown of walking possibilities in both countries makes an excellent companion guide to *Bolivia – a travel survival kit*. It gives Bolivia second billing, but does include detailed trekking information and some invaluable advice for keen hikers and trekkers.

South American River Trips (Bradt Publications, 1982) and *Up the Creek* (Bradt Publications, 1986); travellers planning river trips on their own will find some useful practical advice in these guides, especially if they want to skip the cities.

South American Handbook, edited by John Brooks (Trade & Travel Publications); this voluminous and pricey guide covering everything between the Darien Gap and Tierra del Fuego is one of the best general guides around. The 1992 edition thankfully cleaned up much of the confusing mash of updates from readers' letters.

Travel Survival Kits: if you'll be travelling in other Latin American countries, Lonely Planet has Travel Survival Kits for *Brazil, Colombia, Argentina, Uruguay & Paraguay, Chile* and others. See the back of this book for more details.

Maps

A number of maps are available in La Paz, Cochabamba and Santa Cruz through Los Amigos del Libro. Other bookshops and stationery stores sell national cartographic publications and, in many places, street vendors even hawk poster-like thematic maps of the country. However, the quality of most locally produced maps isn't very good. The colour plates have often been badly misaligned and in some cases, blue rivers and red highways become green and orange lines on yellow backgrounds, and city names are plopped down far enough from their locations to cause confusion.

A widely available road map called *Red de Caminos* (Highway Network) seems to be the result of an optimistic highway commissioner's game of connect the dots. Many of the roads indicated haven't even been planned, and those in the planning stages are depicted as major routes.

Instituto Geográfico Militar, the government mapping office, is in an unassuming cubbyhole at Avenida 16 de Julio 1471, in La Paz. This office has good topographic sheets covering most of the country, available to the public for B35 each. Unfortunately, they are frequently out of the more popular ones, such as Cordillera Real treks and peaks, Lake Titicaca, etc. Photocopies of those which are in greatest demand are available at a discounted price. This office also publishes an excellent map of the entire country which is available in several sizes. The smallest costs B35 and shows significant populations, political divisions, transport routes and physical features. This is the best map available in Bolivia, but it's often in short supply.

These government maps are sometimes available in bookshops. They're easily recognisable because they contain the name of the president in power when the map was commissioned. Before buying, check the publication date as there are still a lot of 1937 and 1952 maps floating around!

City street plans are available from tourist offices in major cities. All have been produced on low budgets, most are outdated and the results vary in quality and accuracy. In smaller cities, street plans may be purchased at the *alcaldía* (municipal hall) for about B35. They are often quite optimistic and emphasise economic and civic accomplishments rather than facilities of interest to tourists.

Climbing maps of major Bolivian peaks are available from Club Andino Boliviano (☎ 324682) at Calle México 1638, La Paz. Their mailing address is Casilla 1346, La Paz, Bolivia.

In the USA, *Maplink* (☎ (805) 965-4402), 25 E Mason St, Dept G, Santa Barbara, CA 93101, is an excellent and exhaustive source for maps of Bolivia and just about anywhere else in the world. A similarly extensive selection of mapping is available in the UK from *Stanfords* (☎ (071) 836-1321), 12-14 Long Acre, London WC2E 9LP.

For general mapping of South America with excellent topographical detail, it's hard to beat the sectional maps published by International Travel Map Productions (Canada). Coverage of Bolivia is provided in *South America – South* (1987); *South America – North East* (1989); *South America – North West* (1987); and *Amazon Basin* (1991).

MEDIA
Newspapers & Periodicals

Cochabamba, La Paz, Potosí, Oruro and Santa Cruz all have daily newspapers which include *Presencia, El Diario, Hoy* and *Última Hora* in La Paz, *La Patria* in Oruro, *El Mundo* and *El Deber* in Santa Cruz, *El Correo del Sur* in Sucre and *Los Tiempos* in Cochabamba. Of these, *Presencia* and the two major Santa Cruz papers are generally the best. Associated Press, Deutsche Presse Agentur, Reuters and United Press International all have representatives in La Paz.

Newsweek, the *International Herald Tribune*, *Time* and the *Miami Herald* are sold at some street kiosks in the major cities and at Los Amigos del Libro in La Paz and Cochabamba.

It may be worthwhile picking up the latest copy of the monthly publication *Guía Boliviana de Transporte y Turismo* which contains airline schedules and directories of services in major cities. It costs B22 per issue and is available in La Paz at GBT (☎ 328559), Plaza del Estudiante 1920, and in Santa Cruz at GBT (☎ 346854), Sucursal Calle Junín esq 21 de Mayo, Galería Casco Viejo #103. GBT also has branch offices in other large cities.

The organisation called CEDOIN in La Paz publishes a newsletter called *Bolivia Bulletin*. It focuses on progressive Bolivian themes, including energy development, conservation, the parallel economy and medicine. For further information, contact them at Calle Ismael Montes 710, Casilla 20194, La Paz.

Another entity known as Pro-Dem promotes improvement of the Bolivian economy at the grass roots level by providing micro loans for cholas who may want to get started in business, an alternative to corruption-plagued International Monetary Fund loans and handouts. They publish *Inside* magazine which reports on the progress of their projects. If you're interested in the concept, contact them at Calle Almirante Grau 625 in La Paz.

Radio & TV

The country has 125 radio stations broadcasting in Spanish, Quechua and Aymará. The seemingly inordinate number may be explained by the mountainous nature of the terrain – signals don't reach very far.

Bolivia has two government and five private TV stations operating in La Paz, Cochabamba, Trinidad, Oruro, Potosí, Tarija and Santa Cruz which are watched on the country's 650,000-odd TV sets. Most of the programming is foreign.

FILM & PHOTOGRAPHY
Film & Equipment

Cameras are available in Bolivia but import duties are exceptionally high, so photographers should bring all necessary equipment from home. Certain types of film, such as Kodachrome or Polaroid, are difficult or impossible to find, although Fujichrome, Agfachrome and print film are available at pleasantly low prices in some markets and from street vendors.

If you're travelling on a budget, bear in mind that a lot of photographic paraphernalia may become quite a liability. Consider carefully which lenses, filters, tripods and attachments are indispensable and which ones will be used only infrequently. Don't take anything you can't risk losing. Your equipment is as safe in Bolivia as it would be in Los Angeles or Sydney, but as in any part of the world, if theft of valuable equipment is convenient, someone may seize the opportunity.

Whatever combination of lenses and accessories you decide to bring, make sure they're carried in a sturdy bag which will protect them from the elements, the dust and the hard knocks they're sure to receive. It's also important to ensure that your travel insurance policy includes camera gear in case of theft.

Repairs & Processing

Casa Kavlin at Calle Potosí 1130 in La Paz is reputable and will repair and service Kodak products. Japanese cameras must be taken to Fuji two blocks away on the same street. Technicians tend to be available only in the morning.

The quality of film processing in Bolivia is poor, and although the postal system is generally reliable, you may not wish to subject precious film to postal uncertainties. In La Paz, there are courier services, including UPS, who ship parcels of less than one kg for approximately B120.

Photographing Scenery

Photographers will quickly learn that Bolivian landscapes swallow celluloid; don't be caught out without a healthy supply of film. Keep in mind, however, that the combination of high-altitude ultraviolet rays and light reflected off snow or water will conspire to fool both your eye and your light meter. A polarising filter will be essential when photographing the Altiplano and will reveal the dramatic effects of the exaggerated UV element at high altitude.

Unless there's a haze to filter sunlight, avoid taking photos during the brightest part of the day when the rays are shorter, the light is harshest and the shadows are blackest. An hour after dawn or an hour prior to sunset are the optimum times because light rays are long and red, shadows are diffused and the light is softened by filtering through many layers of atmosphere.

The lowland rainforests, however, are surprisingly dim and difficult to photograph due to humidity, haze and leafy interference. For optimum photos, you'll require either fast film (200 or 400 ASA) or a tripod which will allow long exposures.

Photographing People

The average Bolivian doesn't indulge in photography as a hobby but does recognise the inherent value of camera equipment. If you carry a camera, especially a swanky model, you won't be able to escape the wealthy foreigner label. This isn't necessarily a problem, but it does set you apart. If you carry a camera, more people will try to sell you things, and those who are superstitious about photography will react differently toward you.

While some Bolivians will be willing photo subjects, others – especially traditional women – may be put off by your attempts to get that perfect 'people shot'. They may harbour superstitions about your camera or suspicions of your motives. Once in a remote village, a colorfully dressed local girl burst into angry tears when a trekker snapped a photo of her. She explained that the mountain people were tired of being exploited by photographers who would sell photos of them and not share any of the profit.

Visitors should be sensitive to the wishes of locals, however photogenic or colourful, who may be superstitious or camera-shy for one reason or another. Ask permission to photograph and don't insist or snap a photo anyway if permission is denied. There'll be plenty of willing subjects who can provide equally interesting 'people shots'.

Photographing Wildlife

For serious wildlife photography, a single-lens reflex camera and telephoto lenses are necessary. If all you have is a little 'aim and shoot' sort of camera, you may as well not bother. Some of the more sophisticated ones have a maximum focal length of 70 mm or so, but that's still not sufficient for decent shots.

Zoom lenses are probably the best for

Hitches with Witches

While working on the first edition of this book, I sneaked a few photos of the Mercado de Hechicería (Witches' Market), in La Paz. One of the vendors, an older woman, saw me and angrily warned that I'd regret the indiscretion. A month later, all my exposed film of Bolivia, about 30 rolls, was stolen and tossed into the Amazon in Brazil. Of course this may have been a simple coincidence, but...you've been warned! Since then, we've received several letters from travellers who took photos of the Mercado de Hechicería and its wares without any hitches. ∎

wildlife photography since you can frame your shot easily and work out the optimum composition. This is important since wildlife is often on the move. The 70 to 210-mm zoom lenses are quite popular, and you'll need at least 200 mm for good close-up shots. The only problem is that with so much glass inside, they absorb about 1.5 f-stops of light and will require higher ASA film (200 to 400) for photos in anything but broad, bright daylight.

A straight telephoto – that is, a long lens with a fixed focal length – will yield better results and greater clarity than zoom lenses, but you're limited by having to carry a separate lens for each required focal length. A 400 or 500-mm lens will bring the action up close but you'll still require fast film.

Another option is to carry a 2x teleconverter, a small adaptor which fits between the lens and camera body, to double the focal length of your lens. This is a good, cheap way of getting the long focal length without having to purchase expensive lenses. It does, however, have a couple of disadvantages: it requires fast film and, depending on the camera and lens, can be difficult to focus quickly and precisely – a real drawback when it comes to wildlife photography.

When using long, heavy lenses, a tripod can be very useful, and with anything greater than about 300 mm, will be essential unless you have an exceptionally steady hand.

HEALTH

Travel health depends on predeparture preparations, day-to-day attention to health-related matters, and the correct handling of medical emergencies if they do arise. Although the following health section may seem like a who's who of dreadfully unpleasant diseases, your chances of contracting a serious illness in Bolivia are slight. You will, however, be exposed to environmental factors, foods and sanitation standards that are probably quite different from what you're used to, but if you take the recommended jabs, faithfully pop your anti-malarials and use common sense, there shouldn't be any problems.

This rundown of health risks includes some preventative measures, symptom descriptions and suggestions about what to do if there is a problem. It isn't meant to replace professional diagnosis or prescription, and visitors to the developing world should discuss with their physician the most up-to-date methods used to prevent and treat the threats to health which may be encountered.

Predeparture Preparations
Health Insurance A travel-insurance policy to cover theft, loss and medical problems is a wise idea. Before heading abroad, travellers should get up-to-date information. A wide variety of policies is available; contact your travel agent for further information. When buying a policy, it's important to check the small print:

Some policies specifically exclude 'dangerous activities' which can include, motorcycling or even trekking. If these activities are on your agenda, such a policy would be of limited value.

You may prefer a policy which pays doctors or hospitals directly rather than requiring you to pay first and claim later. If you must claim after the fact, however, be sure you keep all documentation. Some policies ask you to phone (reverse charges) to a centre in your home country where an immediate assessment of the problem will be made.

Check on the policy's coverage of emergency transport or evacuation back to your home country. If you have to stretch out across several airline seats, someone has to pay for it!

Travel Health Information In the USA you can contact the Overseas Citizens Emergency Center and request a health and safety information bulletin on Bolivia by writing to the Bureau of Consular Affairs Office, State Department, Washington, DC 20520. This office also has a special telephone number for emergencies while abroad: ☎ (202) 632-5525.

Read the Center for Disease Control's (CDC's) *Health Information for International Travel* supplement of *Morbidity & Mortality Weekly Report* or the World Health Organization's (WHO's) *Vaccination Certificate Requirements for International Travel*

A	B
C	D
E	F

A: (RS)   D: (RS)
B: (RS)   E: (RS)
C: (DS)   F: (DS)

Top Left: Fruit vendor - Tupiza Market (RS)
Top Right: Bored Bolivian boar - Río Tuichi (RS)
Bottom Left: Mercado de Hechicería (Witches' Market) - La Paz (TM)
Bottom Right: A vegetarian's nightmare - Sucre Market (TM)

& *Health Advice to Travellers*. Both of these sources are superior to the *Travel Information Manual* published by the International Air Transport Association.

The International Association for Medical Assistance to Travelers (IAMAT) at 417 Center St, Lewiston, New York, NY 14092 can provide travellers with a list of English-speaking physicians in Bolivia.

In the UK, contact Medical Advisory Services for Travellers Abroad (MASTA) (☎ 071-6314408), Keppel St, London WC1E 7HT. MASTA provides a wide range of services including a choice of concise or comprehensive 'Health Briefs' and a range of medical supplies. Another source of medical information and supplies is the British Airways Travel Clinic (☎ 071-8315333).

In Australia, make an appointment with the Traveller's Medical and Vaccination Centre in Sydney (☎ (02) 221-7133) or Melbourne (☎ (03) 650-7600) for general health information pertaining to Bolivia and requisite vaccinations for travel in South America.

Medical Kit It's a good idea to carry a small, straightforward medical kit which may include:

- Aspirin or paracetamol – for pain or fever
- Antihistamine (such as Benadryl) – useful as a decongestant for colds and allergies, to ease itching from insect bites, or to prevent motion sickness
- Antibiotics – useful if you're travelling off the beaten track. Most antibiotics are prescription medicines
- Kaolin and pectin preparation such as Pepto-Bismol for stomach upsets and Imodium or Lomotil to bung things up in case of emergencies during long-distance travel
- Rehydration mixture – for treatment of severe diarrhoea. This is particularly important when travelling with children.
- Antiseptic liquid or cream and antibiotic powder for minor injuries
- Calamine lotion – to ease irritation from bites and stings
- Bandages and Band-aids
- Scissors, tweezers, and a thermometer – but remember that you cannot transport mercury thermometers on airlines

- Insect repellent, sunscreen (15+), suntan lotion, chap stick and water purification tablets (or iodine)
- Sterile syringes are recommended for travel in Amazonia (especially Brazil!) due to the AIDS risk. Be sure you have at least one large enough for a blood test – those normally used for injections are too small. For sources of requisite medical supplies, refer to the Travel Health Information section.

Ideally, antibiotics should be administered only under medical supervision and should never be taken indiscriminately. Overuse of antibiotics can weaken your immune system and reduce the drug's efficacy in the future. Take only the recommended dosage at the prescribed intervals and continue using the antibiotic for the prescribed period, even if you're feeling better sooner. Antibiotics are quite specific to the infections they will react with, so if you're in doubt about a drug's effects or suffer any unexpected reactions, discontinue use immediately.

When buying drugs anywhere in South America, be sure to check expiry dates and storage conditions. Some drugs available there may no longer be recommended, or may even be banned, in other countries.

Health Preparations Make sure you're healthy before embarking on a long journey, have your teeth checked and if you wear glasses or contacts, bring a spare pair and a copy of your optical prescription. Losing your glasses can be a real problem, although in larger Bolivian cities, you can have a new pair made with little fuss.

At least one pair of good quality sunglasses is essential, as the glare is terrific and dust and blown sand can get into the corners of your eyes. A hat, sunscreen lotion and lip protection are also important.

If you require a particular medication, take an adequate supply as it may not be available locally. Take the prescription with the generic rather than brand name so it will be universally recognisable. It's also wise to carry a copy of the prescription to prove you're using the medication legally. Customs and immigration officers may get excited at the sight of syringes or mysterious powdery preparations. The organisations listed under Travel Health Information can provide medical supplies such as syringes, together with multilingual customs documentation.

Immunisations Vaccinations provide protection against diseases you may be exposed to during your travels. A yellow fever vaccination and related documentation is strongly recommended for every traveller in Bolivia, and is legally required for travel in Santa Cruz Department. In addition, Brazilian authorities will not grant entrance from Bolivia without it. The vaccination certificate remains effective for 10 years. Other commonly recommended jabs for travel to South America are typhoid, tetanus DPT, polio and meningitis vaccines as well as gamma globulin as protection against hepatitis. Some physicians will also recommend a cholera vaccine, but its effectiveness is minimal.

Cholera – Although many countries require this vaccine, it lasts only six months and is not recommended for pregnant women.
Tetanus DPT – Boosters are necessary at least every 10 years and are highly recommended as a matter of course.
Typhoid – Protection lasts for three years and is useful if you are travelling for longer periods in rural tropical areas. The most common side effects from this vaccine are pain at the injection site, fever, headache, and a general unwell feeling.
Gamma Globulin – Gamma globulin is not a vaccination but a ready-made antibody which has proven successful in reducing the chances of contracting infectious hepatitis (hepatitis A). Because it may interfere with the development of immunity, it should not be given until at least 10 days after administration of the last vaccine needed and as near as possible to departure due to its relatively short-lived effectiveness – normally about six months.
Yellow Fever – Protection lasts for 10 years and is recommended for all travel to South America. You usually need to visit a special yellow fever vaccination centre. Vaccination isn't recommended during pregnancy, but if you must travel to a high risk area, it is still probably better to take the vaccine.

Pharmacies & Medications

It's not necessary to take with you every remedy for every illness you might conceivably contract during your trip. Just about everything available at home can also be found in Bolivian pharmacies, and pharmaceutical drugs are available without a prescription. They are a bit lax about storage, however, so be sure to check expiry dates before buying. It's also a good idea to take a sufficient supply of any prescriptions that you must take habitually, including contraceptive pills and vitamin tablets.

In addition, all travellers should be aware of any drug allergies they may have and avoid using these drugs or their derivatives while travelling in Bolivia. Since common names of prescription medicines in Bolivia are likely to be different from the ones you're used to, ask a pharmacist before taking anything you're not sure about.

Pharmacies in Bolivia are known as *farmacias* and medicines are called *medicamentos*. The word for doctor is *médico* and medicine tablets are known as *pastillas*.

Basic Rules

Food & Water Care in what you eat and drink is the most important health rule; stomach upsets are the most common travel-health problem, but the majority of these upsets will be minor. Don't be paranoid about sampling local foods – it's all part of the travel experience and shouldn't be missed.

As a general rule, Bolivian tap water isn't potable. The simplest way to purify suspect water is to boil it for eight to 10 minutes. Simple filtering won't remove all dangerous organisms, so if you can't boil suspect water, it should be treated chemically. Chlorine tablets (Puritabs, Steritabs and other brand names) will kill many, but not all, pathogens. Iodine is very effective, and is available in tablet form (such as Potable Aqua) but follow the directions carefully and remember that too much iodine is harmful.

If you can't find tablets, tincture of iodine (2%) or iodine crystals may be used. Add two drops of tincture of iodine per litre or quart of water and let stand for 30 minutes. Iodine crystals can also be used to purify water, but this is a more complicated and dangerous process since you first must prepare a saturated iodine solution. Iodine loses its effectiveness if exposed to air or damp so keep it in a tightly sealed container. Flavoured powder will disguise the normally foul taste of iodine-treated water and is an especially good idea for those travelling with children.

When it's hot, be sure to drink lots of liquids. Excessive sweating can lead to loss of salt and cause muscle cramping. Failure to urinate or dark yellow urine is a sign of dehydration. Always carry a bottle of water on long trips.

Reputable brands of bottled water or soft drinks are normally fine although water bottles are sometimes refilled and resold – check the seals before buying. In rural areas, take care with fruit juices, since water may have been added. Milk should be treated with suspicion as it is often unpasteurised. Boiled milk is fine if it's kept hygienically. Yoghurt is always good. Tea or coffee should also be OK since the water will probably have been boiled.

Vegetables and fruit should be washed with purified water or peeled where possible. Ice cream is usually OK but beware of ice cream that has melted and been refrozen. Thoroughly cooked food is safest but not if it has been left to cool or if it has been reheated. Take great care with shellfish or fish, and avoid undercooked meat. If a place looks clean and well run and the vendor also looks clean and healthy, then the food is probably all right. In general, look for places that are packed with locals.

Diseases of Insanitation

Diarrhoea Few travellers escape the inevitable misery of *Montezuma's Revenge* and there is very little you can do to prevent the onslaught. Also called *turista* and a dozen other descriptive nicknames, there is no escaping the fact that plain old travellers' diarrhoea can happen to you anywhere.

This problem is not caused by lack of sanitation or 'bad' food, but primarily by a change in diet and a lack of resistance to local strains of bacteria. The first thing to remember is that every case of diarrhoea is not dysentery, so don't panic and start stuffing yourself with pills. If you've spent all your life living out of sterilised, cellophane-wrapped packets and tins from the supermarket, you'll have a hard time until you adjust.

Flies live on various wastes produced by humans and other animals. In many places, local people shit fairly indiscriminately whenever the urge takes them. Rural facilities are rare or unspeakable and sewage treatment isn't always top rate. Most gut infections stem from the connection of food and shit via flies. There are very few public lavatories in rural areas and facilities at bus stops and roadside restaurants are rarely sanitary. If you need to make use of the bush, ensure that no paper or sanitary products are left behind.

If and when you get a gut infection, avoid rushing off to the chemist and loading up on antibiotics. In this case, taking antibiotics can do more harm than good. If the bacteria in your body are able to build up an immunity to them, the antibiotics may not work when you really need them. Try to starve out the bugs first. If possible, eat nothing, rest and avoid travelling (or pop an Imodium or Lomotil to plug the drain). Drink lots of liquids – diarrhoea will cause dehydration and may result in stomach cramps due to a salt imbalance in the blood. Chewing a small pellet of paregoric, a stronger version of Milk of Magnesia, will relieve the pain of the cramps.

If you can't hack starvation, keep to a light diet of dry toast, biscuits and black tea. To keep up your liquids, drink bottled water or lemonade. Once you're headed toward recovery, try some yoghurt, but stay away from sweets, fruit, and dairy products. If you don't recover after a couple of days, it may be necessary to visit a doctor to be tested for other problems which could include giardia, dysentery, cholera, and so on.

It's interesting that, in addition to the initial 'shakedown' most people experience upon arriving in South America, they experience a similar readjustment upon arriving home. One therefore suspects that South Americans may have similar discomforts when they visit other countries (the Yankee Quickstep or the Wallaby Hops?) thanks to unfamiliar diet and bacteria.

Giardia This is prevalent in South America and is first characterised by a swelling of the stomach, pale-coloured faeces, diarrhoea, frequent gas, headache and later by nausea and depression. Many doctors recommend Flagyl (metronidazole) tablets (250 mg) twice daily for three days. Flagyl, however, can cause side effects and some doctors prefer to treat giardiasis with two grams of Tinaba (tinadozole), taken in one fell swoop to knock the bug out hard and fast. If it doesn't work the first time, the treatment can be repeated for up to three days.

Dysentery This serious illness is caused by contaminated food or water and is characterised by severe diarrhoea, often with blood or mucus in the stool, and painful gut cramps. There are two types: bacillary dysentery, which is uncomfortable but not enduring; and amoebic dysentery which, as its name suggests, is caused by amoebas. This variety is much more difficult to treat and is more persistent.

Bacillary dysentery hits quickly; because it's caused by bacteria it responds well to antibiotics and is usually treated symptomatically with a kaolin and pectin or a bismuth compound. On the other hand, since the symptoms themselves are actually the best treatment – diarrhoea and fever are both trying to rid the body of the infection – it may be best to just hole up for a few days and let it run its course. If activity or travel is absolutely necessary during the infection, you can take either Imodium or Lomotil to 'plug the drain', so to speak, until reaching a more convenient location to R & R (rest and run).

Amoebic dysentery, or amoebiasis, is a much more serious variety. It is caused by protozoans, or amoebic parasites, called *Endamoeba histolytica* which are also transmitted through contaminated food or water. Once they've invaded, they live in the lower intestinal tract and cause heavy and often bloody diarrhoea, fever, tenderness in the liver area and intense abdominal pain.

If left untreated, ulceration and inflammation of the colon and rectum can become very serious. If you see blood in your faeces over two or three days, seek medical attention. If that's not possible, try the antiparasitic Flagyl (metronidazole). You'll need three tablets three or four times daily for 10 days to rid yourself of the condition. Flagyl should not be taken by pregnant women.

The best method of preventing dysentery is, of course, to avoid eating or drinking contaminated items.

Cholera The cholera vaccine is between 20 to 50% effective according to most authorities, and can have some side effects. Vaccination is not usually recommended, nor is it legally required by Bolivian authorities. If you're travelling further afield, it may be worth getting a jab before you leave.

During 1991, a major cholera epidemic was reported in South America, particularly in Peru and the upper reaches of the Brazilian Amazon. One Bolivian advised us that '*El cólera no ha llegado en Bolivia porque el impuesto en la aduana es muy caro*' (Cholera hasn't arrived in Bolivia because the import tax is too high). Bolivia has been accused of fabricating its few reported cholera cases in order to qualify for international aid. No one really knows whether the country was affected or not, although we recently heard from a traveller that cases have been reported in Cochabamba. In any case, be particularly wary of shellfish or other seafood, which may have come from infected regions of Peru or Chile.

At the time of writing, health certificates were required of travellers entering Bolivia from Peru. This was clearly adopted as a temporary measure following the cholera epidemic of 1991, but may continue in force for some time. At the present time, we strongly recommend that travellers to Peru and Bolivia have the cholera jab recorded on their yellow vaccination certificate prior to travel. Keep up to date with information by contacting travellers' clinics or vaccination centres, and avoid areas where there are outbreaks.

Cholera is characterised by a sudden onset of acute diarrhoea with 'rice water' stools, vomiting, muscular cramps and extreme weakness. You need medical attention but your first concern should be rehydration. Drink as much water as you can – if it refuses to stay down, keep drinking anyway. If there is likely to be an appreciable delay in reaching medical treatment, begin a course of tetracycline which, incidentally, should not be administered to children or pregnant women. Be sure to check the expiry date, since old tetracycline can become toxic.

Viral Gastroenteritis This is not caused by bacteria, but is, as the name implies, a virus. It is characterised by stomach cramps, diarrhoea, vomiting and slight fever. All you can do is rest and keep drinking as much water as possible.

Hepatitis This incapacitating disease is caused by a virus which attacks the liver. Type A can be caught by eating food, drinking water or using cutlery, crockery or toilets contaminated by an infected person. The victim's eyes and skin turn a sickly yellow and urine, orange or brown. An infected person will also experience tenderness in the right side of the abdomen and a loss of appetite.

If you contract infectious hepatitis (hepatitis A) during a short trip to South America, you probably should make arrangements to go home. If you can afford the time, however, and have a reliable travelling companion who can bring food and water, the best cure is to stay where you are, find a few good books and only leave bed to go to the toilet. After a month of so, you should feel like living again. Drink lots of fluids and keep to a diet high in proteins and vitamins. Avoid alcohol and cigarettes absolutely.

The best preventative measure available is a gamma globulin jab before departure from home and booster shots every three or four months thereafter while you're away (beware of unsanitary needles!). A jab is also in order if you come in contact with any infected person; and if *you* come down with hepatitis, anyone who has been in recent contact with you should take the shot too.

Hepatitis B, formerly known as serum hepatitis, can only be caught by having sex with an infected person or by skin penetration such as tattooing or using the same syringe. If type B is diagnosed, fatal liver failure is a real possibility and the victim should be sent home and/or hospitalised immediately. Gamma globulin is not effective against hepatitis B.

A vaccine does exist for hepatitis B, but it is not readily available and is extremely expensive. It consists of a course of three shots over a period of six months.

A variant of the B strain, called hepatitis C, now also exists. Transmission and symptoms are similar to hepatitis B; however, there is presently no vaccine against hepatitis C. It is not very common, though, and should not be of too much concern to travellers.

Typhoid Contaminated food and water are responsible for typhoid fever, another gut infection that travels the faecal-oral route. Vaccination against typhoid isn't 100% effective. Since it can be very serious, medical attention is necessary.

Early symptoms are like those of many other travellers' illnesses – you may feel as though you have a bad cold or the flu combined with a headache, sore throat and fever. The fever rises slowly until it exceeds 40°C, while the pulse slowly drops. These symptoms may be accompanied by nausea, diarrhoea or constipation.

In the second week, the fever and slow pulse continue and a few pink spots may appear on the body. Trembling, delirium, weakness, weight loss and dehydration set in. If there are no further complications, the fever and symptoms will slowly fade during the third week. Medical attention is essential, however, since typhoid is extremely infectious and possible complications include pneumonia or peritonitis (burst appendix).

When feverish, the victim should be kept cool. Watch for dehydration. The recommended antibiotic is chloramphenicol, but ampicillin causes fewer side effects.

Insect Borne Diseases

Malaria If you will only be travelling in highland Bolivia, that is, above 1500 metres or so, antimalarial precautions are not necessary. In Bolivia, the areas of greatest risk include the Amazon Basin, the Chaco and the eastern lowlands.

Malaria is caused by the blood parasite *plasmodium* which is transmitted by the nocturnal *anopheles* mosquito. Only the females spread the disease, but you can contract it through a single bite from an insect carrying the parasite. Malaria sporozites enter the bloodstream and travel to the liver where they mature, infect the red blood cells and begin to multiply. This process takes between one and five weeks. Only when the infected cells re-enter the bloodstream and burst do the dramatic symptoms begin. For this reason, malaria can be extremely dangerous because the victim by this time has often left the malarial area, so the disease is not suspected and therefore is improperly treated.

There are four types of malaria: plasmodium falciparum, the deadliest, plasmodium malariae which is still universally sensitive to chloroquine, and plasmodium vivax and plasmodium ovale which are both harboured outside the blood and can recur. The drug-resistant status of different malarial strains in different parts of the world is constantly in flux.

Diagnosis is confirmed by a blood test in which the plasmodium and its strain may be identified. Some strains, particularly plasmodium falciparum, can be fatal if not immediately and properly treated. Malarial symptoms include (in this order) gradual loss of appetite, malaise, weakness, alternating shivering and hot flashes, diarrhoea, periodic

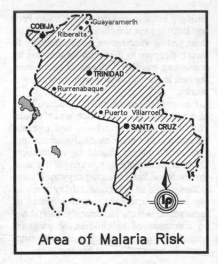

Area of Malaria Risk

high fever, severe headache, vomiting and hallucinations.

The most effective form of malaria prevention, of course, is to avoid being bitten. Since the mosquitoes bite at dusk, you can avoid bites by covering bare skin and using an insect repellent. Sleep under a mosquito net or at least light a mosquito coil. Next best – but hardly 100% effective – is a course of antimalarials which are normally taken two weeks before, during and several weeks after, travelling in malarial areas.

The malaria parasite mutates rapidly and although pharmacology manages to keep one step ahead of it, advice on which antimalarials you'll need to take goes out of date very quickly. Your doctor or travellers' health clinic will have access to the latest information. Currently, the recommended prophylaxis is chloroquine. If you develop malarial symptoms, seek medical advice immediately. If you have plasmodium falciparum and reach the headache stage, you may be in serious danger. If you are not within reach of medical attention, the treatment for all strains (until you can reach a doctor) is one single dose of four tablets (600 mg) of chloroquine followed by two tablets

(300 mg) six hours later and two tablets on each subsequent day. As an alternative (requisite for chloroquine-resistant strains) take a single dose of three tablets of Fansidar. *Never* use Fansidar as a prophylaxis. If you have previously been taking Lariam (mefloquine), don't take chloroquine, as these make a toxic and potentially dangerous combination.

Chagas Disease There is a very small possibility of contracting this disease. It is caused by a parasite which lives in the faeces of the *vinchuca* beetle which inhabits the thatching of dirty huts (up to 2800 metres, but primarily in the lowland and Chaco regions).

The disease, transmitted through the bite of this beetle, more ominously called the assassin bug, causes progressive constriction and hardening of blood vessels, which places increasing strain on the heart. At present there is no cure and Chagas is always fatal over a period of years.

Mind-boggling estimates suggest that up to 25% of Bolivia's population suffers from this disease. Whether this is true or not, researchers in developed countries seem to be largely unaware of this serious disease. The best prevention is to use a mosquito net if you'll be sleeping in thatched buildings. If you are bitten, wash the affected area well and don't scratch the bite or the parasite may be rubbed into the wound. It's only treatable if caught immediately, so if you think you've been bitten, get to the Chagas Institute at the university in Cochabamba for testing and treatment.

Haemorrhagic Fever Incidences of this illness have been reported in low-lying jungle areas, especially in Beni and Pando departments. It's transmitted by mosquitoes and can be prevented by using the same mosquito protection recommended for malaria.

The most salient symptom is an odd pin-prick-type rash which is caused by capillary haemorrhaging. Accompanying symptoms include chills, fever, fatigue, congestion and other influenza-like symptoms. It can be very dangerous, and professional attention, preferably in a hospital, should be immediately sought.

Worms Worms are common in most humid tropical areas and a stool test when you return home isn't a bad idea if you think you may have contracted them. They can live on unwashed vegetables or in undercooked meat, or you can pick them up through your skin by walking barefoot. Infestations may not be obvious for some time and although they are generally not serious, they can cause further health problems if left untreated. Once the problem is confirmed, over-the-counter medication is available to rid yourself of it.

The most common form you're likely to contract are hookworms. They are usually caught by walking barefoot on infected soil. The worms bore through the skin, attach themselves to the inner wall of the intestine and proceed to suck the blood, resulting in abdominal pain and sometimes anaemia.

Threadworms, or *strongyloidiasis*, are also found in low lying areas and operate very much like hookworms, but symptoms are more visible and can include diarrhoea and vomiting.

Worms may be treated with thiabendazole or mabendazole taken orally twice daily for three or four days. You should seek medical advice, however, because the symptoms of worms so closely resemble those of other, more serious, conditions.

Myiasis This very unpleasant affliction is caused by the larvae of tropical flies which lay their eggs on damp or sweaty clothing. One of the most common offenders in lowland Bolivia is the botfly. The eggs of this fly hatch and the larvae burrow into the skin, producing a painful lump (or, if it becomes infected, an ugly boil) as they develop. To kill the invader, place drops of hydrogen peroxide, alcohol or oil over the boil to cut off its air supply, then squeeze the lump to remove the bug. However revolting the process, at this stage the problem is solved.

Yellow Fever Yellow fever is endemic in much of South America, including the Amazon Basin and southern lowland areas. This viral disease, which is transmitted to humans by mosquitoes, first manifests itself with fever, headache, abdominal pain and vomiting. There may appear to be a brief recovery before it progresses into its more severe stages when liver failure becomes a possibility. There is no treatment apart from keeping the fever as low as possible and avoiding dehydration. The yellow fever vaccination, which is highly recommended for every traveller in South America, offers good protection for 10 years.

Typhus Typhus is spread by ticks, mites or lice and begins as a severe cold followed by a fever, chills, headache, muscle pains and rash. There is often a large and painful sore at the site of the bite and nearby lymph nodes become swollen and painful.

Trekkers may be at risk from cattle or wild game ticks. Seek local advice on areas where ticks are present and check yourself carefully after walking in those areas. A strong insect repellent can help and regular bushwalkers should consider treating boots and trousers with repellent.

Cuts, Bites, & Stings

Cuts & Scratches The warm, moist conditions of the tropical lowlands invite and promote the growth of 'wee beasties' that would be thwarted in more temperate climates. Because of this, even a small cut or scratch can become painfully infected and lead to more serious problems.

Since bacterial immunity to certain antibiotics can build up, it's not wise to take these medicines indiscriminately or as a preventative measure. The best treatment for cuts is to frequently cleanse the affected area with soap and water and apply Mercurochrome or an antiseptic cream. Where possible, avoid using bandages, which keep wounds moist and encourage the growth of bacteria. If, despite this, the wound becomes tender and inflamed, then use of a mild, broad-spectrum antibiotic may be warranted.

Snakebite Although threat of snakebite is minimal in Bolivia, travellers walking around the forested northern areas may wish to take precautions. The most dangerous snakes native to Bolivia are the bushmaster and the fer-de-lance which inhabit the northern and eastern lowlands. To minimise chances of being bitten, wear boots, socks and long trousers when walking through undergrowth. A good pair of canvas gaiters will further protect your legs. Don't put your hands into holes and crevices and be careful when collecting firewood. Check shoes, clothing and sleeping bags before use.

Snakebites do not cause instantaneous death and antivenenes are usually available, but it is vital that you make a positive identification of the snake in question, or at the very least, have a detailed description of it.

If someone is bitten by a snake, keep the victim calm and still, wrap the bitten limb as you would for a sprain and then attach a splint to immobilise it. Tourniquets and suction on the wound are now comprehensively discredited. Seek medical help immediately, and if possible, bring the dead snake along for identification (but don't attempt to catch it if there is a chance of being bitten again). Bushwalkers who are (wisely) concerned about snakebite should carry a field guide with photos and detailed descriptions of the possible perpetrators.

Insects Ants, gnats, mosquitoes, bees and flies will be just as annoying in Bolivia as they are at home. If you're going to be walking in humid or densely foliated areas, wear light cotton trousers and shoes, not shorts and sandals or thongs. Regardless of temperature, never wear shorts or thongs in the forest, and remember to carry an effective insect repellent. Bee and wasp stings are usually more painful than dangerous. Calamine lotion offers some relief and ice packs will reduce pain and swelling.

Body lice and scabies mites are also common in South America, and a number of shampoos and creams are available to eliminate them. In addition to hair and skin, clothing and bedding should be washed thoroughly to prevent further infestation.

Diseases Spread by People & Animals

Tetanus This potentially fatal disease is found in underdeveloped tropical areas and is difficult to treat but is easily prevented by vaccination. Tetanus occurs when a wound becomes infected by a bacterium which lives in human or animal faeces. Clean all cuts, punctures, and bites. Tetanus is also known as lockjaw and the first symptom may be difficulty in swallowing, a stiffening of the jaw and neck followed by painful convulsions of the jaw and whole body.

Rabies Throughout Bolivia, but especially in the humid lowlands, rodents and bats carry the rabies virus and pass it on to larger animals and humans. Avoid any animal that appears to be foaming at the mouth or acting strangely. Bats, especially vampire bats, are common in the Amazon Basin and are notorious carriers of rabies. Be sure to cover all parts of your body at night, especially your feet and scalp. Dogs are also particularly notable carriers. Any bite, scratch or even lick from a mammal should be cleaned immediately and thoroughly. Scrub with soap and running water and then clean with an alcohol solution. If there is any possibility that the animal is infected, help should be sought. Even if the animal isn't rabid, all bites should be treated seriously as they can become infected or result in tetanus. A rabies vaccination is now available and should be considered if you spend a lot of time around animals.

If you do get bitten, try to capture or kill the offending animal so that it may be tested. If that's impossible, then you must assume the animal is rabid. The rabies virus incubates slowly in its victim, so while medical attention isn't urgent, it shouldn't be delayed. Rabies vaccinations are available at the Unidad Sanitario Centro Piloto in La Paz (see the Medical Services section in the La Paz chapter for further details). Anyone bitten or scratched by a suspicious animal must take daily vaccinations for seven subsequent days and three more over the next two months.

Meningococcal Meningitis This disease is spread by close contact with people who carry it in their throats and noses. They probably aren't aware they are carriers and pass it on through coughs and sneezes. This very serious disease attacks the brain and can be fatal. A scattered blotchy rash, fever, severe headache, sensitivity to light and stiffness in the neck preventing nodding of the head are the first symptoms. Death can occur within a few hours, so immediate treatment with large doses of penicillin is vital. If intravenous administration is impossible, it should be given intermuscularly. Vaccination offers reasonable protection for over a year, but you should check for reports of recent outbreaks and try to avoid affected areas.

Diptheria Diptheria can appear as a skin infection or a more serious throat infection. It is spread by contaminated dust coming in contact with the skin or being inhaled. About the only way to prevent the skin infection is to keep clean and dry – not always easy in South America. The throat infection is prevented by vaccination.

Gonorrhoea & Syphilis Sexual contact with an infected partner spreads a number of unpleasant diseases. While abstinence is 100% effective, use of a condom will lessen your risk considerably. The most common sexually transmitted diseases are gonorrhoea and syphilis, which in men first appear as sores, blisters or rashes around the genitals and pain or discharge when urinating. Symptoms may be less marked or not evident at all in women. The symptoms of syphilis eventually disappear completely, but the disease continues and may cause severe problems in later years. Antibiotics are used to treat both syphilis and gonorrhoea.

AIDS AIDS is another issue. Although it hasn't yet reached staggering proportions in Bolivia, it is prevalent in neighbouring Brazil to a degree unfamiliar to most Western travellers, and should be a major concern to all visitors. At present, AIDS is a death sentence and will continue to be until a cure is found – and that may not be for a while. Although in the West it is most commonly spread through intravenous drug abuse and male homosexual activity, in South America it is transmitted primarily through heterosexual activity.

Most people affected by the AIDS virus are not aware they have it and hospitals are likely to diagnose their symptoms as something more mundane. The obvious way to best avoid the disease is to remain celibate. Not everyone can – or is inclined to be – so if you do have sex in South America, cut the risk by using a condom. Even then you are far from 100% safe.

You can also pick up AIDS through blood transfusions and it is possible to contract the virus through injection with an unsterilised needle. If you must have an injection, either provide your own sterilised syringe or make absolutely sure it's either new or properly sterilised.

Altitude & Climate-Related Illnesses
Soroche (Altitude Sickness) Due to extreme altitude, the oxygen density in the highland and Altiplano regions is much lower than most foreigners are accustomed to. The atmospheric density at Potosí, at 4070 metres, is less than ⅔ its value at sea level; and at Chacaltaya near La Paz, the summit of which lies at 5600 metres, it is only about half. Water on the Altiplano boils at about 90°C, and planes landing at La Paz's airport reach stall speed at nearly twice the velocity they would in Santa Cruz at only 437 metres.

The human body is also affected by an increase in altitude. On a rapid ascent to high altitude, say a flight from Lima at sea level to La Paz at 3686 metres, the body is not given time to adapt to the lower oxygen concentration. Newly arrived visitors will invariably experience a condition known as *soroche* or simple altitude sickness, and should take it easy for the first few days until their bodies have acclimatised.

As the body attempts to compensate for the decreasing availability of life-sustaining oxygen, respiration is deepened and accelerated. At first, this hyperventilation causes an overabundance of carbon dioxide in the blood. This imbalance causes a feeling of fatigue and lethargy until the kidney kicks into action to correct it.

Mental capacity is reduced and the victim experiences a persistent headache, loss of appetite, weakness and shortness of breath after even minor activity. These symptoms are sometimes accompanied by nausea and vomiting. Chewing coca leaves or drinking *mate de coca* (coca leaf tea) will relieve some of the discomfort, but the best remedy is a day or two of rest while the body begins its acclimatisation process. Drinking large quantities of water – about two or three litres daily – is essential.

After a week or so at high altitude, 80% of the acclimatisation process is complete. After about two more weeks, the bone marrow is stimulated to produce more red blood cells and the oxygen-carrying capacity of the blood is increased by 25%. Further acclimatisation goes on over longer periods of time, but nobody reaches more than about 95% of their sea-level capacity.

If you're travelling quickly to high altitudes (eg from Lima to La Paz) and won't have the opportunity to acclimatise, a drug called Diamox (Acetazolamide) will prevent altitude discomfort. It should be taken in 250-mg doses four times daily, four days before and six days after ascent. In order to prevent the formation of kidney stones, drink lots of water (at least 1½ litres) after the first dosage each day. For altitude-related discomfort, especially on brief ascents to over 4500 metres, Micoren tablets, which are available in Bolivian pharmacies, may be taken two or three times daily. They stimulate the respiratory functions and relieve immediate symptoms. For headache, a non-aspirin pain-reliever such as paracetamol (called acetaminophen in North America) may be used.

Most of Bolivia's population lives above 3000 metres. The most lofty city is Potosí and the highest population is a small group of scientists living at 5300 metres on the slopes of Chacaltaya. This is at the outer limit of human endurance; above this altitude, the body will not adapt sufficiently to allow permanent habitation.

Acute Mountain Sickness (AMS) A more serious condition than soroche, AMS is experienced among climbers and hikers who spend time above their acclimatisation threshold. Above 5600 metres or so, tiny blood vessels in the retina and the brain begin to haemorrhage slightly and vision or brain function can temporarily be affected. Abnormal clotting of blood can also affect the brain and the heart. The only treatment is administration of oxygen and immediate descent to a lower altitude. There is a great variation in different people's susceptibility to AMS; Some people begin feeling ill as low as 2450 metres; other feel fine at 6000 metres. In general, AMS is rare below 2450 metres.

Anyone planning to ascend to altitudes of over 5000 metres for any length of time (longer than a few hours of skiing at Chacaltaya) should first seek medical advice and be familiar with methods and rules used by expedition climbers to deal with AMS. Those with a history of cardiac, pulmonary or circulatory problems should consult a physician before travelling to Bolivia.

There are two types of AMS: benign and malignant. Benign AMS is the more common and milder form but can herald the onset of the severe form. Telltale signs include loss of appetite, headache, dizziness, insomnia, nausea and vomiting (especially in children), disorientation, loss of judgement and general malaise.

Malignant AMS is very serious and can rapidly be fatal. It may occur without warning or may be preceded by symptoms of benign AMS. Breathing becomes laboured due to pulmonary oedema, a concentration of fluids in the lungs. Brain cells may also retain water (cerebral oedema) which eventually leads to unconsciousness and death. Symptoms of pulmonary oedema include extreme breathlessness, coughing,

white frothy sputum and blue lips. Cerebral Oedema is characterised by the following: severe headache, drowsiness, unsteady movement, abnormal behaviour, disorientation and a progressively reduced level of consciousness.

If AMS is suspected, get the victim down to a lower altitude immediately! Descend even if it is the middle of the night – every minute counts. If they're unconscious and vomiting, place them on their side so that the vomit does not enter the lungs. If oxygen is available immediately, then administer it, preferably at four to six litres per minute by a close-fitting mask.

If someone is suffering from malignant AMS in La Paz or elsewhere on the Altiplano, they must get down to the lowlands – Santa Cruz or Trinidad for example – as soon as possible, preferably by air.

Minimising Risk The best way to minimise the risk of AMS is to ascend slowly. Ascending to about 3000 metres normally presents no problem, but above that, the body needs time to acclimatise. A gain of about 300 metres per day would be ideal, but since that may be difficult, rest days between ascents are recommended.

Trekking at high altitudes will cause dehydration due to increased sweating and loss of moisture through accelerated respiration in cold, dry air, so it will also help to increase intake of liquids. Eat light meals high in energy-rich carbohydrates and avoid tobacco since smoking produces carbon monoxide which reduces the amount of oxygen the blood can carry. Alcohol should also be avoided since it increases urine output and results in further dehydration. Furthermore, avoid sedatives which may mask symptoms of AMS.

Most importantly, do not trek alone. AMS reduces good judgement and symptoms are often ignored or not perceived by the victim. If you are suffering from any symptoms of benign AMS, don't go any higher and avoid exertion until they have disappeared. Light outdoor activity is better than bed rest.

Hypothermia Hypothermia is a dangerous lowering of the body temperature. It is caused by exhaustion and exposure to cold, wet or windy weather, which can occur anywhere in Bolivia. Hypothermia is a threat whenever a person is exposed to the elements at temperatures below 10°.

The best treatment is of course to get the victim to shelter and give them warm drinks and a hot bath if possible, which it probably won't be in Bolivia. Wet clothing should be changed or removed – no clothing at all is better than wet garments.

The patient should lie down, wrapped in a sleeping bag or blanket to preserve body heat. Another person may lie down with them in order to provide as much warmth as possible. If no improvement is noticed within a few minutes, seek help but don't leave the victim alone while doing so. The body heat of another person is immediately more important than medical attention.

Sunburn The Altiplano and much of the highland regions of Bolivia lie within the tropics at elevations greater than 3000 metres. The atmosphere there is too thin to screen out much of the dangerous ultraviolet radiation that is absorbed and deflected at lower altitudes. It may be cold and windy or even overcast, but the UV effect is still hazardous and the use of a strong sunscreen is essential: serious burns can occur after even brief exposure. Don't neglect to apply sunscreen to any area of exposed skin, especially if you're near water or snow. On Lake Titicaca and in the high mountains, reflected rays can burn as severely as direct rays.

Sunscreen is unfortunately quite expensive in Bolivia, and it's also difficult to find one with a rating high enough for fair skin, so you may want to bring some from home. In addition, a hat will serve to shade your face and protect your scalp, and sunglasses will prevent eye irritation (especially if you wear contact lenses).

Some people also experience a rash caused by photosensitivity in high altitudes. This can be treated with light applications of cortisone cream to affected areas (never use cortisone near your face, however).

Prickly Heat Prickly heat is an itchy rash caused by excessive perspiration trapped under the skin. It usually strikes travellers newly arrived in a hot climate whose pores have not opened enough to accommodate profuse sweating. Frequent baths and the application of talcum powder will help relieve the itch.

Heat Exhaustion In the tropical lowlands, Yungas and Chaco regions, heat combined with humidity and exposure to the sun can be oppressive and leave you feeling lethargic, irritable and dazed. A cool swim or lazy afternoon in the shade will do wonders to improve your mood. You'll also need to drink lots of liquids and eat salty foods in order to replenish your supply of these products lost during sweating.

Serious dehydration or salt deficiency can lead to heat exhaustion. Take time to acclimatise to high temperatures, and again, be sure to drink sufficient liquids. Salt deficiency, which can be brought on by diarrhoea or nausea, is characterised by fatigue, lethargy, headaches, giddiness and muscle cramps. Salt tablets will probably solve the problem. Anhidrotic heat exhaustion, caused by inability to sweat, is quite rare but can strike even those who have spent some time in hot climates.

Heatstroke This serious, sometimes fatal, condition can occur if the body's thermostat breaks down and body temperature rises to dangerous levels. Continuous exposure to high temperatures can leave you vulnerable to heatstroke. Alcohol intake and strenuous activity can increase chances of heatstroke, especially in those people who've recently arrived in a hot climate.

Symptoms include minimal sweating, a high body temperature (39 to 40° C), and a general feeling of unwellness. The skin may become flushed and red. Severe throbbing headaches, decreased coordination, and aggressive or confused behaviour may be signs of heatstroke. Eventually, the victim will become delirious and go into convulsions. Get the victim out of the sun, remove clothing, cover with a wet towel and fan continually. Seek medical help as soon as possible.

Motion Sickness

If you're susceptible to motion sickness, come prepared, because the roads and railroads in Bolivia aren't exactly smooth. If Dramamine works for you, take some along. Eating very lightly before and during a trip will reduce the chances of motion sickness. Try to find a place that minimises disturbance – near the wing on aircraft or near the centre on buses. Fresh air almost always helps, but reading or cigarette smoking (or even being around someone else's smoke) normally makes matters worse.

Commercial motion-sickness preparations, which can cause drowsiness, have to be taken before the trip; after you've begun feeling ill, it's too late. Dramamine tablets should be taken three hours before departure and scopolamine patches (which are available only by prescription in most places) should be applied 10 to 12 hours before departure. This will dilate the pupils if it accidentally comes in contact with the eyes and has been known to cause drowsiness, so caution should be exercised. Ginger can be used as a natural preventative and is available in capsule form.

Women's Health

Gynaecological Problems Poor diet, lowered resistance due to use of antibiotics, and even contraceptive pills can lead to vaginal infections when travelling in hot climates. To prevent the worst of it, keep the genital area clean, wear cotton underwear and skirts or loose-fitting trousers.

Yeast infections, characterised by a rash, itch and discharge, can be treated with a vinegar or lemon juice douche or with yoghurt. Nystatin suppositories are the usual medical prescription. Trichomonas is a more serious infection which causes a discharge and a burning sensation when urinating.

Male sexual partners must also be treated and if a vinegar and water douche is not effective, medical attention should be sought. Flagyl is the most frequently prescribed drug.

Pregnancy Most miscarriages occur during the first trimester of pregnancy so this is the most risky time to be travelling. The last three months should also be spent within reasonable reach of good medical care since serious problems can develop at this stage as well. Pregnant women should avoid all unnecessary medication, but vaccinations and malarial prophylactics should still be taken where possible. Additional care should be taken to prevent illness and particular attention to diet and proper nutrition will significantly lessen the chances of complications.

WOMEN TRAVELLERS

Bolivia is still very much a man's country, and for a woman travelling alone, this can prove frustrating. The mere fact you seem to be unmarried and far from your home and family may cause you to appear suspiciously disreputable. For your part, keep in mind that modesty is expected of women throughout Spanish-speaking Latin America and particularly in such a traditional society as Bolivia. Short sleeves are more or less acceptable but hemlines shouldn't be above knee level and trousers should be loose-fitting. In general, the lower the altitude in Bolivia, the more liberal the dress code. The best advice is to watch what well-dressed Bolivian women are wearing and follow their example.

Because most young South American men have become acquainted with foreign women through such reliable media as girlie magazines and North American films and TV, the concept of *gringa fácil*, which roughly means 'loose chick', has developed. Since Bolivia has cultural roots in southern Europe, it has been subjected to over four centuries of machismo. Many men consider foreign women – especially those travelling alone – to be fair and willing game.

Most of the ridiculous comments and passes lone women must endure are harmless. The only time I experienced a more serious situation was when a gang of five teenagers began throwing stones in a residential area of Santa Cruz. However, it was a relatively minor incident.

When subjected to machismo, many female travellers simply ignore it or flash a disgusted expression, which is the reaction expected of 'well-bred' Bolivian girls under similar circumstances. It unfortunately gives the impression, however, that the perpetrator is being taken seriously. A woman who simply mutters *casada* and continues on her way leaves the guys wondering whether she would welcome their advances were she not trapped by marriage. The hopeful lads then set about finding an unmarried woman.

It may be useful to remember that at least some of the time, the problem behaviour is the consequence of simple ignorance. Insults or blatant arrogance on a woman's part may derail obnoxious suitors, but more often, it will provide a source of amusement and reinforce the behaviour. Those who prefer to respond civilly may explain that women expect to be treated with more respect. Childish responses will almost certainly be covering up the embarrassment you've caused them.

One option which is 100% effective is to find a male travelling companion. For those women who insist upon travelling alone for whatever reason, it's a good idea to avoid such male domains as bars, sports matches, mines, construction sites and the like. It's all right to catch a lift on a *camión* (truck), especially if there are lots of other people waiting, but otherwise, women should never hitch alone in Bolivia.

DANGERS & ANNOYANCES

The main security problems you're likely to encounter are petty crime and the odd unscrupulous official. Violent crime against foreigners is not common and the following sections offer some suggestions for mitigating or foiling attempted theft or the irregular conduct of officials. Remember, even though you may consider yourself an impecunious traveller, locals will automatically measure you according to the common belief that foreigners have lots of money and expensive cameras. Even if you don't fit this category, as you will be visibly unfamiliar with the turf and possibly the language, you'll be easy to pick out in a crowd.

Many foreign visitors to Bolivia are apprehensive about safety and security. Since many readers may not have previously experienced the methods of petty crime or the extent of corruption evident in parts of South America, this section has been written in detail to heighten awareness. However, it is neither necessary nor helpful to become paranoid – Bolivia is one of the safest Latin American countries. Our intention is to demonstrate that there are many things travellers can do to reduce the minimal risks.

Predeparture Precautions

If you work on the elements of vulnerability, you can significantly minimise risks. For starters, take with you only those items which you are prepared to lose or replace. Travel insurance is essential for replacement of valuables and the cost of a good policy is a worthwhile price to pay for minimum disturbance or even abrupt termination of your travel plans. Loss through violence or petty theft is an emotional and stressful experience which can be reduced if you think ahead. The less you carry with you, the less you have to lose.

Don't bring jewellery, chains or expensive watches; if you do wear a watch, use a cheapie worth a few dollars. Even better, buy your cheapie watch in a Bolivian market and keep it in your pocket, not on your wrist. It may be considered an insensitive affront to the less fortunate if tourists stroll around flaunting expensive jewellery, watches and cameras.

Be prepared for the worst – make copies of your important records: a photocopy of your passport (page with passport number, name, photograph, location where issued and expiration date; all visas); travellers' cheque numbers; credit-card numbers; airline tickets; contact addresses, etc. Keep one copy with you, one with your belongings and the other with a travelling companion.

By law you must carry a passport with you at all times, but many travellers opt to carry a photocopy (preferably certified) whilst they amble about town, and leave the passport locked up somewhere safe. A passport is worth several thousand dollars to some people, so keep a close eye on it. If you do lose it, photocopies of the lost passport and a copy of your birth certificate can usually speed up the issuing of a new passport at embassies and consulates. US citizens should keep in mind that replacement passports may be purchased only with cash US dollars.

Credit cards are useful in emergencies and for regular purchases. Make sure you know the number to call if you lose your credit card, and be quick to cancel it if it's lost or stolen. New-style credit-card coupons do not have carbon-paper inserts and offer more protection against misuse. If you sign an old-style coupon, be sure to ask for the carbon inserts and destroy them after use. Similarly, destroy any coupons which have been filled out incorrectly. These are worthwhile precautions against unwanted duplication of your credit card!

Cabling money is time-consuming, difficult and expensive. You must know the name and address of both the bank sending (record this and keep this with your documents) and the bank receiving your money.

Security Accessories

Make sure your backpack is fitted with double zippers which can be secured using small combination locks. Padlocks are also good, but are easier to pick. A thick backpack cover or modified canvas sack improves protection against pilfering, 'planting' of drugs, and general wear and tear. Double zippers on your daypack can be secured with safety pins to reduce the ease of access favoured by petty thieves. A bicycle combination lock or padlock (steel or chain) is recommended for chaining luggage to racks in buses, trains, and to hotel fixtures. A medium-size combination lock or padlock is useful to replace the

padlock on your hotel door. Rubber wedges are handy to prevent access to doors or windows. To deter thieves operating with razors, you can line the inside of your daypack (and even your backpack) with lightweight wire mesh. This will be especially useful if you'll be visiting Peru.

Don't keep all your valuables together: distribute them about your person and baggage to avoid the risk of losing everything in one fell swoop. Various types of money belt are available which can be worn around the waist, neck or shoulder. Those made of leather or cotton material are more comfortable than the synthetic variety. Money belts are only useful if worn *under* clothing – pouches worn outside clothing are easy prey and attract attention. Determined thieves are wise to conventional money belts, and some travellers now also use cloth pouches sewn into trousers or attached under clothes with safety pins. Other methods include belts with a concealed zipper compartment, and bandages or pouches worn around the leg.

If you wear glasses, secure them with an elastic strap to deter petty theft. Better still, wear contact lenses.

Finally, the extra pair of eyes provided by a travelling companion is an obvious asset!

Security Precautions

There are certain key things you can do to reduce attention from criminals. Your style of dress should be casual and inexpensive. If you carry a daypack, wear it local fashion: strapped in the front like a kangaroo pouch! Whether you're in a bus terminal, restaurant, shop or elsewhere, whenever you have to put your daypack down, put your foot through the strap. Both these ploys make things more difficult for furtive fingers or bag-slashers.

If you have a camera, don't wander around with it dangling over your shoulder or around your neck – keep it out of sight as much as possible. It's also unwise to keep it in a swanky camera bag which is an obvious target. In risky areas, we carried cameras in a sturdy plastic bag from a local supermarket.

Get used to keeping small change and a few banknotes in a shirt pocket, so that you can pay for bus tickets and small expenses without extracting large amounts of money which could quickly attract attention. This easily accessible money is also useful in the rare event that you should be assailed by a mugger. If you carry a wallet, try to keep it in a zippered or buttoned inside pocket and don't use it on public transport or in crowded places where it might attract unwelcome attention.

Changing money on the street is not recommended, but if you have no other option, then you should bear in mind the advice given in the Money section earlier in this chapter.

Before arriving in a new place, make sure you have a map or at least a rough idea about orientation. Try to plan your schedule so you don't arrive at night, and use a taxi if this seems the appropriate way to avoid walking through high-risk areas. A travelling companion is useful since solo travellers are more easily distracted. Be observant and learn to move like a street-smart local.

Favourite Scams

Distraction is a common tactic employed by street thieves. The 'cream technique' is now very common throughout South America, and Bolivia is no exception. The trick commences when you're walking down the street or standing in a public place, and someone surreptitiously sprays a substance on your shoulder, your daypack or anything else connected with you. The substance can be anything from mustard to chocolate or even dog muck. An assistant (young or old; male or female) then taps you on the shoulder and amicably offers to clean off the mess...if you'll just put down your bag for a second. The moment you do, someone makes off with it like a flash. Ignore any such attempt or offer and simply endure your mucky state until you can find a safe place, such as your hotel, where you can wash.

Another distraction technique involves one or more people working to divert you or literally throw you off balance. This trick usually happens when you're standing in the street or somewhere busy like a bus terminal; it happened to us in Yacuiba outside a casa de cambio. One or more characters suddenly ask you a question, 'bump' into you or stage an angry discussion or fight around you, and whilst you are off balance or diverted, there'll be an attempt to pick your pockets or whip your gear.

Druggings have also been reported. Exercise caution when you're offered cigarettes, beer, sweets, etc by strangers. If the circumstances make you suspicious or uneasy, the offer can be gently refused by claiming stomach or other medical problems.

These scams are continuously being developed and imported or exported across borders. Peruvian scams are common in the border areas and may spread. Stay aware of changes by talking to other travellers. In our experience, theft and security are sources of endless fascination and stories: some are true, some are incredible, and some are taller than Illimani! If you think this section is useful and would like to forewarn other travellers about new developments, we'd appreciate your feedback. You might even derive consolation from letting off steam and satisfaction from steering other travellers out of the clutches of criminals.

Streets & Public Transport Thieves watch for people leaving hotels, bus terminals, railway stations, casas de cambio, tourist sights – places with lots of foreigners – then follow their targets. If you notice you're being followed or closely observed, it helps to pause and look straight at the person(s) involved, or, if you're not alone, simply point out the person(s) to your companion. This makes it clear that the element of surprise favoured by petty criminals has been lost.

Don't advertise the fact that you're a foreigner by flashing big bills or wearing jewellery. Keep your watch out of sight in your pocket. Don't carry much money in the streets and even less on the municipal buses. Carry just enough money on your person for the evening's entertainment and transport and keep it discreetly stashed in a money belt, sock, secret pocket or shoe.

Muggings are very rare in Bolivia. Don't carry weapons: in many cases this could make matters much worse. In any case, if you've prepared for your trip along the lines mentioned earlier in this section, you'll probably feel happier just letting the unpleasant event pass.

If you ride the buses, have your change ready before boarding. You may want to avoid the super-crowded city buses. If you have valuables, take taxis rather than buses.

Buses and bus terminals have dedicated scams and scampsters; almost all work according to the distraction technique. An Australian couple told us how they had been sitting in their bus waiting for departure, when someone knocked on their window and held their attention whilst they tried to work out the message. Meanwhile, an accomplice inside the bus had edged up beside them and used the diversion to sneak off with their video camera which had been on the overhead rack. The following variation on this theme is quoted from a reader's letter:

Beware of scam duos, one claiming to be a passenger with a bag, the other claiming to be a bus company employee. I encountered such a duo in La Paz bus terminal as I was about to depart on a bus run by the CISNE bus company.

Before we departed, the 'passenger' sat alongside engaging me in animated conversation. The 'employee' entered the bus and politely asked everyone to store daypacks handily out of the way in the overhead rack. The 'passenger' quickly obliges. I, without thinking, quickly followed suit. More engaging conversation whilst the 'employee' happily rearranges the overhead rack with a razor. In the rush and bustle of people filing off, I suspected nothing at the time. The 'passenger' suddenly remembers he's on the wrong bus and flees. I lost my camera.

This cannot happen with those companies that post a guard at the front of their buses who demands to see a ticket before allowing passengers to enter.

Mark Stambovsky, USA

Long-distance bus and train travel is usually well organised. If you hand over luggage to be placed in the baggage compartment, make sure you receive and keep your receipt. Two or more items can be padlocked together. If you place luggage on the overhead racks inside, padlock it to the rack. If you have to place baggage on the roof of the bus, secure it with a padlock. These last two points are especially important during night trips.

Although Bolivian taxi drivers are no different than their counterparts worldwide when it comes to arbitrary fare augmentation, taxi-related problems are very rare in Bolivia. Still, if you're travelling for a while in South America and plan to take taxis, there are a few guidelines which may help smooth your trip along:

When entering or leaving a taxi, it's advisable (particularly for solo travellers) to keep a passenger door open during the loading or unloading of luggage – particularly if this is being done by someone other than the driver. This reduces the ease with which a taxi can drive off with your luggage, leaving you behind! A neater solution for those who travel light is to fit luggage inside the taxi rather than in the boot.

Also, when entering or leaving a taxi, always remember to watch your luggage (slip your foot or your arm through the appropriate strap). Opportunistic thieves are quick to make off with items whilst you are distracted by price-haggling or baggage arrangement. If you're travelling as a pair (or larger group), it's a good general precaution to always have at least one person remain close to the open passenger door or inside the taxi whenever luggage is still in the taxi.

Before starting, immediately question the presence of any 'shady' characters accompanying the driver, and don't hesitate to take another taxi if you feel uneasy. If there are mechanical or orientation problems en route, do not allow yourself to be separated from your luggage. When you arrive at your destination, don't hand over your luggage to a person who tries to help you out of the car and offers to carry something, unless you are quite positive about their identity. Otherwise, you may see your luggage disappearing down the street.

In Hotels If you consider your hotel to be reliable, place valuables in its safe and get a receipt. Make sure you package your valuables in a small, double-zippered bag which can be padlocked, or use a signed seal which will easily show any tampering. Count money and travellers' cheques before and after retrieving them from the safe – this should quickly identify any attempts to extract single bills or cheques which might otherwise go unnoticed.

Check the door, doorframe and windows of your room for signs of forced entry or unsecured access. If your hotel provides a padlock, it's recommended to use your own combination lock (or padlock) instead. A hotel padlock obviously increases the number of people with access to your room. Although it's not recommended to leave valuables in your room, some travellers padlock baggage to room fixtures or tape items in concealed places. If you tape things, don't leave them behind as a windfall for the cleaner!

Police & Fake Police Scams If something is stolen from you, report it to the police. No big investigation is going to occur, but you will get a police form for your insurance company. The police aren't to be trusted, however, and sometimes require a large payment just to fill out the forms. Bolivian police have been known to plant drugs and sting gringos for bribes. The bribes are like pyramids: the more people involved, the larger the bribe becomes. Due to a recent push to improve Bolivia's image, this practice is fortunately less prevalent that it was just a few years ago.

There is a series of scams associated with police and characters purporting to be police or similar officials responsible for law enforcement. If you are stopped on the street, in a bus terminal or railway station, etc, by one or more of these characters, insist that they produce full proof of their identity. Under *no* circumstances should you agree to use a taxi to go to the police station. Make a note of the police officers' ID details; insist on phoning the police station or going on foot; and preferably find a travelling companion or witness to go with you. Any attempt to persuade you to do otherwise, for example, using a compliant stooge who just 'happens' to be passing to verify their identity or good intentions, should be politely ignored.

In this book, we've included requisite phone numbers for tourist police whenever available. As a general rule, in most parts of Bolivia you should dial 110 to contact the Radio Patrulla (Police Patrol). Whilst researching this edition, we found that police were starting to crack down on these fraudulent characters as a public-relations gesture. Outside La Paz, relatively few travellers have reported problems with 'fake' police.

The most common scenario is as follows: a traveller is stopped on the street by characters with a fake ID (they typically keep their thumb over the photo or ID number), who request that the traveller accompany them in a taxi to the police station. Inside the taxi, the traveller's belongings are 'inspected' and valuables 'confiscated'. A reader in the UK writes:

Twice in La Paz I was asked to show my passport to non-uniformed men carrying stolen or faked police ID. This is apparently a pastime growing in popularity in Bolivia because in Potosí and Cochabamba I saw official notices posted in hotels, post offices, etc, warning tourists of these false policemen. (The notices) advise you to tell anyone asking to see passports, dollars or other documents that you will only show them your documents at the police station to which you must walk, refusing lifts in cars. The notices also say that it is unlikely you'd be asked to show your documents by anyone but a uniformed policeman. In any case, on the occasions when I met the false policemen, they soon disappeared at any mention of police stations.

On one occasion when I was asked for ID, I had a close scrape. I was in a taxi with other Bolivians who handed over their documents without any problem which almost convinced me to do the same. Fortunately, a little common sense got me out of the situation. I also believe that as the Bolivians are fairly new in dealing with tourists and not that adept at tricking them, they are not particularly good at it. I found it quite easy to read on their faces when they were lying.

Travellers crossing the Peruvian-Bolivian borders, Yunguyo/Copacabana in particular, have reported that their Bolivian entry stamp had been dated one day *ahead* of the actual day of entry. Once these travellers arrived in Copacabana and found a hotel, they were visited by police doing a 'routine' search who 'discovered' the 'infringement' (in other words, the date stamp irregularity)...and required a fine. The obvious advice is to check your date stamp carefully at the border and, if incorrect, insist that it is corrected.

Villazón is notorious for plain-clothes police who stop foreigners in the streets, alleging that they must confiscate any 'illegal' US dollar notes the travellers may be carrying. Of course, dollars are not illegal anywhere in Bolivia – this is just another racket in the endless repertoire of Bolivian officialdom, but since few foreigners want to stay in town long enough to raise much of a fuss about it, it's a difficult one to eliminate. Any problems you have should be reported to the officer's superiors, but the best bet is to avoid the situation in the first place. Hide your cash well, leave it in your room, or tell the offender that you only carry travellers' cheques (this worked for us) and hope for the best. If they do find cash, it may help to let them know that there will be serious repercussions should they insist on carrying out such highway robbery.

Another obnoxious scam takes advantage of good-natured foreigners. A packet of money or an unidentifiable package is 'accidentally' dropped by a passer-by in front of a traveller – perhaps in the street or even inside a taxi. When the foreigner follows Good Samaritan instincts and picks up the package, the person who dropped it immediately accuses them of robbery and grabs a police officer – who just happens to be nearby – so that the foreigner can be caught red-handed with the 'stolen' goods. Only after a substantial 'fine' is paid is the alleged offender allowed to go free. It's probably best not to 'find' anything or even try to be helpful by picking up a dropped item.

In parts of Bolivia, hotel managers inform foreign guests that the hotel is subject to a fine unless guests register with the local police. If you comply, it becomes obvious that this is really nothing more than a police attempt to extract charges for a stamp. One method, learnt from experience, is to tell the hotel manager that you'll be seeing the police soon; repeat this as often as the request is repeated. This happened to us in Rurrenabaque, Oruro and San José de Chiquitos. In Camiri, the police stamp appears to be legitimate.

Drug Plants Some unscrupulous and poorly paid officials look for methods of extorting money from anyone who may be caught off guard. If you appear wealthy enough to cough up a few thousand dollars to avoid spending a year in prison awaiting trial, you may be victimised, especially if you're alone.

During a routine search, when you're not paying attention, an officer may triumphantly 'find' a container of suspicious-looking white powder in your luggage. You'll probably never know whether it's actually cocaine because such things as laboratory tests are not considered important. The officer says it's cocaine and so it is, and will, at this point, offer to make a deal: you pay a 'fine' of US$5000 and the officer will agree to overlook the matter. For what it's worth, I haven't actually heard of anyone going to prison because they couldn't pay. Officials will normally be happy with whatever you've got.

Principled individuals who have gone to prison rather than admit to a crime they did not commit, often agree to pay the fine after a few days of incarceration. Unfortunately this only fuels the flame of corruption, and since foreign embassies seem to want nothing to do with drug-related charges, innocent victims are more or less on their own.

This practice is fortunately very uncommon, and while you'll probably never confront it, some precautions are warranted. Whenever you're subjected to customs or police searches, especially at Santa Cruz (Viru Viru) Airport where this practice has been reported, watch carefully while officers are pawing through your luggage. If possible, keep a friend on hand who could serve as a witness and make conversation with the official conducting the search. If you're carrying a piece of luggage on public transportation, lock all latches and zips to prevent tampering when you're not looking.

If things still manage to go awry, don't touch the contraband they've 'found' in your luggage, don't sign anything that might be an admission of guilt and ask for the name of the offending officer. Most importantly, don't panic. This isn't easy, but you'll need to be thinking clearly. Remember, both you and the police officer know that you're innocent. If someone you know is a victim of this scam, report and publicise it to consulates, government officials and other travellers who may be venturing into the jurisdiction of such corruption.

Above all, don't let this remote possibility prevent you from travelling to Bolivia. Chances of this happening are very slim indeed and an alert individual can practically be guaranteed that no such thing will occur.

Drugs

Cocaine Bolivia may be the land of cocaine, but rumours that a cheap and abundant supply is readily available to the general public are untrue. Refined cocaine is highly illegal in Bolivia and unless you have a healthy supply of cash to pay off the arresting officer, it's best left alone.

The big guys get away with processing and exporting because they pay. Backpacking foreigners and coca-producing Indians become statistics to wave at foreign governments as proof, if you will, that Bolivia is doing something about the drug problem. Although foreign travellers are searched less frequently than a few years ago (perhaps the police have realised they don't carry all that much money), it's still not wise to carry drugs of any kind, even in small quantities. The consequences are too costly.

If you choose to ignore this advice and the worst happens – you're caught with drugs and arrested – the safest bet is to pay off the arresting officer(s) before more officials learn about your plight and want to be cut in on the deal. If this seems unethical, you've never seen the inside of a Bolivian prison.

It's best not to call the payoff a bribe per se. Ask something like: '¿Como podemos arreglar este asunto?' ('How can we put this matter right?'). They'll understand what you mean.

If the officer refuses, then you're on your own. Foreign embassies aren't usually interested in such hard-luck stories. They may provide a lawyer to ensure you're treated as fairly as any Bolivian would be under the same circumstances, but beyond that, they're powerless. Details about drug plants have been provided earlier in this section.

Coca Leaves While cocaine, marijuana, hashish and other drugs are illegal, the coca leaf, which is the source of cocaine and related drugs, is chewed daily and even venerated by indigenous peoples. Mama Coca is the daughter of Pachamama, the earth mother. Coca was considered a gift to the people to be used to drive evil forces from their homes and fields. Both the Quechua and Aymará make sacrifices of coca leaves when planting or mining in order to ensure a good harvest or a lucky strike. The yatiri, or witch doctors, use them in their healing and exorcising rituals, and in remote rural areas the leaves are often used in place of money. If you're walking in the mountains or countryside, carry some along as a gift to helpful locals. The gesture will be enormously appreciated.

Coca is an appetite suppressant and a central nervous system stimulant. The conquering Spanish found that those who chewed the leaf became more dedicated workers so they promoted its use among the peasants. Today, nearly all campesinos and cholas, men and women alike, take advantage of its benefits.

The Indians use it while working to lessen the effects of altitude and eliminate the necessity of a lunch break. They also chew it recreationally and socially in much the same way people smoke cigarettes or drink coffee. Among Bolivian miners, the 'coca break' is an institution. Bolivians of European origin, however, still regard chewing coca as a disgusting 'Indian' habit and generally avoid its use.

The leaf itself grows on bushes which are cultivated in the Yungas and Upper Chapare regions at altitudes of between 1000 and 2000 metres. They are sold by the kg in nearly every market in Bolivia along with legía, an alkaloid usually made of potato and quinoa ash, which is used to draw the drug from the leaves when chewed. There are two kinds of legía: *achura*, which is sweet, and *cuta*, which is salty.

The effects of coca-chewing are not startling by any description. It will leave you feeling a little detached, reflective, melancholy or pleasantly contented. The Indians normally chew about 30 to 35 leaves at a time. If you want to try it, the process involves placing a few leaves, say, five to 10, between your gums and cheek until they soften. Repeat the process placing a little legía between the leaves. Don't start chewing until you've stuffed in the desired amount. Once you've chewed it into a pulpy mess, you're supposed to swallow the bitter-tasting juice, which will numb your mouth and throat. (Novocaine and related anaesthetics are coca derivatives.)

Mushrooms & Cacti *Psilocyben* or 'magic mushrooms' are available, as they are in most parts of the world, in places where livestock leave things lying around. They're not illegal – South Americans don't seem to even be aware of them – but make a positive identification before partaking.

Choma, or San Pedro cactus, grows throughout the deserts of south-western Bolivia. It may be found most conveniently in the Valle de la Luna (Valley of the Moon), near La Paz. The natives report that, after being boiled for several hours, the juice of its flesh will 'send you flying' – not surprising since the active ingredient is mescaline. Currently, its use is also quite legal (or rather, it's not criminal) in Bolivia. If you're interested, ask a local to point it out for you.

Beggars

For many, one of the most disconcerting aspects of travel in Bolivia is the constant presence of beggars. With no social welfare system to sustain them, the elderly, blind, crippled, mentally ill and jobless take to the streets and try to arouse sympathy in any way possible.

Since giving even a pittance to every beggar encountered will be financially impossible for most visitors, everyone has a

Gift Giving

When travelling around Bolivia, particularly in rural areas, visitors are frequently shocked by the often apparently primitive conditions they encounter. In response, some are moved to compare the locals' lot with their own. They experience pangs of conscience and outrage at inequalities. Hoping to salve the guilt or inspire goodwill, they indiscriminately distribute gifts of sweets, cigarettes, money and other foreign items to local children and adults.

What foreigners in their high-technology, fast-paced Western societies fail to realise is that in Bolivia, the lack of money, TV, automobiles, mod cons or expensive playthings does not necessarily indicate poverty. The people of rural Bolivia have crops, animals and homes which provide sufficient food, clothing and shelter. They live out their lives in a peaceful environment amid the mountains, free from most of the threats of world conflict. They work hard with the land and in turn, it takes care of them.

While it would be difficult for most Westerners to become accustomed to this lifestyle, the proud and independent highland Bolivians have known nothing else for well over 1000 years and they are as comfortable with it as foreigners are in their own element. When we condescendingly hand out sweets or cigarettes, we cause dental and health problems which they cannot remedy; and when we give money, we impose on them a foreign system of values and upset a well-established balance.

While it's undoubtedly well meaning, the long-term consequences of indiscriminate gift-giving are undeniable; please don't turn proud, independent and self-sufficient people into grovelling beggars! The slums which ring La Paz are evidence of the number of campesinos who have migrated to the city in search of money and material goods, and in doing so have traded a relatively prosperous life for one of real poverty: hunger, disease, squalor and a life of begging. If you wish to be accepted as a friend and fellow human being, perhaps share a conversation, teach a game from home, or show a photograph of your friends or family. If a gift becomes appropriate, share something that won't disrupt local culture or lifestyle, such as a piece of fruit or a few coca leaves. ∎

different idea about what constitutes an appropriately humanitarian response. Some travellers choose to give only to the most pathetic cases or to those enterprising individuals who provide some value for money, such as by singing or playing a musical instrument. Others simply feel that contributions only serve to fuel the machine that creates beggars, and ignore the whining cries that haunt Bolivian footpaths.

All we can offer on this issue is a couple of guidelines; the rest must be left to individual consciences. The physically impaired are always underemployed, frequently left to sell lottery tickets and telephone tokens, but they do manage to earn something. The mentally indigent or the elderly who would appear to have no other possible means of support may be especially good candidates. Keep in mind, however, that many families simply set their older members on the pavement with a tin bowl hoping to generate a little extra income. For those who go begging for bones, scraps and leftovers, or others who are truly trying to change their situations, a bowl of soup or a nutritious hot meal will go a long way.

Regarding the numerous children who beg, it's best not to give money since it will lead to their exploitation by unscrupulous adults and will give the impression that something can be had for nothing. Bolivians like to complain that money given to begging children winds up in the video game parlours. For a child who appears truly hungry, a piece of fruit or other healthy snack will be appreciated; if such gifts are refused and money is demanded, it should be fairly obvious what's really going on.

Plumbing

Most Bolivian plumbing is jerry-built or poorly installed and inferior to what developed nations consider acceptable. Bathtubs are rare outside expensive tourist hotels, as is hot and cold running water. It is possible, however, to have hot (or tepid) showers, thanks to a frightening and deadly looking device that attaches to the shower head and electrically heats the water as it passes

through. Bare wires dangle from the ceiling or run into the shower head. The dangling variety indicates that you're not going to get a hot shower because the device is broken, as many are. Don't bother getting undressed until you've verified that it's working.

On the wall, you'll find a lever that suspiciously resembles an old-time electrocutioner's switch. You have to flip the switch after the water is running, so it's best to leave your shoes on and not get wet until this is done. When the heater is activated, it will begin to emit an electrical humming sound and the lights in the room will dim or go out altogether due to the great deal of electricity required to operate the contraption effectively.

The water temperature can then be adjusted by increasing or decreasing its flow; a larger volume of water cannot be adequately heated in the time it takes to pass through the shower head, so often a shower of a bearable temperature is nothing but a pressureless drip.

When it's time to turn the water off, don't touch the controls until you have your shoes on. This may be tricky, especially if the shower stall is small. Before turning the water off, flip the switch on the wall and then close the valve.

The WC is usually called *el baño* but it's also often misnamed *servicio sanitario* or *servicio higiénico*. Usually neither sanitary nor hygienic, facilities can be unspeakable.

In markets and transportation terminals, use of the facilities will normally cost B.20 to B.50. This investment will yield two sheets of one-ply toilet paper which will generally not be enough. Toilet paper is almost never provided in public facilities, not even in top-class restaurants (or the Bolivian Embassy in Washington, DC, for that matter!), so Bolivians carry a roll wherever they go.

Since water pressure is very weak, the toilets often cannot even choke down shit, let alone such things as tampons or toilet paper. Therefore, a wastebasket is normally provided; if there is no receptacle or if it's already full, toss the used toilet paper on the floor and someone may get around to cleaning it up. In rural areas, toilets tend to be more basic: a hole in the ground or a corner of a pig sty. So much for eating pork...

Incorrect Information

If you're in need of information or directions, be aware that Bolivians will often provide incorrect answers or directions rather than give no response at all. They're not being malicious; they merely want to please you and appear helpful and knowledgeable. It's therefore best not to take spontaneous answers at face value. Ask several people the same question and if one answer seems to stand out above the others, it's probably as close to correct as you'll find.

WORK

There are a vast number of volunteer organisations at work in Bolivia and quite a few international companies with offices in the country, but those looking for paid work on the spot probably won't have much luck. Qualified English teachers interested in working in La Paz and several other cities may want to try the professionally run Centro Boliviano Americano (☎ 351627), Avenida Aniceto Arce at Parque Zenón Iturralde, La Paz. Alternatively, phone Señor Alandia or Señora Miranda at the *Pan American English Language Centre* (☎ 340796), 2308 Avenida Aniceto Arce, to arrange an interview.

If you are interested in voluntary work in Bolivia with an emphasis on environmental protection, contact Earthwatch (☎ (617) 926-8200, 680 Mt Auburn St, Box 403, Watertown, MA 02272, USA.

HIKING, TREKKING & MOUNTAINEERING

Hiking, trekking and mountaineering are among the most rewarding ways to gain an appreciation for the Andes and their many moods and facets. Like the Himalaya, the mountain backbone of South America is not a wilderness area and has been inhabited for thousands of years by farmers and herders. While most of the popular hikes and treks in

Bolivia begin near La Paz, traverse the Cordillera Real along ancient Inca routes, and end in the Yungas, many areas of the country are suitable for hiking. In the text, we've included information on most of the popular alternatives, but we haven't begun to exhaust the possibilities.

If you're interested in pure Andean cultures and interaction with the locals, choose your trip carefully. In the more popular trekking areas, many well-meaning visitors who have passed before have indiscriminately bestowed gifts of sweets, cigarettes and money. As a consequence, foreigners are often pestered with persistent and sometimes threatening demands for material goods by both adults and children. For a few related guidelines, see the Gift Giving aside under Dangers & Annoyances in this chapter. For details on major trekking routes, refer to the Cordilleras & Yungas chapter. Further information on hiking, trekking and mountaineering in Bolivia is available from Club Andino Boliviano in either La Paz or Sorata (see relevant chapters for details).

Serious hikers and trekkers may want to pick up the 4th edition of *Backpacking and Trekking in Peru and Bolivia* by Hilary Bradt. The most recent edition (1989) has been updated and augmented by readers and contains lots of background information on the Cordillera Real as well as general backpacking tips and suggestions pertinent to the mountain areas. It also includes detailed descriptions of trips varying in length from one hour to more than a week.

Mountaineering

The following mountaineering and climbing information was prepared by Todd Miner, the director and coordinator of Alaska Wilderness Studies at the University of Alaska, Anchorage, who has led numerous climbing expeditions in South America.

Climbing in Bolivia, like the country itself, is a lesson in extremes. The weather can be as impossibly wet or as dry as any in the world. Even dry-season temperatures may fluctuate over 40°C in a single day. Roads pass within easy striking distance of many of the fine peaks, but in a land of transport strikes, crowded public transport and constant flux, finding the right camión or bus to get you there can lead to headaches rivalling those caused by soroche.

Whatever the frustrations, the beauty and variety of the aptly named Cordillera Real more than makes up for them. Most people who wish to explore Bolivia's mountains will find the 150-km-long range just east of La Paz offers the easiest access and most spectacular climbing of any in the country.

Providing delightful contrast, the range separates the stark Altiplano on its west from the fertile green Yungas falling away to the Amazon on its east. To the north lies the less accessible Cordillera Apolobamba and to the south, the Quimsa Cruz, which boasts Bolivia's best climbing rock. Six peaks of the Cordillera Real rise above 6000 metres and there are many more gems in the 5000-metre range. Due to the altitude, glaciers and ice or steep snow, few are 'walk-ups', but most are well within reach of the average climber.

During the dry season, May to September, the cordillera is blessed with some of the most stable weather a hiker or climber could ask for. Precipitation is minimal and winds are mild. Due to the elevation and lack of cloud cover, however, temperatures are extreme, with daytime highs of up to 30°C at the lower elevations and nighttime lows of -15°C above 5000 metres. These conditions lead to incredibly stable snow conditions, so the Real is a good place to learn snow climbing on the peaks or to perfect technique on one of the steeper faces or gullies.

The few dangers of climbing in Bolivia mainly relate to the altitude and the lack of any kind of rescue possibilities. Because the cordillera is relatively easy to access, there isn't sufficient time to acclimatise on the approach and soroche is a constant threat. *Mountain Sickness*, by Peter Hackett, is one of the most practical books available, as it's field-oriented and easily transportable. I carry it when I climb to high altitude.

Luckily, those spending much time in Bolivia before climbing will have a head start on acclimatisation. Those just arriving

would do well to spend at least a few days to a week in La Paz or hiking in the surrounding area, staying as high as possible.

Once you're acclimatised to the Altiplano's relatively thin air, remember there are still 2500 more metres of even thinner air lurking above, so climb smart. Drink plenty of fluids (three to four litres daily), sleep as low as possible and descend at any sign of serious altitude sickness *before* a headache, troubled breathing or lethargy turn into life-threatening pulmonary or cerebral oedema. Read the discussion on Altitude & Climate-Related Illnesses in the Health section earlier in this chapter.

Don't forget to treat your water. I don't know how many times I've been miles from any habitation or road, just below the peaks, thinking the water would be safe from animal wastes, only to see llamas or alpacas way above, even as high as the snowfields and glaciers. Far from any roads or towns is no place to get the trots.

If you should get sick or injured, rescue cannot be expected. While many of the routes are frequently climbed, solitude is still one of the joys of Bolivian alpinism, so be prepared to get yourself out of trouble. Club Andino Boliviano now has a mountain rescue service staffed by volunteers, but it's pitifully short of funds and equipment. Helicopter rescue is probably out of the question.

Maps & Guides Planning can be one of the most frustrating parts of climbing in Bolivia. Maps are of poor quality, are miserably small scale and are often difficult to obtain. Even the elevations of the peaks are murky with reported altitudes varying as much as 600 metres.

Maplink in Santa Barbara, CA, and Stanfords in London (for addresses, see the Books & Maps section earlier in this chapter) sometimes carry topographical maps useful to the aspiring alpinist in Bolivia. Michael Kelsey's *Guide to the World's Mountains* (310 East 950 South, Springville, UT 84663 USA) has helpful maps and trip descriptions. The *American Alpine Club Journal* is also a good source for particular route information.

For alpine history of the area look for the long-out-of-print *Climbing and Exploration in the Bolivian Andes* by W M Conway or *Summit* magazine between the July-August 1982 and the July-August 1983 issues. Further technical information and guiding services are available from Club Andino Boliviano; see under Hiking & Climbing Clubs in the La Paz chapter.

Maps are now easier to obtain inside Bolivia than previously, when climbers had to visit the intimidating Instituto Geográfico Militar headquarters. The civilian map office in La Paz is at the corner of Colombia and 16 de Julio in the Edificio Camara Nacional de Comercio. Also check Los Amigos del Libro, 1430 Calle Mercado, in La Paz, for the *Southern Cordillera Real*, a dated but excellent climbing guide, or if you have a working knowledge of Spanish, *La Cordillera Real de los Andes, Bolivia*. For information on some specific climbs in Bolivia, see the Cordilleras & Yungas chapter.

Equipment Scrambling in the Bolivian Andes can be done with little more than what the average traveller normally carries – a sturdy pair of shoes, a good layering of clothes, hat and gloves, water bottle, daypack, etc. If higher peaks beckon, however, more serious equipment will make climbing safer and easier. Bring any climbing gear with you since that found in Bolivia is generally expensive or poor quality. Remember, you'll have to carry this stuff on the plane, bus, camión, mule or on your back, so 'light is right'. While you're not climbing, your gear can be left with a reliable hotel. Following is a list of general recommendations for clothing and gear.

Clothing
    Loose fitting layers are best for the constantly changing temperatures. A sturdy, dark, wind coat that can take the abuse of buses, camiones, mules and the resulting constant dust is important. Bolivia is one of the few places in South America where down is practical.
Camping
    Ensolite pad – important for insulating from cold or rocky ground.

Sleeping bag – down or synthetic, good to -5°C (you can always put on more clothes if it gets colder!).
Tent – useful for occasional snotty weather; adds warmth.
Backpack – a large capacity, internal frame (external frames exposed to Bolivian buses don't last long).
Water bottles – at least two one-litre containers.
Head lamp – important for those pre-dawn starts; bring plenty of batteries and bulbs – locally available ones are of poor quality.
Food
    While the convenience food you may be used to is not easily available, perfectly adequate dried foods such as Knorr soups, rice, instant coffee, etc, can be bought locally. Those going to Bolivia for just a few weeks' climbing may want to bring freeze-dried food; otherwise, buy it at the markets.
Cooking
    Stove – kerosene or multi-fuel stoves such as MSR are best as white gas and butane gas cartridges are difficult to obtain.
    Utensils – large pot for melting snow and another for cooking (mixing the two can produce some pretty funny-looking water which means you don't drink as much which can lead to dehydration which can lead to mountain sickness which – you get the picture). A Teflon frying pan is a nice luxury for frying up the ubiquitous potato.
Water purification
    Remember giardia, dysentery, hepatitis and all their ilk lurk in the mountains, too. See the Health section earlier in this chapter for more information.
Climbing
    The amount and kind of gear you'll need will obviously depend on just how serious you want to get, but the following would suffice for the normal routes on almost any peak in the Cordillera Real. Remember, most routes are over snow and/or ice, often in glacier form. This gear won't do you any good if you don't know how to use it. Climbing and camping gear can often be sold to locals or other travellers for more than you could get back home:

    Harness or webbing
    Three to five carabiners, one locking
    Ice axe and protector
    Crampons and protectors
    Nine or 11-mm rope
    Two or three ice screws and snow pickets or flukes
    Ice hammer – particularly for the more difficult climbs (Condoriri, Illampú, Illimani, Ancohuma).
    Prusiks – for crevasse rescue.

Sun protection
Top-quality sunscreen and glasses are essential: don't scrimp here! A baseball hat with bandana makes an effective 'Lawrence of Arabia' sun shield.

HIGHLIGHTS

The following sights, places and activities are some of our favourites in Bolivia. Although taste is subjective, those with limited time might find this section helpful to get the most from their trip. The first name given is that of the attraction, followed by its location(s).

Churches

San Lorenzo (Potosí); Jesuit mission churches (San Miguel de Velasco, San Rafael de Velasco and San José de Chiquitos); cathedral (Copacabana); and San Francisco (La Paz).

Museums

Chuchini (near Trinidad); Museo Arqueológico (Cochabamba); Museo Arqueológico de Tiwanaku (La Paz); Museos Universitarios (Sucre); and Casa Real de la Moneda (Potosí).

Historical & Archaeological Sites

Tiahuanaco (near La Paz); Cerro Rico mines, (Potosí); Islas Huyñaymarkas (Lake Titicaca); Isla del Sol (Lake Titicaca); Jesuit Mission Circuit (Santa Cruz Department); and Incallajta (near Cochabamba).

Fiestas

La Diablada (Oruro); Phujllay (Tarabuco); Festividad de Neustro Señor Jesús del Gran Poder (La Paz); Alasitas (La Paz); Fiesta de San Roque (Tarija); Fiesta del Santo Patrono de Moxos (San Ignacio de Moxos); Virgen de Candelaria (Copacabana); and Virgen de Urcupiña (Quillacollo).

Music

Bolivia has no bad music except, perhaps, that of unpractised brass bands and the traditional music which has been adapted for lifts and dentists' offices! Our favourite peña is at Don Lucho in Potosí.

Natural Attractions & Activities

Salar de Uyuni (south-western Bolivia); Río Tuichi (Rurrenabaque); Laguna Colorada and Laguna Verde (south-western Bolivia); Río Mamoré river trip (Beni); Tupiza area (Potosí Department); Parque Nacional Noel Kempff Mercado (Santa Cruz Department); Parque Nacional Torotoro (near Cochabamba); Perseverancia and Reserva de Vida Salvaje Ríos Blanco y Negro (Amazon region); Zongo Ice Caves walk (near La Paz); and Cordillera Real treks.

Small Towns

Coroico; Copacabana; Rurrenabaque; Sorata; and San Ignacio de Moxos.

Colonial Architecture

Colonial architecture is in evidence in Sucre, Potosí and La Paz.

Local Food

Lake Titicaca trout; *jugo de tumbo* and other fresh fruit juices (try Sucre Market); *salteñas* (try Confitería Cecy in Cochabamba!); *charque kan* (Altiplano); *surubí al ajo* (try Churros Amadeo in Santa Cruz); *sopa de quinoa* (Altiplano); and Amazon region fish dishes. For more details, see the Food section later in this chapter.

Restaurants

Piccolissimo (Sucre); La Taverne (Sucre); Don Lucho (Potosí); La Casa (Coroico); El Rodeo (Coroico); Only Restaurant (Guayaramerín); El Solar (Tarija); Churros Amadeo (Santa Cruz); Crêperie El Boliche (Santa Cruz); La Suisse (La Paz); La Cantonata (Cochabamba); and Snack La Mejicana (Cochabamba).

Low to Middle-Range Accommodation

Hostal Kory (Coroico); Hostal República (La Paz); Residencial Elisa (Cochabamba); Residencial Charcas (Sucre); Hostal Sucre (Sucre); and Residencial Los Reyes (Riberalta).

ACCOMMODATION

In this book, the Places to Stay sections are broken down into top-end, middle and bottom-end accommodation. A top-end hotel will typically cost more than B90 for a double and will include nearly everything rated with three or more stars on the Bolivian rating scale. Middle-range hotels will run from approximately B35 to B90 for two people, whether the rate is charged per person or per room. Anything less than about B35 double will be considered bottom end. Above average hotels or those that are recommended or frequented by budget travellers will be identified as such.

In some larger cities, you may notice an odd two or three-tier pricing structure in effect. Bolivians, called *nacionales* on price lists, pay one price; in some cases, other South Americans, who are presumed to be richer than Bolivians, pay a slightly higher price; and non-Latin Americans, called *extranjeros*, who are of course very rich, pay the highest price of all. Whatever the grouping, rooms and service are the same for everyone – only the prices vary. The only difference we noticed since the first edition of this book is that the practice of multiple level pricing has become more clandestine.

The majority of hotel owners are friendly, honest people and demand the same of their staff. Competition is such that a hotel can't afford a bad reputation, so your belongings should be safe in the room. Although we've heard tales, in all our travels in Bolivia, we've never had anything stolen from a hotel room. It's still a good idea not to leave valuables in sight. Money or jewellery may be checked at the hotel desk (always get a receipt and package it tightly to avoid tampering!), but would probably be safer stored in some obscure corner of a locked pack.

In many lower-priced hotels, doors will not lock from either side and there's sometimes a window beside the door that can be easily opened from the outside. Decide whether you can trust the proprietor to keep an eye on things whilst you're away.

In some cities, visitors are requested to register with the police upon their arrival. No one has ever provided a viable reason for this, and in only one town, Camiri, will hotel owners refuse you a room without police sanction. In some towns, proprietors are required to provide the police with lists of guests and their personal document numbers. Especially in Cochabamba, police used to make routine searches of hotels where foreigners tended to stay, often at excruciatingly early hours of the morning. This practice is now regulated by law and appears to have become less prevalent.

Nearly all hotels will watch your luggage for a few days if you plan to travel further afield. This service ranges from an informal area behind the counter to a locked luggage room; naturally, the latter is preferable.

Lone travellers should note that *simples*, or single rooms, are sometimes not available or cost only slightly less than a *doble*, or double room. In some cases, if you are given a double you will be expected to pay for both beds. In less expensive places *camas matrimoniales*, or double beds, are also scarce. Rooms with three or four beds are frequently available, but they will cost the same per bed as smaller rooms unless you can talk the owner into a specially tailored high-occupancy discount.

Room availability should be no problem except during major fiestas when prices double and rooms are quickly occupied by visiting nationals. At such times, private homeowners will often let rooms.

Water and electric utilities throughout the country are often sporadic. Most inexpensive hotels only turn on the power and water to the rooms for several hours in the morning and evening. Some establishments expect you to advise them when you want a shower so that they can make the necessary arrangements.

Some final advice – never accept a room without inspecting it first. The most cheery reception areas can shelter some pretty dank and dingy rooms, some without windows. If you're not satisfied with the room you're first shown, ask to see another. Most proprietors welcome travellers and are eager to please.

Types of Accommodation

Dinatur has a hotel rating system that rates hotels with zero to five stars and divides other accommodation into categories which include, in descending order, *hostales* (hostels), *casas de huéspedes, residenciales* (guest houses), *alojamientos* (lodges) and *posadas* (inns).

Bolivia is not a country for accommodation snobs. There are only a handful of five-star hotels in the country, and even these would probably rate about three stars on a worldwide scale. Nevertheless, you can expect clean rooms, acceptable restaurants with bars and entertainment, room service, laundry service (albeit expensive), hot and cold running water, a telephone, refrigerator and all the usual amenities – for about half the price you'd pay at such an establishment in London or Sydney.

A one-star hotel, on the other hand, may offer only cold water – possibly with a hot shower attachment (see the section called Plumbing under Dangers & Annoyances in this chapter), a snack bar, shabby but clean linen and an overall rather 'seedy' appearance. Two to four-star hotels, of course, fall somewhere in between. No stars at all would indicate that the establishment is called a hotel but may actually belong in a lower category. Heating or air-conditioning are unheard of below the three-star level.

Hostales, casas de huéspedes and residenciales all serve as finer budget hotels. A guest will have the option of a *baño privado* – private bath, or *baño común* – shared bath, which will have a hot-water attachment on the shower head. Rooms will also have flush toilets, some sort of laundry sink or even a cleaner, who will do your laundry for a very reasonable rate, and sometimes a restaurant or snack bar where you can buy coffee, breakfast or sandwiches. These hotels cost between B35 and B75 for a double with a private bath, and about 30% less without.

Alojamientos are basic budget accommodation alternatives. 'Alojamiento' means 'lodge', and that's just what these establishments are: places to crash. Few have hot water, some are clean and some are less than speakable. They rarely have private baths or restaurants, though sometimes a laundry sink is provided. Rates are normally charged per person rather than per room so there's no advantage to turning up with a large group. Double beds are sometimes hard to find. Prices range from around B4 per person in Copacabana to B25 in the Amazon Basin.

Posadas are the dirt-cheapest basic roof and bed you're going to find. They vary in quality, but usually that means from bad to worse. In all fairness, there are a few clean ones, but in most you could scrape off the scum with a putty knife. Few have showers and you'll wish they also lacked toilets; costs are kept down by closing the loo door and forgetting that they exist. Posadas range in price from B4 to B10 per person for a bed that may have been slept in for a month without a change of sheets – another cost-cutting measure. You'll have to be on the tightest of bare-bones budgets to appreciate such conditions.

Another type of hotel found mostly in rural areas is the *hotel prefectural*. The idea behind these government-run hotels is to provide minimal luxury in small towns of tourist interest, tucked away in the countryside at the fringes of populated areas. They are normally sterile-looking buildings and may remind you of well-groomed mental institutions, but they offer a relatively comfortable level of accommodation.

Camping

Camping is fairly easy in rural areas around Bolivia, but don't expect chains of caravan parks with clubhouses, showers and all the trimmings. Although a couple of organised campsites have sprung up recently, campers should be self-sufficient with a tent, sleeping bag, light source, stove and other gear.

Although it's difficult to camp near large cities, we've included some suggestions for campsites near a couple of large population centres for those who'd like to escape all the bustle and infernal horn-honking. In most cases, there'll be no safe or reliable water supply nearby, so campers must carry sufficient water for their stay.

If you are hiking or trekking along mountain routes, you'll find that camping is possible just about anywhere except someone's pasture or potato field. Alternatively, ask around in villages – locals will often put travellers up for a small fee. If you're sleeping in huts in the more humid areas, read the warnings about Chagas Disease in the Health section.

Minimum Impact Camping The following guidelines are recommended for those camping in the wilderness or other fragile areas of Bolivia:

• Select a well-drained campsite and, especially if it's raining, use a plastic or other waterproof groundsheet to prevent having to dig trenches.
• Along popular routes, set up camp in established sites.
• Biodegradable items may be buried but food residue and cigarette butts should be carried out, lest they be dug up and scattered by animals.
• Use established toilet facilities if they are available. Otherwise, select a site at least 50 metres from water sources, and bury wastes in a cat-hole at least several cm deep. If possible, burn the used toilet paper or bury it well.
• Use only biodegradable soap products (you'll probably have to carry them from home) and to avoid thermal pollution (the creation of non-natural temperatures in a natural environment) use natural temperature water where possible. When washing up dishes with hot water, either let it cool to outdoor temperature before pouring it out or dump it in a gravelly, non-vegetated place away from natural water sources.
• Wash dishes and brush your teeth well away from watercourses.
• When building a fire, try to select an established site and keep fires as small as possible. Use only down dead wood and when you're finished, make sure ashes are cool and buried before leaving. Again, carry out cigarette butts.

FOOD
Bolivia's food is as diverse as its regions and although its cuisine won't win any international awards, Bolivians have derived an admirable versatility from a few staples. The fare of the Altiplano tends to be starchy and loaded with carbohydrates while in the lowlands, fish, vegetables and fruits feature more prominently.

Meat of some kind will invariably dominate meals and will usually be accompanied by rice, potatoes (or another starchy tuber such as oca) and shredded lettuce. Sometimes the whole affair will be covered with *llajhua*, a hot sauce made from tomatoes and *locotos* (small, hot, yellow, green or red pepper pods) or another spicy sauce. In the Amazon Basin, and occasionally elsewhere, the tuber will be replaced by steamed or fried plantain or *yuca* (manioc).

Meals
Breakfast is called *desayuno* and often consists of nothing more than coffee and a bread roll or some kind of pastry. Around mid-morning, Bolivians eat a snack of *salteñas*, which are described under Fast Foods later in this section.

Lunch is the main meal of the day and restaurants will offer an *almuerzo completo*, the daily special, which normally consists of soup, bread, *segundo* (main course), coffee or tea and, most of the time, a simple dessert. The almuerzo completo changes daily and is normally dirt cheap. If you don't like what they're serving, you can order something from the regular menu for about twice as much as the special.

La cena is the evening meal and operates similar to lunch, but is less elaborate. It is usually eaten after 7 pm.

Fast Foods
The original Bolivian mid-morning snack food is the *salteña*, Bolivia's contribution to fine baking. These meat and vegetable pies are shaped like rugby balls and are stuffed with chicken or beef, olives, eggs, potatoes, onions, peas, carrots and whatever else might have been on hand. They're normally heavily spiced and are absolutely delicious.

Empanadas, ubiquitous throughout South America, are filled with varying quantities of beef *(empanadas de carne)*, chicken *(empanadas de pollo)* or cheese *(empanadas de queso)*, and are either baked in bread or deep-fried in fat. Sometimes other ingredients, such as those which go into salteñas, are added to the meat varieties.

Humintas (often spelt *humitas*) are cornmeal tamales filled with spiced beef, vegetables and potatoes. They are wrapped in a maize husk and fried, grilled or baked. A similar concoction, called a *relleno*, resembles a corn fritter.

Meat & Fish

The most common dishes are derived from beef, chicken or fish. The poorer campesinos eat a lot of mutton *(cordero)*, goat *(cabrito)* or llama. Pork *(carne de chancho)* is considered a delicacy and is only eaten on special occasions.

Typical beef dishes include barbecued or grilled beef *(parrillada* or *asado)* in various cuts like *lomo*, *brazuelo* and *churrasco*. Dried jerked beef is called *charque*; when served with mashed maize, it's known as *charque kan*. In the lowlands, charque with mashed plantain and/or maize is known as *masaco*.

Other concoctions include *thimpu*, spicy lamb and vegetable stew, and *falso conejo* (false rabbit?), a very greasy and rubbery substance that appears to be animal-based. Another popular way to serve meat or chicken is *milanesa*, a greasy wiener schnitzel. When the meat is pounded even thinner and allowed to absorb even more grease, the result is known as *silpancho*.

A dish called *pique a lo macho*, chunked grilled beef and sausage served with potatoes, lettuce, tomatoes, onions and locoto is popular in Sucre and Potosí. *Anticuchos* (beef-heart shish-kebabs) and *fricasés* (pork soup) are specialities in La Paz. *Rostro asado*, or sheep's head, is popular in Oruro.

Chicken is either fried, broiled or grilled and is commonly served as *pollo a la canasta* – chicken in the basket, with mustard, chips and *ají*, a *picante* or hot sauce made from long yellow or red pepper pods.

The most popular types of fish *(pescado)* are *trucha*, or trout from Lake Titicaca, and a host of other fresh-water varieties such as the *dorado, sábalo* and *surubí* found in the Oriente and Amazonia. Surubí, a kind of catfish caught throughout the lowlands, must be one of the best tasting fish around.

In addition, armadillo, jochi (or agouti; a delicacy), alligator and a multitude of other endearing forest critters are eaten to the brink of extinction in some areas of the lowlands.

Dairy Foods

Sheep's milk cheese is made all over the Altiplano and is delicious provided it doesn't contain too much salt. Vendors will normally let you have a sample before buying. It is cheaper and (we believe) better than cow's milk cheese which is considered more prestigious among campesinos.

Chaco cheese from eastern Tarija and western Santa Cruz departments is coveted all over Bolivia as the finest produced in the country. The Mennonite colonies of Santa Cruz Department make some very nice European-style cheeses.

Fresh milk is available through PIL, the national dairy, in the largest cities. In some places, however, it's rather difficult to find. Any store displaying a picture of a happy cow licking its lips will have milk for sale. Some markets also sell raw (unpasteurised and unhomogenised) milk.

Tubers

Tuberous plants make up a great percentage of the vegetable diet of most Bolivians. Potatoes come in nearly 250 varieties, most of which are small and colourful. Freeze-dried potatoes, called *chuños* or *tunta*, are sometimes eaten as snacks or with meals. Chuños are made by leaving potatoes out in the winter cold for four consecutive nights. They're then pressed to extract the water, peeled and dried. Tunta, or bleached chuño, is a little more complicated and requires the packing of chuño in straw and leaving it in running water for at least a month before drying. Most foreigners don't like either variety because they have the appearance and consistency of polystyrene.

Ocas are tough, purple, potato-like tubers. They taste pretty good when they're fried or roasted, but boiled ocas will take some getting used to. Another tuber sold in markets everywhere is the *añu*, a purple, yellow and white stalagmite-shaped thing that tastes like a parsnip and is usually boiled.

In the lowlands, the potato and its relatives are replaced by plantain or the root of the ubiquitous yuca (also known as manioc or cassava), which is good if it's cooked long enough.

Cereals

Two other common foods include *choclo*, a large kernel maize which is eaten everywhere on the Altiplano, and *habas*, the beans of the *palqui* plant, which grow wild and are eaten roasted or added to stews. They are also used to make a coffee-like beverage.

Quinoa and *tarhui*, grains unique to the area, are high in protein and are used to make flour and thicken stews. Quinoa is similar in most respects to sorghum or millet, but it grows on a stalk and looks a bit like caviar when it's in the field. It was first cultivated in the Andes several thousand years ago but the Spanish conquistadores forced the Indians to adopt European grains and thereafter, quinoa was rarely used.

It has recently been rediscovered and analysis has revealed that it contains a unique balance of fat, oil and protein. It is the only edible plant that contains all essential amino acids in the same proportions as milk, making it especially appealing to vegetarians. The best is said to be *quinoa blanca*, or *quinoa real*, which is produced on the Southern Altiplano in Potosí and Oruro departments. Although quinoa is now grown in western USA and is available in Europe and North America, its trendy value is being exploited to the maximum by health-food companies.

For further information or a list of quinoa recipes, contact the Asociación Nacional de Productores de Quinoa (ANAPQUI) (☎ 353872), Avenida 16 de Julio 1456, Edificio Prudencio 3er Piso, Casilla 2354, La Paz, Bolivia.

Fruits

In addition to familiar fruits like oranges and bananas, many other varieties are cultivated, some of which are unfamiliar outside South America. *Chirimoya*, or custard apple, is a green, scaly looking fruit which is available in markets around the country. The flesh looks and tastes like custard pudding.

The fruit of the prickly pear cactus *(tuna)* is eaten in the highlands. In the lowlands, there are scores of exotic tropical fruits; *ambaiba*, which is shaped like a hand, and *guaypurú* are quite good as is *tumbo* (also known as *maracuya*) or passion fruit. There are also variations on the orange and the banana: *mandarinas* (mandarins), *plátanos* (plantains) and *guineos* (finger bananas) are available everywhere.

Sweets

Perhaps the most interesting Bolivian sweets are *confites* which are associated with holidays. These festive candies may only be made by traditional rural confectioners after a *cha'lla* (offering) to Pachamama, the earth mother, has been conducted. The candies are made of blue, pink, red or green boiled sugar syrup, hardened around a filling of nuts, aniseed, fruits, biscuit or desiccated coconut. There are also ceremonial confites which are intended as religious offerings and are not meant to be eaten.

Another sweet popular with children is *tojorí*, an oatmeal-like concoction of mashed corn, cinnamon and sugar. In Potosí, you can get *tawa-tawas*, a relative of the doughnut and similar to *buñuelos* which are available around Bolivia.

For a real treat, Bolivia's own Breick chocolate rivals that of Switzerland and in my opinion, is better than Cadbury. See for yourself!

Restaurants

Restaurants in Bolivia don't tend to serve that vast array of health foods, ethnic cuisines, fast foods and buffets that travellers may be accustomed to at home, and few Bolivians have heard of quiche, salad bars, teppan-yaki and the like. However, the variety available in some larger urban centres will yield some unexpected surprises.

Restaurants serving typical European or North American foods are usually found near large tourist hotels, embassies and wealthy neighbourhoods. There are also several pseudo fast-food joints in La Paz and Cochabamba, including a couple that try very hard to look like some popular US-based chains.

Chifas, or Chinese restaurants, exist in all the major cities and even some more exotic cuisines (for Bolivia), such as Indian, Mexican, Swiss and Japanese, are represented.

Local restaurants range from *confiterías*, where you can get a snack or a cup of coffee, to classy sidewalk cafés where you can sit beside a palm-lined boulevard and eat steak. There are back-street cubbyholes, greasy-spoon truckstops and hundreds of Mom & Pop operations of varying quality in every population centre. In smaller informal establishments there are no menus; the day's offerings are normally written on a chalkboard posted at the entrance. If they do have a menu, it's often just a list of what the owner wishes was available rather than a true representation of what's cooking. In some cases, it's better to ignore the menu and enquire what they do have.

If you're travelling on limited funds or would enjoy sampling a bit of local culture, the markets in every city and town have food stalls where filling and usually tasty bargain-basement meals are served. If you're planning to eat this way, keep in mind that your internal plumbing will need a while to adjust to the idea. Don't give up on market food just because you get the runs the first time you try it.

DRINKS
Nonalcoholic Drinks
Apart from the usual black tea, coffee and chocolate, you'll find other hot drinks such as *mate de coca* (coca leaf tea) and *mate de manzanilla* (chamomile tea).

Many of the usual soft and bubbly imports like Coke, Sprite, Pepsi and Fanta are avail-able. Locals have also been known to enjoy a sugar rush known as Inca Cola, a soft drink which tastes like liquefied bubble gum. Yuck!

A favourite at bus stops is called simply *refresco* or 'refreshment', an anonymous fruit-based juice with a fuzzy ball in the bottom of the glass. The fuzzy ball, known as *despepitado* or *mocachinchi*, is actually a dried and shrivelled peach. Other favourite drinks include *tostada* (known as *aloja* in southern Bolivia) which is made of corn, barley, honey, cinnamon and cloves. A delicious walnut-based drink, which was originally made popular in Central America, is known as *horchata*.

Alcoholic Drinks
When drinking stronger alcoholic beverages, keep in mind that altitude intensifies the effects. In La Paz, you can get good and laid out after just three beers, and may well be unconscious after the fourth.

Another warning: when Bolivians gather to drink alcohol, whether it's beer, wine, *chicha* or whatever, it's serious; they intend to get plastered. Before accepting an invitation to drink with locals, consider that you'll be expected to do the same. In fact, Bolivians seem to take offence if any person in their party is able to walk out of a bar under their own steam.

Beer There are several excellent Bolivian beers: Pilsener and Paceña are brewed in La

"El Inca" drink label

Paz and Santa Cruz, and Sureña comes from Sucre.

Wine & Singani Grapes are grown in the vicinity of Tarija and some palatable wines are produced. A very popular and inexpensive low-grade wine (it's actually drunk more as a spirit) called *singani* is made from poor quality grapes and grape skins. A favourite singani-based drink is known as *chuflay*, singani mixed with lime and ginger ale. Around Cochabamba, you can sample such alcoholic concoctions as *guarapo*, a speciality in Sipe-Sipe, and *garapiña*, which is popular in Quillacollo.

Chicha Undoubtedly, the favourite alcoholic drink consumed by the masses is an industrial-strength maize liquor known as *chicha cochabambina*. Its production is centred around Cochabamba, and those white plastic flags you see flying on long poles indicate a *chichería*, a place where chicha is sold. There are a lot of rumours flying around Bolivia concerning its ingredients; ignore them if you plan to drink it. It's quite good and is guaranteed to produce an effect.

Much milder are the numerous other incarnations of chicha, which are made from a variety of items and may or may not contain alcohol. In Copacabana and La Paz, *api* is served during or after meals. Normally served hot, api is a very syrupy form of chicha made from *maíz morada* (sweet purple maize), lemon, cinnamon and staggering amounts of white sugar. A less sweet and lightly alcoholic form of *chicha de maíz* may be made from *maíz blanco* or white maize. *Chicha de maní* is made from peanuts. In the Amazon region, a favourite drink is *chicha de yuca*, a light and refreshing yuca beverage that tastes like an Indian lassi. In San Ignacio de Moxos, *chicha de camote*, sweet potato chicha, is served as an accompaniment to meals. Rich and not too sweet, it's actually a lot better than it sounds.

contemporary craft design

Getting There & Away

AIR

Many people fly into another South American country and travel overland to Bolivia. Those flying into Peru, Brazil or Colombia will need an onward ticket before they'll be admitted to any of those countries. A Miscellaneous Charges Order (MCO), a voucher good for the equivalent value in travel on any IATA (International Air Transport Association)-approved carrier, should suffice. If unused, it can be cashed in when you get home.

Buying a Plane Ticket

Your plane ticket will probably be the single most expensive item in your budget, and buying it can be an intimidating business. There is likely to be a multitude of airlines and travel agents hoping to separate you from your money, and it is always worth putting aside a few hours to research the current state of the market. Start early: some of the cheapest tickets have to be bought months in advance, and some popular flights sell out early. Talk to other recent travellers – they may be able to stop you making some of the same old mistakes. Look at the ads in newspapers and magazines (not forgetting the press of the ethnic group whose country you plan to visit), consult reference books and watch for special offers. Then phone round travel agents for bargains. (Airlines can supply information on routes and timetables; however, except at times of inter-airline war, they do not supply the cheapest tickets.) Find out the fare, the route, the duration of the journey and any restrictions on the ticket. Then sit back and decide which is best for you.

You may discover that those impossibly cheap flights are 'fully booked, but we have another one that costs a bit more...' Or the flight is on an airline notorious for its poor safety standards and leaves you in the world's least favourite airport in midjourney for 14 hours. Or they claim only to have the last two seats available for that country for the whole of July, which they will hold for you for a maximum of two hours. Don't panic – keep ringing around.

Use the fares quoted in this book as a guide only. They are approximate and based on the rates advertised by travel agents at the time of going to press. Quoted airfares do not necessarily constitute a recommendation for the carrier.

If you are travelling from the UK or the USA, you will probably find that the cheapest flights are being advertised by obscure bucket shops whose names haven't yet reached the telephone directory. Many such firms are honest and solvent, but there are a few rogues who will take your money and disappear, to reopen elsewhere a month or two later under a new name. If you are suspicious about a firm, don't give them all the money at once – leave a deposit of 20% or so and pay the balance when you get the ticket. If they insist on cash in advance, go somewhere else. And once you have the ticket, ring the airline to confirm that you are actually booked on the flight.

You may decide to pay more than the rock-bottom fare by opting for the safety of a better known travel agent. Firms such as STA, who have offices worldwide, Council Travel in the USA or Travel CUTS in Canada are not going to disappear overnight, leaving you clutching a receipt for a nonexistent ticket, but they do offer good prices to most destinations.

Once you have your ticket, write its number down, together with the flight number and other details, and keep the information somewhere separate. If the ticket is lost or stolen, this will help you get a replacement.

It's sensible to buy travel insurance as early as possible. If you buy it the week before you fly, you may find, for example, that you're not covered for delays to your flight caused by industrial action.

Air Travellers with Special Needs

If you have special needs of any sort – you've broken a leg, you're vegetarian, travelling in a wheelchair, taking the baby, terrified of flying – you should let the airline know as soon as possible so that they can make arrangements accordingly. You should remind them when you reconfirm your booking (at least 72 hours before departure) and again when you check in at the airport. It may also be worth ringing round the airlines before you make your booking to find out how they can handle your particular needs.

Airports and airlines can be surprisingly helpful, but they do need advance warning. Most international airports will provide escorts from check-in desk to plane where needed, and there should be ramps, lifts, accessible toilets and reachable phones. Aircraft toilets, on the other hand, are likely to present a problem; travellers should discuss this with the airline at an early stage and, if necessary, with their doctor.

Guide dogs for the blind will often have to travel in a specially pressurised baggage compartment with other animals, away from their owner, though smaller guide dogs may be admitted to the cabin. All guide dogs will be subject to the same quarantine laws (six months in isolation, etc) as any other animal when entering or returning to countries currently free of rabies such as the UK or Australia.

Deaf travellers can ask for airport and in-flight announcements to be written down for them.

Airlines will usually carry babies up to two years of age at 10% of the relevant adult fare, and some carry them free of charge. Reputable international airlines usually provide nappies (diapers), tissues, talcum and all the other paraphernalia needed to keep babies clean, dry and half-happy. For children between two and 12 years of age, the fare on international flights is usually 50% of the regular fare or 67% of a discounted fare. These days, most fares are considered to be discounted. 'Skycots' should be provided for infants by the airline if requested in advance; these will take a child weighing up to about 10 kg. Push chairs can often be taken as hand luggage.

Student Travel

Worldwide, there are a number of student travel organisations which offer bargain-basement airfares to out-of-the-way destinations the world over, including Latin America. Organisations which offer student services include:

Australia
STA, 224 Faraday St, Carlton, Victoria, 3056 (☎ (03) 347-6911)
STA, 1A Lee St, Railway Square, Sydney, NSW (☎ (02) 212-1255)
Canada
CHA 333 River Rd, Vanier, Ottawa, Ontario K1L 8H9
Canadian International Student Services, 80 Richmond St W #1202 Toronto, Ontario M5H 2A4 (☎ (416) 364-2738)
New Zealand
STA, 10 High St, Auckland (☎ 390458)
UK
STA, 74 Old Brompton Rd, London SW7 3LQ (☎ (071) 937-9971)
USA
Whole World Travel, Suite 400, 17 East 45th St, New York, NY 10017 (☎ (212) 986-9470)
Council on International Educational Exchange, 205 East 42nd St, New York, NY 10017
STA, 166 Geary St, San Francisco, CA 94108 (☎ (415) 391-8407)
STA, Suite 507, 2500 Wilshire Blvd, Los Angeles, CA 90057 (☎ (213) 380-2184)

To/From the USA

In the USA, the best way to find cheap flights is by checking the Sunday travel sections in major newspapers such as the *Los Angeles Times*, *San Francisco Examiner* or *Chronicle* on the west coast and the *New York Times* on the east coast. The student travel bureaux – STA or Council Travel – are also worth a go but in the USA you'll have to produce proof of student status and in some cases be under 26 years of age to qualify for their discounted fares.

North America is a relative newcomer to the bucket-shop traditions of Europe and Asia, so ticket availability and the restrictions attached to them need to be weighed against what is offered on the standard Apex or full economy (coach) tickets. Do some homework before setting off. The magazines specialising in bucket-shop advertisements in London (see the discussion under To/From Europe) will post copies so you can study current pricing before you decide on a course of action. Also recommended is the newsletter *Travel Unlimited* (PO Box 1058, Allston, MA 02134) which publishes details of the cheapest airfares and courier possibilities for destinations all over the world from the USA. Courier flight prices from Miami

---

Air Travel Glossary

Apex Tickets Apex stands for Advance Purchase Excursion fare. These tickets are usually between 30 and 40% cheaper than the full economy fare, but there are restrictions. You must purchase the ticket at least 21 days in advance (sometimes more) and must be away for a minimum period (normally 14 days) and return within a maximum period (90 or 180 days). Stopovers are not allowed and if you have to change your dates of travel or destination, there will be extra charges to pay. If you have to cancel altogether, tickets are not fully refundable – the refund is often considerably less than what you originally paid for the ticket. To avoid loss, take out travel insurance to cover you should you have to cancel your trip unexpectedly – for example, due to illness of yourself or your travelling companion.

Baggage Allowance This will be written on your ticket: usually one 20-kg item to go in the hold, plus one item of hand luggage.

Bucket Shops At certain times of the year and/or on certain sectors, many airlines fly with empty seats. This isn't profitable and it's more cost-effective for them to fly full even if that means having to sell a certain number of drastically discounted tickets. They do this by off-loading them onto 'bucket shops', travel agents who specialise in discounted fares. The agents, in turn, sell them to the public at reduced prices. These tickets are often the cheapest you'll find but you can't purchase them directly from the airlines. Availability varies widely, of course, so you'll not only have to be flexible in your travel plans, you'll also have to be quick off the mark as soon as an advertisement hits the press.

Most of the bucket shops are reputable organisations, but there will always be the odd fly-by-night operator who sets up shop, takes your money and then either disappears or issues an invalid ticket. Be sure to check what you're buying before handing over the dough.

Bucket-shop agents advertise in newspapers and magazines and there's a lot of competition – especially in places like Bangkok, Amsterdam and London which are crawling with them – so it's a good idea to telephone and ascertain availability before rushing from shop to shop. Naturally, they'll advertise the cheapest available tickets, but by the time you get there, these may be sold out and you may be looking at something slightly more expensive.

Bumped Just because you have a confirmed seat doesn't mean you're going to get on the plane – see **Overbooking.**

Check In Airlines ask you to check in a certain time ahead of the flight departure (usually 1½ hours on international flights). If you fail to check in on time and the flight is overbooked, the airline can cancel your booking and give your seat to somebody else.

Confirmation Having a ticket written out with the flight and date you want doesn't mean you have a seat; first the agent has to check with the airline that your status is 'OK' or confirmed. Meanwhile you could just be 'on request'.

Economy-Class Tickets Buying a normal economy-class ticket is usually not the most economical way to go, though they do give you maximum flexibility and the tickets are valid for 12 months. If you don't use them, most are fully refundable, as are unused sectors of a multiple ticket.

Lost Tickets If you lose your airline ticket an airline will usually treat it like a travellers' cheque and, after enquiries, issue you with another one. Legally, however, an airline is entitled to treat it like cash, in which case if you lose it then it's gone forever. Take good care of your tickets.

No Shows No shows are passengers who fail to show up for their flight, sometimes due to unexpected

recently quoted in this magazine included US$450 (return flight, stay up to 21 days) for Rio (Brazil); US$250 (return flight, stay up to 21 days) for Quito (Ecuador); and US$250 (return flight, stay up to 14 days) for Caracas (Venezuela).

Non-Discounted Tickets Due to excessive competition between carriers and a lot of governmental red tape in determining fare structures, flights originating in the USA are subject to numerous restrictions and regulations. This is especially true of bargain tickets; anything cheaper than the standard

---

delays or disasters, sometimes due to simply forgetting, sometimes because they made more than one booking and didn't bother to cancel the one they didn't want. Full-fare passengers who fail to turn up are sometimes entitled to travel on a later flight. The rest of us are penalised. See the cancellation details under **Apex Tickets**.

On Request An unconfirmed booking for a flight. See **Confirmation**.

Overbooking Airlines hate to fly empty seats, and since every flight has some passengers who fail to show up, they often book more passengers than they have seats available. Usually the excess passengers balance those who fail to show up, but occasionally somebody gets bumped. If this happens guess who it is most likely to be? The passengers who check in late.

Reconfirmation At least 72 hours prior to departure time of an onward or return flight you must contact the airline and 'reconfirm' that you intend to be on the flight. If you don't do this, the airline can delete your name from the passenger list and you could lose your seat. It doesn't hurt to reconfirm more than once. You don't have to reconfirm if your stopover is less than 72 hours.

Round-the-World Fares Round-the-world (RTW) tickets have become all the rage in the past few years; basically there are two types – airline tickets and agent tickets. An airline RTW ticket is issued by two or more airlines that have joined together to market a ticket which takes you around the world on their combined routes. Within certain time and stopover limitations, you can fly pretty well anywhere you choose using their combined routes as long as you keep moving in approximately the same direction east or west. Compared to full-fare tickets, which permit you to go anywhere you choose on any IATA airline as long as you don't exceed the maximum permitted mileage, these tickets are much less flexible. They are, however, normally much cheaper.

The other type of RTW ticket, the agent ticket, is a combination of cheap fares strung together by an enterprising travel agent. These may be cheaper than an airline RTW ticket but the choice of routes will be limited. Most RTW tickets you'll find which include South America will be of this latter type.

Student Discounts Some airlines offer student-card holders 20 to 25% discounts on their tickets. The same often applies to anyone under the age of 26. These discounts are generally only available on ordinary economy-class fares. You wouldn't get one, for instance, on an Apex or a RTW ticket, since these are already discounted.

Transferred Tickets Airline tickets cannot be transferred from one person to another. Travellers sometimes try to sell the return half of their ticket, but officials can ask you to prove that you are the person named on the ticket. This is unlikely to happen on domestic flights; on an international flight tickets may be compared with passports.

Travel Agencies Travel agencies vary widely and you should ensure you use one that suits your needs. Some simply handle tours, while full-service agencies handle everything from tours and tickets to car rental and hotel bookings. A good one will do all these things and can save you a lot of money, but if all you want is a ticket at the lowest possible price, then you really need an agency specialising in discounted tickets. A discount ticket agency, however, may not be useful for other things, like hotel bookings.

Travel Periods Some officially discounted fares, Apex fares in particular, vary with the time of year. There is often a low (off-peak) season and a high (peak) season. Sometimes there's an intermediate or shoulder season as well. At peak times, when everyone wants to fly, both officially and unofficially discounted fares will be higher, or there may simply be no discounted tickets available. Usually the fare depends on your outward flight – if you depart in the high season and return in the low season, you pay the high-season fare. ■

tourist or economy fare must be purchased at least 14 days, and sometimes as much as 30 days, prior to departure.

In addition, you'll have to book departure and return dates in advance and these tickets will be subject to minimum and maximum stay requirements: usually seven days and six months, respectively. It's often cheaper to purchase a return ticket and trash the return portion than to pay the one-way fare. From the USA, open tickets which allow an open return date within a 12-month period are generally not available, and penalties of up to 50% are imposed if you make changes to the return booking.

Most of the good deals from the USA are out of Miami. If you want to fly directly to Bolivia from Miami, American Airlines flies three times weekly to La Paz and Lloyd Aero Boliviano (LAB) flies every day to Santa Cruz via some combination of Panamá (Panamá), Caracas (Venezuela) and Manaus (Brazil). The cheapest fares are currently US$751 between Miami and La Paz and US$744 to Santa Cruz.

From the USA the major carrier gateway cities are New York, Los Angeles and Miami. All have basically the same fare structure. Economy fares must often be purchased two weeks in advance, with a requirement of a minimum stay of two weeks and a maximum stay of three months usually applied. For this type of return ticket to Rio, a rough starting point for prices would be around US$600 (ex Miami); US$700 (ex New York); and US$800 (ex Los Angeles). A popular choice for budget travellers is the cheap Miami to Rio de Janeiro flight operated via Asunción by Lineas Aereas Paraguayas (LAP). Equatoriana also offers a US$409 fare between Miami and Quito (Ecuador).

Some of the cheapest flights between Brazil and the USA are charters between Manaus, Belém, Rio de Janeiro or São Paulo (all in Brazil) and Miami (the Disney World express!). Manaus, which lies halfway between Rio and Miami, is a useful gateway city if you plan to make a long circuit around South America.

From the US west coast to Lima (Peru),

the best fare is on VARIG which offers return-only Apex fares of US$915. VARIG flies on Sunday and Wednesday. It would be less expensive to travel via Miami using a Super Saver ticket from Los Angeles than to fly to South America directly from Los Angeles.

To/From Canada

Travel CUTS has offices in all major Canadian cities. The *Toronto Globe & Mail* carries travel agents' ads. The magazine *Great Expeditions* (PO Box 8000-411, Abbotsford BC V2S 6H1) is useful. Travellers interested in booking flights with Canadian courier companies should obtain a copy of the *Travel Unlimited* newsletter mentioned in the To/From the USA section.

To/From Europe

Finding Discounted Tickets There are bucket shops by the dozen in London, Paris, Amsterdam, Brussels, Frankfurt and a few other places. In London, several magazines with lots of bucket-shop ads can put you on to the current deals. In these magazines, you'll find discounted fares to Lima, Quito and Rio de Janeiro as well as other parts of South America. A word of warning, however: don't take the advertised fares as gospel truth. To comply with advertising laws in the UK, companies must be able to offer *some* tickets at their cheapest quoted price, but they may only have one or two of them per week. If you're not one of the lucky ones, you'll be looking at higher priced tickets. The best thing to do is begin looking for deals well in advance of your intended departure so you can get a fair idea of what's available. Following is a list of publications and organisations which have travel information for budget travellers:

Trailfinder

This magazine is put out quarterly by Trailfinders (☎ (071) 938-3939/3366) from 9 am to 6 pm Monday to Friday UK time or fax (071) 938-3305 anytime), 42-48 Earls Court Rd, London W8 6EJ, UK. It's free if you pick it up in London but if you want it mailed, it costs UK£6 for four issues in the UK or Ireland and UK£10 or the equivalent for four issues in Europe or elsewhere (airmail). Trailfinders can fix you up with all your ticketing requirements as well. They've been in business for years, their staff are friendly and we highly recommend them.

Time Out
Tower House, Southampton St, London WC2E 7HD (☎ (071) 836-4411). This is London's weekly entertainment guide and contains travel information and advertising. It's available at bookshops, newsagents and newsstands. Subscription enquiries should be addressed to Time Out Subs, Unit 8, Grove Ash, Bletchley, Milton Keynes MK1 1BZ, UK.

TNT Magazine
52 Earls Court Rd, London W8, UK (☎ (071) 937-3985). This free magazine can be picked up at most London Underground stations and on street corners around Earls Court and Kensington. It caters to Aussies and Kiwis working in the UK and is therefore full of travel advertising.

Globe
Globe is a newsletter published for members of the Globetrotters' Club (BCM Roving, London WC1N 3XX). It covers obscure destinations and can be handy to help find travelling companions.

Look also for travel agents' ads in the Sunday papers, travel magazines and listings magazines such as *City Limits*.

To initiate your price comparisons, you could contact travel agents such as Journey Latin America (JLA) (☎ (081) 747-3108) which publishes a very useful *Flights Bulletin*; Trailfinders (☎ (071) 938-3939)/3366); STA (☎ (071) 937-9971); and South American Experience (☎ (071) 379-0344), all in London; or the highly recommended Travel Bug (☎ (061) 721-4000) in Manchester. For courier flight details, contact Polo Express (☎ (081) 759-5383) or Courier Travel Service (☎ (071) 351-0300).

Prices for discounted flights between London and Rio start at around UK£300 one way or UK£550 return – bargain hunters should have little trouble finding even lower prices.

On the continent, the newsletter *Farang* (La Rue 8 á 4261, Braives, Belgium) deals with exotic destinations, as does the magazine *Aventure au Bout du Monde* (116 rue de Javel, 75015 Paris).

Non-Discounted Tickets The cheapest

direct flight from Europe to Bolivia is currently the weekly LAP flight from Brussels to Santa Cruz, Bolivia, and Asunción, Paraguay. Another possible way to go is via Miami. On Virgin Airways or whatever bargain-basement trans-Atlantic carrier is currently operating, you can hop to New York for about US$130 one way. The Apex return fare between New York and Miami is normally around US$99 on several carriers, but if you're pressed for time and don't want to sit around in New York for 14 days, Delta, United, British Airways and Virgin Airways all offer a US$459 return fare on direct flights between London and Miami. For information on flights from Miami, see To/From the USA.

To/From Australia & New Zealand

Travel between Australasia and South America is not cheap. It makes sense for Australasians to think in terms of a RTW ticket or a return ticket to Europe with a stopover in Rio de Janeiro, Buenos Aires or Santiago. RTW tickets with various stopovers can still be found for as little as A$2100, but these tend to include only northern hemisphere stopovers; surcharges are levied if the traveller wants to include Latin America or the South Pacific. The best publications for finding good deals are the Saturday editions of the daily newspapers such as the *Sydney Morning Herald* and the Melbourne *Age*. Alternatively, try STA which has branches at universities and in all state capitals.

One option is to take advantage of Qantas or Air New Zealand's Apex fares between Sydney or Auckland and the US west coast which are currently about A$1500 return, with up to three stopovers. From LA or San Francisco it's a matter of overlanding or finding a cheap Apex ticket to Miami.

Aerolineas Argentinas flies over the South Pole once a week via Sydney, Auckland, Buenos Aires and Rio de Janeiro. Lan Chile flies Sydney, Papeete, Easter Island, Santiago and Rio de Janeiro for US$2387. Qantas flies from Sydney to Rio de Janeiro via Los Angeles for US$2350. The LA-Rio leg is on

VARIG; stopovers are allowed (US$50 each) in Papeete and Honolulu.

To/From Asia

From the Orient, the hot tickets are on Japan Airlines (JAL) and Singapore Airlines. JAL flies from Tokyo to Rio de Janeiro and São Paulo via Los Angeles and they have reasonable fares to Rio from the west coast of the USA.

To/From Elsewhere in South America

To/From Argentina LAB has a service from Buenos Aires to La Paz via Santa Cruz on Tuesday, Friday and Sunday. Fares are US$295 to La Paz and US$244 to Santa Cruz. Once weekly, this flight also serves Salta, Argentina.

To/From Brazil LAB has flights between Rio de Janeiro, São Paulo and La Paz on Monday, Wednesday, Friday and Sunday, stopping in Santa Cruz en route. The fare between Rio and La Paz is US$341 one way and to Santa Cruz, US$273 one way. VARIG/Cruzeiro flies the same route on Tuesday, Thursday, Friday and Saturday. On Friday, Aero Perú flies between La Paz, Santa Cruz, Rio de Janeiro and São Paulo. In addition, LAB does a Thursday run between Manaus and Santa Cruz for US$207 one way. There is a US$16 departure tax on international flights originating in Brazil.

To/From Chile LAN Chile flies to La Paz from Santiago, stopping in Arica and Iquique, on Monday, Wednesday, Friday and Sunday. LAB flies to and from Arica and Santiago on Tuesday, Thursday and Saturday for US$180. Passengers departing Chile are subject to a departure tax of US$12.50.

To/From Paraguay LAB and American Airlines fly between Asunción, La Paz and Santa Cruz on Friday. One-way fares are US$156 from Santa Cruz to Asunción and US$211 from La Paz to Asunción.

To/From Peru LAB, Aero Perú, American Airlines and Lufthansa fly between Lima and La Paz. LAB has a service on Tuesday, Thursday, Saturday and Sunday and costs US$162 one way. Aero Perú flies on Wednesday and Friday. American Airlines and Lufthansa both fly on Thursday.

There is a ticket tax of 21% for Peruvian residents and 7% for non-resident tourists.

LAND

The inexpensive and popular route between North and South America along the 'Gringo Trail' includes eight fascinating countries between the Río Grande and the Colombian border; Belize and Costa Rica are currently on top of the tourist heap. Several other Central American countries, however, are experiencing well-publicised internal difficulties, often accompanied by violence, military action and general paranoia. In the interest of personal safety, El Salvador and the Honduras/Nicaragua border region should be either avoided or put behind you as quickly as possible. Panamá is especially notorious for crime and general security problems.

Because the Pan-American Highway is broken in Eastern Panamá, travellers are obliged to either fly into Colombia or overland past the Darien Gap using a combination of methods, all of which include at least a seven to 14-day slog through the rainforest.

For all the details on this route, see Lonely Planet's *Central America on a shoestring*.

To/From Argentina

Via La Quiaca From Salta or Jujuy in northwestern Argentina, there are buses leaving every couple of hours during the day for La Quiaca, opposite the Bolivian town of Villazón. It takes about 30 minutes to walk between the Argentine and Bolivian bus terminals. Alternatively, you can take a taxi.

From Villazón, there are buses to Tupiza and Potosí and trains to Uyuni, Oruro and La Paz. There's now a direct rail service between La Paz and Buenos Aires, but you'll still have to walk or take a taxi between the Villazón and La Quiaca railway stations – about 40 minutes with luggage.

La Quiaca and Villazón are covered in the Southern Altiplano chapter.

Via Orán This is a minor border crossing with immigration formalities in the hamlet of Aguas Blancas, one hour by bus from Orán. Aguas Blancas lies on the Río Bermejo opposite Bermejo, Bolivia. Access across the river is by ferry. From Bermejo, several bus companies do daily runs to Tarija. See the Chaco & South Central Bolivia chapter for details.

Via Pocitos The border crossing at tiny Pocitos is just a short distance south of Yacuiba, Bolivia, and north of Tartagal, Argentina. The walk across the border between Pocitos, Argentina, and Pocitos, Bolivia, takes about 10 minutes. There are taxis between Pocitos and Yacuiba and buses to and from Tartagal.

From Tucumán in north central Argentina, take a bus to Embarcación and Tartagal, and from there to Pocitos on the frontier. Between Yacuiba and Santa Cruz, there are trains and *ferrobuses* (buses on bogies) as well as buses to and from Tarija. See under Pocitos and Yacuiba in the South Central Bolivia & The Chaco chapter for further information.

To/From Brazil
Via Corumbá Corumbá, opposite the Bolivian border town of Quijarro, has both rail and bus connections from São Paulo, Rio de Janeiro, Cuiabá and southern Brazil. It is the busiest port of entry between Bolivia and Brazil.

From Corumbá, take a bus to the frontier and from there a taxi to the railhead at Quijarro. From Quijarro, a train leaves daily for Santa Cruz during the dry season. During the wet, there may be waits of several days.

From Cáceres, south-west of Cuiabá, you can cross to San Matías in Bolivia and from there either take a bus to San Ignacio de Velasco or fly to Santa Cruz (via Roboré) to connect with terrestrial transport.

For further information, see under Corumbá and Quijarro in the Eastern Lowlands chapter.

Via Northern Brazil From Brasiléia in the state of Acre, you can cross into Cobija, Bolivia. Previously it was necessary to fly from there to other Bolivian cities, but by the time this book hits the shelves, the new Cobija-Riberalta road should be open. From Riberalta there is now a dry-weather road all the way through to La Paz.

A more popular crossing is by ferry from Guajará-Mirim in Brazil across the Río Mamoré into Guayaramerín, Bolivia. From there, a road goes to Riberalta, from where you can take the long dusty route southward toward Rurrenabaque and La Paz.

From Guayaramerín, it's possible to take a 10-day (or longer) river trip up the Río Mamoré and Río Ichilo to the highway at Puerto Villarroel, which has a highway link with Cochabamba, or, when the water is high, from Riberalta up the Río Beni to Rurrenabaque. Alternatively, LAB has flights from Guayaramerín and Riberalta to cities in central and southern Bolivia.

Further details may be found under Guayaramerín, Guajará-Mirim, Cobija and Brasiléia in the Amazon Basin chapter.

To/From Chile
Via Arica There are trains and ferrobuses between La Paz and Arica, with immigration formalities at the border crossing between Visviri and Charaña. This is a very cold and uncomfortable proposition.

By bus, Flota Litoral does the very rough route between Arica and La Paz, via the Chungará/Tambo Quemado border crossing, twice weekly from Calle Chacabuco in Arica:

If you like torture, do the bus trip from Arica to La Paz. The journey took 18 hours including some time waiting at the border. Passengers were shaken up and down all the time on the Bolivian side, 'sitting' in air most of the time. Myself, two Japanese travellers and a British man all agreed that this was the worst journey in the world. They had done some bad trips in the Sudan and Pakistan but this took the prize. We were hoping that the bus would break down to give us a break.

Rolf Wrelph, Sweden

Agencia Martinez, also in Arica, runs a bus service from Arica to connect with Bolivian trains, going only as far as the frontier. Since Bolivian trains don't operate to a reliable schedule, the Martinez bus does a run whenever a train is expected to arrive at Charaña. See Getting There & Away under La Paz for more details.

Via Antofagasta/Calama Going to Bolivia from Antofagasta, you must take a two-hour bus ride to Calama (US$3) from where there's one train weekly to Ollagüe, eight hours *uphill* from Calama on the Bolivian border. In Ollagüe, you have to walk across the border to Abaroa in Bolivia, and connect with the Bolivian train to Uyuni and Oruro.

At the rail office in Antofagasta you can buy a combination bus and train ticket all the way to La Paz. As on all routes between Chile and Bolivia, warm clothes are essential! See under Oruro and Uyuni in the Southern Altiplano chapter.

To/From Paraguay
The route overland into Bolivia from Paraguay is very rough and probably isn't worth considering unless you don't mind long waits. See under Boyuibe in the South Central Bolivia & The Chaco chapter for further information.

Coming from Paraguay, it's much easier to cross into Brazil at Ponta Porã from Pedro Juan Caballero and travel by bus or train to Corumbá in Brazil (18 hours with a change at Campo Grande). At Corumbá, you can cross to Quijarro, Bolivia.

Another option is to catch the boat along the Río Paraguaí from Asunción to Corumbá on the Brazil/Bolivia frontier. Details are provided under Corumbá in the Eastern Lowlands chapter.

To/From Peru
Via Puno There are basically two routes from Puno into Bolivia. The quickest but least interesting is by *micro* from Puno to the frontier at Desaguadero where you can connect with a Bolivian bus to La Paz.

The other route, which is far more scenic and interesting, is via Copacabana and the Estrecho de Tiquina (Straits of Tiquina). Micros leave from Puno and enter Bolivia at Yunguyo, 11 km from Copacabana. There you connect with another micro, or with a bus company, for the four to five-hour trip to La Paz. The entire run from Puno to La Paz can be easily done in a day, but it's worth stopping off at Copacabana for a couple of days to explore the area. See under Copacabana and Puno in the Lake Titicaca chapter.

Other There are other very obscure border crossings such as the one from Puerto Acosta north of Lake Titicaca and a couple of ports of entry along the rivers of the north, but they require some effort and there's no public transport available. Details on crossings from far northern Bolivia are found under Cobija in the Amazon Basin chapter.

Driving
For details about driving to and within Bolivia, see the Car section in the Getting Around chapter.

TOURS
Overland Companies
Overland trips are very popular, especially with UK and Australasian travellers, but they aren't for everyone. They are designed primarily for first-time travellers who feel uncomfortable striking out on their own or for those who prefer guaranteed social interaction to the uncertainties of the road. If you have the slightest inclination toward independence or would feel confined travelling with the same group of 25 or so for most of the trip (quite a few normally drop out along the way), think twice before booking something like this.

If you'd like more information or a list of agents selling overland packages in your home country, contact one of the following South America overland operators, all of which are based in the UK (Exodus and

Encounter also have offices in Australia, New Zealand, the USA and Canada):

Dragoman
    Camp Green, Kenton Rd, Debenham, Suffolk IP14 6LA (☎ (0728) 861133, fax (0728) 861127)
Encounter Overland
    267 Old Brompton Rd, London SW5 9JA (☎ (071) 370-6845)
Exodus Expeditions
    9 Weir Rd, London SW12 0LT (☎ (081) 673-0859, fax (081) 673-0779)
Guerba Expeditions
    101 Eden Vale Rd, Westbury, Wiltshire BA13 3QX (☎ (0373) 826611, fax (0373) 838351)
Hann Overland
    201/203 Vauxhall Bridge Rd, London SW1V 1ER (☎ (071) 834-7337, fax (071) 828-7745)
Top Deck
    Top Deck House, 131/135 Earls Court Rd, London SW5 9RH (☎ (071) 244-8641, fax (071) 373-6201)

Environmental Tours
UK The boom in ecotourism worldwide has prompted the creation of groups and organisations to monitor the effects of tourism and provide assessments and recommendations for those involved. For more information on ecotours, contact the Centre for the Advancement of Responsible Travel (☎ (0732) 352757); Tourism Concern (☎ (081) 878-9053); and Green Flag International (☎ (0223) 893587).

USA Assessments and information about ecological and other types of tours can be obtained from the following organisations: North American Coordinating Center for Responsible Tourism, 2 Kensington Rd, San Anselmo, CA 94960; One World Family Travel Network, PO Box 4317, Berkeley, CA 94703; and Travel Links, Co-op America, 2100 M St NW, Suite 310, Washington DC 20036.

Earthwatch organises trips for volunteers to work overseas on scientific and cultural projects with a strong emphasis on protection and preservation of ecology and environment.

Other organisations which provide tours with a similar emphasis include Conservation International and The Nature Conservancy. For the addresses of these and other environmental organisations, see the Ecology & Environment section in the Facts about the Country chapter.

LEAVING BOLIVIA
Departure Tax
On international flights, the departure tax is US$15, but Bolivian residents and anyone who's been in the country for more than 90 days must pay B100 for flights to neighbouring countries and B150 for flights elsewhere.

Getting Around

AIR

Air travel in Bolivia is inexpensive and is the quickest and most reliable means of reaching out-of-the-way places. It's the only means of transport that doesn't wash out during the wet season, and although schedule disruption does occur, in theory planes can get through even during summer flooding in northern Bolivia.

Bolivia's national carrier is Lloyd Aereo Boliviano (LAB) which flies to the remotest corners of the country as well as to Miami, Panamá and most major South American cities. During the dry season, flights run more or less on schedule and fares are very reasonable.

Service is basic but adequate and LAB is proud of its perfect safety record and its pilots who are familiar with Bolivia's difficult terrain. LAB has ticket offices in every town it serves and, except around holidays, seats are usually available the day before the flight. Other than in the smallest towns,

LAB's ticketing system is less complicated and technologically more advanced than any other we've seen. If there's no queue, the entire process takes less than two minutes: you book the flight, pay at the ticket window and collect the ticket as it pops out of the computer. This is perhaps one of the benefits of not being affiliated with IATA and all its rules and regs!

We were recently advised by some travellers of a special deal with LAB called a 'Vibol Pass'. This air pass, which costs US$150, must be purchased outside Bolivia through a travel agent or LAB office. It allows you to fly to all cities serviced by LAB, beginning and ending in the same city of your choice. It is only possible to visit each city once.

The military airline, Transportes Aereos Militares (TAM), is Bolivia's second notable internal carrier. As with most military operations, schedules change frequently, flights are often cancelled and reservations are ignored. They aren't as reliable as LAB but they do fill in LAB's schedule gaps.

TAM operates smaller planes, such as the Fairchild F27 Turbo-prop, which fly closer to the ground than the big jets. If you're interested in the view or aerial photography, this may be worth considering.

Both LAB and TAM allow 20 kg of luggage, excluding carry-ons, without additional charges. If your flight isn't full, sometimes you'll get away with a bit more.

The airline AeroXpress serves several cities, and is the only airline which has flights to Potosí.

Domestic Air Taxes

AASANA, the government agency responsible for airports and air traffic, charges B8 tax on domestic tickets which is payable at the AASANA desk on check-in for the flight. Many airports also charge a municipal airport tax on internal flights which is not included in the ticket price and must also be paid when checking in.

See the Leaving Bolivia section in the Getting There & Away chapter for details about international departure tax.

BUS

If you're interested in meeting the Bolivians, their children, their luggage and their animals, this is the way to go. Long-distance bus lines in Bolivia are called *flotas*. Large buses are called *buses* (BOO-says) and small ones are known as *micros* (MEE-cros). If you require directions to a bus terminal, ask for *el terminal terrestre*.

The best news is that buses are convenient. Between any two cities, you should have no trouble finding at least one bus leaving every day. On the most popular routes like La Paz-Oruro, numerous flotas do eight to 10 runs daily.

If you can manage to travel by daylight, you'll be treated to an eye-level view of the spectacular landscapes and the serene farms and villages that are the essence of the country.

Nearly everyone will travel by bus sometime during a trip through Bolivia and it is the favoured form of transport among middle-class Bolivians. While buses are inexpensive and allow a down-to-earth experience of the people and landscape, they do have a few drawbacks which should be considered:

• Most flotas depart in the evening and arrive at their destination early in the morning, sometimes too early to get a hotel without paying for the previous night. It also seems that regardless of how many companies service a run, the majority leave at the same time of day, so schedule options are limited.

• Although most buses travel at night, conditions are not optimum for sleeping. If you have a seat – fortunately most flotas do accept advance seat reservations – you'll soon discover the bus was designed with capacity rather than comfort in mind. The floors, racks and roof will be packed to overflowing with bags, boxes, tins, animals and Bolivians. With a little arithmetic, you can calculate that the locals travel with an average of 16 pieces of luggage per person, which leaves pitifully little room for your feet.

• Add to that the obligatory radio or tape player that invariably blares at concentration-shattering volumes throughout the night, frequent highway police stops and narcotics searches, and the inevitable equipment failure that plagues most runs, and you'll be lucky to even close your eyes, let alone sleep.

• It also seems the Bolivian highway budget takes low priority. The word 'highway' can be applied to only a handful of routes around La Paz and Cochabamba. Elsewhere, the word 'track', or in some cases 'rut', would be more appropriate. Given the incredibly rugged and steep terrain, however, the Bolivians have done an admirable job of opening up inhospitable territory.

• During the rainy season from November to March, any or all modes of public transport, including airlines, may suspend service for weeks at a time without explanation. Hillsides come crashing down, bridges collapse into swollen rivers, roads turn into quagmires and mudpits or wash away altogether, and travellers become frustrated as carefully worked schedules go awry. *Mañana*, they'll mutter – 'maybe tomorrow'. A good rule of thumb is that any bus journey over unsurfaced roads, even under optimum conditions, will take half as long again as scheduled. During the rainy season, plan on double or triple the time.

• Equipment must also be reckoned with. Buses range from sagging, sputtering, dilapidated wrecks to large and relatively comfortable coaches with *pullman* seats and ample leg room for the average foreigner. Unfortunately, many companies run both types and a few in between, so it's difficult to be assured of a good one. Generally, any flota with the name 'pullman' attached will run nicer buses. Some roads in Bolivia, however, are so bad that companies will only run expendable equipment over them.

• Drunken driving is a serious problem. Although it's officially prohibited, don't be surprised to see your driver swill a couple of litres during a single rest stop. If you're nervous, you may prefer to travel by air or rail.

What to Carry

It's a good idea to take along food and something to drink on long bus journeys, especially if you're travelling in remote areas. Rest stops are unscheduled and depend largely upon the whims and bodily necessities of the driver.

At some stops, such as police searches, intermediate stations and toll posts, buses are normally invaded by vendors selling anything from parrots to shish kebab to shampoo. Most offer food, however, and you can buy a complete meal or just bread and fruit. Refresco and other drinks are available everywhere. For a suspiciously oily and spotty glass full, you'll pay B.30 or so.

Essential on any highland bus trip, day or night, is twice as much warm clothing as you expect to need. At night, it can get surprisingly cold even in lowland areas and Altiplano nights can be unimaginably bitter! If your alpaca pullover is packed safely away on the roof of the bus, you may suffer, and even with it inside, you'll wish you had two pairs of thermal underwear and an Arctic parka to go with it.

Although temperatures aren't so extreme during the day, changes in altitude will necessitate addition and subtraction of clothing. Once you've done it a few times, you'll understand why the Bolivians all seemed so overdressed when they boarded the bus in 30°C heat!

Major Routes
Major long-distance routes include service between the following: La Paz and Oruro; La Paz and Copacabana; La Paz and Cochabamba; Cochabamba and Sucre; Cochabamba and Santa Cruz; Potosí and Sucre; Potosí and Oruro; Cochabamba and Oruro; Villazón and Potosí; Tupiza and Tarija; La Paz and the Yungas (Coroico, Chulumani or Guanay); La Paz and Rurrenabaque, Riberalta and Guayaramerín; Riberalta and Cobija (new route; scheduled services should be in operation when this book hits the shelves); and Santa Cruz and Trinidad.

Other long-distance routes are constructed with connections between one or more of these and may require waits and changing buses. Getting to Santa Cruz from La Paz, for example, will normally entail an eight to 10-hour stop at Cochabamba.

Colectivos
Colectivos are minibuses, and are found predominantly in La Paz. See the La Paz Getting Around section for more details.

TRAIN
Empresa Nacional de Ferrocarriles (ENFE) is the Bolivian National Railroad, the crown jewel of all that's inefficient and disorganised in the country. In the Oriente, where the train serves more or less as a lifeline, a favourite pastime is to swap stories about ENFE; they're always good for a laugh.

As always, the rainy season may cause delays. In most cases a rail washout will be repaired in 24 hours, and flooded tracks will reappear as soon as it hasn't rained for a while. If a bridge washes out, however, the line will be closed indefinitely, so it's time to find an alternative form of transport.

When travelling internationally by rail to Chile, Brazil or Argentina, you will have to get off, pass through both Bolivian and the other country's immigration formalities and carry your luggage across the border. With the exception of the La Paz to Arica *ferrobus* and the topmost-class carriage to Buenos Aires, trains don't cross international boundaries.

If you require directions or transport to a train station, ask for *la estación de ferrocarriles*.

Tickets & Timetables
Although there's an official timetable, it's meaningless. Arrival and departure times are written on a chalkboard at the station as soon as it appears something may happen. In small stations – where things rarely happen – tickets are not sold until the train is actually sitting in the station, thus confirming an arrival. Even in major stations, tickets cannot be reserved until the day of expected departure. Each station is allotted a certain number of seat reservations (although some smaller stations receive no seats at all) and they go on sale as soon as ENFE employees get around to opening up. When the window opens, however, the only sense of urgency is with the crowds clamouring to buy tickets.

Despite signs prohibiting sleeping in the railway stations, hundreds of people queue up on the previous day – or sooner – to wait for tickets (foreigners should beware of summary 'fines', however). In extreme cases, this necessitates multiple queues: those waiting for today's tickets, those

Bolivian Railway System

waiting for tomorrow's, for the next day's and so on. When the day's allotment of tickets is sold out, the window is lowered and that's it. Lucky ticket-holders settle in to await their journey and others begin re-forming the queue for the following day.

If you do reach the ticket window, you must present the personal documents of each person for whom you are buying tickets. This is done to prevent scalping, which, under the circumstances, could prove quite lucrative.

Normally, 2nd-class tickets don't include seat reservations and may be purchased from the conductor, who'll sell you a ticket for a

mere 10 to 20% more than it would cost at the window, but without the hassles of queueing.

Train Trips

If you do get a seat reservation and the train does arrive, the trip itself will be a continuation of the adventure. The following is a description of a journey Deanna took from Uyuni to Potosí:

The chalkboard announced that the train would depart at 7 pm so I arrived shortly before. I boarded, only to find that my seat had already been occupied and it required a shouting match and the help of the conductor to displace the offender. I stowed my luggage on the rack and settled in. Then the locals began arriving, each with their usual 16 pieces of luggage.

Despite the crescendoing influx of humanity, the temperature in the coach dropped steadily. At around midnight, five hours after it was scheduled to depart, the train had still not left the station. It was below zero and ice was forming on the windows; there was no light and everyone shivered and huddled beneath piles of blankets.

A family of four occupied the two seats across from me and parts of the 150-kg campesina who'd sat down beside me spilled over her seat and half of mine. All her luggage was packed into the floor space between the seats, and a man and his young daughter had settled in on top of it. The campesina was chewing coca leaves and spitting green juice onto the luggage. The family on the seat opposite us, who had been on a shopping spree in Argentina, were surrounded by all sorts of electronic gadgetry, and as there was no room on the floor, they asked us to hold some of it for them.

Finally, at 4 am, the station bell sounded: the train was finally ready to depart! The bell sounded again at 5 am. At 6.15 am, we finally pulled out of Uyuni, but 10 km out of the station we made an unexplained 2½-hour stop in the Altiplano desert. By this time, the temperature had fallen well below zero and people got off the train and set the bush on fire to keep warm. When we finally started again, the accompanying jolt sent luggage crashing down from overhead racks onto the passengers. The entire 14-hour journey to Potosí was a series of bone-crunching jolts and unexplained delays.

Thanks to the incredible piles of luggage and hundreds of unfortunate folk who'd been unable to buy reserved seats, it was impossible to reach the loo. Just as well though; one can only imagine what it must have looked like! I arrived in Potosí that night with my good nature fraying. Cold and disoriented, I felt as though I'd been spat out of a meat-grinder. A visit to a loo had become a matter of urgency and my hotel was a long, uphill, high-altitude crawl from the railway station.

The most incredible thing was that the locals – once they'd left the train – were smiling, chatting and acting as if nothing were amiss. In actual fact nothing *was* amiss; it had been another normal run for ENFE.

Fortunately, short of avoiding the train altogether, there are several ways to avoid the worst of it. Bolivian trains have 1st and 2nd-class coaches, but the only apparent difference is the price. The facilities themselves look just about the same (the trip I recounted was 1st class; the 2nd-class passengers were on the floor!) and the distinction is made only to separate the poorer campesinos from the wealthier classes.

In addition to coaches, some trains carry *bodegas*, or boxcars, and 2nd-class passengers are permitted to ride in them. On most runs, there is space to spread out and relax, adequate ventilation and, because the doors are left open, a good view of the passing scenery.

If you do choose to travel in the bodegas, extreme heat and extreme cold are matters to be reckoned with. Also, be sure to take something to sit on; the bodegas are only cleaned by the bottoms of passengers. It's also a good idea to make sure the boxcar is actually going all the way to your destination to avoid having to shift later.

If you're travelling from the Brazilian or Argentine frontiers, you'll have to be on hand when the cars open in order to stake out a place to sit. These runs are crowded with merchants and their wares, mostly contraband (noodles, wine, flour, etc), being brought unofficially into the country.

Another option which we don't recommend is to ride on the roof of the train. In warmer climes, it can be quite pleasant but it entails obvious risks (remember the jolting starts and stops) and if you fall off, ENFE won't stop to pick you up.

Ferrobus

The best option of all, however, is the *ferrobus*. This bus on bogies is ENFE's redeeming achievement. It runs more or less on time, is fast and comfortable, and ticket sales are limited to available seats in both 1st and 2nd class (pullman and especial). On some runs, tickets are even sold before the day of departure.

Ferrobus service is a bit more expensive than the normal trains, but that serves to eliminate some of the competition for tickets and consequent queueing problems. Demand for tickets still far exceeds supply, however, so you'll have to be quick. Often the military reserves large blocks of seats, so the general public loses out.

Major Lines

Major railway lines in Bolivia operate between La Paz, Oruro and Villazón, (and on to Buenos Aires, Argentina); La Paz and Charaña (and on to Arica, Chile); La Paz and Potosí/Sucre; Oruro and Cochabamba; Uyuni and Abaroa (and on to Calama, Chile); Santa Cruz and Quijarro; and Yacuiba and Santa Cruz.

TAXI

Other than in Beni and Pando departments, taxis are relatively inexpensive. Few taxis are equipped with meters and the driver and passenger merely agree on the price to a specific destination. The price will usually be the same regardless of the number of passengers, although the driver may charge extra if you have a lot of luggage. It's useful to carry enough small change to cover the fare. Drivers often plead a lack of change in the hope that you'll give them the benefit of the difference. If you don't, they'll have to run around trying to break a B10 or B20 note.

When first arriving in a city, ask a merchant or other local in the transport terminal what the usual taxi fare is to your destination before you agree on a price with the driver. Many drivers think that tourists can be taken for a ride, in more ways than one. Taxi prices will be inflated by up to 50% at bus terminals or railway stations; walk outside the terminal area and hail a taxi in the street.

Collective taxis in Bolivia are called *trufis*, and they follow set routes. These vehicles display coloured flags which represent their destination. They are always cheaper than taxis and are nearly as convenient. A trufi driver will usually deviate from the set route in order to get you to your destination.

A taxi may also be chartered for longer distances. This method is particularly useful if you want to visit places near major cities which are outside local transport areas but too near to be covered by long-distance bus networks. An example is the popular return trip to Zongo near La Paz.

CAR

Unless you're feeling adventurous, have a lot of time and money and/or just want to 'prove it can be done', driving in Bolivia as an exclusive means of transport is not recommended. It's possible to enter Bolivia by road from Chile, Peru, Argentina and Paraguay. The route from Chile is poor, and the one from Paraguay should be considered only with careful preparation.

The advantages of a private vehicle are, of course, schedule flexibility, access to remote areas, and the ability to seize fleeting photographic opportunities. The disadvantages, however, are numerous and should be carefully considered.

Few roads in Bolivia are sealed and most are in varying stages of deterioration, so high speed travel is impossible (unless, of course, you're a Bolivian bus driver). Bolivian roads are narrow and winding, following mountain contours and rocky riverbeds. In southern Bolivia, I once saw a little stone barn beside a river. Four hours later, I saw the same barn again, this time from the other side of the river. Instead of building a bridge, the builders had routed the road *around* the river!

Also, the November to March rainy season must be considered. Mud, flooding, washouts, landslides, avalanches and rockfalls may render roads impassable for weeks, and overland transport grinds to a halt until repairs can be made. When I visited the Chapare region in 1986 after flooding had destroyed all the highway bridges, vehicles were being dragged across some hefty rivers behind tractors. Bridges have now been rebuilt but they remain susceptible to annual flooding.

If you remain undaunted, carry a set of tools, extra petrol, oil and water and every spare part that might conceivably give out en route. Auto parts are a rare commodity outside cities, so if there is a breakdown, plan on hitching into a larger city in search of parts that may or may not be available. If you're travelling off major routes, a 4WD high-clearance vehicle and several spare tyres and wheel rims may come in handy. Always carry camping equipment and plenty of food and drinking water. Petrol in Bolivia is low grade, and is available in all major towns. At the time of writing, it cost B.89 per litre.

Driving Regulations

An international driving licence is required to operate a motor vehicle in Bolivia (motorbikes excluded). They can be obtained from the automobile club in your own country.

When entering Bolivia, a circulation card, called an *hoja de ruta*, must be obtained from the Servicio Nacional de Tránsito at the frontier or in the Bolivian city where the trip begins. These two documents must be presented and stamped at all police posts, variously known as *trancas*, *tránsitos* and *controles*, along the routes.

Peajes or 'tolls' are sometimes charged at these checkpoints and vehicles and luggage may be searched for contraband, although this practice is fortunately becoming quite rare. Sometimes you'll get a receipt for tolls paid; if not, you're almost certainly being overcharged. The Bolivian Consulate in Washington, DC, warns against unofficial trancas set up by unauthorised individuals who try to extort money and possessions from unwary motorists. As soon as you're identified as a foreigner, the police may not be able to resist stopping you; expect to be cited for a few alleged infractions and to pay a few bogus fines.

As in most of the Americas, Bolivians keep to the right except on the Yungas road from La Paz where oncoming vehicles pass each other on the left. Traffic regulations are more or less similar to those in the USA and Europe. Speed limits are infrequently posted, but in most cases, road conditions will prevent you from exceeding them anyway.

In the cities, all the cacophonous horn-honking you'll hear isn't to get traffic moving or to intimidate pedestrians; when two cars approach an uncontrolled intersection (with no police officer or functioning signal) from different directions, the driver who honks first has the right-of-way if they intend to pass straight through. Turning vehicles, of course, must wait until the way is clear before doing so. Keep in mind that this system sometimes doesn't work in practice. While timidity may cost some time, it may be better for your sanity until you're accustomed to Bolivians' driving habits.

When two vehicles meet on a mountain road not wide enough to allow both to pass, the vehicle headed downhill must back up until there's enough room for the other to overtake. Again, this doesn't always work in practice and loud, animated and violent discussions sometimes occur before one driver finally concedes. In the meantime, traffic is blocked in both directions and tempers flare.

Car Rental

Although things are constantly improving, don't put too much faith in Bolivian rental vehicles. Many of them aren't regularly serviced and the vehicle insurance bought from rental agencies may cover only accidental damage. Breakdowns are normally your own problem, but even where they are covered, the logistics of making repairs must be handled by the driver. Sort out the policy and get it in writing *before* accepting the vehicle!

Rental agencies will require an international driving licence, a major credit card or cash deposit and, in most cases, accident insurance. You'll be charged a daily rate and a per km rate (some will allow a set number of free km, after which the rate will apply). You'll also be required to buy petrol and may be liable for any non-accident related vehicle malfunctions which occur during the rental period.

MOTORBIKE

In the lowland areas of Bolivia where roads are scarce, motorbikes are a popular means of getting around in towns. They can be hired for B75 to B90 per day, and are a great way to explore those areas which are not served by public transport. There's now a motorbike rental agency in La Paz.

To hire a bike, head for the motorbike taxi stands normally found on or near the main plaza of most northern Bolivian towns. Motorbike taxi drivers can make a lot more money by hiring out their bikes than by working, and while you're using their bike, they have the day off.

Needless to say, there's a lot of competition, so negotiate the price – which should be payable upon return of the vehicle. All you need is a driver's licence from your home country; no other special licences or permits are required. Bear in mind that many travel insurance policies will not cover you for injuries arising from motorbike accidents; check your policy carefully.

HITCHING

Hitching in Bolivia is easy. In fact this is one thing in the country that is organised. The majority of the population, basically the poorer people, use it as their primary means of transport, while private and commercial vehicle owners use it as a means of lowering their costs. If you want to get off the main routes, it's an excellent option.

Carros (cars), *camionetas* (pickups) and *camiones* (open-bed trucks), all accept paying passengers. Often passengers will be loaded aboard far beyond the practical (and far, far beyond the comfortable!) capacity of the vehicle. For their trouble, drivers usually charge about 75% of the price of the standard bus fare on the same run, or more if no buses service the run. Be sure to ask your fellow passengers the correct price; drivers will assume you are rich and will adjust the fare accordingly, not understanding that in your country, rich people don't normally climb into the back of rattle-trap trucks loaded with chickens, oil drums, noodles and 42 other passengers!

Every town has a market, street or plaza where camiones and camionetas await passengers. When they're full by the driver's definition, they leave. It gets to be quite a contest. Once a few passengers have assembled, the driver will announce that the vehicle will leave *ahorita* – 'right away'. If the passengers feel that it's taking too much time, they all shift to another waiting vehicle. At this point, all other passengers in all other waiting vehicles also shift.

The lucky driver of the nearly 'full' vehicle keeps trying to recruit a few more for as long as the passengers will tolerate it. As soon as they begin to climb down, imminent departure is announced and, wonder of wonders, the vehicle begins to move. After a quick spin around the block, the vehicle returns to the spot where it was waiting before the 'departure'. When collective patiences again begin to wear thin, say after another 15 or 20 minutes, the vehicle actually departs.

A less trying method is to take a taxi or micro to the tranca, a highway police post outside every entrance to every town. All vehicles must stop at these posts, and it's a convenient place to ask drivers where they're headed. The drawback is that at this point you've lost the option of choosing a place to sit.

Soon after sunrise, I climbed into the back of the Cochabamba-bound cargo truck already packed with bags of rice, maize, a large pile of firewood and a Volvo engine block.

[In addition to] my 15 tired-looking Bolivian fellow passengers...were six pigs of various sizes and squeals and one ornery goat who persisted in butting anything or anyone that happened to slide into its territory, which happened to be anywhere *it* happened to be at any particular time...

Meanwhile, it suddenly became apparent to the smallest pig that this was *not* the Disneyland Express, and he stubbornly began mounting and humping away at any other pig within reach.

By the time the noontime sun began baking my brains...the goat had terrorised the shit (literally) out of every pig, and goat pellets were rolling freely amongst the passengers according to the whimsy of the highly eroded road. It was twilight before I saw the lights of Cochabamba. They never twinkled so good!

Mike Stambovsky, USA

While most Bolivians ride in the back of camiones and camionetas because of the economic savings, many drivers will give foreigners (especially women) VIP treatment and allow them to ride in the cab. Even if they don't, you can volunteer to pay 30% or so more and ride inside anyway. This isn't nearly as interesting as riding *atrás* (in the bed of the camión), but if it's raining, you'll appreciate the option.

This brings us to another problem: rain

damages cargo and for this reason, every camión carries a handy piece of tarpaulin called *la carpa*. It covers everything, including passengers, and it's difficult to adequately describe the discomfort caused by this device. It's not only dark beneath it, it's also claustrophobic, and because it rests on your head, it seems quite heavy. Worst of all, it traps the diesel fumes emitted by the vehicle and forces passengers to breathe them in nauseating and health-threatening quantities. The only escape is to face the elements and take to standing on the bumper of the vehicle.

It's wise to have a variety of clothing on hand before riding atrás in camiones and pickups, especially when travelling from the lowlands to higher elevations. Even if you're sitting atop your luggage, it may be wedged tightly and inaccessibly beneath cargo, luggage and other passengers.

BOAT

The most relaxing means of getting around in the Amazon region is by river. You can lie in a hammock for days on end and read, sleep, relax and just watch the world go by. More adventurous types can build a raft or hire a dugout canoe to explore lowland rivers under their own steam, but you'd need a measure of expertise in wilderness survival and would have to be familiar with the hazards of navigation on multi-channelled tropical waterways.

There is no scheduled passenger service in Bolivia's portion of the Amazon Basin and most travellers must rely on cargo transport. The quality, velocity and price you find will largely depend on the luck of the draw, but most river transport will be on cargo vessels. Passenger comfort was the last thing the boat builders had in mind, but although accommodation will probably be tight, it's still superior to that offered on many of the 'cattle-boats' that ply the Amazon proper.

While the riverside scenery is interesting, it changes little, so a couple of good long books are recommended. Don't expect to be bored, however. Shipboard acquaintances develop quickly and the fact that the Bolivian passengers have ventured into this frontier region of their country provides them with a sort of kinship with foreign travellers.

Wildlife Viewing

The Bolivian Amazon Basin is actually more interesting than the Amazon proper. For a start, the rivers are narrower and therefore the boats travel nearer the shore, allowing better observation. Secondly, because the area is little developed and has a much lower population density, opportunities for viewing wildlife are better than along the heavily populated Brazilian rivers.

The Río Beni isn't much of a wildlife river, but on the Mamoré and Ichilo, you'll almost certainly see sloths, monkeys, capybaras, rheas, turtles, many species of birds and butterflies, and hundreds of pink river dolphins. On the Mamoré, I've seen giant river otters and there is also a good chance of spotting alligators and even anacondas in the water. If you're very lucky, you'll catch a glimpse of an anteater.

Food & Accommodation

Passages will typically include food and although onboard cooks tend to show little imagination, the fare is life sustaining. Breakfast will invariably consist of masaco, a mash of manioc root, plantains, charque (dried meat), oil, maize and salt – you have to acquire a taste for it. Other meals will consist of rice or noodles, more charque and fried or steamed plantains. On some runs, passengers may be offered turtle eggs or soup made from turtle meat. In the interest of the turtles, who are threatened in parts of the Bolivian Amazon, you may want to avoid partaking, and perhaps may wish to express concern about their diminishing numbers. On boats which transport lemons, bananas, grapefruits and oranges, fruit is plentiful. Coffee is made from river water and sugar is added unsparingly until it reaches a syrupy consistency. Take along a supply of goodies to complement your diet and relieve your taste buds.

On some boats, a hammock will be required for sleeping due to limited floor space. On others, you can stretch out in a sleeping bag on the deck, the roof or even on the cargo. On one trip between Puerto Barador and Guayaramerín, the decks were full and I was permitted to sleep on the roof of the boat, witness to the sunset, stars and the raucous night-long jungle symphony, all of which were missed by passengers sleeping under the roof and nearer to the noisy engines.

It can get chilly at night and there's always a heavy dew. Some sort of mosquito protection (a net or a good repellent) is essential, especially if you're on a boat that ties up at night. If you're required to spend a lot of time outside, use a strong sunscreen. It's also wise to carry either bottled drinking water or water purification tablets, preferably iodine-based, to treat the murky river water available aboard cargo boats.

The majority of boats are equipped with toilet facilities, but showers and clothes washing facilities are rare. Laundry is done in the river and passengers generally bathe there too. Piranhas and alligators don't seem to pose much of a threat (everyone swims) but check with locals before jumping in.

Routes

The most popular routes are from Puerto Villarroel to Trinidad; Rurrenabaque to Riberalta; and Trinidad to Guayaramerín. There's also the less frequented route from Río Grande (Puerto Banegas) to Trinidad. All of these trips will require a minimum of three to five days – if things go well.

Lake Titicaca

Water travel in Bolivia is not limited to the rivers. Lake Titicaca, shared with Peru on Bolivia's western boundary, is traditionally the highest navigable lake in the world. At an altitude of 3810 metres, it bustles with all sorts of watercraft including the world-famous totora reed boats which Thor Heyerdahl used on his Ra II Expedition from North Africa. These sturdy canoes have plied the waters of Titicaca since pre-Columbian times.

In the more recent past, steamers, which were carried piece by piece from the sea to landlocked Bolivia, ferried passengers between Guaqui and the Peruvian ports, linking the railroad terminals of the two countries. This service was discontinued in 1985, however, when the port of Guaqui disappeared under the waters of the rising lake.

A ferry service operates between San Pedro and San Pablo, across the narrow Estrecho de Tiquina (Straits of Tiquina). This is along the most well-travelled route between La Paz and Copacabana, Puno and Cuzco (the latter two are in Peru).

To visit the several Bolivian islands of Lake Titicaca, there are launches, sailboats and rowboats for hire in Copacabana and Huatajata. Prices are reasonable, especially if you can muster a group. The cost is the same for one person or 15 people.

Cruise ship service is provided by Transturin Ltda, of La Paz. It is relatively expensive, however, compared to other modes of transport on the lake. Crillon Tours, also of La Paz, offers hydrofoil excursions between Huatajata, Copacabana, Isla del Sol and the Peruvian ports of Juli and Puno. Further details are provided in the Lake Titicaca chapter.

TOURS

A growing number of foreign and Bolivian tour operators are cashing in on Bolivia's appeal. Tour options range from half-day familiarisation tours in or near major cities to fully guided, multi-week excursions which include food, transportation, accommodation, transfers, etc. The latter are usually purchased outside Bolivia.

The typical package tour will include a hydrofoil excursion on Lake Titicaca, a tour of the Tiahuanaco ruins, a drive to Chacaltaya, and museum visits and shopping in La Paz. Some even visit mines in Potosí or Oruro. While this is a comfortable way to 'see the sights', it's also a confining and expensive way to travel, and isn't for everyone.

The shorter tours are arranged through hotels, agencies and tourist offices and if you're in a hurry, they're a convenient way to quickly visit a sight you'd otherwise miss. They're also relatively inexpensive, averaging US$20 for a daytrip and less for a half-day trip.

This is an excellent way to visit Tiahuanaco, for instance. An English-speaking guide is normally included and the ruins can become something more than an impressive 'pile of rocks'. A short tour is also useful if you want to visit the Chacaltaya ski slopes or the Zongo ice caves, which are difficult to access on your own. Similarly, longer excursions to such remote attractions as Laguna Colorada or the Cordillera Apolobamba are most conveniently done through tour agencies.

For the more adventurous, who nevertheless don't want to strike out into the wilderness alone, there are a number of outfits which offer trekking, mountain climbing, river running and jungle exploration packages.

Following is a list of major tour outfitters and their prime destinations:

Abotours
    Calle Ayacucho 378, La Paz (☎ 329707, fax (591-2) 391225); this unique tour agency specialises in adventure, natural history, geology and cultural tours; specifically, they offer tours with emphasis on such things as Andean weaving, Andean astronomy, Amazonian national parks and wildlife, anthropology and archaeology, Andean natural medicine, and Bolivian music. Their postal address is Casilla 11133, La Paz.

Amazonas Adventure Tours
    Calle Andrés Manso (René Moreno), Santa Cruz (☎ 324099, fax (591-3) 337587); this company specialises in the remote Reserva de Vida Salvaje Ríos Blanco y Negro and the remote resort at Perseverancia. Their postal address is Casilla 2527, Santa Cruz.

Fremen Tours
    Calle Belisario Salinas 429, La Paz (☎ 327073) and Casilla 1040, Calle Tumusla 0-245, Cochabamba (☎ 47126, fax (591-42) 48500); a bit upmarket; Fremen's speciality is the Amazon area, including the Chapare region, Parque Nacional Isiboro-Securé, La Puente – a wilderness resort near Villa Tunari and the Reina de Enin riverboat which is based in Trinidad. See under Travel Agencies in the Cochabamba chapter and under Villa Tunari in the Amazon Basin chapter for further information on Fremen's offerings.

Colibri
    Calle Sagárnaga 309, La Paz (☎ 371936, fax (591-2) 323274); this company offers a wide variety of trekking and climbing expeditions at some of the lowest rates in town; the operator can arrange tours according to your needs. They run excursions to the salares de Uyuni and Coipasa, do a five-day climb of Volcán Sajama and arrange a complete circuit through south-western Bolivia to the salares, Laguna Colorada and Laguna Verde, as well as climbs of two 6000-metre volcanoes. They also hire out trekking and mountaineering equipment.

Guarachi Andes Expeditions
    Plaza Alonzo de Mendoza, Edificio Santa Anita 314, La Paz (☎ 320901); Guarachi specialises in adventure tours to out-of-the-way destinations, including hikes along the Camino de Oro (Gold Trail), Taquesi and Yunga Cruz trails, and in the Cordillera Apolobamba; climbing Volcán Sajama and the peaks of the Cordillera Real; and exploration of south-western Bolivia. Their postal address is Casilla 12287, La Paz.

Paititi
    Avenida 20 de Octubre 2668 or Calle Sagárnaga 213, Galeria Chuquiago 12, La Paz (☎ 341018); services are similar to those of Guarachi. Paititi's postal address is Casilla 106, La Paz.

TAWA Tours
    Calle Sagárnaga 161, La Paz (☎ 329814) and Rosendo Gutiérrez 701 (☎ 325796, fax (591-2) 391175); we've had both rave reviews and pans about TAWA; their specialities include trekking and jeep tours through the Cordillera Real and Cordillera Apolobamba and trips into the lowlands where they maintain their own resorts and campsites.

Toot Ostveen
    C/o Camilo Andrade, Casilla 17-12-513, Quito, Ecuador (☎ (2) 520263, fax (2) 549144); this Dutch biologist and tourist guide is recommended for individualised adventure tours in Bolivia and Ecuador. She specialises in the Amazon Basin national parks and the Reserva Biosférica del Beni.

La Paz

The home of more than a million Bolivians, over half of whom are of Indian heritage, La Paz is the nation's largest city, its de facto capital and its centre of commerce, finance and industry. A visitor's first view of La Paz will never be forgotten; its setting rates in the company of such spectacular cities as Rio, Capetown, San Francisco and Hong Kong!

Those arriving from the Altiplano, which includes all air, rail and highway passengers (except those sneaking in from Amazonia via the Yungas), may look with distaste and pity upon the poor and littered upper suburbs which flank the city's bleak approaches. The muddy roads, which appear to have avoided much attention since Inca times, are lined with auto repair shops and junkyards; unkempt children play in muddy potholes, and nearby, Indian women pound laundry in a sewage-choked river.

Then suddenly, La Paz appears. The earth drops away as if all the poverty and ugliness has been obliterated, and there, 400 metres below, is the city, filling the bowl and climbing the walls of a gaping canyon nearly five km from rim to rim. On a clear day, the snow-capped triple peak of Illimani (6402 metres) towers above it. If you're fortunate enough to arrive on a dark night, La Paz may appear like a mirrored reflection of a glittering night sky.

Since La Paz is nearly four km above the sea, warm clothing will be essential throughout the year. During the summer the climate can be harsh, rain falls daily in the afternoon and the canyon fills with clouds. Frequent hailstorms pelt the city with icy golfballs from heaven and the steep streets become torrents of runoff. Daytime temperatures hang around 18°C but the dampness makes it seem much colder. In the winter, days are slightly cooler, but the crisp, clear air is invigorating. While the sun shines, the temperature may keep to the mid-teens, while at night, it often dips below freezing. In a city where central heating systems are practically unknown, the cold can seem oppressive and debilitating. Occasionally, rain and even snow fall during the winter.

La Paz is the best place in Bolivia to kick back and watch urban Bolivians circulating through their daily tasks and routines. You can spend hours gazing at the passing crowds: the cholas with their obligatory bowler hats and voluminous skirts; the white-shirted businessmen and politicians; the beggars and the machine-gun toting military.

In addition to life and colour, La Paz has a wide range of hotels, restaurants, entertainment and activities for the visitor, and the longer you stay, the more you will realise just how much there is to see and do.

History

The city was founded on 20 October 1548 by a Spaniard, Captain Alonzo de Mendoza (under orders of Pedro de la Gasca, to whom the Spanish king had entrusted rule over the former Inca lands) and named La Ciudad de Nuestra Señora de La Paz – The City of Our Lady of Peace. The first site chosen by Mendoza was at present-day Laja on the Tiahuanaco road. Shortly after its founding, La Paz was shifted to its current site, a valley called Chuquiago Marka, which was previously occupied by a community of Aymará miners and goldsmiths. Although Mendoza is given the credit, the original inhabitants of Bolivia's largest city were actually indigenous.

The 16th-century Spanish historian Cieza de León remarked of the new city:

This is a good place to pass one's life. Here the climate is mild and the view of the mountains inspires one to think of God.

Despite León's rather lofty assessment (one wonders if he didn't accidentally get off in Cochabamba!), the reason for the city's founding was much more down to earth. The

La Paz

To Airport, Lake Titicaca, Zongo Valley & Oruro

To Oruro, Uyuni, Charaña, Villazón, Cochabamba, Potosí & Calama

0   200   400 m

see Central La Paz map

■ PLACES TO STAY

5   Duendes Hostal
14 Residencial Illimani
25 Hotel Plaza
28 Hotel El Dorado
35 Hotel La Paz

▼ PLACES TO EAT

19 Eli's
30 Amadeus
34 La Suisse

OTHER

1   Veloz del Norte & Minibuses
    Trans–Yungas & Flota 13 de Mayo
2   Flota Yungueña
3   Trucks to the Yungas
4   Main Bus Terminal
6   Railway Station
7   Trucks to Sorata
8   Flota Ingavi
9   Transportes Manco Capac
10 Transportes 2 de Febrero
11 Trucks to Zongo Valley
12 Cemetery
13 Plaza Garita de Lima
15 Disco Papillón
16 Disco Love City
17 Stadium
18 Templete Arqueológico
    Semisubterráneo
20 Argentine Consulate
21 Magri Turismo (American Express)
22 Plaza Sucre
23 Prison
24 Club Andino Boliviano
26 Museo Archeológico de Tiwanaku
27 Plaza de los Estudiantes
29 Universidad Mayor de San Andres
31 Museo Marina Nuñez
32 Brazilian Consulate
33 Goethe Institut
36 Peruvian Consulate
37 Alliance Française
38 German Consulate
39 Canadian Consulate
40 Plaza Isabel la Católica
41 Centro Boliviano–Americano
42 Immigration
43 UK Consulate

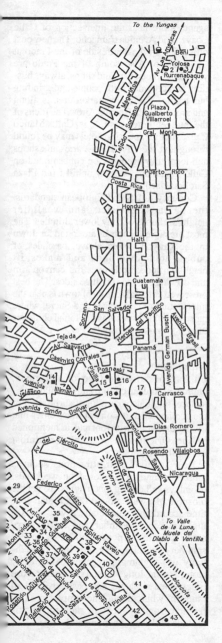

Spanish had always had a weakness for shiny yellow metals and the Río Choqueyapu, which now flows beneath La Paz, seemed to be full of them. The Spanish quickly seized the gold mines, of course, and Mendoza became the first mayor of the new city. The conquerors also imposed their religion and lifestyle on the Indians, and since most of the colonists' women remained in Spain, unions between Spanish men and Indian women soon gave rise to the area's primarily mestizo population.

The site of La Paz in the depths of a rugged canyon seemed to indicate an unpromising future for a successful metropolis based on anything other than gold. However, the protection this position provided from the fierce Altiplano wind and weather – and the fact that it was on the main trade routes between Lima and Potosí – offered La Paz some hope for survival and possible prosperity after gold was no longer an issue. Much of the Potosí silver bound for Peruvian ports on the Pacific passed through La Paz, and by the time the rail lines were built, the city was well enough established to command continuing attention.

On 1 November 1549, Juan Gutiérrez Panaigua was given the task of urban design. He was to lay out plazas and public lands and designate sites for public buildings. La Plaza de los Españoles, now known as Plaza Murillo, was to be the site of the cathedral, royal homes and government buildings.

The logo on the city's coat of arms, commissioned in 1555 by King Carlos V, extols the virtues of La Paz's peaceful foundations. Even so, the City of Peace has known precious little of it since those days. Spain controlled La Paz with a firm grip and the Spanish king had final say in all matters political. He once denied the job of mayor of La Paz to a certain petitioner called Miguel Cervantes de Saavedra, although it was probably just as well. The rejected candidate stayed home and wrote *Don Quixote* instead. Some Bolivians feel, however, that given the opportunity, he would have written it anyway, but to the glory of Bolivia rather than Spain.

Twice in 1781, for a total of six months, a group of Aymará Indians under the leadership of Tupac Katari laid siege to La Paz, destroying public buildings and churches before the uprising was quelled. Another period of unrest took place 30 years later when high plateau Indians laid a two-month siege on La Paz.

Since Bolivia's independence in 1825, Plaza Murillo in La Paz has been centre stage for other revolutions and protests. Bolivian presidents (and more recently, generals) were considered 'endangered species' owing to the abnormally high mortality rate that accompanied high office. As recently as 1946, the then president of Bolivia, Gualberto Villarroel, was publicly hanged in the Plaza Murillo by 'distraught widows', and the presidential palace on the plaza is now known as the Palacio Quemado (Burned Palace), due to its repeated gutting by fire.

Orientation

It's almost impossible to get lost in La Paz. There's only one major thoroughfare, the Prado, which follows the path of least resistance down the canyon along the course of the Río Choqueyapu (which, fortunately for people's olfactory systems, flows mostly underground these days). This main street changes names several times, so it would be handy to familiarise yourself with all of its appellations. From top to bottom they are avenidas Ismael Montes, Mariscal Santa Cruz, 16 de Julio and Villazón. At the lower end, it splits into Avenida 6 de Agosto and Avenida Aniceto Arce.

Away from the Prado everything is steeply and narrowly uphill, and many streets are cobbled or unpaved. Above the downtown skyscrapers, the adobe neighbourhoods and accompanying informal commercial areas climb toward the canyon's rim. If you've become lost and want to return to the Prado, just head downhill.

The centre of commerce and finance extends through the few blocks below Plaza Murillo and north of the Prado. The government offices are naturally centred around Plaza Murillo. Many of the travel and tour agencies are near the intersection of Calle Loayza and Avenida Camacho. The new post office lies on the south side of the Prado at Calle Oruro. Also south of the Prado are various markets, bars and shops, always bustling and crowded with people and grinding bus traffic. The main market area is along and around Calle Buenos Aires. The focus of the budget hotel district is Calle Manco Capac, but inexpensive hotels may be found throughout the city. Tourist artesanía shops and local tour agencies are concentrated on Calle Sagárnaga, steeply uphill from Plaza San Francisco.

Contrary to US and European standards, the business districts and wealthier neighbourhoods occupy lower altitudes. The most prestigious suburbs are found far down in the canyon, while above, cascades of cuboid mud dwellings and makeshift neighbourhoods spill over the canyon rim and down the slopes on three sides. The best preserved colonial section of town is near the intersection of calles Jaén and Sucre, where narrow cobbled streets and colonial churches offer a glimpse of early La Paz.

Information

La Paz has no shortage of museums, churches, Andean culture and colonial architecture, but it also has a lot of surprises. For the acclimatised, it's one of those cities that invites exploration on foot and, as mentioned in the Orientation section, it's almost impossible to get lost.

Bear in mind that attractions such as museums tend to be closed on weekends, Mondays and during lunch hours. To get the most out of a walk around La Paz, plan your time accordingly. Especially if you're visiting between November and April, carry some sort of rain protection. A lovely summery morning may turn into a torrentially wet nightmare by noon. Also, carry along a warm, long-sleeved sweater for those times when a blazing sun passes behind an innocent white cloud. The temperature difference from moment to moment at this altitude will seem phenomenal!

Tourist Information Dinatur (☎ 358213) has its La Paz office on the 18th floor of Edificio Ballivián at Calle Mercado 1328. It's open Monday to Friday from 8.30 am to noon and 2.30 to 6.30 pm.

They have a message box and a book of visitor recommendations and distribute a host of other brochures dealing with La Paz and the entire country, some in English, French and German. The original Spanish versions, however, may make more sense than the mildly amusing and often indecipherable translations. This phenomenon was explained by a brochure we found later from a La Paz translation service which advertised 'accurate traductions' ('translation' in Spanish is *traducción)* from Spanish into English. They must do a booming business with the tourist office!

Don't forget to take your camera; you'll get superb views of the city and equally great photos of Illimani through the windows on either side of the 18th floor lifts. Similarly good views may be had from the restaurants on the top floors of the Hotel Plaza or Hotel Gloria.

The El Lobo restaurant at the corner of Calle Illampú and Avenida Mariscal Santa Cruz has books of travellers' recommendations in both English and Hebrew, so if you have something to add or are interested in finding out where everyone else is going, avoiding, or turning into a travellers' ghetto, you may want to check it out.

Maps The best city maps are *La Paz Información* and *La Paz – the Map & Guide* sold by the tourist office. We hesitate to recommend the latter, however; it isn't really worth the price and its publisher takes a rather cavalier attitude toward copyright. Larger hotels and travel agencies often distribute free city maps marking the location of their establishment in relation to points of interest in La Paz.

National maps and topo sheets may be bought from the Instituto Geográfico Militar (IGM) at Avenida 16 de Julio 1471. You select the map you want, pay the bill and they will have it ready for collection on the after-

noon of the following day. City and national maps of lower quality may be found at bookshops and in the kiosks at the main post office. The post office kiosks are open from 9 am to noon and 3 to 7 pm Monday to Friday.

If everyone seems to be out of the map you need or you can't wait overnight for map delivery to the Avenida 16 de Julio IGM office, try the IGM head office on the corner of Saavedra and Subrieta in Miraflores. In order to avoid a potentially nasty scene, ask the guard at the gate where you'll need to enter to buy a map. The military can be rather sticky about formalities so you'll need your passport to enter this restricted compound. Be prepared for a bit of red tape. Topographic sheets with scales of 1:50,000 are available for the area around La Paz.

Money Several casas de cambio are found on calles Ayacucho and Colón on the block just above Avenida Camacho. The process of exchanging currency in these establishments involves few hassles. Casa de Cambio Sudamer on Calle Colón changes travellers' cheques and is open from 9 am to noon and 2 to 5 pm on weekdays. They also sell Peruvian and Chilean currency (when it's available), often at better rates than you can get in those countries. Casa de Cambio Silves at Calle Mercado 979 and Cambio d'Argent at Calle Mercado 1328 have also been recommended; they'll change travellers' cheques to cash US dollars for 1% commission while Cambio Latino on the Avenida 16 de Julio tourist beat charges a whopping 3%!

One of the most interesting and popular places to exchange money is at the Shampoo Shop on Yanacocha near Calle Mercado. That's not its real name, but it sells shampoo (there's an impressive display of dandruff combatants, hair creams and conditioners in the window!) and has been known to travellers for years. The operation may remind you of a bookie joint in an old-time gangster movie. Go to the register and tell them you want to exchange money and a uniformed guard will escort you around the counter to

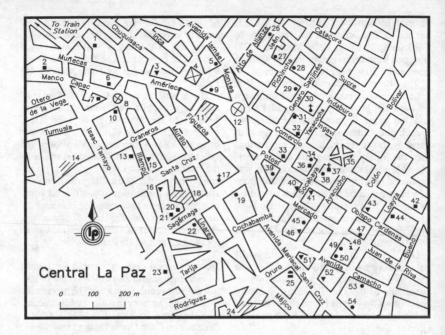

Central La Paz

0   100   200 m

a plush office in a back room where your transaction will take place. They change cash at a good rate and travellers' cheques fetch the same rate as other exchange houses offer for cash. For a mere 1% commission, they will also change travellers' cheques to cash dollars and certify the legitimacy of each dollar note with a rubber stamp.

On Saturdays, you can change cash or travellers' cheques at either the Hotel Gloria or the Unitours travel agency near the corner of calles Loayza and Mercado, but expect a slightly lower rate than is available on weekdays.

Along Avenida Camacho *cambistas* (street changers) will change cash for about the same rate given by the casas de cambio, which at the time of writing was about B3.6 per US$1. Due caution should be exercised in dealing with street changers. See the relevant discussion under Money in the Facts for the Visitor chapter.

If you'd like to purchase travellers'

cheques, try Citibank at Avenida 16 de Julio 1434. For anything up to US$1000 in cheques, they charge US$10 commission. American Express (Magri Turismo) sells cheques for 1% commission, payable in cash or with an American Express card.

VISA cash withdrawals of up to US$300 daily are available in 20 minutes with no commission and a minimum of hassle from the Banco de Santa Cruz at Calle Mercado 1077. Banco Mercantil on the corner of calles Mercado and Ayacucho offers similar services without commission as does Banco Nacional de Bolivia at the corner of Calle Colón and Avenida Camacho. Banco de La Paz charges 1.75% commission on cash draws.

Post The sparkling new main post office is on Avenida Mariscal Santa Cruz and Calle Oruro. If you're posting an international parcel, take it downstairs to the customs desk and have it inspected before sealing it up and

■	PLACES TO STAY	9	Museo Tambo Quirquincho
1	Hostería Florida	11	Mercado Lanza
2	Hotel Panamericano	12	Plaza Pèrez Velasco
6	Hotel Italia	14	Mercado Negro
7	Hotel Andes	17	Iglesia de San Francisco
10	Hotel Continental	18	Mercado de Hechicería
13	Residencial Rosário	19	Peña Naira
20	Hotel Sagárnaga	22	Museo del Charango (Museo de
21	Hotel Alem		Instrumentos Nativos)
23	Hotel Milton	24	Plaza Belzu (Bus to Ventilla)
32	Hostal Austria	25	Main Post Office
33	Hotel Gloria	26	Museos de Metales Preciosos Pre-
36	Hotel Torino		Columbinos, Litoral, Cos-
42	Hostal República		tumbrista Juan de Vargas &
44	Hotel Viena		Casa de Don Pedro Domingo
			Murillo.
▼	PLACES TO EAT	27	Peña Marka Tambo
		28	Cinemateca Boliviana
3	El Palácio de Pescado	29	Teatro Municipal
15	La Hacienda	30	Iglesia de Santo Domingo
16	El Lobo	31	Museo de Etnografía y Folklore
40	Super Salteña	34	Museo Nacional del Arte
41	Confitería Marilín	35	Plaza Murillo
43	Manjari	37	Cathedral
46	Clap	38	Museo de la Catedral
51	Confitería Club de La Paz	39	Shampoo Shop
52	Café Verona	45	ENTEL (Telephone Office)
		47	Los Amigos del Libro
	OTHER	48	Dinatur Tourist Office & Policía
			Turística
4	Plaza Alonzo de Mendoza	49	USA Consulate
5	TAM	50	Casa de Cambio Sudamer
8	Plaza Vicenta Juariste Eguino	53	LAB
		54	Instituto Geográfico Militar

taking it to the parcels desk. Parcels to Bolivian destinations should be taken to the desk marked Encomiendas. Postcards, envelopes, maps, packing materials and greeting cards are available in the half-dozen shops at the far end of the main lobby. Hours are 8.30 am to 6 pm Monday to Saturday, and both poste restante and philatelic services are available.

If you're sending letters or parcels overseas, you should consider certifying them for B1 apiece. While this won't ensure delivery, it will certainly increase their chances of arriving. Expreso service is available for domestic mail and is in theory speedier than the regular post.

Magri Turismo, the American Express representative in La Paz, will hold mail for travellers carrying an American Express card or travellers' cheques. For their address and phone number, see under Organised Tours later in this chapter.

Telecommunications The ENTEL office at Calle Ayacucho 267 between Calle Mercado and Avenida Camacho is open 24 hours for local, national and international telephone calls. Public telephones are found in the ENTEL lobby and in hotels, restaurants and some street stalls. ENTEL also has telegram and telex services, and has recently opened a new but laboriously inefficient fax office. The public fax numbers in La Paz are 391784 and 367625.

Foreign Embassies & Consulates Holidays and opening hours of foreign consulates vary depending on the country and the sort of services required; it's wise to phone in advance for information so that you don't waste a trip:

Argentina
    Edificio Banco de la Nación Argentina, 2nd floor, (☎ 353089)
Australia
    Australian residents are represented by the UK Embassy
Austria
    Edificio Petrolero, 7th floor, #1 (☎ 326601)
Belgium
    Avenida Hernando Siles 5290 esq Calle 7, Obrajes (☎ 784925)
Brazil
    Avenida 20 de Octubre 2038, Edificio Foncomin, Pisos 9, 10, 11 (☎ 322110)
Canada
    Avenida Aniceto Arce 2342 (☎ 375224)
Chile
    Avenida Hernando Siles 5843, Calle 13, Obrajes (☎ 785275)
Colombia
    Plaza Abaroa 2427 (☎ 359658)
Finland
    Calle Mercado 1004 (☎ 350900)
France
    Avenida Hernando Siles 5390, Calle 8, Obrajes (☎ 786189)
Germany
    Avenida Aniceto Arce 2395 (☎ 390850)
Israel
    Avenida Mariscal Santa Cruz, Edificio Esperanza, 10th floor (☎ 358676)
Italy
    Avenida 6 de Agosto 2575 (☎ 323597)
Japan
    Calle Rosendo Gutiérrez 497 esq Lima (☎ 366859)
Netherlands
    Avenida Aniceto Arce 2031, Edificio Victoria, 2nd floor (☎ 356153)
New Zealand
    New Zealand residents are represented by the UK Embassy
Norway
    Calle Alfredo Ascarrunz 2547, Sopocachi (☎ 322528)
Paraguay
    Avenida Aniceto Arce, Edificio Venus, 7th floor (☎ 322018)
Peru
    Avenida 6 de Agosto, Edificio Alianza mezzanine (☎ 352031)

South Africa
    Calacoto, Calle 22 7810 (☎ 792101)
Spain
    Avenida Aniceto Arce esq Cordero Edificio Guanabara, 1st floor (☎ 357203)
Sweden
    Avenida Aniceto Arce 2856 (☎ 377849)
Switzerland
    Avenida 16 de Julio, Edificio Petrolero, 6th floor, #1 (☎ 353091)
UK (also representing New Zealand and Australia)
    Avenida Aniceto Arce casi Campos 2732 (☎ 329401)
USA
    Potosí esq Colón 1285, Edificio Tobias, 2nd floor (☎ 320494)

Cultural Centres The following centres all offer cultural programmes and reading rooms with films, magazines, books and news from their sponsoring countries: Centro Boliviano Americano (☎ 351627) on Avenida Aniceto Arce at Parque Zenón Iturralde; Goethe Institut (☎ 391369) at Avenida 6 de Agosto 2118; and Alliance Française (☎ 324075) with offices at the corner of Calle 20 de Octubre and Fernando Guachalla, and also at the corner of Calle Ingavi and Pichincha.

Bookshops There are quite a few bookshops in La Paz but the majority would only be of interest if you're looking for comics, cheap and trashy novels or Bolivian school texts. A good, complete selection of Spanish language literature and reference books is available at Gisbert & Cia, Calle Comercio 1270.

Los Amigos del Libro, near the corner of calles Mercado and Colón, has a selection of popular English and German-language paperbacks and souvenir books, as well as dictionaries and Spanish-language books. They also sell *Time*, *Newsweek*, *Der Spiegel* and the *Economist*.

Souvenir books and guidebooks are available at appropriately sky-high prices in the bookshop at El Alto Airport.

Laundry Most middle and high-range hotels offer laundry services. As a general rule, the lower the room rates, the lower the laundry rates. If you'd rather do it yourself, there's a coin-operated laundrette at the corner of Avenida Ecuador and Calle Rosendo Gutiérrez.

Film Fujichrome colour slide film is widely available at about B22 per roll; be cautious about purchasing film at street markets where it is exposed to strong sun all day. Fujicolour is the most widely available print film.

For processing of both slides and print film, only two laboratories are reliable: Casa Kavlin at Calle Potosí 1130 and Foto Linares in the Edificio Alborada on the corner of Calle Loayza and Juan de la Riva. The latter also sells a selection of Agfa film.

If you have problems with your camera, the person to see is Rolando Calla. You'll find him in Idem-Fuji Color (☎ 327391) at Calle Potosí 1316 between 10.30 am and noon, and at his home (☎ 373621) at Avenida Sánchez Lima 2178 from 3 to 7 pm.

Camping Equipment You'll find camping equipment at Ballivián Asociados, Limitada, Calle Murillo 999, near the corner of Cochabamba. If you'd rather just hire equipment, Carmoar Tours at the corner of calles Bueno and Federico Zuazo rents tents, sleeping bags and backpacks for around B20 per item per day. The day of rental and return are free. Guarachi Andes Expeditions and Colibri (see Tours in the Getting Around chapter) hire mountaineering equipment at considerably higher rates. Stove fuel is unfortunately not available in Bolivia, and cannot be carried on aircraft. You will only be able to bring it into Bolivia if you are travelling overland from a neighbouring South American country.

Medical Services The Unidad Sanitario Centro Piloto near the brewery just off upper Avenida Ismael Montes is open from 8.30 am to noon and 2.30 to 6.30 pm. Those heading for the lowlands may pick up yellow fever vaccinations and free chloroquine to be used as a malaria prophylaxis. Don't take the chloroquine, however, if you've previously been taking Lariam (mefloquine). They make a toxic and potentially dangerous combination.

Rabies vaccinations are available for B3. Anyone bitten or scratched by a suspicious animal must take daily vaccinations for seven subsequent days and three more over the next two months.

If you're in need of an English-speaking doctor, try Clínica Americana (☎ 783371) at 5409 Avenida 14 de Septiembre, Calle 9 in the Obrajes district. The German clinic, Clínica Alemana (☎ 329155), is at Avenida 6 de Agosto 2216.

Anyone who's interested may want to check out the Clínica de Medicina Natural Wancollo (Wancollo Clinic of Natural Medicine), 20 minutes east of Tiahuanaco. It certainly looked like an intriguing option.

Police If you've been robbed, go to the Policía Turística (☎ 367441 or 361138) on the 18th floor of Edificio Ballivián, 1328 Calle Mercado (the same place as the tourist office). They won't provide much help recovering stolen goods but they'll take an affidavit *(denuncio)* for insurance purposes. The phone number for Radio Patrulla (Radio Patrol), as in all major Bolivian cities, is 110.

Immigration For visa extensions, go to immigration (☎ 370475) in the Edificio Ministerio del Interior at Calle Gonsalves between avenidas Aniceto Arce and 6 de Agosto. They reportedly cost as much as B70 for up to 90 days.

Dangers & Annoyances La Paz is a great city to explore on foot, but don't be in too much of a hurry or the altitude will take its toll, especially when you're walking uphill. If you're arriving in La Paz from the lowlands, you may want to read the section on Altitude & Climate-Related Illnesses in the Health section of the Facts for the Visitor chapter.

During the first three-quarters of the 20th century, political unrest in La Paz was so commonplace it scarcely rated as newsworthy. Visitors nowadays shouldn't consider it a matter of much concern, at least as far as safety is concerned. The days of the revolving door on the presidential palace and the fires, gallows and flying bullets on Plaza Murillo seem to be over, replaced by scheduled, peaceful and democratically sanctioned changes of government.

Although student demonstrations were commonplace in the late 1980s (in one 1986 demonstration, angry students blocked the Prado by stopping city buses and summarily dismantling their engines!), political unrest seems to have subsided for the time being.

Churches

Iglesia de San Francisco The hewn stone basilica of San Francisco, on the plaza of the same name, stands out above all others in La Paz. Its décor and architecture form an interesting blend of mestizo and Spanish styles. Construction began in 1549 after its foundation the previous year by Fray Francisco de los Ángeles. Although the original structure collapsed under heavy snowfall around 1610, reconstruction began in 1744 and was completed in 1753. The second building was constructed entirely of stone quarried at nearby Viacha, and the façade is decorated with stone carvings representing such natural themes as chirimoyas, pine cones and tropical birds.

Indian weddings are traditionally scheduled for Saturday mornings; the finery worn on these occasions is both colourful and beautiful to see.

After looking at the church, turn toward the bizarre and ambitious sculpture that stands in mid-construction on the upper portion of Plaza San Francisco. It's intended to represent and honour three cultures – Tiahuanaco, Inca and modern – but funds ran out and it sits in suspended animation with a few rock pillars and several half-emerged stone faces staring at the aluminium fence that imprisons them.

Cathedral Although it's a recent addition to La Paz's collection of religious structures, the 1835 cathedral on Plaza Murillo is an impressive structure – mostly because it is built on a steep hillside. Its base at the top on Calle Comercio is 12 metres higher than its base on Calle Potosí. The sheer immensity of the building, with its high dome, hulking columns, thick stone walls and high ceilings, is overpowering, but the altar is relatively simple. Inside, the real attraction is the profusion of stained-glass work throughout; stained-glass windows behind the altar amusingly depict a gathering of Bolivian generals and presidents being blessed from above by a flock of heavenly beings.

Beside the cathedral is the Presidential Palace and on the Plaza Murillo opposite them stands a statue of ex-president Gualberto Villarroel. In 1946, he was dragged from the palace by vigilantes and publicly hanged from a lamppost in the square.

Iglesia de Santo Domingo Like the Iglesia de San Francisco, the façade of Santo Domingo on the corner of Yanacocha and Ingavi displays evidence of baroque and mestizo influences. The rest of the structure is of limited interest.

Museums

La Paz, as Bolivia's de facto capital, has its share of cultural and historical museums. In one of the city's best preserved and restored colonial neighbourhoods, on Calle Jaén near Calle Sucre, are four museums which may be visited and absorbed in one shot: Museo Costumbrista Juan de Vargas, Museo del Litoral, Casa de Don Pedro Domingo Murillo and Museo de Metales Preciosos Pre-Columbinos. The combination entry ticket, which may be purchased at Museo Costumbrista, covers entrance to all four museums. Admission costs B2.50 for foreigners and B1.50 for Bolivians. On Saturday, admission is free for everyone. The museum is open Tuesday to Friday from 9.30 am to noon and 2.30 to 6.30 pm. On Saturday and Sunday, it's open from 10 am to 12.30 pm.

Museo Costumbrista Juan de Vargas Museo Costumbrista Juan de Vargas, the

Hillside Neighbourhoods - La Paz (RS)

Top: Accounting Bolivian Style - La Paz (WH)
Left: Young Girl - La Paz (WH)
Right: Aymará Women on Calle Graneros - La Paz (WH)

most interesting of the 'four-in-one' museums, contains art and photos of old La Paz, as well as some superb dioramas of old La Paz made up of ceramic figurines. One of these is a representation of *akulliko*, the hour of coca-chewing; another portrays the festivities surrounding the Día de San Juan Batista on 24 June; yet another depicts the hanging of Murillo in 1810. Colonial artefacts and colourful dolls wearing traditional costumes are also on display.

Museo del Litoral Sometimes called Museo de la Guerra del Pacífico, this small museum contains some relics from the 1884 war in which Bolivia lost its department of Litoral, its only outlet to the sea. The collection is mostly made up of historical maps which hope to advertise to the world Bolivia's emotionally charged claims to Antofagasta and Chile's Segunda Región.

Casa de Don Pedro Domingo Murillo Once the home of Pedro Murillo, a leader in the La Paz Revolution of 16 July 1809, the house now exhibits some colonial art and furniture, textiles, medicines, musical instruments and household items of glass and silver that once belonged to Bolivian aristocracy. Other odds and ends include a collection of Alasitas miniatures. Murillo was publicly lynched by the Spanish on 29 January 1810, in the plaza now named after him. Oddly enough, one of the paintings on display in the house is entitled *The Execution of Murillo*.

Museo de Metales Preciosos Pre-Columbinos This museum, also known as the Museo del Oro, houses three impressively presented salons of pre-Conquest silver, gold and copper works. A fourth salon in the basement contains examples of ancient pottery.

Museo de Etnografía y Folklore On the corner of Ingavi and Calle Genero Sanjinés, the Ethnography and Folklore Museum is a must for Bolivian anthropology buffs. It's housed in the home of the Marquez de Villaverde, constructed between 1776 and 1790. Exhibits cover the customs and artistry of two of the more obscure Bolivian ethnic groups, the Chipayas of western Oruro Department and the Ayoreos of the Beni lowlands. See also the collection of photos and artefacts from the Chipayas, a group whose language, rites and customs differ greatly from those of neighbouring cultures. Some theories place them as descendants of the vanished Tiahuanaco culture. This museum is open Monday to Friday from 8.30 am to noon and 2.30 to 6.30 pm. Admission is B1.

Museo de Mineralogía The worthwhile Mineralogy Museum houses a complete collection of Bolivian gems, metals and minerals, and even a few from elsewhere. It has recently moved to the Banco Minero at Avenida 6 de Agosto 2382 near Calle Belisario Salinas. Hours are Monday to Friday from 9 am to 1 pm and 2.30 to 4.30 pm. Admission is free.

Templete Arqueológico Semisubterráneo Also known as the Museo al Aire Libre, this open pit opposite the stadium is a replica of the Templete Semisubterráneo at Tiahuanaco. It contains restorations of statues found at Tiahuanaco, and if you aren't planning to visit the actual site, it's worth a quick visit.

Museo Arqueológico de Tiwanaku The Museo Nacional de Arqueología, which is called the Museo Tiwanaku (both spellings, 'Tiwanaku' and 'Tiahuanaco' are correct) on most maps, is on Calle Tiwanaku just two blocks from the Prado. It contains a small but well-sorted collection of artefacts which illustrate and explain the most interesting aspects of the Tiahuanaco culture's five stages. (See the Tiahuanaco entry in the Around La Paz section of this chapter for the historical background on the Tiahuanaco culture.)

The presentation isn't overwhelming and can be easily digested in an hour. Many of Tiahuanaco's treasures were stolen or damaged during the colonial days. Some of the ancient stonework disappeared into Spanish construction projects, while valuable pieces – gold and other metallic relics and artwork – found their way into European museums or treasuries. Most of what remains in Bolivia – pottery, figurines, trepanned skulls, mummies, textiles and metal objects – is housed in this one room.

Admission is still a bargain at B1 and it's open Tuesday to Friday from 9 am to noon and 2.30 to 7 pm, and on Saturday and Sunday from 10 am to 12.30 pm and 2.30 to 6.30 pm.

Museo de la Catedral The Cathedral Museum at Calle Socabaya 432 is open Tuesday and Thursday from 10 am to noon and 2.30 to 6 pm. Adult admission is B1. The museum consists mostly of typical religious paraphernalia, but there are two unusual mother-of-pearl coffins and individual portraits of the 12 apostles which are quite well done.

Museo Tambo Quirquincho Tambo Quirquincho at the corner of Plaza Alonzo de Mendoza and Calle Evaristo Valle once served as a *tambo*, which in Quechua refers to a wayside inn and market area selling staple items. It has been converted into a museum housing an exhibit of weird and colourful Diablada masks, drawings of 1845 Bolivia by Neman Regendas, old-time clothing, silverware, paintings, sculptures, photos and festive items. It's open Tuesday to Friday from 9.30 am to 12.30 pm and 3.30 to 7 pm, and on Saturday and Sunday from 10 am to 12.30 pm. Admission is free.

Museo del Charango Also known as the Museo de Instrumentos Nativos, the Museo del Charango (☎ 355776) at Calle Linares 900 near the corner of Calle Sagárnaga is the home of charango master Ernesto Cavour. On display are all possible incarnations of charangos as well as numerous other indigenous instruments. If you'd like to visit, phone in advance to arrange an appointment and when you arrive, speak with the friendly woman who keeps the music shop on the premises.

Museo de la Historia Natural La Paz's Natural History Museum on the university campus in Cotacota, Calle 26, has exhibits on the geology, palaeontology, botany and zoology of Bolivia. It's a bit inconveniently located, but is worthwhile if you're in that area anyway. It's open Tuesday to Sunday from 10 am to 5 pm. From the Prado, take micro 'Ñ' or colectivo 21 headed downhill.

Museo Nacional del Arte The National Art Museum, on the corner of calles Comercio and Socabaya near Plaza Murillo, is housed in the former Palacio de Los Condes de Arana. The building was constructed of pink Viacha granite in 1775 and was restored to its original grandeur by architects Teresa Gisbert and José de Mesa.

In the centre of a huge courtyard, surrounded by three storeys of pillared corridors, is a lovely alabaster fountain. The 1st floor is dedicated to contemporary artists, including one salon which contains only the work of sculptress Marina Nuñez del Prado. The 2nd floor of the museum is devoted to the late-renaissance works of Melchor Perez de Holguín and students of his Potosí school and the 3rd floor displays works of other Latin American artists. Visiting exhibits are shown in the outer salon.

The museum is open Tuesday to Friday between 9.30 am and 12.30 pm and 3 and 7 pm, and on Saturday from 9.30 am to 1.30 pm.

Museo Marina Nuñez This museum (☎ 324906) is dedicated exclusively to the work of Marina Nuñez del Prado, whose sculptures focus on subjects relating to the Quechua and Aymará cultures. Located in her former home at Avenida Ecuador 2034, it contains her personal collection of cultural paraphernalia and numerous examples of her work. It's scheduled to open from 9 am to noon and 2 to 6 pm Tuesday to Friday and between 9 am and noon on Saturday, but these hours are not strictly adhered to so it would be wise to phone ahead for information and schedules.

Prison Visits

It is becoming increasingly popular among travellers to pay a visit to one's own (or someone else's) compatriots imprisoned in La Paz, most of whom were accused of drug-trafficking. It may seem disagreeable to some; many who've gone report that it is almost like visiting a surreal sort of closed society. Nevertheless, most of the foreign prisoners appreciate the company and a word or two in their own language. Items in short supply at the prison include cigarettes, books, fruit and snack goodies, like yoghurt and bananas.

The prison is on Plaza Sucre (also known as Plaza San Pedro). Visitors are only permitted inside on Sunday between 9 and 10 am, but may visit any day if they don't mind chatting through the bars. Also on Plaza Sucre is a shop which sells articles produced by the prisoners.

Cemetery

One British traveller wrote and suggested we include more about La Paz's interesting cemetery:

I suppose that in hindsight, an interest in the cemetery is a little bizarre, but the cemetery in La Paz is so different from those in England and the USA. Bodies are buried normally and then within 10 years are disinterred and cremated. Families purchase/rent glass-fronted spaces in walls to keep the ashes and put up plaques, keep mementos of the dead and place flowers behind the glass door. There are dozens of these doors in each wall, of which there must be hundreds. The cemetery is a place of activity with people leaving fresh flowers, children providing water for them and people visiting their relatives. Some of the walls have been expanded upwards to such an extent that they appear to be apartments with three or four storeys.

There are also huge family mausoleums as you'd find in France, areas dedicated to mine workers and their families and a number of common graves for fallen soldiers who fought in Bolivia's battles with her neighbours. I was told, but never saw myself, that there were professional mourners who dressed in black to follow the coffin around with suitable wails and tears.

The cemetery is certainly worth at least a half-hour visit. On 1 November, the Día de los Muertos (Day of the Dead), nearly everyone visits their dead relatives, and the cemetery is full of people all day.

T B Burgess, UK

Markets

The market exists in Latin American society as an arena for socialising as well as a place to buy goods. If you're interested in meeting the people or just observing the rhythms of local life, one of the best places would be one of the city's dozen or so markets. There's an artesans' market, a witchcraft market, a food market, a flower market and a black market. Anything available in La Paz – from phonograph records to toothpaste to strawberry jam – may be found somewhere in the markets of La Paz.

Mercado de Hechicería The most colourful and unusual market in La Paz thrives along Calle Linares between Calle Sagárnaga and Calle Santa Cruz. It's also known as Mercado de los Brujos, or the Witches' Market. In Aymará, it's called *laki'asina catu*. What they're selling isn't exactly witchcraft as we would envision it. The merchandise includes herbs and folk remedies as well as a few more unorthodox ingredients intended as means of manipulating and supplicating the various good and bad spirits that populate the Aymará world.

If you're planning a new home or office building, for example, you can buy a dead llama foetus to bury beneath the cornerstone as a cha'lla (toast or offering) to Pachamama, thereby encouraging her to bring good luck therein. If you or someone you know is feeling ill, or is being pestered by unwelcome or bothersome spooks, you can purchase a colourful plateful of herbs, seeds and assorted critter parts to remedy the problem. As you wander through the market, look for wandering yatiri who wear dark hats and carry coca pouches and circulate through the area offering fortune-telling services. Foreigners, however, don't seem to be welcomed as clients.

Photography is discouraged around this market.

Mercado Negro The Black Market along upper Calle Graneros between Calle Isaac Tamayo and Maximiliano Paredes is a place to pick up undocumented merchandise and just about anything else you may hope for. Most of it isn't stolen, exactly, although some of it is bootlegged, and in the case of music tapes, vendors make no effort to conceal that fact; the album covers are merely photocopies of the originals! This is a good place to find inexpensive Fuji and Agfa film, including slide film.

Mercado Lanza Between Plaza Perez Velasco and Calle Figueroa, Mercado Lanza is La Paz's largest food market. It sells all manner of fruits, vegetables, juices, dairy products, breads and tinned foods. There are also numerous stalls where you can pick up

Street Market

a sandwich, soup, salteña, empanada or a full meal.

Mercado de Flores The Flower Market, appropriately located opposite the cemetery at the top of Avenida Tumusla, is a beautiful splash of colour amid one of La Paz's drabber areas. Unfortunately, it also sits alongside a festering open sewer and garbage dump. It's all very confusing to the nostrils.

Buenos Aires From the Plaza Perez Velasco uphill toward the cemetery, the streets are crowded with vendors and market stalls selling practical items from clothing and fast foods to groceries, health-care products and cooking pots. The focus of activity is near the intersection of Calle Buenos Aires and Maximiliano Paredes, especially on Wednesday and Saturday. This part of town, which has a largely indigenous population, is always bustling, with traffic honking its way through the narrow cobbled streets, pedestrians jostling with sidewalk salespeople and cholas rushing about socialising and making purchases.

Mercado La Ceja If you're looking for excellent value artesanía, try the Thursday and Sunday La Ceja Market which spreads along the main thoroughfare and across Plaza 16 de Julio in El Alto. There you'll find workshops producing articles for the Calle Sagárnaga shops and market stalls, which are for sale at a fraction of in-town prices. This market opens at 6 am and winds down around 3 pm.

Arts Fair Although it's not a market, per se, on Sunday local artists stage a tasteful arts exhibition on Plaza Humboldt in Calacoto. It merits a browse around if you're passing through on your way to Valle de la Luna, and there's an interesting Japanese garden opposite the plaza which is also worth a look. From the centre, take micro 'Ñ' which goes right past it.

Activities

Hiking & Climbing Clubs Founded in 1939, Club Andino Boliviano (☎ 324682), an outstanding organisation of climbers, backpackers, skiers and other outdoor enthusiasts, is dedicated to the conservation of Bolivia's wilderness and natural resources. The club is happy to provide brochures and answer questions regarding outdoor activities you may wish to pursue in Bolivia, particularly in the La Paz area. They not only organise popular weekend ski trips to Chacaltaya, but also lead ski expeditions to the lesser known peaks of Condoriri and Mururata. If you're interested in backpacking, trekking or technical climbing in the Bolivian Andes, the club also organises guided expeditions and hires out climbing or camping equipment.

Club groups scale all the major Bolivian peaks at least once a year. For the schedule of climbs or other information, write to the President, Señor Huáscar Pacheco Muñoz, care of the club. The club office is at Calle México 1638. The mailing address is Casilla 1346, La Paz. For further information on club activities, refer to the discussion of Chacaltaya in the Around La Paz section of this chapter.

A second La Paz club is Club de Excursionismo, Andinismo y Camping (☎ 352666) at Calle Sagárnaga 207 esq Murillo, a society of outdoor enthusiasts who occasionally organise 10-day excursions to the Salar de Uyuni and Laguna Colorada, and expeditions into the Cordillera Real. Their mailing address is Casilla 3817, La Paz.

Golf & Tennis If you're interested in a round of golf or a game of tennis, you may have to join a club because public facilities do not exist. La Paz has two tennis clubs: the Club de Tennis La Paz (☎ 793930) Avenida Arequipa-La Florida; and the La Paz Sucre Tennis Club (☎ 324483) Avenida Busch 1001. If you just want to get in a couple of games, you may be able to phone and arrange a few hours' access to the courts for a reasonable price.

Those who would like to try their skills on the world's highest golf course at Malasilla can expect to pay at least B35 for a caddy and a round of 18 holes. Private equipment is necessary.

Skiing Skiing is possible at Chacaltaya; refer to the Around La Paz section.

Language & Arts Courses

Spanish language courses are available at the Centro Boliviano Americano (for the address, see the Cultural Centres section under Information in this chapter) or at the Carrera Linguística on the 13th floor of the Universidad Mayor de San Andrés.

If you speak Spanish and are looking for musical instruction on traditional Andean instruments – zampoña, quena, charango, etc, see Profesor Heliodoro Niña at the Academía de Música Helios, Calle Illampú 816. He charges approximately B5 per hour.

The Dirección Nacional de Juventúd (Dinaju) on Calle Ayacucho between calles Potosí and Mercado (above the old post office) can provide further information on traditional weaving courses and instruction on Bolivian musical instruments.

Organised Tours

Most of Bolivia's tour operators are based in La Paz – the city supports at least 100 of them. Some are clearly better than others and

many specialise in specific interests or geographical areas.

Most of the tours are moderately priced and sightseeing around the city – to Tiahuanaco, Copacabana, Zongo Valley, Chacaltaya, etc – will be more comfortable than it would be on crowded and inefficient local buses. A tour to Puno is undoubtedly the most straightforward way of getting into Peru, and it's not at all expensive.

You can also arrange excursions to other places that may interest you, including hard-to-reach attractions like Laguna Colorada or the Cordillera Apolobamba. If you want to go climbing in the marvellous snow-capped peaks of the cordilleras, there are tour operators who will organise a customised expedition, including equipment, porters and even a cook. Alternatively, they'll provide guide service only. If you need hiking or trekking equipment to participate in one of their tours, they'll hire out whatever is necessary.

In most cases, operators will only run a tour if a specified minimum number of people are interested, so keep this in mind when you're looking at more out-of-the-way destinations. If you can't muster a group of the requisite size, you may have to pay at least partial fares for the number lacking.

Following is a list of some of the better tour companies, and a rundown of their services. For information on adventure tours and expeditions further afield, see the section on Tours in the Getting Around chapter.

Balsa Tours
    Avenida 16 de Julio 1650, Edificio Alameda, Casilla 5889 (☎ 356566, fax (591-2) 391310); among other things, Balsa Tours run cruise excursions around the Islas Huyñaymarkas, Isla del Sol, Isla de la Luna and Copacabana. They also operate the Complejo Nautico Balsa, a resort hostel in Puerto Perez on the shores of Lago de Huyñaymarka, the south-east extension of Lake Titicaca.
Crillon Tours
    Avenida Camacho 1223, Casilla 4785 (☎ 374566, fax (591-2) 391039); Crillon operates upmarket hydrofoil trips between Huatajata and Puno on Lake Titicaca. They've also set up their own tourist-class hotel in Huatajata. In

1991, Crillon purchased at auction the boat *The Volga* which had been presented, complete with wolf-skin rugs and Georgian silver brandy cups, to Richard Nixon by Leonid Breshnev in 1972. After removing the opulent décor and rechristening it *Glasnost Arrow*, it was added to Crillon's seven-boat fleet and put into service ferrying tourists around Lake Titicaca.

Diana Tours
    Calle Sagárnaga 328, in the Hotel Sagárnaga (☎ 358757); this company has city tours, and tours to Tiahuanaco, Valle de la Luna, Chacaltaya and the Yungas. It also has among the cheapest tours to Copacabana and Puno.

Magri Turismo, Limitada
    Avenida 16 de Julio 1490, Edificio Avenida, 5th floor (☎ 341201, fax (591-2) 366309); Magri Turismo is the American Express representative in Bolivia, and although they sell sightseeing tours, they're primarily concerned with airline bookings and overseas reservations.

Transturin
    Avenida Mariscal Santa Cruz 1295, 3rd floor, Casilla 5311, La Paz (☎ 320445, fax (591-2) 391162); this company offers enclosed catamaran trips to the Lake Titicaca highlights, including Copacabana, Isla del Sol and Puno, Peru.

Other Tour Companies
    Similar services to those of Dianna Tours are offered by Vicuña Tours (☎ 323504) in the Hotel Viena at Calle Loayza 420; Combitours (☎ 375378) in the Residencial Copacabana at Calle Illampú 734; Nuevo Continente (☎ 373423) in the Residencial Los Andes at Avenida Manco Capac 366; and Turisbus (☎ 325348) in the Residencial Rosário at Calle Illampú 704. Turisbus also has recommended tours to the Salar de Uyuni, Laguna Colorada and Laguna Verde.

Fiestas

La Paz enjoys several local festivals and holidays during the year, but El Gran Poder and Alasitas will be of particular interest to visitors.

El Gran Poder La Festividad de Nuestro Señor Jesús del Gran Poder takes place in La Paz around the end of May or the beginning of June. It began in 1939 as a candle procession led by an image of Christ through the predominantly campesino neighbourhoods. The following year, the local union of embroiderers formed a folkloric group to participate in the event.

Over the years, the festival inspired the

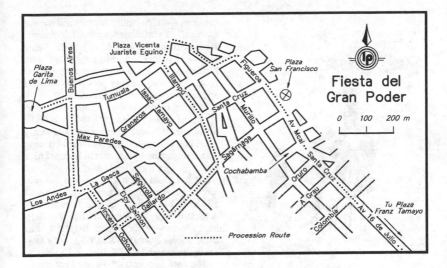

Fiesta del Gran Poder

0   100   200 m

.... Procession Route

establishment of other folkloric groups and the celebration grew larger and more lively. It has now developed into a strictly Paceño festival (a Paceño is a resident of La Paz), with dancers and folkloric groups participating from around the city. The embroiderers prepare elaborate costumes for the event and the performers practise for weeks in advance.

A number of dances, such as the *suri sikuris* in which the dancers are bedecked in ostrich feathers, the lively *Kullasada*, and the *Inkas* which duplicates ancient Inca ceremonial dances, have been perpetuated by these festivities.

El Gran Poder is a wild and exciting time in La Paz and offers a glimpse of Aymará culture at its festive finest. If you're around in early June and would like to catch the procession, go early to stake out a place along the route (see map) but beware of stray or unruly water balloons. The tourist office can provide dates and other specifics about a particular year's celebration. If you can't make it to the festivities, Gran Poder masks, costumes and accessories are made and embroidered in shops scattered around the area above Avenida Buenos Aires.

Alasitas The origin of the festival of abundance, or Alasitas, dates back to Inca times when it coincided with the spring equinox on 21 September. Historians generally agree that the current 24 January Alasitas Fair, though based on the original, began in La Paz around the time of Tupac Katari, the Indian who led the siege of the city in 1781. During the colonial period, it was moved from the equinox to 20 October in honour of the city's founding. After the siege, Governor Sebastián Segurola again changed it, this time to 24 January, a date on which the Festival of Our Lady of Peace had previously been celebrated.

Traditionally, the Alasitas Fair was intended to demonstrate the abundance of the fields. The campesinos weren't pleased with the changes nor with the January date imposed by the Spanish, and turned the celebration into a corny mockery of the original; 'abundance' was redefined to apply not only to crops, but also to homes, tools, cash, clothing and lately, cars, trucks, aeroplanes and even 12-storey apartment complexes. The little god of abundance, Ekeko, made his appearance and the modern Alasitas traditions began.

Ekeko, whose name means 'dwarf' in Aymará, is the household god and the keeper and distributor of material possessions. During the Alasitas Fair, his devotees collect miniatures of everything they'd like to acquire during the year and heap them on small plaster images of the god. He's loaded down with household utensils, baskets of coca, airline tickets, wallets and trunks full of cash (in US$!), lottery tickets, liquor, chocolate and other material goods. The more optimistic devotees buy buses, Toyota 4WDs, airline tickets to Miami, Volkswagen beetles and three-storey suburban homes!

If you can't attend the Alasitas Fair and would still like a glimpse of Ekeko, there's a statue of him near the intersection of Calle Comercio and Avenida Mariscal Santa Cruz.

Places to Stay – bottom end

La Paz has dozens of low-cost hotels and residenciales, the vast majority of which lie in the area between Calle Manco Capac and Avenida Ismael Montes (the Prado), but others are scattered around the city. Most bottom-range hotels have a midnight curfew.

A new entry in La Paz is the *Duendes Hostal* (☎ 351125) at Avenida Uruguay 470 between Avenida Ismael Montes and the bus terminal. It's affiliated with Club Andino Boliviano and has applied to join the Youth Hostel Association. Single rooms with private bath cost B25, while larger dorm rooms are considerably less. Hot showers and laundry services are available.

If being central is your primary consideration, the *Hotel Torino* (☎ 341487) at Calle Socabaya 457 near Plaza Murillo is still a good bet, although it has become a bit surly – an unfortunate by-product of its reputation as *the* budget travellers' haunt. Regardless, it's still a clean place to crash and has nice electric showers from 6 am to 1 pm. There's also a book exchange (open in the morning), a locked baggage room and a free left-baggage service for guests. Single/double/triple rooms cost B17/B23/B30, with low-season prices about 15% less.

The amusing central courtyard contains a replica of Potosí's Casa Real de la Moneda Bacchus and there's a rather noisy bar which is frequented by a consistently plastered bunch of regulars. Fortunately, this closes at 9 pm and things quiet down. Breakfasts of rolls, salteñas and fruit juices are available, and set dinners cost B6. Intending trekkers may buy large bags of granola for B3.

Another popular and centrally located place is *Hostal Austria* (☎ 351140) at 531 Yanacocha near Plaza Murillo. They have electric showers and one to four-bed rooms with shared bath for B12 per person.

Alojamiento Universo at Inca 175 has been recommended as a bargain-basement option at B16 for a double. It's clean, friendly and secure, and has electric hot showers and a left-luggage service. Rooms on the ground floor are nicer than those upstairs.

From the outside, *Hotel Italia* (☎ 325101) at Calle Manco Capac 303 looks more expensive than it is. Although it is set back from the street, the nicest rooms, which are at the front, are still quite noisy. There's a folk music peña on Friday nights at 9 pm. Single/double rooms with shared bath cost B17/24 while rooms with private bath are B27/34.

Just up the street at Calle Manco Capac

364 is the *Hotel Andes* (☎ 323461). It has lots of rooms and although the lifts rarely function, it's a friendly and increasingly popular digs for budget travellers. Single/double rooms cost B25/36 with bath or B16/24 without. Practically next door to the Andes is the very basic *Residencial Central* (☎ 356304) at Calle Manco Capac 384. They sometimes have hot water, but no private baths are available. Rooms cost B10 per person.

A good huff and puff from the centre is the *Hotel Panamericano* (☎ 378370) at Calle Manco Capac 454 near the railway station. It's clean and is still good value for money, catering to organised groups that don't want to pay for the Sheraton. Clean single/double rooms with private baths and hot water cost B20/32. For an additional B3.50, you'll get a continental breakfast of juice, coffee, rolls and condiments.

One of the most pleasant inexpensive places to stay in La Paz is the *Residencial Illimani* (☎ 325948) at Avenida Illimani 1817 not far from the stadium. It's a bit further from the centre of things and a fairly long way from transportation terminals, but it's quiet and friendly and is popular with more laid-back travellers. There's hot water a few hours a day, a laundry sink, a patio sitting area where cooking is also allowed, and the señora will pleasantly admit you if you arrive or return after lock-up time at midnight. Single/double rooms without bath cost B12/B22. There's also a nice view of Illimani from the roof.

At Calle Sagárnaga 334, in the heart of artesanía alley, is the very pleasant *Hotel Alem* (☎ 367400). Singles/doubles cost B20/28 without bath and B35/45 with bath. Rooms with private bath also include breakfast.

Just a couple of doors from the Residencial Rosário at Calle Illampú 734 is *Residencial Copacabana* (☎ 367896). With private bath, singles/doubles cost B24/31 and with shared bath, B17/24. It's not bad but could be better.

An exceptional place to stay in La Paz, with the entire city at its feet, is the friendly *Hostería Florida* at Calle Viacha 489. As yet, it's almost unknown to travellers, probably due to its location amid shabby cheapies and because from the outside, it appears· to be quite expensive. It's a 10-storey modern building with comfortable rooms, all of which have private baths and hot water, for B20 per person. Ask for a room on one of the upper floors with views over the city and near the spacious common lounge where you can rest or watch TV.

You may want to avoid *Hostal Yanacocha* at Yanacocha 540 near Plaza Murillo. This boarding-house-style hotel, which has water only occasionally, is noisy and full of drunks and questionable ladies. The *Alojamiento Metropoly* also has serious problems; although the owner is friendly, her staff are insufferable and even travellers accustomed to basic accommodation consider the toilets unthinkable.

Another less than welcoming place is *Alojamiento Illampú* at Calle Illampú 635. It's run down, but at B10/18 for a single/double, it is economical and there's an especially good view from the top floor.

Places to Stay – middle

It seems the much lauded (and equally scorned!) *Residencial Rosário* (☎ 325348) at Calle Illampú 704 has let success go to its top floor. The staff have become a bit blasé about service, prices have been raised, and all available space has been turned into a rabbit warren of stairways and passages to accommodate its enormous popularity. Even so, it remains ultra-clean and pleasantly quiet: a sort of travellers' capsule with Bolivia just outside the door. Plus points include a sunny courtyard, a travel agency on the ground floor and an excellent restaurant serving such gringo-trail specialities as crêpes, oatmeal, granola, cream of asparagus soup and banana pancakes.

The reservation system has a lot of holes – don't even hope to get a double bed – but advance booking is essential these days. Single/double rooms cost B33/37 without bath. Rooms with private bath are reserved primarily for tour groups and are priced accordingly: a budget-boggling B65 for a double room. Those staying in rooms without bath must pay a B5 deposit on towels. Be warned that Rosário showers are infamously tepid; water hot enough to melt the La Paz chill is available only after midnight in the 1st-floor shower stall!

Down the street at Calle Illampú 626, near Plaza Vicenta Juariste Eguino, is the two-star *Hotel Continental* (☎ 378226) which has placed itself in direct competition with the Rosário. Travellers seem to like it and prices aren't bad: B25/35 for single/double rooms without bath and B35/50 for rooms with bath. Another recommended option is the *Hotel Milton* (☎ 368003) at Calle Illampú 1224. It's clean with good hot showers and costs B36/54 for single/double rooms with bath.

Hotel Sagárnaga (☎ 350252) at Calle Sagárnaga 326 is a pleasant and central option on a bustling street. Rooms cost B47/59 for a single/double with bath, and B28/36 without. A continental breakfast is included in the room price and discounts of 10% are available during periods of low occupancy. If you request it, you can have a TV and telephone in your room. Off the lobby is Diana Tours which offers excursions to sites in the vicinity of La Paz.

The clean *Hostal República* (☎ 357966) at Calle Comercio 1455 near Calle Bueno is in a magnificent historical building which was the home of a former Bolivian president. It has two large courtyards, a garden and a warm reception area with a small library of foreign-language books. They'll also store your luggage and valuables while you travel further afield. Single/double rooms cost B36/54 with private bath and B22/32 without bath. Triple rooms are also available.

An interesting middle-range hotel is *Hotel Viena* (☎ 326090) at Calle Loayza 420, a baroque-style building with immense high-ceiling rooms. If you're interested in unique accommodation, check out the suites; one reader recommends room 113. Double rooms with private baths cost B40 while with shared bath, they're only B30.

Places to Stay – top end

At the bottom of the top end is the *Hotel Gloria* (☎ 370010) at Calle Potosí 909, towering above the snarling traffic of the Prado. Singles/doubles cost B86/161, 30% less for Bolivian residents. Breakfast is included, but is widely bemoaned as not up to snuff for a hotel in this price range. In a similar price range is the *Hotel El Dorado* (☎ 363355) on Avenida Villazón at the Plaza de los Estudiantes. It can be booked toll-free from the USA on (☎ (800) 223-5652).

The Hotel Presidente (☎ 391862) at Calle Potosí 920 bills itself as the highest five-star hotel in the world, which is accurate since the equally five-star *Hotel Plaza* (☎ 378311) at Avenida 16 de Julio 2675 and *Hotel La Paz* (☎ 356950) on Avenida Aniceto Arce are just a few metres lower, further down the Prado. Singles/doubles in any of these will cost in the vicinity of B250/305. If you're after a bit of luxury, these options are bargains considering the prices of comparable accommodation in most other world capitals! Expect such amenities as health clubs, swimming pools, pubs, coffee shops and discos.

For any of these more expensive hotels, reservations should be made in advance through a travel agent or by writing or phoning ahead to confirm room availability.

Places to Eat

La Paz has a wealth of restaurants ranging from street kiosks to fine dining. The latter aren't all posh and pricey 42nd-storey affairs either; most are quite reasonable, and some of the finest are relatively inexpensive.

In the cheapest ranges, don't expect too much variation from the local standards. With only a few exceptions, nearly all specialise in – or serve exclusively – some sort of beef or chicken. The greatest variety lies in quality and price.

Breakfast Most restaurants which serve breakfast don't open until 9 or 9.30 am. If you're an early riser and desperate for a caffeine jolt before you can face the day, the markets always have stalls that sell bread rolls and muddy coffee concentrate for about B1.

A good place to find the most popular Bolivian breakfast food is *Super Salteñas* on Calle Socabaya. They're billed as the world's best salteñas, but they're rather pricey and some of those available in the markets at a third of the price would be equal contenders for the title. Alternatively, try the salteñas at the *Tokio* (not to be confused with the New Tokyo) on the Prado or the *San Luis* beside the main post office.

For a hefty English breakfast, nothing beats the restaurant in the Residencial Rosário which serves ham, eggs, breads, cheese, pancakes, orange juice and excellent cocoa and cappuccino. Non-guests are welcome. For doughnuts, try the rather overpriced *California Donuts* on Avenida Camacho and wash them down with rich hot cocoa and gooey additives.

For healthy vegetarian breakfasts of porridge, yoghurt, juice, granola and crêpes, go to *El Vegetariano* on Calle Loayza between calles Potosí and Comercio. They begin serving at 9.15 am.

At *Eli's* on the Prado, you can get a continental breakfast, including juice, toast, marmalade and coffee, for B3 or a more hefty morning meal for B6 to B9. If you just want to grab a quick coffee and a roll or salteña, try the *Confitería Club de La Paz*, a literary café and haunt of politicians and escaped Nazi war criminals, at the sharp corner of avenidas Camacho and Mariscal Santa Cruz. It's known especially for its strong espresso and lemon meringue pie. *Confitería Marilín* at the corner of calles Potosí and Socabaya is repeatedly recommended, but their coffee should be avoided.

Snacks A serious favourite is *Kuchen Stübe* in the Edificio Guadalquivir on Calle Rosendo Gutiérrez. You can stuff yourself with decadent European coffee, pastries, biscuits and other sweets, then work it off climbing back up the Prado to the centre. Another friendly coffee shop is the *Pierrot* on the ground floor of the Hotel Gloria.

Lunch Lunch specials are found all over town and every Mom & Pop cubbyhole in the city serves some sort of bulk meal. The menu will be outlined on a chalkboard in the doorway and if you're not too picky, you'll find something appealing. Try the recommended *Snack El Diamante* at Calle Manco Capac 315 or *La Hacienda*, diagonally opposite the Residencial Rosário on Calle Illampú, which is known for its home-made chicken soup.

If you don't mind a hectic setting, the cheapest place for a quick lunch is in the markets. They have takeaway snack stands selling empanadas and chicken sandwiches, and restaurant stalls with covered sitting areas. If you don't expect too much in the way of sanitation, a filling meal of soup, a meat dish, rice, lettuce and oca or potato will cost about B3.

Bolivian specialities such as *charque kan*, *chorizos*, *anticuchos* and *chicharrón* are available as executive lunches at *Típicos*, which is on the 6th level of the Shopping Norte arcade at the corner of calles Potosí and Socabaya.

A favourite lunchtime venue – and rightfully so – is the previously mentioned Eli's. Their lunch specials are superb but they must vie for stomach space with a selection of showcased European pastries tempting everyone in the main dining area.

Café Verona on Calle Colón near Avenida Mariscal Santa Cruz is frequently recommended for its sandwiches which will set you back about B6. Pizza costs B10, and set lunches B13. *Amadeus* opposite the university on Avenida 16 de Julio below the Plaza de los Estudiantes serves light meals and specialises in real Mexican tacos.

For a reasonable burger, *California Burgers* (in the same building as California Donuts) on Avenida Camacho is a possibility. You may also want to try those at the unfortunately named *Clap* with three locations – on Avenida Aniceto Arce; Calle Ayacucho; and Belisario Salinas. One reader has even cited them as Bolivia's best hamburgers. For quick chicken, try *Pollo Copacabana* where you'll get a quarter roast chicken, chips and fried plantain smothered in ketchup, mustard and ají for B7. There are two locations, one on Calle Potosí and one on Calle Comercio. Beside the former is a wonderful sweets shop selling Bolivia's own Breick chocolate, indisputably some of the world's best!

El Vegetariano, described under breakfast, also does vegetarian lunches for B3. Another excellent vegetarian restaurant has recently opened in the Hotel Gloria at Calle Potosí 909. They serve set lunches for B5 but it's very popular so arrive before 12.30 pm or risk missing out.

For German-style lunches – sausages, smoked pork chops, sauerkraut and the like – try *Max Bieber's* at Avenida 20 de Octubre 2080. Lunches are rather expensive at B12 to B16 but if you feel like a splurge, they're quite good. It's closed on Tuesday.

Dinner Many of the places listed under lunch also serve dinner. Again, a particularly nice place to eat is the Residencial Rosário. They serve such goodies as cream of asparagus and french onion soup, crumbed chicken (unheard of elsewhere in Bolivia!), and pasta dishes, all nicely done.

An excellent option for Italian food is the small, relaxed and cosy *Pronto Ristorante* on Calle Jáuregui half a block from Avenida 6 de Agosto. All their pasta is home made and their reasonable prices make it accessible to nearly everyone.

The *Manjari Restaurant* at Calle Potosí 1315, near Calle Colón, has hearty vegetarian lunch and dinner specials. For just B4 you get soup, salad, segundo, dessert and tea served in what some travellers have described as 'prison trays'. Unfortunately, Manjari no longer bakes its trademark bread. Never mind; the food is still worthwhile. Another restaurant with vegetarian specialities is *Nutricentro* on Calle Comercio between Calle Socabaya and Yanacocha.

For fish, go to *El Palácio de Pescado* on Avenida América. You'll pay an average of B6 for *surubí, pacu, trucha, pejerrey, sábalo,* etc. When we were there, the day's 'catch', flown in frozen from the Beni, was stacked on the floor in the middle of the dining room!

Inexpensive lunches or dinners are also available at the popular *El Lobo* at the corner of calles Santa Cruz and Illampú. They specialise in chicken and the curry is particularly nice. For some entertaining reading (or writing) while you're there, check out their book of travellers' recommendations.

The majority of La Paz's nicer and higher-priced restaurants are concentrated in the lower end of town around avenidas 20 de Octubre, 6 de Agosto and 16 de Julio (it must be easy to remember historical dates in La Paz!). One of the best is *La Suisse* (☎ 353150) on Avenida Aniceto Arce near the Hotel La Paz. It's actually two restaurants – an Italian and seafood area on the ground floor and a 'gourmet' section upstairs serving copious Swiss grill for B27.50 per person. Raclette with pickled onions and cucumbers, whole wheat bread and assorted veggies costs B25. What's more, the coffee they serve is some of the best in Bolivia. If you want the grill or fondue, it's a good idea to book in advance.

If you don't mind paying for atmosphere, try the *Utama Restaurant* on the top floor of the Hotel Plaza. It's overpriced, but most people find it relatively elegant and the view overlooking the twinkling lights of La Paz makes up for the expense.

The *New Tokyo Restaurant* at Avenida 6 de Agosto 2900 serves Bolivian Japanese food but one couple who wrote to us were less than impressed:

The sake was stale and the chicken was rubbery. We paid B75 for two and felt outrageously ripped off. But the food was only one downer; the real problem lay with the double Yamaha big-screen videos they insisted on blaring throughout our meal. First it was Elvis Presley, a mere shadow of his former self, flinging sweaty scarves at screaming fans in Hawaii. But then the owner put on a video of – no kidding – high speed motorbike crashes. As our main course arrived, we were treated to a stupefying series of clips of riders being smeared on pavement, flying into walls and tumbling head over heels at 80 mph. We asked the owner if he might play something more palatable but he refused.

Another couple recommends the *Nuevo Oruro* on the 2nd floor of Ingavi 773 near the Pichincha steps. They write:

Inside are fantastic ceiling murals and good views from the window tables. We had the Plato de la Casa for B12, which was a platter with steak, chicken, blood sausage, chorizo, intestines, kidneys, whole potatoes and a large salad. Easily a meal for two, but we didn't know this so we also ordered *brazuelo de cordero* which was a huge roast shoulder of mutton on top of creamed chuño and potatoes, also at B12. We ate leftover steak and chicken all the way to Potosí on the bus.

Tom Harriman & Jan King

The odd combination in the plato de la casa is a dish known as El Intendente after the finicky government official who habitually requested this bizarre ensemble from restaurant owners. Needless to say, you'll have to be rather carnivorous to fully appreciate the option!

Several of the La Paz peñas serve dinners. For a rundown, see the discussion under Peñas in the following entertainment section.

Entertainment
Peñas If you want a taste of Bolivian folk music, try to attend at least one *peña*, an Andean or highland Bolivian folk music show which may include dancing. The music is usually played on typical Andean instruments such as quenas, zampoñas and charangos. Shows featuring only guitars, singing, comedy or a combination of these are also common. In all cases, the music gets better as the bottles get emptier, and to get you started the admission charge will generally include your first drink. Although most peñas ambitiously advertise action six nights a week, when there aren't enough patrons, they scale them back to just two or three nights a week, most often Thursday to Saturday.

Peña Naira (☎ 325736), which exists exclusively for the benefit of tourists and Bolivian business people, is at Calle Sagárnaga 161 just above Plaza San Francisco. It plays nightly except Sunday from 10.30 pm to 2 am and costs B18. The attached restaurant specialises in fondue which, however good, is overpriced at B50 for two. Fortunately, there are several better value options on the menu. Note the remarkable table settings.

A less expensive – and some claim more traditional – peña is the Marka Tambo at Calle Jaén 710. Although the restaurant is worthless, the music is great and costs only B15.

Another popular peña is staged at La Casa del Corregidor (☎ 363633), a beautiful old colonial building at Calle Murillo 1040. It plays Monday to Saturday at 9 pm and costs B20, but come earlier and enjoy a meal of their delicious trout, chicken or vegetable dishes.

The peña at Los Escudos (☎ 322028) on Avenida Mariscal Santa Cruz (in the same building as Café Club de La Paz) rounds out the list of larger tourist peñas. It's a bit more upmarket than the others: although the cover charge is only B15, including the first drink, the accompanying meal costs a set B43. It plays Monday to Saturday.

You may also want to check the La Paz paper for advertisements and details about smaller unscheduled peñas and musical events which are staged occasionally.

Bars & Pubs Don't expect too much from bars in La Paz. Unless you don't mind being cursed and slobbered on by incoherent drunks, you may want to avoid bars altogether. Bolivians go to a bar not to dance or carry on semi-intelligent conversation, but to drink and get drunk. In order to avoid trouble and remain intact, most bars close down at midnight or earlier; most of their patrons are tipsy by 6 pm and the following six hours do nothing to improve their condition.

Nicer places to buy a drink are known as *wiskerías*. If you'd like the sort of atmosphere found in a slightly more upmarket saloon or pub, try El Socavón at Avenida 20 de Octubre 2174. It's patronised by a good blend of Bolivian and foreign clientele and they occasionally put on live entertainment. Another good option is the Chilean-run La

Cueva Bar on Calle México just uphill from the main post office. It hops to the beat of salsa and rock music and has become quite popular with foreigners. If you're interested in hearing Bolivian bands attempt Pink Floyd, here's your opportunity.

For a more upmarket option, El Bodegón de Cinti at La Casa del Corregidor, Calle Murillo 1040, opens at 10 pm. The Chuquisaqueño theme dictates southern specialities and drinks based on singani from Cinti province in Chuquisaca Department.

Discos La Paz has several discos which appeal to the young and restless at heart. Forum at Calle Victor Sanjinés 2908 near Ricardo Mujía in Sopacachi has been recommended for its diversity; each night of the week it focuses on different musical themes. Other discos include the Updown at Avenida 6 de Agosto 299 and the Beverly Steer Ranch at Avenida Mariscal Santa Cruz 1223. Near the stadium are two other favourites, Disco Papillón and the optimistically (or ominously!) named Disco Love City.

Cinemas There are numerous cinemas scattered all over the city. Most films are shown in English with Spanish subtitles, but sound systems are poor and crackly and nobody bothers to keep quiet for the foreign dialogue, anyway, so a knowledge of Spanish will help. The pictures shown aren't generally top quality. Most of them came and went quickly in other countries several years earlier, but if you happen to enjoy the Girls' Dorm, Ninjas from Space and Rocky Meets Rambo sort of pictures, you can spend a lot of time in La Paz cinemas.

There is an erudite cinema, Cinemateca Boliviana (☎ 325346), at the corner of Pichincha and Calle Indaburo. It shows subtitled foreign films daily at 4 and 7.30 pm for the same B2 admission price charged by other cinemas.

Theatre Dramatic, dance and musical performances are staged at the Teatro Municipal at the corner of calles Indaburo and Genero Sanjinés. It's a great old restored building

with a round auditorium, elaborate balconies and a vast ceiling mural. The newspapers and tourist office will have information about what's on. The average ticket price is around B12.

Spectator Sports
Futbol, professional football, is as popular with Bolivians as it is elsewhere in Latin America. Matches are played at Hernando Siles Stadium on Sundays year round as well as on Thursday evenings during the winter. Check newspapers for times and prices. Hotels and the tourism office also keep abreast of other upcoming sports events.

Things to Buy
Although prices will naturally be lower at the point of original production, any type of artesanía available in Bolivia may also be found somewhere in La Paz. Prices will vary, of course, depending on quality, but expect to pay around B40 for a passable alpaca sweater and up to B80 for a very good one. A *chullo* (woollen hat) will cost around B8 and a very nice poncho, up to B80 or B90. Prices for just about everything will be slightly higher in La Paz than in Puno or Cuzco, Peru, or elsewhere in Bolivia, but the prevailing quality of the items justifies this.

Along the steep Calle Sagárnaga hill between Avenida Mariscal Santa Cruz and Calle Isaac Tamayo is the main tourist shopping area, where expensive shops compete with street vendors. As a general rule, the nearer an operation is to the Prado, the higher the prices they'll demand; many tourists are willing to pay for the luxury of not having to climb so far uphill! As a rule, shopkeepers will generally not haggle over prices as much as will street vendors, whose prices are lower to begin with. One suspects that the trendier shops do much of their business with tourists who may feel uncomfortable with bargaining.

All sorts of clothing, including ponchos, chompas, chullos, vests, jackets and mufflers, are available in wool, llama and alpaca, or any combination of the three. Alpaca is the finest and is therefore the most expensive.

Some pieces are hand-dyed and woven or knitted, but others are obviously machine-made. Learn to tell the difference and never take an overzealous shopkeeper's word for it. Many would tell you it was made of solid gold if it would result in a sale.

We beg you, however, not to select anything represented as vicuña, a small wild camelod of the Altiplano which is endangered in Bolivia. Vicuñas are strictly wild animals and are too skittish to be domesticated and raised for their valuable wool, so every vicuña product represents dead animals.

Some shops sell Andean musical instruments. The most popular are zampoñas and quenas, as well as drums and armadillo-shell charangos. Other shops specialise in wood-carvings and ceramics from the Oriente, and silver items from Potosí. Some deal in rugs, wall-hangings, woven belts and pouches which carry the designs and artistic personality of the artesan. Quite a few shops sell tourist kitsch, an art form unto itself. You'll find ceramic ashtrays with Inca designs, fake Tiahuanaco figurines, costume jewellery, T-shirts and all manner of mass-produced woollens. Music tapes and recordings are available in small shops and stalls along Calle Evaristo Valle.

Buying a Charango Professional musician Daniel Harvey of Portland, Oregon, tramped around La Paz in search of the perfect charango. Here's what he found:

Although it's rumoured that Bolivia's best charango makers reside in central Bolivia, La Paz offers the widest variety of fine instruments. Once you wade past the herd of made-for-tourist charangos, two classes of instruments remain.

In the US$100 to US$200 category, the work of Juan Achá Campo stands out. His one-piece constructions of fine materials and consistent quality can be found at either of the two shops of La Casa de Charangos at Calle Sagárnaga 177 and 213 in La Paz. Also at Calle Sagárnaga 213 at locale #10, the work of René Gamboa is showcased. Gamboa's charangos play well although their necks are of two-piece construction. At Galería Artesanal #3 near the Iglesia de San Francisco, a charango maker called Rumillajta sells fine one-piece, squarish-necked instruments.

If you're looking to spend less money and are willing to invest more time, it's possible to buy a charango directly off the workbench. The quality of charangos in made-to-order shops varies greatly from luthier to luthier and instrument to instrument. Unlike the work of Achá and Rumillajta, these small shop artesans utilise two-piece construction which may not offer the durability of one-piece instruments; however, a fine instrument at one of these shops may be obtained for as little as US$35.

The most common complaint with smaller shops is their reluctance to tune instruments. Most artesans prefer building instruments to tuning them and because new strings stretch so much, tuning them is very time consuming. The conventional tuning is D (re), G (sol), B (ti), E (mi) and B (ti). The B strings are tuned one octave apart. Once a charango is to pitch, listen carefully to determine whether the frets are placed at proper intervals.

The brothers Bernardino and José Torrico work at Calle Linares 818 (Arte Aiquileño) and 820 (Yachay) in La Paz. José produces the most amazing small charangos called *hualaichos* as well as fine larger instruments. Bernardino's charangos are labelled *sumakj llajta* and consist of some of the most beautiful woods to be found, but watch their intonation. Bernardino carves interesting and elaborate designs on the backs of some of his soundboxes, and both brothers are also adept at charango repair and reconstruction.

Only 30 metres away at 270 Calle Santa Cruz is the shop of Phuju Pampa. Sadly, most of his instruments are constructed with quirquinchos. These creatures have legs to run from charango makers while trees are victims paralysed by roots but I believe that Pachamama prefers the sacrifice of sap rather than blood in the production of music. Besides, *charangos de quirquincho* are less sonorous and more fragile than wooden instruments. Pampa does construct some wooden charangos and although his work appears sloppy, the charango I tested had exceptional voice.

Although these notes are far from exhaustive coverage of charango crafting in Bolivia, I hope my research will assist you in your own search for a high quality instrument.

Daniel Harvey, USA

Buying Wind Instruments Many La Paz artesans specialise in quenas, zampoñas, tarkas and pinquillos, among other traditional woodwinds. There's a lot of low-quality or merely decorative tourist rubbish around; take care to visit a reputable workshop where you'll pay a fraction of gift shop prices and contribute directly to the artesan rather than to an intermediary.

There are clusters of artesans working

along Calle Juan Granier near Plaza Garita de Lima, a couple of blocks below the cemetery. Other recommended shops include those found on Calle Isaac Tamayo near the top of literally breathtaking Calle Sagárnaga, and those at Calle Linares 855 or 859.

Getting There & Away

Air La Paz's El Alto Airport sits on the Altiplano at an elevation of 4018 metres, 10 km from the city centre. It's the world's highest commercial airport, which will be obvious if you arrive or leave from there. The larger planes need several km of runway to take off and must land at higher speeds than usual to compensate for the lower density atmosphere. Stopping distance is much greater, too, and planes must be equipped with special extra-durable tyres in order to land in La Paz.

The airport doesn't have much in the way of facilities. There's no place to change money and the only eatery is an overpriced coffee shop. There's little else apart from a few souvenir kiosks, a bookshop and a duty-free shop which is available to passengers departing internationally.

Domestic flights are serviced by LAB, TAM and AeroXpress. LAB has the widest network and flies to just about every corner of the country. TAM is a bit cheaper but flights must normally be booked well in advance. AeroXpress serves several cities but is most useful for its exclusive service to Potosí. Another option for reaching Potosí by air from La Paz is outlined under Getting There & Away for Potosí.

The following is a sample of one-way airfares to or from locations around Bolivia; these include a 4.2% domestic tax: Santa Cruz – B253; Cochabamba – B117; Sucre – B160; Tarija – B199; Trinidad – B160; Yacuiba – B266; Riberalta – B320; Guayar-amerín – B320; Rurrenabaque – B115; Camiri – B245; Cobija – B417; Puerto Suárez – B506.

The following list contains some of the airlines which have representatives in La Paz. Specific schedules and fares change regularly so it's best to contact individual carriers for details. For information on international flights, refer to the Getting There & Away chapter:

Aerolineas Argentinas
    Avenida 16 de Julio 1486, Edificio Alameda, ground floor (☎ 391059)
Aero Perú
    Avenida 16 de Julio 1490, Edificio Avenida, 2nd floor (☎ 370002)
AeroXpress
    Plaza de los Estudiantes 1920 (☎ 343154)
American Airlines
    Edificio Mariscal de Ayacucho, 3rd floor, 305-306 (☎ 372008)
British Airways
    Plaza de los Estudiantes 1920 (☎ 355541)
Japan Airlines (JAL)
    Edificio Ballivián, 4th floor, 407 (☎ 375251, 376310)
KLM
    Avenida Aniceto Arce, Edificio Cobija 104 (☎ 366887, 390710)
LAN Chile
    Avenida 16 de Julio, Edificio Mariscal de Ayacucho, ground floor (☎ 366563)
Lineas Aereas Paraguayas (LAP)
    Edificio Colón, #4 (☎ 320020, 377595)
Lloyd Aereo Boliviano (LAB)
    Avenida Camacho 1460 (☎ 353606, 353054)
Lufthansa
    Avenida Mariscal Santa Cruz 1328, Edificio Hansa, 7th floor (☎ 372174, 321501)
Qantas
    Avenida 16 de Julio 1800 (☎ 376001, 322047)
Transportes Aereos Militares (TAM)
    Avenida Ismael Montes 728 (☎ 379285)
VARIG/Cruzeiro
    Edificio Cámara de Comercio, Avenida Mariscal Santa Cruz 1392 (☎ 367200)

Bus The majority of long-distance bus traffic arrives and departs from the main bus terminal, the Terminal Terrestre Ciudád de La Paz, on Plaza Antofagasta, 1½ blocks uphill from Avenida Ismael Montes, but there are several smaller terminals for specific destinations scattered throughout the city.

Flotas from La Paz to Oruro leave approximately every half hour. We recommend Nobleza for their comfortable buses and agreeable attitude. The trip takes three hours and costs B10. Flota Bustillo has a direct service to Llallagua daily at 6 pm; from

Oruro, there are seven daily departures to Llallagua.

Plenty of buses go to Cochabamba, most leaving between 8 and 9 pm, though a couple depart in the morning. The trip takes eight to 10 hours and costs around B20. Many of these buses continue on to Santa Cruz; however, the ones which leave La Paz in the evening don't depart from Cochabamba until late in the afternoon of the following day. If you purchase a ticket to Santa Cruz from La Paz on one of these buses, you'll have to occupy yourself in Cochabamba all day and will arrive in Santa Cruz in a zombie state on the morning of the second day. The fare from Cochabamba to Santa Cruz will be negotiable; plan on around B25 for the 10 to 12 hour trip.

All buses to Sucre pass through Cochabamba. They leave in the evening from La Paz and again, you must wait the entire day there for a night departure on to Sucre.

Nine flotas operate between La Paz and Potosí, all departing between 6 and 6.30 pm for the 10 to 12-hour journey, which will cost about B25. Be sure to carry warm clothing. Expreso Cochabamba has been recommended as the most commodious.

To Tarija, the flotas San Lorenzo and Velóz del Sud both leave at 5 pm daily.

To/From Peru & Lake Titicaca The easiest bet for travelling between La Paz and Peru will probably be with a tour company. For suggestions, see under Organised Tours earlier in this chapter. Most of them offer a daily service to Puno (Peru) via Copacabana for around B60 and will collect you from your hotel. Although you'll have to change vehicles in Copacabana near the border, connections are nearly always convenient and straightforward. There are many minibuses doing the run between Puno, Copacabana and La Paz. If a company doesn't fill its bus, they 'sell' the passengers to another company so that no one has to run half-empty buses. You may therefore find that you are not actually travelling with the company who issued your ticket.

Nearly all companies will allow a stop-over in Copacabana. Return trips to Copacabana from La Paz cost only around B35. Since this is such a popular route, it's a real opportunity for scam operators, so be sure to select a reputable company. A surprising number will collect your money and not deliver the transport. Readers recommend against Tur Latino América, Belho Tours and Profian Tours.

Alternatively, you can arrange your own transport to Puno, which involves travelling first to Copacabana on either Transportes Manco Capac (☎ 350033) at José María Aliaga 670, or Transportes 2 de Febrero (☎ 377181) at José María Aliaga 287. Both of these companies are just off Avenida Baptista near the cemetery and quite a long way from the hotel areas. They each have two departures daily, the former at 8 am and 3 pm and the latter at 7 am and 1.30 pm. From Copacabana, you'll have to either find a truck or a *colectivo* (minibus) headed toward Peru.

Flota Ingavi (☎ 328981) provides regular services along the southern route into Peru. Buses leave several times daily from their terminal on Calle José María Asín, and go via Guaqui and Tiahuanaco in Bolivia to Desaguadero in Peru. This route is relatively uninteresting and the border crossing is less straightforward than the one between Copacabana and Yunguyo.

Buses to Huatajata and other eastern Lake Titicaca towns and villages leave about every half hour between 4 am and 5 pm from near the corner of calles Manuel Bustillos and Kollasuyo, also near the cemetery. To return to La Paz from these places, flag the bus down on the highway.

To Tacna, Peru, Flota Litoral leaves on Sunday at 7 am and returns to La Paz on Wednesday. There are no immigration posts at the frontier so pick up a Bolivian exit stamp at immigration in La Paz. Peruvian formalities must be handled at Tacna.

To/From Sorata From Calle Angel Babia near the cemetery, Transportes Larecaja goes to Sorata twice daily at 6.30 and 7 am. Tickets go on sale at 2 pm the previous day.

To/From the Yungas & Amazon The terminal for Flota Yungueña (☎ 312344), which is the most popular scheduled transport to the Yungas and the Amazon region, is found in the *barrio* (district) Villa Fátima steeply uphill from the stadium area. It's a good idea to reserve your seats in advance. Their office is open from 9 am to 1 pm and 2.30 to 7 pm Monday to Friday and from 9 am to 2 pm Saturday and Sunday.

Flota Yungueña buses leave for Coroico on Tuesday, Thursday, Friday and Saturday at 8.30 am, and leave Coroico for La Paz on Monday, Wednesday and Friday at 8 am and Sunday at 1 pm. The trip takes about 3½ hours and costs B12 each way. To Chulumani, they leave on Friday and Saturday at 8.30 am. Going to Rurrenabaque, they leave on Monday and Saturday at around 1 pm and cost B40 for the 18-hour trip. Alternatively, during the winter dry season you can take a Wednesday or Friday bus bound for Riberalta and Guayaramerín and get off in Rurrenabaque. There's also a weekly service to San Borja and Trinidad on Saturday.

Several new transport companies have sprung up in Villa Fatima opposite and around the corner from Flota Yungueña, so it will pay to shop around for the best fare and most convenient departure. Veloz del Norte goes to Caranavi at 8.30 am and 2.30 pm, to Coroico at 8 am and to Chulumani and Guanay at 8.30 am and 2.30 pm, all daily. Trans-Yungas micros depart for Caranavi via Yolosa (the turnoff to Coroico) at 9.30 and 10.30 am and at 2.30 and 4.30 pm daily. During the dry season, Transportes 16 de Noviembre leaves at noon on Monday, Thursday and Saturday for Rurrenabaque, Reyes and Santa Rosa, and on Thursday to San Borja via Yucumo. Approximately every second week they go to Riberalta and Guayaramerín, passing Yucumo at 5 or 6 pm.

Camiones to the Yungas leave from just above the petrol station beside the Flota Yungueña office.

To/From Chile Flota Litoral leaves on Monday and Friday at 5 am for the very, *very* rough journey to Arica in Chile. The trip will take between 18 and 22 hours (possibly even longer, depending on the amount of time spent at the Tambo Quemado immigration post). The fare is B65. Buses from Arica to La Paz leave from Calle Chacabuco in Arica on Monday and Friday at 1 am. Agencia Martinez, also in Arica, connects with the Bolivian train at the Visviri/Charaña border crossing for US$7.50.

See the To/From Peru & Lake Titicaca section for information about flotas to Tacna, the Peruvian coastal town opposite (and easily accessible to) Arica, Chile.

Train The railway station on upper Calle Manco Capac is relatively close to, but steeply uphill from, the city centre. Three rail lines run out from La Paz. One goes southward to Oruro, Uyuni, Tupiza and Villazón, connecting with Argentine rail in La Quiaca. Branches from this line cut off at Uyuni for Calama (Chile), at Río Mulatos for Potosí/Sucre, and at Oruro for Cochabamba. If you're headed south toward Uyuni, Villazón or Abaroa, take a bus to Oruro and purchase onward passage there. They add extra coaches to the train at Oruro and securing a rail ticket in La Paz can be a real travesty: nerve-wracking at best and in some cases, impossible. Another line goes to Arica in Chile; and the third, which is not currently in use, goes to Guaqui on Lake Titicaca.

From La Paz to Cochabamba, there are three weekly ferrobuses, one on Monday and Friday at 8 am and a second one on Friday at 9 pm. They cost B29 in pullman class and B23 in especial (2nd class), taking eight hours.

To Villazón on the Argentine border, trains run via Oruro, Uyuni and Tupiza on Monday and Thursday at 4.10 pm, arriving at 12.15 pm the following day. Don't count on the timetable, however, and be sure to bring lots of warm and woolly clothing for this journey. The pullman/especial fares to Uyuni are B29/22, to Tupiza, B41/31 and to Villazón, B47/35. ENFE has recently inaugurated a system of buses which connect Tarija with Tupiza around the rail schedule. For further information, see Getting There & Away under Tarija.

The newly upgraded service Expreso del Sur connects La Paz with Buenos Aires, Argentina, by rail. Passengers must still disembark at Villazón and walk several km across the border to La Quiaca, but the trains *do* connect and the 1st-class car is actually pushed across the border. This service runs on Tuesday and Friday at 7 pm, arriving at Retiro Station in Buenos Aires at 1.25 pm *three days* later.

To Potosí and Sucre, there's a ferrobus on Monday and Saturday at 6 pm and another on Wednesday at 4.10 pm. Fares to Potosí in pullman/especial are B34/26 and to Sucre, B66/53.

The ferrobus to Arica, Chile, departs Monday and Friday at 7 am and costs B49 in pullman (there is no 2nd class on this run). In the opposite direction, the ferrobus (known in Chile as *coche motor*) leaves Arica on Tuesday and Saturday at 8 am. In La Paz, book tickets through El Dorado, at Edificio Avenida, 10th floor, Avenida 16 de Julio 1490. In Arica, bookings may be made at their office at Calle 21 de Mayo 51.

The train to high, windy and freezing Charaña on the Chilean border departs on Tuesday at 10 pm and costs B16. From there, you'll have to connect with either Chilean bus or rail services into Arica which, in theory, meet the Bolivian train.

To Abaroa/Ollagüe, you'll have to take a bus to Oruro and catch the train from there. It pulls out of Oruro on Wednesday at around 7.25 pm and arrives at the border 12 hours later where the Bolivian train connects with Chilean rail service to Calama, Chile. Plan on long delays in Uyuni, however, and bring warm clothing and a sleeping bag if you hope to cope with the normally subzero overnight temperatures along this journey.

Car & Motorbike Driving in La Paz with all its steep, winding and one-way streets may be a bit trying for the uninitiated, but if you want to do longer daytrips into the immediate hinterlands, hiring a car isn't a bad idea.

Motorbikes may be hired from Moto-Rent

(☎ 366234) at Avenida Busch 1255. They charge B72 per day with unlimited mileage.

A popular car hire agency is Rent-a-Car Imbex (379884) at Avenida Aniceto Arce 2303. The daily rate for a car or a 4WD jeep is B90 with an additional B.25 per km. For a 4WD with enclosed cab, you'll pay B144 per day and B.40 per km. Collision damage waiver insurance is included in the rental fees.

Other agencies, which all charge similar prices, include International (☎ 357061) at Calle Federico Zuazo 1942, Oscar Crespo (☎ 350974) at Avenida Simón Bolivar 1845 and Kolla Motors (☎ 351701) at Calle Rosendo Gutiérrez 502.

Getting Around

To/From the Airport El Alto International Airport is on the Altiplano 10 km from the city centre. There are two roads to the airport, the *autopista* or toll road which costs B3 and the sinuous 'other road'.

The cheapest method is to take a micro for B.60 to La Ceja Market at the brow of the canyon and then walk the two remaining 'level' km to the airport. Airport taxis cost a set B25 to the airport; don't let them talk you into paying more!

If you're going to town from the airport, colectivo minibuses cost B2.80 per person, considerably cheaper than the taxis. Taxi drivers lie in wait for arriving foreigners and will try to pester them into agreeing to an exorbitant fare. The colectivos, which wait just across the parking lot, will drop you at Plaza San Francisco or further down the Prado.

Bus La Paz city buses, which are called micros, are grinding, smoke-spewing, sputtering wrecks, most of which appear to be rapidly wheezing their way toward the junkyard. They mock the law of gravity and defy the principles of brake and transmission mechanics as they struggle fully packed up and down the hills of the city. One suspects that many of them were driven several hundred thousand km in the USA before even making their debut in Bolivia. They do, however, provide cheap but slow (and coronary-free!) transport for the city's masses, who are spared from having to negotiate the steep slopes of the canyon on foot.

Foreigners new to South America may learn the meaning of the word 'masses' on La Paz city buses. Since there's only one door, bodies don't circulate from front to rear. Instead, they push, shove, crawl and climb over each other when the bus arrives at their respective stop. If you feel uncomfortable being aggressive, you could be on the bus all day. An obvious corollary is that it's not a good idea to transport a lot of luggage on city buses; it also follows that caution should be taken with jewellery or valuables.

Women should be especially watchful when travelling on the micros; more than a few female travellers have reported skilful checking of their anatomy.

In addition to a route number or letter, micros plainly display their destination on a signboard posted in the front window. This eliminates the hassle of sorting out and memorising a lot of numbers. Bus stops are not well marked, but most people don't bother to use them anyway. Doors are usually left open, either for ventilation or because the entry is blocked with passengers. Traffic is such that the bus is stationary more often than it's moving, anyway, so you can hop (or squeeze) on just about anywhere en route. The price for most buses is B.60.

Trufis & Colectivos Colectivos in La Paz are minibuses and trufis are cars. For the benefit of those who don't read, colectivos all carry small urchins with big lungs who cry out their destinations every few seconds. Trufis indicate which route they're taking by the colour of the dual flags flying from the bonnet of the car. At the time of writing, the cost of travelling on colectivos and trufis was B.70 per person.

Taxi Although just about everything worth seeing in La Paz lies within reasonable walking distance of the hotels, most people won't want to do much walking while burdened with a lot of luggage. Both the rail and bus terminals are near to, but rather steep climbs from, the main hotel areas, and considering the altitude of La Paz, struggling up the hills through traffic beneath a heavy pack is not fun.

Fortunately, taxis aren't very expensive; expect to pay about B1.30 per person within the central area, which roughly corresponds to the area covered on the (large) La Paz map in this book. If there's a lot of uphill travel involved, drivers will often try to coerce you into paying a bit more. Don't be too upset if the driver hedges profits by picking up additional passengers – it seems to be a standard practice – but do encourage them to be fair about your dropoff order unless you don't mind being taken on a tour of the city en route to your destination.

Taxi drivers aren't always well versed in the geography of the city, so have a map handy and be able to explain to them roughly where you want to go. The name of a budget hotel normally isn't good enough. They'll know where the Hotel Plaza is, but the Residencial Rosário may draw a blank. If you can tell them it's near the intersection of calles Graneros and Illampú, they'll have a better idea, and if you can direct them, then you'll arrive even more quickly at your destination.

To get a taxi, just flag one down. If they all appear to be occupied, try anyway. Drivers will often fill up with passengers and drop them off in the order in which they climbed aboard. While this may seem a slow process, it's actually much faster than waiting for a vacant taxi during times of heavy demand. Be sure to arrange a fare with the driver in advance, and always carry enough change to pay close to the correct fare.

Long-distance taxis gather at the Centro de Taxis on Avenida Aniceto Arce near the Hotel La Paz above Plaza Isabel la Católica. Prices are negotiable; as a general rule, plan on about B150 per day.

Around La Paz

VALLE DE LA LUNA

The Valle de la Luna (Valley of the Moon) isn't a valley at all, but a bizarre eroded hillside maze of miniature canyons and pinnacles technically known as badlands. This amazing lunar landscape and its vegetation are quite desert-like, inspiring the imagination and inviting exploration. Several species of cactus grow in the valley, including the hallucinogenic choma, or San Pedro cactus.

Since vegetation is sparse and the earth material silty and unconsolidated, exploring on foot requires caution. The pinnacles collapse easily and some of the canyons are over 10 metres deep. The soil is slippery, so it's important to wear good walking or hiking shoes and not to venture in alone. Because the valley is a maze, of sorts, you may become disoriented, but it would be very difficult to become lost because the road practically encircles it and a fairly clear trail crosses it. Be sure to carry drinking water; desert hiking quickly depletes body fluids.

Valle de la Luna is in the same canyon as La Paz, 11 km below the city in the Río Abajo area. For a quiet break from urban La Paz, it may be easily visited in a morning or combined with a hike to nearby Muela del Diablo to fill an entire day. If you'd like to stay overnight, search for hidden level spots to camp in the badlands opposite the football field near Mallasa.

Getting There & Away

If you go to Valle de la Luna with any of the numerous agencies offering it as part of an organised tour, you'll get no more than an unimpressive five-minute photo stop. On your own, however, you'll be able to explore the intriguing formations and surrounding areas on foot.

To get there from the Prado in La Paz, take micro 11 headed downhill and get off at its final stop at Barrio Aranjuéz. Alternatively, take any micro marked 'Calacoto', get off at

Plaza Humboldt and wait near the corner to catch micro 11 to Barrio Aranjuéz. At this point, cross the bridge to your right and follow a rather nondescript trail across a ditch and up the hill on your left. (You can also walk up the road but it's quite a bit further.)

· After about 10 minutes, you'll arrive at the *cactario* or cactus gardens. They're not marked as such but are easily identifiable as a slightly artificial-looking stand of cactus. Across the garden there's a poor and rather frightening foot bridge across a gully. This track winds through the Valle de la Luna and emerges at the football pitch near the village of Mallasa. The walk from the cactario to the football pitch should take about 30 minutes. In Mallasa you will find several stores selling snacks, beer and soft drinks. Since the rains drastically alter this fragile landscape, it's possible that portions of the track will wash out in years to come and the route may change. However, if you enter the valley at the cactus garden and keep walking uphill, you'll eventually arrive at the road.

If you turn right along the road at the football pitch – away from Mallasa village – you'll eventually reach Malasilla Golf Course, the world's highest course.

MUELA DEL DIABLO

The Muela del Diablo (Devil's Molar), a prominent rock outcrop which is actually the plug of an extinct volcano, lies on the north side of the Río Choqueyapu – also known as the 'Omo River', due to the amount of laundry soap flowing along with it. A hike up to its base makes a pleasant daytrip from La Paz, and the view of the city and the cordillera is quite good. This hike may be easily done in conjunction with a trip to Valle de la Luna.

Getting There & Away

To get there, take colectivo 213 from Plaza Murillo or the lower Prado to its final stop at the base of the Muela del Diablo track. Alternatively, you can take micro 'Ñ' past Calacoto and Plaza Humboldt. If you're coming from Valle de la Luna, catch it at

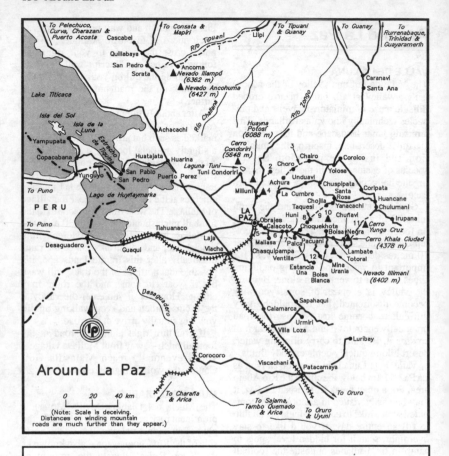

Around La Paz

0   20   40 km

(Note: Scale is deceiving.
Distances on winding mountain
roads are much further than they appear.)

1 El Camino de Oro Trek	7 Cañón del Huaricunca
2 Zongo Ice Caves	8 San Francisco Mine
3 La Cumbre to Coroico Trek	9 Taquesi Trek
4 Chacaltaya	10 Nevado Mururata (5868 m)
5 Valle de la Luna	11 Yunga Cruz Trek
6 Valle de las Ánimas	12 Illimani Base Camp

Plaza Humboldt. Ask the driver to let you off at the trail to Muela del Diablo or look for a sign which identifies Calle 80.

The trail enters a canyon and then climbs rapidly through a series of rather confusing intersecting tracks. In less than two hours you'll come to a pleasant grassy area which has a superb view of Muela del Diablo. From there, the trail descends through a hamlet and again climbs toward the peak; after about half an hour, you'll reach its base. With extreme caution, you can carefully pick your way up to the cleft between the double summit, but without technical equipment

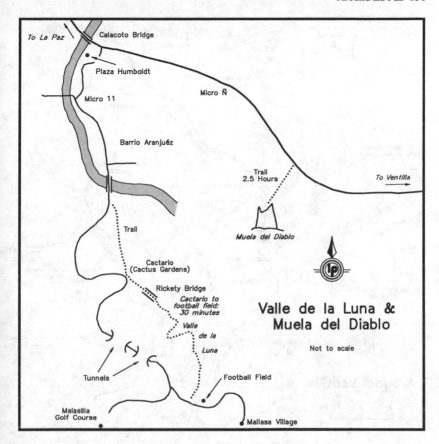

To La Paz

Calacoto Bridge

Plaza Humboldt

Micro 11

Micro Ñ

Barrio Aranjuéz

Trail
2.5 Hours

To Ventilla

Trail

Muela del Diablo

Cactario
(Cactus Gardens)

Rickety Bridge

Cactario to
football field:
30 minutes

Valle
de la
Luna

**Valle de la Luna &
Muela del Diablo**

Not to scale

Tunnels

Football Field

Malasilla
Golf Course

Mallasa Village

and expertise, it's inadvisable to climb further.

AROUND VENTILLA
Valle de las Ánimas & Cañón del Huaricunca

To reach the start of this highly worthwhile day excursion from La Paz, take micro 'Ñ' past Muela del Diablo toward its final stop at Chasquipampa. You can get off anywhere and walk along the track that parallels the road up through the Valle de las Ánimas (Valley of the Spirits). You'll get good close-up views of 6402-metre Illimani and be able to explore fantastically eroded organ-pipe scenery similar to Valle de la Luna but on a grand scale.

At Chasquipampa, the route then turns south and follows a jeep track along the Río Huni, passing the village of Huni before dropping dramatically into the magnificent Cañón del Huaricunca, also known as Palca Canyon, where you'll pass a large and prominent obelisk 100 metres high. After exiting the canyon, the track winds along the Río Choquekhota (also known as Río Palca) through gentle farmlands and ends in the village of Palca, a gold-mining settlement

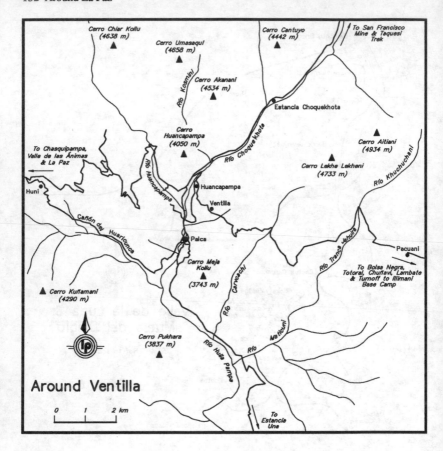

Around Ventilla

0   1   2 km

where the rocks and rivers are still worked by hand. The hike from Chasquipampa to Palca takes between four and five hours, but you may want to allow longer for side trips and exploration.

From Palca there's occasional transport back to La Paz, but don't count on anything after 3 pm. Ask around in Palca for a place to sleep if it becomes necessary, or hike to Ventilla, about an hour's walk away through a eucalyptus plantation. If you have the gear there'll be no problem camping in either Palca or Ventilla, but ask permission before setting up in a field or pasture.

Camiones and an occasional bus do the trip from Ventilla back to La Paz. Naturally, it's also possible to return to Chasquipampa the way you came and take micro 'Ñ' from there back to town.

If you haven't yet had your fill of hiking, however, you can set off from Ventilla along the Taquesi Trek, a two-day route over an ancient Inca road into the Yungas. For a map and further details, see the Cordilleras & Yungas chapter.

CHACALTAYA

The world's highest developed ski area lies

atop a glacier on the slopes of Chacaltaya, the name of which is derived from the Aymará words *chaka* meaning 'bridge' and *thaya* meaning 'cold'. The ski run, between 5200 and 5400 metres elevation, lies just a 90-minute ride from central La Paz. The easily accessible summit of the mountain is 5600 metres above sea level. The Chacaltaya slope itself is a bit steep, and during the dry season, can be extremely icy. There's no 'bunny hill', but even beginners can have a good time if they're not afraid of a few bumps.

If you're coming from the lowlands, it'll be wise to wait a few days in La Paz before attempting a visit to this altitude. See the Health section in the Facts for the Visitor chapter for information on ways to avoid or cope with soroche (altitude sickness). Paracetamol and/or microen tablets, available in La Paz pharmacies, will adequately relieve discomfort during short-term visits to high altitudes.

Intending skiers and hikers should be sure to eat well the previous day, but go easy during the trip because digestion at this altitude requires a great deal of the energy you'll be needing for other activities. Snacks and hot drinks are available at the lodge; if you want anything more substantial, you'll have to bring it from town. Be sure to bring warm (preferably windproof) clothing, sunglasses and sunscreen.

Club Andino Boliviano will be your best bet if you're planning to ski. A number of La Paz tour agencies take groups to Chacaltaya, but tour groups must pay B5 per person for access to the club warm-up hut. During periods of heavy snow, especially between March and early June, the road to Chacaltaya may become impassable, so check the situation before deciding on a tour that can't arrive at its destination! For some suggestions for tour agencies, refer to the discussion of Organised Tours earlier in this chapter.

Skiing
Club Andino Boliviano (☎ 324682) takes ski tours to Chacaltaya on Saturdays and

Sundays. To reserve a spot, give them a call or drop by their office at Calle México 1638. The office is open weekdays from 9 am to noon and 3 to 7 pm.

Ski trips leave from the club office at 8.30 am and arrive at Chacaltaya sometime before 10 am. You ski until 5 pm and are back in La Paz by 7.30 pm. Transport costs B35, equipment rental is an additional B35, and the cable-tow costs B13.

The club has long considered replacing the utterly confounding cable-tow now in operation at Chacaltaya, but they've been discussing it for at least five years and nothing has transpired. Wear expendable clothing; it will suffer assault by the cable.

When you're choosing your ski equipment, be sure to get a good tow hook with a complete U-shaped curl to it, or you won't be able to negotiate the cable-tow. The equipment rental shop is in the main warm-up hut. If they don't have the right size boots, ask them to get some from the club. If you don't insist, you may have to accept boots that don't fit, an uncomfortable and dangerous situation.

Hiking
If you're not interested in skiing, a trip to Chacaltaya can still be a rewarding experience. The views of La Paz, Illimani, Mururata and 6088-metre Huayna Potosí are spectacular. It's a relatively easy, although steep, climb of one km at high altitude from the lodge to the summit of Chacaltaya. Take plenty of rests, say a 30-second stop every 10 steps or so and longer stops if needed, even if you don't feel tired. If you begin to feel light-headed, sit down and rest until the feeling passes. If it doesn't, it's very likely that you are suffering mild altitude sickness. There is only one remedy for this – descent to a lower altitude. Carry warm clothing and water.

It's also possible to climb to the third false summit above the ski area and wind your way down past a turquoise lake into Zongo valley where you'll meet up with the road. Turn right and follow the road from there to the trail which cuts off toward the Zongo Ice

Caves a couple of km further down the valley.

Places To Stay

If you'd like to stay overnight at Chacaltaya, you can either sleep in Club Andino's warm-up hut or ask the club equipment dispenser if there might be room in the laboratory just below the ski lodge. The latter is heated, and the friendly scientific personnel welcome visitors. A warm sleeping bag, food, and some sort of headache remedy will be necessary for an overnight stay in either location.

Getting There & Away

If you go to Chacaltaya with the club on a Saturday and decide to stay overnight on the mountain, there should be no problem catching a lift down with them when they return to La Paz after the Sunday daytrip, if the bus isn't full. On other days, there will normally be tour groups with space for an extra person, but you may have to pay at least half the tour price to join them.

ZONGO VALLEY ICE CAVES

The beautiful Zongo valley between Chacaltaya and the spectacular peak of Huayna Potosí drops from 4624 metres to 1480 metres within 33 km. It contains the starkly anonymous mining village of Milluni and the hydro-electric generating station of the Bolivian Power Company.

The best access to the caves is with an organised tour from La Paz; see the Organised Tours section earlier in this chapter for suggestions. Alternatively, you can take a taxi from the Centro de Taxis on Avenida Aniceto Arce for about B150 for up to five people. Be sure that the driver understands that you want to go to Zongo valley via Milluni. Many taxi drivers expect you to ask for Chacaltaya and may try to take you there anyway.

To reach the caves trailhead, continue about five km past Milluni, which will be visible downhill on your left. You may want to have a look at the interesting Indian cemetery on the roadside above the mine area. If

you're travelling by vehicle, you'll reach Laguna Zongo, an artificial lake with milky blue-green water, and the Compañía Minera del Sur gate a few minutes later. On your right will be the caves trailhead. From there, the road winds downward into Zongo valley. If you're in a taxi, make sure the driver realises it is necessary to wait while you walk up to visit the caves; allow a minimum of three hours for the return walk.

The hike begins at 4600 metres. From the parking area, strike off uphill to the right. After about 100 metres, you'll see an aqueduct which you should follow for about 50 minutes along a treacherous precipice. Watch on your left for the plaque commemorating an Israeli's final motorbike ride along this narrow and vertigo-inspiring route. Several years ago, two Israelis hatched a reckless scheme to rent motorbikes in La Paz and ride to the ice caves. The plaque marks the spot where one of them plunged to his death.

After you cross a large bridge, walk 20 metres and turn right along a vague track leading uphill, following the cairns which mark the way. You'll pass a beautiful turquoise lake, Laguna Cañada, with impressive views of Huayna Potosí which is often shrouded in clouds and mist.

The caves, which aren't nearly as impressive as the walk to them, lie 100 metres higher than the bridge, approximately 35 minutes climbing. The entrance, a large opening at the foot of a tiny glacier, is easy to spot. The cave itself is about 50 metres deep, two metres high and four metres wide. The walls capture the sunlight and you can see the layers of clear and cloudy blue ice, smoothed and rounded into unusual shapes. Watch your feet; this cave is formed by running water and it's extremely slippery.

LAJA

The tiny village of Laja, formerly known as Llaxa and Laxa, lies between La Paz and Tiahuanaco. When the Spanish captain Alonzo de Mendoza was charged with locating a new rest stop and founding a city along the route from Potosí to the coast at Callao in Peru, he set out toward the north-west. On 20 October 1548, he arrived in Laxa and declared it his chosen location. He soon changed his mind, however, and the site was quickly shifted to the gold-bearing canyon where La Paz is today.

In Laja's plaza there's an impressive church built in commemoration of Spanish victories over the Incas. The interior of the church is ornamented with gold, silver, wooden carvings and colonial artwork. Most of the organised tours going to Tiahuanaco make a brief stop at Laja.

TIAHUANACO

Little is actually known about the Tiahuanaco people who constructed the great ceremonial centre on the southern shore of Lake Titicaca over 1000 years ago. Archaeologists generally agree that the civilisation that spawned Tiahuanaco rose around 600 BC. The ceremonial site was under construction around 700 AD, but after about 1200 AD the group had melted into obscurity, becoming another 'lost' civilisation. Evidence of its influence, particularly in the area of religion, has been found throughout the vast area that later became the Inca Empire.

The treasures of Tiahuanaco have literally been scattered to the four corners of the earth. Its gold was looted by the Spanish and early stone and pottery finds were sometimes destroyed by religious zealots who considered them pagan idols. Some of the work found its way to European museums; farmers destroyed pieces of it as they turned the surrounding area into pasture and cropland; the church kept some of the statues or sold them as curios; and the larger stonework went into Spanish construction projects, and even into the bed of the La Paz-Guaqui rail line which passes just south of the site.

Fortunately, a portion of the treasure was preserved and left in Bolivia. A few of the larger anthropomorphic stone statues have been left on the site, or are displayed in the Museo al Aire Libre in La Paz. The ruins were so badly looted, however, that much of the information they could have revealed about their builders is lost forever. Pieces from the earliest Tiahuanaco periods are kept in an onsite museum which is opened only infrequently to the public. Pieces from the three later epochs may be found scattered around Bolivia, but the majority are housed in the archaeological museums in La Paz and Cochabamba.

History

Although no one is sure whether or not it was the capital of a nation, Tiahuanaco was undoubtedly a great ceremonial centre. At its height it was a city of possibly 20,000 inhabitants, encompassing approximately 2.6 sq km. Although only a very small percentage of the original site has been excavated, and what's left of it is less than overwhelming, Tiahuanaco includes the most imposing megalithic architecture of pre-Inca South America.

The civilisation's development has been divided by researchers into five distinct periods, numbered Tiahuanaco I through V, each with its own outstanding attributes.

Tiahuanaco I is placed between the advent of the civilisation and the middle of the 5th century BC. Significant finds from this period include multicoloured pottery and human or animal effigies in painted clay. Tiahuanaco II, which ended around the beginning of the Christian Era, has been hallmarked by ceramic vessels with horizontal handles. Tiahuanaco III was prominent over the following 300 years, producing geometrically designed tricolour pottery which was often decorated with images of stylised animals.

Tiahuanaco IV, also known as the Classic Period, developed from 300 to 700 AD. The large stone structures which dominate the site today were constructed during this period. The use of bronze and gold during this period is considered evidence of contact with groups further east in the Cochabamba valley and further west on the Peruvian coast. Tiahuanaco IV pottery is largely anthropomorphic; archaeologists have uncovered some in the shape of human heads and faces with bulging cheeks, indicating

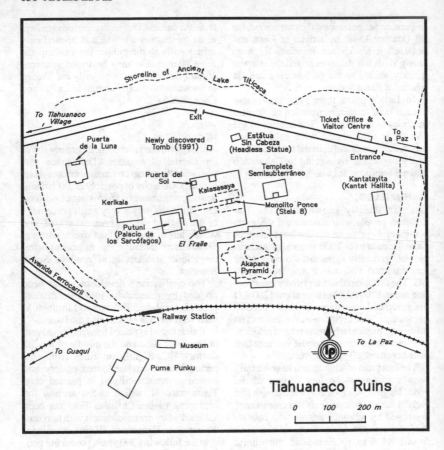

Tiahuanaco Ruins

0   100   200 m

Labels in map:
- Shoreline of Ancient Lake Titicaca
- To Tiahuanaco Village
- Exit
- Ticket Office & Visitor Centre
- To La Paz
- Puerta de la Luna
- Newly discovered Tomb (1991)
- Estátua Sin Cabeza (Headless Statue)
- Entrance
- Puerta del Sol
- Templete Semisubterráneo
- Kantatayita (Kantat Hallita)
- Kalasasaya
- Kerikala
- Monolito Ponce (Stela 8)
- Putuni (Palacio de los Sarcófagos)
- El Fraile
- Akapana Pyramid
- Avenida Ferrocarril
- Railway Station
- To Guaqui
- Museum
- Puma Punku
- To La Paz

that the coca leaf was already in use at this time.

Tiahuanaco V, or the Expansive Period, is marked by a decline that lasted until Tiahuanaco's utter disappearance around 1200 AD. Pottery grew less elaborate, construction projects slowed and stopped and no large-scale monuments were added after the early phases of this period.

When the Spanish arrived in South America, local Indian legends stated that Tiahuanaco had been the capital of the bearded white god Viracocha, and from his city he had reigned over the civilisation.

For more detailed information on the rise and fall of Tiahuanaco, you may want to pick up the English translation of the book *Discovering Tiwanaku* by Hugo Boero Rojo, available from Los Amigos del Libro in La Paz.

Visiting the Site

There are stone slabs weighing as much as 175,000 kg strewn about the site in jumbled heaps. Oddly enough the nearest quarries that could have produced these basalt megaliths are on the Copacabana peninsula, 40 km away across the lake. Even the sandstone

and andesite. It measures 130 metres long by 120 metres wide. The blocks are precisely fitted to form a platform base three metres high. Monolithic uprights flank the massive entrance steps up to the restored portico of the enclosure, beyond which is an interior courtyard and the ruins of priests' quarters.

Other stairways lead up to secondary platforms where there are other monoliths including the famous El Fraile. At the far north-west corner of Kalasasaya is Tiahuanaco's best known structure, Puerta del Sol (Gateway of the Sun). This megalithic gateway was carved from a single block of andesite and archaeologists assume that it was associated in some way with the sun deity. The surface of this fine-grained, grey volcanic rock is ornamented with low-relief designs on one side and a row of four deep niches on the other. Some believe these may have been used for offerings to the sun, while others maintain that the stone served as some kind of a calendar. The structure is believed to weigh over 44,000 kg.

There's a smaller, similar gateway carved with zoomorphic designs near the western end of the site, which is informally called Puerta de la Luna (Gateway of the Moon).

blocks had to be transported from a site over five km away. It's no wonder then that when the Spanish asked local Indians how the buildings were constructed, they replied that it was with the aid of the leader/deity Viracocha. They could conceive of no other plausible explanation.

The most outstanding structure on the site is the Akapana pyramid, which has been constructed on an existing geographical formation. It is a roughly square hill, over 16 metres high, its base covering a surface area of about 200 sq metres. In the centre of its flat summit is an oval-shaped sunken area which some sources attribute to early, haphazard Spanish excavation. Others, due to the presence of a stone drain in the centre, believe it was used for water storage. Because much of Akapana's original construction material went into construction of nearby homes and churches, the pyramid is now in a rather sorry state.

North of the pyramid is Kalasasaya, a ritual platform compound whose walls are constructed of huge blocks of red sandstone

Near the main entrance to Kalasasaya, a stairway leads down into the Templete Semisubterráneo, a red sandstone pit structure measuring 26 by 28 metres with a rectangular sunken courtyard and walls adorned with small carved stone faces.

West of Kalasasaya is a 55 by 60-metre rectangular area known as Putuni or Palacio de los Sarcófagos, which is still in the process of excavation. It is surrounded by double walls and you can see the foundations of several houses.

The heap of rubble at the eastern end of the site is known as Kantatayita. Archaeologists are still trying to deduce some sort of meaningful plan from these well-carved slabs; one elaborately decorated lintel and some larger stone blocks bearing intriguing geometric designs are the only available clues. It has been postulated – and dubiously 'proven' – that they were derived from universal mathematical constants; however, some archaeologists simply see the plans for a large and well-designed building.

Across the rail line near the Tiahuanaco site is the excavation of Puma Punku, (Gateway of the Puma), a large temple area where megaliths of over 440,000 kg have been discovered. Like Kalasasaya and Akapana, there is evidence that Puma Punku was begun with one type of material and finished with another; part was constructed of enormous sandstone blocks, and during a later phase of construction, notched and jointed basalt blocks were employed. Unfortunately, the site museum at Puma Punku is open only sporadically.

Admission to the Tiahuanaco site is B5 for foreigners, which includes entrance to the tiny visitor centre at the ticket office. Guides and people selling ceramic trinkets (don't pay more than B.50 for these imitation artefacts!) are no longer permitted inside the ruins area. Guides are available outside the fence for around B10, but you'll have to bargain them down to that price.

Places to Eat

There are good restaurants and an incredibly colourful Sunday market in the village of Tiahuanaco, which is one km beyond the ruins. If you take a tour, bring your own lunch unless you don't mind being herded into a restaurant and charged three times the fair price to cover your tour guide's kickback. The museum opposite the ruins isn't bad but as would be expected, prices are commensurate with the captive and thirsty tourist clientele. There's also a basic but clean alojamiento in the village which charges B5 per person.

Getting There & Away

Bus Flota Ingavi leaves about eight times daily from Calle José María Asín in La Paz. From the Prado, take any micro marked 'Cementerio' and get off at the flower market opposite the cemetery. From there, the terminal is one block uphill and two blocks to the right. The trip costs B3 each way.

Buses are crowded far beyond comfortable capacity, so plan on waiting an hour or two at the office for a seat reservation or the trip will be rather disagreeable. Even when people are hanging out the windows and doors, drivers still call for more passengers.

To return to La Paz, either flag down a passing micro – which will probably already be filled to overflowing before it reaches the ruins – or walk into town and catch one along the main street.

Micros continuing to Guaqui on the Peruvian border leave from the main plaza in Tiahuanaco village or may be flagged down just outside town. Again, expect crowds. For further information on Guaqui, refer to the Lake Titicaca chapter.

Tours Dozens of La Paz tour agencies offer reasonably priced guided full and half-day tours to Tiahuanaco. Daytrips are remarkably inexpensive – about B45 including transport and guide – and are probably worth it to avoid the trouble and discomfort of local buses. A list of tour agencies can be found under Organised Tours in the La Paz section.

Taxi Taxis to Tiahuanaco may be hired from the Centro de Taxis in La Paz for B75 to B90 return.

URMIRI

In the Valle de Sapahaqui, three hours southeast of La Paz, are the Termas de Urmiri (Urmiri Hot Springs) where the La Paz Prefectura operates a resort hotel. There are two outdoor pools, one lukewarm and another smaller, warmer one. For use of these pools, which are maintained by the hotel, nonguests pay B10 per person.

Places to Stay

Urmiri's only formal accommodation is the *Hotel Prefectural*. Rooms (including three meals and use of the hot springs) cost B40 per person. Best of all, each room adjoins a large – and private – hot bath! Make accommodation and transport reservations at least two days in advance. The hotel office (☎ 374-586) is on the 2nd floor of the La Paz Prefectura at the corner of calles Comercio and Ayacucho.

Camping is possible outside the village and, although it's chilly, those luscious hot springs are never far away!

Getting There & Away

Urmiri lies at an elevation of 3800 metres, 30 km east of the La Paz-Oruro highway. The easiest way to get there is with the hotel shuttle vehicle which charges B30 for the return trip. Transport reservations should be made when reserving your room. The shuttle departs La Paz in the morning from Plaza Perez Velasco.

Alternatively, take a bus or camión from La Paz toward Oruro and get off near the bridge in Villa Loza at Km 70. Turn left and walk or hitch (although you may not have much success with the latter) east along the dirt road. If you can't get a lift, you are in for a long walk. After five km or so, you'll pass a cluster of chullpas (Kolla funerary towers) and begin seeing superb views of the Cordillera Real as you wind down into the fruit-growing area of the Valle de Sapahaqui. After approximately 20 more km, you'll reach the crossing at the settlement of Lurjavi where you'll turn right for the final three and a bit km into Urmiri.

LURIBAY

At the end of a long and twisting road northeast of Patacamaya on the La Paz-Oruro highway is Luribay which in 1983 was the base of operations for a short-lived guerrilla organisation. It was crushed and all its leaders captured before it ever got off the ground. The following account of a visit to Luribay speaks for itself:

I think I have found a more hair-raising road than the one to Coroico – it's to a place called Luribay which is three hours south-west of La Paz along the super-boring Oruro road and then left at Patacamaya at the sign pointing to Luribay. Following this for two more hours is rough but then you reach the best part – you drop 2000-odd metres in eight km by way of 53 (yes, 53!) hairpin bends. This is on a narrow dirt track of a road which is treacherous in the rainy season and has passing places for that oncoming uphill truck that you always meet just when you are least expecting it! You drop from harsh Altiplano to lush lowlands in a valley with its own micro-climate. The best is that there are no tourists and the locals are very friendly. There are wonderful hikes up and down the valley and the scenery is really spectacular. In the Autumn, there is fruit for the picking everywhere and the vegetables grown in this rich valley are some of the tastiest I've had.

Unfortunately, it's a place for the hardy – no running water or electricity, and big wood stoves for cooking since very few people have gas cooking or heating. There is a village latrine five minutes away which is cleaned sporadically and there are some nice churches, plain but simple and very beautiful, nearby. So far there have been hardly any tourists, and hopefully, writing this won't spoil it completely. It's calmer than Coroico but it doesn't have swimming pools, etc. Maybe that's why Carnival time is such a ball here with the usual water-throwing and general merriment.

Ms Alex Rossi, UK

Places to Stay

Luribay has no formal accommodation so visitors must go prepared to camp or arrange lodging in private homes.

Getting There & Away

There is no public transport into the village; you'll have to hitch down the heart-stopping hill with trucks from the Luribay turnoff at Patacamaya. If you do find your way to this rather remote spot, please be sensitive to the local way of life. Tread lightly.

The Cordilleras & Yungas

The Cordillera Real (Royal Range) is Bolivia's most prominent cordillera and one of the Andes' loftiest and most impressive. The bulk of the country's popular hiking and trekking routes follow ancient roads through the Cordillera Real, connecting the high Altiplano with the steamy Yungas (Valleys). It also serves as a venue for Bolivia's best mountaineering.

Lying beneath the Cordillera Real are the Yungas. Here, steep jungle-covered cliffs loom above humid, cloud-filled gorges, forming a distinct natural division between the cold and barren Altiplano and the level Amazon rainforest which covers most of northern Bolivia. The short (distance-wise, anyway!) trip from the 4600-metre La Cumbre pass into the Alto Beni entails a loss of 4343 metres elevation. (Parts of the Cordillera Real and Yungas are included on the Around La Paz map in the La Paz chapter.)

North of Lake Titicaca lies the remote Cordillera Apolobamba with scores of little known valleys and traditional Aymará villages. Here live the renowned Kallahuaya medicine men who employ a blend of herbs and magic to cure ailments. This area also includes the Parque Nacional Ulla-Ulla, a vicuña reserve abutting the Peruvian border. Access to the Apolobamba, which is well off the beaten track, is difficult and tourism is still relatively unknown. There are, however, some wonderful trekking opportunities in this area.

Despite the lethargy-inspiring humidity and precipitation evident in the Yungas, settlers have long been attracted to this area for a number of reasons. While the climate overall is much more agreeable than on the Altiplano, and the physical beauty of the place is astonishing, to say the least, pure economic considerations have been the main motivations for settlement of this area.

The first major draw to the Yungas, in the early days of the Inca Empire, was the discovery of gold in the valleys of the Río Tipuani and Río Mapiri. Naturally the gold-crazed Spanish got involved as soon as they could and forced the local population to labour along the Yungas streams. The Spanish found a fortune in this incredibly lucrative area, and even today there are still a few prospectors haphazardly extracting a living.

Most of the inhabitants currently involved in agricultural activities live in the intermediate altitudes, roughly between 600 and 1800 metres. Sugar, citrus fruits, bananas and coffee are grown in large enough quantities to adequately supply the highlands with these products, and transportation is plentiful even if the route is difficult.

The Yungas are also a primary area of coca production in Bolivia. This activity is centred on the village of Coripata and extends toward the south Yungas capital of Chulumani. The sweet Yungas coca is primarily consumed locally, while leaves from the Chapare region further east serve more infamous purposes.

The climate of the region is humid and rainy throughout most of the year. The bulk of the heavy precipitation falls between November and March; winter rains are much gentler. The average temperature is about 18°C, but daytime temperatures in the 30s are common, often accompanied by motivation-stifling humidity.

The Yungas consist of two political provinces of the La Paz Department, Nor and Sud Yungas, as well as bits of other provinces further east and west, with Coroico and Chulumani as the principal centres of transportation, commerce and administration. They serve as lowland resort areas for chilly highlanders, and are also favourites with foreign travellers.

LA CUMBRE TO COROICO (CHORO) TREK

The La Cumbre to Coroico Trek (also known as the Choro Trek), north-east of La Paz, is

Top: Guaqui - Lake Titicaca (TM)
Left: Horca del Inca observatory - Copacabana (DS)
Right: Totora reed boat, Huatajata - Lake Titicaca (WH)

Top: Entrance to Moorish cathedral - Copacabana (DS)
Left: Face in Templete Semisubterráneo - Tiahuanaco (RS)
Right: Virgen de Candelaria cathedral - Copacabana (DS)

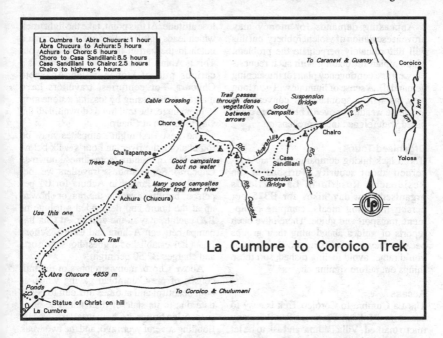

La Cumbre to Abra Chucura: 1 hour
Abra Chucura to Achura: 5 hours
Achura to Choro: 6 hours
Choro to Casa Sandillani: 8.5 hours
Casa Sandillani to Chairo: 2.5 hours
Chairo to highway: 4 hours

To Caranavi & Guanay

Coroico

12 km

4 km

7 km

Trail passes through dense vegetation between arrows

Suspension Bridge

Good Campsite

Cable Crossing

Choro

Chairo

Rio Huarinilla

Casa Sandillani

Yolosa

Cha'llapampa

Good campsites but no water

Trees begin

Suspension Bridge

Rio Chairo

Rio Cascada

Many good campsites below trail near river

Achura (Chucura)

Use this one

La Cumbre to Coroico Trek

Poor Trail

Abra Chucura 4859 m

Ponds

Statue of Christ on hill

La Cumbre

To Coroico & Chulumani

the premier hike in Bolivia. It begins at La Cumbre, the highest point on the La Paz-Coroico highway, and climbs to Abra Chucura (Chucura Pass) at 4859 metres before descending 3250 metres into the steaming Yungas to the village of Chairo. Along the various stages of the walk there are distinct differences in dress, dwellings, crops and herds.

Energetic hikers can finish the walk in two days, but most people prefer to take more time to enjoy the incredible variety of landforms and vegetation found throughout the different altitude zones. The trek can be done quite comfortably in three days, but those unaccustomed to long-distance hiking should allow four.

Be sure to carry water purification tablets; while good surface water is plentiful, human and animal life exist throughout the length of this trail and contamination does occur. Also, come prepared for a wide range of climates. On the first day you'll need winter

gear, but on the second and third days, it will be peeled off layer by layer. On the lower trail, wear light cotton trousers or similar to protect your legs from sharp vegetation and biting insects.

Warning

Since the first edition of this book, begging, theft and robbery have increased along this route. In 1990, a Swedish hiker was killed during a robbery on the ridge north of Choro and her companion was shot and badly injured. He was able to crawl to the village but was refused first aid until he produced a hidden stash of money. The incident attracted outside attention and although the frequency of aggressive or violent robbery has since declined significantly, petty theft remains a problem. Camp away from the trail – out of sight if possible – and don't leave anything outside your tent at night if you can't afford to lose it. Avoid camping near Choro, where most thefts occur.

Appeasing demands for money may prevent escalation of violent robbery, but this will unfortunately perpetuate the problem. Make a plan for dealing with such requests (as well as a contingency plan for threatening demands!). A sense of humour will go a long way, as will a spontaneous conversation about the weather or even a blank stare combined with feigned incomprehension.

Organised Tour

If you lack hiking companions or are concerned about security, Turisbus at the Residencial Rosário in La Paz leads organised four-day hikes for B375 per person including meals, camping equipment, transport and guide. There have been reports of guides abandoning their groups because they were walking too slowly, so if you'd rather avoid feeling rushed, sort these things out before signing on.

Access

The La Cumbre to Coroico Trek is easy to access and follow. From La Paz, take any micro marked 'Villa Fátima' and ask to be let off at the Flota Yungueña office. Several companies based within a block of there run buses and micros to the Yungas at least once daily, with the first departures around 8 am. They charge B5 to drop you at the high point of the Yungas road where the trek begins.

Behind the service station near the Flota Yungueña office, you'll find camiones leaving for the Yungas every few minutes between about 7 am and early afternoon. They charge B3 per person to the pass. Start early if you want the best chances of good views from the pass. The road climbs steeply out of Villa Fátima and less than an hour out of La Paz at the crest of the La Paz-Yungas road is La Cumbre, marked by a statue of Christ.

The Route

Get off at the statue and follow a well-defined track to your left for about one km. There, a smaller track turns right and passes between two small ponds. Follow this up the hill until it curves to the left and begins to lose altitude. At this point, take the light track which leads uphill to the right and through a notch in the barren brown hill before you. This is Abra Chucura. At the high point is a curious pile of stones called Apacheta Chucura. For centuries, travellers have marked their passing by tossing a stone atop it. From there, the trail trends downhill all the way to its end at Chairo.

The best first-night campsites may be found along the river, an hour's walk below the village of Achura (sometimes known as Chucura). Some tentless travellers we met stayed with a family in Achura for B1 per person, but that evening the mayor showed up at the home and demanded a tribute of B20 each to stay in the village. At Cha'llapampa between Achura and Choro, Señora Ivana has established a guest house of sorts and charges B2.50 per night.

Above Choro, many stretches of the trail consist of pre-Columbian paving which is both beautiful and at times difficult to negotiate due to its state of disrepair. The good suspension bridge at Choro was destroyed by flooding several years ago, and the two weak twig-and-vine structures which were constructed to replace it have also headed downstream. The latest crossing method is a cable and pulley contraption tenuously strung several metres above the water. An attendant will haul you across for B3 per person; you will initially be asked for a lot more, so you'll have to negotiate this more or less reasonable price; as you may suspect, Bolivians pay considerably less. Alternatively, you can wade the river and have your pack ferried across for B1.

From the crossing, turn right. The trail climbs steeply to the ridge above town and enters dense trail-swallowing vegetation. Campsites are plentiful between this point and Chairo, but in most cases, it's necessary to bring water from elsewhere. Due to numerous incidences of theft along this stretch, it would be better to continue at least 1½ hours beyond the village before setting up camp.

From the ridge above Choro, the trail plunges and climbs alternately from sunny hillsides to vegetation-choked valleys. It passes streams and waterfalls and at one point, crosses the deep gorge of the Río Cascada with the help of a crude but effective suspension bridge.

Near the trail's end, about 2½ hours from Chairo, you'll encounter a curious and unexpected sight: an oriental home surrounded by beautifully manicured gardens. It's called Casa Sandillani and the friendly Japanese owner, Mr Tamiji Hanamura, is full of trail news and enjoys visitors who stop by to chat and sign his guestbook. He's happy to let you camp in his garden; you may want to bring along some stamps or postcards from home to augment his by now extensive collections.

From Casa Sandillani, it's seven easy downhill km to Chairo from where there are very occasional camiones to Yolosa or Coroico. There's also other light, intermittent traffic. If you need to stay over in Chairo, it's possible to sleep on the veranda of the school or camp near the trail across the suspension bridge. Meals and supplies are available from the small shop on the main street; the owners are some of the friendliest people you're likely to meet.

It's also possible to walk the relatively level 12 km from Chairo to the highway, but this involves a rather hairy river-fording and due caution should be exercised, especially after periods of heavy rain. Plan on four hours for the walk and carry water. Once you reach the main road, it will be easy to find a camión going to Yolosa, four km away, and a lift up the hill to Coroico seven km away or, if you're in a hurry, back to La Paz.

YOLOSA

Travelling between Coroico and La Paz or the Beni, you'll have to pass through Yolosa, at the road junction in the valley seven km below Coroico. Along with numerous street stalls selling fast snacks to truckers, you'll find the Spaguetti Restaurant, which serves (no, not spaghetti) excellent chicken and chips. Note the immense mural on the wall which provides evidence that, yes, there are Bengal tigers in the Bolivian rainforest. If you find yourself planted overnight, there's a place to crash above the restaurant opposite the Spaguetti for B5 for a double.

The tranca at Yolosa closes between 1 and 5 am, impeding overnight traffic between the Yungas and La Paz. Transport awaiting passengers to Coroico queues up on the hill beside the Spaguetti Restaurant. The local price is B1.50 per person but foreigners won't get away paying less than B2.

COROICO

Coroico, the Nor Yungas provincial capital, is a serene little town at a pleasantly tropical altitude of 1500 metres. Perched eyrie-like on the shoulder of Cerro Uchumachi, it commands a far-ranging view of forested canyons, cloud-wreathed mountain peaks, patchwork agricultural lands, citrus orchards, coffee plantations and dozens of small settlements. When the weather is clear, the view stretches to the snow-covered summits of the Cordillera Real.

The town's tranquillity is the prime attraction and the slow pace leaves plenty of time for relaxing, swimming, lying in the sun or walking in the surrounding hills. Coroico is warm year-round with rain almost daily in the afternoon and powerful downpours during the summer. Fog is common at any time, but especially in the afternoon when it rises from the deep valleys and swirls around the streets of town.

Information

Money There's no place to change travellers' cheques, but several businesses in town will change cash dollars. To be on the safe side, bring any cash you'll be needing in the Yungas, especially if you're travelling north into the Amazon Basin.

Post & Telecommunications The post office is open Tuesday, Thursday, Friday and Saturday from 9.30 am to noon and 2.30 to 5 pm. On Sunday, it's open between 9.30 am and noon.

To phone La Paz or elsewhere, go to the DITER office on the plaza between 9 am and 1 pm or 5 and 8 pm, Tuesday to Friday. Calls cost B1 per minute. From COTEL opposite

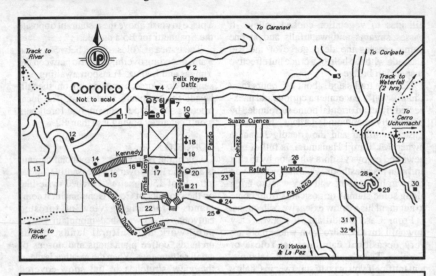

To Caranavi

Track to River

To Coripata

Coroico
Not to scale

Felix Reyes Dañz

Track to Waterfall (2 hrs)

To Cerro Uchumachi

Suazo Cuenca

Kennedy

Monseñor Thomas Manning

Tomás Manjón

Sagárnaga

Pando

Deheza

Rafael

Miranda

Pacheco

Track to River

To Yolosa & La Paz

■ PLACES TO STAY

3 Hotel & Restaurant Don Quijote
6 Residencial Coroico
7 Hotel Lluvia de Oro
11 Alojamiento Paiyuan
13 Hotel Prefectural
15 Residencial & Restaurant La Casa
16 Hostal Kory
21 Residencial 2 de Febrero
30 Hostal Sol y Luna

▼ PLACES TO EAT

2 El Rodeo Restaurant
4 La Tasca Bar
31 Rancho Beni (Dany & Patricio
   Horse Rental & Café)

OTHER

1 Chapel
5 Flota Yungueña & Comedor
   Municipal
8 Transportes Adán
9 Post Office
10 Veloz del Norte Bus Terminal
12 Lavandería Benedita
14 Madres de Clarissa Convent
17 Artesanía Arco Irís
18 Iglesia
19 COTEL Public Telephone
20 Flota Trans-Santiago Lucho
22 Mercado Municipal San José
23 Cinema
24 COTEL Office & Photocopies
25 Tranca
26 Ch'aka Khuyta'asiri
   Wind Instruments
27 Iglesia Calvario
28 Military Base
29 Cemetery
32 Hospital

the tranca and in the main plaza you can *only* phone La Paz. It's open from 8 am to noon and 2 to 10 pm, Monday to Saturday.

There are basically only two telephones in Coroico so to make hotel reservations, you

must phone COTEL (☎ 813260) and leave a message and your phone number. They'll contact the person or establishment you're wanting to speak with and have them phone you back.

Laundry Try the Lavandería Benedita on Avenida Monsignor Thomas Manning below the Hotel Prefectural.

Walks

For a good panoramic view of Coroico and the surrounding countryside, walk up to the Iglesia Calvario on the hill. From there, you can climb straight up to the summit of Cerro Uchumachi, but wait for a fine day or the spectacular view will be irrelevant. Alternatively, turn left at the church and follow a prominent trail that winds around the hillside. It follows a water pipe across some flowery hillsides, occasionally plunging into mini-rainforests. After two hours, you'll reach a refreshing waterfall above the village of Coripata.

The tracks leading down to the Río Coroico are more complicated and difficult to follow because part of the trip involves road walking. The easiest one leads from the north-west corner of the plaza down to Puente Mururata. There are some lovely swimming holes just upstream from the bridge.

When walking through the bush, especially along the river track, use insect repellent and wear long trousers as protection against the nasty little yellow flies in this region that can make your life miserable for several days. On the brighter side of the insect world are the blue morphos and numerous other species of butterflies which are frequently observed on this walk. Watch also for toucans and other colourful tropical birds.

Horse Rental

French folk Dany and Patricio at Rancho Beni hire horses for B15 per hour. They're located beside the new hospital, about 20-minutes' walk uphill from the town centre. If you're arriving on a weekend, make reservations through Dolly Travel (☎ 373435, fax (591-2) 352906 La Paz), Avenida 20 de Octubre 2463, Casilla 14462, La Paz.

Places to Stay – bottom end

Hotels are completely booked out on Friday and Saturday nights, so make reservations in advance (see under Post & Telecommunications for instructions). On Monday, the town more or less closes down to recover from the Sunday tourist rush. Several lower-end Coroico hotels have swimming pools, but the colour of the water will limit your appreciation of them: they're not exactly brilliant chlorine blue.

The *Hostal Kory* is quick to point out that *kory* means 'gold' in Quechua and from the look of things, it lives up to its name! The view, which includes everything between the valleys and the cordillera peaks, makes it the travellers' favourite in Coroico. Rooms cost B12 per person, showers are good and hot and there's a swimming pool available to guests. Unfortunately, there's been some robbery reported and things have gone missing from the laundry line. Take care with your valuables.

The new *Residencial La Casa* just below the Restaurant La Casa is exceptionally clean and offers rooms with shared bath for B10 per person.

Another favourite is the German-run *Hostal Sol y Luna*, which has a luxuriant garden setting, 30 minutes' walk from town. Double cabañas cost B30; each additional person is B10 extra. Dorm rooms with sheets included cost B6 per person, and campsites are B4 per person. You'll enjoy the novel open-air showers, the swimming pool and the breezy snack-bar area. The owner, Sigrid Fronius, will provide 50 minutes of Japanese massage (nirvana for those coming off the Choro Trek!) for B20. Book at least a week in advance through Dolly Travel (☎ 373435, fax (591-2) 352906), La Paz.

Although it's gone downhill, the *Hotel Lluvia de Oro* is still hanging in there with its sundeck, patio, green swimming pool and faded garden. They've installed electric hot showers, but you can forget about the restaurant. Rooms cost B16/25 for a single/double with bath or B8 single without bath. Quite a bit better is the friendly *Residencial 2 de Febrero* attached to the Las Peñas restaurant. On weekends they charge B10/16 for a single/double; the rest of the week it's B8/15.

The very basic *Alojamiento Paiyuan* has a good view and could be used as a last resort, but it's not recommended. Rooms cost B5 per person without hot water. Similarly, the *Residencial Coroico* is another bottom-of-the-barrel option. Rooms cost B8 per person, but the showers don't work and it's grimy. The best low-budget choice is the *Alojamiento* beside the Veloz del Norte bus terminal. It's clean and sunny, and costs only B7 per person.

Places to Stay – middle

The large red-roofed *Hotel Prefectural* (☎ 312391, La Paz) is downhill from town near the football pitch. It gets two stars under the Bolivian rating system and the view is nearly as good as the Hostal Kory's. Unfortunately, there are two rooms per bath and the room doors don't lock; one couple reported drunks wandering into their room at night. With the three-meal plan, rooms cost B50 per person, or without the meal plan, B20. A double bed costs B35.

A new addition to Coroico's hotel scene is the *Hotel Don Quijote*, 700 metres from town. It looks more expensive than it is; rooms cost only B44 per person with a three-meal plan or B20 per person excluding food. It's friendly, quiet and super clean. Book through Flamingo Tours (☎ 358723) in La Paz.

Camping

Secluded spots may be found near the church on the hill above town. *Hostal Sol y Luna* has campsites for B4 per person.

Places to Eat

Food fans will have plenty of choices in Coroico and may want to stick around long enough to exhaust all the possibilities.

The German/Bolivian-run *Restaurant La Casa* down the stairs from Coroico's main plaza is as fondly anticipated by foreign visitors as the Madres de Clarisa Convent just opposite it! For breakfasts, fondues, coffee, chocolate, pancakes, and local or continental dishes, it's hard to beat. If you're geared up for fondue, you'll need a minimum of two people and an advance booking. A wonderful fondue bourguignonne or raclette costs just B18 per person, including a range of salads and appetisers! Like most things in Coroico, La Casa is closed on Mondays.

Almost as good is the laid-back dining room cum travellers' rap session at the Hostal Kory, the place to go if you're after a dozen tales of the La Cumbre to Coroico Trek. Recommended specialities include Yungas coffee, American breakfast, fish, spaghetti alla carbonara and that ubiquitous travellers' icon, the banana pancake.

Along the road to Caranavi 100 metres out of town is the rather ethereal outdoor garden restaurant, *El Rodeo*. Diners overlook one of Bolivia's most memorable views with orchestration provided by flocks of resident turkeys, chickens and ducks and a couple of clearly disturbed dogs. It's open for lunch and dinner and offers exceptional food for ordinary prices. As with most Coroico restaurants, the coffee is great. We recommend the chop suey, Spanish tortillas, stir-fry enchilada and filet mignon.

An extraordinary treat if you have a group – or can muster one – is the *luna llena*, an Indonesian buffet for eight to 20 people at the German-run *Sol y Luna* on the hill. It costs an accessible B9 per person, but must be booked a day in advance.

Another foreign option up the hillside is the French-run *Rancho Beni*, which has an inspiring view and a verdant open-air setting. Here Dany and Patricio serve up superb Yungas coffee, chocolate mousse, cakes and other goodies.

The *Madres de Clarisa Convent* opposite Restaurant La Casa is renowned for its delicious brownies, orange cakes, peanut butter, biscuits (chocolate, vanilla, coconut, honey and peanut butter!) and local wines. It's open from 8 am to 8 pm; knock on the door and they'll let you into the shop area.

An inexpensive local place with pretty good food and an ordinary menu is the *Safari Restaurant & Disco* at the Veloz del Norte bus terminal. Alternatively, make a selection from the crop of food stalls in the Comedor

Municipal. You'll find good vegetarian food as well as standard Bolivian favourites.

Getting There & Away

The Yungas Road Although rumour has it that a road more terrifying than the one between La Paz and the Yungas exists somewhere in Zanskar or Bhutan, we won't believe it until we see it.

Those up for an adrenalin rush will be in their element, but if you're unnerved by unsurfaced roads just wide enough for one vehicle, sheer 1000-metre dropoffs, hulking rock overhangs and waterfalls which spill across and erode away the highway, your best bet is either to walk to Coroico or to bury your head and don't look until it's over. There may be some comfort in taking a minibus; they're smaller and therefore presumably safer than camiones or even buses.

Upon leaving La Paz to cross La Cumbre, you'll notice a most curious phenomenon: various and sundry dogs are posted at 100-metre intervals like sentinels, presumably awaiting handouts. Camión drivers feed them in hopes that the *achachilas* (mountain gods) will encourage gravity to be merciful during their trip down. At La Cumbre, drivers also perform a cha'lla for the achachilas, sprinkling the vehicle's tyres with alcohol or meths before beginning their descent.

Perhaps it's these insurance policies that encourage drivers to travel at often suicidal speeds with horns blaring, brakes squealing and loads lurching out over the Great Abyss. A number of crosses, described as 'Bolivian *Caution* signs', line the way and testify to frequent tragedies. The most renowned took place on 24 July 1983, when driver Carlos Pizarroso Inde drove his camión over the precipice, killing himself and more than 100 passengers. It was the worst accident in the history of Bolivian transport.

Those who do travel in an open camión and keep their eyes open will be rewarded with some of the most stunning vertical scenery South America has to offer. Take an arctic-to-tropical range of clothing and raingear for drenching mists and waterfalls;

the road drops (or gains) 3000 metres during the two-hour trip between La Cumbre and Coroico!

NB: Although Bolivian traffic normally keeps to the right, oncoming traffic on the Yungas road passes on the left. That is, downhill traffic must manoeuvre onto the precarious turnout ledges and wait while uphill traffic squeezes past, hugging the cliff. If you're driving, don't become confused!

Bus All companies charge B12 for the 3½-hour trip to or from La Paz. Flota Yungueña does the run to Coroico on Tuesday, Thursday, Friday and Saturday at 8.30 am. On other days, take any Caranavi bus, get off at Yolosa and catch a lift the seven km uphill to Coroico.

Because Coroico is so popular, it's a notorious place for getting stuck; if you want to leave on a Sunday bus, reserve a place the moment you arrive (otherwise, you may have to rely on camiones). Flota Yungueña goes to La Paz on Monday, Wednesday and Friday at 8 am, and on Sunday at 1 pm. Their office is in the Comedor Municipal which is open 2 to 5 pm and 7 to 9 pm.

Trans-Yungas leaves for La Paz on Sunday at 2.30 pm and Flota 16 de Noviembre leaves on Sunday at 1.30 pm. Veloz del Norte goes to La Paz daily at 2.30 pm and Arapata minibuses leave at 8 am on Thursday. Trans-Yungas is your easiest bet for getting to Caranavi.

Guests at the Hotel Prefectural have access to the Trans Tours minibuses which provide transport to and from La Paz daily. The bus leaves Coroico at 9 am and returns in the afternoon, departing La Paz at 3 pm; the fare is B13 per person. For reservations phone La Paz: ☎ 312391.

Camión Camiones from La Paz to Coroico leave regularly until mid-afternoon from the street behind the Villa Fátima petrol station.

From Coroico, the first step is getting to Yolosa. All vehicles headed down the hill must stop at the tranca office near the town entrance so it's best to wait there for a lift. Drivers all seem to stop for a snack in Yolosa, so if your lift isn't carrying on to your destination, this is a good opportunity to chat with other drivers about onward lifts. There should be no problem finding transport to Caranavi, Guanay or La Paz, but to Puerto Linares you'll first have to go to Caranavi and then find another vehicle from there.

To reach Chulumani, head back toward La Paz and change vehicles at the bleak Chuspipata road junction. For a trip through Bolivia's main coca-growing region, take a camión from Yolosa to Arapata, another from Arapata to Coripata, and yet another to Chulumani. Don't be in too much of a hurry.

Walking Many people walk to Coroico from La Cumbre. For details, see the La Cumbre to Coroico Trek described earlier in this chapter.

TAQUESI TREK

Also known as the Inca Trail or Inca Road, the Taquesi Trek is one of the most popular walks in the Andes. The route was used as a highway not only by the early Aymará but also by the Incas and the Spanish, and it still serves as a major route to the humid Yungas over a relatively low pass in the Cordillera Real. Nearly half the trail's 40 km consists of expertly engineered pre-Inca paving, more like a highway than a walking track. The walk itself will take only 12 to 14 hours, but it's best to plan on several days due to transport uncertainties to and from the trailheads.

Naturally, the dry season between May and October is best for this trip. In the rainy season, the wet and cold combined with ankle-deep mud may contribute to a less-than-optimum experience. Since trail's end is in the Yungas, however, plan on some rain at all times of the year.

Access

The easiest way to reach the upper trailhead is to hire a long-distance taxi at the Centro de Taxis near Plaza Isabel la Católica on Avenida Aniceto Arce in La Paz. They'll charge a reasonable B50 for up to four people

all the way to the trailhead near the San Francisco mine.

If you prefer to use buses and camiones, your first destination will be Ventilla. There's an elusive Bolsa Negra bus which leaves for Ventilla and Bolsa Negra between 9 and 9.30 am from Plaza Belzú in Barrio Belén, just two blocks uphill from the main La Paz post office. There are no signs announcing your arrival in Ventilla so make sure the driver – and anyone else you may want to tell – knows that that's where you want to get off.

Another option is to take micro 'Ñ' from Plaza Murillo in La Paz to the Ovejura tranca or Chasquipampa. From there, you can either hope for a lift along the road or trek through the beautiful Valle de las Ánimas (Valley of the Spirits) and Cañón del Huaricunca (Palca Canyon) to Palca and then to Ventilla. This route, which will add an extra day to the trip, is outlined in the Around La Paz section of the La Paz chapter.

Transport is sparse between Ventilla and the San Francisco mine at the start of the Taquesi Trek so it's best to begin walking. If you're extremely lucky, a vehicle may pass and offer a lift.

The Route

About 150 metres beyond Ventilla, take a left turn and follow the rough road uphill toward the San Francisco mine. After 1½ hours of climbing, you'll reach the village of Choquekhota which may remind you of something in the remotest regions of North Wales. On foot, it's another two to 2½ hours of climbing to the trailhead. Shortly after a stream crossing, the main road continues another km to the San Francisco mine but you should turn right onto a smaller track.

After an hour of climbing, you'll reach the final ascent, a switchbacking half-hour climb to the pass at 4650 metres. There, you'll find the *apacheta* (travellers' rock pile) and a spectacular view of 5868-metre Nevado Mururata. Just beyond is a mine tunnel which may be explored with a torch. If you've walked all the way from Ventilla, you may want to camp the first

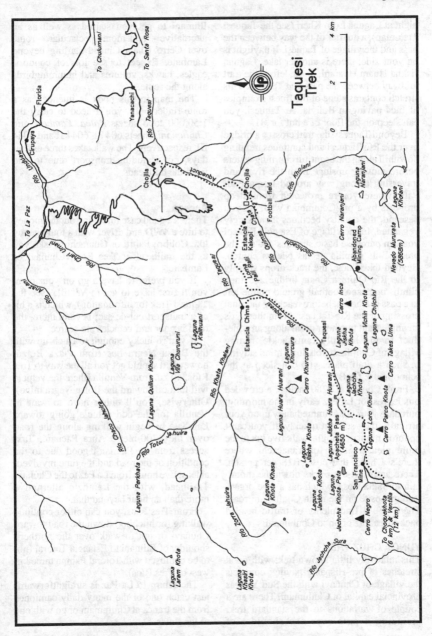

Taquesi Trek

4 km
3
2
1
0

To Chulumani
To Santa Rosa
Florida
To La Paz
Cirupaya
Yanacachi
Río Taquesi
Río Unduavi
Cholla
Río Chari Umani
Río Anazani
Aqueduct
Choquekota
Río Kholani
Laguna Naranjani
Laguna Kholani
Football field
Estancia Kakapi
Loma Palli
Palli Khota
Río Quimsa Chata
Río Sochocachi
Cerro Naranjani
Abandoned Mining Camp
Nevado Mururata (5868m)
Cerro Inca
Laguna Chijchini
Cerro Vichin Khota
Cerro Takes Uma
Laguna Murata
Estancia Chima
Río Taquesi (Jankhuni)
Taquesi
Laguna Jiska Khota
Laguna Khurcura
Laguna Huara Huarani
Cerro Khurcura
Laguna Jachcha Khota
Laguna Jiskha Huara Huarani
Cerro Parco Khota
Río Khala Khatari
Laguna Villa Chorurani
Laguna Kalihuani
Laguna Quillun Khota
Laguna Huara Huarani
Laguna Jiskha Khota
Apacheta Pass (4650 m)
Laguna Lara Kheri
Río Chaco Jahuira
Jahuira
Río Zora Jahuira
Río Totor
Laguna Perkhata
Laguna Khasa
Laguna Khota Khota
Laguna Jankho Khota
Laguna Jiskha Khota Pata
San Francisco Mine
Cerro Negro
To Choquekhota (6 km) & Ventilla (12 km)
Laguna Larum Khota
Laguna Khasiri Khota
Laguna Jachcha Sura

night at Laguna Loro Kheri (see the Taquesi Trek map), a quarter of the way between the pass and the village of Taquesi. If daylight is on your side, there is another lake, Laguna Jiskha Huara Huarani, to the left of the trail midway between the pass and Taquesi. This stretch contains some of the finest examples of Inca paving in Bolivia. At Taquesi, you can sleep on the floor of a hut for B1.

Beyond Taquesi, the trail crosses a bridge over the Río Taquesi and continues trending downhill along the beautiful churning waters before moving upslope from the river and traversing a long way around Loma Palli Palli where you're protected from steep dropoffs by a pre-Columbian wall. As you descend, the country becomes increasingly vegetated. In the village of Estancia Kakapi you can purchase basic supplies and see the pretty little Capilla de las Nieves church. Beyond the village, the track drops sharply to the Río Quimsa Chata bridge and then climbs up past a football ground on the left to a pass at Chojila, before reaching the final crossing of the Río Taquesi. From there, it's an unpleasant two hour grunt along an aqueduct to the horridly ramshackle mining village of Chojlla. If you don't mind staying in such a drab place, you can sleep at the schoolhouse for B1.

From Chojlla at 2280 metres, a crowded bus leaves for La Paz early in the morning; purchase your ticket immediately upon your arrival – they sell out quickly. If you can't endure a night in Chojlla, walk five km to the more pleasant town of Yanacachi where there's a hotel that costs B18 per person. There are short-cut tracks down the mountain to Santa Rosa, which has a nice organised campsite on the main Chulumani road. There you'll find plenty of traffic headed back to La Paz or on to Chulumani.

YUNGA CRUZ TREK

This relatively little known trek, with good stretches of pre-Hispanic paving, connects the village of Chuñavi with the Sud Yungas provincial capital of Chulumani. There are a couple of variations to the standard trek, including a pass over one shoulder of

Illimani to get you started as well as an alternative – and more spectacular – route over Cerro Khala Ciudad starting beyond Lambate. Expect to see lots of condors, eagles, hawks, vultures and hummingbirds along the route.

The map in this book is intended as a route-finder only; you'll need to carry the 1:50,000 topo sheets *Palca*, *Lambate* and *Chulumani*, sheets 6044 I, 6044 II and 6044 III, respectively. The walk takes three or four days, not including transport time to and from the trailheads.

Access

There's a good case for laying out the money to hire a 4WD and driver with a tour agency like Colibri, Paititi or Guarachi to take you to the trailhead at Tres Ríos, Chuñavi or Lambate.

If you prefer to have a go on your own, you'll first have to get to Ventilla (see the Taquesi Trek for information), which is a bit of a transport cul-de-sac; beyond there, the road is poor and vehicles are scarce.

If you're lucky enough to catch up with the Bolsa Negra bus from Plaza Belzú, however, it should get you all the way to Tres Ríos, 40 km from Ventilla (there the vehicle will turn off toward the Bolsa Negra mine). Otherwise, you'll either have to wait in Ventilla for the odd vehicle going toward Lambate or begin walking along the road over the 4700-metre Abra Pacuani. Taxi access from La Paz isn't good due to the condition of the road and the time involved: at least five hours from La Paz to the Chuñavi Trailhead, with the Lambate alternative more than an hour beyond that.

From Tres Ríos, you can either continue walking (or hitching) down the road toward Chuñavi or opt to walk over the northern shoulder of Illimani to Estancia Totoral (not to be confused with Totoral Pampa three km west of Tres Ríos).

The return to La Paz is straightforward; just catch one of the many daily camiones from the tranca at Chulumani or go with one of the flotas.

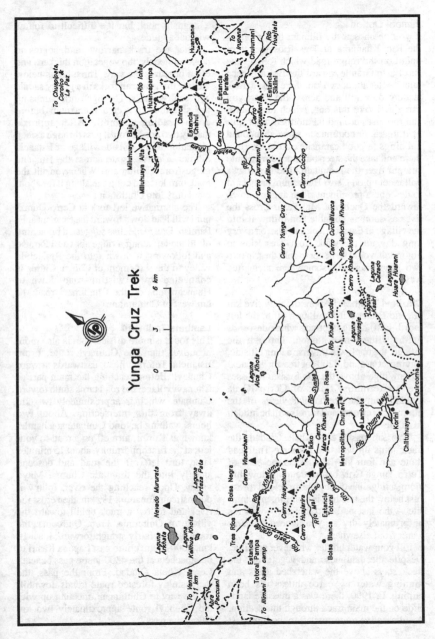

Yunga Cruz Trek

0   3   6 km

Illimani Option

If you've chosen the Illimani option, cross the Río Khañuma at Tres Ríos then turn uphill on the rough road which follows the Río Pasto Grande toward the Bolsa Blanca mine. After about two km, there'll be a track leading downhill and across the river; you can either take this one, which turns north and traverses around the northernmost spur of Illimani, or continue to some abandoned buildings (a good campsite), cross the river there and take the steep but more direct route straight over the mountain. The two tracks will meet up on Cerro Huaychuni and begin to descend a prominent ridge angling down toward the Quebrada Mal Paso. Cross the river as soon as possible and follow it into the village of Estancia Totoral. Plan on a very long day for the walk from Tres Ríos to Totoral; it would be better to split the trip into two days, camping somewhere along the way.

Chuñavi Trailhead Approximately five km beyond Estancia Totoral, turn off to the left (north-east) along the track which descends to the village of Chuñavi. Through the village, the track will traverse a long hillside, staying at around 4200 metres for the next 30 km, high above the Río Susisa. It passes the westernmost flank of Cerro Khala Ciudad, but the spectacular views of the mountain's cirques and turrets will be hidden from view.

Two km past Cerro Khala Ciudad, the track joins up with the Lambate Trailhead route and four km later, skirts the peak of Cerro Yunga Cruz before trending downhill along a ridgeline through heavy cloud forest. Just below the tree line is a prominent campsite – the last before trail's end – but it's unfortunately dry so you'll need to carry water from elsewhere.

Fill your water bottles whenever possible. Despite the dampness and vegetation, the track stays above the watershed areas and running water is scarce unless it's been raining. In 1990, there was a massive landslide on the main track through this section. An alternative route cuts off to the right past a stagnant pool, but it's difficult to follow without a guide.

After the track narrows and begins to descend steeply, the vegetation thickens and often obscures the way. Three hours below the tree line, the trail forks in a grassy saddle between two hills. The right fork climbs up the shoulder of Cerro Duraznuni before again heading downhill. After approximately two hours, you'll pass through a steep plantation to the hillside village of Estancia Sikilini, a citrus estate across the Huajtata gorge from Chulumani. When you hit the road, turn left and continue along it for about two hours into Chulumani.

The alternative left fork at Cerro Duraznuni will lead down toward the estancia at El Paraíso. One reader has suggested branching off to the left along a ridge above El Paraíso and following it down into the Río Ichila valley to the settlement of Chirca. Chirca is connected by a twisting road down to Huancapampa on the Chulumani road, 12 km west of Chulumani.

Lambate Trailhead

This route is more difficult but is also more beautiful than the Chuñavi route. From Estancia Totoral, head eastwards toward Chuñavi. Before reaching the main part of Chuñavi village, the road turns south toward Lambate, which is approximately two km away from this intersection. About two hours' walking beyond Lambate at a hamlet known as Korini, turn off on a road to your left; at the first opportunity, about 15 minutes later, turn left off the road and descend steeply into the dramatic Chunga Mayu valley. Upon reaching the river, follow it downstream for about 1½ km, then cross the river and follow a track uphill toward the village of Quircoma. From Quircoma, the route will be fairly straightforward; it's a 10 km, 2000-metre climb past Laguna Kasiri to the apacheta at the 4300-metre pass beneath Cerro Khala Ciudad. From the pass, the increasingly forested route trends downhill all the way to Chulumani, meeting up with the Chuñavi route approximately two km below the pass.

CHULUMANI

Chulumani, the capital of Sud Yungas, is another relaxing town with a view, and is a centre for growing coffee, bananas and Yungas coca. Locals claim the town's name is derived from *Cholumanya* (Tiger's Dew), to commemorate a jaguar's visit to the town's well...hmmm, maybe.

Rebels during the 1781 La Paz revolt escaped to the Yungas and hid out in the valleys around Chulumani until things calmed down. There is large population of African-Bolivians living in the Chulumani area, descendants of the slaves brought to work in the Potosí mines.

Currently the town sees very few visitors except during the week following 24 August when the town stages the Fiesta de San Bartolomé and lots of highlanders turn up to join in the festivities.

For those with some time to spare, one reader has recommended the two to three-hour (each way) walk from Chulumani along

the Irupana road to the lovely village of Ocabaya.

Places to Stay

The *Hotel Bolivar* just up from the main plaza is clean and costs B10 per person. They have cold showers but often there's no water at all. The *Hotel García* is a very friendly place and has a nice restaurant on the terrace overlooking the surrounding countryside. Rooms with private bath cost B18 per person.

The friendly *Residencial El Milagro* is quite pleasant with a beautiful garden, an antique-furnished reception area and a great view. A one or two-bed double costs B50 with a private bath and a room with six beds and a bath goes for B110. There are no single rooms.

At B18 per person, the *Hotel Prefectural* below the market is bearable but lacks character. Reservations should be made in La Paz at least two days in advance. The hotel office

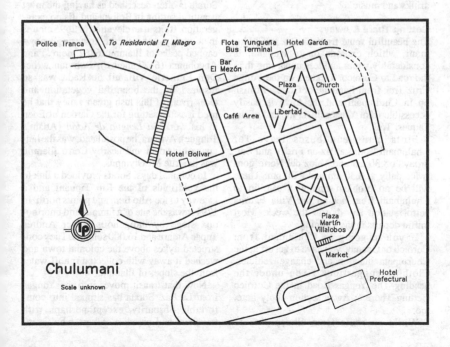

Chulumani

Scale unknown

(☎ 374586) is on the 2nd floor of the La Paz Prefectura at the corner of Calle Comercio and Calle Ayacucho.

The most upmarket option is the *Hotel San Bartolomé*, which provides minibus transport from La Paz on weekends. It may be booked through the Hotel Plaza (☎ 378314) in La Paz.

Places to Eat

The market in Chulumani may well be the cleanest in Bolivia. It's especially good for breakfast, as local coffee is available, but if you're not a coffee fan, try their delicious cocoa.

The restaurant at the *Hotel García* serves all the Bolivian stand-bys, and is probably the best in town. Prices are reasonable for the quality and their patio dining room overlooks a very pastoral slice of the Yungas.

Numerous small cafés are scattered around and just uphill from the Plaza Libertad. *Bar El Mezón* is recommended for drinks and music.

Getting There & Away

The beautiful route from La Paz to Chulumani, which extends on to Irupana, is considerably wider and less unnerving than the road to Coroico. Trekkers on the Yunga Cruz Trek from Lambate or Chuñavi finish up in Chulumani and the town is easily accessible from Yanacachi, at the end of the Taquesi Trek.

Flota Yungueña buses leave for Chulumani from La Paz on Friday and Saturday at 8.30 am and Veloz del Norte goes twice daily at 8.30 am and 2.30 pm. There will be no problem finding a camión to Chulumani from behind the Villa Fátima petrol station any day of the week. Most traffic departs in the morning.

If you're going to Chulumani from Coroico or Guanay, you have to get off at the Chuspipata junction and change vehicles. Clothing suggestions given under the heading The Yungas Road in the Coroico Getting There & Away section apply here, too.

While en route from Chuspipata to Chulumani, keep an eye out for the wispy Bridal Veil Falls on the left side of the road and the unusual Castillo El Chaco, a castle-like home 60 km from the Chuspipata junction.

Camiones from Chulumani to La Paz or other Yungas towns may be boarded at the tranca near the Residencial El Milagro. The trip takes eight or nine hours. Once again, be sure to have proper highland clothing on hand before setting out.

PUENTE VILLA

The small village of Puente Villa lies at the intersection of the La Paz and Coripata roads, 30 km from Chulumani. The only reason to stop there is to stay at the Hotel Tamampaya, the Yungas' nicest hotel and an affordable place to relax and soak up some serenity. To make a reservation, contact Safra Limitada, Casilla 1314, La Paz.

SORATA

Sorata is often described as having the most beautiful setting in Bolivia and it's no exaggeration. It sits at an elevation of 2695 metres in a valley beneath the towering snow-capped peaks of Illampú (6362 metres) and Ancohuma (6427 metres). Bolivian writer Don Emiterio Villamil de Rada was so inspired by the bountiful vegetation and clear rivers of this lush green valley that he used it as the setting for the Garden of Eden in his work *La Lengua de Adán* (Adam's Tongue). Aymará, he postulated, was the language of Adam and nearby Cerro Illampú was the true Mt Olympus.

In colonial days, Sorata provided a link to the goldfields of the Río Tipuani and a gateway to the Alto Beni and points north. In 1791 it was the site of a famous and unorthodox siege by indigenous leader Andrés Tupac Amaru and 16,000 soldiers. They constructed dykes above the colonial town and washed it away with collected runoff water from the slopes of Illampú.

Now that transit moves into the Yungas from La Paz, Sorata has slipped into comfortable obscurity, except perhaps with travellers and paradise-seekers who've re-routed the Gringo trail to include this formerly off-the-beaten-track destination. We've never met anyone who doesn't like the place.

Sunday is market day in the town, and the main fiesta, a riotous affair, is held on 14 September.

Gruta de San Pedro

Most visitors make a daytrip of the 10-km hike to the Gruta de San Pedro (San Pedro Cave) near the village of San Pedro, two to 2½-hours walk from Sorata. To get there, walk downhill from Sorata's main plaza. The street becomes a winding rocky trail which will take you to the village of San Pedro; you've arrived when you see the village church and football pitch. The cave is about 1 km beyond the village, 15 metres above the new jeep track (the construction of which is making a rocky mess of the walking route). There's always someone on hand to rent a torch. Expect to pay about B1.50.

From the entrance, you can walk several hundred metres to a cold underground lake which impedes further exploration. Watch out for the cave's batty residents.

Club Sorata

Club Sorata at the Hotel Copacabana is the local branch of Club Andino Boliviano. The Swiss and Norwegian guides at the club lead walking and trekking expeditions for B35 per person per day, including food. They've done a lot of research and come up with a variety of three to seven-day trekking options from Sorata. The club sells maps and hires camping and climbing equipment, including mountain bikes. If you prefer to strike out on your own, they're happy to provide directions and other information about the most popular trips.

If your time is limited, an exhausting but recommended 12-hour return hike will take you to the beautiful sacred lake, Laguna Chilata (Inca Marka in Aymará), surrounded by peaks and glaciers. Locals tend to be quite sensitive about this glorious place so it's best to go with an organised group and to tread as lightly as possible.

Mountaineering

Sorata is the base to use for scaling Illampú (known as Hualpacayo (Hen's foot), in Aymará), or Ancohuma. For more info on Ancohuma, see the Climbing in the Cordillera Real section near the end of this chapter. Your best sources of information will be the Club Sorata guides or Edward at Hotel Copacabana.

Places to Stay

Sorata's most popular travellers' digs is the German-run *Hotel. Copacabana* downhill from the plaza on the route to San Pedro. It boasts hot showers, excellent food and a swimming pool nearby. The clean rooms are a bargain at B9 per person. Owners Edward and Diana are video fiends and their growing collection is available to guests who are tired of the great outdoors and want a bit of couch potato-type vegetation. Only hotel guests are welcome to partake but if you're desperate, offer a couple of bolivianos and see what happens!

Another good option is the *Hotel Paraíso* near the plaza which offers comfortable rooms with private bath for B16 per person. The *Hotel San Cristóbal* charges B6 per person with good food and cold water. *Hotel Central* on the plaza is even cheaper at B5 per person but the showers are dodgy.

The *Residencial Sorata*, in a rotting old mansion just off the main plaza, is a bit grimy around the edges these days but the owner is friendly. There's a nice garden and a great view of the cordillera. Rooms cost B8 per person with communal bath only.

Places to Eat

If you're after quality, shell out for the restaurant at the Hotel Copacabana. If your budget doesn't stretch that far, go for the small inexpensive restaurants around the plaza; a filling set meal will cost only B2.50. The Hotel Paraíso restaurant has also been recommended.

As we were going to press, Italian reader Mario Morpurgo wrote to recommend Sorata's newly opened *Ristorante Italiano*. It's run by a 'friendly gentleman from

Bologna who offers Italian cuisine and even a good espresso in a paradise-like garden with orange trees and grape vines'. Sounds irresistible.

Getting There & Away

Sorata is a long way from the other Yungas towns. There's no road connecting it directly with Coroico or Chulumani, so access from La Paz is a 4½-hour trip via Huarina and Achacachi near Lake Titicaca. From La Paz, Transportes Larecaja leaves for Sorata from Calle Angel Babia 1556 near the cemetery at 6.30 and 7 am daily and returns to La Paz from Sorata's main plaza, departing at 12.30 pm. Going either direction, buses get crowded so arrive as early as possible. Tickets go on sale at 2 pm the previous day and cost B10.

Alternatively go to Huarina near Lake Titicaca on the Huatajata or Copacabana bus and catch a camión bound for Sorata. If you're going to Copacabana from Sorata, take the La Paz bus as far as Huarina (unfortunately, you'll have to pay the full La Paz fare) and connect with a Copacabana-bound bus at the Huarina police tranca.

EL CAMINO DE ORO (THE GOLD TRAIL)

If the current road-building trend continues, the popular trek between Sorata or Ancoma and the Río Tipuani goldfields may last only a few more years. This Inca road has been used for nearly 1000 years as a commerce and trade link between the Altiplano and the lowland goldfields. Indeed, the Tipuani and Mapiri valleys were major sources of the gold that once adorned the Inca capital at Cuzco.

Today, however, the fields are worked primarily by bulldozers and dredges owned by mining cooperatives. They scour and scrape the landscape for the shiny stuff and dump the detritus which is picked over by out-of-work Aymará refugees from the highlands. Horrid little settlements of plastic, banana leaves and sheet aluminium have sprung up along the rivers, the banks of which are staked out for panning by wildcat miners. It's projected that gold will soon replace tin as

Bolivia's greatest source of mineral export income.

Fortunately, the upper part of the route remains magnificent and nearly everything above Chusi has been left alone, including some wonderfully exhausting Inca staircases and dilapidated ancient highway engineering. When planning your schedule, keep in mind that this trek is more challenging than the Taquesi, La Cumbre to Coroico, or Yunga Cruz routes; if you want to get the most from it, plan on six or seven days' walking between Sorata and Llipi, less if you opt for a jeep to Ancoma. At Llipi, you should find transport to Tipuani or Guanay so as to avoid a walking pace tour through the worst of the destruction.

Although it's unlikely the road will push up the valley as far as Ancoma, the aesthetics of the lower valley and its landscape have already been irreparably scarred and eroded by large-scale mining and road building. A new mining cooperative has started up at Wainapata near the trail's halfway mark; this may well be the road's ultimate destination.

Access

Due to its downhill trending, nearly everyone does the route from Sorata down the valley to Tipuani and Guanay. It's a shame, too, because the end of the walk passes through largely devastated landscapes and some of the ugliest settlements imaginable. Nevertheless, we'll be true to tradition and describe the walk from the top down. You may want to consider doing it in reverse.

For the route between Sorata and Ancoma there are three options. First, you can hire a jeep in Sorata and cut at least two days off the trek. Second, for a more challenging alternative, you may prefer to walk the very steep route from Sorata up the Río Challasuy to the 4800-metre pass four hours above Ancoma. The third option is to strike out from Sorata along the slightly shorter track leading to the village of Lacathiya, trek over the 4741-metre Abra de Illampú and meet up with the road about 1½ hours above Ancoma.

Allow a minimum of two days for either

El Camino de Oro
(The Gold Trail)

Not to scale

of the latter options and seek advice on routes and conditions at Hotel Copacabana or Club Sorata (see under Sorata for further information) before setting out.

The Route

Once you're in Ancoma, the route is fairly straightforward. Leave the jeep track and follow the trail along the southern bank of the Río Tipuani. At a wide spot called Llallajta, about half a day's walk below Ancoma, it crosses a bridge and briefly follows the north bank before recrossing the river and heading toward Sumata. Another

Inca-engineered diversion to the north bank has been avoided by bridge washouts, forcing hikers to follow a spontaneously constructed but thankfully brief detour above the southern bank. Just beyond is the village of Sumata. A couple of hours later you'll reach Wainapata, and an hour beyond there, passing through lush vegetation, you'll reach an interesting ancient tunnel drilled through rock. There's a campsite at Pampa Quillapituni, half an hour further along.

Four hours after crossing the swinging bridge at the Río Cooco you'll reach the new settlement of Mina Yuna where the trail is routed through a less-than-inspiring mine pit. An hour further down is Chusi, just four hours before your first encounter with the road. As you follow the road, the scene grows increasingly depressing. For a final look at relatively unaffected landscape, take the shortcut trail to the Río Santa Ana toll bridge. It issues back onto the road at Baja Llipi. Pay your B1 to cross, climb up the hill and look for camionetas or land cruiser transport to Tipuani and Guanay. Camionetas between the Río Santa Ana bridge and Unutuluni cost B5 per person; to continue on to Tipuani or Guanay is an additional B15.

Basic supplies are available at Ancoma, Wainapata, Mina Yuna, Chusi and Llipi, as well as all the lower settlements along the road. Spartan accommodation may be found in Unutuluni, Chima (more rough and ready than most and not recommended!), Tipuani and Guanay, all of which are along the road.

There's been word that an alternative Inca trekking route from Sorata to Guanay is currently receiving attention and that a jeep track has now been bulldozed through to the lowland gold-mining settlement of Mapiri. The route reportedly strikes out from Consata (accessed from Sorata via Quillabaya) and follows the Río Mapiri to the town of the same name. The major drawbacks seem to be horrendous mud, road construction and some hairy unbridged river crossings. If you can get a jeep as far as Consata, the trip to Mapiri should entail about five days' walking. From there, you can hire a motorised dugout down the river to Guanay.

GUANAY

Guanay serves as a base for interesting excursions into some of the gold-mining operations along the Río Mapiri and Río Tipuani. The miners and panners along the way are generally relaxed and courteous and if you can excuse the utter rape of the landscape they've perpetrated for the sake of gold, a visit will prove an interesting experience.

Guanay and points upriver are certainly frontier settlements, and few visitors fail to be reminded of the Old West of film and legend. Gold is legal tender and saloons, gambling, prostitutes and large hunks of beef seem to form the foundations of local culture.

River Trips

Access to the gold-mining areas is by jeep up the road toward Llipi on the Río Tipuani or by motorised dugout canoes which may be hired in Guanay for travel up the Río Mapiri. The Mapiri trip is easier to organise because boats leave more or less daily. The trip to Mapiri takes five hours upstream and costs B35 per person. The three-hour trip back to Guanay costs only B25. The river passes through dense jungle, and some sort of insect repellent is necessary. If you want to spend the night, Mapiri has a pleasant alojamiento.

Places to Stay & Eat

The *Hotel Estrella Azul*, which has clean, inexpensive rooms, is probably the nicest place in town. *Hotel Los Pinos* and *Hotel Santos* are also fine, but avoid *Hotel Mexico*; it's a real dump.

For large steaks and fresh juices, try *Las Parrilladas* on the road which leads down to the port. *Lila's* between the Hotel Mexico and the port has also been recommended.

Getting There & Away

Bus Flota Velóz del Norte in the La Paz suburb of Villa Fátima serves Caranavi and Guanay twice daily at 8.30 am and 2.30 pm, but camión traffic is plentiful and less expensive. From La Paz to Caranavi takes seven hours, then it's four more hours to Guanay. A road now links Caranavi with Rurrenabaque, Riberalta and Guayaramerín.

Walking For information on the walking track from Sorata, see the Camino de Oro trek description earlier in this chapter.

A jeep track has reportedly been bulldozed through to Consata and Sorata but transport is highly unreliable. Alternatively, a recently cleared Inca trail links Mapiri with the highlands.

Boat From Guanay, it is possible to travel by outboard canoe down the Río Beni to Rurrenabaque; make arrangements through the Agencia Fluvial in Guanay. These canoes will generally accommodate up to 10 people and their luggage, but the fewer the passengers, the more comfortable the trip will be. It's probably best to insist on paying half the fare in advance and half once you've arrived, or they'll continuously pick up and crowd in more passengers.

On river runs between Guanay and Rurrenabaque, make it absolutely clear to the boat owner/captain that you expect to arrive the same day or you will pay less for the passage. Boat owners are notorious for making very short-lived departure-time promises.

When the owner of our boat decided all gringos are not created equal, charging more for some of us than others, we switched to another boat whose owner promised a uniform lower price per head and 'immediate' departure.

We certainly did leave immediately – only to stop for two hours just five minutes downstream. Due to our turtle-like pace once we did depart, we didn't make Rurrenabaque that night and almost capsized in the pitch darkness trying to navigate over and around the many rockbeds of the river.

The 'captain' somehow managed to pull us off a particularly nasty rockbed and then led the boat to the riverbank. With no explanation at all, no apology, no nothin', we quickly realised we would be spending the night on the muddy bank. No one was prepared for this – some of us had no tent or sleeping provisions whatsoever.

We left at daybreak and reached Rurrenabaque by mid-morning. For the broken promise, disorganisation and a carelessness that could have ended in catastrophe, we jointly decided to lower the trip price by 25%. The captain was furious and went to the police, but we prevailed.

These guys have to be held accountable for their behaviour or they'll continue these dangerous games. The going rate was B700 to rent an entire boat for the normally 10-hour trip from Guanay to Rurrenabaque. Know the correct going rate! A group of Japanese tourists that preceded us forked over B1000 *each* for the trip.

Mark Stambovsky, USA

PUERTO LINARES

Although it was once a jumping-off point for river trips along the Río Beni to Rurrenabaque and Riberalta, cargo transport from Puerto Linares is now cut off by the Sapecho bridge near Caranavi. You can still arrange motorised canoe trips down the river from Puerto Linares, but there's no other reason to visit the area. To get there from La Paz, first take a bus or camión to Caranavi and find another camión to Puerto Linares from there.

CLIMBING IN THE CORDILLERA REAL

There are an increasing number of La Paz travel agencies which organise technical climbs and expeditions into the Cordillera Real and to Volcán Sajama near the Chilean border, Bolivia's highest peak. For a list of recommended agencies, see under Tours in the Getting Around chapter. Alternatively, contact the *American Alpine Institute* (☎ (206) 671-1505) at 1212 24th St, Bellingham, Washington 98225 USA.

In addition, Señor Alfredo Martinez Delgado (☎ 324682, home ☎ 300658) of the Club Andino Boliviano, one of Bolivia's foremost mountain guides, leads expeditions to all the higher peaks of the Cordillera Real for very reasonable rates: approximately B150 per day for up to four people. For the club address, see Hiking & Climbing Clubs under Activities in the La Paz chapter.

The following section is a rundown of some of the more popular climbs in the Cordillera Real. There are many other peaks to entice the experienced climber and whether you choose one of those described here or one of the lesser known and less travelled ones, climbing in the Bolivian mountains is always an adventure.

For further information on mountaineering in Bolivia, see the Hiking, Trekking & Mountaineering section in the Facts for the Visitor chapter. The Around La Paz map in the La Paz chapter can be used in conjunction with this section on the Cordillera Real.

Illimani

Illimani, the 6460-metre giant overlooking La Paz, is probably the most famous of Bolivia's peaks. It was first climbed by a party led by W M Conway, the pioneer alpinist of the 19th century. Although it's not a difficult climb, the combination of altitude and ice conditions warrant serious consideration and caution. Technical equipment should be used above the snow line; caution is especially warranted on the descent from the summit to Nido de Condores.

Access There are essentially two routes to the base camp from La Paz. The first is from Palca to Estancia Una and then cross country to the foot of the mountain. On your own, you can try to catch the buses and camiones which go several times weekly from Plaza Belzú to Estancia Una at around 6 am (expect to pay around B10 per person), then hire mules and porters for the three to four-hour walk via Estancia Pinaya to base camp. Club Andino Boliviano offers five-day expeditions, including transport between La Paz and Estancia Una, horse-packing to the base camp and a mountain guide on the climb.

More experienced mountaineers can make their own arrangements. For around B300 you can hire a 4WD and driver from the Guarachi, Colibri or Paititi agencies in La Paz (again, refer to Tours in the Getting Around chapter) to get you to Estancia Una or (by the second route) all the way to base camp.

The second route requires first going to Ventilla (see Access under the Taquesi Trek). If you manage to get the elusive Bolsa Negra bus, get off at the turnoff to the Urania mine, about 15 km east of Ventilla and four km east of Pacuani. Otherwise, you'll probably have to slog to the Urania turnoff: head east from Ventilla toward Estancia Totoral Pampa and upon reaching the turnoff, turn right and follow the deteriorated road. After about 27 km you'll arrive at base camp beside an old bridge with a hut ruin above. Here you can hire porters to carry your gear to the first night's camp at Nido de Condores. If there's snow, however, and you can't provide the porters with jackets and shoes – and you can't find any porters who have their own – you may want to forego this option.

The Route The normal climb is straightforward. Follow the faint path up through rock and scree to the major ridge between the glaciers. Stay to the right of the scree slope at first, then get onto the ridge crest. After about six to eight hours, you'll gain a plateau called Nido de Condores (Nest of the Condors; it's marked 'Campo de Nieve' on the 1:50,000 topo sheet), at 5600 metres. This is the normal camping spot.

The next day is more difficult and involves a two-hour ascent of a steep and narrow snow ridge. Exercise *extreme* caution in periods of low visibility; many of the deaths on Illimani have been in this section. At 6000 metres, you'll have to skirt a large icefall; the normal route around it seems to be on the left but we found a more direct bypass on the right. From the ridge top, turn south for an easy if breathless stroll to the summit, avoiding the yawning crevasses opening up to your right. Plan on about seven or eight hours for the climb from Nido de Condores to the summit.

Huayna Potosí

Huayna Potosí, 6088 metres high, is probably the most popular major peak in Bolivia due to ease of access and imposing beauty. It is also the easiest of the climbs described in this section, and is suitable for beginners, although prospective climbers will still require technical equipment: ropes, crampons, ice axes and knowledge of glacier travel technique.

Access Access is by taxi or by hitching on camiones which infrequently run to Milluni via El Alto above La Paz. From Milluni it's about six km to Abra Zongo (Zongo Pass) and another two to Laguna Zongo along a relatively well-travelled road. Club Andino Boliviano will provide transport to and from the base for B125 each way and also leads three-day expeditions to the summit.

The Route From the lake, cross the dam and follow the pipe through a boulder field to a creek flowing out of a small reservoir. It will ascend a moraine and then turn onto a slippery scree slope. Stay left of the icefall; after about 45 minutes following the cairns, you'll gain the glacier where you should rope up. Keep to the right and ascend the snow ridge.

Between 5500 and 5700 metres there are several places to camp (the higher ones receive more sun); the most popular is the plateau known as Campo Argentino about four hours from the base of the mountain.

It's about six hours from there to the summit, so get an early start. There are deep crevasses to the left of the route so it's a good idea to rope up and keep as far to the right as possible.

Condoriri

Condoriri is a beautifully sculpted mountain with twin wing-like ridges flowing from either side of the summit pyramid. At 5648 metres it is the smallest of the peaks discussed here, but arguably the most difficult. Without a vehicle, access is not easy.

Access Take a taxi or camión to Milluni via El Alto above La Paz. From there, charter a vehicle or walk 24 km west along the jeep track to Laguna Tuni. There's also a 17-km walking track to Laguna Tuni from Estancia Chaca Pampa in the Zongo valley, 12 km north of Laguna Zongo. Club Andino Boliviano in La Paz charges B180 for transport all the way to base camp.

The Route From Laguna Tuni, follow the rough road which circles south around the lake and continues up a drainage trending north. Follow this to a second lake where there are several good campsites. A saddle to the left (west) of the slopes above the lake will allow you to skip the icefall and thereby provides easy access to the glacier. Head back toward the summit pyramid to access a gully in front of the east face. This will take you through a rock band to a notch, and from there to the summit ridge and on to the top. The summit ridge is very exposed with huge, airy sheets of rime.

Ancohuma

This is the highest peak in the Sorata massif, towering 6427 metres on the remote northern edge of the Cordillera Real. It was not climbed until 1919 and still remains very challenging.

Access The peak is accessed via Sorata. From this lovely little town you can hire a jeep for the long traverse to the Candelaria mine where the fun begins. A few km beyond the mine is the quiet village of Cooco where a llama train can be hired to take you to the lake basin east of the peaks at about 4500 metres. It will take at least two days for these various transportation arrangements to get you to the lakes. Further advice and information are available in Sorata. For details, see under Sorata earlier in this chapter.

The Route From the lakes, head west up to the glacier following the drainage up through loose moraine. Camp should be made below the north ridge, the normal route. After a circuitous path through a crevasse field, a steep pitch or two of ice will gain the north ridge. An exposed but fairly easy ridge walk will take you to the summit.

A fascinating way back to La Paz is via the Camino de Oro, exposing an incredible cross-section of Bolivia from the glaciated heights to the jungle lowlands. For further information, see under El Camino de Oro earlier in this chapter. It's best to have the climbing gear sent back to Sorata so that you don't have to heave it all the way out the up-and-down route to Llipi.

Nevado Ancohuma

Cordillera Apolobamba

The remote Cordillera Apolobamba, hard by the Peruvian border north of Lake Titicaca, is slowly opening up as a new hiking, trekking and climbing option. It must be stressed, however, that this region remains extremely remote and isn't set up for tourism. There are no services to speak of, transport is sporadic at best and the people maintain a fragile traditional lifestyle. We highly recommend that visitors go only with an organised group.

If you're in the area around 5 August, try to arrange a visit to the village of Italaque, north-east of Escoma, for the Fiesta de La Virgen de las Nieves, which features a potpourri of traditional Andean dances: Kena Kenas, Morenos, Llameros, Choquelas, Kapñis, Jacha Sikuris, Chunchos, etc.

Charazani

Charazani, also known as Villa General José Perez, is the administrative town of Bautista Saavedra province. The surrounding area of the upper Charazani valley is the home of the Kallahuaya, the wandering medicine men who are versed in the art of natural healing with herbs, potions, amulets and incantations.

Hallmarks of the Kallahuaya are the *huincha*, the woven headband worn by women, and the *alforja* or medicine pouch carried by the men. The people of Charazani region are known for their colourful weavings which typically bear natural designs, both zoomorphic and anthropomorphic, and for their *llijllas*, striped women's shawls with bands of colour representing the landscape of the town of origin.

The Kallahuaya The origins and age of the Kallahuaya tradition are unknown, although some claim they are descended from the apparently vanished Tiahuanaco culture. The Kallahuaya language, however, which is used exclusively for healing, is derived from Quechua, the language of the Incas. Knowl-

edge and skills are passed down through generations, although it's sometimes possible for aspiring healers to study under acknowledged masters.

The early Kallahuaya were known for their wanderings and travelled all over the continent in search of medicinal herbs. The most capable of today's practitioners will have memorised the properties and uses of 600 to 1000 different healing herbs, but their practices also involve magic and charms. They believe that sickness and disease are the result of a displaced or imbalanced *ajallu* or 'life force'. The incantations and amulets are intended to encourage it back into a state of equilibrium within the body.

The Kallahuaya's legacy has been recorded by several anthropologists and medical professionals; German university psychiatrist Ina Rössing has produced an immense four-volume work called *El Mundo de los Kallahuaya* about her ongoing research and Frenchman Louis Girault has compiled an encyclopaedia of herbal remedies employed by the Kallahuaya entitled *Kallahuaya, Curanderos Itinerantes de los Andes*.

Places to Stay & Eat There's an alojamiento in Charazani on the plaza just to the right of the church. Basic food supplies are normally available but they arrive only sporadically, so carry reserves.

Getting There & Away Despite the number of foreign researchers passing through, very few locals speak Spanish and sensitivity to local culture is requisite in this highly traditional area. Individualised tours may be organised through any of the La Paz travel agencies which know the Cordillera Apolobamba. For suggestions, see under Tours in the Getting Around chapter.

You can also catch the Pelechuco camión (see the Pelechuco section later in this chapter), and get off at Abra Pumasani (this is the Charazani turnoff). From there, walk the long and winding 30 or so km to Charazani or try for a lift with the occasional

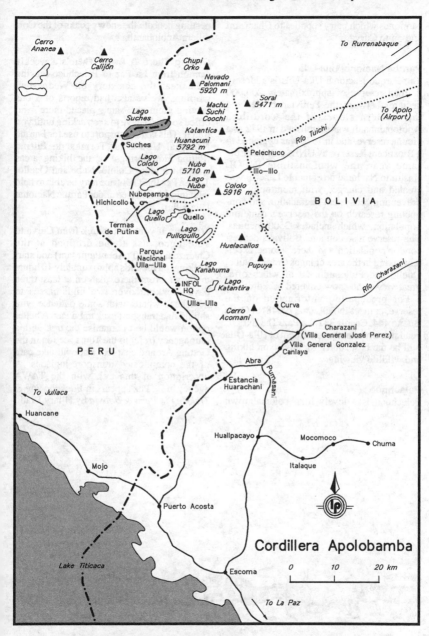

Cordillera Apolobamba

camiones which carry supplies to Charazani and on to Curva.

Parque Nacional Ulla-Ulla

The Parque Nacional Ulla-Ulla is a loosely defined reserve of approximately 200,000 hectares between the Peruvian border and the western slopes of the Cordillera Apolobamba. It was established in 1972 as a vicuña reserve, and in 1977 was upgraded to a Biosphere Reserve by UNESCO. Later the same year, the wool institute INFOL (Instituto Nacional de Fomento Lanero) was created and charged with monitoring and preventing ecosystem degradation and conducting research on the reserve's cameloid population, which includes 2500 vicuñas. The reserve also contains Bolivia's densest condor population and there's some excellent hiking in the area of lagos Cololo, Nube, Quello and Pullopullo, all of which offer great views and snow-covered backdrops.

For predeparture information on the reserve, contact INFOL (☎ 379048) at Calle Bueno 444, Casilla 732, La Paz. The INFOL headquarters near the settlement of Ulla-Ulla will be the best source for advice on hiking and wildlife viewing.

Pelechuco

Pelechuco is a lovely little colonial town nestling beneath the snowy peaks of the Cordillera Apolobamba.

Getting There & Away There's a weekly camión from La Paz to Pelechuco leaving from near the cemetery on Wednesday morning. We've also had reports of a bus leaving from the same place; there's no office so you'll have to keep asking until you find it. This is the transport to use for Parque Nacional Ulla-Ulla, Termas de Putina (Putina Hot Springs) or the hiking areas around the lagos Cololo, Nube and Quello. The La Paz INFOL office may be able to help with information (see under Parque Nacional Ulla-Ulla).

Trekking If you want to trek from Curva to Pelechuco, ask to be dropped at the Charazani turnoff (Abra Pumasani) and start walking; on foot, it's approximately 10 hours to Curva. From there, plan on at least three days' trekking over two high passes to Pelechuco where, with some patience, you should find transport back to La Paz. A better option would be to organise the trek with a tour agency (refer to the Tours section in the Getting Around chapter) who will take care of the complicated transport logistics. A description of this trek with the TAWA agency in La Paz appears in *Backpacking & Trekking in Peru & Bolivia* by Hilary Bradt.

Lake Titicaca

Lake Titicaca, the deep sapphire-blue lake which straddles the Peru-Bolivia border, sits amid rolling, scrub-covered hills in the heart of the Altiplano north-west of La Paz. At an altitude of 3810 metres, it's traditionally regarded as the highest navigable body of water in the world (although there are higher lakes in both Peru and Chile which can be navigated by small craft).

This immense lake is South America's inland sea. Its current dimensions are 233 km measured from north-west to south-east and 97 km from north-east to south-west. With a surface area of over 9000 sq km, it is South America's second largest lake, after Venezuela's Lake Maracaibo. Long thought to be 'bottomless', its depth was recently measured at 457 metres. During the flooding of 1985-86, the waters of Titicaca rose several metres and inundated an additional 1000 sq km.

History
The pre-Inca peoples of the Altiplano believed that the sun itself and also their bearded, white leader/deity Viracocha had both risen out of its mysterious depths, whilst the Incas believed it to be the birthplace of their civilisation. When you first glimpse its gem-like waters beneath the looming backdrop of the cloud-covered Cordillera Real in the clear light of the Altiplano, it should be easy to imagine why the early inhabitants of the area connected it with such mystical events.

Titicaca Island, renamed Isla del Sol (Island of the Sun) by the Spanish, lies in Bolivian waters near the mainland village of Yampupata. In the early 1600s, Spanish chronicler Garcilaso de la Vega sceptically wrote of its renown:

The Incas say that on this (Titicaca) island, the Sun placed his two children, male and female, when he sent them down to instruct the barbarous people who dwelt on the Earth...They say that after the deluge, the rays of the Sun were seen on this island, and over the great lake, before they appeared in any other part.

The first Inca, Manco Capac, taking advantage of the ancient legend and assisted by his own genius and wisdom, seeing that the Indians venerated the lake and the islands as sacred things, composed another legend saying that he and his wife (Mama Ocllo or Huaca) were children of the Sun and that their father had placed them on that island that they might thence pass through the country, teaching the people.

The Incas Amautas, who were philosophers and learned men of the State, reduced the first legend to the second, teaching it as prophecy. They said that the Sun, having shed his first rays on that Island whence to illuminate the world (in the original Creation), was a sign and a promise that on the same spot he would place his own children, whence to go forth instructing the natives and drawing them away from the savage condition in which they lived, as those (Inca) kings actually did later. With those and similar legends the Incas made the Indians believe that they were children of the Sun.

When the Spanish arrived in the mid-1500s, legends of treasure began to surface, including the tale that the Incas, in desperation, had flung their gold into the lake to prevent the Spanish from carting it off. Due to the obvious fluctuation of the water level, other rumours maintained that entire ruined cities existed beneath the surface of the water.

Although no one has turned up any underwater cities, underwater archaeology has uncovered some interesting finds in the vicinity of Isla Koa north-west of Isla del Sol. These include 22 large stone boxes, a silver llama, some shell figurines and several types of incense burners, but they haven't provided any conclusive evidence of their origins.

Changes in water level from year to year are not uncommon and previous fluctuations may have inundated many more ruins and artefacts. In the floods of 1985-86, highways, docks, fields, pastures and city streets disappeared beneath the rising waters; adobe homes turned to mud and collapsed, and 200,000 people were displaced. It took several years for the the Río Desaguadero,

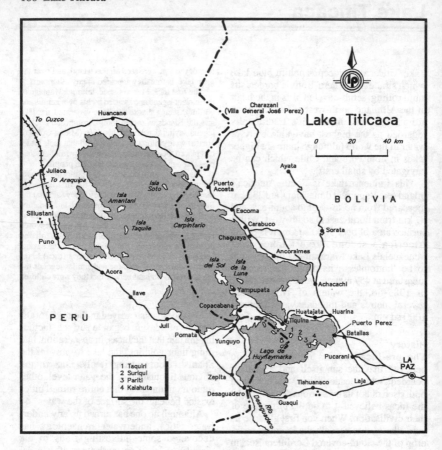

Lake Titicaca

0   20   40 km

BOLIVIA

PERU

1 Taquiri
2 Suriqui
3 Pariti
4 Kalahuta

the lake's only outlet, to drain off the flood waters.

It will probably be apparent that life around the lake hasn't changed much since the days when the Incas were capturing the imaginations – and the lands – of the Aymará inhabitants with dazzling tales of their origins.

Organised Tours

A number of guided excursions of Lake Titicaca originate in La Paz and include a stop in Copacabana, usually around lunchtime. You have a choice of hydrofoils,

catamarans, motor launches and land transport of all descriptions. For those with limited time and unlimited funds, this is a quick way to 'do' Titicaca. They are best arranged from La Paz but if there is space, one of the Copacabana tour agencies may be able to get you onto a tour there when the boat stops for lunch.

For suggestions, see the listing of companies under Organised Tours in the La Paz chapter. The most popular companies are Crillon, which has a hydrofoil service, and Transturin, which has covered catamarans. Expect to pay around B350 for a day of cruising around the lake, stopping at some combination of the following: Suriqui, Huatajata, Isla del Sol, Copacabana, Puno and possibly one of the Peruvian islands.

PUERTO PEREZ
Puerto Perez, only 65 km from La Paz, is the site of Balsa Tours (☎ 356566, fax (591-2) 391310, La Paz) lake resort, Complejo Nautico Balsa (☎ 350597, La Paz). Using the hostel at the resort as a base, they operate tours to the islands of Kalahuta (Queguaya), Suriqui and Pariti for B95 per day. For further information on these islands, refer to the discussion of the Islas Huyñaymarkas later in this chapter.

HUATAJATA
The tiny community of Huatajata lies on the shore of Lake Titicaca's southern extension, Lago de Huyñaymarka, about midway between Copacabana and La Paz. The only yacht club on the lake has been turned into the headquarters of Crillon Tours which operates hydrofoil services to Copacabana and Puno and has installed a three-star hotel.

There's really not much to see in the town itself – it mainly serves as a base for trips to the Islas Huyñaymarkas – but it's a pleasant place to experience day-to-day life in a typical lakeside community where very little ever changes. Each morning the fisherfolk take their boats out on their daily run and each afternoon, return with the day's haul, while the women spend their days repairing nets, caring for children, weaving, cooking and cleaning, and selling the previous day's catch.

Museo Altiplano Eco
This new museum at the Inca Utama Hotel is operated by Crillon Tours and focuses on the history and cultures of the Altiplano as well as the natural features of the Lake Titicaca region.

Fiestas
In late spring or early summer, depending on the year, the small lakeside community of Compi, midway between Huatajata and the Estrecho de Tiquina (Straits of Tiquina), stages a folk festival with dancing, feasting and bicycle racing.

Places to Stay
The Catari Brothers run *Alojamiento Inti Karka* a pleasant alojamiento where you can stay for B9 per person. It's right on the shore and has magnificent views of the lake, especially at sunset. There's a sign for it on the main highway but not near the building itself; just look for a three-storey white house on the waterfront. Anyone in town will be able to direct you.

For the same price you can stay at the imposing *Alojamiento Wiñay Marka*, half a block from the highway.

The new three-star resort hotel *Inca Utama* (☎ 350363, fax (591-2) 391039, La Paz) is run by Crillon Tours. Midway between Huatajata and Huarina, nearer La Paz, is the relatively luxurious *Hotel Titicaca*. Reservations should be made through the Hotel Libertador (☎ 355080, La Paz).

Places to Eat
Inexpensive meals are available at the two alojamientos. Their specialities are – you guessed it – fish. Near the Inca Utama are two more elegant options, the *Lago Azul* and the *Las Playas*.

Getting There & Away
From La Paz, the buses which go through to Copacabana will not sell you an advance ticket if you're only going to Huatajata. Instead, you have to catch a bus from the corner of calles Manuel Bustillos and Kollasuyo near the La Paz cemetery. They leave about every half hour between 4 am and 5 pm and also service other lakeside communities as far as Achacachi.

To return to La Paz, just flag down any bus heading east along the main highway. The last one runs at about 6 pm.

ISLAS HUYÑAYMARKA
The three most visited islands in Lago de Huyñaymarka are Kalahuta, Pariti and

Suriqui, which are easily seen in a few hours. It's also possible to camp overnight, especially on the more sparsely populated islands of Pariti and Kalahuta.

Isla Kalahuta

Kalahuta, which in Aymará means 'stone houses', served as a cemetery for the Incas. The entire island is dotted with stone tombs several metres high. Superstitious locals are afraid to live outside the island's one town of Queguaya and are also reluctant to venture anywhere at night due to legends of horrible fates befalling those who so desecrate the cemetery. If you dare to camp there, you'll have most of the island to yourself.

The shores of Kalahuta are lined with beds of *totora* reed, the versatile building material for which Titicaca is famous. By day, fisherfolk ply the island's main bay in totora reed boats while others come in to the shoreline to gather reeds for canoe construction.

Isla Pariti

Like Kalahuta, much of Pariti is surrounded by marshes of totora reed. This small and friendly island offers little more than a view of the tranquil lifestyle of its inhabitants. The Indians there trade cheese, fish and woollen goods in Huatajata for items from the Yungas and La Paz. Their sailboats, used for fishing, are beautiful to watch as they slice through the Titicaca waters in search of a bountiful catch.

Isla Suriqui

Suriqui, the best known island in Lago de Huyñaymarka, is world-renowned for its totora reed boats which are still constructed on a relatively large scale and figure prominently in the daily lives of islanders.

The construction process is quite simple. Green reeds are gathered from the lake shallows and left to dry in the sun. Once they're free of all moisture, they're gathered into four fat bundles and lashed together with strong grass. Often a sail of reeds is added. These bloated little canoes don't last very long as far as watercraft go; after six months of use, they become waterlogged and begin

to rot and sink. In order to increase their life span the canoes are often stored on the lakeshore.

In the early 1970s Dr Thor Heyerdahl, the unconventional Norwegian explorer and scientist, solicited the help of the Aymará shipbuilders of Isla Suriqui to design and construct his vessel the *Ra II*. Dr Heyerdahl wanted to test his theory that early contact and migration occurred between the ancient peoples of North Africa and the Americas. He planned to demonstrate the feasibility of travelling great distances using the boats of the period.

Four of the Aymará shipbuilders accompanied him on the expedition from Morocco to the Barbados, and one of them, Paulino Esteban, an interesting and humble person, enjoys chatting with visitors interested in his work. Esteban's Museo San Pablo, a small museum near the dock in Suriqui, contains all sorts of paraphernalia about *Ra II* and the other Heyerdahl expeditions which employed ancient design watercraft, such as the *Ra I*, *Tigris* and the *Kon Tiki*. Displays also include the various types of boats he himself has designed and built, and small, meticulously constructed models are for sale. Señor Demetrio Limachi Corani on Suriqui will construct full-size balsa reed boats to order for B75.

Unfortunately, the once lovely island of Suriqui has become quite a depressing place, tragically corrupted by tourism. Foreign visitors are now besieged by beggars, many of them children, who whine for sweets and money. When tourism reduces once proud people to such a tragic condition, it's time to re-examine its motives. *Please* read the warning under Gift Giving in the Dangers and Annoyances section of the Facts for the Visitor chapter.

Isla Incas

Legend has it that this tiny, uninhabited island near Suriqui was part of an Inca network of underground passageways, reputed to link many parts of the Inca Empire with the capital at Cuzco.

Getting There & Away

Any of the Aymará fisherfolk in Huatajata will probably be happy to take a day off to shuttle tourists around the islands. The most knowledgeable and economical guides are the Catari Brothers. Ramon Catari takes up to 15 people to Kalahuta, Pariti and Suriqui for about B110 and will provide an informative running commentary on the legends, customs, people, history and natural features of the lake. He'll allow as much time as you'd like on each island and introduce you to friends who will provide insights into the Aymará way of life. If you'd like to camp overnight on one of the islands, you can arrange to be picked up the following day.

Organised cruises to the islands are available through Balsa Tours, Transturin and Crillon Tours in La Paz. For details, see under Organised Tours in the La Paz chapter.

COPACABANA

The bright town of Copacabana on the southern shore of Lake Titicaca was established around a splendid bay between two hills. This agreeable stopover along the Tiquina route between La Paz and Cuzco has served as a site of religious pilgrimage for centuries, beginning with the Incas. The most animated times are during the several fiestas which bring this ordinarily sleepy place to life with pilgrims and visitors from all over Bolivia.

Copacabana's climate is generally pleasant and sunny, receiving most of its rainfall in mid-summer (December and January). At an altitude of 3800 metres, however, Copacabana is subject to bitterly cold nights and water-cooled winds from the lake.

History

After the fall and disappearance of the Tiahuanaco culture, the Kollas or Aymará rose to become the dominant group in the Titicaca region. The primary deities of their religion were not only the husband and wife combination, the sun and moon, but also Pachamama, the earth mother, and the achachilas, or mountain spirits. Among the idols erected along the shoreline of what is now known as the Manco Capac peninsula

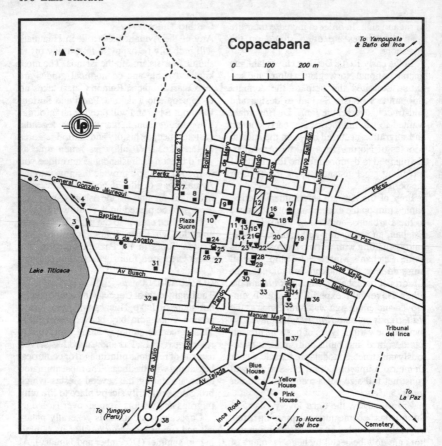

was *Copacahuana* (Place of the Precious Stone), an image with the head of a human and the body of a fish. It was placed at the site now known as Asiento del Inca.

After the Aymará had been subsumed into the Inca Empire, the settlement of Copacabana was founded by Inca Emperor Tupac Yupanqui as a wayside rest for pilgrims en route to the *huaca*, the site of (gulp!) human sacrifice at *Titicaca* (Rock of the Puma), on Isla del Sol in Lake Titicaca.

Before the arrival of the Spanish Dominican and Augustinian priests in the mid-1500s, the Incas had divided local inhabitants into two distinct groups. Those who were faithful to the empire were known as Hanansaya and were placed in positions of power. Those who resisted, the Hurinsaya, were relegated to manual labour. This went entirely against the grain of the community-oriented Aymará culture, and the floods and crop failures that befell them in the 1570s were attributed to this social aberration.

A direct result was the rejection of the Inca religion and the partial adoption of Christianity and establishment of the Santuario de Copacabana. This resulted in a mishmash sort of religion which combined aspects of

■ PLACES TO STAY

5	Alojamiento Aroma
7	Alojamiento Urinsaya
8	Hotel Ambassador
9	Residencial Copacabana
13	Residencial La Porteñita
14	Alojamiento El Turista
24	Hotel Playa Azul
26	Residencial & Pensión Aransaya
28	Residencial Boston
30	Hospedería
31	Alojamiento Kota Kahuaña
32	Hotel Prefectural
36	Alojamiento Sucre
37	Alojamiento Emperador

▼ PLACES TO EAT

4	Beach Restaurants
10	La Merced
11	Tito Yupanqui
15	Restaurant Colonial
19	Snack Restaurant Napoles

22	Puerta del Sol
23	The Tourist Palace
27	Snack 6 de Agosto
29	El Turista
34	Snack Cristal

OTHER

1	Cerro Calvario
2	Naval Base & Ferry Dock
3	Boat Landing
6	Bicycle Rental
12	Market
16	Transportes 2 de Febrero Bus Terminal
17	Post Office
18	Museo en Miniatura
20	Plaza 2 de Febrero
21	Transportes Manco Capac Bus Terminal
25	Minibuses to Puno & La Paz
33	Cathedral
35	ENTEL
38	Bolivian Customs

both traditional and Christian doctrines. The populace elected La Santísima Virgen de Candelaria as its patron saint and established a congregation in her honour. Noting the lack of an image for the altar, Francisco Tito Yupanqui, a direct descendant of the Inca emperor, fashioned an image of clay and placed it in the church, but it was deemed unsuitable to represent the honoured patron of the village, and was removed.

The humiliated sculptor went to Potosí to study arts and find the perfect model for the image he wanted to create. Feeling suitably inspired, he began carving a wooden image in June 1582, completing it after eight months. On 2 February 1583, La Virgen Morena del Lago (The Dark Virgin of the Lake) was placed on the adobe altar at Copacabana and the miracles began; the number of healings effected are reported only as 'innumerable' and Copacabana consequently developed into a pilgrimage site.

In 1605, the Augustinian priesthood determined that the community should construct a cathedral sufficiently opulent to house the image. The altar was completed in 1614 but work on the building continued for 200 years. It wasn't until 15 April 1805, that the mudéjar cathedral was consecrated, and construction was finally completed in 1820. On 10 August 1925, Francisco Tito Yupanqui's image was canonised by the Vatican.

Information

Money The Banco del Estado beside the Playa Azul Hotel on Calle 6 de Agosto is reportedly open Wednesday to Sunday mornings. The fanciful travellers' cheque stickers plastered on the tellers' windows are apparently only decorative – no one in Copacabana changes travellers' cheques! Be sure to carry a supply of cash from either La Paz or Peru.

The Hotel Playa Azul changes Peruvian *soles* and cash US dollars, as does the dispensary beside the cathedral. Slightly better rates are available around the plaza in Yunguyo, just beyond the Peruvian frontier.

Post & Telecommunications The post office is on Calle Hugo Ballivián, just off the

Plaza 2 de Febrero. It's open whenever its sole employee is there. Try late morning.

ENTEL, beside the library on Plazuela Tito Yupanqui, is closed on Sundays. If you're phoning Copacabana from elsewhere in the country, you must go through ENTEL and dial 7 prior to the local number.

Film With a constant influx of tourists, both national and foreign, Copacabana is a good place to buy film. The cholas in front of the cathedral sell 36-exposure Kodak, Fuji or Agfa print film for B7 per roll, and 36-exposure Fujichrome for B18.

Dangers & Annoyances Police and tranca officials posted at the entrance to town have been known to charge arriving tourists and pilgrims a 'tax' for the upkeep of the sanctuary and the Virgin. A notice in the cathedral states that neither the church nor the sanctuary gets one cent of this opportunistic scam. Refuse to pay and if there are problems, smile knowingly and report that you've seen the notice posted in the cathedral: *He visto el aviso en la catedral.*

Natural Considerations Since the air is so thin, it conducts scorchingly high levels of ultraviolet radiation, so remember to wear a hat, especially when you're out on the water, and use a reliable sunscreen. If you're going walking in the hills around Copacabana, beware of a particularly insidious variety of thorn bush which shreds skin on contact. Watch what you're brushing against!

Cathedral

Built between 1605 and 1820, the brilliant white Moorish cathedral with its mudéjar domes and colourful *azulejos* (decorative tiles) dominates the town. The beautiful church courtyard is usually ablaze with the colours of wild and domestic flowers.

Virgen de Candelaria The cathedral is a repository for both European and local religious art, including the Virgen de Candelaria. The black statue was carved in the 1580s by the Indian artist Francisco

Yupanqui, grandson of the Inca Emperor Tupac Yupanqui (see the History section in the Copacabana intro). It's encased in glass above the altar upstairs in the cathedral; follow the signs to the Camarín de la Virgen. The statue is never moved from the cathedral, as superstition has it that its disturbance would precipitate a devastating flooding of Lake Titicaca. The *camarín* (niche in which a religious image is displayed) is closed from noon to 1 pm daily.

Museo de la Catedral The cathedral museum contains some interesting articles. Don't miss the ostrich vases or the hundreds of paper cranes donated by a pregnant Japanese woman hedging her bets with the Virgin in hopes of bearing an intelligent child. It's open from 8.45 am to noon on Sundays only and costs B1.

Museo en Miniatura

This museum on the north-eastern corner of the plaza contains an immense collection of all sorts of miniatures – bottles, dolls, furniture and even ceramic Bolivian market scenes. It's open from 9 am to 5 pm daily. Admission costs B1.

Cerro Calvario

A trail to the summit of Cerro Calvario, the hill to the north-west of town, begins near the church at the end of Calle Destacamento 211, climbing past the Stations of the Cross. From the summit, you'll have a superb view of both the lake and the town. Even with frequent altitude-inflicted rests, it may be reached in less than half an hour.

Niño Calvario (Kesanani) & Horca del Inca

The hill just to the north of the saddle is called Niño Calvario (Little Calvary), also known by its original name of Kesanani. Its weirdly rugged rock formations and oddly arranged piles of boulders are worth exploration. A trail leads uphill from the end of Calle Murillo to the Horca del Inca (Inca Gallows), an odd trilithic gate perched on the hillside. Actually a pre-Inca observatory, it is surrounded by pierced rocks which at the solstices allow the sun's rays to pass through onto the lintel.

The higher hill behind Niño Calvario is dotted with Inca *asientos* (seats), ancient agricultural terraces and numerous unrestored and little known ruins. To get there, follow Calle Murillo to its end where, between two brightly coloured houses, it turns into a cobbled Inca road. Fifty metres or so beyond this point, a crumbling stone aqueduct leads off to the left. The entrance is a metre or so above the road level, so look carefully. The easiest access to the mountain is from the saddle at the summit of the aqueduct.

Intikala (Tribunal del Inca)
Just below the cemetery off the La Paz road is a field of artificially sculpted boulders known as the Tribunal del Inca (Inca Tribunal). The original purpose of this place is unknown. There are about seven carved stones with asientos, basins and niches for idols. During the rainy season, the place is hopping with thousands of small frogs.

Kusillata & Baño del Inca
A two-km walk along the Titicaca shoreline from the end of Calle Hugo Ballivián will bring you to a colonial manor building known as Kusillata which has been converted into a small museum. Beside the manor you'll find a pre-Columbian tunnel which was used as access to the underground water supply. The carved stone water tank on the site is known as El Baño del Inca (The Inca Bath).

Market
Local specialities include: handmade miniatures of Lake Titicaca reed boats; huge mutant peanuts; a variety of Andean potatoes; and *pasankalla* (puffed choclo with caramel), a South American version of popcorn which, if crispy, can be quite tasty. You'll also find shops which produce the dark-coloured felt derby hats worn by local women. Kitsch vehicle adornments, miniatures and religious paraphernalia are available in the numerous street stalls in front of the cathedral. If you're after miniatures, they're sold en masse atop Cerro Calvario.

Cha'lla
The word cha'lla is used for any ritual blessing, toasting or offering to the powers that be, whether Inca, Aymará or Christian. On Sunday morning in front of the cathedral, cars, trucks and buses of pilgrims, visitors and even flota companies are decked out in garlands of real or plastic flowers, coloured ribbons, model reed boats, flags and even stuffed ducks. Petitions for protection are made to the Virgin and a ritual offering of alcohol is poured over the vehicles' tyres and bonnets, thereby consecrating them for the journey home.

When we were last in Copacabana, one La Paz flota had brought a newly purchased fleet of buses for the 'spiritual' baptism to prepare them for Bolivian highways.

Fiestas
Copacabana hosts three major fiestas during the year. On the first two days of February, the Fiesta de la Virgen de Candelaria is celebrated in honour of the dark wooden image created by Francisco Tito Yupanqui. Although this fiesta is celebrated to varying degrees throughout the country, Copacabana puts on an extra big bash with pilgrims and dancers coming from both Peru and Bolivia.

On Good Friday the town fills with *peregrinos* (pilgrims) who've travelled to Copacabana to do penance at the Stations of the Cross on Cerro Calvario. Many of them journey on foot from La Paz, 158 km away. Once on the hill's summit, they light incense and buy miniatures in hopes that the Virgin will bless them with the real thing during the year of their pilgrimage.

Beginning at dusk from the cathedral, pilgrims join a solemn candlelit procession through town, led by a statue of Christ in a glass coffin and a replica of the Virgen de Candelaria, the patron saint of Bolivia. A local priest relates the significance of the holiday through a microphone, a military band plays dirges and city hall's audio system blares *Ave Maria* for all to hear.

From Good Friday to the end of Easter, the cars and camiones that carry the pilgrims home are consecrated by the cha'lla; they're decorated with bright plastic garlands and blessed with alcohol for the journey ahead.

Copacabana stages its biggest bash during the week of Bolivian Independence Day (the first week in August). The most animated of the town's annual festivities, it's characterised by pilgrimages, dancing, around-the-clock music, parades, fireworks and an amazingly high, and continuous, consumption of alcohol. Although Copacabana is relatively free of petty thievery during the remainder of the year, this is a time to beware of light-fingered lifters who may prey on careless celebrants.

Places to Stay

For a town of its size, Copacabana is well-endowed with hotels, residenciales and alojamientos. Unless you arrive at the height of a fiesta, when rooms fill up and rates double, you should have no trouble finding acceptable, inexpensive accommodation.

Despite the proximity of the lake, the water supply is normally functional only in the morning. The water and electric utilities are also unpredictable and often fail. When hotels claim to have electric hot showers, interpret this as a chance of having a shower whenever the water and electric services coincide.

Copacabana is the least expensive town in Bolivia, but there's no single outstanding place to stay. Nearly all the tour groups wind up at the overpriced *Hotel Playa Azul* (☎ 227 in town, ☎ 320068 in La Paz). Rooms cost B45 per person with private bath and a three-meal plan. Rooms without meals aren't available, which is a shame, as Copacabana has several restaurants worth trying.

The *Hotel Prefectural* (☎ 256), near the beach, affords a lovely view of the lake and surrounding mountains. It's utterly dead during the week but springs to life on weekends. There's a nice restaurant with live entertainment on weekends and upstairs are table-tennis and billiards tables. Some rooms even have sundecks overlooking the lake. Clean but stark rooms cost B45 per person with the three-meal plan and B25 without.

The *Alojamiento Urinsaya* at Calle Destacamento 211, 390 looks shabby from the outside but it's still good, friendly value and is highly recommended. Try for one of the super-clean, airy rooms upstairs (one room is a six-bed dormitory) which cost B5 per person. Hot water is available in the morning and there's a laundry sink and sundeck.

The *Hotel Ambassador* (☎ 216 in town, ☎ 343110 in La Paz) around the corner on Calle General Gonzalo Jáuregui is a bit grotty but offers reasonable value at B8 per person with bath or B5 without. Space heaters are available upon request. This place is the acting youth hostel in Copacabana.

A sunny new establishment in town is the *Residencial Aransaya*, affiliated with Copacabana's famous trout restaurant, the Pensión Aransaya. Comfortable rooms cost B7 per person with shared bath. If you crave conversation, turn to Carlos, their chatty bird-brained parrot who entertains diners with his acrobatics above the patio.

An oddly designed but quiet, friendly and pleasant new place with the best view in town is the *Alojamiento Aroma*. Room Nos 1 to 4 are a stiff climb from the ground floor, but they open onto a lovely open patio/balcony – a superb perch above the lake and the town. Beware of the loos, however; one has an exceptional two-way view of the stairwell! Rooms cost only B5 per person.

The budget travellers' choice is currently the *Alojamiento Emperador* (☎ 250) at Calle Murillo 235. This upbeat and colourfully speckled place charges B5 per person with shared bath, and if you're in need of reading material, there's a travellers' book exchange. The helpful staff also provide visitor information.

Residencial Copacabana (☎ 220 in town, ☎ 784130 in La Paz) isn't the nicest accommodation in town but it's adequate for fiesta lodging if all other places are full. Singles/

doubles cost B7/10. The *Residencial La Porteñita* also has clean rooms at B7/14 for a single/double. *Alojamiento Sucre* on Calle Junín has been recommended for its friendliness, washing facilities and good value accommodation. *Residencial Boston* on the lake side of the cathedral has also been praised as a good, clean option, but doubles cost a rather steep B18.

For a totally different alternative, try the *Hospedería*. The rooms are gloomy mediaeval cells and lack beds, but if you have a sleeping bag and some sort of ground protection, you can stay for as little as B2 per person. The building itself, an old mansion with plenty of rooms overlooking a marvellous flowery courtyard, makes up for any discomfort.

The *Alojamiento Kota Kahuaña* at Avenida Busch 15 advertises a 'beautiful lake view' but some of the rooms don't even have windows; check your room before signing in!

Alojamiento El Turista (☎ 223) at Calle Pando 378, between Calle General Gonzalo Jáuregui and Calle 6 de Agosto, was gaining a favourable reputation but there have been reports of things going missing from the rooms; furthermore, the staff are less than friendly and the restaurant is reportedly unspeakable.

The *Alojamiento Las Playas* on Calle 6 de Agosto near the beach is also not recommended. Although it has a good view, it has received several nominations as the filthiest place to stay in Bolivia.

Camping
Although the slopes around Copacabana are generally steep and rocky, there are several excellent campsites in the area. The field opposite the beach is fairly private and comfortable and the summits of both Niño Calvario and its neighbouring hill have smooth, grassy saddle areas suitable for tent camping. They also provide magnificent views of the lake, the surrounding farms and villages, and the Andean Cordillera. Another pleasant campsite is the high point of the Inca road toward Yunguyo at the foot of Cerro Copacte, less than a km beyond the end of Calle Murillo.

Places to Eat
There is unfortunately little originality in preparation methods in Copacabana; all main courses are served with dry rice, fried potatoes and lettuce. The real highlight of eating in Copacabana is Lake Titicaca trout. The fish were introduced in 1939 by foreign pisciculturists in order to improve the protein content in the local diet. For many years the trout were also tinned and exported, but that ended when fish stocks became severely depleted. Nowadays, however, the lake produces the world's largest rainbow trout and some of the most delicious.

Our favourite restaurant is *Pensión Aransaya* on Calle 6 de Agosto which is, surprisingly, accessible to tight budgets. The food is especially good, of course, and service is friendly. Plan on paying about B9 for a meal of trout, trimmings and a tall, cold beer.

Snack 6 de Agosto just up the street is also very good value, with huge portions of trout for a remarkable B7. Unfortunately, it closes at 6 pm. *Snack Cristal* on Calle Murillo also specialises in trout and is repeatedly recommended for inexpensive meals. For breakfast, try *Snack Restaurant Napoles* on Plaza 2 de Febrero, which also serves trout and other standards, but ascertain prices before ordering, make sure the bill coincides with these, and count your change.

The *Puerta del Sol* at the corner of the plaza and Calle 6 de Agosto serves good trout and pejerrey. Restaurant *Tito Yupanqui* at Calle General Gonzalo Jáuregui 119 is known for its good vegetable soup.

The overpriced *Restaurant Colonial* on the plaza is heated so it's a viable option on those evenings when you just can't warm up. They serve trout and pejerrey but always seem to be out of everything else on their impressive menu; ask for the story behind their *desayuno Japonés* (Japanese breakfast).

The *Tourist Palace* on Calle 6 de Agosto has a menu with a table of contents. They serve continental and English breakfasts as well as three local trout dishes, delicious pejerrey and all the other standards. An unnamed parrot provides background sound effects.

On Calle General Gonzalo Jáuregui near 3 de Mayo is *La Merced*, a lovely courtyard restaurant with friendly owners. It's a great place to spend a mellow afternoon drinking a Paceña or two and delving into journal or letter writing. Naturally, they serve trout...

On sunny days, *El Rey* and several other restaurants at the beach have tables outside where you can have a drink and observe quintessential Bolivian beach life, such as it is.

As usual, the bargain basement of the Bolivian food scene is the market food hall where numerous small operations compete fiercely for your business. You can eat a generous meal of trout or beef for a pittance, while a contingent of the town's canine population patiently awaits handouts. If you're up for an insulin shock in the morning, treat yourself to a breakfast of hot api morado and syrupy buñuelos.

Getting There & Away

Bus Tourist micros provide the best sightseeing opportunities along the dramatic road between Copacabana and Tiquina and are the most hassle-free option for crossing the border into Peru. The journey between La Paz and Copacabana is impressive, following a magnificent route across the Altiplano and along the shoreline to the Estrecho de Tiquina. The barges which ferry vehicles across the strait between San Pedro and San Pablo have been known to flip in the water so passengers are ferried across separately on launches. The fare across is a very reasonable B.70 per person, payable at the ticket office at the dock. Even passengers on public buses must pay.

To/From La Paz Numerous tourist micros depart from the Pensión Aransaya for La Paz at around noon. Book tickets in advance through the Pensión Aransaya, the Hotel Playa Azul or one of several tour agencies

around town. On Saturday and Sunday, the services are extremely crowded so advance bookings are essential. The fare is B20 per person. Ferry availability will determine whether the trip takes four or five hours.

Two major bus companies also run between La Paz and Copacabana. Transportes 2 de Febrero (☎ 377181, La Paz) departs from the Plaza 2 de Febrero in Copacabana, Monday to Saturday at 8 am, noon and 3 pm. On Sunday, there are additional departures at 1 and 2 pm. Most locals use either this or the other line, Transportes Manco Capac (☎ 350033, La Paz), which leaves at 7 and 11.30 am and 1 and 2 pm Monday to Saturday with additional departures at 4 pm on Friday and Saturday. On Sunday, they leave at 7 and 10 am, and hourly between 1 and 4 pm. The fare on Transportes 2 de Febrero is B8, and on Manco Capac, B7.50.

Crossing the Border A number of tourist bus companies operate between Copacabana and Puno, Peru. Transport to Puno can be booked at the Pensión Aransaya, Hotel Playa Azul or a tour agency. Micros depart from the Pensión Aransaya around noon; any minibus with Peruvian number plates will be going to Puno. The B10 to B12 trip takes two or three hours depending on the whims of immigration. Buses to Yunguyo cost B1 and depart when full – approximately every half hour or so – from immigration. Have your exit stamp ready.

All transport from Puno departs between 8 and 9 am. If you're entering Bolivia and require a visa, there are consulates in both Puno and Yunguyo (the former is not recommended). Non-Bolivian Latin Americans entering Bolivia at Yunguyo must register with the police before crossing the border. For further information on travelling between Bolivia and Puno, refer to the Puno Getting There & Away section later in this chapter.

Getting Around

Bicycle rentals are available at Calle 6 de Agosto 125 or on the beach. They're great for zipping up and down the beach or around town, but foreigners are expected to pay several times the local rate: B4 per hour, B15 for six hours and B25 for a full 12-hour day (6 am to 6 pm). Negotiate!

COPACABANA TO YAMPUPATA TREK

From Copacabana, an interesting and enjoyable method of reaching Isla del Sol is to trek along the lakeshore to the village of Yampupata, just a short rowboat ride from the ruins of Pilco Kaima on Isla del Sol. The four to five-hour walk is highly recommended for its scenery, and when combined

with a couple of days on the island, makes a fabulous trip.

The Route

From Copacabana head north-east along the road which runs across the flat plain. Continue along the coastal track for nearly an hour until you reach the isolated Hinchaca fish hatchery and reafforestation project on your left. Just beyond the hatchery, leave the track and cross the stream on your left, following the obvious Inca road up the steep hill. Part way up you'll pass the Gruta de Lourdes, a cave which for locals evokes

Copacabana to Yampupata Trek

0   1   2 km

1 Gruta de Lourdes
2 Hinchaca Fish Hatchery
   & Reforestation Project
3 Kusillata & Baño del Inca
4 Cerro Calvario
5 Tribunal del Inca

images of its French namesake. This stretch shows some good Inca paving and makes a considerable short cut, rejoining the track at the crest of the hill.

Continue along the track until you reach a fork in the road; take the left turning which descends back to the shore and leads on through the village of Titicachi. From here, you're walking through more populated areas. Keep going through Sicuani, resisting offers to take you to Isla del Sol for an exorbitant B60.

Approximately four hours from Copacabana, you'll arrive at the village of Yampupata, a tiny collection of mud houses. You can hire a rowboat here to the Escalera del Inca (Inca Steps) on Isla del Sol for B8. Either arrange for the boat owner to wait, or better, to collect you at a later date.

To return from Yampupata to Copacabana, there are three possibilities: hop on one of the boats that leave for Copacabana between 8 and 9 am every Thursday, Saturday and Sunday for B4 per person; take the Saturday camión which costs B2 per person and leaves in the early to mid-afternoon – the trip may take more than two hours since it stops to sell produce along the way; or walk back to Copacabana the way you came.

ISLA DEL SOL

Isla del Sol (Island of the Sun), was known to early inhabitants as Titicaca (Rock of the Puma), from which the lake takes its name. The Isla del Sol has been identified as the birthplace of all sorts of important entities, including the sun itself. There the bearded white leader/deity Viracocha and the first Incas, Manco Capac and his sister/wife Mama Ocllo, mystically appeared under direct orders of the sun. Modern-day Aymará and Quechua of Peru and Bolivia accept these legends as fact.

Isla del Sol has a population of around 5000. The island's main settlement is Cha'llapampa, often referred to as Cha'lla, which unfortunately causes confusion because there's another settlement called Cha'lla on Bahía Kea about two km southeast of Cha'llapampa. The other major village is Yumani which wraps around a small headland north of Fuente del Inca.

Exploring the Island

The numerous ruins on Isla del Sol are worth a good look but it's also pleasant to visit the tiny traditional villages; explore the island's dry slopes, which are covered with sweet smelling *koa* (incense) brush; or hike over the ancient *pampas* (terraces) which are still cultivated by the island families.

There are no vehicles on Isla del Sol so all your exploration will have to be done on foot or by boat. Most private transport from Copacabana and Yampupata and all the tour boats land at the Inca steps/Fuente del Inca complex where fresh water pours from a natural spring and through three artificial stone channels into a rough basin.

From there, it's a short walk south to the island's most prominent ruins complex, Pilco Kaima. The best known site is the two-level Palacio del Inca; its rectangular windows and doors have thresholds which are wider than their covering lintels. The arched roof vault was once covered with flagstone shingles and reinforced with a layer of mud and straw.

Heading back north past the Inca steps and the small Iglesia de San Antonio, you'll come to the village of Yumani, where you can climb up onto the ridge for a view down to Bahía Kona on the western shore and the village of Japapi. Continue north along the ridge until it reaches a junction: to the left the track leads to the shore at Bahía Kona; straight ahead it continues along the ridge; and to the right the track drops down to Bahía Kea, continuing from there northward to Cha'llapampa. North-west of Cha'llapampa along the track is the Templo del Inca, and further along at the north-west corner of the island lies Titicaca, the sacred rock of the Inca creation legend.

Places to Stay

Camping is possible just about anywhere on the island but it's best to set up away from villages, avoiding cultivated land. The wild

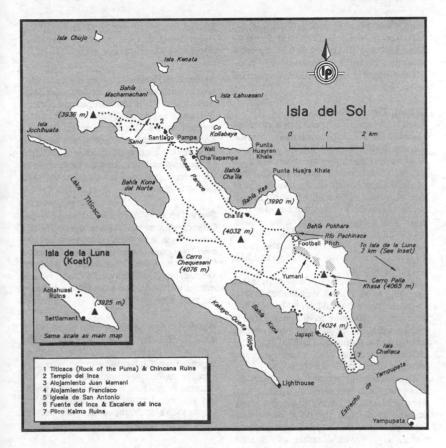

1 Titicaca (Rock of the Puma) & Chincana Ruins
2 Templo del Inca
3 Alojamiento Juan Mamani
4 Alojamiento Francisco
5 Iglesia de San Antonio
6 Fuente del Inca & Escalera del Inca
7 Pilco Kaima Ruins

and practically uninhabited western slopes are particularly inviting.

Increasing tourism has prompted several islanders to set up informal alojamientos in their homes. The nicest and most popular is *Alojamiento Juan Mamani* right on the lake beside the school at Cha'llapampa. It charges B4.50 per person with beds, blankets and a stove. Juan is probably the best source of information on island ruins and hiking routes.

Alternatively, for B3 you can sleep on the floor of a warehouse full of flour sacks. It's rented by the rather surly Señora Ticoma who lives in the brightly painted green and white house on the main route through Cha'lla. Not the most pleasant of options!

Near the upper end of Yumani village, north of the Fuente del Inca, is the *Alojamiento Francisco*, a modern home with two rooms upstairs: a double and a dorm room which will accommodate up to five people for B3 per person. The outdoor loos are straight out of the Middle Ages.

Places to Eat
At the Fuente del Inca, villagers prepare potatoes, eggs and cheese to sell to arriving

tours. Juan Mamani in Cha'llapampa and Francisco in Yumani can provide the same items and soft drinks as well. Very basic cooked meals will cost approximately B3.

Lake water should be boiled or purified before drinking.

Getting There & Away

From Copacabana, there are numerous launches and sailboats available for the journey to either Isla del Sol, Isla de la Luna, or to both islands. Arrange your length of stay with the pilot in advance or you may find yourself short of time on the islands. Carry food and water since it's not possible to visit the ruins *and* the villages in a half-day trip. If you plan to spend the night on the islands, remember to arrange return transport before you go. A good sunscreen will also prove invaluable; the sun was born here, and he's still going strong.

The biggest drawback to these trips is that they only allow a short visit to each island. To remain more than an hour on Isla del Sol, for example, you may have to pay extra. If you're keen to spend more time, either arrange one-way transport and have the pilot pick you up at a later time, or organise return transport whilst you're on the island.

There are unfortunately some unscrupulous pilots who will settle on a price, then when it's time to return to the mainland, demand more than the price negotiated. Stand your ground! The pilot has to get back home, too! If you'd rather avoid such unpleasantries, ask other travellers and local business people to recommend reputable boat owners; don't pay the full amount for the trip until you've returned to Copacabana; and, if you're not staying on Isla del Sol, carry just enough money for the day.

Launches To hire a boat, turn up on the beach in Copacabana between 6.30 and 8 am. To visit Pilco Kaima on Isla del Sol and the ruins on Isla de la Luna by small boat, you'll have to do some negotiating. Plan on B150 per day, including pilot, for a motorised launch holding up to 12 passengers. If you want to visit the northern end of

Isla del Sol, expect to pay a bit more. If you forego Isla de la Luna, it may be possible to negotiate a slightly lower price.

Sailboat & Rowboat Alternatively, a rowboat or sailboat and pilot for five people will cost around B80 to Isla del Sol and perhaps B30 more to add Isla de la Luna. These are probably more pleasant than the launches because they're silent and if you wish to exercise the biceps, the pilot will certainly oblige! In a sailboat, the trip can be done in six hours, but allow a bit longer as the wind can be fickle.

Ferry The ferry from Cha'llapampa to the Copacabana naval station costs B7 per person each way; locals are given priority over foreigners if space is limited. It departs Cha'llapampa for Copacabana at 8 am on Wednesday, Saturday and Sunday and returns to Isla del Sol from Copacabana on the same days at 2 pm.

Walking Although there have been lots of miracles at Lake Titicaca, you can't really walk to Isla del Sol. It is possible, however, to walk from Copacabana to the village of Yampupata on the mainland, just a short distance by rowboat from the island's southern tip. For further information, see the Copacabana to Yampupata Trek section earlier in this chapter.

ISLA DE LA LUNA

The Island of the Moon, formerly known as Koati, was the place where Viracocha commanded the moon to rise into the sky. This peaceful little island is surrounded by clear aquamarine water. There are ruins of an Inca era temple, Acllahuasi – a 'nunnery' for the Vírgenes del Sol – in an amphitheatre-like valley on the north-east shore. It's constructed of well-laboured stone seated in adobe mortar.

The walk up to the summit eucalyptus grove, where shepherds graze their flocks, is rewarded by a spectacular vista of Illampú and the entire snow-covered Cordillera Real.

Places to Stay

It's possible to camp anywhere on the small island away from the settlement but expect a bit of curious – and mercenary – attention.

Getting There & Away

See under Getting There & Away for Isla del Sol.

THE NORTH-EASTERN SHORE

If you're heading north-west from Huatajata toward the Peru-Bolivia border area at Puerto Acosta, there are a couple of sites of marginal interest.

About 90 km north of La Paz along the road to Sorata is the large market town of Achacachi. The church in Ancoraimes, about 20 km north of Achacachi, features a lovely ornamental screen above the altar; the colonial township of Carabuco has a colourful Sunday market; and from Escoma (165 km north-west of La Paz) you can strike off toward the Cordillera Apolobamba.

There are occasional buses from La Paz to Puerto Acosta, near the border, but beyond there, you'll have to rely on camiones. For information on the Cordillera Apolobamba region north of Lake Titicaca, refer to the Cordilleras & Yungas chapter.

THE SOUTHERN SHORE
Guaqui

Three hours by bus from La Paz, Guaqui sits beside, and partially under, Lago de Huyñaymarka, the southern extension of Lake Titicaca. It lies only 20 minutes by micro beyond Tiahuanaco near the Peruvian frontier at Desaguadero. This tranquil little Altiplano town has a truly beautiful church with a silver altar and some colonial artwork inside. Most of the excitement Guaqui ever sees is during the riotous Fiesta de Santiago during the final week of July.

Evidence of the 1986 flooding, in which half town was left in ruin, is still apparent. There's no longer a rail service from La Paz, and the famous lake steamer which once chugged between Guaqui and Puno was discontinued when the lake port disappeared beneath rising flood waters.

Places to Stay

Residencial Guaqui is really the only accommodation in town. It was damaged in the flooding but has since undergone repairs.

Getting There & Away The Tiahuanaco bus from La Paz continues on to Guaqui. From there, you can catch a colectivo to Desaguadero, Peru, for B.70 or a camión all the way to the border. After completing the normally quirky immigration formalities at Desaguadero, you can continue up the lakeshore to Puno or cut off toward the border town of Yunguyo and back into Bolivia at Copacabana.

The last bus back to La Paz leaves from the main avenue in the lower part of town between 4 and 5 pm and costs B6.

Peruvian Lake Titicaca

Half of Lake Titicaca lies within Peru and there are quite a few worthwhile places to visit. With inflation running rampant in Peru, there's no telling what will happen pricewise. Violence is on the increase and security is a real problem, especially in Puno, Juliaca and along the gringo trail to Cuzco. Don't let your guard down for an instant; trains and railway stations are notorious for organised rip-offs.

PUNO (PERU)

Puno is the principal settlement on the Peruvian shore of Lake Titicaca and most excursions begin there. Although the city was founded on 4 November 1668, there are few colonial buildings apart from the cathedral, and the town itself has a rather drab flavour. Fortunately, the environs are full of interesting and worthwhile sites making it a pleasant side trip or stop en route between Bolivia and Cuzco/Machu Picchu.

Information
Tourist Office The tourist office (☎ 351449) is at Arequipa 314.

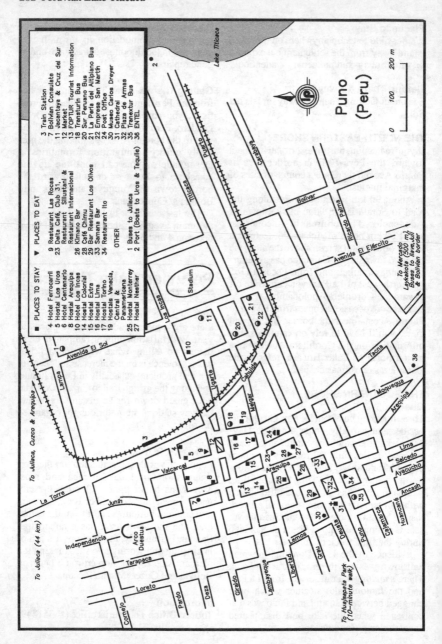

Puno (Peru)

PLACES TO STAY
4 Hotel Ferrocarril
5 Hostal Los Uros
6 Hotel Centenario
8 Hotel Arequipa
10 Hotel Los Incas
14 Hotel Colonial
15 Hotel Extra
16 Hotel Lima
17 Hostal Torino
19 Hostals Venecia,
   Central &
   Panamericana
25 Hostal Monterrey
27 Hostal Nesther

▼ PLACES TO EAT
9 Restaurant Las Rocas
23 Delta Café, Club 31
26 Restaurant Sillustani &
   Restaurant Internacional
26 Kimano Bar
28 Café Chimu
29 Bar Restaurant Los Olivos
33 Samana Bar
34 Restaurant Ito

OTHER
1 Buses to Juliaca
2 Port (Boats to Uros & Taquile)
3 Train Station
7 Bolivian Consulate
11 Ucantaya & Cruz del Sur
12 Market
13 FOPTUR Tourist Information
18 Transturin Bus
20 Sur Peruano Bus
21 La Perla del Altiplano Bus
22 Empresa San Martín
24 Post Office
30 Museo Carlos Dreyer
31 Cathedral
32 Plaza de Armas
35 Tranextur Bus
36 ENTEL

Money Bolivianos can be exchanged in Puno for Peruvian soles. Money changers hang out in front of the banks on Calle Lima and give better rates than the latter. Casas de cambio operate intermittently. Some of the hotels change money, particularly if you're staying there. Try the hostals Monterrey and Arequipa.

Bolivian Consulate The Bolivian Consulate is on the top floor of the building at the back of a courtyard at Arequipa 136. In theory, it's open from 8.30 am to 12.30 pm and from 2.30 to 4.30 pm Monday to Friday and visas may be obtained from the consulate within 24 hours. We've received reports that service is unreliable, so unless there's a change in organisation, you may want to secure your visa in Yunguyo.

Museo Carlos Dreyer
Puno's major museum, open from 9 am to 7 pm Monday to Friday, is just off the plaza. Admission is US$.50c. It's best to go in the morning.

Parque de Huajsapata
This little hill 10 minutes' walk south-west of town is topped by a statue of Manco Capac looking out over the lake. The views of the town and the lake are excellent, but the park is unfortunately dirty. Another good spot for views is the balcony beside the arch on Calle Independencia.

Fiestas
The department of Puno has a wealth of traditional dances featuring ornate and imaginative costumes often worth more than an entire household's ordinary wardrobe. See the tourist office for fiesta information. The best celebrations in Puno include the Virgen de Candelaria (2 February), Alasitas and Santa Cruz (2 to 4 May), Santiago (25 July, Taquile island), Nuestra Señora de la Merced (24 September), and the town festivities (1 to 7 November).

Places to Stay
Hotels fill up quickly when the evening train

arrives and prices rise during fiestas or times of increased demand. There are plenty of cheap hotels near the corner of Libertad and Tacna, but most are none too clean and have only cold showers. One of the best cheapies is *Hostal Torino* with singles/doubles for US$1/2.

Other similarly priced dive options include hostals *Venecia*, *Central* and *Centenario*. The *Hostal Colonial* isn't too bad and sometimes has hot water. For a few cents more, the *Hostal Extra* sometimes has hot water in the evenings and has a reasonably attractive courtyard.

A frequently recommended hotel is the *Hostal Los Uros*, the best of a generally bad bunch. They have hot water in the evenings and a cafeteria which is open for breakfast. Triple and quadruple rooms will work out to about US$1.75 per person. In a similar price range is the *Hotel Los Incas* with occasional hot water.

Clean singles/doubles are available at the *Hostal Nesther* for US$2/3.25, and one of the nicest budget options is the *Hostal Monterrey*. In a similar price range is the clean and central *Hostal Lima* with hot water most of the day.

Places to Eat
There is a choice of restaurants on the corner of Moquegua and Libertad. The *Delta Café* is cheap and recommended for early breakfasts. The *Restaurant Sillustani* and *Internacional* are among the best in town. *Club 31* is cheap and uncrowded, and the *Restaurant Las Rocas* has good food and is reasonably priced.

There are other inexpensive restaurants along Avenida Lima – the *Restaurant Ambassador* is good. The *Café Chimu* has been recommended for breakfasts and pastries. The *Kimano Bar* and *Bar Restaurant Los Olivos* are popular with locals. The *Restaurant Ito* on the corner of the plaza has been recommended but hours are erratic. The Hotel Ferrocarril has a medium-priced Italian restaurant.

Entertainment

For nightly folk music, try the Hotel Ferrocarril peña at 7.30 pm. The Samana Bar has a pleasant atmosphere and there is live music most weekends with a cover charge of about US$.50c.

Getting There & Away

Bus The roads are poor around Puno and most people prefer the train but if you insist on the bus – which is more secure than the train – try flotas Cruz del Sur or Jacantaya. Between them, they have four or five daily buses to Cuzco. These companies also have services to Lima, Nazca and Arequipa. Empresa San Martín has buses to Tacna on the Chilean border three times weekly.

Buses to Bolivia leave from the Avenida El Ejército side of the Mercado Laykakota and dozens of tour agencies along the main street have minibuses headed for Copacabana. They trade off services so you may not actually go with the company you've booked with. Never mind; they're all about the same, anyway.

Buses to Juliaca leave frequently from the corner of Lampa and El Sol.

Train From Puno, rail lines head north to Cuzco and Machu Picchu, and south-west to Arequipa where connections can be made to Lima and the rest of coastal Peru. The first few km of the journey to Cuzco follow the shores of Lake Titicaca and the views are good. The train departs daily except Sunday at 7.25 am. The Arequipa train leaves daily at 7.45 pm. Be alert for thieves in the railway station, and once you board the train, either wrap your body around your luggage or protect it somehow from slashing and padlock it to the shelves.

You should purchase your ticket the night prior to your journey, although sometimes, especially for the Cuzco train, the numbered 1st-class tickets are sold out early. It is difficult to purchase tickets earlier than the day before travel and queues are always long. If all else fails, check tour agencies; they operate a racket selling tickets at 25% commission.

Colectivo & Taxi A colectivo leaves frequently for Juliaca from in front of the railway station. The fare is about US$.80c per person for the 45-minute trip. There are also shared taxi services to Arequipa which cost about US$9 per person and depart in the morning.

AROUND PUNO

There are several attractions around Puno which merit attention if you're heading for Cuzco or spending a couple of days in Peru to renew a Bolivian visa.

Sillustani

The southern 'quarter' of the Inca Empire was known as Kollasuyo after the Kolla tribe, which was later absorbed into the empire. The noble Kolla dead were buried in funerary towers called *chullpas* which may be visited at Sillustani, a beautiful hilltop site on a peninsula overlooking Lago Umayo. The tallest chullpas are some 12 metres high, and look quite impressive against the lonely landscape.

Getting There & Away A daily Tranextur bus makes the 30-km run from Puno's Plaza de Armas; tickets are available at numerous tour agencies in town. It leaves at 2.30 pm and costs US$2 for the 3½-hour return trip, allowing 1½ hours at the ruins. Admission to the ruins costs an additional US$2 and the small onsite museum charges US$.20c.

Los Uros

The excursion to the floating islands of the Uros people has become somewhat over-commercialised. Despite this, it remains popular, as, with the exception of the floating islands of Mesopotamia's Tigris and Euphrates deltas, there is nothing quite like it anywhere else.

The Uros people have intermarried with Aymará-speaking Indians so no pure-blooded Uros remain. They have always been a small tribe and began their unusual floating existence centuries ago in an attempt to isolate themselves from the Kollas and the

Incas. The islands' current population is approximately 300.

The lives of the Uros are completely interwoven with the totora reed which grows in abundance in the Lake Titicaca shallows. They harvest these reeds and place them on the surface of the islands, replacing those which have rotted away on the bottom. The 'ground' is soft and springy so step carefully!

The Uros also construct their balsa canoes from tightly bundled reeds. If they are well-constructed, these canoes will last up to six months, and can carry an entire family. For a fee, you can take a ride on the boats or snap a photograph. Begging and hard-selling is rampant. If you must give something, bring oranges or other fruit from the mainland.

Getting There & Away Boats to the Uros depart from the Puno docks hourly (or as soon as there are 20 to 30 passengers) between 7 am and early afternoon. The standard tour takes about four hours, visiting the main island and perhaps one of the others. The fare is about US$2.50 per person.

Isla Taquile

Taquile is a fascinating island with colourfully costumed Quechua-speaking people with a strong group identity. The island lacks roads and electricity, there are no vehicles and, surprisingly, no dogs.

The island is six or seven km long and has several hills with Inca terracing and minor ruins. Visitors can wander around exploring these ruins, soaking up the scenery and the peaceful environment.

From the dock it takes 20 minutes, if you are acclimatised, to climb the steep stairway to the centre of the island. Due to the high altitude, take your time and rest if you begin to feel lightheaded.

The Fiesta de Santiago (25 July) is the big feast day on Taquile, with the requisite dancing, music and general carousing continuing until the beginning of August when the locals traditionally make offerings to Pachamama. New Year's Day is also festive and rowdy.

Places to Stay & Eat There are no hotels on Taquile; after arriving at the dock, individuals or small groups of visitors will be assigned to families who will put them up in their homes. The charge is approximately US$1 per person, but gifts of fresh foods from Puno are also appreciated.

Although they provide blankets, a sleeping bag will probably be more comfortable because nights can get extremely cold. Visitors do what the locals do, washing from a bucket of cold water and using the fields as a latrine. Bring a torch!

The island has a few simple restaurants. If you're lucky, there'll be fresh trout. Otherwise, expect boiled potatoes. You may want to bring some munchies from the mainland just in case. Bottled drinks are normally available and boiled tea is usually safe to drink, but it's worth carrying bottled water or purification tablets if you're concerned.

Change is limited on the island so carry small notes. You may also want to bring sufficient cash to pick up some of the unique and irresistible woven or knitted woollens produced and sold by local women.

Getting There & Away The Taquile boat departs from the Puno docks daily at around 8 or 9 am, but turn up at 7.30 am to ensure a place. The 24-km passage takes four hours, including a brief stop at the Uros, and costs US$4 for the return trip. The boat back to Puno leaves at 2.30 pm allowing about two hours on Taquile, but if you plan to stay overnight on the island, you may use the return portion on another day. Bring sunscreen, since the high-altitude sun and reflections off the lake can be fierce.

Isla Amántani

This island a few km north of Taquile is less frequently visited and has fewer facilities. Basic food and accommodation are available for about US$2 per day or you can eat in one of the cooperative restaurants. Boats leave from Puno's dock between 7.30 and 8.30 am on most days. The round trip costs US$4.

YUNGUYO (PERU)

Yunguyo is the Peruvian border town opposite Copacabana. Buses for Yunguyo from Puno depart from the Mercado Laykakota and take three hours. It's far less problematic to arrange a minibus directly to Copacabana with one of the numerous tour agencies in Puno. They'll wait while you exchange money in Yunguyo and while you complete immigration procedures on both sides. If you have a minute, note the whimsical topiary on the plaza. Sunday is market day in Yunguyo.

Money changers may be found around Yunguyo plaza and at the border two km away, but use extreme caution changing with them. Casas de cambio generally give poor rates changing Peruvian soles or US dollars into bolivianos, but they're often better than in Copacabana where there are no official exchange facilities.

Getting There & Away

Crossing the Border The border, where you pass through immigration procedures, is open between 8 am and 6 pm. Once across, you still have to reach Bolivian customs at Copacabana, nine km away. If you're entering Bolivia, make certain that the date stamped on your passport matches the calendar date. Immigration officials are notorious for setting up sting operations in which they deliberately misstamp your passport then track you down and impose a fine for the irregularity.

Be warned also that the *impuesto turístico* (tourist entry tax), requested at the border when coming from Peru is unofficial and optional. It's an alternative to requesting a tip and any money paid slides right into the pockets of immigration officers.

At the time of writing, proof of vaccination against cholera and/or a health certificate stating that the bearer is cholera-free was required of anyone entering Bolivia from Peru. Selling health documents to foreign travellers has become quite a profitable racket on the streets of both Puno and Yunguyo, but Bolivian officials have wised up. Have a cholera jab before you travel and get an official certificate from the clinic in Yunguyo; minibus drivers will wait while you complete the formalities.

contemporary craft design

Southern Altiplano

Stretching south from La Paz all the way to the Chilean and Argentine frontiers and beyond is a harsh, sparsely populated wilderness of scrubby windswept basins, lonely peaks and glaring, nearly lifeless salt deserts. This is the archetypal Altiplano, a Tibet-like land of lonely mirages and indeterminable distances. Though the air retains no warmth, the land and sky meet in waves of shimmering reflected heat and the horizon disappears. Stark mountains seem to hover somewhere beyond reality and the sense of solitude is overwhelming. The nights are just as haunting, with black skies and icy stars. As soon as the sun sets, you'll quickly learn that this air has teeth.

Geologically, the vast plateau was a deep intermontane valley during the Cretaceous period some 100,000,000 years ago. Erosion in those mountains filled the valley with a 15,000-metre-deep deposit of sediment to create the base for the present-day Altiplano. With such porous alluvial soil, the basin's fertility is predictable, but the presence of salts, lack of adequate moisture and a rocky surface character make agriculture a challenging venture.

The few inhabitants of the region are among the hardiest souls on earth, living at the ragged edge of human endurance. They contend with wind, drought, bitter cold, and high altitude without modern conveniences which make such things bearable in harsh climates elsewhere. They labour unceasingly throughout their lives to wrest an existence from this land. The campesino miners, farmers and herders of the Altiplano deserve a great deal of respect for their accomplishments.

Even given the opportunity of relative prosperity in the developing lowlands, few Aymará have chosen to leave their ancestral homes. This is the same hardy group of people that managed to resist efforts by the Incas to assimilate them, body and soul, into the empire. They refused to accept the Quechua language and the culture of the conquerors from the West and were the only conquered tribe to get away with it.

Fiercely proud and stubborn, the Aymará seem as harsh and cold as the land they inhabit. This is spawned by a deep suspicion of the motives of foreigners who venture in with what seems to be a lot of money and no visible means of support. People who work hard at meagre survival can't fathom someone trotting around the globe rather than attending to work, religious and family responsibilities at home (some of your relatives may feel the same way!). With patience and diplomacy, however, the icy barrier can sometimes be broken and you can catch a glimpse of a world and lifestyle harsh beyond imagining.

The mineral-rich Southern Altiplano produces a large portion of Bolivia's non-illicit exports. Oruro and Llallagua are the centres of tin production and an enormous tin smelter operates at Vinto, near Oruro. Throughout southern Potosí Department are numerous remote and antiquated mining operations which dip into the area's rich concentrations of antimony, bismuth, silver, lead, zinc, copper, salt, sulphur, magnesium and other buried treasures.

The country is wisely protective of these mineral-rich remote border regions. However, due to lack of capital and expertise, many of Bolivia's resources in these areas are either ignored or underexploited. One Bolivian put it this way: 'Bolivia is like a donkey loaded with silver – all this potential wealth is nothing but a liability'.

The sheltered and spectacular red rock country of the Tupiza area in south-eastern Potosí Department represents a gentler side of south-western Bolivia. Its population is currently swelling with *mineros despedidos* (unemployed miners), victims of layoffs and labour strife in the mines of Oruro and Potosí.

Climatically, the best time to visit is

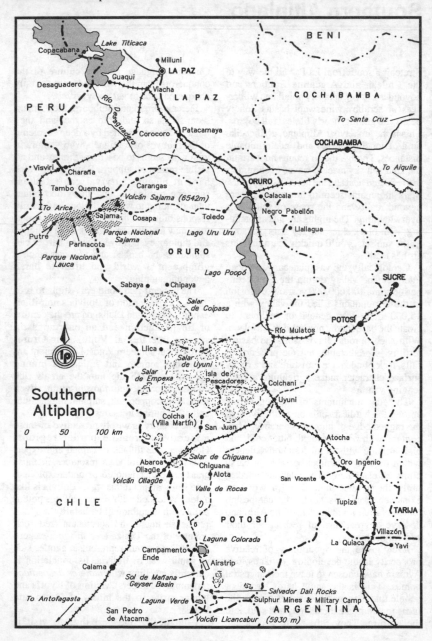

Southern Altiplano

0   50   100 km

between the months of April and July. Although the area experiences an arid climate, it does receive rain between November and March. Winds blow year-round but are at their most violent in late winter and early spring. At any time of year, bring protection against both sun and wind and for winter nights, dress as you would for Outer Mongolia or Alaska's North Slope and you can't go wrong; Altiplano night time temperatures combined with a good stiff wind can bring the wind chill down to -40°!

ORURO

Oruro, the only city of the Southern Altiplano, lies immediately north of the salty lakes Uru Uru and Poopó, three hours by bus south of La Paz. It sits at the intersection of the rail lines between Cochabamba, La Paz and Chile/Argentina, crowded against a colourful range of mineral-rich low hills at an altitude of 3702 metres. The 150,000 to 170,000 inhabitants of Oruro, of whom 90% are of pure Indian heritage, are for some reason known as *quirquinchos* (armadillos).

Visitors are rarely indifferent to Oruro – they either love it or hate it. Although it's one of Bolivia's most culturally colourful cities – it's known as the 'Folkloric Capital of Bolivia' – for tourists it is neither a friendly nor welcoming place and recent mining difficulties seem to have made matters worse. Don't arrive expecting the worst, however; if you can demonstrate that you pose no threats, people may open up, and if you manage to attend La Diablada, a wild annual fiesta which takes place during Carnival, you certainly won't regret it.

Once upon a time, visitors had to register with the police upon arrival in Oruro if they planned to stay overnight. This is no longer required, but hotels still recommend it.

History

Founded in 1606, Oruro owes its existence to the hills that form its backdrop. Chock full of copper, silver and tin, they occupy only 10 sq km and rise to an average height of just 350 metres above the surrounding Altiplano.

Early activities focused almost exclusively on silver extraction, but when production declined in the early 1800s, Indian workers moved on in search of more lucrative livelihoods, and the community was more or less abandoned. Oruro's importance as a mining region was revived during the late 19th and early 20th centuries, when demands for tin and copper rose on world markets. By the 1920s, Bolivia's exploding tin-mining industry was controlled by three major capitalists. The most powerful was Simon I Patiño, the Indian from Cochabamba valley who disputably became the world's wealthiest man.

La Salvadora tin mine east of Oruro near the village of Uncia had been purchased by Patiño in 1897 and became the world's most productive. Patiño's success snowballed into capitalistic mania and by 1924 he had taken ownership of the rich mines at nearby Llallagua, thereby gaining control of about 50% of the nation's tin output. Now secure in his wealth, he set up in England, where he began buying up European and North American smelters and tin interests. As a consequence of this defection, not only was the tin being exported from Bolivia, the profits were also. Public outcry launched a series of labour uprisings and set the stage for nationalisation of the mines by Victor Paz Estenssoro in 1952.

The two other 'tin barons', Carlos Victor Aramayo from Tupiza and Mauricio Hothschild, a Jew of European extraction, kept their centres of operations in Bolivia, but the 1952 revolution stripped them of their wealth and Aramayo fled to Europe to escape the ill will of his compatriots.

The government has now turned the mining interests over to the private sector and the resulting turmoil – accompanied by low world tin prices, stiff competition from abroad, and turbulent labour unrest – has left the already fluctuating population of Oruro in a state of uncertainty. Due to unstable conditions, high unemployment and low wages, the city's population is currently decreasing, and many residents believe Oruro is dying. Others take a more optimistic

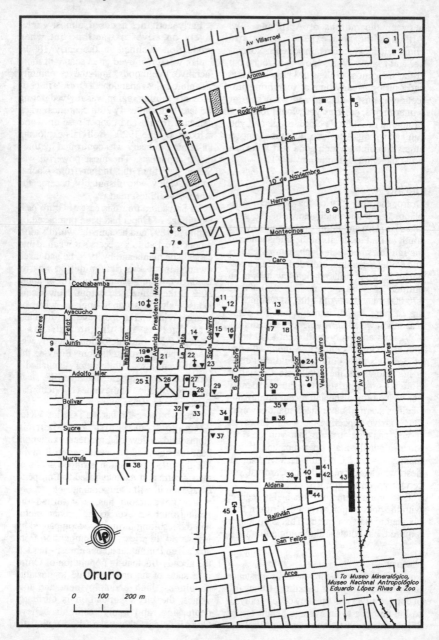

Oruro

0   100   200 m

■ PLACES TO STAY

2	Hotel Terminal
4	Residencial Bolivia
5	Hotel Lipton
13	Alojamiento Scala
17	Alojamiento Ayacucho
18	Alojamiento Pagador
30	Residencial Ideal
34	Hotel Sucre
36	Hotel Repostero
38	Hostal Osber
41	Alojamiento San Juan de Diós
42	Alojamiento Copacabana
44	Hotel Prefectural

▼ PLACES TO EAT

12	Rabitos
14	El Chef 312
15	Super Salteñas
16	Coral
21	La Casona
23	Confitería Paris
29	Heladería Alemana
32	Le Grill
35	El Huerto

| 37 | Burger Queen & Indianapolis Driving School |
| 39 | Nayjama |

OTHER

1	Bus Terminal
3	Diablada Masks & Costumes
6	Iglesia de Conchupata
7	Parque Abaroa & Teatro al Aire Libre
8	Stop for Micro to Hot Springs
9	Museo Etnográfico Minero & Santuario del Socavón
10	Mercado Fermín López & Iglesia de Santo Domingo
11	Museo Patiño (Casa de la Cultura)
19	LAB
20	Post Office
22	Iglesia San Francisco
24	Ferretería Findel
25	Tourist Office
26	Plaza 10 de Febrero
27	Librería Elier
28	ENTEL
31	Mercado Campero
33	Farmacia Santa Marta
40	Lavandería Alemana
43	Railway Station
45	Church

approach and maintain that it's only experiencing a transition period.

Information

Tourist Office The poor old tourist office (☎ 51764) is open weekdays from 9 am to noon and 2 to 6 pm, and on Saturday and Sunday from 9 am to noon. It tries to be helpful, but without any maps, brochures or pamphlets – not even photocopies – it finds it fairly difficult to make much of an impression. In response to our various questions, a single lonely office employee at a bare desk scrawled out responses (which we later verified to be commendably accurate) with the stub of a pencil – we had to supply the paper. Go and give this fellow a vote of confidence!

The booklet *Carnaval de Oruro Bolivia – Guia Turística 1991* by Elias Delgado Morales will be a good source of information if you read Spanish. You'll find it at the Librería Elier at the corner of Adolfo Mier and La Plata.

Money Only a couple of places change travellers' cheques and the rate is much lower than for cash. Try the Farmacia Santa Marta on Calle Bolivar opposite the ENTEL office or the Ferretería Findel on the corner of Adolfo Mier and Pagador, facing the market. Any of the shops displaying *compro dólares* signs will exchange cash dollars; there are a few along Adolfo Mier. Street changers can be found on the corner of 6 de Octubre and Aldana near Plaza Ingavi.

Post & Telecommunications The ENTEL office, one of the nicest modern buildings in Oruro, is near the corner of Soria Galvarro and Bolivar, just below the main plaza, Plaza 10 de Febrero. The public fax number in Oruro is (052) 50574.

The post office is just north of the tourist office near the main plaza. If you're planning to post a parcel, have it inspected at the Aduana Nacional on Velasco Galvarro between Ayacucho and Calle Junín before taking it to the post office.

Foreign Consulate For some unfathomable reason, there's a German Consulate on Adolfo Mier just below the main plaza. It's open weekday mornings until 11 am.

Laundry Laundry service is available at Lavandería Alemana, opposite the Hotel Prefectural.

Mines

Several mines in the hills behind the city are open to tourists. The most popular is Mina San José, high on the mountain behind the city, which claims to have been in operation for more than 450 years. To get there take micro 'D' (yellow) marked 'San José' which leaves from the north-west corner of Plaza 10 de Febrero near the tourist office. Arrive at 7 am and visit the Superintendencia de Minas for a permit to enter. There are no guides and no admission charges; just wander in and look around – cautiously, of course. Non-employees aren't permitted on the lower levels. Itos, another mine south-west of town, is reached by micro 'C' marked 'Sud'.

Churches

The cathedral just below the main plaza has nice stained glass work above the altar. The Santuario de la Virgen del Socavón, on Cerro Pie de Gallo (Rooster Foot Hill) above town, offers a view over the city and figures prominently in the Diablada as the site where good ultimately defeats evil (see the discussion of La Diablada under Fiestas). For the energetic, there's also a good view from the Capilla de Serrato, accessible from the end of Calle Washington. Iglesia de Conchupata at the top of Avenida Presidente Montes is much easier to reach for a great view across the town.

Museums

Museo Patiño (Casa de la Cultura) The university-administered Museo Patiño in the Casa de la Cultura is on Soria Galvarro north of Ayacucho. It's housed in the old Patiño mansion, and his furniture and personal effects, and an ornate stairway are on display. The museum is open weekdays from 8.30 am to noon and 2 to 6 pm. Visiting exhibitions are featured in the downstairs lobby. Admission is free.

Museo Etnográfico Minero Adjacent to the Santuario de la Virgen del Socavón is the Mining Museum, an actual mine tunnel, which reveals the various aspects and methods of mining in Bolivia: tunnels, 'mailboxes', tailing dumps, chimneys, 'El Tío' (the devilish character who legend has it owns the minerals), etc. It's open daily from 9 am to noon and 3 to 5.30 pm. Admission is B2.

Museo Mineralógico The worthwhile Mineralogy Museum, upstairs in the prominent multistorey building on the university hill, has minerals, precious stones, fossils and crystals from around the world. It's open from 9 am to noon and 2.30 to 6 pm Monday to Saturday; if it's locked, go to the Departamento de Minas at the university or knock on the door and the janitor may let you in. From the patio outside is a nice view of Lago Uru Uru, several km away.

To get to the museum, catch micro 'A' (green) marked 'Sud' from the YPFB petrol station opposite the railway station and get off at the end of the line. Admission is free.

Museo Nacional Antropológico Eduardo López Rivas The National Anthropological Museum at the south end of town has been newly remodelled and upgraded with local contributions and the help of the German government. The focus is on the Oruro area and displays include artefacts and information on the early Chipayas and Uros tribes. To get there, take micro 'C' (orange) marked 'Sud' from the north-west corner of the main plaza or opposite the railway station and get off just beyond the tin-foundry compound. Museum hours are from 10 am to noon and 3 to 6 pm Tuesday to Sunday. Admission is B1.50.

Zoo

Oruro's marginally interesting but nauseatingly unkempt zoo is just near the children's playground opposite the Museo Antropológico. Its only redemption is a large aviary where you get a close-up view of Andean condors, but interest pales when you realise such large and stately birds would prefer to be soaring over remote Andean crags. It's open from 10 am to noon and 3 to 6 pm Tuesday to Sunday and costs B1. From the plaza, take micro 'C' (orange) marked 'Sud'.

Old Trains

There are a number of old and decomposing steam locomotives and rail cars moored along the tracks at the north end of town. The railyards are off limits to outsiders, but you can catch a glimpse of them through the fence.

Fiestas

La Diablada The Diablada (Dance of the Devils) has become the most renowned and largest annual celebration held in Bolivia. If you plan to be on hand for La Diablada, reserve accommodation early or plan to camp. Prices will go up automatically during the Diablada but beware of excessive 'gringo' pricing.

In the broadest sense, the Carnival festivities can be described as the triumph of good over evil, but it is so interlaced with threads of both Christian and Indian myths, fables, deities and traditions that to oversimplify it in this way detracts from its uniqueness.

The origins of a similar festival may be traced back to 12th-century Cataluña (Spain), although Orureños maintain that it commemorates an event that occurred during the early days of Oruro. Legend has it that one night a thief called Chiruchiru was seriously wounded by a traveller he'd attempted to rob. The Virgin of Candelaria

La Diablada Dancer

gently helped him reach his home near the mine and succoured him at the base of Cerro Píe de Gallo before he died. When the miners found him there, they saw hanging over his head the Virgin's image. Today, the mine is called Socavón de la Virgen (Grotto of the Virgin). This legend has been combined with the ancient Uros tale of Huari and the struggle of Michael the Archangel against the seven deadly sins into the spectacle that is presented during the Oruro Carnival.

The design and creation of Diablada costumes has become an art form in Oruro and several Diablada clubs consisting of members from all levels of Oruro society are sponsored by local businesses. Groups number anywhere from 40 to 300 dancing participants. Costumes, which may cost several hundred dollars each, are owned by individual dancers, and rehearsals of their diabolical dances begin on the first Sunday in November, several months in advance of the Carnival.

Festivities begin the first Saturday before Ash Wednesday with a glorious *entrada* or opening parade led by the brightly costumed Michael the Archangel character. Behind him, dancing and marching, come the

La Diablada Mask

famous devils and a host of bears and condors. The chief devil, Lucifer, wears the most extravagant costume, complete with a velvet cape and an ornate mask. Faithfully at his side are two other devils, including Supay, the Andean god of evil that inhabits the hills and mineshafts.

The procession is followed by vehicles adorned with jewels, coins and silver service in commemoration of the achura rites in which the Incas offered their treasures to Inti (the sun) in the festival of Inti Raymi, and the miners offer the year's highest quality mineral to El Tío, the devil who owns the mines.

Behind them follow the Incas and a host of conquistadores, including Francisco Pizarro and Diego de Almagro. When the Archangel and the fierce-looking devilish dancers arrive at the football stadium, a series of dances unfold the ultimate battle between good and evil. When it becomes apparent that good has triumphed, the dancers retire to the Santuario de la Virgen del Socavón and a mass is held in honour of the Virgen del Socavón, who pronounces that good has prevailed.

For three days following the entrada, other dance groups perform at locations throughout the city. Each group has its specific costume and performs its own dance. For a brief rundown of the dances, refer to the discussion of Dance in the Arts & Culture section of the Facts about the Country chapter.

Places to Stay – bottom end

Most of the accommodation in Oruro falls into the bottom-end range. Alojamientos *Scala* (☎ 52553), *Pagador* (☎ 54985) and *Ayacucho* (☎ 50567) all seem to be cast in the same unfriendly mould. To foreigners, they're normally 'full', anyway. The Pagador is the least objectionable of the lot. They all charge B9/16 for a single/double. As in most of Oruro, hot water is unheard of and blankets are jealously rationed.

Alojamiento Copacabana (☎ 54184) at Velasco Galvarro 6352 and *Alojamiento Ferrocarril* (☎ 60079) at Velasco Galvarro 6278, both near the railway station, are slightly more welcoming, although they are far from clean and are not really good-value options. *Alojamiento San Juan de Diós* (☎ 53083) at Velasco Galvarro 6344 is friendlier and a bit nicer. All charge B9/16 for very basic single/double rooms.

Slightly better, but far from ideal, is the *Residencial Ideal* (☎ 52863) on Calle Bolivar which has hot water and charges B11/13 for single/double rooms. Another step up is *Hostal Osber* on the corner of Calles Murguía and Washington.

The *Hotel Repostero* (☎ 50505) at Calle Sucre 370 is Oruro's friendliest and most relaxed hotel. Singles/doubles with bath and hot showers cost B29/55 or B17/32 with shared bath.

A popular place with travellers is the *Hotel Lipton* (☎ 41583) at the corner of Avenida 6 de Agosto and Rodriguez. It's a good option if you want to stay near the bus terminal but would rather avoid the rip-off Hotel Terminal. Spartan rooms without bath cost B15 per person and unfortunately the shared loos don't receive much attention and can get quite aromatic. Double beds with private bath and electric hot water cost just B40.

Near the Hotel Lipton is the *Residencial Bolivia* on Rodriguez between Velasco Galvarro and Avenida 6 de Agosto. Rooms without bath cost B20/30 for singles/ doubles. Alternatively, try the relatively friendly *Hotel Sucre* (☎ 53838) at Calle Sucre 510. Rooms with bath and electric showers are B28/50 while without bath, they cost B18/30.

Places to Stay – middle

As far as amenities are concerned, the *Hotel Terminal* (☎ 53127) above the bus terminal is probably the nicest of a bad lot in Oruro. It has private baths, heating and hot showers, but their pricing structure is a revolting scam. Bolivians pay B35/50 for single/double rooms and foreigners must pay B61/81. One British business traveller wrote that his Bolivian colleagues were most embarrassed at this clear case of discrimination.

A better choice would be the *Hotel Prefectural* (☎ 60588) at the corner of Aldana and Pagador. They have a restaurant, laundry service, and electric showers. Singles/ doubles with bath cost B30/50. Without bath, you'll pay B18/30.

Camping

There aren't any organised sites, but it is possible to camp in the low hills immediately behind the university where it won't be too difficult to find a secluded place to pitch a tent with views of the city and Lago Uru Uru. There's no surface water so carry all you'll be needing.

Places to Eat

If you're hoping for anything but a market breakfast, you'll probably be out of luck. Most places don't open until 11 am or later and the few that open earlier don't seem to have anything worthwhile. *Heladería Alemana* which opens at 9 am, for example, serves salteñas and Pepsi and absolutely nothing else, not even coffee, until lunchtime. The best salteñas are found at *La Casona* on Avenida Presidente Montes just

off the main plaza, opposite the post office, and *Super Salteñas* on Soria Galvarro. Both these places serve pizzas in the evening.

For bargain lunch specials check out such eateries as *Beirut*, *El Turista* and *San Juan de Diós* opposite the railway station. Even better are *Coral* on Calle 6 de Octubre, *Rabitos* on Ayacucho and *Le Grill* on Calle Bolivar. *Nayjama* on the corner of Pagador and Aldana has good lunches and a variety of typical dishes for under B12. The railway station has a passable bar and, although it's not saying much, the bus terminal confitería serves the best coffee in town.

About the only recommended Oruro restaurant is *El Chef 312* at Calle Junín 676 between La Plata and Soria Galvarro. Daily lunch specials may include such exotics as pizzas and pasta, as well as old Bolivian stand-bys. Vegetarian dishes are available at *El Huerto* on Calle Bolivar.

If it's ice cream you're after, try *Heladería Suiza* on Calle Bolivar or *Confitería Paris* at the corner of Adolfo Mier and Soria Galvarro. The Suiza also serves salteñas, hot drinks and pastries, and the Paris extends itself as far as banana splits, snacks and quickie meals.

Altiplano Campesino

For fast food, try the marginal *Burger Queen* beneath a borrowed Burger King logo. You can't miss it; it's just next door to the Indianapolis Driving School where, it seems, all Oru256os have honed their driving skills.

Market food stalls in both the *Mercado Campero* near the railway station and *Mercado Fermín López* on Calle Washington are the cheapest places to eat. They feature noodles in all forms (imported from Argentina!), falso conejo, mutton soup, beef dishes and thimpu de cordero – boiled potatoes, oca, rice and carrots over mutton, smothered with hot llajhua sauce.

Things to Buy

The most unique items available in Oruro relate to La Diablada. Along Avenida La Paz there are many small shops where artesans sell embroidered wall hangings, devil masks and costumes of all descriptions for B10 to B1000.

Llama and alpaca wool bags and clothing are found at artesanía shops in the town centre, but similar, less expensive articles are sold inside the north-east corner of the main market. Zampoñas, charangos and other indigenous musical instruments are sold at sidewalk kiosks in front of the railway station.

Getting There & Away

Bus Oruro serves as a transportation hub between La Paz and the highland valleys region. The Terminal de Omnibuses Hernando Siles claims to be one of Bolivia's most modern; it may be only a few years old, but it's already falling into disrepair.

There are departures every half hour for the three-hour journey between La Paz and Oruro. The fare is B10. About midway between La Paz and Oruro, look for a shallow lake about 100 metres east of the highway; it's normally teeming with flamingos.

Buses to and from Cochabamba are nearly as frequent. The trip costs B8 and takes six hours. Service onward to Santa Cruz requires several hours' layover in Cochabamba, even

on flotas offering 'direct' service. The only company which goes straight through to Sucre, an 18-hour trip, is Transportes Oruro, with an hour stop in Cochabamba.

To Potosí, the flotas Alianza and Universo leave at 7 pm daily for the rather rough overnight trip. Seven times daily, Flota Bustillo goes to Llallagua for B5.50.

Train Thanks to its mines, Oruro is a railroad centre and for what it's worth, has one of the most organised and efficient railway stations in Bolivia. In fact, the schedules for Bolivia's western rail network are devised here and the proud planners have produced an impressive printed timetable – the only one found anywhere in the country – with schedules showing precision to the minute. However, comparison with the chalkboard announcements at the station will reveal that the document is no more than a recording of a moment in history: the one in which the schedule was elaborated.

Oruro marks the beginning for most rail journeys toward Chile or Argentina. Because rail service between La Paz and Oruro is slow and difficult to arrange, most people travel by bus from La Paz to Oruro and begin their rail journey there.

From Oruro, you can travel to Uyuni, where the rail line splits; one line goes to Tupiza and Villazón and the other to Chile. Going east, there are lines to Cochabamba, and to Potosí and Sucre via Río Mulatos.

To/From Cochabamba There are ferrobuses doing the five-hour journey from Oruro to Cochabamba on Monday and Wednesday at 12.10 pm, on Saturday at 1.10 pm and on Wednesday, Friday and Sunday at 8.15 am. For the schedule from Cochabamba to Oruro, see Getting There & Away under Cochabamba. The fare in pullman is B17 and in especial, B13. On Thursday, there's a train going to Cochabamba at 8.20 am. The fare is B15/11 for 1st/2nd class.

The rail trip between Cochabamba and Oruro is one of the great rail trips of South America. It runs along the river valley for two hours past small, otherwise inaccessible, villages, then crosses the river and zigzags up 5000 feet onto the Altiplano. The views of the valley below and the rock formations at sunset are quite majestic.

Kevin Bell

To/From Potosí & Sucre Trains leave for Potosí and Sucre on Wednesday at 9 pm and cost B22/16 in 1st/2nd class to Potosí and B33/25 to Sucre. The ferrobus leaves on Tuesday and Saturday at 10 pm and costs B32/26 for pullman/especial to Potosí and B48/38 to Sucre. The trip to Potosí takes seven hours, and to Sucre, 12 hours.

To/From Southern Bolivia There is a ferrobus going as far as Tupiza on Tuesday and Saturday at 11.30 am. To Uyuni, Tupiza and Villazón, trains leave at 9 pm on Monday and Thursday and on Wednesday and Sunday at 7.25 pm (the Wednesday train splits at Uyuni; part goes to Chile, the rest to Villazón). The trip to Uyuni ideally takes about six hours, to Tupiza, 12 hours and to Villazón, 15 hours.

To/From Chile The rail trip from Oruro to Calama, Chile, will take anywhere from 18 to 27 hours. Once in Calama, you will need to board a bus for the two to three-hour trip to Antofagasta on the coast, as although there is a rail line, there is currently no rail service on this route. It's sometimes possible to change money in Uyuni or Ollagüe but it's best not to count on it. Casa de Cambio Sudamer in La Paz gives the best and most reliable rate for Chilean pesos.

The route passes through some interesting and spectacular scenery and the journey is highly worthwhile if you come prepared for uncomfortable conditions. Temperatures in the coaches fall well below zero at night so a sleeping bag or woollen blanket and plenty of warm clothing will be essential. There's no dining car, so bring plenty of food as well. You can't carry fruit, meat, or cheese across the border into Chile so try to eat it up before reaching customs at Ollagüe.

Between Uyuni and the border, the line crosses vast saltpans, deserts and rugged barren mountains. Flamingoes, guanacos, vicuñas and wild burros are common, and thanks to a startling mirage effect, so are a host of other assorted things. *Remolinos* (dust devils or willy-willys) whirl across the stark landscape beneath towering snow-capped volcanoes. One type of vegetation that flourishes is *yareta*, a combustible salt-tolerant moss that oozes a turpentine-like jelly and is used by the locals as stove fuel. It appears soft and spongy from a distance but is actually rock-hard. Yareta grows very slowly; a large clump may be several hundred years old. The plant is now an officially protected species in Chile.

Bolivian exit stamps are given on the train as soon as it leaves Uyuni: passports are collected in bulk, stamped and returned coach by coach in the last coach of the train. The Chilean immigration procedures at Abaroa/Ollagüe, a windy, dusty and unprotected outpost in a broad pass through the Andes, can be trying. You must queue up for your entrance stamp and again for a luggage search. All this takes place outside, and at night it's a miserable exercise in endurance.

At the border post, travellers must change to the Chilean coaches, which are in surprisingly worse repair than their Bolivian counterparts. Windows are broken and the coaches lack light and heating. Some have wooden benches instead of seats, cold winds whistle through loose boards and the toilets are actually outside, exposed to the elements.

The Calama-bound train departs Oruro on Wednesday at 7.25 pm and costs B61 for the only class available. Expect unexplained delays, especially at Uyuni.

To/From Argentina Going toward Argentina, you can take the Expreso del Sur which goes to Retiro Station in Buenos Aires in just under three days, including a walk across the border between Villazón and La Quiaca. Prepare for a lengthy stop in Uyuni and read the cold weather warnings under To/From Chile. The train from Oruro runs on Tuesday and Friday at 7 pm and from Buenos Aires on Thursday at 6 pm. The total fare is B281.

For border crossing information, see Getting There & Away under Villazón.

Getting Around

Oruro city micros and minibuses cost B.50 and connect the city centre with outlying areas. They're lettered A, B, C and D but each micro may do several different runs. One micro 'D', for example, goes to the Vinto smelter and is marked 'Vinto ENAF'. Another micro 'D' goes to the San José mine and is marked 'San José'. Oruro micros are small and crowded so don't carry luggage aboard.

Taxis from the transportation terminals to the centre, or between the transportation terminals, cost B1.50 per person. Prices aren't negotiable and many charge an additional B1 if you have a lot of luggage. Don't let the cabbies talk you into paying more than the standard fare, which they will surely try to do.

AROUND ORURO
Complejo Metalúrgico Vinto

This US$12,000,000 tin smelter was constructed in the early 1970s during the presidency of General Hugo Banzer Suárez. By the time it was put into operation, the Bolivian tin industry was already experiencing a steady decline.

It's eight km east of the centre, and may be visited between 9 am and noon on weekdays. To get there, take micro 'D' marked 'Vinto ENAF' from the north-west corner of Plaza 10 de Noviembre and apply at the office for permission to tour the operation.

Lago Uru Uru (Lago del Milagro)

To visit this large shallow lake just south of town, take micro 'A' marked 'Sud' to its terminus at the university. From there, walk three km or so along the highway to the lake. There's good fishing for pejerrey and you'll also see flamingoes in the shallow water. There's a small restaurant and a cabaña at the shore where you may hire boats for fishing or exploring the lake.

Capachos & Obrajes

The hot springs of Capachos and Obrajes are 16 and 23 km from Oruro along the Cochabamba road. Both resorts have covered hot pools and individual baths. To get there, catch the micro which costs B2 and leaves when full from Avenida 6 de Agosto, between Herrera and Montecinos. Admission to either of the springs is B2 per person.

Calacala

The archaeological site at Calacala lies approximately 20 km east of Oruro along the road toward Negro Pabellón. The rock paintings and engravings are in a rock shelter at the base of a hulking monolith. The llama theme is most prominent, but there are also a puma and some roughly human figures painted in white and earth tones. As yet, no definitive theory of their origin has been formulated, but some investigators credit an Inca-era cameloid cult.

On 14 September, there's a pilgrimage and fiesta in honour of the Señor de Lagunas at the church in Calacala.

Getting There & Away On Saturday and Sunday, micros run from Oruro to Calacala; alternatively, you can get a taxi. Once in Calacala, you'll have to track down the park guard who will unlock the gate to the site and act as a guide.

LLALLAGUA

Originally belonging to the Chilean Llallagua Company, the town of Llallagua was bought out by tin baron Simon Patiño in 1924 after he gained sufficient capital from his success in nearby Uncia. The area's most famous mine, Siglo XX, grew into one of Bolivia's most productive, and remains the largest tin mine in the country, with 800 km of underground passages.

History

With the nationalisation of mining interests in 1952, control of Llallagua passed into the hands of COMIBOL (Corporación Minera de Bolivia). It was then operated by the federal government until the mid-1980s when Victor Paz Estenssoro (the same president who had initiated the 1952 mining reform!) decided during his third non-consecutive term of office to return the project to private, miner-owned cooperatives.

Visiting the Mines

A large sign posted outside the Siglo XX mine states that foreigners must obtain permission from COMIBOL headquarters in Catavi before they will be admitted as visitors. Strikes, layoffs and the drop in tin prices have turned Llallagua into a near ghost town. Given the confusion resulting from the transition-related strife, catering to curious tourists is the least of the miners' concerns. Often, promised severance pay hasn't materialised and many destitute, out-of-work miners have emigrated from the region en masse.

The miners that remain in Llallagua, though mostly illiterate and largely ignorant of world affairs, passionately try to keep abreast of the Bolivian political situation that so profoundly affects their lives, and will happily engage willing listeners in a discussion of their favourite topic.

One foreign traveller who had business in Llallagua has written of his experiences:

Being involved in a tin project in Bolivia has been frustrating because of the disastrous drop in the tin price to around US$3 per pound. The offices of COMIBOL in La Paz reflect the state of things; offices are old and run down and the mines I visited were the most dangerous I've ever seen, mainly because safety measures cost money that is not available. It is certainly a case of production first and everything else second. Some mines are being renovated with foreign loan money in a very professional manner, which means that Bolivia has some excellent engineering staff.

Llallagua was very interesting and I can recommend the book by Domitila Barrios de Chungara, *Let Me Speak*, as a good description of what it's like to live and work in Siglo XX. There's no problem visiting the area once you're through the security gate. The cooperative miners are friendly and are quite happy to tell you about their work on the tailings dumps and in the rivers. They are proud that their work is respected enough by others to ask questions. This must be the only place in the world where mining

methods are the same as they were centuries ago and the miners are happy to have their photos taken.

The profit margin on these small-scale operations is almost nil and it is very hard work. It is not possible to visit the town or the plant without permission granted by the COMIBOL general manager who has some control over the area; he lives near the Patiño theatre and was very friendly, allowing my group to see anything we wanted.

Fiesta

On the 14th and 15th of August is the fiesta of the Virgen de la Asunción with processions and drunken tinku fighting.

Places to Stay & Eat

The friendly but basic *Hotel Llallagua* costs B7 and the restaurant will cook up anything that happens to be available in the market.

Getting There & Away

Llallagua lies 95 km by road south-east of Oruro. Flota Bustillo has a service from Oruro seven times daily. Llallagua is also served daily at 6 pm by Flota Minera from Cochabamba.

COROCORO

Corocoro, just east of the Río Desaguadero near the La Paz-Arica rail line, is another major Southern Altiplano mining town. The Corocoro mines produce nearly all of Bolivia's copper and Corocoro is one of the two major sources of native copper in the world today, the other being on Michigan's Upper Peninsula on the US shore of Lake Superior. Since the copper is found in nugget form and not in ore which must be smelted, the early native peoples of the Altiplano used it long before anyone knew what to do with ore copper. The Museo de Metales Preciosos Pre-Columbinos in La Paz displays some examples of their work.

PARQUE NACIONAL SAJAMA

Loosely defined and undeveloped Parque Nacional Sajama occupies approximately 80,000 hectares abutting the Chilean border. It was created on 5 November 1945 for the protection of the hulking volcano Nevado Sajama, disputably Bolivia's highest peak, at

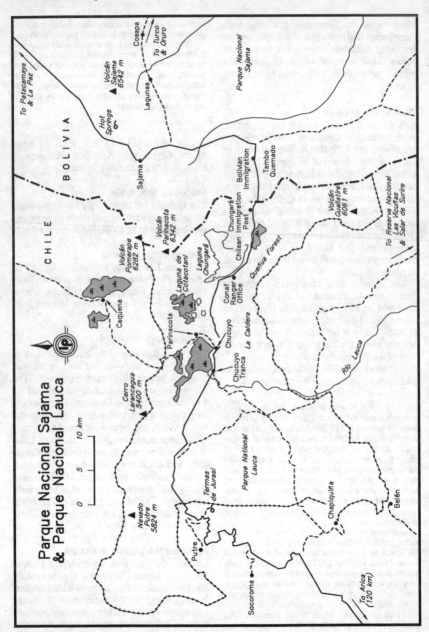

Parque Nacional Sajama
& Parque Nacional Lauca

6542 metres, the *queñua* tree, and the wild-life that inhabits this northern region of the Atacama desert.

The world's highest forest covers the foothills flanking the impressive Volcán Sajama. This forest consists of dwarf queñua trees, a species unique to the Altiplano, but they're nothing to get steamed up about unless you're into checking off superlatives. These 'trees' have the size and appearance of creosote bushes. Unfortunately, depredation of the park has already eliminated the puma, Andean deer, viscacha and guanaco; only the vicuña, condor, flamingo, rhea and armadillo survive, but in very limited numbers.

Volcán Sajama

This mountain is unquestionably the centrepiece of all it surveys. Those who'd like a crack at mountaineering may wish to try their luck on Sajama with its glaciers and wildly eroded slopes. There are no trails per se so hiking in the park will be strictly backcountry. Carry an ample supply of water on all hikes.

Although it's a relatively easy climb, Sajama's altitude and difficulty of access make it somewhat challenging. If you're going on your own, talk with the foreigner living in Sajama village who has climbed the mountain many times and has a record of his routes. Alternatively, you may want to consider a guided expedition with the American Alpine Institute or one of the several La Paz tour agencies offering climbs of Sajama. For suggestions, see under Tours in the Getting Around chapter.

Access to the mountain is from the Tambo Quemado-Patacamaya road near the village of Sajama or from the Oruro-Turco-Lagunas road near Lagunas. Experienced climbers can commence their assault on the mountain from the north, south (from Lagunas), or west (from Sajama); allow two or three days to reach the summit and plan on extremely cold and windy conditions. Dust and sand will make for uncomfortable conditions when the wind kicks up. Carry lots of water, though once on the snow cap there'll be plenty available in the form of ice.

For general mountaineering tips and guidelines, refer to the Hiking, Trekking & Mountaineering section in the Facts for the Visitor chapter.

Places to Stay & Eat

Camping is fine just about anywhere in this sparsely populated region, so a tent and a good cold-weather sleeping bag are highly recommended. If you're not camping, ask around in Sajama village for lodging in a private home; you'll still need a warm sleeping bag and many layers of clothing for the typically cold and windy nights. Only basic supplies are available.

If you'd like to warm up, there are some hot springs five km from the village of Sajama on the skirt of the mountain. Ask locals to point you in the right direction.

Getting There & Away

Flota Litoral buses leave La Paz for Arica, Chile, on Monday and Friday at 5 am and pass over an excruciatingly rough road through Parque Nacional Sajama. Plan on eight to 12 hours for the journey, depending on current road conditions. During the rainy season it may not be passable at all. If the bus is crowded, you may have to pay the full Arica fare of B65.

To travel onwards into Chile, flag down a passing bus on Monday or Friday evening. Returning to La Paz, the flota passes in the early afternoon on Monday and Friday, but there may not be a seat. Camiones do pass infrequently and will accept paying passengers. Once you've come this far, a visit to Chile's spectacular and well-organised Parque Nacional Lauca is highly recommended.

Crossing the Border The border crossing between Tambo Quemado, Bolivia, and Chungará, Chile, is quite straightforward. At Tambo Quemado, however, no one is in much of a hurry so expect delays.

PARQUE NACIONAL LAUCA (CHILE)

Across the frontier from Sajama is Chile's 137,000-hectare Parque Nacional Lauca, with a marvellously intact Andean ecosystem. It was declared a national park by the Chilean government in 1970. There is a profusion of wildlife including flamingoes, vicuñas, Andean geese, condors, guanacos, llamas, alpacas, rheas, viscachas, foxes, armadillos and Andean deer (huemules); and some unusual plants like the dwarf queñua trees and clumps of yareta moss.

Near the Bolivian border beneath the volcanoes Pomerape and Parinacota, known collectively as Las Payachatas (both with elevations of over 6000 metres), is Lago Chungará, a lovely alpine lake. At 4517 metres, it's one of the world's highest. Visitors may walk at will, but conditions, due to the altitude, combined with wind, cold and swampy ground, can be fierce. Snow is possible at any time of year.

Parinacota

The lovely pre-Hispanic stone village of Parinacota sits at an elevation of 4400 metres beside the marshy Laguna de Cotacotani, situated along the silver route between Potosí and Arica. Conaf (the Chilean National Parks department) operates a visitor centre and museum at the eastern end of the village.

The most imposing structure is the whitewashed stone church in the centre of the village. It was originally built in the 1600s but was reconstructed in 1789. The interior walls are decorated with 17th-century frescoes depicting religious figures.

Places to Stay & Eat

There is a Conaf campsite at the Lago Chungará ranger headquarters. In this *refúgio* are a couple of beds and a warm stove, and backpackers are normally welcome to stay for a nominal fee. The Conaf visitors' centre and museum at the eastern end of Parinacota village offers rough accommodation for tourists. At Putre near the park's western entrance are two hosterías, *Las Vicuñas* and *San Martín*.

Chucuyo at the Parinacota turnoff has a viable restaurant with set meals. They also sell locally produced alpaca chompas, gloves, hats and scarves.

Getting There & Away

The easiest way to reach Lauca is with one of the popular guided tours operating from Arica (Chile). The best is probably Jurasi Tour (☎ 251696, Arica) at Bolognesi 360-A in Arica. Alternatively, try Vicuña Tour (☎ 222971, Arica) at 18 de Septiembre 399, #218, Arica.

The route from Arica follows the lovely oasis-like Lluta valley and climbs into the Atacama hills past ancient petroglyphs and the interesting adobe church and cemetery at Poconchile. Between 1300 and 1800 metres, you'll see the appropriately named candelabra cactus which grows just five mm annually and flowers for just 24 hours. It virtually never rains in the Atacama so the cactus has to take its moisture from the fog.

If you want to visit Lauca on your own, Flota Litoral operates between Arica and La Paz and passes right through the park. For details, see the Getting There & Away section under Parque Nacional Sajama.

South-Western Bolivia

The south-western corner of Bolivia is the most remote highland area of the country. With few roads or inhabitants, unpredictable weather conditions, only a few scattered settlements and unreliable transport, travel into and around the region becomes an exercise in patience and creativity. Its boundaries are more or less defined by the rail lines between Uyuni and the Chilean and Argentine frontiers and by the minor ranges known as the Cordillera de Lipez and Cordillera de Chichas. Nearly treeless, the country and villages south of the Salar de Uyuni are occupied only by a few miners, military personnel and some very determined Aymará.

For visitors, the area will prove a paradise. Bleached deposits of brine provide an occasional splash of white amid the prevailing browns. The surreal landscape is punctuated by steaming, towering volcanic peaks; dozens of hot pools and springs; flamingo-filled lakes stained by minerals and algae into a palette of rainbow hues; and the featureless salt deserts that are considered to be some of the world's flattest terrain. Transport is scarce and expensive and amenities are few, but visitors will be rewarded with a first-hand view of this fascinating and unearthly geology.

History

The prehistoric lakes Minchín and Tauca which once covered most of this high plateau country evaporated some 10,000 years ago and left behind a parched landscape of brackish puddles and salt flats.

Human history hasn't left much of a mark on the region either. Sometime during the mid-1400s, the reigning Inca Pachacuti sent his son Tupac Inca Yupanqui southward to conquer all the lands he encountered. He was apparently a clever PR man because the south-western extremes of Bolivia and the deserts of northern Chile were taken bloodlessly. The conquerors marched on across the wastelands to the northern bank of Chile's Río Maule, where a fierce tribe of Araucanian Indians forced them to stake out the southern boundary of the Inca Empire and sent them packing back to Cuzco.

Due to the unbelievably harsh conditions encountered in the deserts, the Incas never effectively colonised the area. Little has changed since then; the landscape is dotted with only mining camps, health and military outposts and geothermal projects.

Travelling in South-Western Bolivia

The remoteness and difficulty of individual travel in this area cannot be overstressed. Flexibility is the key if you're relying on lifts in camiones or jeeps. Days and weeks pass without a sign of activity so prepare for considerable waits for transportation going your way.

Puestos sanitarios (health posts) are dispersed around the area for the benefit of local miners, military personnel and campesinos, but their medical supplies and expertise are basic and shouldn't be counted on. Friendly locals and miners will usually do what they can to provide a place to crash and even share their limited food, but it's unfair to rely on them. You may want to bring along small gifts for stranded officials and workers who may prove helpful, such as coffee, fruit, magazines, coca, etc, which aren't locally available, to share in reciprocation. If you want to explore on your own, come equipped with a tent, torch, warm sleeping bag, fuel, a reliable stove, a compass, sunglasses, sunscreen, water and maps. It's also a good idea to carry twice as much food as you expect you'll need, as well as clothing for subzero temperatures. Soroche can be a problem (see guidelines in the Health section), especially for hikers, and snow may fall at any time.

The best time to travel in south-western Bolivia is between late March and October when the days are cold but dry. During the remainder of the year, the roads deteriorate and transportation is sparse. Visiting at this time is not recommended.

Organised Tours

The easiest way to explore the region will be with an organised tour from La Paz, Potosí or Uyuni. Most tours take in some combination of the Salar de Uyuni, Laguna Colorada, Laguna Verde and the Salar de Coipasa and, in theory, include some combination of transport, guide, lodging and food.

Every company is different, but cutting corners seems to be the name of the game. Think twice before paying extra for a tour that includes lodging and food. Chances are the 'lodging' will be a space on the earthen floor of a drafty adobe hut and 'meals' may be four-day-old bread rolls and boiled potatoes.

Your most important lifeline will be the vehicle. Make sure it will stand up to the harsh conditions to be meted out by tracks which are ideally negotiated with 4WD. Ascertain that the guide is carrying sufficient oil and petrol for the journey; beyond Uyuni, there's no reliable supply. Vehicles are unfortunately not well maintained and breakdowns are common, so carry enough food and extra water for several days beyond the projected length of your trip.

Finally, in order to ensure the trip goes smoothly, pay only half the negotiated fee in advance and the remainder when you've returned. This is normal in Bolivia so don't let the guide bamboozle you with a sob story about expenses, as you'll almost certainly regret it.

The following are the options from Uyuni. For further choices, see Tours in the Getting Around chapter and under La Paz and Potosí:

Tours Uyuni
Hotel Avenida, Avenida Ferroviario; they charge B1450 for four people, for a five-day tour to the Salar de Uyuni, Laguna Colorada and Laguna Verde, excluding food and lodging.

Voyage Tours
Calle Camacho, Ferroviario 2 (☎ 838), Uyuni (attention Arlina Valdivia T); tours of up to six people cost B1270 to the Salar de Uyuni, Laguna Colorada, Laguna Verde and Sol de Mañana, excluding food and lodging. If you want to continue to San Pedro de Atacama (Chile) from Laguna Verde, advise them and they'll telex Nativa Tours in San Pedro to come and pick you up. (This is an *extremely* expensive option.) You must check out of Bolivia at Uyuni immigration and check into Chile at San Pedro.

Andes Tours
Calle Camacho 92, Casilla 18, Uyuni (☎ 320901, La Paz, fax (591-2) 320901, attention Celina Ignacio); Andes Tours offer several different itineraries, including four or five-day trips from Uyuni. To the Salar de Uyuni and Laguna Colorada only, including food, they charge B1260 for up to six people; if you add Laguna Verde, the price goes up to B1620.

UYUNI

Uyuni is the Alaska of Bolivia; mention it to a Bolivian and the first words you're likely to hear in response are *mucho frío* (very cold). Yes, it is bloody cold in this unattractive desert community, and there seems to be no escape from it. The wind bites through clothing, buildings are drafty and nobody has indoor heating. Well, almost nobody; the jefe (official) at the railway station has a space heater, but he quickly shoos away anyone trying to steal a bit of the warmth.

Uyuni's 5000 people are employed in two major enterprises: government and mining.

The former includes railway workers, military and police personnel and city officials. The latter are almost exclusively involved in salt extraction on the Salar de Uyuni, one of Bolivia's most unique and impressive sights. The town is known affectionately as *La Hija Predilecta de Bolivia* (Bolivia's Favourite Daughter), due to its succouring of the Bolivian troops returning from the Guerra del Pacífico, the war in which Bolivia lost its only outlet to the sea to Chile.

Fiesta

During the first week in July is the festival commemorating the town's founding. This entails torch parades, speeches, dancing, music and naturally, lots of drinking.

Places to Stay

Unfortunately, Uyuni hotels welcome visitors with little more than an unpleasant scowl. The climate again? Whatever, the least disagreeable is the recently upgraded and expanded *Hotel Avenida* diagonally opposite the railway station. For single/ double rooms with bath, they charge B20/40. Without bath, they're B8/16. If you want them to thaw out a shower, it costs an additional B2.50.

Unless the Avenida is full, the alternatives aren't worth a glance. The *Alojamiento Uyuni*, *Alojamiento Urcupiña* and *Alojamiento Copacabana* (the worst of the lot) should be avoided. If you have no other options, they all charge B6 per person with cold water and no showers.

It's possible to sleep in the *salón de espera* at the railway station; it's free and with all the bodies normally crashed out there, it's one of the warmest spots in town. It's also next door to the jefe's office and some of the warmth from his space heater leaks through the wall. Unfortunately, people wander in and out all night long and forget to shut the door. The Bolivians seem to ignore the cold and you may find yourself up and down all night trying to retain the heat. As an alternative to the railway station, the officials at the

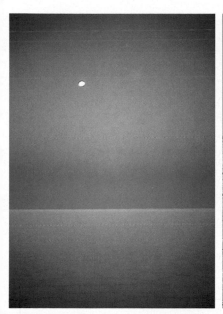

Left: Moon over Salar de Uyuni (DS)
Right: Salt extraction - Salar de Uyuni (DS)
Bottom: Salar de Uyuni from Isla de Pescadores (RS)

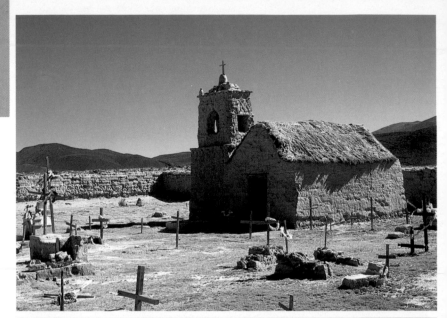

Top: Church - San Juan (DS)
Bottom: Jesuit Mission church - San José de Chiquitos (DS)

alcaldía (municipal hall) are friendly and may allow you to spread out on the floor there if you appear reputable.

Places to Eat

Uyuni's favourite food haunt is *El Rosedal* on the plaza; check out the unique heating system mentioned in the walking tour and watch out for lions, tigers and bears! There's also a decent restaurant at the Hotel Avenida which serves breakfast as well as other meals.

Also on the plaza is the *Restaurante 16 de Julio* which leaves the door open but will provide a charcoal brazier when icicles begin to form on your nose. The food is rather bland; expect some combination of rice, potatoes and oatmeal soup seasoned with cabbage and sausage. For a dose of charque kan or chicken and chips washed down with Bolivia's own Doble Cola, try the *Snack Ducal*.

As usual, the most economical meals are available at the market food stalls.

Getting There & Away

Bus Transportes Quijarro runs a daily bus to Potosí at 12.30 pm for B18. Buy your ticket early. From Potosí, the bus to Uyuni departs at noon.

Train Uyuni sits at the junction of the rail lines to Antofagasta (Chile), Villazón and Oruro, and lies just south of Río Mulatos where the Potosí and Sucre line branches off the main north-south route.

Trains passing through Uyuni are typically running very late when they arrive, and are even further behind schedule when they depart. Although the official timetable

Surreal Uyuni Walking Tour

On first glance, Uyuni could be the set for an erudite post-nuclear apocalypse film. On second glance, there seems to be something intangibly weird about the place. Maybe it's the climate – or the dust...or maybe it's something in the water. Who knows. We arrived in Uyuni late on a cold, dark and dusty night (like all nights in Uyuni) and way beyond the lights of town, our headlamps caught a glimpse of a brass band marching through the desert. Perhaps they knew we were coming.

Oh, yes, the walking tour...

First, visit the Hotel Avenida to look for a room; you enter the lobby through the owner's bedroom and there he is in bed, huddled beneath the blankets attempting to maintain normal body temperature. Visit the loo where you'll trip over a charcoal brazier strategically placed under the plumbing to foil the ice blocks holed up inside.

Then take a stroll down Avenida Ferroviario. In front of the hotel you'll find masterfully crafted evidence that Uyuni sits at the cutting edge of cultural revolution: a monument of a coverall-clad worker lugging an immense wrench while a faithful cog rolls merrily along at his heels. It would be the envy of any park in Pyongyang (North Korea).

If you're hungry, wander out for a meal and discover Uyuni's contribution to *haute cuisine* – charque kan: dried shredded llama meat and mashed hominy – but wear your winter woollies; Uyuni eateries operate on the premise that unless the door is wide open, no one will realise they're doing business. If you're really going in style, spring for a churrasco at the heated El Rosedal on the plaza, where a weak blue flame is kept alive on an intravenous kerosene drip lashed to the ceiling, while ceramic raised relief tigers and gorillas look on from the walls.

When you're up for some shopping, visit the Harrod's outlet beside the Hotel Avenida where you can browse among boxes of Chilean fruit juice, wine, teddy bears, Scottish Highlander dolls, eight brands of Chilean loo paper and an impressive glass display case brimming with 25-watt light bulbs.

Then, when you're ready for some sightseeing, take a stroll down the dusty, half-deserted streets which are wide enough to U-turn a 20-mule team without asking the mules to do anything unusual. Note the locomotive that has chugged into the centre of appropriately named Avenida Ferroviario (Railway Avenue) and decided to stay. Now that your appetite for railway paraphernalia has been whetted, rush over to the railway station where you can gaze wistfully at the three-metre-high corrugated aluminium barrier that encloses the compound containing Uyuni's crowning attraction: a magnificent – and off-limits – collection of dilapidated steam locomotives. ∎

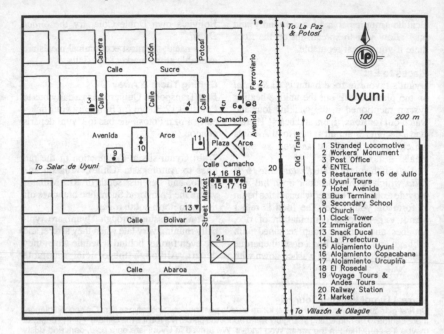

To La Paz & Potosí

Uyuni

0   100   200 m

To Salar de Uyuni

To Villazón & Ollagüe

1 Stranded Locomotive
2 Workers' Monument
3 Post Office
4 ENTEL
5 Restaurante 16 de Julio
6 Uyuni Tours
7 Hotel Avenida
8 Bus Terminal
9 Secondary School
10 Church
11 Clock Tower
12 Immigration
13 Snack Ducal
14 La Prefectura
15 Alojamiento Uyuni
16 Alojamiento Copacabana
17 Alojamiento Urcupiña
18 El Rosedal
19 Voyage Tours & Andes Tours
20 Railway Station
21 Market

schedules stops of just 20 minutes, I've never spent less than four hours there. In my experience, and according to railway officials, the average train runs six to 12 hours behind schedule.

The following is an account of one traveller's experience with the Bolivian rail system:

I walked straight into a six-day-old strike/industrial dispute. The [officials]...at the ticket office sold us tickets knowing full well that a strike was in progress (this particular strike didn't make headlines until we passengers kicked up a fuss). We got as far as Uyuni (a one-horse town if there ever was one) with only about 60 people on the train, but as you know, Bolivians travel with an obligatory 16 bags each as well as 20 *pan dulces*, 16 red acrylic chompas, 100 sausages, 20 pairs of Reeboks, 15 coats, 12 blankets, half a case of Coke or other sickly bubbly liquid, two flasks, half a tonne of makeup, a grandmother, 20 toys and tonnes of sweet distractions for the bawling kids...and in Uyuni we stayed.

Aware of the fact that Bolivian railways are not reliable for the reality of their timetables, we all waited four hours to discover that we had walked into a strike. We could not pass, as engines and train parts had been piled across the tracks. The [male passengers] (being Latin and macho) went out to try and lift the trains off the points to clear the tracks so we could move on. While they were doing this, the workers...began throwing stones at us. What to do?

We, the women, children and older passengers, decided to go and denounce the workers to the police. We walked to the station but the commissioner had mysteriously 'gone to La Paz'. We went to the Army and as they saw us walking down the street you could see the panic in their faces. Luckily for them, they'd brought their musical instruments and they bought themselves three minutes of thinking time by striking up the national anthem. Everyone stood stock still while they played it in its entirety with a couple of extra verses in there for good measure. A ridiculous scene – furious passengers being placated by the national anthem. This is why we have armed forces!

At the end of this farce, they told us they couldn't interfere with this civil affair and to go back to our train. NO WAY! How do you solve a strike in South America? Certainly not by coercion or doing physical battle. We threatened radio/TV publicity, international retribution, hellfire and damnation, and none of these worked.

In the end, the gentle hand of femininity and frailty won out. The women and children went to the union bosses and pleaded that they be allowed to get through as they were starving and had children to feed and a train compartment was no place to raise children (much less in Uyuni) and we were miraculously let through. Fourteen hours we waited there. I was the only tourist on the train; obviously some people have wised up to this route!

Ms Alex Rossi, UK

If you're ready for a real rail trip, catch the weekly *tren tortuga* (turtle train) to Potosí. It's slow going but it crosses the scenic pass at El Condor, the highest point on the Bolivian rail lines and also one of the world's highest at 4786 metres. It leaves Uyuni at about 6 pm on Friday.

From Oruro, there are trains on Monday and Thursday at 9 pm and Wednesday and Sunday at 7.25 pm, and a ferrobus Tuesday and Saturday at 11.30 am. All these trains continue to Tupiza and Villazón except the Wednesday evening train, which goes to Abaroa/Ollagüe on the Chilean border.

To Oruro, trains leave at 11.20 pm on Tuesday and Friday, 12.10 am on Monday and Thursday and 3.15 pm Saturday. The ferrobus runs at 12.10 pm Wednesday and Sunday.

Those are the wishful thinking schedules. For more realistic ones, check the chalkboard at the station on the day you want to depart and join the clamour for a ticket.

SALAR DE UYUNI

The 12,106-sq-km Salar de Uyuni which covers nearly all of Daniel Campos province is Bolivia's largest saltpan. When there's a little water on the flats, it reflects perfectly the blue Altiplano sky and the effect is positively eerie. When they're dry, the salar becomes a blinding white expanse of the greatest nothing imaginable.

The Salar de Uyuni is now a centre of salt extraction and processing, particularly around the settlement of Colchani, 20 km up the rail line from Uyuni. The estimated annual capacity of the Colchani operation is 19,700 tonnes, 18,000 tonnes of which is for human consumption while the rest is for livestock. There remain at least 10 billion tonnes of salt in the Salar de Uyuni, but the only takers thus far are the Colchani campesinos who hack it out with picks and shovels. There's a salt treatment plant near the Colchani railway station, and when trains pull in, vendors board to sell small parcels of salt for domestic use.

History

In recent geological history, this part of the Altiplano was covered entirely by water. Around the ancient lakeshore, two distinctive levels of terraces are visible, indicating the succession of two lakes; below the lower one are fossils of coral in limestone. From 40,000 to 25,000 years ago, Lago Minchín, whose highest level reached 3760 metres, occupied much of south-western Bolivia. When it evaporated, the area lay dry for 14,000 years before the appearance of short-lived Lago Tauca, which lasted for only about 1000 years and rose to 3720 metres. When it dried up, it left a couple of puddles, lagos Poopó and Uru Uru, and two major salt concentrations, the salares de Uyuni and Coipasa.

This part of the Altiplano is drained internally, with no outlet to the sea; the salt deposits are the result of the minerals leeched from the mountains and deposited at the lowest available point.

Isla de Pescadores

The magnificent Isla de Pescadores in the heart of the Salar de Uyuni is the normal destination of salar tours. It's a remarkably otherworldly place, a hilly cactus-covered outpost surrounded by a flat white sea of hexagonal salt tiles. A large population of stranded viscachas populates its rocky slopes.

Places to Stay

It's possible to cross the salar to the village of Llica, the unlikely site of a teachers' college (which serves as accommodation). There's also a basic new alojamiento in the village or you can sleep at the alcaldía for B3.50.

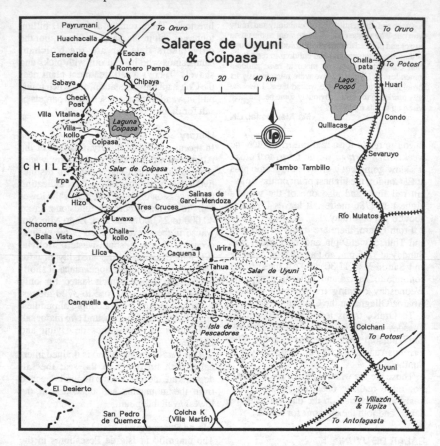

Getting There & Away

If you travel by rail from Uyuni to Potosí or Oruro, you'll glimpse the salar during the stop at Cochani, but to fully appreciate the place, you need to get out onto the salt.

The only easy access will be with an organised tour. If you're keen to visit on your own, there are camiones which connect Uyuni with Colchani on the eastern shore of the salar. You'll have the most luck between 7 and 9 am. Some salt workers living in Uyuni commute daily to Colchani in private vehicles or on motorbikes, and for a small fee you may be able to hitch along.

Alternatively, you can hire a taxi in Uyuni for a half-day trip to Colchani and back for about B35, but if you really want to reach the heart of the salar, you'll have to hire a 4WD vehicle and driver and it won't be cheap. Speak with any of the tour agencies listed under Organised Tours in the introduction to the South-Western Bolivia section.

Walking We received the following correspondence from a reader who stayed a week in Uyuni and environs and took exception to the harsh assessment of Uyuni in the first edition:

The amazing natural beauty of the place was the part I enjoyed most. One day, I walked from Colchani to Uyuni; despite its being perfectly flat, it was one of the most amazing walks I've ever taken. I found a stone arrowhead and one of the rounded stones fashioned by the wind. To the east, there's a hill, Yana Polera, with a cross on top and Stations of the Cross leading to it. The top is covered with hairy cacti which locals call *vicuñita*. There is a good view of the surrounding area from the top. As I was coming down around sunset, there was a very interesting optical illusion; the mountains in the distance across the salar had their mirror images sprouting from their tops. It would appear and disappear as I was descending and my angle of observation changed. This hike takes three to four hours.

Dan Golopentia, USA

Getting Around

Infrequent unscheduled camiones from Uyuni make the trip to Llica in a couple of hours and from there, often continue further into the south-west region, carrying supplies to sulphur mines. You may have long waits for a lift back to Uyuni.

If you're driving on the salar, carry a compass, food, water, extra fuel, tools, spare parts and a means of warming up. Drivers often become lost on the white expanse, and without reference points, they drive in circles until the vehicle runs out of petrol. For anyone lost away from the main routes across the salar, chances of rescue and survival are slim.

Contrary to what you may read elsewhere, long-time locals assure us that there has never been enough liquid in the salar, at least in the last millennium, to support a boat of any description across to Llica.

SALAR DE COIPASA REGION

The more remote Salar de Coipasa, the great salt desert north-west of the Salar de Uyuni, was part of the same prehistoric lakes which covered the area over 10,000 years ago. The road to the Salar de Coipasa is extremely poor and vehicles are subject to bogging in deep sand, so you'll need a 4WD. The village of Coipasa sits on an island in the middle of the salar.

Chipaya

Immediately north of the Salar de Coipasa, on the Río Sabaya delta, live the Chipaya Indians, who occupy a single desert village of circular mud huts. The Chipaya are conjectured to be the remnant of the lost Tiahuanaco civilisation. Some anthropologists say the Chipaya language, vastly different from either Quechua or Aymará, closely resembles Uros (most likely) while others note similarities to Mayan, Arabic and North African tribal languages.

Chipaya tradition states that the people descend from the builders of the chullpas scattered around Lake Titicaca. Their religion deifies, among other things, phallic images, stones, rivers, mountains and animal carcasses. Their most revered deity is the phallic village church tower.

Within a 15 km radius of the settlement are nine whitewashed sod cones which serve as receptacles for appeasement offerings to keep evil spirits from invading the village. Petitions are also offered to the Volcán Sajama, the home of another revered spirit.

Tourists aren't particularly welcome, although a few culturally sensitive individuals have visited and developed a superficial rapport with the people. If you don't go to gawk or take photos, you'll have a better chance of being accepted. The Indians are traditionally quite superstitious about cameras, but nowadays, some willing models have taken to charging for photos. We understand that the head man in Chipaya has begun charging tourists an exorbitant fee for 'photography permits'. However, these permits don't seem to make the locals any less camera shy, and we recommend that visitors abstain from photographing people in the Chipaya area.

Chipaya may be reached from Llica across the Salar de Coipasa or from Oruro via Toledo, Corque and Huachacalla. Hitching will be slow.

SOUTH-WEST CIRCUIT
Salar de Uyuni to Laguna Colorada

The normal tour route from Uyuni is via Colchani, 20 km to the north-west, then 40 km west across the salar to Isla de Pescadores (see under Salar de Uyuni earlier in this chapter). After a stop to explore the island, the route turns south and 40 km later, reaches the edge of the salar. After 10 more km is the village of Colcha K (pronounced COL-cha-KAH), also known as Villa Martín, where there's a lovely adobe church and rudimentary accommodation in a private home and shop just 100 metres up the cobbled street. Here, you'll pass through a military checkpoint. Less than 15 km further along is San Juan, with another interesting church and cemetery. Accommodation is provided at an upmarket hostel or in several private homes.

At San Juan, the route turns west across the Salar de Chiguana where the landscape opens up and snow-capped Ollagüe, an active volcano straddling the Bolivian/Chilean border, appears in the distance. There's a rough road leading to a field of steaming fumaroles and sulphur lakes at the 5000-metre level near the summit and it's possible to catch a ride up with miners who work at sulphur camps.

At Chiguana, where the road crosses the Uyuni-Calama rail line, passports will be scrutinised by a crowd of gawking military people. There, the route turns south and climbs into high and increasingly wild terrain, passing mineral lakes filled with flamingoes and mountains resembling spilt chocolate sundaes. After approximately 170 km of rough bumping, you'll wind down a hillside to Laguna Colorada at 4400 metres.

Laguna Colorada

Laguna Colorada, a fiery red lake about 25 km from the Chilean border, is inhabited by rare James flamingoes. On its western shore is Campamento Ende and beside it, there's a squalid little meteorological station where visitors without tents will find a place to crash. For a very marginal bed in a drafty unheated room, they charge B6 per person. If you're relegated to the adobe floor, you'll pay only B3. We spoke with some visitors who pitched their tent at the base of the hills and were charged the same price because they were within view of the camp.

The clear air is bitterly cold and at night the temperature drops below -20°C. Just as well; if the temperature ever rose above freezing, the stench of the shit and animal carcasses strewn about the place would be unbearable. Instead, the air is perfumed with the scent of the yareta moss which is burned for fuel despite the region's practically boundless geothermal, wind and solar power potential.

Sol de Mañana

Most transport you find along the tracks around Laguna Colorada will be supplying or servicing mining and military camps or the developing geothermal project 50 km south at Sol de Mañana.

The real interest at Sol de Mañana is the 4800-metre-high geyser basin with bubbling mud pots, hellish fumaroles and a thick aroma of sulphur fumes. Be extremely careful when approaching the site; any damp or cracked earth is potentially dangerous and cave-ins do occur, sometimes causing serious injury.

Laguna Verde

Laguna Verde, a stunning blue-green lake at 5000 metres, is tucked into the south-western corner of Bolivian territory 92 km from Sol de Mañana. Behind the lake rises the cone of 5930-metre Volcán Licancabur, whose summit shelters an ancient Inca crypt. On this and many other peaks in the vicinity, young Inca men were marched to the summit, exposed to the cruel elements and forced to freeze to death as a sacrifice to the gods in commemoration of significant events within the empire.

There are two approaches to Laguna Verde. Where the route splits about 60 km south of Sol de Mañana, the left fork climbs up and over a 5300-metre pass, then up a hillside resembling a freshly raked Zen garden with rocks meticulously placed by Salvador Dali. Down the opposite slope are two sulphur mines and a military camp where the army normally welcomes overnight guests. From there, it's approximately 10 km to the lake. The slightly shorter right fork winds along a relatively level route and around a caramel-coloured range of hills to the lakeshore.

Crossing the Border

The nearest petrol is at San Pedro de Atacama in Chile; a Bolivian military stamp from the Laguna Verde military camp, 10 km from the lake, should suffice to get you out of Bolivia and in again.

If you're not on a tour and want to enter Chile, you must have picked up an exit stamp from Bolivian immigration in Uyuni. By road, the distance from Laguna Verde to the border is a bitterly cold and windy 25 km at 5000 metres elevation, and there's practically no transport so you'll have to walk. On the Chilean side, you can stop one of the mining trucks which run between the mining camps and San Pedro de Atacama, three hours away, where you can check in with Chilean immigration.

Valles de Rocas

The route back to Uyuni turns north-east a few km north of Laguna Colorada and winds through more high, lonesome country and several valleys of bizarre eroded rock formations. Petrol is available sporadically at the village of Alota and from there, it's a trying six-hour jostle back to Uyuni.

TUPIZA

In the background looms the Tupizan range, very red, or better, a ruddy sepia; and very distinct, resembling a landscape painted by an artist with the animated brilliance of Delacroix or by an impressionist like Renoir...In the tranquil translucent air, flows the breath of smiling grace...

Carlos Medinaceli, Bolivian Writer

Tupiza, in the heart of some of Bolivia's most spectacular countryside, is a real gem. Anyone who loves the desert landscapes of the American Southwest, Australia's Kimberley Ranges or south-western Africa will also love Tupiza. The capital of Sud Chichas, a province of Potosí Department, Tupiza is among the most literate and educated cities in Bolivia, with over 90% of the population able to read and write. It's also a compara-

tively young city – half of its 20,000 inhabitants are under the age of 20 and its growth rate is one of the country's highest.

It lies in the narrow valley of the Río Tupiza at an altitude of 2950 metres, surrounded by the rugged Cordillera de Chichas. The climate is mild year-round, with most of the rain falling between November and March. In July and August, the days are hot, dry and clear, but night-time temperatures can drop to below freezing.

Economically, the town depends primarily on agriculture and mining. Area mines produce antimony, lead, silver, bismuth, and some tin. A YPFB (Yacimientos Petrolíferos Fiscales Bolivianos) refinery five km south of town provides employment, and the only antimony smelter in Bolivia operates along a dry tributary of the Río Tupiza.

The main attractions of Tupiza are natural – multi-hued rocks, mountains, chasms, spires and pinnacles; clear rivers; dry washes; cactus forests; dramatic sunsets; brilliant skies; and lots of room to wander. A reddish colour predominates, but brown, sepia, cream, green, blue, yellow and violet are all found in the landscape. Although tourists have recently begun trickling into Tupiza, the Chichas area is still well off the rutted track.

History

The tribe that originally inhabited the valley and surrounding mountains called themselves Chichas. They left archaeological evidence of their existence but very little is known about their language and culture. It's assumed they were a unique group, separate from the tribes living in neighbouring areas of southern Bolivia and northern Argentina, but anything unique about them was destroyed between 1471 and 1488 when the Incas, under the leadership of Tupac Inca Yupanqui, annexed the region into the Inca Empire. The Chichas were used by the Incas as a military nucleus from which to gather forces and organise armies to conquer the Humahuaca, Diaguitas, and Calchaquíes tribes of northern Argentina.

Once the Inca Empire had fallen at the

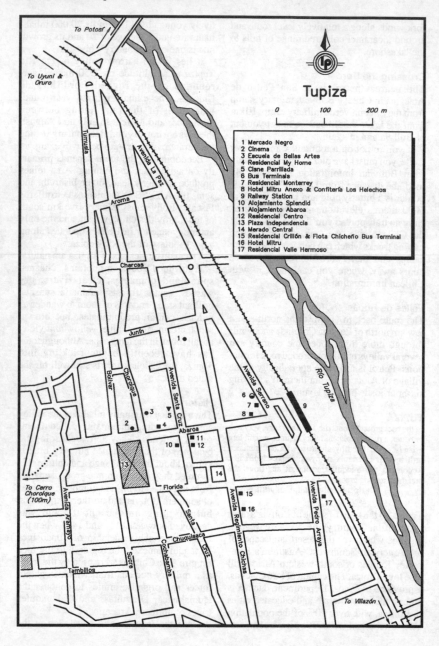

Tupiza

0   100   200 m

1 Mercado Negro
2 Cinema
3 Escuela de Bellas Artes
4 Residencial My Home
5 Cisne Parrillada
6 Bus Terminals
7 Residencial Monterrey
8 Hotel Mitru Anexo & Confitería Los Helechos
9 Railway Station
10 Alojamiento Splendid
11 Alojamiento Abaroa
12 Residencial Centro
13 Plaza Independencia
14 Mercado Central
15 Residencial Crillón & Flota Chicheño Bus Terminal
16 Hotel Mitru
17 Residencial Valle Hermoso

hands of the Spanish, the entire southern half of the Viceroyalty of Alto Peru was awarded to Diego de Almagro by decree of King Carlos V of Spain. When Almagro and company arrived in the Tupiza valley on a familiarisation expedition in October 1535, the Chichas culture had been forgotten, absorbed entirely into that of the Quechuas. Almagro stayed briefly in the valley, and then moved southward toward Chile, bent on exploring the remainder of his newly acquired spoils.

Although the town was officially founded on 4 June 1574 by Captain Luis de Fuentes (who also founded Tarija), this date is pure conjecture. The origin of the name is similarly hazy. The current spelling was derived from *Tope'sa* or *Tucpicsa* but no one knows what that Chichas word meant. It has been suggested that it probably referred to 'red rock' since that seems to be the salient feature of the area, but this is just a guess.

In 1781, the region took part in the tumultuous Campesino Rebellion. Luis de la Vega, who supported the peasants, mobilised the local militia and proclaimed himself governor of Chichas, Lipez, Cinti and Porco, encouraging resistance against Spanish authorities. The mob was successful in executing the Spanish *corregidor* (chief magistrate) of Tupiza and levelling his estate, but the rebellion was squashed before it really got underway. At the time of the Tupiza revolt, 4000 Indian troops were marching toward the village under the leadership of Pedro de la Crúz Condori. They'd been charged with organising and carrying out terrorist acts against the government, but were intercepted by Spanish forces before reaching their destination.

On 7 November 1810, the Battle of Suipacha just east of the Tupiza valley brought about the first victory in Alto Peru's struggle for independence from Spain. Similarly, the deciding battle of the 15-year War of Independence took place at Tumusla in the northern Chichas on 9 December 1824.

From the time of founding through the War of Independence the Spanish population of Tupiza grew steadily, lured to the area by the favourable climate and suitable agricultural and grazing lands. Later, the discovery of minerals in the Cordilleras de Chichas and Lipez attracted even more inhabitants, and with them came Indians to do the manual labour. The current residents of Tupiza are of predominantly Spanish descent, although the Quechua and Chichas influence is evident. In 1840, Argentine revolutionaries fleeing the tyranny of dictator Juan Manuel Rosas escaped into Tupiza and were incorporated into the community. More recently, campesinos have been moving into town from the countryside, and many out-of-work miners and their families have already settled there. If there's a resurgence of mining unrest and layoffs, more can be expected to arrive. The favourable climatic and economic conditions are also attracting migrants from other parts of Bolivia.

Information

Money You'll see lots of compro dólares signs around town. Try the Cooperativa El Chorolque on the Plaza Independencia or in the two hardware stores, Ferretería Cruz on Avenida Santa Cruz and Ferretería Marco Hermanos on the corner of Avenida Santa Cruz and Florida. There's no place to change travellers' cheques, but in an emergency, ask around for Señor Umberto Bernal who may be able to help out.

Finca Chajrahuasi

Across the river just out of town is the abandoned farmstead of tin baron Carlos Victor Aramayo. Today it's overgrown with weeds and in the later stages of disrepair. Aramayo, who had maintained his business in Bolivia using Bolivian labour, was heaped into the same category as the absentee Simon Patiño and when his mines were nationalised in 1952, the estate was confiscated and Aramayo fled to Europe to escape the backlash. Chajrahuasi now serves as a rough football pitch but it's apparent that it was once quite a comfy residence.

Escuela de Bellas Artes

The Escuela de Bellas Artes (School of Fine

Arts) occupies the 16th-century mansion of the Eguía family. It's pretty dilapidated but there are efforts underway to renovate it. Inside is a small art museum and a small but beautiful library of old literary works and reference books in Spanish, English and French.

Cerro Chorolque

The short trail to the summit of Cerro Chorolque, flanked by Stations of the Cross, is a pleasant morning or evening walk when the low sun brings out the fiery reds of the surrounding countryside. The hill, which is crowned by a statue of Christ, affords a good overall view of the town.

Markets

The Mercado de Ferias takes place on Monday, Thursday, and Saturday mornings along Avenida Regimiento Chichas. The Mercado Negro (Black Market), where you'll find a mishmash of consumer goods, occupies the block between Avenida Regimiento Chichas, Avenida Santa Cruz, Junín and Abaroa. It's open daily.

Places to Stay

The *Residencial Centro* (☎ 352) on Avenida Santa Cruz costs B10/15 for a single/double with private bath. It's clean but don't put too much faith in their claim to having hot water.

Another popular good-value option is the cosy-sounding *Residencial My Home* at Abaroa 288. Rooms cost B14 per person with private bath and B7 without bath.

The bright and airy *Hotel Mitru* (☎ 444) seems to take back seat to the affiliated *Hotel Mitru Anexo* (☎ 425), where most of the enterprise's resources are being channelled. Both are good choices but their showers aren't as hot as they'd have you believe. Rooms cost B15 per person with private bath and B10 without bath.

The *Residencial Monterrey*, opposite the railway station and amid the bus terminals, costs B7/14 for a single/double with common bath. Slightly cheaper is the *Residencial Valle Hermoso* which asks B6 per person for rooms without bath.

Moving down the scale are the alojamientos *Abaroa* and *Splendid* on Avenida Santa Cruz. Simple beds cost B4 per person. Don't expect much and you won't be disappointed. The *Residencial Crillón* on Avenida Regimiento Chichas near Florida is basic and cheap at B5 per person.

Places to Eat

There isn't a large selection of eating establishments in Tupiza and most of the restaurants are associated with residenciales. The dining room at Residencial My Home and the Hotel Mitru both serve palatable set meals. Residencial Centro has a very pleasant-looking attached restaurant that never seems to open.

Confitería Los Helechos at the Mitru Anexo sets the scene with a cactus skeleton done up in coloured Christmas lights. It's the only restaurant that keeps reliable hours, but behind the glittering sign and bright dining room lie some very greasy omelettes and overpriced pizza slices. Their burgers and chicken are superb, however, as are the fruit *licuados* (milkshakes) which come in strawberry, banana, peach and papaya. Brekkies are also very nice and are served with quince jam and real coffee. The full restaurant next door, which is also associated with the Mitru Anexo, serves well-prepared and filling dishes.

For carnivorous appetites, try the interesting *Cisne Parrillada* which is through the courtyard and up the stairs from the sign marking its location.

In the afternoon, street vendors in front of the railway station set up little open-air food stalls where you can get a filling meal of salad, potatoes, rice and a main dish for B3. Salteñas and humintas are sold by street vendors along Abaroa between the railway station and Avenida Regimiento Chichas. Similar meals may be found in the cubbyhole restaurants around the bus terminals; the *Pensión Familiar* is recommended. The market food stalls are cheap and are especially good for breakfast. *Heladería Mil Delicias* on Abaroa has snacks and ice cream.

Getting There & Away

Bus All the bus terminals except Flota Chicheño are on Avenida Serrano opposite the railway station. Chorolque and Trans-Bolivar go to Villazón daily. Boquerón departs for Potosí daily at 5.30 pm with connections to Sucre, Cochabamba and La Paz. Panamericano goes to Potosí every second night and Trans Gran Chaco connects Tupiza with Tarija every second night. The fare to Potosí is B20.

Train Plan on hassles and long queues when buying rail tickets. The trains do carry bodegas (boxcars) as far as Uyuni but it would be a bitterly cold ride and you'd probably prefer the ticket queue to a night of shivering in a cold bodega.

There are trains to Uyuni and Oruro departing at 5.20 pm on Tuesday and Friday and 6 pm Monday and Thursday. The 1st and 2nd-class fares to Uyuni are B12/9 and to Oruro, B28/21. The ferrobus runs on Wednesday and Sunday at 8.20 am. The pullman/especial fares to Uyuni are B23/18 and to Oruro, B57/46.

There are trains to Villazón on Monday, Tuesday, Thursday and Friday for B7/5 in 1st/2nd class. The train to Potosí and Sucre via Uyuni and Río Mulatos leaves on Friday at 12.10 pm and returns the following day, departing from Sucre at 5.30 pm.

The Expreso del Sur between Oruro and Buenos Aires leaves Oruro at 7 pm on Tuesday and Friday, arriving in Tupiza at 10 am the following morning. Headed north, it leaves Tupiza at 6.15 pm and arrives in Oruro at 5.15 am the following morning.

AROUND TUPIZA

Tupiza's real appeal lies in the surrounding landscape. Thanks to mining activities on the Altiplano west of town, there's a relatively good network of crisscrossing roads. There's no public transport, but you can hitch lifts with the camiones which service the mines, foundries, geologic camps and health posts scattered between Tupiza and the Chilean frontier.

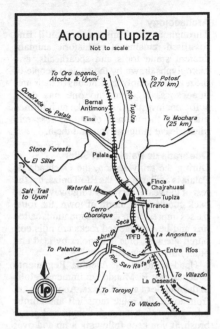

Hiking opportunities are numerous and up the Quebrada de Palala (Palala Wash) within three or four km of town you can get a good idea of what the country has to offer. In addition to the roads and tracks there are ridges, dry washes and canyons which provide rewarding daytrips into the wilderness. If you're venturing away from the tracks, carry a compass and wear shoes that can withstand assault by all sorts of prickly desert vegetation. You can purchase topographic maps at the Instituto Geográfico Militar in La Paz, but even without a map, anyone experienced in cross-country travel won't get lost.

Carry all the water you'll be needing – at least two litres per person per day in this dry desert climate. If it looks like rain, avoid the dry washes; flash flooding is a real danger. It will be possible to pitch a tent just about anywhere, but again, avoid canyons and dry washes.

Archaeology

Throughout the Tupiza area you'll find fossilised remains of prehistoric animals, ancient stone tools and spearheads, and hieroglyphs drawn by the ancient people of the region, possibly the Chichas or their predecessors. It seems no one has done sufficient investigation to make an informed guess. In the interest of future research, please leave things as you find them.

Quebrada de Palala & El Sillar

During the rainy season, the Quebrada de Palala is a tributary of the Río Tupiza, but the rest of the year it serves as a highway into the back country. Just north of town, the route passes impressive red rock formations called *fins* and beyond the red rocks are hills coloured greenish blue and violet by lead and other mineral deposits.

Head north along Avenida Regimiento Chichas past El Mundo, an immense globe in the middle of a small plaza. About five km from town, the route turns left and climbs into a dry wash through cactus and scrub brush. If you keep following it up and over the mountain, you'll reach a place called El Sillar (The Saddle) where the road straddles a narrow ridge between two peaks. Throughout this area are rugged amphitheatres of pillars and eroded spires which resemble China's Stone Forest. The distance from Tupiza to El Sillar is 16 km.

This walk is part of a centuries-old trade route and along the way, you'll pass trains of llamas, alpacas and donkeys carrying blocks of salt mined in the Salar de Uyuni to market in Tarija, a total distance of 300 km.

In Tupiza you can arrange a taxi for up to five people to El Sillar or other sites in the area for about B60 – not bad if you have a group – and the drivers accommodate as many photo stops as you'd like. Try Radio Taxi la Joya (☎ 473) at Avenida Santa Cruz 306.

Waterfall Walk

A good short walk from town heads out along Calle Chuquisaca past the military barracks (the route will be obvious from the summit of Cerro Chorolque). The road narrows to a track paralleling the mountains and crosses a dry wash. Here you should turn left and follow the wash for a short distance toward the red hills, turning again into the first tributary wash on your right. You'll pass some spectacular fin formations similar to those in Quebrada de Palala. If there's been some rain, you'll find a small waterfall in the canyon at the end of the track.

Quebrada Seca

South of town near the YPFB plant the road turns right into Quebrada Seca meaning simply 'dry wash'. Unfortunately, the lower reaches of Quebrada Seca now serve as Tupiza's rubbish tip but if you continue up the wash, the trash thins out and the route passes through some spectacular red rock country. At the intersection, the right fork climbs the hill toward the village of Palaniza and the left fork crosses the Río San Rafael, eventually getting lost in the side canyons opening into the main channel. This is a particularly beautiful route and I've seen condors soaring above Quebrada Seca.

During the dry season, you can turn left before the Río San Rafael bridge (10 km from Tupiza) and follow the river's northern bank to Entre Ríos where you'll have to wade across the Río Tupiza. From there, you can return to town via the road coming from Villazón.

La Angostura & Entre Ríos

About eight km south of Tupiza, the Río Tupiza narrows to squeeze through La Angostura (The Narrows), a tight opening in the rock. Inside the rock tunnel constructed for the Villazón road, there's a view through to the churning waters below. Along the route to La Angostura notice the diggings in the yellowish soil along the road; gold is found in profitable quantities in this soil, and the locals often pick through it. As you approach La Angostura from Tupiza, watch along the ridge west of the river for the formation known as Bolívar, a rock outcropping which resembles a profile of the liberator.

A nice view across the confluence of the Ríos Tupiza and San Rafael can be had at the lay-by at Entre Ríos, 10 km south of Tupiza.

La Deseada

The name La Deseada means 'The Desired'. This shady little spot beside the Río Tupiza, with a broad flat area for tent camping near the riverbank, serves as a favourite picnic area for the residents of Tupiza. To get there, walk across the Calle Beni bridge from Tupiza and hitch a ride from the tranca (police post) south along the Villazón road. La Deseada is 12 km from Tupiza; the driver should know the right place.

SAN VICENTE

This one mule town wouldn't even rate a mention were it not the village where the legendary outlaws Butch Cassidy and the Sundance Kid supposedly met their untimely demise at the hands of the Bolivian Army in November 1908. Legend has it that the pair came under fire while holed up in the church-yard. Sundance mercy-killed his cohort before committing suicide. Until her death, Butch's sister claimed that he returned to Utah from South America years after his presumed death and that the entire Bolivian encounter was more or less a fabrication embellished over the years into a popular folk legend.

New evidence surfaced in December 1991, however, when forensic anthropologist Clyde Snow uncovered the bullet-riddled corpses of two Caucasian men in the cemetery at San Vicente. The one presumed to be Butch sports a bullet hole through the temple and the other, who suffered a smashed forehead, would be Sundance. The excavation was prompted by the discovery of a 1909 Bolivian government report of a gunfight involving two English-speaking outlaws holed up in a house.

Places to Stay

Until San Vicente becomes a Butch and Sundance pilgrimage destination, there won't be any accommodation in the village, so bring camping equipment.

Getting There & Away

There's no public transport to remote San Vicente but there are rough roads from both Oro Ingenio and Atocha, the first stations north of Tupiza along the rail line. Traffic is sporadic so come prepared for long waits.

One map shows access directly from Tupiza via El Sillar (see the Around Tupiza section), with a northward (right) turning at a village called Nazarenito. We haven't checked it out but suspect that it follows the salt road from the Salar de Uyuni. If you're prepared and feeling adventurous, you may want to have a go.

VILLAZÓN

Villazón, a dusty, uninteresting and haphazard-looking settlement, is the most popular border crossing between Bolivia and Argentina. Coming from the south, it will be a headlong dive into the Andean scene.

Much of Jujuy province in northern Argentina is populated by Bolivian expats. Migration into Argentina continues at a significant rate, giving Villazón the nickname the 'Tijuana of Bolivia'. It sits at an altitude of 3443 metres, a real jump if you're coming directly from Jujuy (Argentina), so soroche is a possibility. The border region experiences typical Altiplano weather patterns: days are normally clear, but strong winds blow almost constantly across the unprotected plain and nights can be extremely cold.

In addition to being a port of entry, Villazón serves as a warehousing and marketing centre for contraband – food products, electronics goods, and alcohol – which is smuggled into Bolivia from Argentina via the *comercio de hormigas* (ant trade). Thousands of kg of goods are carried across the bridge daily on the backs of peasants, forming a continuous human cargo train across the frontier. It all takes place under the noses of customs officials who seem to do a lot of looking the other way. Only selectively do they enforce the law, especially when they notice a passing item that strikes their fancy. A lot of Argentine wine is confiscated this way!

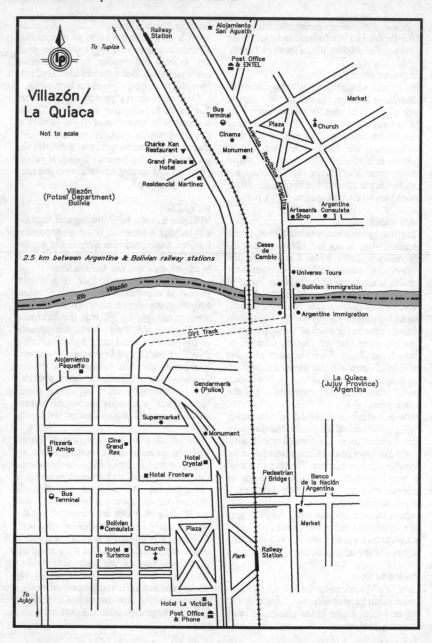

Information

Money If you're changing cash dollars or Argentine pesos into bolivianos, you can get reasonable rates at the numerous casas de cambio along Avenida República Argentina near the international bridge. Not all places offer the same rates, however, so it pays to shop around and even bargain with them. Universo Tours at República Argentina 387 beside the bridge will change travellers' cheques if US dollars are currently in demand. Beware of counterfeit US dollar notes!

Post & Telecommunications There are post and telephone offices on both sides of the border but Argentine service seems to be superior on both counts.

Time Change From October to April, there's a one-hour time change between Bolivia and Argentina (noon in Villazón is 1 pm in La Quiaca). From May to September, the Argentine province of Jujuy, where La Quiaca is located, operates on Bolivian time (only a bit more efficiently).

Foreign Consulate The helpful Argentine Consulate is open Monday to Friday from 10 am to noon and 2 to 5 pm.

Places to Stay

Villazón has a couple of economical hotels and alojamientos. The nicest is the friendly *Residencial Martinez* (☎ 562) near the bus terminal. Double rooms with/without bath cost B33/20.

The *Grand Palace Hotel* (☎ 333), also opposite the bus terminal, is fairly clean. A room with private bath is B15 per person, or B10 per person without bath. *Residencial El Cortijo* has also been recommended.

Near the railway station at Antofagasta 860 is the marginal *Alojamiento San Agustín*, without private baths or hot water. It costs B6 per person.

Places to Eat

There aren't many good meal options in Villazón. Try the *Charke Kan Restaurant* opposite the bus terminal, a rather greasy and grimy place. They're very keen on music, and a bizarre round record player hums away in the background.

There are several other less appealing restaurants near the transportation terminals. The food stalls in the market are cheap but don't offer much variety.

Getting There & Away

Bus Buses headed north all depart from the central terminal. Several buses leave for Potosí at 5 pm and cost B18 with connections to Sucre for B28, Oruro for B32 and La Paz for B36. To Tarija, buses depart at 7 and 8 pm and cost B20.

Several flotas leave for Tupiza between 3 and 5 pm for B6. It's a beautiful trip so go as early as possible to be assured of maximum daylight viewing.

Train Many visitors to Villazón arrive or depart by rail. If you're coming from the south and want to take the train to Uyuni or Oruro, you'll have to walk or take a cab across the border. The distance between the bus terminal in La Quiaca and the railway station in Villazón is two to three km. You can hire a *carretero* to haul your bags across the border for a small and negotiable fee – about B5.

The station chief laughed when we enquired about the rail timetable; apparently it doesn't vaguely represent reality. The window where tickets are sold is meant to open at 8 am on the day of departure but tickets are difficult to secure and the station chief recommends spending the night in the queue at the station.

If you'd rather avoid the ferrocarril frolics, go to Universo Tours (☎ 320) at Avenida República Argentina 387. You'll pay a commission but it's worth it for the minimum of fuss. Don't be tempted to purchase tickets from scalpers outside the station; 90% of the time, the tickets have already been used and they're banking that new arrivals in Bolivia won't know the difference.

Trains to Uyuni and Oruro depart on Wednesday and Saturday at 3.30 pm. From

Oruro to Villazón, the Expreso del Sur leaves on Tuesday and Friday at 7 pm and arrives in Villazón at 1 pm the following day. The fare from Oruro is B88/63 for 1st/2nd class. The 2nd-class pullman cars include breakfast and heating while 1st class includes a cushioned seat and videos as well. To continue on to Jujuy, Tucumán and Buenos Aires, cross the border to La Quiaca and board the connecting El Panamericano, the Argentine counterpart. Less pretentious trains run from Oruro on Monday, Wednesday and Thursday at 4.10 pm.

Crossing the Border For tourists, crossing the border should be no problem at all, but don't get caught up in the contrabandist's procession or you'll be hours getting through. Immigration offices and federal police are stationed on either side of the bridge and formalities here are normally minimal and friendly. If you need an Argentine visa, pick it up at the consulate in Villazón or Tarija. Going the other direction, there's a Bolivian Consulate in La Quiaca.

Despite past disputes, British citizens are now admitted to Argentina and no visas are necessary. Argentina is paranoid about Bolivian drug trafficking through their territory so prepare for thorough and exhaustive searches for coca leaves and harder drugs about 20 km south of La Quiaca. Body searches are common.

Entering Bolivia, the searches are casual, if conducted at all. Bolivian immigration is open from 7 am to 7 pm and doesn't close for lunch. If the Argentine official is working on his own, the post closes for lunch between noon and 2 pm.

LA QUIACA (ARGENTINA)
Villazón's twin village of La Quiaca lies just across the Río Villazón in northern Argentina. The contrast between the two sides is striking; La Quiaca is a neatly groomed town with tree-lined avenues, surfaced streets, nice restaurants and well-stocked shops.

Information
Money If you're entering Argentina at La Quiaca, it's a good idea to exchange just enough cash to get you to Salta or Jujuy where rates will be better. The province of Jujuy issues its own peso banknotes which resemble Monopoly money and may be used only within the province. Only the Banco de la Nación Argentina exchanges cash dollars but at a poor rate; try at the hotels or in Villazón.

Post & Telecommunications The post is generally more reliable than in Bolivia and reverse charge phone calls are accepted to limited areas.

Bolivian Consulate The Bolivian Consulate is open Monday to Friday from 8.30 to 11 am and 2 to 5 pm. On Saturday, it opens from 9 am to noon.

Iglesia de San Francisco – Yavi
If you're continuing into Argentina, a visit to Yavi 15 km east of La Quiaca is recommended. Here you will find the tiny Iglesia de San Francisco, built in 1680, which has an ornately gilded interior and translucent onyx windows. It's open Tuesday from 9 am to noon and 3 to 6 pm, and on Saturday from 9 am to noon. Find the caretaker who'll open the door and show you around. Flota La Quiaqueña departs for Yavi from the La Quiaca bus terminal.

Places to Stay
Bottom end accommodation is available in La Quiaca at the basic *Alojamiento Pequeño* near the frontier. Simple but clean rooms without baths cost US$2.40 per person. A similar option is the *Hotel La Victoria* on the main plaza.

In the mid-range, the *Hotel Crystal* (☎ 255) at Avenida Sarmiento 539 charges US$12 per person for rooms with bath; a double costs only US$18. A room without bath will cost US$5.50. Request the room that shares a wall with the bakery; it's almost as good as having a heater!

The *Hotel Frontera* costs US$4.50 per person with shared bath. There's no heating but you can get an electric shower.

Near the corner of Arabe Siria and San Martín is the clean *Hotel de Turismo* which charges US$24 double. They do have heat radiators but only fire them up in July.

Places to Eat

Food is nicer and better value on the Argentine side of the border. The *Hotel de Turismo* has a lovely dining room with a stone fireplace and a cosy atmosphere. An immense steak with chips goes for US$4.

The unassuming *Confitería La Frontera* at the Hotel Frontera serves luscious *pasta al pesto* with real pesto sauce for US$1.20. Service can be a bit surly but the food makes up for it. Opposite the bus terminal, *Confitería El Buen Gusto* is a good snack option and there's also a restaurant upstairs in the terminal itself. For pizza, go to *Pizzería El Amigo* just a block away.

Getting There & Away

Bus All buses now depart from the new central bus terminal in La Quiaca. The Panamericano bus leaves for Jujuy at least three times daily for US$16 and takes from eight to nine hours, passing through some stunningly colourful and cactus-studded landscapes. From Jujuy (also known as San Salvador de Jujuy), there are frequent connections to Salta, Cafayate, Rosario, Córdoba and Buenos Aires. Atahuallpa buses connect La Quiaca with Salta and Jujuy at least three times daily, with the same connections as Panamericano.

Flota La Quiaqueña serves Yavi and other nearby communities.

Train Tickets for long-distance trains are sold from 8.30 am to noon and 3 to 9 pm on Wednesday and from 11.30 am to 1 pm and 3 to 9 pm on Saturday. The Panamericano bus to Retiro station in Buenos Aires via Jujuy, Tucumán and Rosario departs at 8.35 pm on Wednesday and Saturday.

The slower train to Buenos Aires via Jujuy and Córdoba leaves at 6.45 am on Tuesday, Sunday and Friday. There's also a local train to Güemes on Tuesday, Thursday and Saturday at 9.20 am. Tickets are sold from 8.30 am on the day of departure.

contemporary craft design

Cochabamba

Chicha quiero, chicha busco,
Por chicha mis paseos.
Señora, deme un vasito
Para cumplir mis deseos.

This longing old Bolivian verse cries: 'I want chicha, I search for chicha, for chicha are my wanderings. Lady, give me a glass to satisfy my longing'.

To most Bolivians, Cochabamba is known for one of two things: romantics will dreamily remark on its luscious climate. Hardcore imbibers, such as the author of the above poem, will identify Cochabamba with its luscious chicha cochabambina. Both images of the city are well founded.

The saying: *Las golondrinas nunca migran de Cochabamba* (The swallows never migrate from Cochabamba) aptly describes what Cochabambinos believe is the world's most pleasant climate. With dry, sunny weather similar to that of the Mediterranean lands, Cochabamba physically resembles parts of Spain or Southern California. Throughout the valley and around much of southern Cochabamba Department, you'll see white cloth or plastic flags flying on long poles, indicating that chicha is available. Travelling outside the town, you'll realise just how popular it is and at 2570-metres elevation, it does pack a good punch!

Cochabamba's population is currently over 400,000 and growing. Although it long held the title of Bolivia's second city, the recent push for economic development of the lowlands has transferred those honours to Santa Cruz. The name 'Cochabamba' is derived by joining the Quechua words *kjocha* and *pampa* which mean 'swampy plain'.

The city occupies a fertile green bowl, 25 km long by 10 km wide, set in a landscape of fields and low hills. To the north-west rises 5035-metre Cerro Tunari, the highest peak in central Bolivia. The rich soil of the area yields abundant crops of maize, barley, wheat, alfalfa and orchard and citrus fruits. A large European population inhabits Cochabamba and environs, and only a small percentage of Cochabambinos are of pure Indian extraction.

History

The city was founded in January of 1574 by Sebastián Barba de Padilla. It was named the Villa de Oropeza in honour of the Count and Countess of Oropeza, parents of Viceroy Francisco de Toledo who chartered and promoted its settlement.

During the height of Potosí's silver boom, the Cochabamba valley developed into the primary source of food for the miners in agriculturally unproductive Potosí. Cochabamba came to be known as the 'breadbasket' of Bolivia due to its high volume of maize and wheat production. When Potosí declined in importance during the early 18th century, so did Cochabamba. Grain production in the Chuquisaca (Sucre) area, much closer to Potosí, was sufficient to supply the decreasing demand.

By the mid-1800s, however, the economic crisis subsided and the city again assumed its position as the nation's granary. Elite landowners in the valley grew wealthy and began to invest in highland mining ventures in western Bolivia. Before long, the Altiplano mines were attracting international capital and the focus of Bolivian mining shifted from Potosí to south-western Bolivia. As a result, Cochabamba thrived and its European/Quechua population gained a reputation for affluence and prosperity.

Economically active and growing, the area today offers a clutch of historical and archaeological attractions, and has a progressive atmosphere and a vitality that is visibly absent in the more traditional cities at higher altitudes.

Orientation

The central area of the city is compact and

well laid out, so unless you're travelling to the outskirts, it's easy to walk around Cochabamba. The climate is also conducive to walking, and since the city sits on a level valley floor, there are no hills to climb. The central business district lies roughly between the river in the north and La Coronilla (a hill) and Laguna Alalay in the south-west and south-east, respectively. It's bounded on the east and west by Avenida Oquendo and Calle Tumusla.

The largest market areas are on or south of Avenida Aroma, sandwiched between the Colina San Sebastián and Laguna Alalay, near the new Terminal de Buses. Here also are the railway station and most of the intra-valley bus terminals. Long-distance buses leave from the brand-new Terminal de Buses on Avenida Ayachucho near the intersection of Punata.

Many addresses in the city are measured from the Plaza 14 de Septiembre and are preceded by 'N' (norte), 'S' (sud), 'E' (este), or 'O' (oeste – to avoid alphanumeric confusion, they sometimes use a 'W' here instead). Obviously, these stand for 'north', 'south', 'east' and 'west', respectively.

Information

Tourist Office The Dinatur kiosk is on Calle General Achá in front of the ENTEL building. It's open from 9 am to noon and 2 to 6 pm Monday to Friday. The staff are quite helpful with specific questions and sell photocopied maps of the city for B.50.

Money Librería la Juventud and American Exchange on Plaza 14 de Septiembre change travellers' cheques at reasonable rates. Cambios Universo on Calle España (just off the plaza) also exchange travellers' cheques, but American is a more professional operation and gives a better rate.

Street changers hang out all over town, but their main haunt is on the corner of Avenida de las Heroínas and Calle 25 de Mayo. Their rates are competitive, but they'll only accept cash US dollars and won't give much over the official rates.

Post & Telecommunications The post and telephone offices are both in the large complex on Avenida Ayacucho between Calle General Achá and Avenida de las Heroínas. Postal service from Cochabamba is reliable and the facilities are among the country's finest. Downstairs from the main lobby is a special express post office.

The ENTEL office, on the other hand, is a little disorganised; expect longer than normal waits for international connections. The public fax number in Cochabamba is (042) 48500.

Foreign Consulates Consular representatives in Cochabamba include:

Argentina
    Avenida Pando 1329, 2nd floor (☎ 48268); open 9 am to 1 pm Monday to Friday.
Brazil
    Calle Potosí 1252 (☎ 25529); open 9 am to noon and 2 to 6 pm weekdays.
Chile
    Plazuela 4 de Noviembre, Edificio Los Álamos (☎ 46039); open 9 am to noon Monday to Friday.
Germany
    Calle España N-149 (☎ 25529); open 5 to 6 pm Monday to Wednesday.
Peru
    Avenida Pando 1143 (☎ 46210); open 9 am to noon and 2 to 5 pm weekdays.
USA
    Avenida Libertador Bolivar 1724 (☎ 43216); open 9 am to noon weekdays.

Cultural Centres Alliance Française at Calle Santivañez O-181 and the Goethe Institut at the corner of Calle Sucre and Antezana provide cultural activities and have newspapers and books in French and German, respectively. The reading room of the Instituto Boliviano-Americano, Calle 25 de Mayo N-365 near Plaza Colón, is open weekdays from 9 am to noon and 3 to 9.30 pm.

Travel Agencies Gitano Tours on Avenida de las Heroínas between Calle 25 de Mayo and Avenida San Martín has been recommended as the best place to buy discounted international airline tickets.

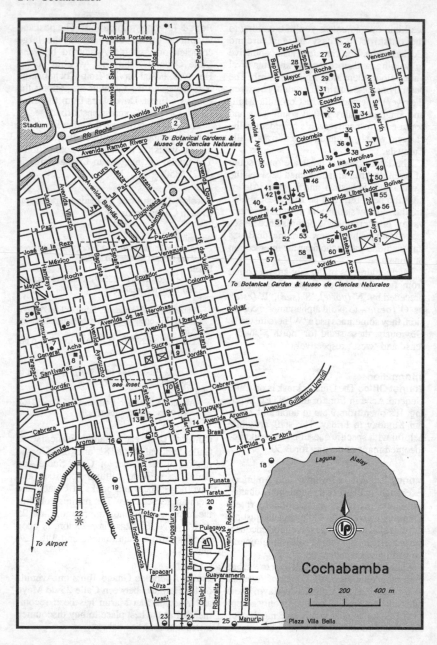

Cochabamba

0   200   400 m

■ PLACES TO STAY

8 Hostal Central
9 Residencial Familiar
10 Residencial Florida
11 Alojamiento Cochabamba
12 Alojamiento Escobar
13 Residencial Escobar
17 Residencial Elisa
30 Gran Hotel Ambassador
33 Residencial Familiar Anexo
34 Hotel Capitol
35 Hotel Boston
46 Uni Hotel
55 Caesar's Plaza
58 Residencial Imperial
60 Gran Hotel Las Vegas

▼ PLACES TO EAT

3 Jamaica
4 Bibossy
27 El Rincón Salón de Te
28 La Cantonata
31 Snack La Mejicana
32 Gopal's Restaurante Vegetariano
37 Tea Room Zürich
47 Heladería Dumbo
48 California Burgers & Donuts
49 Confitería Cecy

OTHER

1 Palacio de Portales
2 Parque Arqueológico
5 Fremen Tours

6 TAM
7 The 'Big Screw'
14 Mercado Cancha Calatayud
15 Old Long-distance Bus Terminals
16 Micros to Quillacollo, Payrumani, Sipe-Sipe, etc
18 Micros to Chapare
19 New Central Bus Terminal
20 Mercado de Ferias Central
21 Railway Station
22 Colina San Sebastián
23 Micros to Tarata
24 Micros to Cliza
25 Micros To Punata & Arani
26 Plaza Colón
29 Caminante Equipo de Camping
36 Museo Arqueológico
38 Casa de la Cultura
39 Los Amigos del Libro II
40 Librería Cervantes
41 Post Office
42 LAB
43 ENTEL
44 Tourist Office (Dinatur)
45 Iglesia de la Compañía de Jesús
50 Iglesia & Convento de San Francisco
51 Los Amigos del Libro
52 American Exchange, Exprinter & Exprintbol (Casas de Cambio)
53 Librería La Juventud
54 Plaza 14 de Septiembre
56 Banco de Santa Cruz
57 Iglesia de Santo Domingo
59 Cathedral
61 Mercado 25 de Mayo

A very useful but slightly upmarket travel agency is the Dutch-operated company, Fremen Tours (Viajes Fremen). They organise excursions to Chapare, Torotoro, Incallajta, Parque Nacional Tunari, Cerro Tunari and the more interesting villages scattered around the Cochabamba valley. If you have a large group, you can get the per person costs down to quite reasonable levels.

Fremen also arranges visits to their Hotel Puente in Villa Tunari (for details, see under Villa Tunari in the Bolivian Amazon chapter) and cruises on the *Reina de Enin* riverboat (refer to the discussion on Trinidad in the Amazon Basin chapter). For information,

contact Fremen Tours (☎ 47126, fax (591-42) 48500), Casilla 1040, Calle Tumusla O-245, Cochabamba, Bolivia.

Bookshops Look for books or maps in Cochabamba at one of the two representatives of Los Amigos del Libro at Avenida de las Heroínas E-311 and at Calle General Achá E-110 diagonally opposite the tourist office. They sell English, French and German-language paperbacks, reference books and souvenir publications. The Librería Cervantes at the corner of Avenida Ayacucho and Calle General Achá is worth seeing for the monumental mural of Don

Quixote and entourage that graces the building, but its selection of books is limited to Spanish-language literature and texts.

A range of marginal quality thematic maps are available from street vendors who set up in front of the LAB office in the post office/ENTEL complex.

Camping Equipment Camping equipment is available at the Caminante Equipo de Camping shop at Calle 25 de Mayo 391.

Film Slide film may be found at Foto Broadway, Calle Colombia 283. On Tuesday and Thursday, they develop E-6 process transparencies.

Dangers & Annoyances At the time of publication, cholera was spreading in Cochabamba at the rate of 100 cases per month. Although the problem may soon be brought under control, visitors should be especially careful with raw produce, animal products and drinking water. For further information, refer to the Health section in the Facts for the Visitor chapter.

Hotel passport checks by immigration officers are fortunately less frequent than they once were and you'll no longer be aroused from your sleep at 5 am. Due to new regulations, officers are only permitted to check passports between 8 am and noon at the hotel reception desk.

The tap water in Cochabamba is contaminated with amoebas and there's a real danger of contracting amoebic dysentery from salads, glasses rinsed in buckets of water, locally produced cheese and thin-skinned fruits such as papayas and mangoes.

If you're travelling in Cochabamba's rural hinterlands, be especially careful to avoid vinchuca beetles, which carry the deadly Chagas disease. If you're interested, the Chagas Institute at the university does tests and distributes free booklets about the beetle and the disease.

Churches
Readers have written that Cochabamba's churches are rarely open during the hours

posted at the tourist office. You'll have the most luck on Saturday afternoons, Sundays and early mornings.

Cathedral The cathedral on Plaza 14 de Septiembre was built in neoclassic style in 1571, making it the oldest religious structure in the valley and the original church of Oropeza. With a myriad of architectural styles added to it over the years, the composition doesn't hang together well, but the frescoes and paintings inside are worth a look.

Iglesia & Convento de San Francisco Constructed in 1581, the Iglesia de San Francisco on Calle 25 de Mayo and Avenida Libertador Bolivar is the second oldest church in Cochabamba. Major revisions and renovation took place in both 1782 and 1925, however, and very little of the original structure remains. The attached convent and cloister were added during the 1600s. So that the pleasant Cochabamba climate could be appreciated, the cloister was constructed of wood rather than stone, as would have been customary at the time. The pulpit displays fine examples of mestizo design. San Francisco normally opens from 6.30 to 8 pm.

Convento de Santa Teresa The Convento de Santa Teresa on Calle Baptista and Plaza Granado is quite beautiful inside if you can ignore the kitsch Christmas lights over the altar. It's the result of combining two churches, one built on top of the other. Work on the first church was begun in 1753 by Jesuits. Santa Teresa is meant to be open from 7.30 to 8 am.

El Hospício El Hospício on Plaza Colón is composed of a blend of baroque, byzantine, and neoclassical architectural styles. It was begun in 1875 and is the newest major church in Cochabamba.

Iglesia de Santo Domingo This church at the corner of Calle Santivañez and Avenida Ayacucho is a rather interesting structure for several reasons. It was founded in 1612, but actual construction wasn't begun until 1778. When its chief promoter, Francisco Claros García, died in 1795, construction was still underway. Its style is roccoco and the interesting main doorway is flanked by two anthropomorphic columns.

Iglesia de la Recoleta The Iglesia de la Recoleta north of the river is a baroque structure begun in 1654. The attraction is a wooden carving called Cristo de la Recoleta, accurately carved from a single piece of wood by Diego Ortiz de Guzmán.

Parks
Plaza Colón is a pleasant little park with well-kept gardens, fountains, bridges and ponds. Unfortunately, however, it is a druggie hangout and should be avoided at night. Just to the north of the plaza is Avenida Ballivián, also known as the Prado, a palm-lined avenue with shops and cafés that will carry you directly to southern California.

The Parque Arqueológico between the nauseating Río Rocha and Avenida Ramón Rivero is full of gruesome stone heads, reproductions of originals housed in the Museo Arqueológico in the centre. Beside this park is an unusual children's playground. Just a few blocks west along the river is the zoo, which is not worth visiting.

Colina San Sebastián, a hill to the south of Avenida Aroma towers over the airport and is a good place to relax and read or watch the planes. From this vantage point, there's quite a nice view over the city. From San Sebastián, a trail leads along a ridge to another nearby hill, La Coronilla, where there's a monument dedicated to the women, children and elderly people who courageously defended the city from the Spanish forces of José Manuel Goyeneche in 1812.

Readers have warned of impromptu passport checks and fines from police in this area; if you're stopped, ask to see the officer's identification and insist that the matter be settled at the police station.

Museums
Museo Arqueológico Cochabamba's Archaeological Museum is probably the most pleasant and complete in Bolivia. The exhibits include thousands of artefacts dating from as early as 15,000 BC and as late as the colonial period. Admission is B5 and the excellent guided tour, conducted in English, French or Spanish, takes about 1½ hours. The museum is on 25 de Mayo between Avenida de las Heroínas and Colombia, and is open Monday to Friday from 9 am to noon and 3 to 7 pm. On Saturday, it opens from 9 am to 1 pm.

Museo de Ciencias Naturales & Botanical Garden The Natural Science Museum, once well-displayed in the Casa de la Cultura, was recently transferred to a tiny outpost in the botanical garden. The large insect collection with thousands of beetles, bugs and butterflies is fascinating, but as it's cramped into an uncomfortably small room, it's difficult to appreciate. The museum also contains some interesting mineral specimens and a pathetic collection of moth-eaten stuffed animals.

Even less interesting is the garden itself, little more than a swathe of dry grass studded with a few sickly shrubs and eucalyptus trees. If you've nothing else to do, it's open from 6 am to 6 pm. Take micro 'H' from Avenida San Martín to Avenida Ramón Rivero at the end of Aniceto Arce.

Casa de la Cultura
The city archives, reading room and art exhibits are on the 3rd floor of the Casa de la Cultura on the corner of Avenida de las Heroínas and Calle 25 de Mayo. It's open to the public from 8 am to noon and 2 to 6 pm Monday to Friday. Admission is free. Ask the curator to show you the recent discoveries from Omereque, a pre-Inca burial site near Aiquile, south-east of Cochabamba. The faces bear an incredibly strong resemblance to the 'little green men' described by victims of UFO encounters around the world!

Palacio de Portales
North of the river is the Palacio de Portales, also known as Centro Cultural Pedagógico

de Portales. Free guided tours are offered between 5 and 6 pm Monday to Friday, on Saturday from 10 to 11 am and Sunday from 11 am to noon. The wealth-supported ego-mania of its builder, tin baron Simon Patiño, cannot be adequately described. The design was the work of French architect Eugene Bliault in 1925. The fireplaces are made of flawless Carrera marble, the furniture and woodwork were carved in wood imported from France, the walls are covered with bro-caded silk, and one very intricate 'painting' is actually a woven silk tapestry. The gardens and exterior are equally representative of inconceivable affluence and extravagance. The house was completed in 1927 but was never occupied, and today is used as a teaching centre, a hall for visiting exhibitions and an arts complex.

The Palacio de Portales is in the barrio of Queru-Queru; take micro 'G' from near the corner of avenidas San Martín and de las Heroínas.

Markets

Cochabamba is the biggest market town in Bolivia, and the larger markets are the best stocked and most nerve-shattering and crowded places you're likely to find in the country. Most of the larger ones occupy open plazas (called *canchas* in Quechua) around the southern part of the city. The largest and most accessible is Mercado Cancha Cala-tayud which sprawls across a wide spot in Avenida Aroma. Here is your best opportunity to see the local costumes, which are strikingly different to those worn on the Alti-plano. Cancha Francisco Rivas and the Mercado de Ferias Central are both near the railway station, and several other minor market areas can be found scattered around the city.

There has been massive expansion and amalgamation of the formerly separate markets in the San Antonio area, near the railway station and the Terminal de Buses. This is a very obvious effect of the 'New Economic Policy' which the Bolivian government has been pursuing since 1985. In practice, privatisation of public services and cuts in public spending have created massive unemployment, and thousands of people are now trying to earn a living as street vendors or market stallholders. The whole San Antonio area is now one massive market, known universally as 'La Cancha'. I can't think of an item that it isn't possible to buy in the cancha; it's incredible and totally ex-hausting. At the south-west end, around the junction of Tarata and Calle Esteban Arce, are two alleys of artesans' wares; one is mostly cloth and ornaments, the other mostly musical instruments. It is reasonably priced and the people are friendly.

Paul L Younger, Bolivia

Cristo Rey

An immense new statue of Cristo Rey (Christ the King), stands on a hilltop behind Cochabamba. It's a few cm higher than the famous Cristo Redentor on Rio de Janeiro's Corcovado, which stands 33 metres high, or one metre for each year of Christ's life. Cochabambinos justify the one-upmanship by claiming that Christ actually lived *33 años y un poquito*, 33 years and a bit.

Language Courses

If you'd enjoy studying Spanish in Cocha-bamba's ideal climate, try the Padres de Maryknoll Instituto de Idiomas, Casilla 550, Cochabamba, Bolivia. Write in advance for info. Another option is the Instituto de Lenguaje Cochabamba (☎ 44868), at Plazuela Busch S-0826 esq Bolivar, Casilla 2966, Cochabamba, Bolivia, which offers Spanish, Quechua and Portuguese courses.

Alternatively, there are quite a few private teachers in town, but although lessons will be more personalised, they're also more expensive – around B18 per hour. If you're interested in learning Quechua, try Jaime Claros (☎ 41241) who charges B12 per hour.

Fiestas

The major annual festival in Cochabamba, Heroínas de la Coronilla, is celebrated on 27 May in honour of the women and children who defended the city in the battle of 1812. It's more of a solemn commemoration than a fiesta, so it's not an occasion for excite-ment.

The fiesta of Santa Veracruz Tatala is cel-ebrated on 2 May each year, in and around a chapel located seven km along the highway toward Sucre. Farmers from around Cochabamba valley gather to pray for fertility of the soil during the coming season. The celebration is accompanied by folk music, dancing and lots of raging drunken activity.

Refer to the discussion of Quillacollo for information on Cochabamba valley's largest celebration, the Virgen de Urcupiña.

Places to Stay – bottom end

One of Bolivia's finest inexpensive digs is *Residencial Elisa* (☎ 27846) at Calle Agustín Lopez 0834 (just off Avenida Aroma). Although this part of town is rather aromatic, to say the least, just inside the door of the Elisa is a different world, with a grassy courtyard and clean, sunny garden tables. The owner is friendly and knowledgeable about Cochabamba, and can help you with any sort of tourist information you may need. Rooms with private baths and electric hot showers cost B18 per person. Without bath, they're B12. All prices include a breakfast of juice, bread, jam, milk and coffee.

Another very pleasant and friendly place is the sparkling *Residencial Florida* (☎ 27787) at Calle 25 de Mayo S-0583 which has a quiet patio and lawn furniture on the main floor and a sunny deck upstairs. Hot water is available until 1 pm and the owner, a very nice lady, cooks a mean breakfast for her guests. It's in a good location midway between the town centre and the bus terminals, and is a good place to meet other travellers. You'll pay B18/12 per person for rooms with/without private baths.

The centrally located *Residencial Imperial* costs B10/20 for a single/double with common baths and hot showers. It's friendly and clean, and they'll watch your luggage while you're out travelling around.

The *Residencial Familiar* (☎ 27988) at Calle Sucre E-554 and the *Residencial Familiar Anexo* (☎ 27986) at Calle 25 de Mayo N-0234 are popular with both Bolivian and foreign travellers. The clean rooms are arranged around a central courtyard and cost B10 per person without private bath. Hot water is available in the showers. The door locks aren't always secure.

The cheapest acceptable accommodation is *Alojamiento Cochabamba* (☎ 25067) at Calle Aguirre S-591. Although it's basically a flophouse, it serves as a popular crash for ultra-low-budget travellers. Singles/doubles with common bath cost B7/14 without breakfast.

Near the old bus terminals but fortunately well off nerve-wracking Avenida Aroma are the *Residencial Escobar* (☎ 29275), which charges B11 per person with common bath, and *Alojamiento Escobar*, 30 metres away, which charges only B8 per person. They're nothing to write home about but they are cheap.

The quirky *Hostal Central* (☎ 23622) on Calle General Achá, three blocks west of the plaza, has been newly renovated. The major plus point is that it's set back from the street and is therefore relatively quiet. Without bath, singles/doubles cost B15/20, while with bath, they're B30/35.

Places to Stay – middle

The mildly faded *Gran Hotel Las Vegas* (☎ 29217) at Calle Esteban Arce S-0352 near the main plaza costs B40/60/80 for a single/double/triple, all with bath. Although the rooms are clean, they've been accurately described as drab and dingy.

Alternatively, at Calle 25 de Mayo 0167 is the *Hotel Boston* (☎ 28530), a reasonable mid-range option with singles/doubles for B60/90.

Very clean and central is the new *Uni Hotel* (☎ 22444, fax (591-42) 24341) at Calle Baptista S-0111, which tries very hard to appear trendy and upbeat. Seemingly in a constant state of renovation and addition, at times it feels like a construction zone. Rooms with private baths and breakfast included cost B52/86/103 for a single/double/triple, or B72 for a double bed.

The *Hotel Capitol* (☎ 24510) at the corner of calles Colombia and 25 de Mayo isn't bad at B40/60 for a single/double with bath. Showers are only lukewarm, however, and rooms are dim and merely functional.

Places to Stay – top end
A good upmarket hotel is *Caesar's Plaza* (☎ 24558, fax (591-42) 22646) at Calle 25 de Mayo S-210. Single/double/triple rooms start at B137/169/227 including breakfast.

The four-star *Gran Hotel Ambassador* (☎ 48777) at Calle España 349 offers single/double rooms for B90/105. Oddly enough, they charge B125 for a room with a double bed and suites are approximately 30% more expensive.

Places to Eat
Breakfast For breakfast, *Confitería Cecy* at Avenida de las Heroínas E-452 serves great orange juice, eggs, toast and chocolate as well as Irish coffee and award-winning cheese, chicken and beef salteñas. *California Burgers & Donuts* does pretty much the same for breakfast as the Cecy, but it doesn't quite measure up. Perhaps the best place for a blowout gringo breakfast is *Kivón Helados* at Avenida de las Heroínas 352 where they pile on the pancakes, french toast, eggs, ham and so on for a predictably elevated price. If you're after an early breakfast, *Heladería Dumbo* in the same area opens before 8 am.

The market is the cheapest place to find coffee and a roll and since Cochabamba is known for its fruit production, you'll also find a nice selection of orchard and citrus varieties. If you're up for something more traditional, try *arroz con leche*, a local breakfast speciality.

Lunch & Snacks For lunch, there is a wide range of places to choose from. One of the most economical is *Bar Pensión Familiar* at Avenida Aroma O-176. For B4 you get a complete meal of salad, soup, a main course and a dessert, and beer is inexpensive. Other good bets for quick traditional lunches are *Anexo El Negro* at Calle Esteban Arce between Jordán and Calama; *Rellenos Calama* on Calama between 16 de Julio and Antezana; and *El Caminante* on Calle Esteban Arce near Cabrera. *Cafe Express Bolivar* at Avenida Libertador Bolivar 485 has been recommended as having the best espresso and cappuccino in Cochabamba.

Avenida de las Heroínas is fast-food row and the aforementioned Confitería Cecy is good for light lunches of burgers, chips, chicken, pizza and the like. The friendly owner speaks good English, having spent many years in the USA, and although he has North American fast-food culture down to an art, he also produces delicious award-winning salteñas. Other fast-food places in the immediate vicinity include *California Burgers* with good strong Irish coffee; *Kivón Helados* at Avenida de las Heroínas 352 which serves snack meals, pastries, flan, and a variety of ice-cream concoctions; *Dumbo* – look for the landmark flying elephant; and the bizarrely decorated *Unicornio*.

When the popular *Govinda* vegetarian restaurant 'went off to Argentina' (as the new tenant describes it), the *El Rincón Salón de Te* moved into Mayor Rocha 355 to take its place. We went in search of Indian curry and wound up with coffee, cheesecake and lemon meringue pie – highly recommended for afternoon tea. Alternatively, try the coffee, doughnuts and eclairs at the *Tea Room Zürich* at Avenida San Martín 143, open daily except Tuesday from 9.30 to 11.30 am and 2 to 7.30 pm.

If you're going walking or want something to munch in your hotel room, stop by *San Marcos* on Ladislao Cabrera between Calle Esteban Arce and Nataniel Aguirre where you can buy large bags of terrific *granola de tarhui* (tarhui is a local grain) for B2.

Full Lunches & Dinners Moving up the price scale, you'll find a string of sidewalk cafés along Avenida Ballivián which offer European, Bolivian and North American fare in a very pleasant environment. If you're really hungry, we recommend *Bibossy* at Avenida Ballivián N-539 near Plaza Colón. Their intimidating lunch portions formidably bury the plate!

Further down the Prado is *Los Inmortales* which serves a few Mexican dishes, but Bolivia's most authentic Mexican food is available at *Snack La Mejicana*. It's owned by a Bolivian who spent 35 years in Los

Angeles perfecting his tortilla technique and margarita magic. If you're craving tacos or enchiladas, don't miss it!

Repeatedly recommended, *Gopal's Restaurante Vegetariano* at Calle España 250 is currently Cochabamba's only vegetarian restaurant. They wash their fruit and veggies in iodine so there's no risk of giardia.

Just half a block away concealed behind rose-coloured stucco is one of the city's best and most upmarket restaurants, *La Cantonata*. It's an exceptionally good splurge where you can sip fine Chilean wine before a roaring fireplace. The menu, as the staff point out, is based on that of the *Porto Bello* in Houston, Texas.

Entertainment

Peña Arahui (☎ 40086) on Avenida América, just beyond the second bridge west of town, features live folk music shows on Friday, Saturday and Sunday evenings. To get there, take a taxi or micro 'J' from Avenida Ayacucho. Phone for information on specific times. There's also Cafe Concert Cuicacalli (☎ 49647) at Calle Junín 800 which serves meals and stages concerts, theatre, traditional music peñas and other cultural events. For information about what's on, phone or look in the newspaper entertainment listings.

For disco, locals frequent Arlequín on Avenida Uyuni. Cochabamba also has eight cinemas, and a good film quite often sneaks in; watch the newspapers for listings.

Things to Buy

If you missed purchasing a locally crafted musical instrument in La Paz, visit Inti Fábrica de Instrumentos Musicales near the corner of calles Tumusla and General Achá. It seems rather tourist-oriented, but may be worth a look.

Locally produced woollens are available at three main outlets: Fortrama on Avenida de las Heroínas; Asarti's at Mayor Rocha 375; and Casa Fisher's at Avenida Ramón Rivero 204. Fortrama also has a bargain factory outlet up the hill above Calacala Circle (the roundabout near the entrance to Parque Nacional Tunari). Cheaper alpaca and llama wool chompas are found in the markets.

Getting There & Away

Air The José Wilsterman Airport is at the south-west end of town below Colina San Sebastián. It is served by both LAB and TAM, each of which connect Cochabamba with La Paz and Santa Cruz. In addition, LAB serves Tarija, Trinidad, Riberalta, Guayaramerín and Sucre. TAM connects Cochabamba with Cobija, Riberalta and Guayaramerín.

The fare to La Paz is B117 one way, to Santa Cruz about B153, and to Sucre, B84.

Bus Long-distance buses now leave from the brand-new Terminal de Buses on Avenida Ayacucho near the intersection of Punata. This terminal replaces the old bus stops which were previously strung out along Avenida Aroma. There may be an additional surcharge on the cost of long-distance bus tickets to pay for construction of the new terminal.

Since it's so central, reaching Cochabamba is fairly easy from just about anywhere in the country and vice versa. Naturally, a great many buses do the run to La Paz, and well over a score depart between 7 and 9 pm daily. The most commodious daytime departure is with Nobleza, which takes 10 hours and costs B18, complete with videos.

Some of the nighttime La Paz buses stop in Oruro, but in addition Oruro is served by Flota Bolivia at 9 am and 5.30 pm. In addition, Unificado, Flota Oruro, Danubio and others serve Oruro at least every half hour in the morning and every hour in the afternoon.

The companies Bolivia, Expreso Mopar and Trans-Copacabana depart for Santa Cruz in the morning and numerous flotas leave for Santa Cruz between 4 and 6 pm. All Santa Cruz runs travel via Chapare. To Potosí, Flota Copacabana departs at 6 pm daily. Several flotas depart for Sucre between 4.30 and 6.30 pm daily.

To Villa Tunari and Puerto Villarroel (Chapare), micros depart from the corner of avenidas 9 de Abril and Oquendo near the lake. The first one is at 6.30 am and thereafter, they leave when all seats are sold. The fare to Chapare is B8. For information on reaching smaller villages near Cochabamba, see the Around Cochabamba Valley section later in this chapter.

Train Cochabamba is served mainly by ferrobus which eliminates a few of the major problems normally associated with Bolivian rail travel (specifically, trains!).

The ferrobus from La Paz leaves on Monday and Friday at 8 am and again on Friday at 9 pm. It leaves Cochabamba for La Paz on Tuesday and Thursday at 8 am and on Sunday at 8.20 pm. Fares are B29 pullman class and B23 especial class.

From Oruro to Cochabamba, there's a ferrobus on Monday and Wednesday at 12.10 pm, Saturday at 1.10 pm and Wednesday, Friday and Sunday at 8.15 am. There's also a train on Thursday at 8.20 am. From Cochabamba to Oruro, ferrobuses depart at 8 am Tuesday and Thursday, 8.30 pm Sunday, and 2.15 pm Wednesday, Friday and Sunday. The train goes on Friday at 8.30 am. Ferrobus fare is B17 pullman and B13 especial, while the train is slightly less.

Getting Around

To/From the Airport The airport taxi costs B5 per person.

Bus Micro buses are lettered and are rather difficult to use since they do not display their destination and bus stops are not marked. Fortunately, help is easy to find and Cochabambinos are happy to direct visitors in the use of their micros, which run to all corners of the city.

Taxi Cab fare to anywhere south and east of the river or north and west of the Laguna Alalay is only about B3. Beyond those limits, it doubles.

PARQUE NACIONAL TUNARI

This national park was created in 1962 to protect the mountain environs of Cocha-

bamba and the forested slopes above the city. Regulations are not enforced, however, and the city has encroached so far into parkland that it's probably too late for controls to do much good. In fact, Parque Nacional Tunari may soon be reclassified as merely an urban green area.

Ten km beyond the entrance tranca (see Getting There & Away under this section), you'll reach a lovely picnic area with *parrillas* (barbeques), a playground and forests of pine and eucalyptus. Another 10 km up the road are the pleasant Lagunas de Huarahuara, small lakes containing trout. From here, it's a day return trip to the summit of El Pirámide for views down the other side of the cordillera. There's a choice of wild camping sites.

The following description outlines an alternative route from the park tranca:

There is a path along the west side of the pink and white housing development used by the campesinos living behind it. Follow the road that passes behind the development between various farms. We left this road after about 300 metres, crossed a ravine to the left and headed (with permission) along the edge of several fields and found ourselves on a dirt roadside with an irrigation ditch upslope of it. The ditch had water in it – running fast! Our general goal was to climb up the valley that constitutes Tunari National Park. Once we found water, we followed it upstream past a small collection works and on up the canyon. The higher we went, the better it got! Eventually, we were in a temperate forest with small waterfalls, wildflowers, ferns and mosses and saw an outrageously beautiful moth. We passed several families of campesinos on their way down loaded with freshly cut herbs. Getting down only took one-sixth of the time getting up. Once down, you can [catch a prearranged taxi]...or just walk back to the main road.

Greg & Katie Cumberford, USA

Getting There & Away

With a private vehicle, the southern extreme of Parque Nacional Tunari is easily accessible from Cochabamba. On foot, you'll need a good day to get there and although you may be able to catch a lift back to town, you may want to carry food, water and camping equipment in case you're stuck.

To reach the park tranca, take the micro marked 'Temporal' from the centre of

Cochabamba. Alternatively, walk north along Calle España and Avenida Ballivián across the river where it becomes Avenida Libertador Bolivar. Continue to the Plazuela de Cala Cala, turn right on Calle Atahuallpa and follow it over Avenida Circumbalación to its end at a pink and white housing development and the national park tranca.

CERRO TUNARI

Snow-capped Cerro Tunari at 5035 metres is the highest peak in central Bolivia. Its flanks lie 40 km from Cochabamba along the road to Independencia. This area is spectacular for camping and hiking but without private 4WD transport, access is difficult.

Trekking enquiries may be directed to Franklin Fuentes at the tourist office who can make recommendations regarding guides and provide the latest transport details. A more upmarket option is to go on an organised trek with Fremen (see Travel Agencies under Cochabamba), a tour agency which leads two-day excursions to the mountain. With a group of two people, you'll pay B360 per person while groups of four pay only B288 per person, all inclusive.

Morochata Route

Take a micro to Quillacollo, a village 13 km from Cochabamba (see under Quillacollo in the Around Cochabamba Valley section for details) and try to hitch to Morochata, the village at the foot of Cerro Tunari on the Independencia road. From Morochata, you can climb up to the summit and down again in a long day, but the stiff high-altitude ascent will be more pleasant if you plan to camp and spend at least two days. You'll need a guide if you'd rather not risk getting lost on the fairly complicated route.

In Morochata, basic lodging is available at the school but you'll need at least a sleeping bag. On the way back to Cochabamba, you may want to stop at the Termas de Luriuni (Luriuni Hot Springs), seven km from Quillacollo, for a good relaxing soak.

AROUND COCHABAMBA VALLEY

Quillacollo

Besides Cochabamba itself, Quillacollo, 13 km away, is the largest and most commercially important community in the Cochabamba valley. Its name is derived from *khella-collu* meaning 'ash hill'. Apart from the *feria dominical*, or Sunday market, there is little of interest, although a pre-Inca burial mound has been discovered beneath a platform in Plaza Bolivar. One reader was inspired by the church in Quillacollo:

Quillacollo has a very interesting church, which houses the shrine of the Virgen de Urkupiña. The shrine is to the right of the altar in a little side chapel. It's a room full of candles and commemorative plaques thanking the Virgin for favours received. The rest of the church has interesting statues, and is in remarkably good condition compared to the majority of older churches in Cochabamba.

Mind out when approaching the church for the squad of women who pin the pilgrim's badges of the Virgin on your shirt first and then ask you for B2!

Paul L Younger, Bolivia

While you're at the market, try garapiña, the Quillacollo area's answer to the dessert drink, which is available only on Sundays. It's a deceptively strong combination of chicha, cinnamon, coconut and *ayrampo*, a local mystery ingredient which makes it red. If you're not visiting Quillacollo or neighbouring villages, you can try garapiña at El Caminante on Calle Esteban Arce near the corner of Cabrera in Cochabamba.

Fiesta de la Virgen de Urcupiña If you're fortunate enough to be in the area around the middle of August, you can catch the Fiesta de la Virgen de Urcupiña, the biggest annual celebration in Cochabamba Department. Folkloric musicians and dancers from all over Bolivia perform at this event and the chicha flows for three days, from 15 to 18 August.

Getting There & Away Micros and trufis to Quillacollo leave Cochabamba from the corner of avenidas Ayacucho and Aroma.

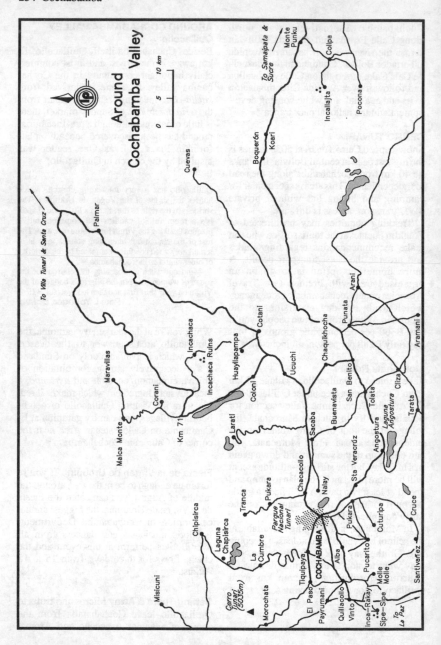

The trip costs around B1.50 and takes half an hour. You'll be let off at Plaza Bolivar.

Sipe-Sipe & Inca-Rakay

Sipe-Sipe, a quiet and friendly village 27 km from Cochabamba, is the site of Inca-Rakay, the most easily accessible of the major Cochabamba area ruins. If you're in Sipe-Sipe on a Sunday between February and May, make a point of sampling guarapo, a sweet grape liquor which is a speciality here.

The ruins of Inca-Rakay are mostly crumbling stone walls these days, but with some imagination one can perhaps conjure up images of how they must once have appeared. The site, in the Serrania de Tarhuani, consists of the remains of several hefty buildings and a large open plaza area overlooking the Cochabamba valley. One odd rock outcrop resembles the head of a condor, with a natural passageway inside leading to the top. Just off the plaza area is a cave which may be explored with a torch. Legend has it that this cave is the remnant of another of those ubiquitous Inca passageways – this one linking Inca-Rakay with Cuzco.

The plaza, which affords a spectacular view of the entire valley on a clear, smog-free day, is an excellent place to set up a tent – a night spent amid these secluded and unattended ruins is quite a haunting experience. If you're staying, remember to bring water since none is available.

If you read Spanish, you may want to pick up a copy of *Inkallajta & Inkaraqay* by Jesús Lara, published by Los Amigos del Libro and available at their shop in Cochabamba for about B22. It contains good maps of both sites and explains in detail theories about their origins and purposes.

Getting There & Away If you're not planning to stay overnight at the site, get an early start out of Cochabamba; the trip will require the better part of a day and you'll want to leave some time for exploring once you reach the ruins.

On Wednesday and Saturday, you can get a micro directly to Sipe-Sipe from the corner of avenidas Ayacucho and Aroma in Cochabamba. The rest of the week, take a micro from the same spot to Plaza Bolivar in Quillacollo and from there, a trufi or a micro to the main plaza in Sipe-Sipe.

On rare occasions, camiones travel up the hill and pass within several hundred metres of Inca-Rakay. If transport isn't available, however, you'll have to walk. If you're coming from the lowlands to Cochabamba, it's advisable to stay in town for a couple of days to acclimatise to the altitude before tackling this uphill hike.

From the main plaza in Sipe-Sipe, take the road which passes the· *colegio* (secondary school). There it narrows into a path and crosses a small ditch. Across the ditch, turn right onto the wider road. At this point you have a choice. If you stay on the road, it's a relatively easy uphill climb that will take about four hours if you are carrying a pack. On the roadside, there's a new sign pointing toward the ruins, which are hidden from view amid rock outcroppings and a clump of *molle* trees, which are similar to willows.

If you opt to follow the more direct route, straight up the mountain, it's a tiring two-hour grunt. This route is not straightforward and is at times very steep. From several hundred metres up the road from town, follow a water pipeline up the hill to the first major ridge. There'll be a large ravine on your left. From there, bear to the right, following the ridge until you see a smaller ravine to the right. At this point, you'll be able to see Inca-Rakay atop a reddish hill in the distance, but from so far away it won't be obvious what you're looking at.

Cross the small ravine and follow it until you can look across and see two small houses. In front of you will be a little hill with some minor ruins at the top. Climb the hill and cross the large flat area on top, then climb up two more false ridges and you'll see the ruins.

Taquiña Brewery

In the hills along the road toward Tiquipaya, 10 km from Cochabamba, is the source of that refreshing brew, Taquiña. On weekends, you may visit one of Bolivia's finest restaurants, with a menu which includes trout, lamb, duck and *lechón* (suckling pig) – washed down, of course, with the prime tipple. It also boasts a delicious view across the valley. If beer is your interest, however, brewery tours are available during the week.

Access from town is by hitching or taxi, which will cost around B7.

Payrumani

If you haven't already had your fill of Patiño's legacy in Oruro and Cochabamba, go to Payrumani where you can tour the tin baron's estate, the home he actually occupied. It was called Villa Albina after his wife, who was apparently as fussy as her husband when it came to surrounding the family with the finest of everything. The elegant French décor of the main house and the Carrera marble mausoleum seem typical of royalty – mineral or otherwise – anywhere in the world. In 1964, the entire estate was donated to the Salesian Congregation (a non-profit organisation) by the Simon I Patiño University Memorial fund which represents the baron's heirs. Today it operates as a museum.

To get to Payrumani take a trufi #211Z from Avenida Aroma in Cochabamba or from Plaza Bolivar in Quillacollo and get off at Villa Albina. The estate is open to tourists only between 3 and 4 pm Monday to Friday so you'll have to plan carefully in order to get there at the right time. Although it's only 22 km from Cochabamba, plan to spend a couple of hours getting there.

Vinto

Not to be confused with the tin smelter of the same name near Oruro, the village of Vinto in the Cochabamba valley is noted for two annual fiestas which are held there. On 19 March the Fiesta de San José (or St Joseph, the patron saint of carpenters) is celebrated. The other festival, Fiesta de la Virgen del Carmen, on 16 July, is celebrated with folkloric groups, masses, parades, and military bands.

The easiest access to Vinto is by trufi 211Z from the corner of avenidas Ayacucho and

Aroma in Cochabamba. On Wednesday and Saturday, there are direct micros from the same corner but on other days, you'll have to go via Quillacollo.

Punata

The small market town of Punata, 48 km east of Cochabamba, is known for the finest chicha in all Bolivia. If you're not going to Punata, you can sample its chicha in Cochabamba from a small shop on the north side of Avenida Aroma between calles 25 de Mayo and Esteban Arce. Market day falls on Tuesday and the town is accessible by micros which depart from Avenida República (the southern extension of Antezana) at Plaza Villa Bella in Cochabamba.

Tarata

Tarata, 30 km from Cochabamba, lives in infamy as the birthplace of the mad president General Mariano Melgarejo. The town has an enormous and interesting church and a worthwhile Thursday market specialising in ceramics. The air in Tarata, a village of potters and pottery painters, is thick with the scent of eucalyptus branches and leaves being burned in cylindrical firing kilns. Micros leave Cochabamba from the corner of Angostura and Avenida 6 de Agosto, five blocks south of the Cochabamba railway station.

Cliza

The Sunday market in Cliza is a good alternative to the utter shutdown in Cochabamba on Sunday. You can also avoid the bone-chilling early morning camión to Torotoro by catching the warm micro to Cliza, and then, after the temperature has risen to a bearable level, catch the Tototoro-bound camión from there. Micros which do the 45-minute journey to Cliza depart from the corner of Avenida Barrientos and Manuripi in Cochabamba.

Arani

Arani, 53 km from Cochabamba, stages a Thursday market specialising in alpaca wool chompas and other locally produced woollen

Top Left: Travelling in south-western Bolivia (RS)
Top Right: Landscape - south-west Bolivia (DS)
Bottom Left: Climber below summit - Illimani (JW)
Bottom Right: Taquesi Trail (the Inca Trail) (JW)

Top: Travel by camión in the Cordillera Real (TM)
Bottom: Shepherd - south-western Bolivia near Sajama (TM)

textiles. The village boasts 500 women who work as artesans creating these colourful and practical articles for export. One km south of Arani is the hamlet of Villa Rivero where men and women weave magnificent carpets in zoomorphic patterns and high relief.

If you're looking for weavings and carpets, bear in mind that purchasing them directly from the source rather than a shop will decrease the price you pay and increase the percentage of the sale going directly to the artesan. For example, a two-metre-sq carpet requiring 15 kg of wool and about 15 days of spinning and weaving sells for around B150, while in Cochabamba, the mark-up will be at least 50%.

Arani is also famous for *pan de Arani*, a bread concocted from a special blend of grains to yield a distinct flavour. Take a look also at the intricately carved wooden altars in the church, formerly the seat of the Bishop of Santa Cruz de la Sierra. On 24 August, Arani stages the Festividad de la Virgen de la Bella which dates from colonial times. Micros leave from the corner of Avenida República and Plaza Villa Bella in Cochabamba.

INCALLAJTA

Bolivia's nearest equivalent to Machu Picchu are the ruins of Incallajta – once the easternmost outpost of the Inca Empire. After Tiahuanaco, they're the country's most significant archaeological site. The name means 'Land of the Inca'.

Incallajta lies 132 km east of Cochabamba on a flat mountain spur above the Río Machajmarka. This ruined city with an immense fortification and more than 50 other structures is believed to have been founded by the Inca Emperor Tupac Yupanqui, who had previously wandered southward to define the southernmost limits of the empire in present-day Chile. The date of his arrival at Incallajta is estimated to have been some time during the 1460s. In 1525, the last year of the rule of Emperor Huayna Capac, the place was invaded and ruined by hordes of Guaraníes, Indians from the southeast.

You may want to pick up a copy of Jesús Lara's book *Inkallajta & Inkaraqay* from Los Amigos del Libro in Cochabamba. His original research was carried out in the 1920s, but it wasn't published until 1967. A basic knowledge of Spanish will be necessary to get something out of the text, but it also contains an excellent map of the site.

Getting There & Away

Without your own transport, getting to Incallajta will prove inconvenient and you'll have to carry camping equipment or take a chance on finding lodging in a private home. If you still want to visit this impressive and infrequently visited site, take any camión or bus headed toward Sucre and get off at Monte Punku, 119 km east of Cochabamba. From there, turn south along the road to Pocona and walk seven km to Collpa, then turn west and continue for about six more km to Incallajta.

You may have to spend the night in Collpa, but since there are no hotels, you'll either have to camp or arrange to stay with a local family. Alternatively, you can set up camp in the vicinity of the ruins. The return trip to Cochabamba probably won't be easy, so carry plenty of water, food and warm clothing.

A couple of travel agencies in Cochabamba occasionally do tours to Incallajta but only if they have a group large enough to make it worth their while. Enquire at the tourist kiosk in Cochabamba.

TOTORA

Totora, the loveliest colonial village in Cochabamba Department, lies in a valley at the foot of Cerro Sutuchira. It's 140 km east of Cochabamba along the Sucre road but unfortunately, few travellers have the opportunity to see it by day because the buses all seem to travel at night.

AIQUILE & MIZQUE

Aiquile and Mizque, two small villages 38 km apart in the Valles Altos region of southeastern Cochabamba Department are destinations for anyone seeking a peaceful and pastoral respite from the noise of the city. Aiquile is known for some of the best charangos produced in Bolivia.

Since these villages lie on the main route between Cochabamba and Sucre, access on public transport is simple enough. The only catch is that most buses arrive in the wee hours of the night when these already soporific little places are soundly asleep.

The dusty little town of Aiquile is the halfway point on the flota route between Sucre and Cochabamba. It is a town near the Tipajara Mayu watershed, complete with a lovely family-run pensión/restaurant called La Tradición and a place offering 15-minute hot showers (B2), saunas, and steam baths called El Cisne. However, avoid the Aiquile Inn on the main street as one of our friends captured a vinchuca beetle there in his bedroom. Aiquile sponsors a lively Sunday market, has a dental and medical clinic and even sports a Correos de Bolivia and telecommunications outpost. The kids in Aiquile are great and there is also a movie house showing old flicks.

If travellers happen to be passing through Mizque, the dustier townlet on the Mizque River north of Aiquile, they will find passable food at Doña Nati's and also from the women who cook on the kerb to the right of the church. Sounds grim but if you're as far out as Mizque, clean food that won't make you sick is considered 'all right'! I personally thought Doña Nati's *sopita de arroz* was delicious.

Lodging in Mizque can be found in a clean, well-lit *dormitorio* with showers, offered by a Belgian Franciscan priest. His place is just south of the *cancha de futbol* (football pitch) on the eastern end of town.

The reasons why anyone would want to venture to Mizque are to experience the beauty of the Río Tucuna valley – the river flows perennially and dumps into the Mizque River just east of the village; to watch a resident flock of over 100 highly endangered red-fronted macaws yak and frolic about in the early morning light; and to consider spending the rest of one's life in a stunningly beautiful and warm pastoral setting. Yes, this is a romantic fantasy, but the Tucuna valley is a place that hatches such ideas.

Red-fronted macaws are large red, blue and green parrots with 22-inch wingspans. If you're used to seeing these sort of birds in cages, it is an utter delight to see them in flocks in the wild.

It's about a 60-minute drive between Mizque and Aiquile. It is possible to thumb a ride on the road from passing camiones or 4WD vehicles. In August, the road is thick with dust. Bring protection! There is a tollgate halfway down the road; my understanding is that it only applies to vehicles carrying agricultural produce. We never paid anything.

Greg & Katie Cumberford, USA

TOROTORO

Torotoro lies in Potosí Department 7½ hours and 198 km by road, south-east of Cochabamba. It's an absolute jewel, but like Incallajta, it's expensive, and difficult or uncomfortable to reach without private transport. This promises to change in the near future, however, with greater interest being generated in the area and more buses and camiones doing the run from Cochabamba.

Information

The largely pristine treasures of Torotoro are now contained in the newly created Parque Nacional Torotoro which is administered from Cochabamba. Although there's no information available at Torotoro itself, in Cochabamba you may contact Roxana Arce or Adelaida Luna at the Asociación Experimental Torotoro (☎ 25843 or 25853), Calle 25 de Mayo 482. They're quite friendly and occasionally offer escorted tours to the caves, tracks and fossil areas.

Dinosaur Tracks

Palaeontology buffs who make the effort to get here won't be disappointed. The town, which sits in a wide spot of a 20-km-long valley at 2600 metres elevation, is flanked on two sides by enormous tilted and layered sedimentary rock formations. On the side of the valley adjacent to the village are numerous incidences of Cretaceous period biped and quadruped dinosaur tracks. As the road flattens out beside the stream to the north-west of Torotoro, it actually crosses the path of a group of three-toed tracks which are medium-sized at about 25 cm long each.

Nearer the town, a few metres before the stream crossing, the largest tracks in the area can be seen just above the waterline. Their size is impressive – 35 cm wide, 50 cm long, and 20 cm deep with a stride of nearly two metres!

Several hundred metres upstream from the road, a group of small three-toed tracks climb out of the water and under a layer of rocks. Five km upstream are more tracks, and dinosaur bone fragments may be found

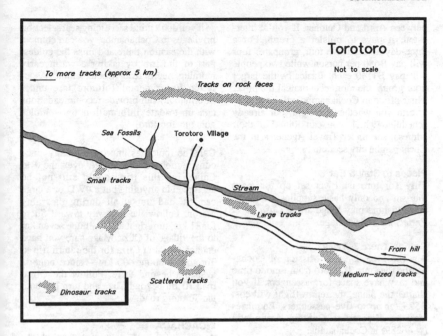

in layers of red earth. Inexplicably, nearly all the tracks seem to lead uphill.

In a little side gully just upstream from the village there is a deposit of sea fossils. To confuse matters even further, limestone and volcanic layers of rock are both present, in addition to the sedimentary layers in which the tracks are found.

Gruta de Umajalanta
Six km north-west of town, the stream disappears beneath a layer of limestone approximately 22 metres thick, forming the two-km long Gruta de Umajalanta. Inside are numerous stalagmite and stalactite formations, an underground lake with blind catfish, the Umajalanta waterfall, and most surprising of all, more dinosaur tracks. This cave is undeveloped and you'll need a torch to explore its deeper recesses.

Fiesta de Santiago
On 25 July, the village of Torotoro stages the Fiesta de Santiago which features sheep sacrifices and tinku fights in which the participants literally beat the hell out of each other with their fists or worse. This may be a good time to look for transportation to Torotoro, but certainly not the best for visiting the natural attractions. One reader writes of his 1991 visit during the Fiesta:

At Torotoro, there was an incredible fireworks display the first night of the fiesta. There were no deaths at this year's tinku although things got out of hand more than a couple of times with vicious fights erupting among the community of spectators. I advise watching from a balcony, if possible, away from the possibility of being caught in a sudden melee.
Mike Stambovsky, USA

Organised Tours
Fremen in Cochabamba organises rather expensive tours to Torotoro, visiting the caves of Chilijusco and Umajalanta as well as the dinosaur tracks. They use air transport in the rainy season and 4WD vehicle

between April and October. If you're interested, it pays to muster a group. For a three-day all-inclusive tour, groups of four will pay B650 per person while two people will pay B1140 each. Basically, the larger your group, the more economical the price. Their office in Cochabamba will be able to inform you whether there's a tour already scheduled which you can join. For their address, see under Travel Agencies in the Cochabamba city section.

Places to Stay & Eat
Tiny Torotoro isn't yet set up for mass tourism and only basic supplies are available. Visitors may lodge at the *Casa de la Prefectura* in the village.

Getting There & Away
Air The Free Swedish Mission of Cochabamba flies into Torotoro from time to time and may have space for passengers. If you charter the plane, the return flight will cost B525 for up to five passengers. Enquiries may be directed to Captain Arvindson (☎ 46289) in Cochabamba.

Bus Buses depart on Thursday and Sunday at approximately 7 am from the corner of Avenida República and Calle Punata in Cochabamba and return on Friday and Monday at 7 am from just off the plaza in Torotoro. The trip takes approximately nine hours and costs B10 per person. One reader warns that during school vacations, student groups sometimes book the entire bus.

Camión Each week, three camiones make the return trip to Torotoro, departing from the same place as the buses. They take 10 to 12 hours each way and probably won't cost any less than the bus. The journey passes through several climatic zones, so unless you're able to arrange a place in the cab, bring a range of clothing for the trip.

All camiones stop in Cliza for breakfast,

so if you don't mind sacrificing seat selection privileges in Cochabamba, you can connect with the camión there and miss the coldest part of the trip by taking a warm early morning micro from Cochabamba. Asociación Experimental Torotoro (see under Information) can provide recommendations and up-to-date information on vehicles going to Torotoro.

Car The route has improved greatly since construction of the bridge over the Río Caine, but this trip should still not be attempted in anything but a 4WD or a large camión, and not at all during the rainy season. Follow the highway toward Sucre for 31 km, turn right and continue seven km to the village of Cliza. Make sure you have enough petrol at Cliza for the return trip to Torotoro – about 400 km – since none is available beyond there. Follow the Oruro road 10 km beyond Cliza and turn left onto the Torotoro road.

INCACHACA
At Incachaca or 'Inca House', in the highlands 93 km along the Chapare road from Cochabamba, an odd microclimate has created an area of tropical rainforest. There's also an interesting waterfall that issues from the Ventana del Diablo (Devil's Window), where an underground river reaches the surface.

Incachaca is accessible from Cochabamba by any bus going to either Santa Cruz or Chapare. The Fremen agency in Cochabamba also organises excursions to Incachaca. See under Travel Agencies in the Cochabamba section of this chapter for their contact details.

CHAPARE
For details on the Chapare region of northern Cochabamba Department, refer to the chapter dealing with the Amazon Basin.

Potosí

I am rich Potosí,
The treasure of the world
And the envy of kings.

The slogan on the city's first coat of arms wasn't far off the mark, but then, any city with a mountain of silver in its backyard is certain to attract attention! In fact, in Spanish, anything that is incredibly lucrative is said to *valer un Potosí* (be worth a Potosí). A good example is the city of San Luís Potosí in central Mexico where silver was discovered in the 1600s. It didn't, however, live up to its Bolivian namesake.

Visitors to Potosí will find remnants of a grand colonial city – ornate churches, monuments, and colonial architecture – in a most unlikely setting. At 4070 metres, Potosí is the world's highest city, a bit of trivia which will hit home as you climb some of its steeper streets.

Set beneath the colourful Cerro Rico and surrounded by barren hills, it's partially protected from the harsh climatic conditions found on the Altiplano, but temperatures do reflect its lofty situation and central heating is unfortunately rare. The wet season often brings damp, rainy and even snowy days, while winter, with generally clear weather, is characterised by a weak but welcome warmth by day and brutally cold temperatures at night.

History

No one is certain how much silver was extracted from Cerro Rico, the 'rich hill' in Potosí's backdrop, over its four centuries of productivity. A popular boast was that the Spanish could have constructed a silver bridge to Spain and still had some left to carry across on it. The Spanish monarchs, who personally received 20% of the booty, were certainly worth more than a few *pesetas*.

Although the story about how all the fuss got started is probably somewhat less than factual, it's an interesting tale. In 1544, a Peruvian Indian called Diego Huallpa was tending his llamas in the area when he realised that two of the beasts were missing. He set off immediately in search of them and while he was still in hot pursuit, night came – and with it, cold – so he stopped to build a fire. The fire grew so hot that the earth beneath it began to melt and a shiny liquid oozed out. Huallpa realised that it was silver, one of the items the conquering Spanish became so steamed up about. He didn't inform them of his discovery but instead, told a friend, another Indian called Huanca, and together they formulated a get-rich plan.

The newly discovered vein proved productive but soon a dispute between the partners developed into a quarrel about division of profits. Huanca, who had become weary of the whole mess, went to the Spanish with news of the mine – and they were interested.

It wasn't long before the conquerors had assessed the magnitude of the discovery and determined that it warranted immediate attention. On 1 April (according to some sources, 10 April) 1545, the Villa Imperial de Carlos V was founded at the foot of Cerro Rico and large-scale excavation began. In the time it takes to say 'Get down there and dig', thousands of Indian slaves had been pressed into service and the first of the silver was on its way to Spain.

The work was so dangerous, however, and so many Indians were dying of accidents and silicosis pneumonia, that literally millions of African slaves were imported to extract the silver. It's been estimated that during the three centuries of the colonial period, 1545 to 1825, eight million Africans and Indians died from the appalling working conditions in the Potosí mines.

In 1572, in order to increase productivity, Viceroy Toledo instituted the Ley de la Mita, a law requiring all Indians and Blacks in Potosí over the age of 18 to work in shifts of

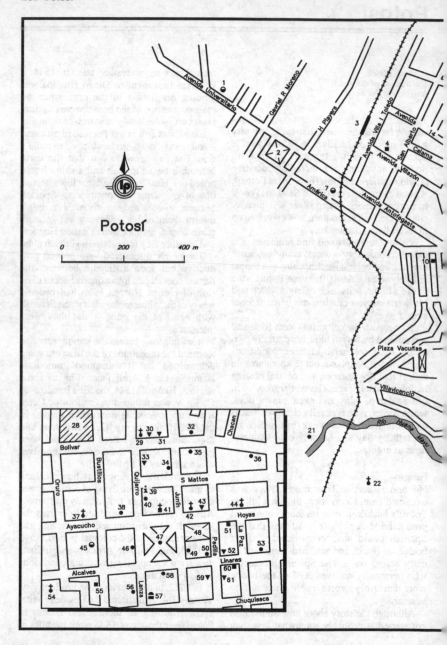

Potosí

0   200   400 m

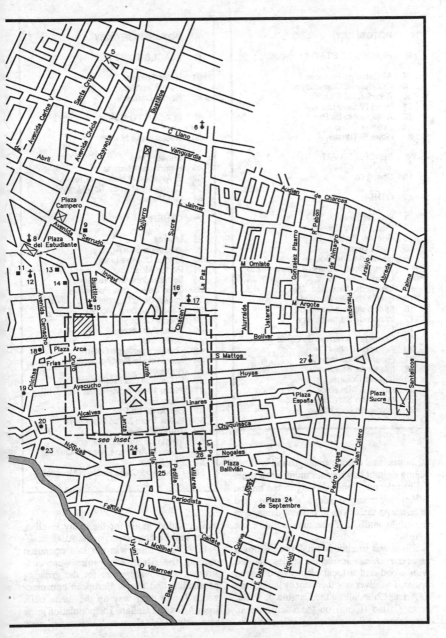

POTOSÍ KEY

■ PLACES TO STAY

4 Alojamiento Ferrocarril
9 Residencial Copacabana
10 Residencial Sumaj
11 Hotel IV Centenario
13 Alojamiento La Paz
14 Posada Oruro
24 Hotel El Turista

▼ PLACES TO EAT

16 Chaplin's

OTHER

1 Bus Terminal
2 Plaza Chuquimia
3 Railway Station
5 Plaza Uyuni
6 Iglesia de San Roque
7 Transportes Quijarro & Camiones to Uyuni
8 Iglesia de Jerusalén
12 Iglesia de San Bernardo
15 Iglesia de San Lorenzo
17 Iglesia de Santa Mónica
18 ENTEL
19 Convento & Museo de Santa Teresa
20 Arcos de Cobija
21 Ribera de los Ingenios
22 Iglesia de San Benito
23 Ingenio Dolores
25 Iglesia & Museo de San Francisco
26 Iglesia de San Juan de Diós
27 Iglesia de San Martín

POTOSÍ INSET KEY

■ PLACES TO STAY

51 Hotel Colonial
55 Hotel Central
60 Hostal Carlos V

▼ PLACES TO EAT

30 Restaurante Marisel
31 Don Lucho
33 Sumac Orko
43 Heladería Alemana
52 El Aldabón & Heladería Tokyo
59 Cherry's Salón de Te & Maxim's
61 Las Vegas

OTHER

28 Market
29 Iglesia de San Agustín
32 Museo Universitario
34 Portón Mestizo
35 Distribuidora Cultural Sud
36 Casa de las Tres Portadas
37 Iglesia de la Compañía de Jesús
38 Casa Real de la Moneda
39 Tourist Office
40 Trans-Amazonas
41 Cathedral
42 Former Iglesia de Belén
44 Iglesia de la Merced
45 Andesbus
46 El Cabildo (La Prefectura)
47 Plaza 10 de Noviembre
48 Plaza 6 de Agosto
49 Banco de La Paz
50 Balsa Tours & Top Wisquería
53 Transtin
54 Iglesia de Santo Domingo
56 Casa de Antonio López de Quiroga
57 Post Office
58 Edificio de Cajas Reales (Alcaldía)

12 hours, and remain underground without seeing light of day for four months at a time, eating, sleeping, and working in the mines. When they emerged from a 'shift', they had to bandage their eyes to prevent damage in the bright sunlight. These miners didn't last long.

Silver was smelted in small ovens known as *huayrachinas* inside the mines, fuelled with wood and a local plant called *pacha brava*. The silver was then sent by llama train to Arica, Chile, along the Camino de Plata, or to Callao (Lima) on the Pacific coast. From there, it was carried by ship to Spain,

and provided spoils for the many English, Dutch and French pirates in the Atlantic.

In 1672, a mint was put into operation coining the silver. Reservoirs were constructed to provide water for the growing population and exotic European consumer goods found their way up the llama trails from Arica and Callao. The population grew to nearly 200,000, over 80 churches were constructed and amidst the mania, Potosí became the largest city in Latin America and one of the largest in the world. One politician of the period put it succinctly: 'Potosí was raised in the pandemonium of greed at the foot of riches discovered by accident'.

As with most boom towns, Potosí's glory was not to last. In the early 19th century, Cerro Rico, the seemingly inexhaustible mountain of silver, began to play out. By the time of Bolivian independence in 1825, the mines were already in decline and in the late 1800s, a severe drop in silver prices dealt a blow from which Potosí has never completely recovered. Tin took over as Bolivia's major metallic export and Potosinos began mining tailings for lead, zinc and tin which had previously been discarded. Silver extraction continued, but on a very limited scale.

The mining reforms of 1952 brought the Pailaviri mine under government control and mining conditions were improved immensely. Most of the Cerro Rico operations, however, remained in the control of miner-owned cooperatives and the revolution had little effect upon them. Nowadays, the government mine is plagued by strikes, protests and general dissatisfaction, while the cooperatives continue operating under conditions that have changed little from the colonial period. In 1987, UNESCO named Potosí a World Heritage Site in recognition of its rich and tragic history and its wealth of colonial architecture.

Information

The IBT tourist office kiosk just above the main plaza is an unmitigated waste of time in a city where there are a number of better things to do. On the rare occasion it's open – Saturday and Sunday from 9 am to noon and 2 to 6 pm – it's of no help at all. Similarly, the office upstairs at the corner of Matos and Calle Quijarro is more interested in collecting the highest possible price for brochures (at least B1 per folder) than dispensing information. It's open from 9 am to noon and 2 to 6 pm Monday to Friday.

Money With cash US dollars, changing money in Potosí is no problem at all; numerous business establishments along Calle Bolívar and Calle Sucre change at a reasonable rate; look for the compro dólares signs. Travellers' cheques may be changed at the Distribuidora Cultural Sud bookshop. If they are short of cash, try the Trans-Amazonas tour agency.

VISA cash advances are available within 20 minutes at Banco de La Paz on the plaza. There's a B5 charge for the telex to determine the card's validity and you can receive the cash in bolivianos or US dollars.

Post & Telecommunications The central post office is on Calle Lanza, a block south of the main plaza. There is an interesting artesanía shop in the lobby which also sells postcards. Less expensive postcards are available at Distribuidora Cultural Sud. Currently, everything posted from Potosí has to travel overland, so the reliability of the service is questionable.

The new ENTEL office is near the corner of Frias and Avenida Camacho. Potosí's public fax number is (062) 24005.

Dangers & Annoyances If someone approaches you (particularly at the bus terminal) claiming to be a police officer and asks to see your passport or money, make a show of carefully scrutinising their ID. If possible, memorise or jot down the name and number and refuse to show anything unless they'll walk with you to the terminal police office or the city police station. They'll probably back down; the scam is most often directed at newly arrived foreigners who don't realise that legitimate passport checks are conducted only inside the terminal police office. If you are harassed by phoney police, report the practice to either Radio Patrulla (☎ 110) or the tourist police (☎ 25288).

Many buses arrive in Potosí before dawn. One traveller wrote that they were intercepted outside their selected hotel early in the morning by a local who claimed that the door was locked. He led them around the back where a 'police officer' mysteriously appeared and demanded to see their money. Realising what was up, the traveller took off.

Museums

Casa Real de la Moneda The Casa Real de la Moneda (Royal Mint) is one of South America's finest and most interesting museums. The building was first constructed on the current site of the Casa de Justicia in 1572 under orders of the Viceroy Toledo. The present building at the corner of Ayacucho and Calle Quijarro near Plaza 10 de Noviembre was constructed between 1753 and 1773 and in places, its oppressive walls exceed one metre in thickness. It functioned not only as a mint but also did a spell as a prison, a fortress, and during the Chaco War, served as the headquarters of the Bolivian Army; it's now preserved as a national monument.

Upon entering the museum, you're ushered into a courtyard where you're greeted by a stone fountain and a gaudy mask of Bacchus, the wine god, placed there by a Frenchman for reasons known only to him. This aberration, which appears to have come straight out of a children's fun fair, has somehow become an icon of the Bolivian tourism industry.

Inside you'll see the first locomotive used in Bolivia, a beautiful salon with religious theme paintings (lots of blood), carriages, silver coins, two amazingly complex safe boxes and war relics from past skirmishes. There is also a collection of shells from Bolivia's lost seacoast, as well as Tiahuanaco artefacts, traditionally costumed dolls, mineral specimens and portraits of Bolivian presidents (only a few; a complete collection could fill an entire museum!).

Upstairs you'll see rooms of colonial-era furniture and the prison-like slave quarters. In the basement are minting machines imported from Philadelphia, USA, in 1869, and still-functional hand-powered minting devices used during the previous 300 years. They also have several interesting horse-powered laminating machines on which horses were worked for three days and nights without food or rest; the average life span for

a horse under such conditions was about eight days, so horses were continuously imported from Argentina.

Visitors are obliged to take a tour since all the exhibits are kept carefully locked. The three-hour tours cost B3 and are conducted in Spanish or English daily at 9 am and 2 pm. Whatever the outside temperature, be sure to wear thermal underwear and several layers of clothing; the huge dungeon-like spaces in this building never feel the warmth of day!

Museo Universitario The highly recommended Museo Universitario Ricardo Bohorquez on Calle Bolivar contains a good mixture of contemporary art, including modern paintings, pottery and local artefacts. It's open Monday to Friday from 9 am to noon and 2 to 6 pm. The B1 admission charge goes toward upkeep of the university.

Museo de San Francisco At the time of writing, the Iglesia de San Francisco was closed for renovation, but it should be open by the time you read this. It was originally constructed in the 1500s and was rebuilt in 1707. Inside is a museum of typical religious art, as well as the remains and a portrait of Antonio Lopez de Quiroga, a wealthy 17th-century philanthropist who donated large sums of money to the Church. A gold-covered altar from this building is now housed in the Casa Real de la Moneda.

Visitors must take the B3 guided tour which lasts about 45 minutes. The highlight comes at the end when you're ushered up through the tower and onto the roof for a grand vista over Potosí. The museum is open from 2.30 to 4.30 pm Monday to Saturday.

Interesting Buildings

A couple of other homes and monuments of note which you may want to visit are the El Cabildo (old town hall) on the Plaza 10 de Noviembre; the home of Antonio Lopez de Quiroga on Calle Lanza; the Casa de las Tres Portadas at Calle Bolivar 1052-1092; the Palacio de Cristal at Calle Sucre 148-156; and the Arcos de Cobija (Arches of Cobija) on the street of the same name. These arches honour not the present-day capital of Pando but the Pacific port of Cobija which now belongs to Chile. Just below the first arch is the Ingenio Dolores which bears a 1787 inscription. The Banco Nacional on Calle Junín has a lovely mestizo-style doorway, marked on the map in this book as Portón Mestizo.

A couple of interesting statues in Potosí are the Monumento al Minero on Avenida Villazón, the Monumento al Minero Revolucionario on Plaza del Minero, and the Monumento a la Madre on Avenida del Estudiante.

Churches

Iglesia San Bernardo This immense former church and convent on Plaza del Estudiante is now occupied by a cinema, but its baroque architecture and ornamented entrance remain impressive. The original structure dates back to 1590, but it was completely renovated in the late 1720s.

Belén This building with a three-tier baroque façade was constructed in 1735 as a church and has also served as a hospital. It is now occupied by Teatro Omiste.

Iglesia de la Compañía de Jesús This Jesuit church, just over a block west of the main plaza on Ayacucho, is renowned for its ornate and beautiful bell tower. It was completed in 1707 after the original church, which had been built in 1590, collapsed. Both the tower and the doorway are examples of mestizo baroque architecture.

Iglesia de San Benito The Iglesia de San Benito was begun in 1711 and completed in 16 years, a colonial construction record. Its byzantine domes and mestizo doorway are probably its most interesting features. The entire building is laid out in the shape of a Latin cross.

Cathedral Potosí's main religious structure is on the Plaza 10 de Noviembre. It was founded in 1572 but was rebuilt with Greek and Spanish neoclassic additions designed by architect Fray Manuel Sanauja, between 1808 and 1838. The interior décor is some of the finest in Potosí.

Iglesia de San Martín This church on Calle Hoyos near Plaza Cervantes was built in the 1600s and is today run by the French Redemptionist Fathers. Inside is a veritable art museum, but it's quite a climb up there and it's often closed.

Iglesia de San Lorenzo The ornate mestizo design portal of San Lorenzo is one of Bolivia's most photographed subjects. It was carved in stone by master Indian artesans in the 16th century, but the main structure wasn't completed until 1744 when the bell towers were added. The main interior attractions are two Holguín paintings and the handcrafted silver work on the altar. The church was renovated in 1987.

Convento de Santa Teresa A visit to the Convento de Santa Teresa is like a taking a step backward in time. The display of religious art is more interesting than most and includes works of Bolivia's most renowned artist, Melchor Pérez de Holguín, as well as morbid disciplinary paraphernalia (fortunately no longer in use), and – as one correspondent put it – 'lots of flagellation'. Ugh!

The B3 admission charge goes to sustain the convent. Buying a ticket can be tricky; the nuns are cloistered so you must go to a wooden turnstile at the back of the courtyard, just uphill from the church. Attract the attendant's attention by pulling a rope hanging from the wall. Once you've bought the ticket, you can gain access to the building by knocking on a big metal door on the street uphill from the church gate. The tour of the convent takes a little over an hour. It's open weekdays from 9 am to noon and 2 to 5 pm Monday to Saturday.

Other Churches Other churches of note in Potosí include Jerusalén with its golden ornamentation, San Juan de Diós, which has stood since the 1600s despite its adobe construction, San Agustín with its elegant renaissance doorway and La Mercéd on Calle Hoyos.

Mines

Cooperative Mines A visit to the cooperative mines is an experience which should not be missed, if for no other reason than to witness working conditions that should have gone out with the Middle Ages. They're difficult to imagine and once the tour is over, you're left in a state of shock.

Contrary to popular rumour, women are admitted to many cooperative mines – only a few miners hang on to the tradition that women underground invite bad luck. Nevertheless, local women are normally consigned to picking through the tailings searching for bits of minerals that may have been missed. These women are known as *pailiris* which means 'those who select' in Quechua.

Since cooperative mines are owned by the miners themselves, they must produce to make their meagre living. All work is done by hand with tools they must purchase themselves, including their acetylene lamps. Each miner must also buy his own explosives, and shops near Cerro Rico sell dynamite, fuses, detonators, ammonium nitrate, and acetylene (as well as such goodies as black tobacco, coca, *legía* and cigarettes to make it all bearable).

Miners prepare for their workday by socialising and chewing coca for several hours, beginning work at about 10 am. They work until lunch at 2 pm when they rest and chew more coca. For those who don't spend the night working, the day normally ends at 7 pm.

Underground, each miner has a personal work area where he carries out the operation from start to finish. Upon locating a vein he chisels out wells in which to place the dynamite, which he packs and detonates himself, paying dearly for any carelessness. The spoils and tailings must be carried on his back up as many levels as necessary in order to deposit them in an area accessible either to an ore cart, to a 'mailbox' for later collection, or to a tailings dump. On the weekend,

he sells his week's production to the buyer for as high a price as he can negotiate.

In most cooperative operations, there is a minimal medical plan in case of accident or silicosis (which is inevitable after seven to 10 years working underground) and a pension of about B72 per month for those so incapacitated. Once a miner has lost 50% of his lung capacity to silicosis, he may retire, if he so wishes. In case of death, a miner's widow and children collect this pension.

Visiting the Cooperative Mines Several young men hire themselves out as tour guides through the cooperative mines but a couple of years ago, the government stipulated that guides could only operate through travel agencies. Since then, tour prices have more than doubled, although they're still good value at B15 for four gruelling hours. Agencies take half the fee, the worthless tourist office gets B2 and the miners' cooperatives get only B1, while the guides, who must pay for transport to the mines, lantern fuel and coca leaves for the miners, take the rest. Most of the tours leave at around 8 am Monday to Saturday, but when demand is high, afternoon tours are conducted as well.

The most frequently recommended guide is Eduardo Garnica Fajardo (☎ 23138, home or ☎ 24708, Koala Tours) whose experience and background well qualify him for the job – he is descended from a family of miners and has worked as a miner himself. Over the years, he has picked up a good deal of English. Although Eduardo does have his good and bad days, he's still the most knowledgeable of the guides in Potosí. Another recommended guide is Raúl Braulio Mamani (☎ 25304, home or ☎ 25786, Potosí Tours), who makes a point of detonating a stick of dynamite at the end of his tour. When either of these guys decides to take a day off, their brothers stand in.

Mine visits are not easy. The ceilings are low and passageways are steep and muddy, so wear old clothing and shoes. Inside, temperatures reach 45°, and the altitude of nearly 4500 metres can be taxing. To make matters worse, you'll be exposed to all sorts of noxious chemicals and gases including silica dust (the cause of silicosis), arsenic gas, acetylene vapours and other trapped mine gases, and the byproducts of combustion and detonation of mining equipment. Anyone with doubts or medical problems should avoid these tours.

The plus side is that you'll have the opportunity to speak with the friendly miners who are happy to share with you some of their insights and opinions about their difficult lot. Surprisingly, most of them are miners by choice, carrying on family traditions by working there. Although gifts are not expected, they will especially appreciate coca leaves and cigarettes, luxuries for which their meagre earnings are scarcely sufficient.

Pailaviri Pailaviri, the state-owned mine which owns the most imposing structure on Cerro Rico, contrasts sharply with the cooperatives. The government provides electric lamps, jackhammers, lifts and superior wages, plus medical and pension plans. If you visit only the state mine, you'll get an artificial picture of mining in Bolivia.

Catch the ENTE #100 bus which leaves for Pailaviri Monday to Friday between 7 and 8 am. Either flag it down on the southern side of the main plaza or wait for it at Plaza 25 de Mayo. Since miners' syndicate strikes frequently disrupt Pailaviri operations, it's not unusual to find the scheduled tours cancelled for indefinite periods. Ascertain in advance whether or not they're running. The official tour of the mine costs a whopping B30 per person.

El Tío During mine visits, you'll undoubtedly notice a small devilish-looking figure occupying a small niche somewhere along the passageways. Around him will be strewn cigarette butts, coca leaves, glasses of alcohol and other small tokens. As most of the miners believe in a God in Heaven, they deduce that there must also be a devil beneath the earth in a place where it's hot and uncomfortable. Since Hell must not be far

from the environment in which they work, they reason that the devil himself must own the minerals they're digging and dynamiting out of the earth. In order to appease this character – they call him Tío (Uncle) (never Diablo) – they set up a little ceramic figurine in a place of honour.

On Friday nights a cha'lla is offered to invoke his luck and protection. A little alcohol is poured on the ground before the statue, lighted cigarettes are placed in his mouth, and coca leaves are placed within easy reach. Then, as in most Bolivian celebrations, the miners smoke, chew coca and proceed to drink themselves unconscious. While this is all taken very seriously, it also provides a bit of diversion from an extremely difficult existence.

Los Ingenios
Beside the Río Ribera in the upper Potosí barrios of Cantumarca and San Antonio are some fine ruined examples of the *ingenios* (smelting mills) used to extract silver from the ore being hauled out of Cerro Rico. The mills were turned by water impounded in the 32 artificial Lagunas de Kari Kari south-east of the city. Some date back to the 1570s. For related information, see under Lagunas & Cordillera de Kari Kari in the Around Potosí section of this chapter.

Organised Tours
There are lots of guided tours on offer from Potosí as well as lots of tour agencies offering them. Apart from the cooperative mine tours, the most popular include the South-western circuit (taking in Laguna Colorada), Potosí area hot springs, Lagunas Kari Kari treks and Hacienda Cayara. Some guides are professional but many are merely fly-by-night options. If you're going to Laguna Colorada, it may help to read the Travelling in South-Western Bolivia section in the Southern Altiplano chapter. The following is a partial list of Potosí tour agencies and their specialities:

Bohemia Tours
Calle Chuquisaca 587 (☎ 26112); Termas de Chaquí (Chaquí Hot Springs), Lagunas Kari Kari and city tours (Laguna Colorada tours not recommended).

Cerro Rico Travel
Plaza Alonzo de Ibañes (☎ 25552); city tours, Torotoro, Tarapaya and Chaqui, Lagunas Kari Kari, Pailaviri, Laguna Colorada & Southwestern Bolivia.

Koala Tours
Calle Hernández 1035, Casilla 33 (☎ 24708); Laguna Colorada & South-western Bolivia, Lagunas Kari Kari, Tarapaya and La Ribera smelters.

Potosí Tours
Plaza Alonzo de Ibañez 16 (☎ 25786); Lagunas Kari Kari, Tarapaya, Chaquí, Salar de Uyuni and La Ribera smelters.

Trans-Amazonas
Calle Quijarro 12 (☎ 27175); Laguna Colorada tours (good but a bit overpriced), Lagunas Kari Kari, Chapare, Tarapaya, Chaquí.

Zungara Travel
Calle Padilla 21 (☎ 26186); city tours, Lagunas Kari Kari, Tarapaya and Chaquí.

Fiestas

Fiesta del Espíritu Fiesta del Espíritu is the most unusual Potosí fiesta. It takes place on the last three Saturdays of June and the first Saturday of August, and is dedicated to the honour of Pachamama, the earth mother, who the miners regard as the mother of all Bolivians.

Campesinos from the surrounding countryside bring llamas to the base of Cerro Rico to hawk to the miners for use in the festival. The entire ritual is conducted according to a meticulous schedule. At 10 am, one miner from each mine purchases a llama and the miners' families arrive to join in the celebrations. At 11 am they move to the entrances of their respective mines, chewing coca and drinking alcohol from 11 to 11.45 am. At precisely 11.45 am, they prepare the llama for sacrifice to Pachamama by tying its feet and offering it coca and alcohol. As you may expect, at high noon, the llama meets its maker. As the throat is slit, the miners petition Pachamama for luck, protection and an abundance of minerals. The llama's blood is caught in glasses and thrown around the mouth of the mine in order to ensure Pachamama's attention, cooperation and blessing.

For the following three hours, the men chew and drink while the women prepare a llama parrillada. The meat is traditionally served with potatoes baked in a small adobe oven along with haba and oca. When the oven reaches the optimum temperature, it is smashed on top of the vegetables which are baked beneath the hot shards. The stomach, feet and head of the llama are buried in a three-metre hole as a further offering to Pachamama, then the music and dancing begin. Later in the evening, truckloads of drunken miners are escorted home in transport provided by the honoured miner who secured the llama for his respective mine's celebration.

Fiesta de San Bartolomé Also known as Chu'tillos, this rollicking celebration normally takes place on the final weekend of August or the first weekend of September and is marked by processions, student exhibitions and folk dancing from all over the country.

Exaltación de la Santa Vera Cruz This festival in honour of Santo Cristo de la Vera Cruz falls on 14 September with activities centred on the church of San Lorenzo and the railway station. Silver cutlery figures prominently, as do parades, duelling brass bands, dancing costumed children and lots of alcohol.

Places to Stay – bottom end

Potosí hotel prices are regulated, so if you feel that a price is too high or that you're being cheated, ask for *la tarifa oficial*, the official price list.

There are several popular budget hotels but the favourite seems to be the *Residencial Sumaj* (☎ 23336), near the Plaza del Estudiante. The appeal of the place escapes most people, but it somehow keeps plugging along. There are two central meeting areas where cooking is permitted and there's even a TV for those who want to catch up on a bit of culture. Since it has a reputation as 'the place where gringos stay', you'll be incessantly pestered by tour guides throwing their sales pitch at every new bod that rolls up; beware of thieves posing as guides.

Small, dark rooms cost B10 per person without private baths and for an additional B3, you'll get a basic breakfast. The hot water situation is hit or miss. Although the Sumaj is a tiring uphill walk from the centre, it's convenient to both the bus and train terminals.

A budding favourite that seems poised to supplant the Sumaj as the backpackers' haunt is the friendly *Hostal Carlos V* (☎ 25121). It's in a cosy old colonial building with a covered patio. Its greatest faults are the tepid temperature of the 'hot' showers and the slightly higher than rock-bottom price. Rooms cost B16 per person.

Moving slightly upmarket, the *Hotel El Turista* (☎ 22492) at Calle Lanza 19 is our favourite in Potosí and worth the splurge. It's exceptionally friendly and clean and offers some of Bolivia's best hot showers between 6.30 and 11 am. The owner, Señor Luksic, who also runs the LAB ticket desk in the lobby, provides the most reliable tourist information in town. Rooms cost B20/37 for a single/double. For a room with a view, request something on the top floor, particularly room 32!

The friendly *Hotel Central* (☎ 22207), only a block from the main plaza, is in a pleasant and quiet old area of town with a traditional Potosino overhanging balcony. Rooms are cold but management will provide as many blankets as you need. Although hot water is available if you request it an hour in advance, it's of little benefit due to the outdoor location of the shower. Rooms cost B10 per person.

If you prefer to avoid lugging a heavy pack uphill from the bus terminal or railway station, try the basic *Alojamiento Ferrocarril* (☎ 24294) on Avenida Villazón. Rooms cost B9 per person.

Basically just a flophouse (with the emphasis on basic), the seedy *Posada Oruro* offers ultra low-budget rooms for B5.50 per person. Showers are available at the public

baths just up the street. The *Residencial Copacabana* (☎ 22712) at Avenida Serrudo 319 is clean and costs B12 per person without private bath. *Residencial San Antonio* (☎ 23566) at Calle Oruro 136 costs B9 per person with barely warmish showers.

An up and coming budget travellers' favourite is the *Alojamiento La Paz* (☎ 22632) at Calle Oruro 262, but it seems everyone has a shocking tale to tell about the showers! Rooms cost B8 per person and the dodgy showers are B1 extra.

The *Hotel IV Centenario* (☎ 22791) is an odd and imposing structure attached to the cinema/church on the Plaza del Estudiante. Even if you don't stay here, it's worth a look to see the interesting sculpted mural of mining in Potosí that hangs in the lobby. Rooms cost B25/40 for singles/doubles.

Places to Stay – middle

The most upmarket hotel in Potosí is the *Hotel Colonial* (☎ 24265), in a lovely old colonial building near the main plaza at Calle Hoyos 8. Singles/doubles with private bath and central heating cost B60/80.

Alternatively, there's the *Hostal Bolivar* (☎ 25647) at Bolivar 772 opposite the market. It's also housed in a colonial home and rooms cost the same as those at the Hotel Colonial.

Places to Eat

It was a pleasant surprise returning to Potosí and finding that the culinary desert had been magically transformed into an oasis!

The best and most innovative meals in town are found at *Don Lucho*. They serve a pretty good lunch for B9 including soup, salad, a main course and dessert. Dinners are even better, ranging from killer pasta to excellent filet mignon with béchamel sauce. On Friday night, they stage a peña (see Entertainment for more info).

Almost as good but a bit expensive is the *Las Vegas* near the corner of calles Padilla and Linares. Their exhaustive four-course lunch specials run at about B13 with a 10% service charge on top, and the house speciality is pique a lo macho. Beware of overcharging here; if you suspect a problem, request an itemised bill (*cuenta detallada* or *cuenta elaborada*).

Next door to the Don Lucho is the *Restaurante Marisel* which has an occasional peña and serves a very standard menu, including pique a lo macho. A good place for lunch specials is *El Aldabón* at the corner of calles Padilla and Linares.

The *Sumac Orko* at Calle Quijarro 46 offers filling lunch specials of soup, potatoes, rice and a meat dish for just B5 as well as more interesting dishes such as *trucha al limón* and *picante de perdíz* – lemon trout and spicy partridge. This place has apparently seen quite a few tourists; after one meal, the waiter chased us down the street demanding a tip!

Another friendly option is *Chaplin's* on Calle Sucre where you can get a delicious vegetarian lunch of vegetable noodle soup, spicy lentils, potatoes, rice, fruit juice and papaya for B3. At night, they sometimes serve good (albeit odd) tacos and two nights a week, they have nachos.

If you're after decadent *apfelstrudel*, chocolate cake and other cakes and pastries, as well as good coffee and tea, try *Cherry's Salón de Te* on Calle Padilla near Calle Linares.

For great salteñas, go to *Café Imma Sumac* at Calle Bustillos 987. In the morning, meatless salteñas Potosinas are available on the street near Iglesia San Lorenzo for B.50 each. Meat empanadas are sold around the market until early afternoon, and in the evening street vendors sell cornmeal humintas.

The market *comedor* (eating area) is probably the best inexpensive place in town to eat breakfast; almost everything else is locked up tight until well into the morning. There are a few *panaderías* (bakeries) which open at 8 am, but there's not a lot to recommend them except three-day-old pastries and coffee from the same era. *Heladería Alemaña* on the corner beside the cathedral is one quick breakfast option, with snacks and ice-cream concoctions available during the rest of the day.

Entertainment
Don't miss the Friday night peña at Don Lucho, the best we've seen in Bolivia. If you're lucky, you'll have the opportunity to hear the lively and driving music of the local group, Arpegio Cinco, as well as some whiny and nasal accompaniment for Potosí Department's own tinku fights.

For dancing, try the popular Disco TK at Calle Junín 7 or the Charlie Fox Club. A recommended upmarket pub is Top Wisquería on Plaza Alonzo de Ibañes, the wide spot in Calle Padilla just above the main plaza.

Things to Buy
Naturally, favoured Potosí souvenirs will include silver articles available in stands near the market entrance on Calle Oruro. Alternatively, try the Mercado Artesanal between Calle Junín and Calle Sucre at Omiste. They sell musical instruments and a wide variety of local crafts but also a lot of touristy junk; it pays to check quality before buying.

Getting There & Away
Air Potosí is too high for most commercial traffic and although a larger airport is currently under construction, the current runway isn't long enough to accommodate the larger planes. The only scheduled airline service, therefore, is on AeroXpress (☎ 26740) which flies to and from Cochabamba on Wednesday and Thursday, to and from La Paz on Monday, Wednesday and Friday and to and from Sucre daily, Monday to Friday. Their office is at the corner of calles Bolivar and Junín.

As an alternative way to travel by air to Potosí, readers David Lynch and Gail Strachan of Glasgow suggest the plane which delivers newspapers from La Paz to that lofty city. It departs La Paz daily at around 9 am and may be booked through Johnny Cederberg at the Transamazonas agency (on the 10th floor directly across the Prado from the Hotel Plaza in La Paz). The flight takes two hours and costs B198 per person.

The LAB office in Potosí (☎ 22361) is in the El Turista hotel at Calle Lanza 19.

Bus Reaching Potosí by bus is fairly easy provided you don't try to do it during the rainy season when rivers rise and water-logged slopes cause massive slides. All routes to Potosí are quite scenic but there are lots of bumps and bounces included in the ticket price. The bus terminal is a long way from the centre so if you're walking, leave at least half an hour to get there.

Buses to Sucre depart from their respective offices near the plaza, not from the bus terminal. Andesbus on Calle Bustillos near Ayacucho leaves daily at 7 am and 5 pm and takes four hours. Lunch is included in the B18 fare. Transtin at Calle Linares 93 and Geminis beside Andesbus leave at 7.30 am and 5 pm, and both cost B14.

The cheapest way to travel between Potosí and Sucre is by camión or micro. They leave from Plaza Uyuni when full, which is basically every few minutes. Between these cities, watch for the picturesque Puente Sucre with its castle-like buttresses just a km or so from the new bridge at the Río Pilcomayo crossing.

Several lines leave from the main terminal for Oruro and La Paz between 6 and 6.30 pm. The trip to La Paz costs B25 and takes 10 to 12 hours. The trip to Oruro takes seven hours and costs B15. Flota Bustillo goes to Llallagua on Wednesday and Saturday at 7.30 am and Veloz del Sud serves Tarija at 7.30 am on Monday and Saturday.

Buses to Tupiza leave between 5 and 5.30 pm from the bus terminal and cost B20. Tupiza is 11 bus hours from Potosí, and Villazón, on the Argentine border, is about 13 hours.

Transportes Quijarro has a daily bus to Uyuni, leaving at noon from the end of Calle América across the railway from town. Camiones leave from the same spot. The route to Uyuni is quite spectacular, passing through some Shangri-la-type valleys with interesting vegetation and landscapes.

Train The railway station is at the bottom of Avenida Villazón below the university. There's a ferrobus to Sucre on Wednesday and Sunday at 5 am and Monday and Friday at 7.30 am for B19/16 in pullman/especial. The train goes on Thursday only at 7.10 am and costs B13/10 in 1st/2nd class. All these services return to Potosí on the afternoon of the same days.

The train to Oruro and La Paz leaves on Thursday at 10 pm, and the ferrobus departs on Wednesday and Sunday at 11.30 pm. The former costs B22/16 in 1st/2nd class and the latter is B32/26 in pullman/especial.

Getting Around

Bus Most local micros provide transport back and forth to the mines on Cerro Rico. but one goes to the rail and bus terminals from the cathedral side of the main plaza, stopping at the university en route.

Taxis Taxis from the centre to either the mines or the transportation terminals will cost around B2.50. If you're coming from the bus terminal, walk across the street and hail one; otherwise, expect to pay double the going rate.

Around Potosí

LAGUNAS & CORDILLERA DE KARI KARI

The artificial lakes of Kari Kari were constructed in the late 16th and early 17th centuries by 20,000 Indian slaves to provide water for the city and hydro power to run the 132 ingenios (smelting mills) operating there. Of the 32 originally constructed, only 25 lakes survive and all are abandoned. In 1626, the retaining wall of Laguna San Sebastián broke and caused a minor flood in Potosí.

The easiest access will be with one of the several Potosí tour agencies; for suggestions, see Organised Tours in the Potosí section. If you prefer to strike out on your own, carry food, water and warm clothing. There are several variations on the walking routes around the lagunas and into the Cordillera Kari Kari. In a long day, you can have a good look around but it will be more rewarding to bring camping equipment and stay overnight in the mountains.

Access is fairly easy. Either hitch out past Cerro Rico along the Tupiza road; you'll begin seeing the lakes on your left about eight km south-east of town, or alternatively, start walking east from Potosí's main plaza along Calle Hoyos. A few blocks beyond the Iglesia de San Martín, you'll take a right fork and eventually reach a track. Follow it south-east up the hill and eventually you'll reach Laguna San Ildefonso.

From here, either follow the track around the right side of the lake and continue up the valley or strike off into the hills. The higher you go, the more spectacular the views become and the area is riddled with open mine entrances and remains of mining equipment.

On the valley route, you'll eventually pass a small ephemeral lake; turn south and climb up a side valley to a pass with impressive views of distant high peaks, about six hours' walking from Potosí. At this point, there are a couple of routes back to town but the most aesthetic is the way you came. Alternatively – with camping equipment – you can keep wandering. There are no difficult summits in the area and as long as you can catch sight of Cerro Rico, the route back to Potosí will be obvious. The only problem will be the altitude which ranges from 4400 to 5000 metres. The Cordillera Kari Kari is included on the IGM topo sheet number 6435, available at the Instituto Geográfico Militar in La Paz.

HACIENDA CAYARA

For a real retreat or some comfortable hill-walking, a stay at the Hacienda Cayara, 25 km down valley from Potosí at an elevation of 3550 metres, will prove ideal. This beautiful working farm, set amid lovely hills, produces vegetables and milk for the city.

Places to Stay

The onsite hostal is like a museum: an opulent colonial mansion furnished with original paintings and period furniture. Guests will have use of the fireplace and extensive library. An English-speaking historian and agronomist will provide information about the site and answer questions about Bolivia and its history. Bookings may be made with Señor Luis Aitken (☎ 26098) or Señorita María Luisa Serrano (☎ 26389) in Potosí. Rooms with private bath cost B72 per person. Meals are available for an extra charge.

Getting There & Away

The booking people will organise your transport from Potosí but it would actually be cheaper to go by taxi, especially if you're in a group; have the driver take the left fork at La Palca instead of heading right through the canyon toward Tarapaya.

BETANZOS

Set in a landscape of rugged mountains, the village of Betanzos lies two hours from Potosí along the road to Sucre. It makes an excellent daytrip, especially on Sundays when the market is in full swing. Many campesinos wearing local dress bring their harvests and handicrafts from the countryside. Unlike the Tarabuco market, it isn't staged for the benefit of tourists so there won't be a lot of artesanía. You may be lucky and catch an unscheduled fiesta during the Sunday market. The surrounding area is said to be filled with the fossilised skeletons of prehistoric animals.

Fiesta

On 4 and 5 April, Betanzos celebrates the Fiesta de la Papa (Potato Festival). While it isn't well known, reports indicate that it's a winner. Major musical groups travel to Betanzos from all over Bolivia to dance and play Andean folk music.

Places to Stay

The best option is the *Hotel Sucre*; the *Hotel Betanzos* is a real dump.

Getting There & Away

Camiones and micros leave for Betanzos

from Plaza Uyuni in Potosí early on Sunday mornings. In addition, any Sucre bus will drop you there.

TARAPAYA

Belief in the curative powers of Tarapaya, the most frequently visited hot springs area around Potosí, dates back to Inca times. It even served as the holiday destination for Inca Huayna Capac, who would come all the way from Cuzco to bathe.

The most interesting site is Ojo del Inca, a perfectly round green lake in a volcanic crater. Locals believe all bathing must be done in the morning since *remolinos* or whirlpools develop early in the afternoon and have caused drownings. Along the river below the crater are several *balnearios* (resorts) with medicinal thermal pools utilising water from the lake.

Places to Stay

Balneario Paraíso has a basic hostel for overnight guests and when we were last there, a hotel was under construction at Balneario de Tarapaya.

If you'd like to camp in this scenic area, there are a number of level and secluded sites near the river; all water should be purified.

Getting There & Away

From Potosí, Tarapaya is a 25-km trip along asphalted highway. There are frequent camiones from Plaza Chuquimia near the bus terminal, charging B2 per person.

Ask the driver to let you off at the bridge where the gravel road turns off. The Balneario de Tarapaya is 400 metres from the bridge along the paved road. Balneario Paraíso is over the bridge and 400 metres down the road to the right. Miraflores lies three km beyond Paraíso.

To reach Ojo del Inca, cross the bridge, turn left and walk about 200 metres. Just past the waterfall on the right, a trail that resembles a washed out roadbed leads uphill. Follow it about 400 metres to the lake. The track may disappear at times into eroded gullies but if you keep walking uphill or

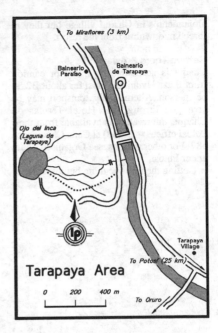

along the streams that flow from the lake, you'll get there.

CHAQUÍ

Another major hot springs site lies several km uphill from the village of Chaquí, two hours south-east of Potosí.

The countryside surrounding nearby Puna and Belén is interesting but transport may be a problem. On Sunday, Potosinos frequently venture this way with loads of sugar, flour, rice and bread to exchange in the markets for potatoes, cheese, and local farm products. The climate here is much more agreeable than in Potosí and superior quality handicrafts, such as weavings and blankets, are available in small villages.

Places to Stay

The *Hotel Termas de Chaquí* has rooms for B13 per person, including use of the hot pools. Non-guests may use the pools and sauna for B3.50. There are a couple of cheap alojamientos in Chaquí village but they're three km downhill from the resort.

Getting There & Away

Chaquí is accessible by micro or camión from Plaza Uyuni in Potosí for about B2.50 per person. Alternatively, transport may be arranged through the Hotel Termas de Chaquí. Information is available from their Potosí office (☎ 22158) at Calle Chuquisaca 587. For other options, see Organised Tours under Potosí.

Getting there is one thing but a spontane-ous return to Potosí will be another. Drivers may be planning to go but if there's insuffi-cient interest, they won't bother. Have a contingency plan or offer enough money to make it worth their while.

DON DIEGO

The hot springs at Don Diego are along the Sucre road and may be reached by micro or camión from Plaza Uyuni or on a Sucre bus. The resort has a hostel which costs B10 per person, including use of the baths.

Contemporary Craft Design

Sucre

Ask any Bolivian who knows Sucre and they'll tell you it's their nation's most beautiful city. They've reverently bestowed upon it romantic-sounding nicknames: the Spanish equivalents of The Athens of America, The City of Four Names, The Cradle of Liberty and The White City of the Americas. At an altitude of 2790 metres, it enjoys a mild and comfortable climate nearly as appealing as that of Cochabamba.

Set in a valley surrounded by low mountains, Sucre remains Bolivia's official or legal capital. Like the Netherlands, Libya and South Africa, Bolivia divides its bureaucracy between multiple capitals. Although La Paz has usurped most of the governmental power, the Supreme Court still convenes in Sucre and with some kind of twisted pride, the Sureños maintain that their city remains the real centre of Bolivian government.

Today, Sucre struggles to retain the flavour of its colonial heritage. All buildings within the central core of the city must be either whitewashed or painted white. Numerous museums have been established in Sucre to house the art and relics of the pre-Columbian, colonial and post-colonial eras, and some of its many churches have been renovated to reflect their former glory. The city remains a centre of learning and both Sucre and its university enjoy their reputations as focal points of liberal and progressive thought within the country. It's worth spending at least a few days absorbing the city's pleasant atmosphere, attractions and pace of life.

History

Throughout its history, Sucre has served as the administrative, legal, religious, cultural and educational centre of the easternmost Spanish territories, and in the 17th century, came to be known as the Athens of America.

Prior to Spanish domination, the town of Charcas, where Sucre now stands, was the indigenous capital of the valley of Choque-Chaca. It served as the residence of local religious, military and executive leaders and its jurisdiction extended to several thousand inhabitants. When the Spanish arrived, the entire area from Southern Peru to the Río de la Plata in present-day Argentina came to be known as Charcas.

In the early 1530s, Francisco Pizarro, the conquistador who felled the Inca Empire, sent his brother Gonzalo to the Charcas region to oversee Indian mining activities and interests which might be valuable to the Spanish realm. Uninterested in the Altiplano, he concentrated on the highlands east of the main Andean Cordilleras. As a direct result, in 1538 the city of La Plata was founded by Pedro de Anzures, Marquéz de Campo Redondo, as the Spanish capital of the Charcas. As his Indian predecessors had done, he chose the warm, fertile and well-watered valley of Choque-Chaca for its site.

During the early 16th century, the Viceroyalty of Lima governed all Spanish territories in central and eastern South America. In 1559, King Phillip II created the Audiencia (Royal Court) of Charcas with its headquarters in the city of La Plata to administer the eastern territories. The Audiencia was unique in the New World in that it held both judicial authority and executive powers. The judge of the Audiencia also served as the chief executive officer. Governmental subdivisions within the district came under the jurisdiction of royal officers known as *corregidores*.

Until 1776, the Audiencia presided over Paraguay, south-eastern Peru, northern Chile and Argentina, and most of Bolivia. When Portuguese interests in Brazil threatened the easternmost Spanish-dominated regions, a new Viceroyalty, La Plata, was established in order to govern and ensure tight control. The city of La Plata thereby lost jurisdiction over all but the former Choque-Chaca, one of the four provinces of Alto Peru, which comprised leftover territories between the

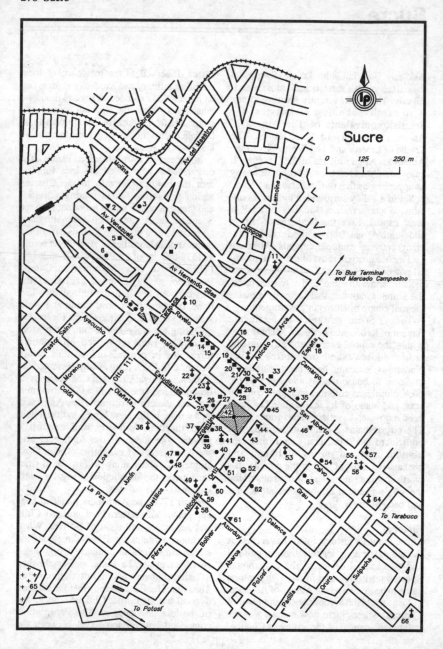

Sucre

0   125   250 m

To Bus Terminal
and Mercado Campesino

To Tarabuco

To Potosí

Viceroyalties of Lima and La Plata. The city's name was changed to Chuquisaca (the Spanish corruption of Choque-Chaca), presumably to avoid confusion between the city and the new Vice-royalty.

The city had received an archbishopric in 1609, according it theological autonomy. That, along with the establishment of the University of San Xavier in 1622 and the 1681 opening of a law school, Academía Carolina, fostered continued growth and development of liberal and revolutionary ideas and set the stage for 'the first cry of Independence in the Americas' on 25 May 1809. The mini-revolution set off the alarm throughout Spanish America and like ninepins, the north-western South American republics were liberated by the armies of the military genius, Simón Bolivar.

After the definitive liberation of Peru at the battles of Junín and Ayacucho on 6 August and 9 December 1824, Alto Peru, historically tied to the Lima government, was technically free of Spanish rule. Historically, however, it had carried on closer relations with the La Plata government in Bueños Aires and disputes arose about what to do with the territory.

On 9 February 1825, Bolivar's second-in-command, General Antonio José de Sucre, drafted and delivered a declaration which stated in part:

The...Viceroyalty of Buenos Aires to which these provinces pertained at the time of the revolution of America lacks a general government which represents completely, legally, and legitimately the authority of all the provinces...Their political future must therefore result from the deliberation of the provinces themselves and from an agreement between the congress of Perú and that...in the Río de la Plata.

Bolivar, unhappy with this unauthorised act of sovereignty, rejected the idea but Sucre stood his ground, convinced that there was sufficient separatist sentiment in Alto Peru to back him up. As he expected, the people of the region refused to wait for a decision from the new congress to be installed in Lima the following year, and rejected subsequent invitations to join the Buenos Aires government.

On 6 August, the first anniversary of the Battle of Junín, independence was declared in the Casa de la Libertad at Chuquisaca and the new republic was christened 'Bolivia' after its liberator. On 11 August, the city's name was changed for the final time to Sucre in honour of the general who promoted the independence movement.

Difficult years followed in the Republic of Bolivia and at one stage, the Great Liberator became disenchanted with his namesake republic. After a particularly tumultuous period of political shuffling, he uttered: 'Hapless Bolivia has had four different leaders in less than two weeks! Only the kingdom of Hell could offer so appalling a picture discrediting humanity!'.

Information

Tourist Office The once efficient IBT tourist office (☎ 35994) in the Caserón de la Capellanía (the old vicarage) is a mere shadow of its former self. It's now hardly worth a visit. From November to April, it's open from 8 am to noon and 2 to 6 pm and from May to October, 8.30 am to noon and 2.30 to 6.30 pm. The tourist police occupy the same office.

The Dinatur office at the airport is consid-erably more helpful but it's a long way to carry casual queries.

In addition to the government tourist offices, there's a most helpful university tourist information centre (☎ 23763) at Calle Nicolás Ortiz 182. There, you'll meet tourism students whose curriculae include arranging and giving guided city tours. If you speak even a little Spanish, a visit will prove worthwhile. You pay only transport expenses and a tip, if you wish.

Money There are a couple of casas de cambio around the main market. Ambar at Calle San Alberto 7 changes travellers' cheques at acceptable rates. For good rates on travellers' cheques, try also Almacén del Sol at Calle Ravelo 74.

Street money changers operate along Avenida Hernando Siles at the back entrance to the main market. There are also quite a few businesses around town displaying compro dólares signs, but they'll only accept cash.

VISA cash advances take 10 minutes at the Banco de Santa Cruz at the corner of calles San Alberto and España.

Post & Telecommunications The ultra-modern ENTEL office on the corner of Calle España and Urcillo opens at 8 am.

The central post office is on Avenida Argentina, less than a block from Plaza 25 de Mayo. Service is normally reliable.

Cultural Centres The Instituto Cultural Boliviano Aleman or Goethe Institut has a selection of current German-language books and newspapers as well as a café and news from the German community. It's open Monday to Friday from 9.30 am to 12.30 pm and 3 to 9 pm and on Saturday from 9.30 am to 12.30 pm.

Similarly, Alliance Française (☎ 23599) at Avenida Aniceto Arce 35 keeps a supply of French-language reading material and news-papers and operates a restaurant, La Taverne. They also show foreign films nightly; for the schedule, check the notice board at the north-west corner of the main plaza.

The Centro Cultural Los Masis at Calle

Bolivar 561 (☎ 23403) is a joint German and North American funded cultural operation which encourages and promotes Bolivian artists and musicians. There's a small museum of local musical instruments and the centre offers Quechua classes and sponsors concerts and other cultural events. It's open Monday to Friday from 10 am to noon and 3.30 to 9 pm.

For further cultural options, see Caserón de la Capellanía later in this section.

Travel Agencies There are several tour agencies in Sucre, but unfortunately, only overpriced Sur Andes offers excursions into the surrounding countryside. We enquired about the places they visited and they responded 'If we tell you about them, people will go on their own and not pay us to take them'. This agency is desperately in need of competition.

Laundry For 90-minute laundry service, go to Laverap at Calle Bolivar 617. It's open Monday to Saturday from 8 am to 8 pm and on Sunday and holidays from 9 am to 1 pm. They charge B10 per kg for washing, drying and ironing.

Immigration If you need a visa extension, the immigration office (☎ 32770) is at Plaza 25 de Mayo 1. This is one of the best places in Bolivia to extend visas. It takes five minutes and at the time of writing extensions of up to 90 days were free of charge.

Dangers & Annoyances Harassment and robbery of tourists by bogus police is increasing in Sucre. If you do have a problem, report it to the tourist police (☎ 25983) or the Radio Patrulla (☎ 110).

Museums
Museo de Santa Clara The old Convento de Santa Clara, founded in 1639, is now a museum. In 1985 it was robbed, and several paintings and gold ornaments disappeared. An item still remaining in the exhibit which receives the most attention is a canvas that was too big to carry off. The robbers sliced a big chunk of material out of the middle and left the rest hanging – and it's still hanging just that way. There's also a very interesting 17th-century pipe organ. It still works and if you like, the guide will give a demonstration.

Admission to the museum is B3. It's open Monday to Friday from 9 to 11 am and 5 to 7 pm. On Saturday, you can visit from 10 am to noon.

Museo de la Catedral The recently renovated Museo de la Catedral beside the Capilla de la Virgen de Guadalupe contains what is probably Bolivia's best collection of religious relics, half of which were donated by one archbishop. In addition to paintings and carvings, there are some priceless gold and silver religious articles set with rubies, emeralds and other precious stones. It's meant to be open Monday to Friday from 10 am to noon and 3 to 5 pm, and Saturday from 10 am to noon, but hours will remain sporadic until security can be beefed up.

Museos Universitarios The three university museums at Calle Bolivar 698 near Dalence make a worthwhile visit. When all is well in Sucre academia, they're open Monday to Friday from 9 am to noon and 2 to 6 pm and on Saturday from 9 am to noon. Admission is B3, with an extra charge of B5 for a photography permit. There is also the affiliated Museo de Anatomía (Anatomy Museum) in the university building near the Supreme Court, and the Museo de Historia Natural (Natural History Museum) on Calle San Alberto.

Museo de Charcas The Museo de Charcas, was founded in 1939 and occupies a home with 21 large rooms. It houses Bolivia's best known works of art, including some by Holguín, Padilla, Gamarra and Villavicencio. You'll also see ornate furniture which was handcrafted by Indians of the Jesuit missions.

Museo Antropológico The Anthropology Museum, founded in 1943, contains separate exhibits dealing with folklore, archaeology and ethnography. Highlights include mummies, skulls, and artefacts from the eastern jungles of Bolivia. There are also the usual collections of pottery, tools and textiles.

Museo de Arte Moderna The best of the three university museums is the Museum of Modern Art, which has good examples of modern Bolivian painting and sculpture as well as pieces from around Latin America. Don't miss the handcrafted charangos by Bolivian artist and musician, Mauro Nuñez, and the section devoted to native art.

Churches
Cathedral The cathedral on the southern corner of the Plaza 25 de Mayo was begun in 1551 and although the original structure was completed 10 years later, major sections were added between 1580 and 1633. Of interest is the bell tower, a Sucre landmark, and the statues of the 12 apostles and four patron saints of Sucre. The interior, however, is overburdened with kitsch.

Around the corner is the Capilla de la Virgen de Guadalupe which was completed in 1625. Encased in the altar is the Virgin de Guadalupe de la Extremadura, named after a similar image in Spain. She was originally painted by Fray Diego de Ocaña in 1601. The work was subsequently coated with highlights of gold and silver and adorned in robes encrusted with diamonds, amethysts, pearls, rubies and emeralds donated by wealthy colonial parishioners. The jewels alone are said to be worth millions of dollars and one wonders why the priceless Virgin's head is ringed with cheap incandescent Christmas bulbs!

The chapel and cathedral are open daily between 7 and 8 am. The Museo de la Catedral is described earlier in this section.

Iglesia de San Francisco The Iglesia de San Francisco at Calle Ravelo 1 was founded in 1538 by Francisco de Aroca soon after the founding of La Plata. It began as a makeshift structure; the current church wasn't completed until 1581. Architecturally, its most interesting feature is the domed mudéjar

ceiling. In the belfry is the Campana de la Libertad, Bolivia's Liberty Bell, which called patriots to revolution in 1825. The church is open daily from 7 to 9 am and 4 to 7 pm, and during mass on weekends.

Convento de San Felipe Neri For an explanation of why Sucre was known as the White City of the Americas, visit the bell tower and tiled rooftop of the Convento de San Felipe Neri at Calle Nicolás Ortiz 165. In the days when San Felipe Neri served as a monastery, asceticism didn't prevent the monks coming to meditate over the view; you can still see the stone seats on the roof terraces. The church was originally constructed of stone but was later covered with a layer of stucco. In the courtyard are gardens of poinsettias and roses, and a nice painting of the Last Supper hangs in the stairwell.

In the catacombs are tunnels where priests and nuns once met clandestinely and where guerrillas would hide and circulate around the city during times of political unrest. The building now functions as a parochial school.

The church and roof are open Monday to Friday from 4.30 to 6 pm. First you must visit the university tourist information office opposite San Felipe Neri and procure a guide (no charge). Admission is B1, payable at the convent.

Iglesia de Santa Monica The Iglesia de Santa Monica at the corner of Arenales and Calle Junín, begun in 1565, is Sucre's best example of mestizo architecture. It's adorned with carvings of seashells, animals and human figures. The inside ceiling woodwork is impressive and the courtyard is one of the city's finest with lawns and a variety of semitropical plants.

The building has recently been converted into a multipurpose civic auditorium.

Iglesia de San Miguel Built between 1612 and 1621, the Iglesia de San Miguel reflects mudéjar influences. Originally a Jesuit church, it was rededicated when the order was expelled from Bolivia. The church contains some very nice period paintings and sculpture. The interior is open from 7 to 8 pm Monday to Friday and during mass on weekends.

Iglesia de la Merced The Iglesia de la Merced on Azurduy, diagonally opposite San Felipe Neri, contains the most beautiful interior of any church in Sucre and possibly in Bolivia. It dates back to approximately 1581. The baroque-style altar and carved mestizo pulpit are decorated with filigree and gold inlay. Several paintings by the esteemed artist Holguín – notably *El Nacimiento de Jesús*, *El Nacimiento de María*, and a self-portrait of the artist rising from the depths of Purgatory – are displayed, as well as sculptures by other artists.

It seems La Merced has been decommissioned due to a shortage of padres, so a visit may prove tricky. It's meant to be open Monday to Friday from 10 to 11.30 am and 3 to 5.30 pm, but this is rarely the case. If it's not open, try knocking on the door during opening hours.

Iglesia de Santo Domingo The Iglesia de Santo Domingo at Calle Calvo 101 was constructed in the mid-16th century by the Dominican Order. The only item of interest is a superb wooden carving of Christ.

Iglesia San Lázaro Iglesia San Lázaro, constructed in 1544 on Calle Calvo between Padilla and Oruro, is the oldest church in the Audiencia de Charcas. Most of the building has been reworked, however, and the primary items of note are the original silverwork on the altar and several paintings attributed to the school of Polanco.

Caserón de la Capellanía
This 17th-century structure on the corner of Potosí and Calle San Alberto once served as a vicarage but is now a cultural centre with itinerant art exhibitions, artistic workshops and a snack coffee shop serving local specialities.

On the inner patio is Proyecto Textíl, a Swiss-funded project which markets locally produced weavings and ensures that all profits go to the artesans. Don't miss their Museo de Textiles Indígenas containing practical and artistic weavings, including complicated patterns from around Bolivia and numerous items from Tarabuco, all beautifully and tastefully displayed in appropriate light and background colours. It's open from 9 am to noon and 2 to 6.30 pm Monday to Friday. Admission is free.

Scheduled cultural events are posted on the notice board at the north-west side of the main plaza.

Cemetery
The enthusiasm that surrounds Sucre's cemetery is completely disproportionate to what's there. Locals anxiously ask tourists whether they've yet seen the cemetery. 'See it,' they urge. 'It's wonderful.' The tourist office reminds visitors not to miss it. Restaurant owners sing its praises.

The fact is there doesn't seem to be anything that should inspire that sort of emotional fervour. There are some arches carved out of poplar trees surrounded by unkempt gardens and mausoleums of wealthy colonial families. By all means go and judge it for yourself, or a lot of proud locals may be disappointed! To get there, take a taxi or walk from the centre.

Casa de la Libertad
The Casa de la Libertad has been designated a national memorial in commemoration of several historical events that have taken place there, particularly the signing of the Bolivian Declaration of Independence on 6 August 1825. The actual document and numerous other mementoes of the era are on display.

The first score of Bolivian congresses were held and doctoral candidates were examined in the Salon, originally a Jesuit chapel. Behind the pulpit hang portraits of Simón Bolívar, Hugo Ballivián and Antonio José de Sucre. General Bolívar said that this portrait by Peruvian artist José Gil de Castro was the most lifelike representation ever done of him.

The museum also includes portraits of presidents, military decorations, old governmental documents, and war and independence-related art and relics. The most memorable is a huge wooden bust of Bolivar carved by artist/musician Mauro Nuñez.

The Casa de la Libertad is open Monday to Friday from 9 am to noon and 4.30 to 6 pm. Admission is B3; a photography permit costs an additional B5.

La Recoleta

The Recoleta, established by the Franciscan Order in 1601, overlooks the city of Sucre from the top of Calle Polanco. It has served not only as a convent and museum but also as a barracks and prison. In one of the stairwells is a plaque marking the spot where, in 1828, President D Pedro Blanco was assassinated. Outside are courtyard gardens brimming with colour and the renowned Cedro Milenario – the ancient cedar – a huge tree that was once even larger than its current size. It is the only remnant of the cedars which were once abundant around Sucre.

The museum is worth a look for its anonymous paintings and sculptures from the 16th to 20th centuries, including numerous interpretations of St Francis of Assisi. One particularly interesting wooden carving of St Francis and another work entitled *Christ Bound to the Column* by Diego Quispe Curo are the best known. You'll also see myriad odds and ends: native arrows from the Bolivian Oriente, crosses from funeral masses and a complete collection of Bolivian currency. Note the denominations from bolivianos to pesos back to bolivianos – they illustrate well the degree of inflation that has plagued Bolivia over the years.

The highlight is the church choir and its magnificent wooden carvings dating back to the 1870s, each one intricately unique. They represent the Franciscan, Jesuit and Japanese martyrs who were crucified in 1595 in Nagasaki, Japan.

The view from La Recoleta over the city is best in the morning, while the forested twin hills of Sica Sica and Churuquella, which form its backdrop, look best in the afternoon. If you get an early start, the summits of these hills make pleasant hiking destinations.

La Recoleta is open from 9 to 11 am and 3 to 5 pm; access is by guided tour only, which costs B3. Check out the pricelist for religious services on the notice board at the entrance!

La Glorieta

After an extended tour of Europe, the wealthy businessman Don Francisco Argandoña decided to build a home reflecting the various architectural traditions he'd seen overseas. He commissioned the architect Antonio Camponovo to design a castle that incorporated a blend of European styles to be built on the outskirts of Sucre. The result was La Glorieta, an imposing mishmash that is difficult to discuss without passing judgement. Now a classic example of faded grandeur, it serves as the Lyceo Militar, the military school. A restoration project is planned.

To get there, take a taxi or Micro 'G' seven km out of town along the Potosí road. It's open Monday to Friday from 9 am to noon and 2 to 6 pm and on Saturdays from 9 am to noon. Admission is free but you must leave your passport at the entrance.

Mercado Campesino

The native market is a great place to wander and soak up a bit of urbanised Chuquisaca country life. Take micro 'A' or 'C' toward the bus terminal and ask to be dropped at the market.

Parque Bolivar

The clean and pleasant Parque Bolivar between the railway station and the Supreme Court is full of shady trees, benches and green lawns. There's also a public tennis court, a swimming pool and children's playground. For homesick French travellers, they have some pathetic miniature replicas of the Arc de Triomphe, Tour Eiffel and the Place de la Concorde obelisk.

Organised Tours

If you'd like to visit or trek around some of the fascinating natural, archaeological and cultural sites in the immediate vicinity of Sucre, contact the friendly and knowledgeable local guides, Lucho and Dely Loredo. They speak Quechua and some English and are acquainted with the customs and daily life of the *campo* (countryside). One to five-day organised treks along Inca trails and byways, including transport, food and drinks, will cost B70 per person per day. With groups of more than four, you'll pay only B55 per day. Accommodation options include lodging in local homes or camping.

There's no phone so you may contact the Loredos by taking a B1.50 taxi ride to their home at Barrio Petrolero, Calla Panamá final esq Calle Comarapa, 127.

Treks

When deciding where you'd like to go and what you'd like to see, refer to the Around Sucre map on which some of the major sites of interest are identified. Trekking on your own isn't really recommended; the routes aren't always clear and few campesinos or villagers speak Spanish.

A particularly interesting trek leaves from Punilla, 25 km north-west of Sucre. It climbs into the Cordillera de los Frailes to Chataquila where there's a stone church and two interesting sets of petroglyphs, Pumamachay and Incamachay. From there, it descends along pre-Hispanic paving to the village of Chaunaca which has an inviting sandy river beach. At this point, you can either head off toward Potolo, source of the famous weavings of red and black animals, or strike out toward Crater de Maragua (Maragua Crater), a source of natural obsidian glass.

From Maragua, the route continues south to the Termas de Talula (Talula Hot Springs) near an impressive gorge on the Río Pilcomayo before turning back toward Sucre. When it again crosses the Cordillera de los Frailes, there's a possible side trip to the summit of Cerro Obispo, a 3500-metre peak with a superb view across mountains and valleys. At that point, you can either head back to Sucre via the track to Cachimayu or via the Marca Rumi petroglyphs near the village of Quila-Quila.

This trip may be done in five or six days.

Fiestas

Fiesta de la Virgen de Guadalupe On the evening of September 8, peasants sing and recite couplets to celebrate this festival. The following day, they dress in colourful costumes and parade around the main plaza carrying religious images and silver arches. It's a worthwhile event if you're in the area.

Mojar con Agua Beware of the pre-Lent water carnivals which take place on Sunday nights in late January and early February, accompanied by processions and booming brass bands. They continue right up to Carnival when they crescendo into madness. The object is to *mojar con agua* – that is, drench every passing thing – with burst water balloons; foreign women are favourite targets.

Fiesta de la Empanada One reader recommended the Fiesta de la Empanada which takes place in late November at the Caserón de la Capellanía. Various chefs and bakers sell a variety of salteñas and empanadas, and prizes are awarded for the best in several categories. The festival includes folkloric music, dancing and costumes, and there are tables selling handicrafts and weavings. The director of the event wants to expand it to take place four times annually.

Places to Stay – bottom end

Sucre is quite popular with visitors so there's a choice of inexpensive accommodation and hotel prices are negotiable. The main budget hotel area focuses on the market and several blocks along calles Ravelo and San Alberto.

Residencial Charcas (☎ 23972) at Calle Ravelo 62 at the upper end of the bottom range is a winner. If you're looking for friendly and inexpensive accommodation, it's clearly the best value for money in Sucre. Showers are combined solar and electric so hot water is available around the clock.

Sparkling clean single/double rooms cost B22/35 with bath or B15/25 without.

The once grand *Grand Hotel* (☎ 22104) at Avenida Aniceto Arce 61 is one of Sucre's friendliest, but it's fading fast. Single/double rooms with bath cost B22/34. Without bath, they're B17/28.

A popular backpackers' haunt is the *Residencial Bustillo* (☎ 21560) at Calle Ravelo 158, just a block from the market. It's comfortable but the shower heads are something else. They charge B12/22 for singles/doubles without bath. Brekkie is an additional B1.80.

The *Residencial Bolivia* (☎ 24346) at Calle San Alberto 42 looks like someone has run amok with remaindered paint. This residencial is centrally located but its facilities are fairly remote from the sleeping quarters, and the breakfast they advertise isn't worth opening your mouth for. Singles/doubles cost B17/25 without bath and B23/35 with bath.

For downmarket accommodation, try *Residencial Oriental* (☎ 21644); it's good value at B10 per person. There are no private baths, but rooms are cleaned daily and there's a popular TV set in the reception area.

Alojamiento El Turista (☎ 23172) in the same area at Calle Ravelo 118 is a mediocre but friendly place, and at B8/12 for a single/double, it's good value for strict budgets. On a sadder note, it seems their friendly talking parrot was bird-napped in 1990 and not a squawk has been heard from him since.

In the middle of nowhere opposite the bus terminal at Avenida Ostria Gutiérrez 456 is the misnamed *Alojamiento Central* (☎ 23935). It's only ten minutes to the city centre on micro 'A', however, from the bus stop at the front door. Rooms without bath cost B9 per person.

The weird *Gran Hotel Londres* appears to be headed down the tubes but readers continue to recommend it. It once had a fine restaurant, cooking facilities and lovely parrilladas in the garden but these are all gone now and about all you'll get is a sour look from the bored desk clerk. Spartan

singles/doubles with bath cost B20/30. Without bath, they're B15/20.

For rock-bottom accommodation, try *Alojamiento Anexo San José* (☎ 25572) on Calle Ravelo beside the El Turista. It's cheap and basic at B7 per person with communal bath. If you prefer to be a bit further from the heart of things, try the quiet *Residencial Avenida* (☎ 21245) opposite the Gran Hotel Londres for B15 per person with bath.

Places to Stay – middle

Hostal Sucre (☎ 21411) at Calle Bustillos 113 gets our vote for Sucre's nicest hotel. It has a lovely antique dining room and a sunny, flowery courtyard to kick back and read or catch up on letters. At B45/65 for single/double rooms, it's a rewarding splurge.

Hostal Libertad (☎ 23101, fax (591-64) 30128) just a block from the plaza at Avenida Aniceto Arce 99 offers TV, telephone, piped music, private baths and a frigobar. Single/double rooms cost B50/75 while a double bed is B65. The spacious suite with huge wraparound windows and lots of light costs B110 and would be ideal for two couples but unfortunately there's a bit of traffic noise.

Places to Stay – top end

The *Hostal Colonial* (☎ 24709) on Plaza 25 de Mayo receives four stars by the Bolivian rating system. In our opinion, it lacks the character of the middle-range Hostal Sucre, but it's as central as a hotel can be. Singles/doubles costs B65/83 and a luxury double suite is B130.

Hotel Municipal Simón Bolivar (☎ 21216, fax (591-61) 24826) at Avenida Venezuela 1052 near Parque Bolivar is an average upmarket option with a lively beer garden called La Rotonda, which provides a bright counterpoint to the dark and pretentious dining room. Single/double rooms cost B72/95.

Places to Eat

Sucre has a pleasant variety of quality restaurants and is a good place to spend time lolling around coffee shops and witnessing university life, Bolivian style.

A good place for breakfast is *Agencias Todo Fresco* at Calle Ravelo 74 (the sign outside says 'Dillmann'). It's a bakery offering great fresh bread, pastries, coffee, tea, etc. In the market just opposite you can have a typical breakfast of *pastel* (pastry) and api, or go for salteñas, for as little as B1. The best places for salteñas are *El Patio* at Calle San Alberto 18 and *Don Sancho* at Calle España 150.

Pizza Napolitana on the plaza seems to do well. It plays good British and US music and serves as a hangout for the under-21 university crowd. It serves ice-cream concoctions during the day and Sucre's best pizzas by night. Drinks and coffee are a bit expensive, but a pizza large enough to fill two people costs only B13.

Alternatively, try *Pecos Bill Pizzería* on Avenida Argentina which thrills pizza freaks by opening at 10 am and serving the coldest Sureña beer in town. For roast chicken, choose from the wide selection of snack restaurants along Avenida Hernando Siles between Tarapaca and Calle Junín.

Plusher restaurants with good fare are *El Solar* at the corner of calles Bolivar and Azurduy and better still, *Piso Cero* at Avenida Venezuela 1241. The latter has excellent international and regional food and a huge portion will cost no more than B15.

For excellent upmarket Italian food, including lasagna, ravioli, canneloni, etc, there's *Piccolissimo* at Calle San Alberto 237. It's about as elegant as Sucre gets and although the extraordinary service tries to be pretentious, it joyfully fails. Plan on spending about B15 to B20 per person, more if you splurge on a bottle of Chilean wine. After the meal, try a cup of coffee – so good one could wax poetic about it!

The frequently recommended *El China*, operated by fun-loving Shanghai Chinese, is upstairs on the corner of Avenida Aniceto Arce and Calle San Alberto. An average meal of stir-fry vegetables with pork or chicken will cost around B9 but ask them to go easy on the oil. *Restaurant Shanghai* on Ravelo,

another chifa, is particularly good at egg flower soup.

The long-running *Las Vegas* on the main plaza is good if you want to hang out in the centre of things, but it's a legend only in its own mind. The primarily meat-based meals are filling and adequate, but are nothing out of the ordinary. Plan on spending about B10 per person without drinks. For a snack, try their famous cheese *cuñapes*.

For a real treat, go to *La Taverne* on Avenida Aniceto Arce just below the plaza. They serve a mean ratatouille for B4.50 as well as coq au vin, quiche lorraine and other continental favourites. And then there are the desserts... We confess this was our favourite Sucre restaurant.

There's also a trio of German-run options. The best is *Bibliocafé* with a dark but cosy atmosphere, good music and stacks of *Geo* and *Der Spiegel* on the shelves. The B8 plate of spaghetti bolognaise is recommended, as is the banana, chocolate and cream crêpe for B4.50. It's only open in the evening and gets very crowded, so come early.

Another German option is *Kultur Café Berlin* at Calle Abaroa 326, a German coffee shop and restaurant, which is open for lunch from 12.30 to 3 pm. For variety try the *Arco Iris* with its weird and starkly modern décor. There's a foreign atmosphere and the menu is great, including such delights as *roeschti*, fondue bourguignonne, mousse au chocolat and head-buzzing cappuccino. Vegetarian food is also available and they show videos and occasionally arrange peñas featuring local bands.

If you prefer a cheaper option, there's *Tahuichi* around the corner from the Residencial Bustillo where you can get a good solid lunch special for only B3.

For a snack, try *Snack Paulista* on Calle Ortíz near the main plaza. Despite their large menu, you won't get much except humintas and chicken empanadas, but they are good. For those who prefer their snacks frozen, *Helados Cri Cri* on Calle Estudiantes serves recommended ice cream. Sucre must be a city of chocoholics: there seems to be a chocolate shop on every street corner. In the late morning, you may also want to visit Convento de Santa Teresa near the corner of Calle San Alberto and Potosí where the nuns sell candied fruit they've prepared.

The fruit salads and other fruit concoctions available in the market are Bolivian highlights. You'll have to search for the correct stalls; they're tucked in an obscure corner of the ground floor. For something different (unless you're coming from Brazil or the lowlands), try *jugo de tumbo*, the juice of maracuya, or yellow passion fruit. Beyond that, they'll mix up any combination of melon, guava, pomelo, strawberry, papaya, banana, orange, lime and so on, throw it in a blender and come up with something indescribably delicious. Upstairs in the market, you'll find good, filling meals in unusually sanitary conditions (for a market, anyway) for B2.50 to B3.

Finally, there's the marvel-ridden *Saico del Sur* supermarket at the corner of Avenida Aniceto Arce and Calle Ravelo. Here you can buy all the nasty prepackaged food items that you may have begun dreaming about (don't deny it!) – taco shells, Cadbury chocolate, Pringle's potato chips, Reese's peanut butter cups – at a premium. Well, it doesn't cost anything to wander in and look.

Entertainment

If you'd like to go dancing and meet the wealthier university crowds, try the recently opened Discoteca Up-Down at the corner of Gregorio Mendizábal and Franz Ruck, two blocks from Parque Bolivar. Although it's a bit snobby and expensive, it's probably the best in town. It's open from Thursday to Sunday and admission costs B10, including your first drink.

Despite the name, don't go to Andy Capp's Wisquería in search of warm beer and pub meals. It's rather basic; more of a red light and local wheeler dealers' hangout than a pleasant pub. The Chinese proprietors sell Brazilian cachaça for only B4.

On Plaza Pizarro, there's an opulent old opera house, the Teatro Gran Mariscal de Ayacucho. Events are announced on the notice board at the north-west corner of the plaza.

Things to Buy

The best shopping option is the Proyecto Textíl in the Caserón de la Capellania. Prices are steep by Bolivian standards, but profits are directed back to the artesans and the degree of artistry and quality of the items justifies the high prices.

Some of the best charango makers are based in Sucre or the surrounding countryside and several shops in town specialise in them. Learning to play one is another matter but if you already play the guitar, you should be able to coax some pleasant sound out of these instruments. The artesan may even give you a quick lesson or two. Try the shops at Calle Junín 1190 and Destacamento 59.

Some recommended artesanías include: Bolivia, Avenida Argentina 31; Calcha, Avenida Aniceto Arce 76; Puerta del Sol, Plaza 25 de Mayo; Tawatinsuyo, Calle Junín 405, local #14; and Inti Punku, Calle Ravelo 44. If you failed to pick up silver goods and jewellery in Potosí, street vendors who hang out on Calle Ravelo near the market offer another chance.

Getting There & Away

Air The LAB office (☎ 21140) is at Calle Bustillos 127; their airport information number is ☎ 24445. TAM (☎ 23534) has an office at Calle Nicolás Ortiz 110. The new AeroXpress office (☎ 21256) is at Calle España 66.

LAB flies to La Paz five times weekly, to and from Cochabamba on Thursday and Saturday, to and from Santa Cruz on Tuesday and Friday (continuing on to Miami), to and from Tarija on Thursday and Saturday and to and from Camiri on Tuesday and Thursday. On Sunday, TAM flies to and from Santa Cruz, Villa Montes, Yacuiba and Tarija. AeroXpress does the 20-minute run to and from Potosí from Monday to Friday. Sample fares include B85 to Camiri, B84 to Cochabamba, B160 to La Paz, B121 to Tarija and B113 to Santa Cruz.

Cerro Rico and rooftops - Potosí (DS)

Left: Miner, Candelaria mine, Cerro Rico - Potosí (DS)
Right: Mineral buyer & miners, Cerro Rico - Potosí (DS)
Bottom: Wash day - Roboré (DS)

Bus The long-distance bus terminal is unfortunately not within comfortable walking distance of the centre. Micro 'A' does the run from Calle Junín, just north-east of Calle Camargo, for B.50 but it's normally quite full and would be a nightmare with luggage. Taxis to the bus terminal run at about B2 per person. There's a B3 tax on tickets for departures from the main terminal.

There are five daily buses to Cochabamba, all leaving around 6 pm and taking about 12 hours. The fare is B20. Direct buses go to Santa Cruz three times weekly and take 18 to 20 hours for B38. Three companies, Transtin, Geminis and Andesbus, leave for Potosí daily between 7 and 7.30 am and at 5 pm from their respective offices for B14 to B18 including a 10-minute stop for a sandwich and Coke. The trip takes 4½ hours and this comfortable and reliable service goes directly to the city centre rather than to Potosí's suburban bus terminal.

If you prefer to continue on to Oruro, Tupiza or Tarija, you may want to get a direct bus from the main terminal. If the road is passable, Flota Chaqueña does the beautiful but excruciatingly rough trip to Camiri twice weekly for B63.

Micros to many of these destinations, particularly Potosí, leave when full from the Indian market near the railroad tracks at Avenida Ostria Gutiérrez. To points southward such as Tarabuco, Padilla, Tomina or Camiri, there are camiones and micros that leave when full from the camión stop about a km out along the Tarabuco road from the top of Calle Calvo.

Train The railway station is across the plaza/traffic circle north-west of Parque Bolivar on Cabrera.

To Potosí and Tupiza, there's a train leaving Saturday at 5.30 pm. From Oruro, there's a service on Wednesday at 9 pm, returning from Sucre on Thursday at 3.30 pm. The fare is B33/25 in 1st/2nd class. The ferrobus leaves Oruro for Potosí and Sucre on Tuesday and Saturday at 10 pm and returns from Sucre at 6.50 pm on Wednesday

and Sunday. Fares in pullman/especial are B48/38.

The *autocarril* (a very odd ferrobus) to Tarabuco costs B8.20 and leaves on Sunday morning at 7 am, returning at 2 pm. The trip takes 2½ hours.

Getting Around
To/From the Airport The airport, nine km north-west of town, is accessed by micro 'F' from Avenida Hernando Siles or by taxi for B5. Unfortunately, LAB no longer provides an airport shuttle.

Bus There are a number of micros which ply the streets of the city and all seem to congregate at or near the market between runs. They're usually very crowded but since the town is so small, you won't have to spend much time aboard. The fare is B.50. The most useful routes are the one which climbs the steep hill to the top of Avenida Grau to the Recoleta one km from the Tarabuco camión stop, and micro 'A' which goes to the campesino market and the main bus terminal.

Taxi Taxis to anywhere around the centre cost B1.50 per person, but watch out for unscrupulous price augmentation.

Around Sucre

TARABUCO
The village of Tarabuco lies a dusty 65 km (three hours by camión) south-east of Sucre at an elevation of 3200 metres. It enjoys a mild climate, just a little cooler than Sucre's.

The majority of Tarabuco's residents are involved in agriculture or textiles and the colourful handmade clothing and weavings produced there are some of the most renowned in Bolivia.

On 12 March 1816 Tarabuco was the site of the Battle of Jumbati in which the village folk defended themselves under the leadership of a woman, Doña Juana Azurduy de

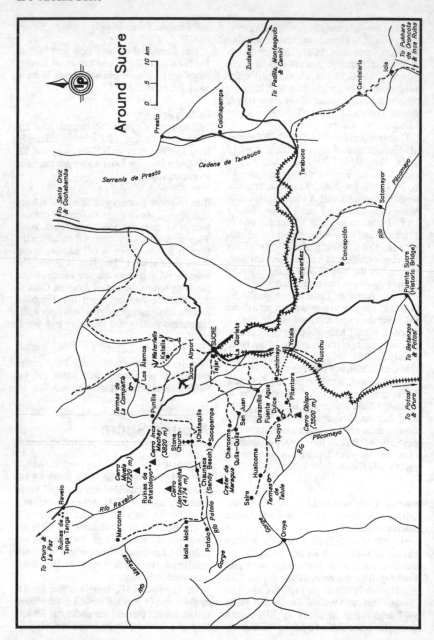

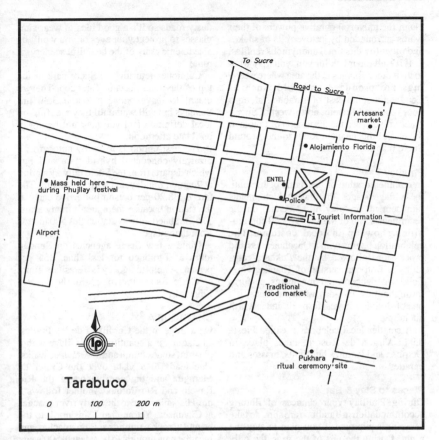

Tarabuco

0   100   200 m

Padilla, and liberated the town from Spanish forces.

Indian Market

Other than during the celebration of Phujllay, the only reason to go to Tarabuco is to visit the colourful Sunday market where you can buy beautiful artesanía – charangos, pullovers, coca pouches, ponchos and weavings featuring geometric and zoomorphic designs. The colourful wares laid out in stalls around the plaza and on side streets lend a festive and lighthearted atmosphere to the entire place. It's worth going to see the

unique costumes of the strolling charango-playing campesinos. The men wear distinct monteras (also known as *morriones*) which are leather hats patterned after those worn by the conquistadores.

It's all very touristy, however, drawing organised groups as well as individual travellers, and even well-bargained prices are high. Come prepared for an onslaught of high-pressure sales tactics; you'll have to learn to appreciate and admire skill and quality while it's being shoved up your nose.

One reader suggests looking for the snake oil vendors in the central market; they proclaim the universal curative powers of their wares surrounded by leftover bits of snakes and other (by this time) anonymous reptiles.

If it's all too much for you, you may want to visit other villages in the area where weavings are produced and sold, such as Candelaria south-east of Tarabuco along a poor road, and Ravelo, north-west of Sucre. Alternatively, see the discussion of Potolo at the end of this chapter. Refer to the Around Sucre map for locations.

Phujllay

In commemoration of the Battle of Jumbati, the village stages Phujllay (which means 'amusement' or 'play' in Quechua) on the second weekend of March. Over 60 communities show up in local costume. The celebration begins with a Quechua mass and procession followed by the Pukhara ceremony, a Bolivian version of Thanksgiving. Folkloric dancers and musicians perform throughout the two-day weekend fiesta. It's one of Bolivia's largest festivals and is worth attending.

A smaller local celebration called Fiesta de la Virgen de Rosario takes place in October, and features bullfights, masses and parades.

Places to Stay & Eat

During Phujllay your chances of finding accommodation in Tarabuco are slim, so take camping equipment if you plan to stay the night. During the rest of the year, the only lodging is at the *Alojamiento Florida*, open sporadically, half a block from the plaza. Rooms cost B5 per person without water. Meals of chorizo, curry, charque kan and soup are available from street stalls during market hours. On the plaza, there are a couple of restaurants.

Getting There & Away

Camiones leave from the parking area one km from the top of Calle Calvo in Sucre (on the Tarabuco road) between 6.30 and 9.30 am on Sundays. They charge B2 to ride atrás (in the bed of the camión) or B4 in the cab. The trip takes at least two hours along very

dusty roads so it's a good idea to wear sunglasses to protect your eyes or you won't be able to enjoy any of the beautiful scenery en route.

Camiones returning to Sucre park at the top of the main plaza in Tarabuco. They're meant to leave between 2 and 3.30 pm Sundays but will wait until they are 'full' by local definition and you may not get away until late afternoon.

The best option is to go by autocarril, a bizarrely concocted hybrid train and bus which departs from the Sucre railway station at 7 am on Sunday and returns at 2 pm. The fare is B8.20 per person but arrive early at the station because there aren't many seats. The Tarabuco railway station lies 500 metres from the village.

Quite a few Sucre agencies do Sunday tours to Tarabuco for less than B65 per person. A helpful agency is Teresita's Tours at Calle San Alberto 13 in the Hostal Libertad.

CHATAQUILA

On a ridge in the Cordillera de los Frailes, Chataquila is a beautiful little village with a pleasant stone church and several nice walks. One leads to a vista over the Crater de Maragua and the confluence of the Río Ravelo and Río Potolo. Another follows a pre-Hispanic route to the sandy river beaches at Chaunaca. Yet another leads north to the beautiful rock paintings at Pumamachay and Incamachay, thought to be at least 1500 years old.

There's no accommodation at Chataquila but camping is possible. As there are no large-scale maps of this area, local guides are highly recommended. For further information, see under Organised Tours in the Sucre section.

POTOLO

Potolo is the origin of some of Bolivia's finest weavings, including the lovely red and black animal weavings for sale throughout the country and as far away as Cuzco, Peru. It lies 60 km north-west of Sucre. Camiones to Potolo depart two times weekly between

May and October from the parking area along Calle Cobija in Sucre.

PADILLA

Padilla is a friendly agricultural mountain town on the road between Sucre and Camiri. The annual highlight is Carnival when each family in town prepares a different dish or beverage (most often chicha) for an immense potluck feast. The only accommodation is at the Residencial Cascada beside the post office on the main plaza. The attached restaurant serves good typical fare.

contemporary craft design

South Central Bolivia & The Chaco

Drier and more desolate than the country further north, the people of the isolated highlands of Tarija Department have historically identified and traded more with Argentina than with the rest of Bolivia. The department bills itself as the Andalucia de Bolivia, in reference to its dry eroded badlands, neatly groomed vineyards and orchards, and white stucco and red-tile architecture, all reminiscent of the Iberian peninsula. The people call themselves Chapacos and speak with the lilting sing-song dialect of European Spanish. Even the river running through their capital is called the Guadalquivir!

In the far eastern regions of Tarija and Chuquisaca departments, the highlands roll down into the petroleum-rich scrublands and red earth of the Gran Chaco. Although other populations exist in these transitional zones, the only city of the true Chaco is Villamontes, a small settlement on the Santa Cruz-Yacuiba railway. It claims the distinction of being literally the country's hottest spot. Further north is the growing but uninteresting oil town of Camiri.

South Central Bolivia

Despite Tarija's grand delusions about spiritual kinship with Andalucia, more urbanised Bolivians regard south central Bolivia as a half-civilised backwater; the tasteless jokes one hears in Europe and North America are retold in La Paz with 'Chapaco' replacing the standard butts of such humour elsewhere. In

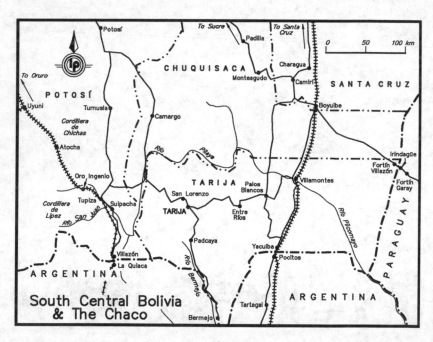

South Central Bolivia & The Chaco

rebuttal, the regionalistic southerners are quick to point out to other Bolivians that in 1810, the year following Chuquisaca Department's 'first cry of independence in the Americas', part of Tarija Department declared independence from Spain and operated briefly under a sovereign government with its capital at Tarija.

In the southernmost 'toe' of Bolivia one finds the oil-bearing veins and the lush sugar-cane producing valleys surrounding the town of Bermejo on the Argentine border.

TARIJA

The distinctly Mediterranean flavour of Tarija is evident in its climate, architecture and vegetation. Around the main plaza grow stately date palms and the surrounding landscape has been wildly eroded by wind and water into badlands that resemble parts of the Spanish Meseta. Chapacos are proud to be accused of considering themselves more Spanish or Argentine than Bolivian; many Tarijeños are descended from Argentine gauchos.

Tarija is a well-educated, clean and friendly city that's free of the flurry of more touristed locales. The city is renowned for its many fiestas and the unique musical instruments used to celebrate them, and the surrounding badlands are chock full of the fossilised remains of prehistoric animals.

The city of 60,000 people lies at an elevation of 1924 metres. The climate of the valley resembles that of Cochabamba, although winter nights may be slightly cooler. As in most of Bolivia, the dry season lasts from April to November.

History

Tarija was founded on 4 July 1574 as La Villa de San Bernardo de Tarixa by Don Luis de Fuentes y Vargas under the orders of Viceroy Don Francisco de Toledo. In 1810, Tarija and the surrounding area declared independence from Spanish rule, but no one took it very seriously. The situation didn't erupt into armed warfare until 15 April 1817, at the Batalla de la Tablada, a battle in which the Chapacos won a significant victory over the

Spanish forces. The departmental holiday is now celebrated on 15 April.

In the early 1800s, Tarija supported Bolivia's struggle for independence, and although Argentina was anxious to annex the area, when the Bolivian republic was established in 1825, Tarija opted to join with Bolivia.

Information

Tourist Office The tourist office (☎ 25948) at Calle General Bernardo Trigo 883, between La Madrid and Calle Ingavi, is helpful with queries regarding sites both within the city and out of town. They no longer distribute maps, but do offer a tourist booklet containing a small map. The airport information desk is useless.

Money The several casas de cambio on Calle Bolivar between Calle Sucre and Daniel Campos take only US dollars and Argentine pesos for Bolivianos. If you have travellers' cheques, go to the Banco del Perú or the travel agencies International Tarija at Calle Sucre N-721 or Pulido at Calle Bolivar O-226. In a pinch, the hardware shop Ferretería El Lorito will change travellers' cheques, but for an extortionate commission of 5 to 10%!

Post & Telecommunications The spanking new central post office is at the corner of Calle Sucre and Virginio Lema. ENTEL is at the corner of Virginio Lema and Daniel Campos. It's open Monday to Saturday from 8 am to midnight and on Sunday from 8 am to 9 pm. Tarija's public fax number is (066) 23402.

Foreign Consulate If you need a visa for Argentina, the consulate (☎ 22661) is at Calle Ballivián N-0699, at the corner of Calle Bolivar. It's open from 8 am to 1 pm Monday to Friday.

Dangers & Annoyances Between 1 and 4 pm, Tarija becomes a veritable ghost town, so transact all business in the morning or you'll have to wait until late afternoon.

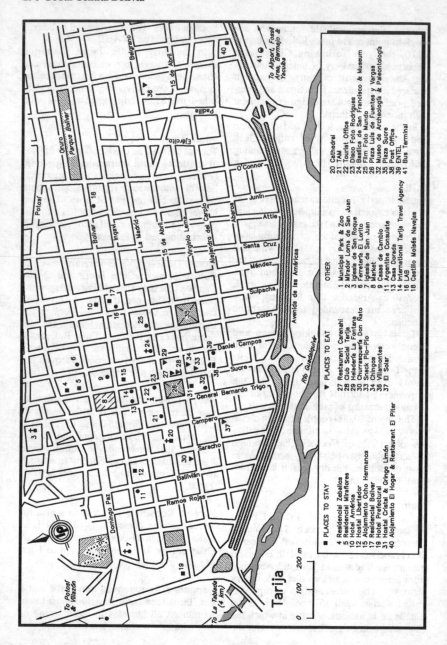

Tarija

PLACES TO STAY
4   Residencial Zeballos
5   Residencial Miraflores
10 Hotel América
12 Hostal Libertador
15 Alojamiento Echo Hermanos
17 Residencial Bolívar
19 Hotel Prefectural
31 Hostal Cristal & Gringo Limón
40 Alojamiento El Hogar & Restaurant El Piter

▼ PLACES TO EAT
27 Restaurant Carenahí
28 Club Social Tarija
29 Heladería La Fontana
30 Churrasquería Don Nato
33 Snack Pío-Pío
34 Villingos
36 Villamontes
37 El Solar

OTHER
1   Municipal Park & Zoo
2   Mirador Loma de San Juan
3   Iglesia de San Roque
6   Ferretería El Lorito
7   Iglesia de San Juan
8   Market
9   Casas de Cambio
11 Argentine Consulate
13 Castellanos
14 International Tarija Travel Agency
16 LAB
18 Castillo Moisés Navajas
20 Cathedral
21 TAM
22 Tourist Office
23 Disco Foto Rodrigues
24 Basílica de San Francisco & Museum
25 Film from Mundo
26 Plaza Luis de Fuentes y Vargas
32 Museo de Archeología & Paleontología
35 Plaza Sucre
38 Post Office
39 ENTEL
41 Bus Terminal

0   100   200 m

Churches

Basílica de San Francisco The Basílica de San Francisco at the corner of Daniel Campos and La Madrid was founded in 1606 and is now a national monument. The attached convent houses the largest library in Tarija, which may be visited with special permission from the Franciscan order. It includes some antique colonial books and archives. There is also a small religious art museum at the basilica which is open from 8 am to 6 pm daily.

Cathedral The cathedral at the end of La Madrid, one block from the Plaza Luis de Fuentes y Vargas, contains the remains of prominent Tarijeños, including Tarija's founder, Luis de Fuentes y Vargas. It was constructed in 1611 and expanded and embellished in 1925. By Bolivian standards, the interior is ordinary.

Iglesia de San Roque Architecturally, Tarija's most unusual church is the Iglesia de San Roque, which sits on the hill at the end of Calle General Bernardo Trigo. It's a recent addition, having been completed in 1887. This imposing structure serves as a prominent landmark visible from all over town. Its balcony once served as a lookout post.

Iglesia de San Juan The Iglesia de San Juan at the top of Calle Bolivar was constructed in 1632 and here the Spanish signed their surrender to the liberation army after the Batalla de la Tablada on 15 April 1817. The garden affords a sweeping view over Tarija and its dramatic backdrop of brown mountains.

Mirador Loma de San Juan

This park area above the tree-covered slopes of Loma de San Juan provides a lovely view over the city and is a favourite with students, who spend their afternoons there studying and socialising. To get there climb Calle Bolivar to its end, turn right behind the hill and climb the footpath up the slope that faces away from the city.

Casa Dorada

Although it could be considered imposing, the Casa Dorada (Gilded House) at the corner of calles Ingavi and General Bernardo Trigo is basically nothing but a large façade sloppily splashed with gold and silver paint and topped with a row of liberating angels. It dates back to 1930 when it was one of the several homes of the wealthy Tarija landowner, Moisés Navajas. The building now belongs to the university and contains the Casa de la Cultura. It's open from 8 am to noon and 2.30 to 6 pm Monday to Friday. Admission is free.

Castillo Moisés Navajas

The Castillo Moisés Navajas, another of Moisés Navajas' homes, is an oddly prominent and rapidly deteriorating mansion on Calle Bolivar between Junín and O'Connor. It is currently inhabited, but the owner does show visitors around. To visit, just ring the bell.

Zoo

The zoo in the park west of town, 15 minutes' walk from the centre, is unkempt and the animals are mostly in poor condition. They've got pumas, monkeys, a bear, a monkey island, a rhea which runs around loose and a cageful of condors (the cage is too small for one bird, let alone seven). Overall, it's quite depressing. The surrounding park, however, is pleasant and there's a nice children's playground. Admission is B.70.

Museo de Archeología & Paleontología

The Archeology and Paleontology Museum, operated by the university, is on the corner of Calle General Bernardo Trigo and Virginio Lema, one block from the main plaza. It provides a convenient overview of the prehistoric creatures and the early peoples that once inhabited the Tarija area. Other sections focus on history and geology.

You can see the well-preserved remains of most of the animals: *megatherium*, a giant ground sloth; *mastodon*; *glyptodon*, a giant prehistoric armadillo, *macrochenia*, a llama/tapir cross; *lestodon*; *scelidotherium*, a small ground sloth; and *toxodon*, a dozy-looking creature with buck teeth. Of note are the nearly complete glyptodon carapace, and the tail and a superb hand of a megatherium. Accompanying the displays are interesting artistic representations of how the animals appeared in the flesh. The archaeological section displays ancient tools, weapons and pottery from all over southern Bolivia.

The museum is open from 8.30 am to 12.30 pm and 2.30 to 6 pm. Admission is free.

Randall Collection

Ronald Randall, the late palaeontologist and fossil expert, was a New Zealander who spent over 25 years in the Tarija area, hunting and collecting specimens all over Bolivia. His wife maintains a small museum of his finds in her home and is happy to show and explain them to interested travellers. To arrange a visit, phone Ms Mavis Randall on ☎ 25108.

Fossils

The Tarija area is a paradise for amateur palaeontologists who'd like to try their hand at finding fossils. The *quebradas* (ravines or washes) near the airport and across the highway along the pipeline are littered with the remains of prehistoric creatures, mainly early horses, mastodons, megatheriums and three-metre long armadillo-like glyptodons. Since the area is severely eroded and each rainfall changes the face of the land, bones have been sloshed around for thousands of years and deposited haphazardly in the sedimentary layers. The more complete fossil bones lie loose or perched on pedestals of sediment, but it's rare to find a complete skeleton.

If you know what to look for, the profusion of specimens will seem overwhelming. The ubiquitous small blue 'stones' are well-fossilised fragments of mastodon bones, tusks and teeth; the crumbly rosettes which lie in heaps or embedded in sediment are bits of glyptodon carapace; and the small and rounded chalk-like 'pebbles' come from the hide of megatherium. Crania, pelvic bones and long bones of all these creatures are common, but due to the lack of water, they normally haven't been well-petrified and are quite fragile. Don't try to unearth them or they'll crumble into dust as soon as the supporting soil is removed.

When you're wandering through the quebradas and badlands, carry water and wear good hiking footwear with lots of tread; the terrain is difficult and the unconsolidated silt is slippery, especially when it's wet. Please leave the specimens as you find them and report any significant discoveries to the Museo de Archeología & Paleontología in town.

La Tablada

Across the Río Guadalquivir four km from Tarija is the historic battlefield of La Tablada where Moto Mendez and his forces defeated the Spanish royal armies in 1817. It's now a pleasant park and national monument. Take micro 'C' from the centre.

Wineries

The Tarija region is known for its wines. We're no wine experts, but in our opinion, it may be awhile before Bolivia produces anything that can be drunk without a spontaneous reaction of the facial muscles. If you want to visit the wineries and cellars or sample the product, visit the offices of the largest companies; the managements are friendly and you may be able to get a lift with the staff. Companies include Kohlberg, whose office is a Calle 15 de Abril O-275; Aranjuéz on Calle 15 de Abril O-241; Casa Real on Calle 15 de Abril O-246; and Rujero on the corner of La Madrid and Suipacha. Only the Aranjuéz vineyard is close to town; Kohlberg and Casa Real are in Santana, 15 km from Tarija and Rujero is near Concepción, 27 km from town.

Kohlberg, Aranjuéz and Casa Real have small shops attached where they sell their wines at factory prices. Rujero has separate shops at Calle Ingavi E-311 and at O'Connor N-642. Besides the wine, they also produce singani.

Fiestas

The traditional La Rueda is danced at all Tarija annual fiestas. Charangos, guitars and flutes, popular elsewhere in the Andes, also figure prominently in the music-making. For a rundown of the unusual Chapaco musical instruments used in Tarija festivities, refer to the Arts & Culture section of the Facts about the Country chapter.

Carnival The Carnival of Tarija is one of the most animated in Bolivia and is well-worth visiting if the one in Oruro proves too touristy for your liking. It's dedicated to good fun and the streets fill with joyful dancing, unusual original music and colourfully costumed country folk who come to town for the event. There's a Grand Ball in the main plaza after the celebration and the entire town turns out for dancing and performances by folkloric groups, bands and orchestras. Water balloons figure prominently in the festivities.

Rodeo Chapaco In keeping with its gaucho heritage, Tarija stages a rodeo in Parque La Tablada (across the river from Tarija) between 15 and 21 April. It includes all the standard cowboy events and prizes for the overall winner. To get there, take micro 'C' from the centre.

Fiesta de San Roque Tarija's best known festival is the Fiesta de San Roque, the patron saint of the city. Although San Roque's feast day falls on 16 August, the celebration actually begins on the first Sunday of September and continues for eight days. Celebrations begin with the *chunchus* procession, a parade of costumed dancers, musical groups and even festively dressed canines (San Roque is also the patron saint of dogs!). The costumes feature brilliantly coloured silk scarves, half-length shirts and headdresses of polychrome feathers and ribbons, topped off with glittering sequins and other small bright objects. Participants masquerade as members of a Chaco tribe which has been recently converted to Christianity.

Fiesta de las Flores Another annual event is the Fiesta de las Flores, a religious celebration dedicated to the Virgen de Rosario. It begins on the second Sunday in October when a procession of the faithful led by an image of the Virgen de Rosario sets off from the Iglesia de San Juan. Along their route, they're showered with flower petals thrown by the spectators. The highlight of the day is a colourful fair and bazaar in which the faithful spend lavishly for the benefit of the Church.

Places to Stay – bottom end

The *Residencial Bolivar* (☎ 22741) at Calle Bolivar 256 is friendly and tidy with hot showers, a TV room and a pleasant and sunny courtyard. Prices are high – B25/35 for singles/doubles with bath – to pay for their recent renovation efforts; however, despite the cost, the windows don't close properly and security is a little dodgy. Breakfast costs an additional B2.50 per person.

Opposite the Bolivar is the *Hotel América* (☎ 22627). You can't miss the obtrusive overkill sign hanging above the street. This place is noisy, dirty and disorganised with a raucous bar downstairs. Single or double rooms without bath cost B12. With bath they're B18.

For recommended low-budget accommodation, try *Alojamiento Ocho Hermanos* (☎ 22111) at Calle Sucre N-782. Tidy and pleasant rooms cost B10 per person with shared bath. *Alojamiento El Hogar* opposite the bus terminal offers similar accommodation and prices but it's a good walk from the centre. More central is the *Residencial Familiar* (☎ 22024) at Calle Sucre 626. Dank and musty double rooms cost B30/20 with/without private bath. The owner is eager to do business, and is prepared to bargain.

The *Residencial Miraflores* charges B9 and B10 for Bolivians and foreigners respectively for dorm-style rooms without baths. Individual rooms cost B11 for Bolivians and B12 for foreigners. The *Residencial Zeballos* (☎ 22068) at Calle Sucre N-966 has bright comfortable rooms and hot water for B25/33 for a single/double with bath.

In quiet Barrio El Molino is *Hostal Carmen* (☎ 23372), Calle Ingavi O-0784, which bills itself as *su segundo hogar* (your second home). It's good value: doubles with private bath, hot water and TV cost only B27.

Places to Stay – middle

A passable central option is *Hostal Libertador* (☎ 24231) at Calle Bolivar O-649. Singles/doubles with bath cost B35/60. Without bath, they're B24/36. TV costs B3 extra.

Even more central is the *Hostal Cristal* (☎ 25534) at Calle 15 de Abril 363, above the Gringo Limón café, on the Plaza Luis de Fuentes y Vargas. Singles/doubles cost B50/70 including breakfast, and all rooms have a private bath.

The most upmarket option is the *Hotel Prefectural* (☎ 22461, fax 22789) at the corner of Avenida de las Américas and La Madrid. Single/double rooms including breakfast, free airport transfer (they have a booth at the airport), private bath and TV cost B60/80.

Camping

If it isn't raining, the best place to camp is in the quebradas and fossil areas near the airport or on the far bank of the Río Guadalquivir, accessible via the bridge near the intersection of Calle 15 de Abril and Avenida de las Américas. The latter area has seen recent population growth so it won't be very secluded.

Places to Eat

For lunch, you're sure to enjoy the *El Solar*, a vegetarian restaurant at the corner of Campero and Virginio Lema. The food is still superb but this once general-interest restaurant has gone a bit freaky, attracting Tarija's New Age fringe with chromotherapy, aromatherapy, geotherapy, natural baths, psychic readings, group yoga sessions, etc, in the office next door. The restaurant experiments with such non-traditional practices as serving the dessert before the meal; you'd think you were in Southern California! Lunch is served from noon to 2 pm for B4 and it's a real cow's delight; you can guzzle green alfalfa juice and graze on avocado salad, oat soup, bulgur wheat, cream of mango puree and straw tea. Get there early to beat the herd.

For more conservative set lunches, try the *Club Social Tarija* at the calles 15 de Abril and Sucre corner of Plaza Luis de Fuentes y Vargas. *Snack Pio-Pio* and *Chingos* near the corner of calles Sucre and 15 de Abril are local youth hangouts. They serve fairly good chicken and chips, but the portions are small. Beneath the Hostal Cristal on the plaza is *Gringo Limón*, an upbeat sort of fast-food café. *Heladería La Fontana* is a good choice for ice-cream confections.

Cheap regional dishes are served at the *Villamontes* at Belgrano E-1054, a rustic place popular with locals. For meat dishes and an aquarium view (a few guppies and a stranded diver), try *Churrasquería Don Ñato* at Calle 15 de Abril 842 where quality is a hit or miss proposition. They serve typical parrillada, *zaraza* (beef stomach), lomo, silpancho (beef pounded paper thin and deep fried in batter) and milanesa de pollo. Beware of grease in indigestible doses.

Much better is the friendly *Restaurant Carenahi* on the plaza. There's no sign; it's beside the Club Social Tarija. Set lunches cost B5.50 and they have an interesting menu including lots of pasta, fish, port and other non-standard items. Meals include a salad bar and prices are reasonable. It's one of the few places where you can sample local wines without having to buy an entire bottle. You may also want to try your luck with *taba*, a regional game popular here.

North-east of the market at the corner of Calle Sucre and Domingo Paz, street vendors sell local pastries and snacks not available in other parts of Bolivia, including some delicious crêpe-like concoctions, known as *panqueques*, for B.10 each.

The only bottled water in town is available at *El Piter* opposite the bus terminal for B2. The locally produced beer, Cerveza Astra, is quite good and is available in lager or malt.

Entertainment

There's a peña on Friday at 9 pm at Los Parrales (☎ 24046), Calle Cochabamba 1154, in Barrio La Loma. Cabaña Don Pepe (☎ 22426) at Daniel Campos and Abaroa occasionally stages a peña at the weekends; phone in advance for times.

Things to Buy

The best handcrafted souvenirs typical of Tarija would naturally be the unique musical instruments played in the area. It would be difficult to carry a caña or a caja around in your pack, but smaller instruments may be posted home.

For the best selection of Chapaco and Bolivian music, go to Disco Foto Rodrigues at the corner of Calle Sucre and La Madrid. We suggest the tape *Tarija y su Música* by various artists, and anything by the groups Los Trobadores Chapacos and Los Sapos Cantores de Tarija, the 'singing toads of Tarija'.

Artesanías Vemar, touted by the tourist office, offers tacky primary school crafts and nothing of real interest. Try the Casa Folklórica on the corner of La Madrid and Calle General Bernardo Trigo.

Getting There & Away

Air The Oriel Lea Plaza Airport is about three km east of town along the main highway. It can be reached by taxi from the centre in 10 minutes. Tarija is served by LAB (☎ 22282) to and from La Paz, Sucre, Cochabamba, Santa Cruz, Bermejo and Yacuiba, and Buenos Aires and Salta, Argentina. Their office is at Calle Ingavi O-0236. TAM (☎ 22734) at La Madrid O-470 flies to Yacuiba, Villamontes, Santa Cruz and La Paz.

Bus & Camión The main bus terminal is at the east end of town on Avenida de las Américas. It's within walking distance of the centre but would be a long way to carry luggage.

Heading toward Bermejo on the Argentine border, Flota Trans Gran Chaco leaves at 7.30 am daily and costs B18 for the seven-hour trip. Trans Gran Chaco has a daily service at 6 pm to Yacuiba, another border town east of Tarija, and Expreso Yacuiba departs daily at 7 pm. Both charge B30 for the 12-hour trip over a beautiful route that is unfortunately travelled at night.

Pullman 10 de Noviembre leaves daily for La Paz at 4.30 pm while Expreso Yacuiba does the same trip at 7.30 am. ENFE, the national railway, offers dubious bus/train connections to La Paz, Oruro, Uyuni and Villazón via Tupiza, leaving Tarija at 7 am on Tuesday and Thursday. To Oruro, Cochabamba, Sucre and Potosí, Expreso San Juan departs daily at 4.30 pm. Expreso Yacuiba and Trans Gran Chaco charge B90 for their Monday and Sunday departures to Santa Cruz.

Between Tupiza and Tarija, Trans-Cristal leaves on Monday, Wednesday and Friday at 7.30 pm and charges B23. To Villazón, the border town opposite La Quiaca, Argentina, Expreso Yacuiba leaves daily at 8 pm and costs B20. If you prefer to travel by day, Trans-Cristal goes on Tuesday and Thursday at 6.30 am.

For a lift to Villamontes, a route served almost exclusively by petrol trucks, wait at the tranca east of town. The road can get dodgy but the scenery is indescribable. Between Entre Ríos and Palos Blancos you'll keep experiencing the strange sensation that you've been transported back to the American West of the late 1800s. Near Villamontes, the road passes through the amazing Cañón de Pilcomayo (Pilcomayo Gorge). During the dry season, plan on 20 hours for this 279-km trip. During the wet, it will be easier to take the long way around through Argentina via Bermejo, Orán, Tartagal, Pocitos and Yacuiba.

An alternative way to reach Villamontes is to take the Yacuiba bus as far as Palos Blancos and hitch a ride from there. All the petrol truck drivers stop at the bar in Palos Blancos to get drunk on Argentine wine before braving the Cañón de Pilcomayo. Now there's a comforting thought!

For camiones to Potosí, Villazón, Yacuiba or Bermejo, take a taxi to the appropriate tranca and wait for a vehicle going your way. Use the north tranca for Villazón and Potosí and the south-east tranca for Yacuiba and Bermejo. Expect to pay only slightly less than you would on the bus.

Getting Around
To/From the Airport A taxi to the centre from inside the airport compound will cost B3.50 per person. If you walk to the taxi ranks outside the airport gates, you'll pay only B3.50 for up to four people. Alternatively, walk 100 metres across the main road and flag down one of the many passing trufis or buses which charge B.60 per person.

Bus City micros cost B.60 per ride.

Taxi Tarija is small so it's possible to walk just about anywhere. Taxis cost only B1.50 within the centre, including to the long-distance bus terminal. To the fossil areas or trancas they'll charge about B5.

AROUND TARIJA
San Jacinto
The new 700-hectare artificial lake of San Jacinto seven km south-west of town provides Tarija with water-related recreation close to home. There's a tourist complex with middle-range cabañas, boat tours, a restaurant and pleasant views. At the time of writing, there was no public transport to San Jacinto, but at the weekends, hitching should be easy. For more information, contact the resort office (☎ 23179) in Comercial Villanueva at Campero 1025 in Tarija.

San Lorenzo
San Lorenzo, a beautiful colonial village 15 km from Tarija, was the home of José Eustaquio 'Moto' Mendez, the hero of the Batalla de la Tablada. His opulent home now houses the Museo Moto Mendez, which contains the personal belongings he bequeathed to the people of Tarija. It's open from 10 am to noon and 3 to 5 pm Monday to Friday.

The popular Fiesta de San Lorenzo takes place on 10 August, featuring Chapaco musical instruments and dances. San Lorenzo lies along the road toward Tupiza. Wait near the zoo for any micro headed in that direction.

Chaguaya
In Chaguaya, 51 km south of Tarija near Padcaya, is the pilgrimage shrine, Santuario de la Virgen de Chaguaya. The Fiesta de la Virgen de Chaguaya begins on 15 August, with celebrations on the subsequent Sunday; alcohol is forbidden at this time. Pilgrims from all over Bolivia arrive during the following month, often on foot. Any Bermejo bus from Tarija will drop you at Padcaya, a short distance from Chaguaya.

BERMEJO
Hot, muggy and dusty (or muddy) Bermejo, Bolivia's southernmost town, is 270 km south of Tarija. It lies on the banks of the Río Bermejo at the south-west end of Bolivia's oil-bearing geologic formation. There's little for the the visitor but an entry/exit stamp to/from Bolivia.

There's a YPFB (petroleum) compound which keeps many of the town's 15,000 or so residents busy. Bermejo also lies in the heart of a major sugar-cane producing region and there's a sugar refinery just outside town. Five km upriver from the YPFB, an international bridge over a canyon provides a highway link with the Argentine side.

The comercio de hormigas (ant trade) described under Villazón in the Southern Altiplano chapter is alive and well here, too. The ludicrous shenanigans can become quite a comedy of errors (and it's something to watch while standing in the queue at Argentine immigration). The Argentine officer feigns ignorance of their intentions as the *contrabandistas* pass through the gate into his country. From time to time, he'll confiscate any suspicious-looking empty sacks, lest they be used for some illicit purpose, such as transporting 'contraband' back across the river. Most of the 'ants' smile, defiantly retrieve the confiscated sacks, and march on through the gate without another word.

Once they've filled their containers with

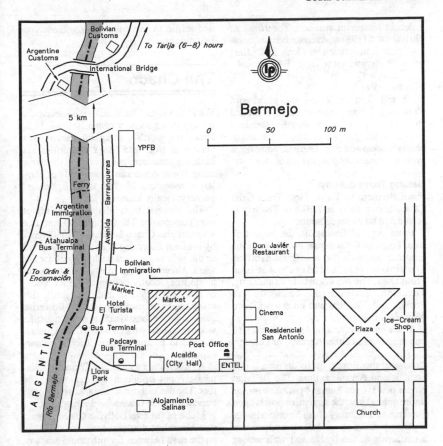

Bermejo

0   50   100 m

wine, noodles, rice and what have you, they play the same game to return to Bolivia, passing through the gate while the officials are conversing or literally looking the other way. Occasionally something is confiscated or a sack of noodles is 'accidentally' broken on the ground but nothing is taken too seriously. They'll be back the next day to try again.

Information

Money The main street is lined with casas de cambio but none change travellers' cheques so be sure to have Argentine pesos, cash

dollars or bolivianos on hand. There are several casas de cambio, so shop around for the best rates.

Dangers & Annoyances The power is turned off overnight in Bermejo, and tap water, drawn straight from the river, is murky and unsafe to drink.

Places to Stay

There isn't much choice of accommodation. The *Residencial San Antonio* is basic but clean, with no private baths. It costs B16 per person. The owners are friendly and there's a decent restaurant attached. The *Hotel El Turista* (☎ 61198) at Avenida Barranqueras 146 near immigration is clean and offers private baths and hot water for B45 a double.

Places to Eat
Both the *Don Javiér* on the plaza and *Residencial San Antonio* serve standard Bolivian favourites for equally standard prices. Nothing is outstanding – just lomo, chicken, soup and rice. There is, however, a good ice-cream shop on the plaza.

Getting There & Away
From Bermejo to Tarija, Flota Trans Gran Chaco leaves daily at 7.30 am. The trip is scenic and takes seven hours.

From Aguas Blancas on the Argentine side, buses to Orán depart hourly from the terminal opposite the immigration office. The trip costs US$2 and takes about an hour. From Orán, you can connect to Salta, Jujuy, Tucumán, Tartagal (the connection to Pocitos and Yacuiba) and once a week, to Asunción, Paraguay.

There are no hotels in Aguas Blancas so you must stay in either Bermejo or Orán.

Crossing the Border Bolivian time is one hour behind Argentine time. The Bolivian border post is open 7 am to 4 pm *más o menos* (more or less), and the Argentine post is open the same hours, from 8 am to 5 pm local time.

After picking up an exit stamp, you can hitch a ride to the bridge and walk across (this is the hard way) or take the ferry across the river to Aguas Blancas. The trip costs B1 and boats leave when full – about every 30 seconds when the contrabandists are active! Get your entrance stamp at the immigration post on the opposite side.

Plan on several thorough searches by customs and police, first at the border crossing and again near Orán. Argentine officials are drug paranoid and no one escapes suspicion. Be careful with cameras, radios, personal cassette players, or other electronic devices; unscrupulous Argentine officials have a habit of trying to confiscate tempting items. Report problems to superior officials and refuse to leave the room without your belongings.

The Chaco

While the level Chaco lacks the spectacular up-and-down scenery of the Bolivian highlands, it's worth visiting for its colourful variety of flora and fauna. Butterflies and birds are abundant, and it's one of the dwindling South American strongholds of some larger mammals like the tapir, jaguar and peccary, locally known as *javeli*.

The unusual flora of the Chaco region won't disappoint. The thorny scrub that characterises the Chaco landscape is enlivened by brilliant flowering trees and bushes such as the yellow *carnival* bush, the yellow and white *huevo* and the pink or white thorny bottle tree, locally known as the *toboroche* or *palo borracho*. In addition, you'll find many species of cactus and the red-flowering *quebracho* or 'break-axe' tree. Its beautiful wood is so heavy that it won't float. Quebracho wood is one of the Chaco's primary exports.

As interesting as it is, the Chaco is unfortunately not optimum for exploration on foot. The dense thorn scrub makes it virtually impenetrable to those who walk upright.

Much of the true Bolivian Chaco is inaccessible unless you're prepared to strike out on the road between Boyuibe and Paraguay. It is possible, however, to skirt its fringes travelling between Camiri, Boyuibe and Villamontes.

History
Before the 1932-35 Chaco War, most of Paraguay north-east of the Paraguay and Pilcomayo rivers – encompassing about 240,680 sq km – and the 168,765-sq-km chunk of Argentina north of the Río Bermejo, lay within Bolivian territory.

The dispute between Bolivia and Paraguay which led to the Chaco War had its roots in Paraguay's formal 1842 declaration of independence which omitted official demarcation of Paraguay's boundary with Bolivia. In 1878, the Hayes Arbitration designated the Río Pilcomayo as the boundary between Paraguay and Argentina, which was duly accepted. The empty land to the north, however, became a matter of dispute between Paraguay and Bolivia. Subsequent attempts at arbitration failed and Bolivia began pressing for a settlement.

After losing the War of the Pacific in 1884, Bolivia more than ever needed the Chaco as an outlet to the Atlantic via the Río Paraguay. Hoping that physical possession would be interpreted as official sovereignty, the Bolivian army set up a fort at Piquirenda on the Pilcomayo.

Arbitration attempts failed because Bolivia refused to relinquish rights to Fort Vanguardia, its only port on the Río Paraguay. Paraguay was unwilling to concede and in 1928, the Paraguayan military seized the fort. Although the situation heated up, both sides maintained a conciliatory attitude, hoping that a military solution would not be necessary.

While negotiations were underway in Washington (the USA never could stay out of a good conflict), an unauthorised action on the part of the Bolivian military erupted into full-scale warfare. Casualties on both sides were heavy but the highland Bolivians, unaccustomed to the subtropical terrain, fared miserably. No decisive victory was reached, but the 1938 peace negotiations awarded most of the disputed territory to Paraguay. Bolivia retained only the town of Villamontes, where, in 1934, it saw its most successful campaign of the war.

YACUIBA

In the transition zone between the Chaco and the Argentine Pampa, Yacuiba is the easternmost border crossing on the Bolivian/Argentine frontier. It's the terminus for both the railway from Santa Cruz and the 10,000-barrel-per-day YPFB oil pipeline from Camiri. The rail line was constructed with Argentine capital according to the terms of a 10 February 1941 treaty between the two countries, in which Bolivia agreed to export its surplus petroleum to Argentina in exchange for a 580-km rail approach to the Buenos Aires-Pocitos line terminus. Although construction began immediately, it wasn't completed until the 1960s.

Yacuiba is a typical border town with lots of shoddy commercial goods for sale and lots of shoppers buying stuff nobody really wants or needs. The town and the surrounding area are really of little interest but you may find yourself here awaiting a train or a bus out.

Information

Money The main north-south street of Yacuiba is lined with several casas de cambio. None will exchange travellers' cheques, so going north you'll have to wait until Camiri or Santa Cruz and going south until Embarcación, Argentina. Be careful changing money: there are lots of counterfeit US dollar notes floating around. US dollar rates are poor, anyway, so stick to pesos and bolivianos, if possible. Calculate the amount you should receive, and count it carefully.

Dangers & Annoyances Due to excessive traffic passing through Yacuiba, pickpocketing and petty thievery is on the increase, especially in the crowded shopping areas.

Places to Stay – bottom end

Yacuiba's number of hotels, bars and restaurants is disproportionate to its size. Passable budget accommodation includes the *Residencial Aguaragüe* which costs B9/14 for a single/double without bath. Alternatively, try the *Residencial Familiar* for B10/16 for a single/double, again without bath. The *Residencial Oriental* has hot showers and private baths for only B18/29 for a single/double. It's marginally clean.

Other cheap dosshouses include the following: *Residencial Gran Potosí*, *Alojamiento Ferrocarril*, *Residencial San Martín*, and *Hotel Select*. They're all very basic with shared baths and cold showers, and charge B9 per person. The *Residencial Yacuiba* costs B11 per person with hot water. Doubles with private bath will cost B36. *Residencial San Pedro* costs B18 for a double without

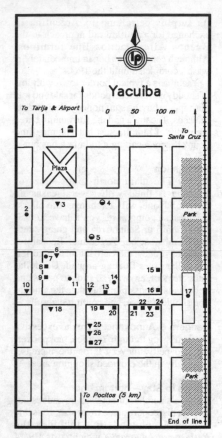

Yacuiba

To Tarija & Airport

0   50   100 m

To Santa Cruz

Plaza

Park

Park

To Pocitos (5 km)

End of line

■	PLACES TO STAY
8	Residencial Familiar
9	Hotel Select
13	Residencial Yacuiba
15	Hotel Valentín
16	Residencial San Martín
19	Residencial Oriental
20	Residencial San Pedro
21	Residencial Gran Potosí
22	Residencial Aguaragüe
24	Alojamiento Ferrocarril
27	Hotel Monumental

▼	PLACES TO EAT
3	Pepito's Café
6	La Pianola
10	Café El Negrito
12	TVO Expreso Café
18	Pizzería Chop
23	Parrilladas Ricardo
25	Swin Restaurant
26	La Alhambra Confitería, El Mesón, Salón de Te San Silvestre

	OTHER
1	Post Office & ENTEL
2	LAB
4	Flota Gran Chaco Bus Terminal
5	Expreso Yacuiba Bus Terminal
7	TAM
11	Casas de Cambio
14	Supermarket
17	Railway Station

bath and B36 with bath. The Hotel Monumental (see below) has a few cheap rooms.

Places to Stay – middle
The nicest accommodation and best deal in town is the new *Hotel Valentín* (☎ 2317) opposite the railway station. There's a bar/restaurant attached and rooms with double bed and private bath cost B50. Singles/doubles without bath are B15/25. A great double suite is a bargain B70.

Alternatively, there's the second best *Hotel Monumental* (☎ 2088), which is older and has a few problems with plumbing and

electricity. In the newer section, singles/doubles cost B30/43. Rooms with more than two beds are B22 per person, all with bath. In the older section (formerly the Residencial Frontera, a real dump), you'll pay B15/25 for single/double rooms without bath and B12 per person for rooms accommodating more than two people.

Places to Eat
For a taste of Argentina north of the border – that means huge slabs of meat – try *Parrilladas Ricardo*. Typical Bolivian meals are available at the unfortunately named *Swin* (which we think was intended to be 'Swing'), *La Pianola* and *Café El Negrito*

(popular with locals). *TVO Expreso Café, Pepito's Café, Pizzería Chop, La Alhambra Confitería* and *Salón de Te San Silvestre* all serve snacks. For a bearable breakfast, try the aforementioned Swin.

Getting There & Away

Air LAB flies to and from Tarija, Bermejo and Santa Cruz on Friday. TAM flies to Villamontes and Santa Cruz at 12.35 pm Saturday and to Tarija and La Paz on Sunday at 1.30 pm. Also on Sunday it flies from Santa Cruz via Villamontes. The fare to Tarija is only B67 and avoids a gruelling 12 hours on the overnight bus. To or from Santa Cruz, the fare is B184. Both airline offices are marked on the Yacuiba map.

Bus & Camión Flota Trans Gran Chaco and Flota San Lorenzo each do a daily run to Tarija for B30. If you'd rather do the scenic route to Villamontes, take the Tarija bus as far as Palos Blancos and hitch a ride with a petrol truck into Villamontes. Alternatively, there are camiones which take the more direct route to Villamontes following the foothills of the Cordillera Oriental. Mini-buses to Villamontes depart Monday to Friday at 10.30 am and leave Villamontes for the return trip at 4 pm. For tickets or further information, go to Galería Copacabana #15 in the Yacuiba shopping district.

For Argentine Veloz del Norte bus tickets from Pocitos to Salta, Jujuy, Tucumán, Buenos Aires or Santiago del Estero, go to the TVO Expreso Café in Yacuiba. The Veloz del Norte bus terminal is in Pocitos, Argentina, just over the border.

Train The railway station ticket window opens at 8 am on the day of departure, but queue up one or two hours earlier. For up-to-date information on rail schedules, phone (☎ 2308). If you have a 2nd-class ticket on one of the trains, you might consider riding in the bodegas to Santa Cruz. It's a bit uncomfortable riding with all the freight, but there are some interesting conversations to be had with the contrabandistas who transport their goods on the train. There's nothing

risky about it – smuggling is considered an honourable profession here.

There's a fast train to Santa Cruz via Villamontes leaving on Thursday at 4 pm, arriving at 5.40 am the following day. Only pullman seats are available and cost B50. Slower trains leave on Tuesday and Saturday at 5.25 pm and on Monday and Thursday at 3.10 pm, costing B32/22 for 1st/2nd class seats. The Monday and Thursday train pulls only 2nd-class carriages.

The ferrobus, which is sometimes booked solid by the military, leaves for Santa Cruz on Thursday, Saturday and Sunday at 9 pm, arriving at 6.10 am the following day. The fares in pullman/cspecial are B72/57.

POCITOS

The tiny village of Pocitos straddles the border of Bolivia and Argentina, five km south of Yacuiba. From the Argentine side, buses depart approximately every two hours to Tartagal and Embarcación where connections may be made to Salta, Jujuy, Orán and Buenos Aires. Remember that Bolivian time is one hour behind Argentine time. There are also rail connections between Pocitos, Argentina, and Buenos Aires. The Argentine bus terminals are just a couple of minutes' walk from immigration.

From the Bolivian side, taxis queue up along the main street awaiting passengers to Yacuiba. The fare is B1.50 per person regardless of the number of people. There's no consulate for either country.

PALOS BLANCOS

Little more than a few bars and scattered houses overlooking a beautiful river, Palos Blancos simply oozes character. It could easily pass for a Hollywood western movie set; standing on the main street, you can almost see Butch and Sundance storming into town in a cloud of billowing dust.

The charming and rustic church is a tumbledown, whitewashed mud building set in a colourful red and green landscape. An arch of cowbells outside is used to call the faithful to worship and the donation box is surrounded by wildflowers and prayer requests.

Places to Stay & Eat

There's no formal accommodation, but campsites abound along the river. Minimal food services are available at stores and bars opposite the church.

Getting There & Away

All transport between Villamontes, Yacuiba, and Tarija must pass through Palos Blancos, so finding a ride in or out should be no problem during the dry season (from March to October).

VILLAMONTES

Villamontes, Bolivia's outpost in the true Chaco, prides itself on being the hottest place in the country – not hard to believe when the mercury rises above the 40° mark and a hot dry wind coats everything with a thick layer of red dust. It is also, as is the entire Chaco, famous for its wildlife, particularly the small buzzing varieties – ravenous flies and mosquitoes thrive.

History

During Inca times, tribes of Guaraníes immigrated to this area from what is now Paraguay and their descendants now comprise most of the town's indigenous population.

This small and lonely outpost continued unnoticed until it emerged as a strategic Bolivian army stronghold during the Chaco War. The Paraguayans considered Villamontes their key to undisputed victory.

In the Battle of Villamontes in 1934, the Bolivian army enjoyed its most significant victory of the war under the command of General Bernardino Bilbao Rioja and Major Germán Busch. The momentum gained in that battle allowed them to recapture portions of the eastern Chaco and some of the Santa Cruz oil fields previously lost to Paraguay.

Cañón de Pilcomayo

The beautiful Pilcomayo Gorge, south of

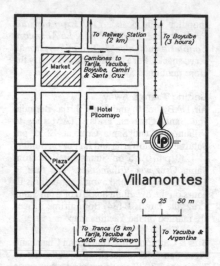

To Railway Station (2 km)

To Boyuibe (3 hours)

Camiones to Tarija, Yacuiba, Boyuibe, Camiri & Santa Cruz

Market

■ Hotel Pilcomayo

Plaza

Villamontes

0   25   50 m

To Tranca (5 km)
Tarija, Yacuiba &
Cañón de Pilcomayo

To Yacuiba &
Argentina

Villamontes, is popular with anglers. At El Chorro Grande waterfall on the Río Pilcomayo, the fish are prevented from swimming further upstream and surubí, sábalo, and dorado are abundant and easily caught. The dorado, with an odd hinge at the front of its jawbone allowing the mouth to open wider horizontally, is particularly interesting. There are great views from the restaurants along the Tarija road seven to 10 km from town. There you can sample local fish dishes for about B10.

To get there, take any Tarija bound bus or petrol truck, or go by taxi to the tranca and hitch or walk from there. Where the road forks, take a right.

Places to Stay

The very basic *Hotel Pilcomayo* has no sign, so ask for the right doorway; rooms cost B9 per person. Alternatively, there's the slightly more expensive *Residencial Raldes* (☎ 2545) near the rail line east of the main plaza. It's not too clean but the grounds are nice and flowery. Rooms costs B18 per person.

The *Hotel El Rancho* opposite the railway station two km north of town is nicer but more expensive.

Getting There & Away

Air TAM flies from La Paz, Tarija and Yacuiba to Villamontes on Saturday. On Sunday, it flies from Santa Cruz and continues on to Yacuiba, Tarija and La Paz at 12.40 pm.

Bus & Camión Camiones going to Tarija, Yacuiba, Boyuibe, Palos Blancos, Camiri and Santa Cruz queue up along the strip marked 'Parada de Camiones' at the north end of the market. If you're heading toward Yacuiba it's worth taking a taxi to the tranca five km south of town and hitching from there.

Train Villamontes lies two hours by rail north of Yacuiba and 10 hours south of Santa Cruz. The railway station, two km north of town, is accessible by taxi for B1.50 per person. There's a ferrobus from Santa Cruz on Thursday, Saturday and Sunday at 8 am and from Yacuiba back to Santa Cruz on the same days at 9 pm. For more information on trains, see Getting There & Away under Yacuiba and Santa Cruz.

BOYUIBE

Scarcely large enough to be called a town, Boyuibe sits on the fringes of the Chaco along the rail line three hours north of Villamontes and seven hours south of Santa Cruz. It serves mainly as a point of transit. There are roads south to Villamontes, west to Camiri and east to Paraguay.

Places to Stay

There are two hotels: the *Hotel Chaqueño* and the *Hotel Guadalquivir*. Either one will provide a basic bed to crash in, but due to scarcity of accommodation and captive audiences, they cost B15 per person.

Getting There & Away

Camiones to Camiri, Villamontes and Yacuiba wait in front of the Tránsito office along the main street. All trains between Santa Cruz and Yacuiba stop in Boyuibe. For information on departure times, see Getting There & Away for Santa Cruz and Yacuiba.

To Paraguay If you're looking for transport into northern Paraguay, plan on spending at least a day or two simmering in Boyuibe then a couple more days enduring repeated immigration, customs, police and military checkpoints before you can settle back and relax in Paraguay.

Camiones leave for Mariscal Estigarribia, the first major town inside Paraguay, more or less once a week during the dry season, but there's no set schedule. Petrol trucks no longer do the run because the fuel costs are now equal in Bolivia and Paraguay, making the trip unprofitable. Passengers from Boyuibe to Mariscal Estigarribia can expect to pay about B75 per person for the 30-hour (under optimum conditions) trip. During the wet season, the otherwise rough and sandy road turns to quicksand and slimy mud, and becomes impassable.

If you have access to a hardy 4WD vehicle, this trip may be attempted independently, but serious and thorough preparations are necessary. There are no spares or fuel available until well into Paraguay, road conditions change with each rainfall, and traffic is intermittent at best. A supply of fuel, water, food, spare parts, tyres and so on is essential.

Before setting out, pick up an exit stamp, which may or may not be free, from the customs office, then proceed to the army post south of town for a second stamp. It's 137 km from Boyuibe to the dusty border post at Fortín Villazón where you'll receive yet another exit stamp.

The Paraguayan entry post is several km further on at Irindagüe but you pick up stamps in the village of Fortín Garay about 15 km further along. Between there and Mariscal Estigarribia, there are a couple more sporadic checkpoints, and upon reaching Mariscal Estigarribia, you'll be subjected to a military inspection.

CAMIRI

On the edge of the Chaco with a favourable climate, Camiri has grown phenomenally in recent years due to lucrative employment opportunities with YPFB, known affectionately as just 'Yacimientos'. Important for the production of petroleum and natural gas, Camiri bills itself as the Capital Petrolífero de Bolivia.

History

In 1955, two pipelines were constructed to carry natural gas and petroleum to Yacuiba on the Argentine frontier. The following year, a 1.5 million dollar natural gas reinjection plant was built by YPFB atop Cerro Sararenda to recover liquid petroleum gas by injecting natural gas into oil-bearing formations. Another plant to process this liquid petroleum gas was built and began functioning in 1968, and a refrigeration and dehydration plant to recover liquid petroleum was put into operation at nearby Taquiparenda in 1983. Decreased production closed it, however, after only three years in operation. Camiri has since experienced ups and downs in the industry but it remains the centre of Bolivia's fossil fuel production.

Information

Money Hotel Ortuño will exchange travellers' cheques at a good rate and the small shop beside it changes cash US dollars.

Dangers & Annoyances Camiri is a military garrison town and visitors staying overnight must register with immigration upon arrival, then report to the military police for a permit. For your trouble, you waste half a page in your passport and suffer sweaty palms while a lineup of military and police officers suspiciously question your motives. The procedures cost B1 each so don't let them talk you out of further 'donations' to their cause. Those with private vehicles must repeat the whole tiresome process for a B10 permit to proceed. Watch closely during any luggage searches; there have been reports of drug plants.

Despite its reputation as an energy town, Camiri lacks sufficient electricity to fulfil its growing demands, so each neighbourhood goes without electricity for several hours a day. The water that oozes from Camiri's taps is filthy and should be avoided.

Things to See & Do

There's not an overwhelming number of things to do in Camiri but the town is proud of its YPFB plant. Although there's no formal tour, if you'd like a look around, turn up at about 8 am and try to appear interested in oil.

Alternatively, climb up to the Christ statue behind the market for a nice view over the town and surrounding hills.

Just north of Camiri about 200 metres off the Sucre road is a wedge-shaped sports centre with racquetball courts. It's popular with locals and military personnel.

Places to Stay

The friendly and recommended *Hotel Ortuño* on Calle Comercio charges B18 per person for rooms without bath. Several of the Ortuño children have attended school in the USA and some English is spoken. The fairly clean *Gran Hotel Londres* (☎ 2326) at Avenida Busch 6 costs B15 per person without bath and B18 with bath and hot water.

The *Residencial Premier* is exceptionally clean. For B27 per person they offer private baths and hot water whenever both water and electricity are available. Similarly priced new options include the *Residencial Las Melissas* (☎ 2614) at the corner of Calle Capitan Manchego and Avenida Busch and the *Residencial Marieta* (☎ 2254), owned by Ana and Federico Forfori, at Avenida Petrolero 15.

Places to Eat

Camiri has only a couple of restaurants. *Pollo Rico* on the plaza serves roast chicken in the evening and *Restaurant Poji* on the corner of Calle Comercio and Avenida Busch does good set lunches of soup, salad, bread, rice and a main dish for B4.50. You can eat at the Hotel Ortuño for a similar price.

The best deals are found at the market on the corner of Avenida Bolivar and Calle Comercio. For breakfast, street vendors outside the market sell coffee, tea, chocolate, bread and delicious fruit and milk frappés.

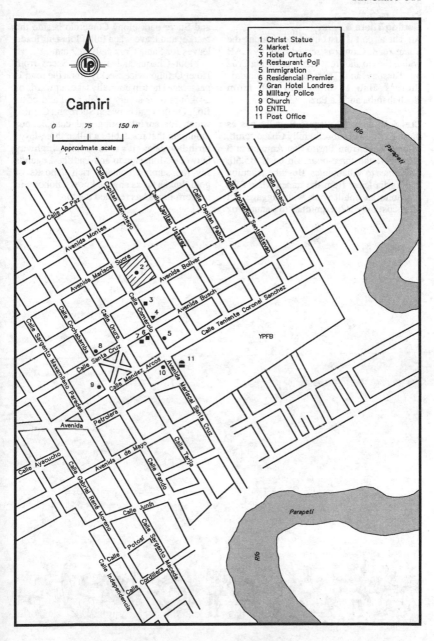

Camiri

0   75   150 m

Approximate scale

1 Christ Statue
2 Market
3 Hotel Ortuño
4 Restaurant Poji
5 Immigration
6 Residencial Premier
7 Gran Hotel Londres
8 Military Police
9 Church
10 ENTEL
11 Post Office

Getting There & Away

Air The airport is just outside town along the Sucre road. Camiri is served only by LAB which flies to and from Sucre and Santa Cruz on Tuesday and Thursday. On Thursday, there's also a service to and from Cochabamba and La Paz.

Bus & Camión The trip to Boyuibe passes through some beautifully hilly Chaco scrub. Micros leave from Barrio San Antonio at 3 pm daily; the three-hour trip costs B5.50. Camiones to Villamontes, Boyuibe, Yacuiba and Tarija leave from the tranca when full. It's quite an uphill walk with luggage but taxis cost only B2. Camiones to Santa Cruz and Sucre park along Comercio beside the market and leave when full. Flota Unificado leaves for Santa Cruz daily at 7 am.

Flota Chaqueña leaves for Sucre from Hotel Ortuño twice weekly when the road is passable. The trip normally takes upwards of 24 hours over a very rough road and costs B63. On the road between Sucre and Camiri, watch for an interesting and conspicuous mountain that resembles a fallen three-layer birthday cake; it's west of the highway between Monteagudo and Padilla. Legends say the summit contains rich deposits of gold, but as far as anyone knows, nobody in modern times has reached the top.

Contemporary Craft Design

Santa Cruz

Since 1950, Santa Cruz has mushroomed from a backwater cattle-producing town of 30,000 to its present position as Bolivia's second city, with over 800,000 people. Despite continuing to grow at a phenomenal rate, this cosmopolitan city retains traces of its dusty past, evident in its wide streets, frontier architecture and small-town atmosphere.

Santa Cruz today is a big city at the edge of a wilderness. Once an isolated agricultural outpost, it has developed into a hub of transportation and trade. It is connected by rail with Argentina and Brazil and by road with Cochabamba, the Chaco and Trinidad. It has an international airport with direct flights to Miami, but forest-dwelling sloths hang in the trees of the main plaza. The area serves as a centre of cocaine-smuggling, but is also Bolivia's primary source of rice, cotton, soybeans and other warm-weather crops.

In Santa Cruz you'll find people from all corners of the earth and many walks of life – Japanese businessmen, Platt-Deutsch-speaking Canadian Mennonites, Sikh agriculturalists, escaped Nazis, Arabs, foreign oil workers, drug traffickers, campesinos from highland Bolivia and environmental activists.

The disproportionate amount of money that flits around Santa Cruz is evident in the number of 12-bedroom homes, Toyota 4WDs, BMWs and a variety of other playthings which are not normally associated with Bolivia.

The climate is considered tropical, but because the city sits in the transition zone between the Amazon rainforest, the highlands and the dry Chaco plains, it enjoys more sun and less stifling temperatures than the Beni. During the winter, rainfall comes mainly in the form of 10-minute downpours, but a single summer deluge can last for days. Santa Cruz also experiences heavy winds that rarely subside. During the winter, cold surazo winds blow from the Argentine Pampa or Patagonia and bring surprisingly chilly temperatures.

History

Santa Cruz de la Sierra was founded in 1561 by Ñuflo de Chaves, a Spaniard who hailed from what is now Paraguay. The town originally lay 220 km east of its current location, but around the end of the 16th century, it proved too vulnerable to attack by local tribes and was moved to its present position, 50 km east of the Cordillera Oriental foothills.

Santa Cruz was founded to supply the rest of the colony with tropical and subtropical agricultural products such as rice, cotton, sugar and fruit. The prosperity lasted until the late 1800s, when transportation routes were opened up between La Paz and the Peruvian coast. Imported goods then became cheaper than those produced in Santa Cruz and hauled over mule trails.

In 1954 the highway was completed, linking Santa Cruz with other major centres, and the city sprung back from the economic lull imposed by its remoteness. The completion of the railway line to Brazil in the mid-1950s opened trade routes to the east and Santa Cruz was suddenly in a position to thrive. Tropical agriculture prospered and the city entered a flurry of growth that would continue unabated to the present day.

Not surprisingly, the area's agricultural potential has attracted not only optimistic settlers from the highlands, but also a rice-growing Okinawan colony, a settlement of Italians, Indian Sikhs and thousands of Mennonites fleeing governmental problems in their former colony in Belize.

Orientation

The city is roughly oval in shape and is laid out in *anillos* or rings. Most commercial enterprises, hotels and restaurants lie within the first ring, which has its focus at the main plaza. The railway station lies within the

Santa Cruz

0   200   400 m

To University
(500 m)

To Río Piray &
Jardín Botánico

To Cochabamba-bound camiones

To Zoo & Viru–Viru Airport

To TAM Office &
El Trompillo Airport

second anillo but is still less than a half-hour walk from the centre. The second, third and fourth anillos are comprised primarily of residential and industrial areas. With the exception of the zoo, the Río Piray and a couple of markets, they contain little of interest to visitors.

Information

Tourist Office The new tourist office (☎ 348644) is upstairs in the immigration building at Avenida Irala 563; you'll have to present your documents to enter the building. The staff are quite helpful with specific

queries and they distribute a small assortment of informative brochures. The office is open from 8.30 am to 1.30 pm, Monday to Friday.

Money Currency exchange is possible at Sudamer, Alemán and Mendicambio, all positioned around the main plaza, or at one of the several exchange houses on Calle Libertad. The most straightforward option seems to be Mendicambio at Plaza 24 de Septiembre 30. All exchange houses charge 3% commission on travellers' cheques. We've had reports of less than scrupulous

■ PLACES TO STAY

6	Alojamiento Santa Bárbara
7	Alojamiento Oriente
8	Hotel Bibosi
9	Hotel Amazonas
13	Hotel Copacabana
19	Residencial Bolivar
26	Hotel Italia
33	Residencial Monte Carlos
34	Alojamiento Lemoine
37	Alojamiento 15 de Octubre
39	Residencial Grigotá

▼ PLACES TO EAT

5	Crêperie El Boliche
12	El Jacuú 85
14	Churros Amadeo
15	El Sirari & Bonanza
18	La Pascana
27	Bar El Tapekua
31	California Donuts
32	The Jungle Restaurant
35	La Bella Napoli

OTHER

1	Museo del Carnaval
2	Parque El Arenal
3	Mercado Los Pozos
4	Buses to Cotoca & Puerto Pailas
10	Banco de Santa Cruz
11	Post Office
16	Plaza 24 de Septiembre
17	Cambios Alemán & Mendicambio
20	Bus Stop for Zoo
21	Lavandería
22	Basílica Menor de San Lorenzo & Museo de la Catedral
23	Casa de la Cultura/Museo de Arte
24	Mercado Siete Calles
25	Magri Turismo (American Express)
28	Uimpex Travel
29	LAB
30	ENTEL
36	Bus Terminal
38	Mercado La Ramada
40	Tourist Office & Immigration
41	Amazonas Adventure Tours
42	Railway Station

dealings by Cambios Alemán, including increasing the 3% commission on travellers' cheques to 10% and refusing to provide a detailed receipt. Keep on your guard!

If you're changing American Express travellers' cheques, you must have them certified at the American Express office (see under Travel Agencies in this section) before presenting them to the casas de cambio. Quick and convenient VISA cash advances are available at the Banco de Santa Cruz at Calle Junín 154 near the main plaza.

Street changers operate along Avenida Cañoto between Ayacucho and Calle Junín; at the intersection of avenidas Cañoto and Irala near the bus terminal; and occasionally around the main plaza.

Post & Telecommunications The post office is half a block from the main plaza on Calle Junín. Beware of overcharging for postal services. Employees have been known to pocket any extra cash they can take in.

The ENTEL office is on Warnes between Calle René Moreno and Chuquisaca. You can send an overseas telegram for B1 per word, including those words which comprise the address. The public fax number in Santa Cruz is (591-3) 350546.

Foreign Consulates Some of the more useful consular addresses in Santa Cruz include:

Argentina
  Plaza 24 de Septiembre, North, Banco de la Nación, Calle Junín 22 (☎ 324153)
Brazil
  Avenida Busch 330, 2nd Anillo (☎ 344400)
Chile
  Calle Elvira de Mendoza 275, 3rd Anillo, northwest (☎ 331043)
Germany
  Cnr El Trompillo & Chaco (☎ 344569)
Paraguay
  Barrio Equipetrol, Avenida San Martín 14 (☎ 325088)
Peru
  Calle Libertad 349 (☎ 330482)

USA
Cnr Calle Ballivián & Chuquisaca, Edificio Oriente (☎ 330725)

Immigration For visa and length of stay extensions go to the immigration office at Avenida Irala 563 between 8.30 am and 1.30 pm, Monday to Friday.

Travel Agencies The American Express representative in Santa Cruz is Magri Turismo Limitada (☎ 345663, fax (591-3) 366309) at Calle Ingavi 14. Before changing American Express travellers' cheques at the casas de cambio, you must first have them certified at this office. They will receive post for American Express customers at Casilla 4438, Santa Cruz.

If you're interested in visiting the wilderness camp at Perseverancia in the pristine Reserva de Vida Salvaje Ríos Blanco Y Negro, contact Amazonas Adventure Tours (☎ 324099, fax 337587) at their office on Calle Andrés Manso (René Moreno) just south of Avenida Irala.

Another useful travel agency is friendly Uimpex Travel (☎ 330785) at Calle René Moreno 226. They organise tours of the Jesuit missions, the Dunas de Palmar, Bermejo and Los Espejillos, and Samaipata. They are also trying to set up a programme for the Parque Nacional Noel Kempff Mercado. Speak to Señora Aida McKenney.

Bookshops If you're desperate for reading material, a few English-language books are sold at the bookshop on Calle René Moreno opposite the cathedral. This shop is, however, quite expensive. Books on ecology, alternative lifestyles and natural health are available at La Alternativa, Cuéllar 175.

Laundry There's an unnamed *lavandería* at Calle Bolivar 490, which offers one-day service. If the door is closed, knock and they'll let you drop off clothes. Washing, drying and ironing costs B3 per kg. There's another laundrette at Calle Abaroa 65.

Camping Equipment You'll find limited camping equipment at La Jara Caza y Pesca, Calle Bolivar 458.

Medical Services The Clínica Japonesa (☎ 352030), on the 3rd Anillo, lado este (east side), is recommended for good, inexpensive medical treatment.

Some travellers have had problems with the US-affiliated Clínica Foianini (☎ 342211) at Avenida Irala 468. It seems they maximise the bill by running tests which aren't required and keeping patients longer than necessary.

Dangers & Annoyances When you're walking around Santa Cruz, carry your passport at all times. If you're caught in the street without documents you'll be required to pay the usual 'fine' of about B180 and will waste several hours at the police station while relevant paperwork is shuffled.

Beware also of bogus immigration officials, especially at the railway station; if someone asks to see your passport, check their credentials. If they want to see your money, insist that formalities be completed at either the police station or immigration offices, both of which are marked on the map. Don't get into a taxi and don't let them lead you astray!

If you're reporting a robbery to the police for insurance or travellers' cheque refund purposes, ascertain the price in advance. Travellers have been charged up to B40 to file an official *denuncio*.

Basílica Menor de San Lorenzo & Museo de la Catedral

Although the original cathedral on Plaza 24 de Septiembre was founded in 1605, the present structure dates back to 1845, and wasn't consecrated until 1915. The artistic woodwork on the ceiling and silver plating around the altar are worth a look.

The cathedral museum is open Tuesday and Thursday from 8.30 am to noon and 2.30 to 6 pm. Admission is B3. Its large collection of religious icons and artefacts includes very little typical art. Most interesting are the numerous gold and silver relics from the Jesuit Guarayos missions north-east of Santa Cruz. There's also a collection of religious vestments and medallions, as well as one of the world's smallest books, a thumbnail-sized volume containing the Lord's Prayer in several languages.

Parque El Arenal

Parque El Arenal, with its pleasant lagoon and landscaping, is a good spot for picnicking or just relaxing under the trees. On an island in the centre of the lagoon is a raised-relief mural with a collage of historical and modern-day aspects of Santa Cruz by renowned Bolivian artist, Lorgio Vaca.

Museo del Carnaval

The new Carnival Museum at Calle 21 de Mayo 581 near the corner of Rafael Peña features Diablada costumes and other festive paraphernalia. It's open Tuesday to Sunday from 9.30 am to 12.30 pm and from 3.30 to 7.30 pm. The museum sponsors a folkloric show on Friday and Saturday from 9 pm to midnight.

Casa de la Cultura\Museo de Arte

The Casa de la Cultura Raúl Otero Reiche has recently relocated from the main plaza to Calle Sucre near the corner of Quijarro. The highlight is the art museum which includes the works of contemporary Bolivian artists such as Lorgio Vaca, Herminio Pedraza and Tito Kurasotto. Originality runs high and it's a breath of fresh air for anyone overdosed on the blood and flagellation frequently evident in other Bolivian museums. It's open daily from 8.30 to noon and 2.30 to 6 pm; admission is free. The museum sponsors frequent live music performances in the evening for an admission charge of B3 per person.

Museo de la Historia Natural

The new natural history museum is on the René Moreno university campus; the main drawcard is an immense collection of insects. If you're interested, ask to speak with Paolo Bettella who is the curator and local bug expert. Admission is free.

Zoo

The Santa Cruz zoo is one of the few in South America worth visiting. The collection is limited to animals indigenous to South America, and all appear to be humanely treated and well fed. The woolly llamas, however, do seem a bit overdressed and irritable in the tropical climate.

You'll also see endangered and exotic species such as tapirs, pumas, jaguars and spectacled bears. Sloths, which are too slow and lazy to escape successfully, are not confined to cages, and hang around in the trees, occasionally mustering enough energy for a slow crawl around the grounds.

To get to the zoo, take micro 11 north from the stop near the corner of calles La Paz and Sucre, or a taxi, which costs B5. Admission is B3.50.

Río Piray

The Jardín Botánico (Botanical Garden) was destroyed in a flood several years ago and plans to renovate it developed into the creation of a park requiring less maintenance. The river banks are good for a picnic, especially on the weekend when local families make an outing of it, and there are stalls and a basic teahouse selling food.

To get there, take micro 6 or 9 along Avenida Cañoto near the long-distance bus terminal and get off at the western end of avenidas Coronado and Roca.

Sports

If you're up for racquetball or swimming, there are several sports complexes in town. The least expensive, however, is at Villa Rosita, five km from the centre. To get there, take micro 50 or 17 along Avenida Grigota.

Places to Stay – bottom end

There isn't any one place that stands out overwhelmingly as *the* travellers' hotel in Santa Cruz, but several are marginally popular. The current favourite seems to be the *Residencial Bolivar* (☎ 342500) at Calle Sucre 131. It's a bit overpriced for what you get, but it's clean, bright and offers good hot showers. Singles/doubles without bath cost

B18/27. Things can get a little noisy if you're in a room near the reception area.

In a quiet neighbourhood near the long-distance bus terminal and the Mercado La Ramada is the *Residencial Monte Carlos* (☎ 347776) at Ghiriguanos 190. Rooms cost B10 per person without bath or B15 with bath. Room 10 is most amazing.

Alojamiento Santa Bárbara (☎ 321817) at Calle Santa Bárbara 151 is simple but clean. Rooms cost B15/20 for a single/double without bath. The similarly priced *Alojamiento 24 de Septiembre* (☎ 321992) at Calle Santa Bárbara 79, is a bit dirty and not particularly friendly but it seems popular with young Bolivians.

The *Hotel Copacabana* (☎ 321845) at Junín 217 is very good value. It's ultra clean and costs only B16/29 for a single/double without bath or B29/41 with private bath. It's a large place and has hot water, a TV lounge and an attached restaurant.

Alojamiento Oriente (☎ 321976) at Calle Junín 364 is marginally clean and the rooms surround a nice, quiet green courtyard. Singles/doubles without bath cost B15/20. Rooms with bath cost B20/30 and include electric showers.

If you don't feel like walking far on arrival at the bus terminal or you're just passing through the city, you can select from several cheap places near the bus terminal. The best among them seems to be the *Residencial Grigotá* at the corner of Avenida Grigotá and Calle Muchurí, two blocks from the terminal. It has fairly clean rooms at B10 per person and has hot water in one of the communal baths. The proprietors are friendly.

Another nearby option is *Alojamiento 15 de Octubre* at Calle Guaraní 33. It costs the same as the Grigotá but is more basic and lacks hot water. Another place in the bus terminal area is the *Alojamiento Lemoine* (☎ 347610) at Calle Lemoine 469. It's in the same class and price range as the Grigotá and sometimes has hot water.

There are lots of similarly inexpensive residenciales, alojamientos and posadas in the back streets around the Mercado Los Pozos, midway between the city centre and the long-distance bus terminal. Some are gloomy and grotty, so look at several rooms before deciding.

Places to Stay – middle

Hotel Italia (☎ 323119) at Calle René Moreno 167 is both clean and central, offering fans, private phones, air-conditioning and hot showers for B30 per person or B55 for a double bed.

The very centrally located *Hotel Bibosi* (☎ 348548, fax (591-3) 348887) at Calle Junín 218 is extremely friendly and has a cheery proprietor, clean, spacious rooms, and a great view from the roof. Rooms with fans, telephones and private baths cost B30/50 for a single/double, including breakfast.

Beside the Bibosi at Calle Junín 214 is *Hotel Amazonas* (☎ 334583). Single/double rooms with TV and private bath cost B30/55.

Places to Stay – top end

The five-star *Hotel Los Tajibos* (☎ 330022, fax (591-3) 333915) is Santa Cruz's most upmarket hotel. With a nightclub, fountains, swimming pools, racquetball courts, a massage parlour and tropical gardens, it's a very appealing option. The major drawback is its location out on Avenida San Martín in Barrio Equipetrol (third anillo), a good distance from the centre.

Slightly less opulent is the *Hotel La Quinta* (☎ 342244) in the Urbarí Perimetral Sur. It has several swimming pools and a deluxe restaurant, but again, it's a taxi ride from the centre.

Places to Eat

When it comes to matters culinary, cosmopolitan Santa Cruz will not disappoint. There are quite a few options and the food is generally of high quality, but at the better places, prices are high.

For an inexpensive breakfast, go to the mercados La Ramada, Siete Calles or Los Pozos for *jugo de papaya*, *guineo* or *naranja con leche* – papaya, banana or orange juice with milk, whipped in a blender and served cold for B1.50. It's hard to tear yourself away after only one glass! The markets also serve meals during the day, but you may be put off by the heat. Mercado Los Pozos is good for a variety of unusual tropical fruits. Try some of the more exotic ones like guaypurú and ambaiba.

If you're interested in roast chicken, churrasco, chips and fried bananas, take a stroll down Pollo Alley (aka Avenida Cañoto) where there are dozens of nearly identical grill restaurants. *Restaurante 30 de Marzo* is recommended.

Unfortunately, Gandhi International and the London Grill, two long-time favourites with travellers, no longer exist. They have changed owners, names, décor and menus. What was the Gandhi, on Calle Junín just off the plaza, is now *El Sirari*, a good place for a B5 set lunch but not much else. The former London Grill at Calle Junín 85 is now *El Jacuú 85* (☎ 323512). Its interior décor has gone from London pub to Rick's Café Americain. They serve good lunches and will prepare Mexican food for dinner if you ring in the afternoon and order it.

For surubí fans, *Churros Amadeo* at Calle 21 de Mayo 86 is unsurpassed. Their prices are reasonable and the food is excellent. Highly recommended are *surubí al ajo*, *ceviche de surubí*, *pique a lo macho* and *majadito* – rice, meat, potatoes, peas and spices covered with an egg and served with plantain. For dessert *pai de limón* (lemon meringue pie) is a must.

Excellent vegetarian meals are available at *Su Salud*, Quijarro 375 near the market. It's open Sunday to Friday for breakfast, lunch and dinner. There's also a health shop, *La Alternativa* at Cuéllar 175, where you can pick up organically grown produce, juices, bread, yoghurt, natural medicines, candles, books and cassette tapes, as well as advice on Bolivia's ecology movement and natural alternative lifestyles.

The popular *La Pascana* on the main plaza is worthwhile if you can spring for the cost. A four course lunch special is B9, but if you're really feeling wealthy, try the *surubí a la thermidor* for B14. The equally popular *El Dorado* at the opposite corner of the plaza

offers good lunch specials for only B4. Yet another plaza lunch option is the quiet *Restaurante Plaza* at Calle Libertad 116 which is especially good for soup and set lunches for B4.50.

La Bella Napoli in a rustic old barn at Calle Independencia 635, six blocks south of the main plaza, offers excellent spaghetti, lasagna, ravioli and other Italian dishes, which are served on chunky hardwood tables. Prices are reasonable, but it's a dark walk back to the centre at night.

Another great dinner choice is *Crêperie El Boliche*, which has a rustic, two-level dining area and interesting décor. It's at Calle Beni 222 near the Air France office. If your budget will stretch this far, you'll find the food here to be one of the highlights of a visit to Santa Cruz. You can choose from crêpe dishes, salads, ice-cream confections, cakes and cocktails for around B35 per person.

A reasonable attempt at Mexican food is available at *The Jungle Restaurant*, Calle Cordillera 346. It's open Tuesday to Sunday from 11 am to 2 pm and 6.30 to 11.30 pm. Authentic Chinese meals may be had at *El Pato Pekin* on Plaza 24 de Septiembre.

The cosy Swiss/Bolivian-owned *Bar El Tapekua* (☎ 343390) at the corner of calles Ballivián and La Paz serves what can only be described as pub meals. The musician owner appreciates good music and on Thursday, Friday and Saturday nights, there are live performances for a B4 cover charge. Phone in advance to find out what's on.

For ice cream and sundaes, locals recommend *Helados Casimba* at the corner of Figueroa and Calle René Moreno, and *Kivon* at Ayacucho 267. At Calle Independencia 481, *California Donuts* serves coffee, burgers and sticky North American doughnuts.

Entertainment

Santa Cruz discos, popular with the more affluent younger folk, are known throughout Bolivia as being some of the country's most liberal. The best are a taxi ride from the central area and entry is generally around B8. If you want to conserve your funds, steer clear of the bar; beer is rarely less than B3.50 and spirits cost much more. Discos normally open at 9 pm and don't start warming up until 11 pm, then continue until 3 am. Among the best known are Champágne on Avenida Ejército Nacional near de Garay, Swing, five km away on the highway to Samaipata, and Fizz, near the zoo in the third anillo.

If you're in Santa Cruz for Carnival, you may want to check out the Mau-Mau in the auditorium at the corner of Ibañez and Calle 21 de Mayo. This annual event, which includes dancing, music shows and the coronation of the Carnival queen, attracts over 10,000 spectators and participants.

Pleasant drinking establishments include the Tijuana Saloon at Velarde 230 and Bar El Tapekua at the corner of calles Ballivián and La Paz. See under Places to Eat for further details.

As you'd expect, Santa Cruz has quite a few cinemas and occasionally, one of them will screen a good foreign film. For schedules, see the daily papers *El Deber* and *El Mundo*.

Things to Buy

There are artesanía shops scattered around town, where you can buy beautiful Western-style clothing made of llama and alpaca wool. Mercado Los Pozos is good for inexpensive basketry, but if you're after genuine indigenous articles, the Altiplano is a better place to look.

Woodcarvings made from the tropical hardwoods, *morado* and *guayacán*, are unique to the Santa Cruz area. They look nice, but they're not cheap. Although morado is less expensive than guayacán, you'll still pay at least B75 for a nice piece of work. Relief carvings on *tari* nuts are also interesting and make easily transportable souvenirs.

Local Indians make beautiful macramé *llicas*, bags of root fibres similar in both use and design to the New Guinea *bilum* bags. Santa Cruz leatherwork is expert, but unfortunately most items are adorned with kitsch designs and slogans. There are also some lovely ceramic pieces for sale, but they're difficult to transport.

Getting There & Away

Air Only TAM still leaves from the old El Trompillo Airport, 10 blocks south of the main plaza. The new Santa Cruz International Airport is at Viru-Viru, 15 km north of town, half an hour by micro from the main bus terminal and slightly less by taxi. The LAB office (☎ 344896) is at the corner of Warnes and Chuquisaca. On Monday, TAM sells tickets for the entire week from their office (☎ 342102) at El Trompillo Airport.

LAB has one to three daily flights to and from La Paz, Cochabamba and Sucre and serves most other Bolivian cities at least several times weekly. Santa Cruz has also become a hub for LAB service between Bolivia and Panamá, the USA, Brazil and Argentina, including several flights weekly to and from São Paulo, Belo Horizonte, Buenos Aires and Salta. At least once daily LAB flies between Santa Cruz and Miami (B1950 one way) with various routings via Manaus (Brazil), Caracas (Venezuela) and Panamá City (Panamá). These flights have gained a reputation for drug trafficking, so if you're going from Santa Cruz to Miami, prepare for a thorough shakedown at Miami Airport.

Lineas Aereas Paraguayas (LAP) flies directly to Asunción; VARIG has flights to Rio de Janeiro and São Paulo; and Aereolineas Argentinas flies to Buenos Aires. Via La Paz, Santa Cruz is served by LAB flights to and from Lima (Peru) and Arica and Santiago (Chile).

LAB flies to Puerto Suárez on Bolivia's eastern frontier opposite Corumbá (Brazil) on Monday, Wednesday and Saturday. The fare is B253 each way. TAM flies to Puerto Suárez for a slightly cheaper fare on Tuesday and Friday, and from Puerto Suárez to Santa Cruz on Tuesday and Saturday. These flights avoid the fuss of travelling by train to Brazil, but they normally book up well in advance, so make reservations and purchase your ticket as far ahead as possible. Alternatively, you can use the backdoor approach to Brazil

Top: Ski Hut - Chacaltaya (RS)
Bottom: Beni home - near Río Tuichi (DS)

Top: Dusty street - Riberalta (RS)
Bottom Left: Trekking through rainforest - Río Tuichi (RS)
Bottom Right: Río Beni - Riberalta (RS)

by taking TAM's flight on Saturday to San Matías and crossing from there to Cáceres (Brazil) where you'll find connections to Cuiabá and the rest of Brazil.

It's also possible to fly with LAB to or from San Ignacio de Velasco in the Jesuit missions area on Monday, Wednesday and Friday for B110.

Bus Most of the flotas represented in the long-distance bus terminal use the new Chapare road to Cochabamba, from where they connect with La Paz, Oruro, Sucre, Potosí and Tarija services. All charge B25 and nearly all depart in the evening between 5 and 7 pm. Jumbo Bus Bolivar is recommended, especially if you're making connections to La Paz; Nobleza also has a good service. A couple of flotas have now begun a morning service to Cochabamba and they're worth taking for the stunning scenery.

If you're going to Sucre and wish to avoid the detour to Cochabamba, Flota Unificado has a service at 5 pm on Monday, Wednesday and Saturday for B40. From Sucre, the bus continues to Potosí. Flota Trans-Copacabana goes directly to Sucre on Wednesday, Friday and Saturday at 5 pm.

There are several evening departures to Trinidad, a journey of about 12 hours under optimum conditions. Although the road is theoretically open year-round, in the rainy season it can become problematic. Flota Trans-Copacabana departs at 6.30 pm.

The Trans-Chaco Boreal bus goes to Yacuiba at 5.30 pm daily, arriving in Camiri at 4 am and in Yacuiba at 8.30 pm. The fare to Camiri is B30, to Yacuiba, B60. Veloz del Sur leaves for Camiri daily at 6 pm. For the two-hour trip to Samaipata, Transportes Vallegrande leaves more or less hourly between 1 and 5 pm daily and costs B6. The buses then continue to either Vallegrande or Mairana.

If there's sufficient interest, Flota Chiquitana and Flota Trans-Oriente depart on Monday, Wednesday and Friday at 7 am and Saturday at 4 pm to San Ignacio de Velasco in the Jesuit missions. From there, they continue to San José de Chiquitos. It's a long, rough and slow trip, made slower if the weather is unfavourable – count on between 28 and 30 hours if it is not raining. The fare is B30 to San Ignacio and B50 to San José de Chiquitos.

Smaller micros and colectivos to the airport, Montero, Mairana, Samaipata, Yapacaní and other smaller communities within Santa Cruz Department also depart regularly from the main terminal.

For a camión to Cochabamba, go to Avenida Grigotá near the third anillo; most cargo traffic still uses the old road. Alternatively, take micro 17 to the tranca 12 km west of town where they all must stop. You'll pay between B11 and B18 for the approximately 16-hour trip. Carry warm clothing!

Train The railway station in Santa Cruz is in the second anillo south-east of the centre. Tickets are hard to come by, especially on the Quijarro run. At the time of writing, it was possible to reserve only ferrobus tickets the day prior to departure. Train tickets could be purchased only on the day of departure.

Whatever anyone tells you about the ticket window at the station, it will not open prior to 8 am and probably won't see any action until much later. If you want a chance at a reserved seat ticket, join the queue in the wee hours of the morning. There's a sign on the wall prohibiting overnight occupation of the railway station and we've had letters from foreigners who've been 'fined' up to US$100 for sleeping overnight in the queue, despite the fact that hundreds of locals were doing the same thing. Once you've joined the queue, be prepared to fight for your place; latecomers show up at the last minute and shove their way to the front. When we were there, the police and military were called in to restore order.

During times of high demand, tickets probably aren't worth the hassle required to secure them. Carriages become so crowded with people and luggage, there's no room to sit, anyway. As an alternative, you may want to stake out a place in the bodegas and purchase a 2nd-class ticket from the acrobatic conductor (for 20% above the ticket window price) when he comes by.

There are plenty of plain-clothes police at the station, so keep your passport handy. For the Quijarro run, they sometimes employ the dirty trick of checking your documents the moment before the train is set to leave. Hoping for a bribe, they'll prevent you from boarding if you don't have an exit stamp from the immigration office in town. This is not necessary; the stamp is picked up at Quijarro. React politely but firmly. If you're worried, get the stamp at immigration beforehand (see Immigration in the Information section earlier in this chapter) or perhaps explain to the officer that you're only visiting Quijarro and have no intention of crossing into Brazil.

To/From Quijarro The rail line between Santa Cruz and Quijarro is known as the Death Train. The journey is beautiful, passing through lush jungle, Chaco scrub and oddly shaped mountains to the steamy, sticky Pantanal area near the frontier. The many cattle ranches, internationally donated soybean elevators, agricultural projects, logging concerns and Mennonite colonies along the railway are all indicators of the current thrust into development of the long-neglected Bolivian Oriente.

Despite all the economic changes and growth in the area, there is still a diverse and abundant supply of wildlife and vegetation. Colourful flowers, birds and butterflies thrive in the warm, moist conditions, and larger species, though rarely seen, still exist in limited numbers. Be sure to have plenty of mosquito repellent on hand, since there are often long and unexplained stops in low-lying, swampy areas. Anticipate delays.

Four classes of service are available – bracha, pullman, 1st and 2nd, but it is sometimes difficult to distinguish between these last two. There's a distinctly bovine feel to this train. The boxcars have their drawbacks but they're still more comfortable than the overcrowded coaches! If you do ride inside, chain your luggage to the racks, especially at night.

Timetables along this route are theoretical at best and more often than not pure fantasy and fabrication, so don't rely on the following descriptions for more than a rough idea:

On Tuesday, Thursday and Saturday, the ferrobus leaves at 6 pm and arrives in Quijarro at 6 am the following day. The fare is B81/65 in pullman/especial. It returns to Santa Cruz from Quijarro at 9 am on Wednesday, Friday and Sunday.

On Monday and Friday at 2.30 pm eastbound and Tuesday and Saturday at 3.30 pm westbound, there's the optimistically named *tren bala* (bullet train) which costs B59 in pullman. It also carries the bracha carriage, a locked, air-conditioned car with videos and marginal food service. The fare is B145 and seats may be booked through Santa Cruz travel agencies. The tren rápido runs on Wednesday and Sunday at 1.30 pm and the tren mixto, which has no delusions about its velocity, departs at 10.30 am on Tuesday and Friday. It pulls only 2nd-class carriages.

For further information, see under Quijarro in the Eastern Lowlands chapter.

To/From Yacuiba Tickets for the Yacuiba train are a bit easier to come by and there's a special window at the railway station. From Santa Cruz the bodegas are just about empty but on the return journey they're brimming with Argentine contraband and not as comfortable. There's a ferrobus to Yacuiba at 8 am on Thursday, Saturday and Sunday, returning to Santa Cruz at 9 pm the same night. Pullman/especial tickets cost B72/57.

The tren expreso leaves at 6 pm on Wednesday; the tren rápido at 5 pm on Monday and Friday; and the tren mixto at 10.30 am Wednesday and Sunday.

Getting Around
To/From the Airport Micros leave for Viru-Viru Airport approximately every 15 minutes and cost B2.50; taxis for up to five people cost B20. In the past, this airport has been notorious for drug plants but the city is trying to improve its image and problems are becoming more infrequent.

Bus There is a good system of city micros connecting the transportation terminals and all the anillos with the centre. The fare is B.60 per ride. Micros and colectivos to small settlements around Santa Cruz leave from the north end of the bus terminal.

Taxi Taxis in Santa Cruz are slightly more expensive than in highland Bolivia, but are cheaper than in the Beni. Expect to pay B3 to any destination within the first anillo. Although drivers may try to convince unsuspecting arrivals to pay B4 per person, taxis to or from the railway station are B4 for up to four passengers.

Around Santa Cruz

DUNAS DE PALMAR
These large sand dunes, 16 km (about 45 minutes) south of Santa Cruz on the road to Palmasola, are popular on weekends. The largest of these is Loma Chivato. There's an artificial lake and freshwater lagoons where locals go to swim, picnic and buzz around on motorbikes. There are plans to improve the road and build facilities at the site, but as yet, nothing has happened.

Getting There & Away
To get there, take the micro marked 'Palmar' from the corner of avenidas Grigotá and Cañoto in Santa Cruz and ask to be dropped off at the turnoff for 'las lomas de arena'. From there, it's an eight-km walk along a 4WD track to the dunes, but if you go on Sunday, there'll be a good chance of catching a lift.

COTOCA
In Cotoca, 20 km east of Santa Cruz, is the shrine of the Virgen de Cotoca, a wooden image discovered in a tree trunk in the mid-1700s by two woodsmen who had been exiled from polite society. A beautiful church was constructed in 1799 and the Virgin's discovery and blessings are celebrated each year on 8 December, drawing thousands of pilgrims from far and wide. Santa Cruz residents grateful for answers to special petitions customarily walk to the shrine overnight from Santa Cruz.

Getting There & Away
Micros leave for Cotoca every ten minutes from in front of the El Deber building at the corner of Oruro and Suárez Arana in Santa Cruz. The trip takes 35 minutes.

PUERTO PAILAS
East of Santa Cruz, a 40-minute trip along the rail line, is Puerto Pailas. The town is a base of operations for a new Sikh colony which is planning to build a new temple in the centre of their agricultural and reafforestation projects. It's a lovely area and although there's no tourist infrastructure, private accommodation is available for about B3.50 per person. On the negative side, on Sunday they stage cock fights at 10 am and horse races at 5 pm. The Sikhs also welcome volunteers for their tree planting and temple building projects.

One reader wrote to tell us that further information and transport arrangements were available through Mr Harpa Minder Singh at El Shalimar Indian Restaurant (☎ 349223), Suárez Arana 244. We were unsuccessful in locating either Mr Singh or the restaurant; if you have any luck, let us know!

Getting There & Away
You can ride the train to Puerto Pailas, take a camión from Cotoca, or take the micro (B.80) from in front of the El Deber building at the corner of Oruro and Suárez Arana in Santa Cruz.

MONTERO
The rapidly growing community of Montero in the flat agricultural lands north of Santa Cruz lies on the new highway between Santa Cruz and Cochabamba. With a population of 60,000, it's one of the largest cities in the Bolivian lowlands. The immediate vicinity of Montero is planted with cash crops such as bananas, sugar cane and rice. Soybeans,

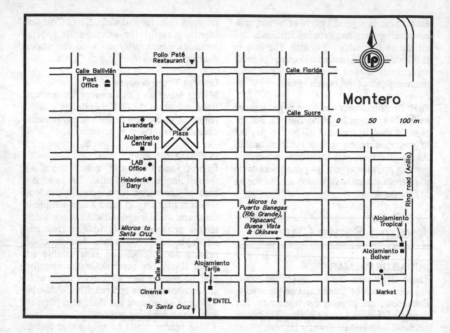

sesame and peanuts, which are used to produce vegetable oils, are also cultivated.

Montero is 50 minutes by micro from Santa Cruz bus terminal but there's little reason to visit except as an inexpensive accommodation option or a jumping-off point for day excursions to points of interest north of Santa Cruz.

Market

The market in this town is incredible; there isn't a doubt that it's the filthiest in Bolivia. If the trash, insects and discarded animal parts don't make you retch, the sewage, dogs and festering stagnant water will. Keep clear unless you just want the experience of seeing something so revolting.

Places to Stay

The only accommodation is in several basic alojamientos which are just over half the price of equivalent accommodation in Santa Cruz. Alojamientos *Central*, *Tarija*, *Bolivar*

and *Tropical* are all marked on the map. The Central appears to be the cleanest and most pleasant of the lot.

Near the Alojamiento Central is a self-service laundrette which may prove useful, especially since clothing hung out in this humid climate will often sour before it's dry.

Places to Eat

There are quite a few cubbyhole restaurants serving the old Bolivian standards. *Pollo Paté* on Calle Florida does pretty good chicken and chips, and ice cream is available at *Heladería Dany* and *Kivón* on the main plaza. If none of this sounds appealing, go to the market where you'll lose your appetite altogether!

Getting There & Away

There's a micro (B3) leaving from the Santa Cruz bus terminal every ten minutes. Micros back to Santa Cruz queue up two blocks south of the plaza and leave when full. The return trip costs only B2.50 because you don't have to pay the terminal tax.

Micros to Puerto Banegas, Yapacaní, Buena Vista, Okinawa and other villages in the area leave from the same street four blocks west of the market.

En route between Santa Cruz and Montero, notice the interesting sculpture in the middle of the Warnes traffic circle, a colourful rendition of a man with an oxen-drawn banana cart known appropriately as 'El Carretero'.

NORTH OF MONTERO
Okinawa
A trip to Okinawa, the Japanese rice-growing colony to the north-east of Montero makes an interesting excursion, but the colony is on the wane as disillusioned settlers migrate to greener pastures. Not far from Okinawa is Puerto Banegas, known locally as Río Grande. When the water level is high, it may be possible to catch a boat to Trinidad, but it's not a well-established cargo route. Micros from Montero to either Okinawa or Puerto Banegas cost B5.

Río Surutú
Río Surutú is a popular excursion for locals. There's a pleasant sandy beach ideal for picnics, swimming and camping during the dry season. From Montero, take the micro to Buena Vista and walk the three km to the riverbend nearest the town. The opposite bank is the boundary of Parque Nacional Amboró.

Yapacaní
Another possible destination is the bridge over the Río Yapacaní on the new Cochabamba road, 85 km from Montero. Along the river is a row of haphazardly built eating establishments serving surubí and other fresh fish from the river. Unfortunately, they also cook up more exotic species like *jochi* (agouti) and *tatu* (armadillo). These buildings are normally washed away by flooding in the rainy season and must be rebuilt each year. Don't bother stopping between November and March.

PARQUE NACIONAL AMBORÓ
The 630,000-hectare Amboró National Park lies in a unique geographic position at the confluence of three distinct ecosystems: the Amazon Basin, the northern Chaco, and the Andes. The park was originally created as the Reserva de Vida Silvestre Germán Busch in 1973 with an area of just 180,000 hectares. In 1984, thanks to the efforts of Bolivian biologist Noel Kempff Mercado, it was given the status of a national park and in 1990, the park was expanded to its present size.

Thanks to its range of habitats, both highland and lowland species are found here. All species native to Amazonia, except those of the Beni savannas, are represented, including the spectacled bear which is now verging on extinction. Jaguars, capybaras and peccaries still exist in relatively large numbers and birdlife is profuse. The unfortunately tasty *mutún* is still native to the area, and even rare quetzals have been spotted. A valuable publication is the 1991 pamphlet *Las Especies Forestales Mas Comunes en el Parque Nacional Amboró*, which has descriptions of the most common plant species in the park. It's available at the Fundación Amigos de la Naturaleza (FAN) office in Santa Cruz (see under Park Ecology below for the address) and park headquarters in Buena Vista.

Park Ecology
While the park's location is an asset, it's also a problem. Amboró lies practically within spitting distance of Bolivia's second largest city and squarely between the old and new Cochabamba-Santa Cruz highways. While the more remote parks of the Amazon lowlands are also threatened, Amboró is in an especially vulnerable position.

Despite a clause in its charter forbidding settlement and resource exploitation, hunters, loggers and campesino settlers continue to pour in, and the north-eastern 20% of the park area is already settled, cultivated and hunted out. Although FAN (the ecology group in charge of park administration) hopes to train committed *guardaparques*

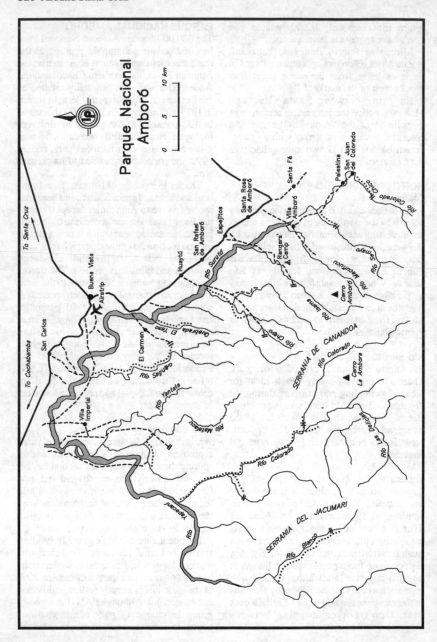

Parque Nacional Amboró

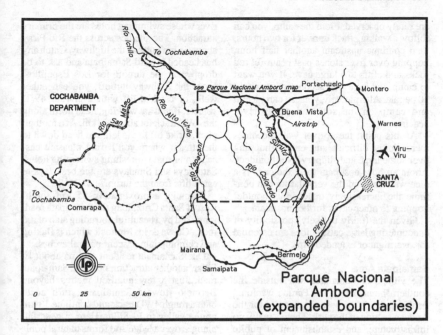

Parque Nacional
Amboró
(expanded boundaries)

(rangers) and educate the populace about the values of wilderness, without stringent measures, more will be lost every year. For further information or updates on the situation, contact FAN (☎ 333806), Casilla 1615, Avenida Irala 421, Santa Cruz, Bolivia.

Buena Vista Area

The park headquarters (☎ 2032) is at Buena Vista, 100 km from Santa Cruz along the new Cochabamba road. Here, you can collect information and plan your visit, hire guardaparque guides for B10 per day, and arrange transport to the park perimeter.

There's one daily bus heading south from Buena Vista along the Río Surutú which forms Amboró's eastern boundary. Along the road, several rough routes and tracks head south-west into the interior and follow tributaries of the Surutú: the Quebrada El Yeso, and the Ríos Cheyo, Isama, Macuñucu, Semayo and Colorado Chico. The rangers

can provide information on the logistics of travelling on any of these routes.

Río Isama & Cerro Amboró The Río Isama route turns off at the village of Espejitos, 28 km from Buena Vista, and provides access to the base of 1300-metre Cerro Amboró, the bulbous peak for which the park is named. It's possible to climb to the summit, but it's a difficult trek and a guide is essential.

Río Macuñucu The Río Macuñucu route, the most popular access into the park, turns off 35 km south of Buena Vista. From there, it's 11 km on a rough track to the rangers' camp at the end of the motorable road. There's a sleeping loft which costs B10 per day including the use of rudimentary cooking facilities.

The primary activity at the camp is sitting beside the river and waiting for wildlife to wander past. Jaguar and puma tracks are seen frequently along the riverbank, but large cats are rarely observed. From the camp, you can follow a walking track upriver for two hours, then continue upstream another half hour, hopping over river stones past beautiful red rocks and cliffs to a large cave. If you want to camp, the cave will accommodate about 10 people. Alternatively, you can carry a tent and camp on the soft and sandy river beaches.

At this point, the upriver walk becomes increasingly difficult and entails hopping over some large and slippery river boulders. About an hour upstream from the cave is a nice waterfall and the very daring can continue the increasingly treacherous boulder hopping to other caves further upstream.

Given the (fairly unlikely) possibility of encountering large cats, guides are essential for overnight or extended trips.

Samaipata Area

The village of Samaipata sits outside the southern boundary of the Parque Nacional Amboró, and is the best access point for the Andean section of the park. There's really no infrastructure, and establishment of public walking tracks is still in the planning stages.

From Samaipata, the guardaparques will take you by motorbike to a cabin at the road's end. From there, it's a four-hour walk to a camping spot near the boundary of the primary forest and Andean cloud forest. It's possible to continue one hour further into the park from there, but you'll need a guide and a good machete! For further information, refer to the section on Samaipata later in this chapter.

Getting There & Away

There are bus and micro services from Santa Cruz to Buena Vista and Samaipata. For further information, see Getting There & Away under Santa Cruz.

LOS ESPEJILLOS, BERMEJO & EL SILLAR

Los Espejillos is a popular retreat 30 km west of Santa Cruz. Its name, which means 'the little mirrors' is derived from the smooth black rock polished by a small mountain river whose swimming holes are the primary attraction. The site lies across the Río Piray about six km north of the highway. Catch any bus headed toward Samaipata and ask to be dropped at the turnoff for Los Espejillos. From the highway turnoff, you can either walk, or catch a lift with a private 4WD vehicle. If you are walking, head north along the 4WD track for about six km. At a football pitch, strike off to the left and head down to the stream where you'll find pleasant cascades and some refreshing swimming holes. Saturdays and Sundays are the best days to catch lifts from the turnoff.

Bermejo, approximately 85 km southwest of Santa Cruz along the Samaipata road, is marked by a beautiful obtruding slab of red rock, 'Cueva de los Monos', which is flaking and chipping into nascent natural arches.

One Samaipata resident told us about El Sillar, another attraction near the Samaipata road. Just a few hundred metres beyond Bermejo (toward Samaipata), turn north onto a rough 4WD track and continue 13 km up the valley to El Sillar. Here, a waterfall plunges over a ledge and forms natural pools along a mountain stream where you can swim. You can reach Bermejo on the Samaipata bus from Santa Cruz, but without a private vehicle, you'll probably have to walk to El Sillar from there. No accommodation is available, so take camping gear.

SAMAIPATA

Samaipata, a tiny settlement in the foothills of the Cordillera Oriental three hours southwest of Santa Cruz, is a popular weekend destination for Santa Cruz school groups and lowland families escaping the heat for a couple of days. This pleasant little town at 1660 metres has recently attracted foreign settlers as well as Bolivians in search of a quiet retreat, and a fairly cosmopolitan society is developing. One German resident is installing a mini-golf course on the hill above town!

It's a good place to hole up for a couple of days, and, if you're coming from the lowlands, staying here gives you an opportunity to begin altitude acclimatisation in degrees.

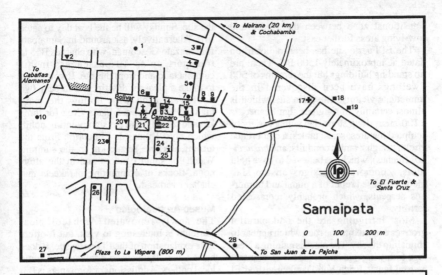

Samaipata

0   100   200 m

To Mairana (20 km)
& Cochabamba

To
Cabañas
Alemanes

To El Fuerte &
Santa Cruz

Plaza to La Víspera (800 m)

To San Juan & La Pajcha

■ PLACES TO STAY

3   Alojamiento Claure
6   Hostería Mi Casa
9   Residencial Don Jorge
11 Alojamiento El Tucano
16 Hotel Fuerte City
18 Alojamiento El Turista & Bus Stop
19 Hotel Pascana
27 Hospedaje La Víspera

▼ PLACES TO EAT

2   Churrasquería-Pizzería El Chancho
    Rengo
15 Hamburguesa Tobby
20 Restaurante El Buen Gusto

OTHER

1   Aeroplane
4   ENTEL
5   Mercado de Artesanía
7   Museo Archeológico
8   Taller de Cerámica (Ceramics Work-
    shop)
10 Proposed Mini-Golf Course
12 Church
13 FAN Office
14 Disco Ché Wilson
17 Hospital
21 Plaza 15 de Diciembre
22 Post Office
23 Lips Disco
24 Market
25 Tourist Information
26 Matadero (Slaughterhouse)
28 Japanese Nursery

Information

Tourist Information For information on hiking and trekking in the Andean sector of Parque Nacional Amboró, your best source of information will be FAN, which has an office one block from the church. They'll provide route advice and can hire out guardaparque guides for B10 per day.

Further discussion is found under Parque Nacional Amboró earlier in this chapter.

El Fuerte

Samaipata's main attraction is El Fuerte, a pre-Inca archaeological site on a hilltop eight km from town. The view from the ruins takes in the characteristic hills and valleys of the transitional zone between the Andes and low-lying areas further east.

The El Fuerte site has been radiocarbon dated at approximately 1500 BC. There are no standing buildings but the remains of 500 dwellings have been discovered in the immediate vicinity. The main site, which is almost certainly of religious significance, is a 100-metre-long stone slab with a variety of sculpted features: seats; tables; a conference circle; troughs; tanks; conduits; and *hornecinos* (niches), which are believed to have held idols. Zoomorphic designs on the slab include a raised relief of a puma and numerous serpents, which probably represented fertility.

Most intriguing are the odd parallel grooves carved into the rock which appear to shoot into the sky. The place is gaining a New Age following – in one of his fits of extraterrestrial fancy, Erich Von Daniken visited El Fuerte and proclaimed the site a takeoff and landing ramp for ancient spacecraft. One can hardly blame him; take a look into the valley below and you'll see a large flying saucer which has landed (and remains) on the grounds of Achira Kamping, a European-style camping complex.

About 300 metres down an obscure track behind the main ruin is El Hueco, an impressive hole in the ground which seems menacing due to its concealment by vegetation and the sloping ground around it. There are three theories about its origin: that it served as a water storage cistern; that it was used as an escape-proof prison; or that it was part of a subterranean communication system between the main ruin and its immediate surroundings. It has been partially explored, but excavators abandoned the project when they heard mysterious sounds emanating from the walls. Openings of suspected passages within the hole are now blocked with earth.

At the time of writing, El Fuerte was open only on weekends, but that may change at any time. Foreigners pay B2 admission, and Bolivians and student-card holders pay B1.

Getting There & Away If you're hitching to the site, Sunday will be the best day to catch lifts. Alternatively, ask around in Samaipata for Gonzalo Geacomán, who charges B15 to transport up to 10 passengers in his camioneta to and from the site. If you prefer to make a pleasant daytrip, it's an easy two hour walk each way. Follow the main highway back toward Santa Cruz for three km and turn right at the sign pointing uphill which says 'Ruinas de El Fuerte'. From the turnoff, it's five scenic km to the summit. Watch for small condors and in the afternoon, flocks of commuting parakeets that chatter overhead.

Museo Archeológico

The newly renovated Archaeological Museum is interesting to visit, but it offers little explanation of the El Fuerte site. It does have a few Tiahuanaco artefacts and some local pottery. Admission for foreigners is B3, whilst Bolivians pay B1.

Japanese Nursery

The Japanese nursery on the hillside above Samaipata has beautiful Japanese gardens, and many varieties of vegetables and flowers are grown here. The two friendly Japanese families living at the nursery are pleased to show visitors around their projects.

La Pajcha

La Pajcha is a series of three beautiful waterfalls on a turbid mountain river. There's a sandy beach for swimming and it is possible to camp here. It lies 42 km (one to two hours by jeep) south of Samaipata toward San Juan, then seven km on foot from the main road. Access is difficult, but you'll occasionally find transport heading in the right direction. Unless you have guaranteed transport back, carry food and camping gear.

Archaeological Sites

The area of Samaipata abounds in painted caves and semi-explored archaeological sites, including examples at Mairana, Pampagrande, Matarral and other nearby areas. Fortunately for the sites, access is difficult. If you're genuinely interested, contact Samaipata archaeologist Señor Omar Claure, for information and/or directions.

Places to Stay – bottom end

The friendly *Hotel Fuerte City* (☎ 6118) is basic but *su arcondicionador es de aire natural* (your air-conditioner is fresh air); the owners have recently installed electric hot showers. Rooms without bath cost B12 per person and the price includes a Brazilian-style breakfast with fruit juice.

The *Alojamiento El Turista* on the main highway charges B7 per person without bath. There's a constant noise problem due to traffic on the highway. Next door is the clean and recommended *Hotel Mily* which charges B15 per person without bath and B20 per person with bath. An especially playful dog enlivens the scene. As with the El Turista, the noise of the passing traffic is a problem. Other cheap options include *Hotel Pascana*, *Alojamiento El Tucano*, *Residencial Don Jorge* and *Alojamiento Claure*.

A pleasant and quiet option is *Hospedaje La Víspera*, situated on an experimental biological farm about 800 metres from town. It's owned by a Dutch couple, Margarita, a tour guide, and Pieter, Bolivia's only piano tuner. They rent horses and can organise trekking around Samaipata or trips further afield.

The guest house may be rented by groups of up to 15 people; during the week it costs B125 for up to six people and B20 for each additional person. On weekends, it's B180 for up to six and B20 for each additional guest. It's clean and warm, there's a great view across the valley, and self-catering is available. Bookings should be made through Tropical Tours (☎ 361428, Santa Cruz) at Calle Ballivián 18 in Santa Cruz. Be sure to carry a torch, as there's no street lighting between the village and the guest house.

Places to Stay – middle

A bit upmarket are the *Cabañas Alemanes*, popular with the more affluent sector of Santa Cruz society. These individual cabins include cooking facilities, refrigerators, private baths, indoor heating, great views

and lots of peace and quiet. Reserve in advance through Uimpex Travel (☎ 330785, Santa Cruz); ask for Señora Aida McKenney or Señor Claudio Holzmann. Prices range from B90 to B160 per night for up to six people, and each additional person up to eight will cost B20 extra. When you arrive in town, hunt up Georg, the German care-taker, and he'll indicate the way and provide you with a key.

On the main street is the *Hostería Mi Casa* (☎ 6061) with a nice garden and passable accommodation. Rooms without bath, including lunch and a choice of breakfast or dinner cost B36 per person.

Camping

Bolivia's leap into European style camping begins at *Achira Kamping* at Km 112, eight km east of Samaipata on the banks of the Río Paredones. They rent out cabañas as well as tent space and provide baths, showers and washing sinks as well as a social hall with a restaurant and games room. For further information and reservations, contact the Urbarí Racquet Club (☎ 343836, Santa Cruz) near the Hotel La Quinta, Barrio Urbarí, Calle Igmirí 590, Santa Cruz.

More basic camping is available at the secluded *Mama Pasquale's*. It's in a beautiful valley 500 metres upstream from the river crossing en route to El Fuerte. Campsites cost B5 per person and a bed in a cabaña is B7.

Places to Eat

The inexpensive *Restaurante El Buen Gusto* on the plaza offers cheap criollo cooking. Similar meals and good sandwiches are available at *El Turista*, which is attached to the Alojamiento El Turista on the main highway.

For snacks, try the hamburgers, chicken and amazing jugo de mandarina at the very friendly *Hamburguesa Tobby*. On Friday, Saturday and Sunday nights, you can get good German baked goods and real coffee at *Postrería Helga* beside the main market.

You'll find great pizza and home-baked goodies at the *Churrasquería-Pizzería El*

Chancho Rengo, but the prices are geared to the wallets of Cruceños on holiday.

Excellent international and criollo dishes are available at *Mi Casa Wisquería-Restaurante* (☎ 6061) at Calle Bolivar 98. Lunch specials cost B12. If you want a major meal, it's wise to reserve in advance. If the door is locked when you arrive, just ring the bell.

Entertainment

A slice of Santa Cruz nightlife is transported to Samaipata each weekend and revived at the loud and popular discos, *Ché Wilson* and *Lips*.

Getting There & Away

There are buses to Samaipata from Santa Cruz hourly between 1 and 5 pm, taking three hours for the 120-km journey. To return to Santa Cruz, stand by the main highway between noon and 5 pm and wait for a bus heading in the right direction. Alternatively, you can pick up a camión at the petrol station.

contemporary Craft Design

Eastern Lowlands

The vast, sparsely populated lowlands of the Bolivian Oriente take in all of crescent-shaped south-eastern Bolivia. They're bounded on the west by the foothills of the Cordillera Oriental; on the north by Llanos de Guarayos; and on the south and east by the international boundaries of Paraguay and Brazil.

The land is generally flat, broken only by long, low ridges and odd monolithic mountains. Much of the territory lies soaking under vast marshes like the Bañados del Izozog deep in the wilderness and the Pantanal along the Brazilian frontier. Mostly, however, it serves as a transition zone between the hostile, thorny Chaco scrubland in the south and the low jungle-like forests and savannas of the Amazon Basin in the north.

The release of the film *The Mission*, which was set in the South American Jesuit missions, spawned an awakening of interest in Jesuit work in the interior regions of the continent. Perhaps the height of mission architecture is represented in the unique and well-preserved churches of south-eastern Bolivia. The most interesting and accessible are found at San Ignacio de Velasco, San Javier, San José de Chiquitos, Concepción and San Rafael de Velasco, north of the railway to Brazil.

Culturally and economically, the Oriente looks toward Brazil rather than La Paz, and the 'Death Train' between Santa Cruz and Quijarro on the Brazilian border is the lifeline. Over this dilapidating link flow all sorts of undocumented imports, commerce and contraband. As the train from the frontier pulls into the outskirts of Santa Cruz, hundreds of baskets, parcels and boxes are jettisoned from the train and retrieved by awaiting transport just prior to arrival – and customs inspections – at the station.

Highway transport in eastern Bolivia is more or less limited to the road circuit through the Jesuit missions. Other mud tracks bulldozed through the forests are unreliable and many are scarcely passable. Few settlements have airstrips, and those that do are only accessible by air taxi or private aircraft.

History

When eastern Bolivia was still unsurveyed and largely unorganised territory, the Jesuits established an autonomous religious state in Paraguay. From there, they spread outward, founding missions and venturing into wilderness previously unexplored by Europeans. The northern areas were inhabited by tribes of hunting and gathering Indians – the Chiquitanos, Moxos, Guaraníes and others.

Each mission became an experiment with community life for groups of people who had lived by their wits from time immemorial. The Jesuits established what they considered the optimum community hierarchy. Each population unit, known as a *reducción*, was headed by two or three Jesuit priests. Attached to the reducciones were military units, and for a time, the Jesuit armies were the strongest and best trained on the continent. These units provided a formidable barrier/buffer zone between the Spanish in the west and the Portuguese in Brazil.

Over the years, a trade network was established with the Quechua and Aymará in the highlands. Cotton, honey, beeswax and artwork were exchanged for raw silver mined in the highlands. The Indians, traditionally hunters and gatherers, were instructed in the principles of agriculture and forcibly settled into an agricultural economy.

In addition to economic ventures, the Jesuits promoted education and culture among the tribes. With Jesuit training, the Indians became accomplished artesans and produced outstanding work in both silver and wood, handcrafting the renowned violins and harps featured today in the Chaco music of Paraguay. At the height of this amazing cultural transition, the Indians were

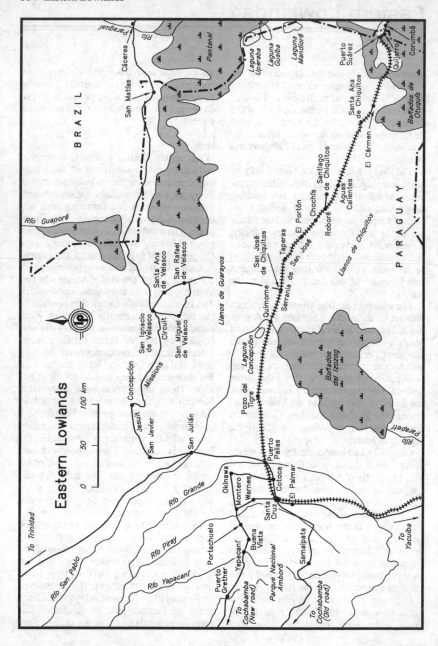

giving concerts and dances and even performing Italian baroque opera in the heart of the wilderness!

Naturally, the Indians were also thrust heart and soul into Christianity. Local rituals and belief systems were suppressed and the people were coerced into European thinking and lifestyle. The coup was so complete that today, very little is known about the pre-Jesuit cultures of the South American interior.

By the mid-1700s, political strife in Europe had escalated into a power struggle between the Church and the governments of France, Spain and Portugal. When the Spanish in South America fully realised the extent of Jesuit influence and got wind of all the wealth being produced in the wilderness, they decided the Jesuits had usurped too much power from the state. In 1767, caught in a crossfire of political babble and religious dogma, the missions were disbanded and the Jesuits expelled from the continent.

During the period leading up to Bolivian independence in 1825, the eastern regions of the Spanish colonies were largely ignored. Possession of the hostile lowlands and the hazy boundaries between Alto Peru, the Viceroyalty of La Plata and Portuguese territory was of little concern. Although agriculture was thriving in the Santa Cruz area, the Spanish remained intent upon extracting every scrap of mineral wealth that could be squeezed from the rich and more hospitable highlands.

SAN JOSÉ DE CHIQUITOS

One of the most accessible of the Jesuit missions, San José de Chiquitos was named for the Chiquitanos Indians who were the original inhabitants of the area. The Jesuits arrived sometime in the mid-1740s, and construction of the magnificent mission church that today dominates the town was begun around 1748.

San José de Chiquitos surprises its few visitors with the atmosphere and beauty of an Old West frontier town complete with dusty streets and footpaths shaded by pillared roofs. Flanked on the south by a low escarpment and on the north by flat soggy forest, San José is developing into the cattle ranching centre of the deep Oriente. Much of its population is involved either in ranching or buying and selling contraband foodstuffs from Brazil.

The toboroche trees on the town's huge plaza shelter noisy parrots and during the rainy season the place is home to thousands of frogs and large toads. Note the rather odd and erotic fountain off to one side; it's safe to say you won't find anything like it in highland Bolivia!

Perhaps the saddest news since the last edition of this book is the disappearance of the plaza's sloths. According to the local gardener, a baby sloth met a tragic death falling from a tree and the adults either emigrated to the nearby hills or died of starvation when the toboroche trees flowered and lost their leaves.

There are currently a few foreigners in town installing a satellite telephone system, and German and North American aid workers maintain an SOS children's village.

Information

Money The small corner store two blocks from the main plaza changes cash US dollars if they have sufficient bolivianos on hand. You'll probably be limited by cash availability to about US$50 at a time.

Dangers & Annoyances The police on the main plaza may want you to register with them upon your arrival in town. This practice serves primarily as an excuse to beg for 'entirely voluntary donations' toward 'stationery, stamps, ink and writing implements' for the police force. Right!

Jesuit Mission Church

Even if you've filled up and maxxed out on ho-hum monuments to New World colonialism, you'll still be impressed by the Jesuit Mission church in San José de Chiquitos, which is unique in South America. Vague similarities to churches in Poland and Belgium have been noted, but there is no conclusive evidence about the origins of its

To Santa Cruz

Railway Station

To Quijarro

Restaurant & Kiosks

Basketball Court

Restaurant ▼ ■ Alojamiento San Silvestre

Football Field

Chiquitano Monument

Hospital ✚

TV Tower & Satellite Dish

Flota Trans—Oriente

To Tranca (700 m), Mennonite Colony (45 km) & Jesuit Missions

Store to exchange cash

Red Cross

Hotel Victoria

Post Office & ENTEL

Police

Jesuit Church Complex

Market ●

Pharmacy ●

Plaza

Hotel Raquelita & Restaurant

● Bank

● Ferro Concrete Nymphs

Plaza to pool (4.2 km)

This Section of road is not in proportion to the rest of the map.

● Old Schoolhouse

San José de Chiquitos

0   50   100 m

Approximate scale

Pool & Trail to Waterfall ●

---

unusual exterior design. The main altar is nearly identical to those found in churches in other nearby Jesuit missions.

The church compound occupies an entire block with several buildings and courtyards arranged inside. The bell tower was finished in 1748, the Death Chapel is dated 1752 and the *parroquio* or living area was completed in 1754. All construction work was done by the Chiquitano Indians under Jesuit direction. The doors, some of the altar work and one magnificent bench seat were hand-carved in wood by expert Chiquitano artesans. Massive renovations and restora-

tions, drawn up by Swiss architects Hans Roth and Ekhard Kühne, are currently underway.

Chiquitano Monument

The people of the area seem to be proud of the indigenous heritage of San José and to prove it they've erected a monument of an archetypal Chiquitano maiden with her obligatory water jar at the entrance to town.

Pool & Waterfall Walk

There's a small resort, of sorts, 4½ km from town, where locals go to cool off in a murky green swimming pool. Admission is B3 per person but the walk itself is more appealing than the pool. Just outside town, the road passes beneath an archway supported by bikini-clad ferro concrete nymphs welcoming you to the Old Santa Cruz Highway (the route to the original Santa Cruz de la Sierra). These beauties were obviously designed by the same person responsible for the Chiquitano maiden and the plaza fountain. Further along are cattle ranches, jungle vegetation, trees squawking with green parrots and even an abandoned schoolhouse from bygone days.

In the forest near the pool is a pleasant waterfall, the source of San José's drinking water. It's a cool, shady spot out of the blistering tropical heat, but swarms of biting insects make it less appealing for a lengthy visit. Carry insect repellent on this walk and wear something substantial on your feet and legs to protect them from ferocious biting ants.

Places to Stay

The *Alojamiento San Silvestre* (☎ 2041) opposite the railway station charges B12 per person for rooms without baths. Beware of the stereo system that swallowed South America.

Opposite the church is the *Hotel Victoria* (☎ 2136) which costs B10 per person. All rooms have frontage onto the living and dining quarters where the vociferous proprietor barks a steady stream of directives at her staff.

Despite its dozy staff, the nicest option is the clean *Hotel Raquelita* (☎ 2037) on the main plaza, which has fans and sparkling loos. Doubles with private bath cost B30 while singles/doubles without bath are B17/24. Rooms for three or more people without bath cost B12 per person.

If you'd prefer to camp out, ask the priest at the church if you can pitch a tent in the courtyard.

Places to Eat

There's a good clean restaurant in the Hotel Raquelita on the main plaza where you can get chicken and beef dishes as well as a mean guineo con leche. It's worth going in to see the unusual wall décor, especially the simian representation of General Idi Amin with brightly painted toenails.

There's also a reasonable restaurant next door to the Alojamiento San Silvestre and some pleasant street restaurants near the railway serving inexpensive lunch and dinner specials. Mineral water is only available at one of the small kiosks near the railway station.

Getting There & Away

Bus & Camión If there's sufficient interest, Flota Trans-Oriente (☎ 2041) and Flota Chiquitano leave for San Rafael de Velasco, San Miguel, San Ignacio de Velasco, Concepción, San Javier and Santa Cruz on Sunday, Wednesday and Friday shortly after the Quijarro train arrives in the station. The fare to San Ignacio de Velasco is B20 and to Santa Cruz, B30.

On Tuesday, Thursday and Saturday at 10 am, there's a micro from the market in San Ignacio de Velasco to San José de Chiquitos, returning to San Ignacio on Wednesday, Friday and Sunday.

If you prefer to take your chances with a camión to the missions, wait at the tranca beyond the rail line 700 metres north of town.

Train The easiest way to reach San José de Chiquitos is on the Death Train from Santa Cruz or Quijarro. For timetables, refer to the departure times under Getting There & Away in the Santa Cruz and Quijarro sections of this book. Nearly all the trains arrive and depart at night, a shame because the area around San José de Chiquitos is the most scenic on the eastern rail line.

The train takes approximately 12 hours to or from Quijarro and eight to 10 hours from Santa Cruz, while the ferrobus takes seven hours from Quijarro and six hours from Santa Cruz.

Ferrobus fares between Quijarro and San José de Chiquitos are B52/43 in pullman/especial and B40/32 to or from Santa Cruz.

Train tickets to or from Santa Cruz cost B28/19/13 in pullman/1st/2nd class and to or from Quijarro, B37/25/17.

Intermediate stations like San José de Chiquitos don't receive ticket allotments. Purchasing a ticket will be difficult or impossible until the train is actually in the station and the station official can verify the availability of seats by checking the passenger list. Plan on long hours hovering around the ticket window.

MENNONITE COLONY

Although preferably not turned into a tourist attraction, the Mennonite colony, 45 km north of San José de Chiquitos, makes for an interesting cultural side trip.

The highly traditional Mennonites belong to a religious sect founded by Menno Simons, a 16th-century Dutch reformer. They speak a German dialect known as Platt-Deutsch, actually more of a hybrid of German and Dutch. Despite this particular colony's Canadian roots, very few of the Mennonites speak English and many don't even speak Spanish. The Menonos, as the locals call them, are easily recognised by their dress. The men all wear hats and identical blue or green overalls, and the women, who are more or less required to blend into the background, wear head coverings and plain monocoloured knee-length dresses. Mennonites live in simple mid-western US-style farmhouses and travel about in horse-drawn carts. Most of the farm work is done by hand or by draught animals.

This is only one of numerous Mennonite colonies in Bolivia; there are others scattered around the entire Oriente, including Santa Cruz and further north toward the Beni, as well as throughout Paraguay, northern Argentina and south-western Brazil.

History

The Mennonites in this colony originally came from Saskatchewan, Canada. They set out from there in search of a place where they could practise their religion, farm their land and live out peaceful and self-sufficient lives without the influences of modern society.

They originally found such a place in Belize, Central America, but hassles with the Belizean government in the mid-70s sent them off again in search of a home.

Recognising the agricultural potential of the Bolivian Oriente, thousands came to the wilderness north and east of Santa Cruz. They cleared vast tracts of forest and recreated a rustic cross between the north German plain and the North American Midwest in the heart of Bolivia. So far the Bolivian government has appreciated the role that the Mennonites have played in opening up previously uninhabited territory, but as more and more highland Bolivians look toward the Oriente as a source of economic possibilities, their unique situation may become threatened.

Getting There & Away

San José de Chiquitos merchants carry on trade with the colony, buying milk, cheese, butter and poultry from the Mennonites on a regular basis. Normally, at least one camión does the run each day. If you'd like to ride along, wait at the tranca north of town before 9 am. The return trip will cost between B10 and B18 per person.

Visitors to the colony should respect the privacy of the colonists. Most prefer not to have their photos taken and many, especially the women, would rather avoid contact with the outside world.

JESUIT MISSIONS CIRCUIT

North of San José de Chiquitos in the Llanos de Chiquitos and Llanos de Guarayos is a road circuit through several of the most important Jesuit missions. Those at San Javier, San Rafael and Concepción were originally designed by Martin Schmidt, a Swiss missionary, musician and architect who worked with the local Indians during the mid-1700s. More detail on the history of the Jesuits in Bolivia is outlined in the introduction to this chapter.

The missions circuit from San José de Chiquitos to Santa Cruz first passes through relatively pristine forest and low-lying wetlands. After 150 km, it leads to the mission complex of Velasco province: San Rafael, San Miguel, Santa Ana and San Ignacio. At San Ignacio, the road turns west, passing through mostly wild, undisturbed forest which gradually gives way to predominantly agricultural and ranching lands around Concepción and San Javier. There, it turns south, crosses the Río San Pablo at San Julián and continues to Puerto Pailas where it crosses the Río Grande and heads west along the final leg into Santa Cruz.

San Rafael de Velasco

Founded in 1696 and constructed between 1740 and 1748, San Rafael was the first mission church to be completed. During the 1980s, it was restored by the same Swiss architects involved in the restoration of the church at San José de Chiquitos. The interior is particularly beautiful with its original paintings and woodwork intact. San Rafael lies 150 km north of San José, about seven hours on the bus under optimum conditions.

Santa Ana de Velasco

The mission at the tiny Chiquitano village of Santa Ana, 25 km north of San Rafael, was established in 1755. With its earthen floor and roof of palm fronds, the church is much more rustic than the others, recalling those constructed by the Jesuit missionaries upon their arrival in the area. Given its age, the original structure remains in remarkable condition, but it's scheduled for renovation in the near future. Santa Ana lies off the bus route.

San Miguel de Velasco

Originally founded in 1721, San Miguel, 39 km (two hours by bus) from San Rafael, is the most accurately restored of the Bolivian missions. Its spiral pillars, carved wooden altar, religious artwork, toy-like bell tower and elaborately painted façade are superb. It was not designed by Martin Schmidt but does reflect his influence and is generally considered the most beautiful of the Jesuit missions in Bolivia.

There's a small alojamiento in San Miguel. If you'd like to camp, speak with the religious community at the church who may be able to direct you to a suitable site.

San Ignacio de Velasco

The original mission church at San Ignacio de Velasco was founded in 1748. It was the largest and perhaps the most elaborate in the missions but was unnecessarily demolished in 1974 and replaced by a modern abomination. The town, still inhabited by Indians, is interesting to visit and not far outside is the new Guapomó reservoir where you can swim or hire a boat and putter around. San Ignacio lies 40 km (three hours by bus over a poor road) from San Miguel.

Accommodation can be found at *Casa Suiza*. The proprietor, Señora Cristina, speaks German and Spanish and will arrange horseback riding, fishing trips and visits to surrounding haciendas. If you prefer to relax, she also has a wonderful library of books. Rooms cost B25 per person, including all meals.

Other lodging possibilities include *Alojamiento Guapomó* and *El Oriental*, both inexpensive. Basic meals are available at *El Riabel* and *Barquito*.

Concepción

Concepción lies 175 km (six to eight hours by bus over a very rough road) west of San Ignacio in an agricultural and cattle-ranching area. The church, which was founded in 1706, has been excessively restored and appears to have fallen prey to kitsch tendencies, with gaudy plastic décor and a Disney-like atmosphere. The only real appeal is the tranquillity of the village.

Concepción's nicest accommodation is *Alojamiento Westfalia*. There are also several recommended restaurants: the *Club Social* with bargain specials, the *Suni* and the *Ismeldia*.

San Javier

The earliest of the area missions was San Javier, 77 km (two hours by bus) from Concepción and 231 km (six hours) from Santa Cruz. It was founded in 1692 on a hilltop with a commanding view over the surrounding hills. The mission church, constructed in the mid-1700s, is currently undergoing renovations. San Javier is also proud of its new cheese factory, and near the town are some pleasant hot springs for bathing. As yet, no one has established a hotel, but there are several alojamientos, a petrol station and a restaurant called the *Snack*.

Organised Tours

Uimpex Travel (☎ 330785) at Calle René Moreno 226 in Santa Cruz offers three-day tours from Santa Cruz to San Javier and Concepción. Prices depend on the number of people interested; groups of four will pay B760 per person, all inclusive.

Getting There & Away

Air LAB flies from Santa Cruz to San Ignacio at 7.30 am on Monday, Wednesday and Friday, and returns to Santa Cruz at 8.35 am on the same days. The one-way fare is B110.

Bus & Camión Flota Chiquitana and Flota Trans-Oriente leave from the main bus terminal in Santa Cruz on Monday, Wednesday and Friday at 7 am and on Saturday at 4 pm. They travel via San Javier, Concepción, San Ignacio, San Miguel and San Rafael to San José de Chiquitos and return to Santa Cruz along the same route on Sunday, Wednesday and Friday shortly after the arrival of the train from Quijarro. The fare to Santa Cruz from San José de Chiquitos is B50, and from San Ignacio, B30.

During the dry season, there are daily micros from San Ignacio to San Matías on the Brazilian border, where you'll find onward transport to Cáceres and Cuiabá in Brazil. There's also a micro leaving from the San Ignacio market for San José de Chiquitos on Tuesday, Thursday and Saturday at around 10 am.

To arrange transport from San José de Chiquitos, wait at the tranca early in the morning. During the dry season, there are camiones going to San Ignacio and the other missions nearly every day. Plan on B80 to

B100 per person between San José de Chiquitos and Santa Cruz, via the missions.

ROBORÉ

The town of Roboré, about four or five hours along the railway east of San José de Chiquitos, began in 1916 as a military outpost and the military presence is still a bit overwhelming. You can probably imagine what happens when a lot of bored soldiers posted in the middle of nowhere encounter tourists in a town that rarely sees outsiders. The situation seems to have improved in the last couple of years, but it's still best not to appear conspicuous.

Río Roboré

The Río Roboré which flows through town is cool and clean and offers some pleasant and refreshing swimming. You may want to move several hundred metres upstream from the bridge to avoid the curious eyes of local crowds.

Los Balnearios

Highly recommended by locals is 'El Balneario', a mountain stream with a waterfall and natural swimming hole. It's a two-hour walk each way from town and you'll need a local guide to find it. Alternatively, there's another closer swimming hole which is accessible by taxi for B5 return.

Santiago de Chiquitos

Santiago de Chiquitos, 20 km from Roboré, is one of the more accessible Jesuit missions in far eastern Bolivia, and, in the cultural sense, is more interesting than San José de Chiquitos. It's in the hills and the cooler climate provides a welcome break from the tropical heat of the lowlands. By taxi, the return trip from Roboré with up to four people costs B60. Camiones and military vehicles occasionally do the run from the east end of town for B5.50 per person each way.

Aguas Calientes

At Aguas Calientes, 31 km east of Roboré, there are 40 to 41°C thermal baths which are

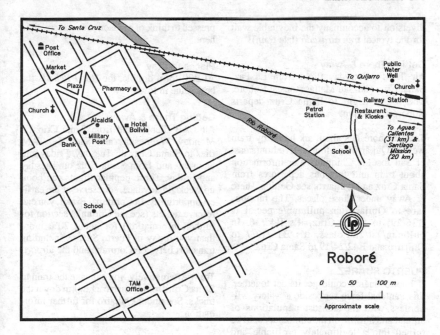

Roboré

0   50   100 m

Approximate scale

reputed to have curative powers and are popular with Bolivian tourists. The Santa Cruz-Quijarro train stops in Aguas Calientes and camiones leave from the east end of town, costing B5.50 per person. Taxis cost B60 for up to four passengers. The baths are best visited on a daytrip since there's no accommodation available.

Chochís
Chochís, two stops toward San José de Chiquitos along the rail line, has a lovely church which has been recently renovated.

El Portón
Toward San José de Chiquitos, the rail line passes through a bizarre and beautiful region of wilderness hills and monoliths, but unfortunately, trains pass only at night. If you're feeling adventurous and are keen to explore the best of it by daylight, the most convenient station is El Portón, just west of the spectacular and oft-photographed formation of the

same name. There are no tourist facilities so carry food and camping gear.

Places to Stay
The only accommodation in Roboré is at the *Hotel Bolivia*, half a block from the plaza. Doubles cost B25 with bath or B15 with a double bed but no bath. If you're waiting for an evening train, they'll let you keep the room for the normal rate less a B5 discount.

Places to Eat
The best place for breakfast is the terrace of the Hotel Bolivia where you'll get coffee, eggs, bread rolls and jam for about B2. For other meals, check out the *Pollo de Oro* restaurant near the station where local dogs have immortalised themselves by leaving paw prints in the blue concrete patio floor. In the evening, this place livens up appreciably; the scratchy stereo system and alcohol-assisted celebrating will provide a bit of

diversion to accompany the inevitable wait for the typical *tren atrasado* (late train)!

Getting There & Away
Air TAM's Saturday flight from La Paz, Santa Cruz and San Matías stops at Roboré. The return flight to Santa Cruz departs Roboré at 1.50 pm.

Train Roboré lies about six hours by train west of Quijarro and four to five hours east of San José de Chiquitos. For information about train and ferrobus departures from Santa Cruz and Quijarro, see Getting There & Away under those places. The ferrobus fare to Quijarro in pullman/especial is B36/29; to Santa Cruz, it's B45/36. In pullman/1st/2nd-class, it's B15/12/7 to Quijarro and B42/24/19 to Santa Cruz.

PUERTO SUÁREZ
If Puerto Suárez could get its act together, this Pantanal town set beside a watery wilderness with the densest populations of animal and birdlife on the continent could be turned into a legitimately profitable and attractive place. Instead, it's infamous as the place where São Paulo car thieves dump their spoils and 80% of the population is in some way involved in illicit dealings. In his book, *The Incredible Voyage*, Tristan Jones describes the place aptly:

...it is fit for neither man nor beast. I will go further and say that it is the asshole of the Americas, North and South. It consists of a few unpainted, rotting wooden shacks slouched around railroad sidings, the lines of which are overgrown with jungle and alive with mosquitoes. On each side of the siding is a noisy fog-ridden swamp of fetid, stagnant water that stinks to high heaven. During the twilight hours millions of mosquitoes rise off it, crowding the night air so thickly that there is hardly room between them to see . the giant moths which smash headlong into every light they can find. Over all this hovers a smothering, dank heat, making for an experience rather like putting your head into an oven full of rotting rats.

This descriptive passage was written fifteen years ago and Puerto Suárez hasn't changed. Bolivia has a lot going for it but this place is certainly a black mark and you'd be hard pressed to think of a reason to spend any time here.

Places to Stay
At B30 for a double, the *Hotel Bebe* is the best value in town.

Getting There & Away
Air LAB flies to and from Santa Cruz on Monday, Wednesday and Saturday. TAM flies to Santa Cruz on Tuesday, Friday and Saturday and from Santa Cruz on Tuesday and Friday. These popular flights can book up weeks in advance, so reserve at the earliest opportunity. In Corumbá, Brazil, you can reserve tickets (see the Corumbá section for further information) for about 20% more than you'd pay in Puerto Suárez, including transport between Corumbá and the airport.

Train Alternatively, you can take the train to Santa Cruz from Quijarro a few km down the tracks. See under Quijarro for further information.

QUIJARRO
Quijarro, a muddy collection of shacks at the eastern terminus of the Death Train, sits on slightly higher and drier ground than Puerto Suárez and serves as the border crossing between Bolivia and Corumbá, Brazil. Visitors headed east will be treated to a wonderful preview of Corumbá; from muddy Quijarro, it appears on a hill in the distance, a dream city of sparkling white towers rising above the vast green expanses of the Pantanal. In Mutún, just south of Quijarro, the richest deposits of iron manganese on the continent are currently being developed.

The Bolivian Pantanal
The Hotel Santa Cruz in Quijarro organises boat tours through the unspoilt, wildlife-rich wetlands of the Bolivian Pantanal and provides an alternative to the well-visited and controversially managed Brazilian Pantanal. A comfortable three-day excursion including transport, food and accommodation (on

the boat) will cost approximately B220 per person.

Places to Stay & Eat

The most pleasant accommodation is at the friendly *Hotel Santa Cruz*, two blocks from the railway station. This place charges B35/40 for clean, air-conditioned single/double rooms. Reservations may be made through the Hotel Amazonas (☎ 334583) in Santa Cruz. More basic accommodation is available for B12 per person at the small alojamientos to the left as you exit the railway station.

Pleasant inexpensive restaurants are found along the street perpendicular to the railway station entrance.

Getting There & Away

Train From Quijarro to Santa Cruz, the tren bala runs on Tuesday and Saturday at 3 pm and the rápido on Monday and Thursday at 12.30 pm. In the opposite direction, there's a tren bala on Monday and Friday at 2.30 pm and a rápido on Wednesday and Sunday at 1.30 pm. By train, the journey will take anywhere from 20 to 25 hours and cost B59/39/27 in pullman/1st/2nd class.

You'll have the same problems buying tickets in Quijarro as in Santa Cruz. Quijarro taxi drivers scalp tickets at inflated prices – B45/35 for 1st/2nd class, but before you buy, ascertain that they're valid for the correct day and train, and that they're not already punched.

The ferrobus runs from Quijarro to Santa Cruz on Wednesday, Friday and Sunday at 8.55 pm and costs B85/68 in pullman/especial. From Santa Cruz to Quijarro, it leaves on Wednesday, Thursday and Saturday at 6 pm. Securing a ticket can be difficult, but again, the taxi drivers in Quijarro may be able to help.

For real Bolivian-style luxury there's the Expreso Especial Bracha, a rapidly deteriorating rail car offering air-conditioning, videos and minimal food service. Westbound, it runs on Tuesday and Saturday and eastbound on Monday and Friday. Tickets may be reserved in Corumbá three or four days in advance through Receptivo Pantanal at Rua Frei Mariano 502. They cost US\$40 per person.

Crossing the Border

When the train pulls into Quijarro, a lineup of taxis waits to take new arrivals to the border two km from the station. Drivers count on foreigners not knowing the distance to be travelled – about two km – so you may have to bargain over their inflated initial rates. The going rate is currently B3.50 per person. Some people have reported being charged for a Bolivian exit stamp but it probably depends on the officer on duty at the time.

Just over the bridge on the Brazilian side, you may be subjected to a customs search and from there, you can get a Corumbá city bus to the centre. Brazilian immigration is at the Polícia Federal post at the Corumbá *rodoviária* (long-distance bus terminal, pronounced 'haw-doo-VYAHR-ya') just a few blocks from the centre. Buses from Corumbá to the Bolivian border depart from the main *praça* (plaza) opposite the cathedral. You'll be able to change cash US dollars or travellers' cheques at the Banco do Brasil, two blocks from the praça.

Technically, anyone entering Brazil from Bolivia must have a yellow fever vaccination certificate. Officials don't always ask for the certificate, but when they do, the rule is inflexibly enforced. In a pinch, there's a high-priced clinic in Corumbá which provides the vaccine.

If you have time, the Brazilian Pantanal near Corumbá is worth a visit. You can spend several hours or several days cruising around this immense marshland, or take a guided motor tour or walking trip to view the diverse wildlife of the area. It's also possible to travel the Transpantaneira Highway across the Pantanal between Corumbá and Cuiabá in the northern part of the Brazilian Mato Grosso. For further information, see the Corumbá section which follows.

If you're entering Bolivia, you can change money at the frontier. Cruzeiros are accepted, but money changers are more interested in US dollars. Unless you relish the attention of onlookers, have your requisite amount readily and discreetly available. It appears that the cruzeiro is following in the footsteps of its hyperinflationary predecessors, so it's impossible to quote a reliable exchange rate. Your best bet will be to ask travellers going the opposite direction for the current rate.

CORUMBÁ (BRAZIL)

The Brazilian port city of Corumbá near the Río Paraguai is the southern gateway to the Pantanal, Brazil's watery wildlife paradise. The city is 403 km north-west of Campo Grande by road or rail. Due to the strategic location near the Paraguayan and Bolivian borders, Corumbá has a reputation for drug trafficking, gun running, poaching and commerce in stolen vehicles, so visitors should exercise caution and avoid suspicious characters or dealings.

History

Corumbá, the Cidade Branca (White City), was founded and named in 1776 by Captain Luis de Albuquerque. By 1840 it was the biggest river port in the world and boasted a dozen foreign consulates. Ships would enter the Río de la Plata in the South Atlantic, sail up the Río Paraná to its confluence with the Río Paraguai and then up to Corumbá. The crumbling but impressive buildings along the waterfront reflect the wealth that passed through during the 19th century. With the coming of the railway, Corumbá lost its importance as a port and went into decline.

Orientation

The *ferroviária* (railway station) and rodoviária (bus terminal) are side by side six blocks from the centre of town. The waterfront lies three blocks from the centre in the opposite direction.

Information

Tourist Office There's not much in the way of government tourist information available, but there are lots of travel agencies in town, most of them promoting Pantanal tours.

Money The Banco do Brasil at Rua 13 de Junho 914 has a *câmbios* division on the 2nd floor offering *turismo* rates for cash US dollars and travellers' cheques. An alternative place to change cash is the store at Rua Antônio Maria Coelho 140, which gives close to parallel rates.

Post & Telecommunications The post office is on Rua Delamare opposite Praça da República. Telems, the state phone company, has a *posto telefônico* (telephone office) on Rua Dom Aquino.

Foreign Consulates The Bolivian Consulate (☎ 231-5606) is at Rua Antônio Maria Coelho 852, near the intersection of Rua América. It's open from 8.30 am to 1.30 pm Monday to Friday. Oddly, intending visitors to Bolivia may have to check out of Brazil before applying for their visas. The Paraguayan Consulate (☎ 231-2030) is on Rua Cuiabá. On the Bolivian side, the nearest Brazilian consulate is in Santa Cruz.

Travel Agencies Some reputable options include Pantanal Safaris (☎ 231-2112) at Rua Antônio Maria Coelho 330, Pantur (☎ 231-4343) at Rua América 969 and Vagáotur (☎ 231-5255) at Rua Dom Aquino 700. Receptivo Pantanal (☎ 231-5797) at Rua Frei Mariano 502 is also recommended.

Polícia Federal For a Brazilian entry/exit stamp, go to the Polícia Federal at the rodoviária. Daily opening hours for the office are 7.30 am to 12.30 pm and 2 to 5 pm. If you're obtaining your Bolivian visa in Corumbá, you may have to get your Brazilian exit stamp before applying for the visa.

Museu do Pantanal

The Museu do Pantanal, on the corner of Rua 13 de Junho and Rua Antônio Maria Coelho, outlines the Pantanal ecosystems and natural history. It's open from 8 to 11 am and 2 to 5 pm Tuesday to Friday and on Saturday from 8 am to noon. As with most Brazilian museums, admission is free.

PLACES TO STAY
1 Hotel Beira–Rio
3 Moderno
4 Condor
5 Salette
10 Santa Monica Palace
11 Alfa
12 Premier
14 Grande Hotel
18 Youth Hostel
19 Nacional
23 Hotel Schabib
24 Hotel Londres

PLACES TO EAT
7 Churrascaria Rodeio
13 Peixaria do Lulu
16 Pizzeria/Restaurante Paladar
22 Bar El Pacu

OTHER
2 Post Office
6 Local Bus Terminal
8 Museu do Pantanal
9 Banco do Brasil
15 Telefônica
17 Casa de Artesão
20 Pantur
21 Bolivian Consulate
25 Rodoviária and Polícia Federal
26 Ferroviária

Corumbá (Brazil)

Airport

To Puerto Suárez (Bolivia) & Quijarro

To Campo Grande

0   50   100 m

Forte Coimbra

Those looking for something different might consider a two-day trip to Forte Coimbra, seven hours by boat from Corumbá along the Río Paraguai. In days past it was a key defence of the Brazilian west, and you still need permission from the Brigada Mista at Avenida General Rondon 1735 to visit it. See Corumbá travel agencies for tour agency details.

The Pantanal

Corumbá's star attraction is the Pantanal.

Although *pantano* means swamp in Portuguese, the Pantanal is not a swamp, but rather a drowned alluvial plain. In geological terms, it is a sedimentary basin of quaternary origin, the remains of an ancient inland sea called the Xaraés which began to dry out 65 million years ago.

The periodically flooded Pantanal – 2000 km from the Atlantic Ocean but only 100 to 200 metres above sea level – is bounded by higher lands: the mountains of the Serra de Maracajú to the east; the Serra da Bodoquena to the south; the Paraguayan and Bolivian

Chaco to the south-west; and the Serra dos Parecis and the Serra do Roncador to the north. From these highlands, the rains flow into the Pantanal and out to the south and east via the Río Paraguai.

During the October to March rainy season, the rivers flood their banks and inundate much of the Pantanal, creating *cordilheiras*, patches of dry land where animals gather. The waters reach their highest – as much as three metres – in January or February, beginning to recede in March and dropping steadily until the rains return some six months later. This seasonal flooding has made systematic farming impossible and severely limited human incursions into the area. It has also provided an enormously rich feeding ground for wildlife.

Wildlife is abundant throughout most of the Pantanal, with the greatest concentrations in the lush meadows between Corumbá and Cuiabá, 10 to 20 km from Porto Jofre. The Pantanal is rich in diverse birds, including toucans, parrots, *tuiuius* (a type of stork), kingfishers and even the rare and beautiful hyacinth macaws. Larger animals, including *jacarés* (caimans), *tatus* (armadillos) and capybaras, are all abundant. Less frequently observed are jaguars, *tamanduas* (anteaters) and small deer. At night, a torch will reveal owls, anacondas and other night creatures.

Climate If possible, visit during the dry season from April to September or October; temperatures are hot by day and cool by night but there's still the occasional rainstorm. The best time for birdwatching is during the latter part of the dry season, from July to September; after the waters have receded and the new green grasses have emerged from the muck, the birds descend on their rookeries in great numbers.

Flooding, incessant rains and sticky heat make travel difficult between November and March; this is also the time when cattle and the larger wild animals huddle together on small islands of remaining dry land. The heat peaks in November and December, when temperatures over 40° C are common, roads turn to mush, mosquitoes stream out in military force and many of the hotels close down. The heaviest rainfall comes in February and March, and once every decade or so, the rains are excessive. In 1988, the city of Corumbá experienced devastating flooding and was submerged for weeks.

Organised Tours Travellers can get a preview of the Pantanal from Morro Urucum (1100 metres) in Corumbá. For a closer look at Corumbá's immediate surroundings, daily boat tours are available from all travel agencies. A daytrip on the boat *Pérola do Pantanal*, for example, will set you back US$25, including lunch. Contact Pantanal Safaris (details under Travel Agencies) for more details. Other packages include sightseeing trips to Bolivia and daytrips by road.

Many budget travellers choose to take cheap three to four-day tours into the Pantanal. These trips, which generally cost around US$20 per person per day, can be rough and ready affairs – imagine a boy scout outing with *cachaça* (a strong and nasty Brazilian cane spirit). Accommodation is in hammocks under thatch or in shacks optimistically referred to as *fazendas*. Food is generally pretty good but you'll have to carry water and allow time for vehicular breakdowns. You'll see lots of birds and plenty of crocodiles, but the mammals are understandably shy, especially when they're being chased by a truck at 80 km/h. Some of the 'guides' are ex-crocodile hunters/poachers, so their attitude toward animals may not be entirely green.

Before signing on for a trip – and certainly before parting with any cash – there are a few things to check carefully. First, find out how far into the Pantanal you'll be going – for the best wildlife viewing, it should be at least 200 km and preferably more. Ask for a rundown of the itinerary, preferably in writing, and ascertain whether it's flexible enough to accommodate mechanical breakdowns and inclement weather. Check out whether the truck is equipped with such emergency supplies as a radio and first-aid kit.

Plan on spending at least one day travelling into the Pantanal and one day for the return, allowing at least two days for wildlife viewing. Your chances of spotting wildlife are greatly increased if you go with a reputable guide who forsakes the 'mechanical chase' approach in favour of foot travel; vehicles should be used for access only. Most people prefer smaller groups – five or fewer participants. The best option will be several days of walking and camping at night (away from filthy fazendas cum drinking dens!), including walks at the optimum times to observe wildlife: before sunrise, at dusk and at night. The ideal trip length, therefore, will be at least five days from Corumbá.

Guides Insist on meeting your guide (or make it clear in writing that you will only go with the designated guide) and avoid signing on through an intermediary. Find out how long the guide has been working in the Pantanal. Those who've spent their entire lives in the area and gained extensive local knowledge and experience will normally speak only Portuguese, while those who advertise foreign-language skills may hail from the city and not be as well-versed in practical skills or wilderness lore.

Beware also of *guias piratas* (pirate guides) who are not registered with the Associação das Guias (Guides' Association). If you have some complaint about them or want a refund, you'll have no recourse. Even on 'official' tours, there's often an annoying amount of cachaça guzzling; perhaps tour guides operate on the premise that cachaça is cheaper than petrol and drunken tourists won't be too upset when the tour doesn't deliver on initial promises. Tales of woe include abandonment in the marshes, assorted drunken mayhem, and even attempted rape. Several travellers have complained about Necolândia Tours, and in particular, about two associated guides called Murilo and Nolasco.

The following guides are recommended: Clovis Carneiro (☎ 231-4473), an elderly guy with excellent local knowledge; Rodrigues (☎ 231-6746); Ico (☎ 231-2629),

president of the Associação das Guias; and Johnny Indiano (231-6835), who has spent his life in the Pantanal and is especially well-versed in local flora and the habits and habitats of wildlife.

Hotel Fazendas If you want a comfortable and well-organised trip – and the idea of buzzing around in a pickup truck terrifying wildlife doesn't grab you – pay a bit more and stay at a hotel-fazenda for a few days. If you're prepared to take it as it comes, it can be a pleasant and relaxing option.

What to Bring There are few shops in the Pantanal, so come prepared with attire for hot days, cool nights, rain and mosquitoes. You'll need sunscreen, sunglasses, a hat, sneakers or boots, light raingear, and something for cooler evenings, as well as long trousers and long-sleeved shirts to discourage mosquitoes. Vitamin B12 may also help. The Brazilian Autan brand repellent is recommended by four out of five Pantaneiros. Some travellers, however, note that Pantanal mosquitoes may have begun regarding Autan simply as a sort of apéritif before the big drill.

You may also want to carry binoculars, especially if you're travelling by vehicle and want to catch a glimpse of animal backsides before they disappear into the bush. An alarm clock will facilitate pre-dawn wildlife viewing and a high-powered torch will help on night walks. Finally – if you're photographically inclined – don't forget to carry a camera, plenty of film, a tripod and a long lens – 300 mm is about right for the wisely timid wildlife.

Places to Stay

In Brazil, *quartos* are simple rooms without baths while *apartamentos* include private baths.

In Town About five minutes' walk from the bus and railway station, the budget travellers' favourite is the *Hotel Schabib* (☎ 231-1404) at Rua Frei Mariano 1153. It's a friendly place, with Spanish, Portuguese,

German, English, French and Arabic spoken – and often all six at once! It's well worth the US$3 tariff. If it's full, close by at Rua Joaquim Murtinho 1021 is *Hotel Londres* (☎ 231-6717) with quartos for US$4 a head and singles/double quartos with fans for US$5/9.

In the centre, there are a number of cheapies located on Rua Delamare between Rua Antônio Maria Coelho and Rua Frei Mariano. *Salette* (☎ 231-3678) has rooms starting at US$5/9 for a single/double. Next door, the clean and friendly *Condor* has quartos with fan for US$3 per person. A couple of doors along at 911 is the *Moderno*, another good-value option, with quartos for US$3.50 a head. There's a youth hostel (☎ 231-2305) at Rua Antônio Maria Coelho 677.

Moving up in price, the *Grande Hotel* (☎ 231-1012) at Rua Frei Mariano 468 has spacious quartos for US$9/12 and apartamentos for slightly more, but breakfast is not included.

An interesting place to stay, though it's a bit out of the way, is on the waterfront at the *Hotel Beira-Río* (☎ 231-2554), Rua Manoel Cavassa 109. Popular with fisherfolk, this place charges US$12 per person for rooms with air-conditioning.

There are three hotels in a row along Rua Antônio Maria Coelho. The *Premier* (☎ 231-4937) at 389, has single/double apartamentos for US$12/15 with air-conditioning and TV, but the rooms are on the small side. Almost next door at 367 is the *Alfa* (☎ 231-6699) which is a bit cheaper, but doesn't have TVs, and nearby at 345 is the two-star *Santa Monica Palace* (231-3001). Singles/doubles with the lot here cost US$23/33.

The *Nacional* (☎ 231-6868) at Rua América 936 is the most expensive hotel in town. Singles/doubles go for US$40/50.

Pantanal Pantanal accommodation is divided into three general categories – fazendas, *pesqueiros* and *botels*. Nicer fazendas are ranch-style hotels which usually have horses for hire and often boats. Pesqueiros are hangouts for fisherfolk, and boats and

fishing gear can normally be rented. A botel, a contraction of boat and hotel, is a floating lodge. Reservations are required for all accommodation, especially in July, when lots of Brazilian tourists spend their holidays in the Pantanal. Agencies in Corumbá can make all necessary arrangements.

Unfortunately, nearly all accommodation is expensive. It usually includes transport by plane, boat or 4WD from Corumbá or Cuiabá, good food and modest lodging. Often, reservations are handled through a travel agent and clients must pay in advance. It's a good idea to call ahead to enquire about weather conditions. The rainy and dry seasons are never exact and proper conditions can make or break a trip.

Places to Eat

Bar El Pacu on Rua Cabral is a good, cheap restaurant and the fish is excellent. It's run by Herman the German, an interesting character who has spent a long time in the Pantanal. Try the delicious local specialty *peixe urucum* (fish with cheese melted on top in a condensed milk sauce) for US$4. *Peixaria do Lulu* on Rua Antônio João is another good fish restaurant. *Churrascaria Rodeio* at Rua 13 de Junho 760 has live music as well as tasty meat dishes. *Pizzeria/Restaurante Paladar* on Rua Antônio Maria Coelho has expensive but good pizza.

Things to Buy

The Casa de Artesão in the old prison at Rua Dom Aquino 405 has a good selection of Indian art, as well as Corumbá's best selection of Pantanal T-shirts.

Getting There & Away

Air The airport (☎ 231-5842) is three km from the town centre. VASP, with offices at Rua 15 de Novembro 392 (☎ 231-4441) and at the airport (☎ 231-4308), is the only major airline flying into Corumbá. They have connections with Brazilian capitals, while air taxis fly to remote points in the Pantanal.

For Bolivian air connections, contact Pantur (see under Travel Agencies earlier in this chapter) which is the agent for LAB and

TAM. The Pantur price for a one-way LAB ticket from Puerto Suárez to Santa Cruz is US$98, including transport between Corumbá and Puerto Suárez. If you arrange your own transport across the border, the price drops to US$78. For TAM tickets, the Pantur one-way fare from Puerto Suárez to Santa Cruz is US$85, including transport between Corumbá and Puerto Suárez, or US$69 if you arrange your own transport.

Bus From the rodoviária, buses run to Campo Grande eight times a day between 8.30 am and midnight. The seven-hour trip costs US$12 and is much quicker than the more relaxing train.

Train To Campo Grande, there are trains every Tuesday, Thursday and Sunday leaving at 9 pm (pullman class, US$8; sleeping berth US$20 for a double); and Monday, Wednesday and Friday at 8 am (2nd class, US$3; 1st class, US$5). Pullman seats *(poltronas leitos)* may only be reserved on the day of travel and there are no ticket sales on Saturday. From Campo Grande to Corumbá, the day train operates on Tuesday, Saturday and Sunday and departs at 6.45 am. The night train departs on Monday, Wednesday and Friday at 9 pm.

For information about the rail journey from Quijarro to Santa Cruz, see Getting There & Away under Quijarro.

Boat The Paraguayan company, Flota Mercantil del Estado, operates riverboat services every second week on Friday along the Río Paraguai between Asunción (Paraguay) and Corumbá. The trip takes five days and costs US$40 for a cabin or US$30 for a hammock. It's much cooler if you take the cheap class and sling your hammock on deck. Meals are not included in the ticket price, but acceptable food is available in the restaurant on board. Some boats travel as far south as Buenos Aires on the Río Paraguai. Information on infrequent boats upriver from Corumbá through the Pantanal is available at the Porto Geral in Corumbá.

Getting Around
A taxi from either the rodoviária or the railway station to the centre will cost about US$1.50. From the centre to the Bolivian frontier, expect to pay US$3.50. The city bus between the centre and the Brazilian border runs about twice an hour and the ticket costs US$0.60. The Polícia Federal at the rodoviária is open for immigration procedures daily from 7.30 am to 12.30 pm; and from 2 to 5 pm.

CÁCERES (BRAZIL) & SAN MATÍAS
The city of Cáceres, Brazil, founded in 1778 on the western bank of the Río Paraguai, is an access point for San Matías, Bolivia, and several Pantanal lodges. It lies 215 km from Cuiabá near the Ilha de Taiamã ecological reserve.

There are rumours of cement barges travelling between Cáceres and Corumbá but you'd have to be very lucky, and without unlimited time to hang around, the idea is best forgotten. Even the port captain has no idea when the boats are likely to arrive.

Places to Stay
Cáceres has a number of modest hotels and restaurants; the best cheapie options are near the bus terminal. Try the friendly *Hotel Avenida* (☎ 221-1553), just around the corner from the bus terminal on Avenida 7 de Setembro, which charges US$4 per person. Nearer the river on Praça Major João Carlos, the *Río Hotel* (☎ 221-1387) is a good option. Apartamentos with fans cost US$7/11 a single/double. Another possibility is the *Hotel Comodoro* (☎ 221-1525) on Praça Duque de Caxias, with single/double apartamentos for US$12/20.

The *Hotel Barranquinho* (☎ 221-2641) at the confluence of the Jauru and Paraguai rivers, 18 km from the Pirapitanga waterfalls, is 72 km and 2½ hours by boat from Cáceres. *Frontier Fishing Safari* (☎ 227-0920, São Paulo) is 115 km by boat from Cáceres.

Places to Eat
Corimba near the river at the corner of Rua

6 de Outubro and Rua 15 de Novembro is a good fish restaurant. *Pilão* in Praça Barão do Río Branco is a decent churrascaria (grill).

Getting There & Away

Buses regularly do the three-hour run between Cáceres and Cuiabá. There are also daily buses which do the 4½-hour trip between San Matías and Cáceres for US$10. TAM operates flights each way between San Matías and Santa Cruz, via Roboré, on Saturdays. There's also a daily bus between San Matías and San Ignacio de Velasco in the Jesuit missions area where you'll find flights and bus connections to Santa Cruz.

Crossing the Border If you're travelling to or from Bolivia, get a Brazilian entry or exit stamp from the Polícia Federal at Rua Antônio João 160.

contemporary craft design

Amazon Basin

Although it lies 1000 km upstream from the Great River itself, Bolivia's portion of the Amazon Basin better resembles and preserves the classic image travellers tend to associate with that river than the real thing does. While the accessible portion of Brazil's rainforest suffers from haphazard depredation, just over the border in Bolivia, the archetypal Amazon is alive and relatively intact. Although it's facing similar problems, the Bolivian Amazon still offers a glimpse of the deep, mysterious and scarcely inhabited Eden (it's also been called the Green Hell!) that calls from the glossy pages of adventure books and magazines. For further information on the state of the Amazon – and a few bright rays – see the Ecology & Environment discussion in the Facts about the Country chapter.

History

Historically, the Beni, Pando and surrounding areas have weathered continuous immigration and boom/bust cycles. Only a few forest-dwelling tribes, the original inhabitants of the region, remain, and even fewer continue their traditional subsistence hunting and gathering lifestyles. Indigenous peoples occupying the western regions of the Bolivian Amazon were conquered early on by the Incas and annexed into the empire.

Next came the Spanish. Like greyhounds chasing the elusive rabbit, they wandered all over the Americas following whispered legends and rumours of the mystical city of unimaginable wealth which they called El Dorado (The Gilded). One such tale was of Paititi, an incredibly opulent land east of the Andean Cordillera near the source of the Río Paraguai. It was said to be governed by a particularly affluent king called El Gran Moxo. Though the would-be looters combed and scoured the region for a trace of the coveted booty, they found nothing but a few primitive and hostile tribes and muddy jungle villages. There was not a single street paved with gold nor a single royal treasury brimming with precious gems and metals. In the mid-1600s, they gave up and went searching elsewhere for El Dorado.

The Jesuits The Spanish may have found nothing that interested them in the Moxos, a region named after the mythical king, but the Jesuits did. The area was rich in souls ripe for the plucking by the messengers of the Christian god. Their first mission in the Moxos was founded at Loreto in 1675. The first significant European penetration of these lowlands was staged by these hardy missionaries who also opened up the eastern lowlands to Christianity and European domination.

The Jesuits set up a society similar to the one they would establish in the Llanos de Chiquitos and Llanos de Guarayos during the following century. They imposed Christianity upon the 'pagan' inhabitants and taught them European ways – metal and leatherwork, weaving, basketry, writing, reading, printing, woodcarving and so on. They imported herds of cattle and horses to the remote outpost, and thanks to the prolific vegetation that grew there naturally, the animals fared well. In fact, the descendants of these herds still thrive throughout most of the Beni Department.

The Jesuits also taught the Indians tropical agriculture. Thanks to their efforts, the Beni today produces bananas, coffee, tobacco, cotton, cacao, peanuts and a host of other warm weather crops.

When the Jesuits were expelled in 1767, the missionaries and opportunistic settlers that followed brought only slavery and disease to the indigenous peoples. The vast steamy forests and plains of northern Bolivia saw little activity for 50 years.

Alcides D'Orbigny, the young French naturalist who explored the South American interior during the early 1830s, observed that those missionaries who arrived to fill the

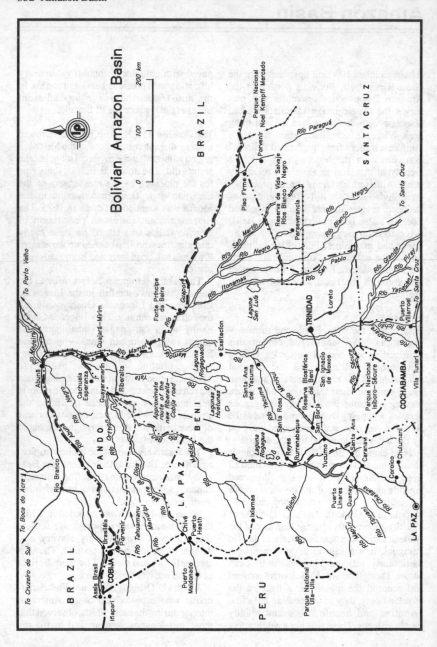

Bolivian Amazon Basin

void left by the Jesuits' expulsion did little more than convert the Beni Indians into Christian slaves. D'Orbigny predicted, however, that the rich potential of the region would someday be exploited on a grand scale.

The Rubber Boom The transplanting of the Suárez family from Santa Cruz to Trinidad in the late 1800s partially fulfilled D'Orbigny's vision. While Suárez senior was occupied with cattle ranching, young Nicolás Suárez set off to explore the inhospitable wilderness of Bolivia's northern hinterlands (at the time, this included a sizeable portion of what is now western Brazil). He became intimately acquainted with the region and developed a substantial business dealing in quinine, an antimalarial remedy derived from the bark of the cinchona tree.

When the natural rubber boom descended upon Amazonian Brazil, it was a simple matter for Suárez to shift his emphasis and arrange a system for transporting rubber around the Mamoré rapids into Brazil and thence down the Río Madeira to the Amazon and the Atlantic. Before the turn of the century, the Suárez family had amassed a fortune and owned about six million hectares of lowland real estate. Unfortunately, a good proportion of these holdings lay in the remote Acre Territory, which Bolivia managed to lose to Brazil in 1903. Although a large percentage of the Suárez fortune was lost with the Acre and the rubber boom came grinding to a halt, the family was by no means devastated.

The Cocaine Trade Less than a century later, a relative of Nicolás Suárez came to control another booming industry and brought worldwide recognition to lowland Bolivia. Coca, the leaf revered by the highland Indians for its ability to stave off the discomforts of altitude, thirst, hunger, discontent and stress, grows primarily in the Yungas north of La Paz and in the Chapare region of northern Cochabamba Department. The Yungas produce the more pala-table leaves while the Chapare crop is more bitter-tasting. Local Indians, therefore, prefer the former for everyday consumption while the Chapare coca has become a matter of worldwide interest. Dried, soaked in kerosene and mashed into a pasty pulp, the leaves are treated with hydrochloric and sulphuric acid until they form a foul-smelling brown base. Further treatment with ether creates the pure white hydrochloride crystals that find their illicit way up nasal passages worldwide.

So profitable is Bolivia's cocaine industry that over 60% (and probably more) of Bolivia's informal gross national product is derived from it and the name of the country has come to be synonymous with large-scale production of illicit substances.

Roberto Suárez Gomez, the great-nephew of former rubber baron Nicolás Suárez, amassed a fortune (surpassing even that of his great uncle) from the cocaine trade. Throughout Bolivia, people perpetuate legends of philanthropic deeds and acts of compassion performed by this man who became an enigma and folk hero among his compatriots. One story had him landing unannounced (which is the way he usually lands) in a Piper aircraft at Reyes Airport, walking into a particularly poor neighbourhood and flinging large quantities of cash into the air to be collected by the local people. From there, he reportedly proceeded to the local drinking establishment and declared open bar for the remainder of the evening.

Other tales speak of his donations to rural schools, development projects and health clinics. And of course now and again he's been known to make significant and self-serving contributions to the federal government.

The life of Suárez Gomez reads like a spy novel in which the hero (or bad guy, depending on your point of view) always stays one step ahead of the CIA – or in this case, the DEA (US Drug Enforcement Administration). In 1980, a couple of his men were caught in a cleverly arranged 'sting' operation and were brought before the US courts.

Although the setup was well-executed, one of the men managed to wriggle his way out of trouble on a technicality and the other jumped US$1 million bail and returned to Bolivia.

By the mid-1980s, US yuppiedom was consuming so much Bolivian cocaine that the North American government decided something had to be done about it. Realising that it would be unpopular to bomb the cocaine users among their own population, the USA pointed an accusing finger at Bolivia, and threatened drastic DEA action should the Bolivian government not cooperate with US military action aimed at curtailing the production of Bolivia's most lucrative export. When Ronald Reagan and his buddies in the Pentagon proposed some joint cleaning up of the remote reaches of the Beni and Chapare regions, Bolivian president Victor Paz Estenssoro agreed to go along with their plans.

The operation was prematurely leaked to the press, however, and the remote processing labs were given sufficient warning to pack up and clear out before the bombs arrived. Only minor damage was done and the US government found itself in a rather embarrassing situation.

In 1987 the Bolivian army failed in its attempt to arrest the elusive Suárez Gomez when it noisily raided his ranch by helicopter, ruining its element of surprise. In Suárez's absence, the Bolivian government sentenced him to 12 years in prison, and in mid-1988, Bolivian soldiers, sent in quietly and under cover of night, managed to arrest the cocaine king while he was sleeping.

Bolivian Amazonia Today Despite all the attention focused on the environment and the drugs issue, northern Bolivia is not all cocaine and rainforest. Cattle ranching is still carried out on a large scale, especially in the savannas north and west of Trinidad. The ancestry of some of the Beni herds traces back to Jesuit times, though most of the cattle raised today are Asian Indian zebu cattle imported from Brazil.

The main highways of the region are the Amazon tributaries – the Mamoré, the Ichilo, the Beni, Madre de Dios and Guaporé, to name but a few – that elsewhere would be considered great rivers in their own right. Along these jungle waterways, riverboats, barges, buckets and bathtubs serve as the primary means of transportation for passengers, freight, vehicles and livestock. Villages are relatively thin on the ground and some remote tribes have had only minimal contact with modern civilisation. All that is bound to change, however, with the recent spate of road construction and subsequent increase in highland settlers, logging activities and land clearance for cattle ranches. Although the lowlands are a very different Bolivia than La Paz and the highlands, what transpires in the Amazon Basin over the next few years will have profound effects upon the remainder of the country.

For further historical information, see the History section of the Facts about the Country chapter.

Chapare Region

VILLA TUNARI

For some spectacular Yungas scenery, travel the road between Cochabamba and Villa Tunari. The trip passes peaks and high mountain lakes before dropping steeply into deep, steaming valleys. Near Villa Tunari, the landscape flattens out into seemingly endless tropical forests. Villa Tunari itself is primarily a tropical resort for cold-weary highlanders. It's a quiet and relaxing spot to rent a cabaña, swim in cool forest rivers and relax.

The flooding of late 1985 and early 1986 that sent Lake Titicaca overflowing its banks also had a profound effect in this region. Most of the bridges along this route were either damaged or washed out altogether. While repairs were going on, traffic just had to plough through several very hairy river crossings without bridges. Although the bridges have been repaired and this road has replaced the Siberia Pass/Samaipata route as the main terrestrial link between Cochabamba and Santa Cruz, the heaps of concrete rubble (and at one point a 30-metre chunk of highway!) that litter the river bottom are sufficient evidence that it could occur again at any time.

Organised Tours

There is a great deal of interest around the area but transport and orientation are difficult so guides are recommended. Villa Tunari is a focus of emphasis for Fremen Tours, a Dutch, Cochabamba-based agency which organises tours, accommodation, river trips and other activities to difficult-to-reach sites in the region. It's more upmarket than most budget travellers will be able to afford, but does provide splurge options.

Possibilities include organised trips to Los Pozos, 14 idyllic natural swimming holes near Fremen's Hotel Puente deep in the forest, and to the Cuevas de los Pájaros Nocturnos (Caves of the Night Birds) to see the *guácheros* (*Steatornis Caripensis*, also known as *oilbirds*), a rare species of nocturnal bird which inhabits the caves. This four-hour excursion includes a slog through the rainforest and a hairy crossing of the Río San Mateo on a single cable. Fremen also runs excursions to the ghost town of Todos Santos, an abandoned Italian colony near Puerto Aurora, now swallowed by lush forest greenery. It's 55 km from Villa Tunari on the Río Chapare. Fremen's future plans include raft trips on the Río Chapare from Villa Tunari to Puerto San Francisco.

For a five-day, all-inclusive tour with cabaña-style accommodation, expect to pay about B1100 to B1600, depending on the season. Note that prices will be considerably lower if you book in Bolivia rather than overseas. Three and four-day trips are also available. For further information, contact Fremen Tours (☎ 47126, fax (591-42) 48500), attention Maria de los Ángeles Ribera, Casilla 1040, Calle Tumusla O-245, Cochabamba, Bolivia.

Places to Stay & Eat

The *Hotel Las Palmas* (☎ 47126, Cochabamba) costs B44 for a double including access to the swimming pool. The attached restaurant serves excellent, locally caught fish. Another option is the *Hotel Las Vegas* which is friendly and also serves good meals. Rooms cost B25 for a double.

Four km from Villa Tunari, Fremen has set up the *Hotel Puente*, a forest retreat which blends magically into the environment near the point where the Río San Mateo and Río Espíritu Santo join to form the Río Chapare. If you can afford it, this is a great place to mellow out, savour the slow and quiet pace and perhaps enjoy a good snout-to-snout chat with the hotel's pet pig, Monty. Single/double cabañas cost B65/85 and family rooms with one double bed and two twin beds are B140.

Getting There & Away

From Cochabamba, any short-distance bus going to Puerto Villarroel or any flota heading for Santa Cruz will pass through Villa Tunari. The fare is B9 and the trip takes about three hours.

From Villa Tunari to Santa Cruz, there are several services in the early afternoon but most of the Santa Cruz traffic departs in the evening. To Cochabamba, there is an 8.30 am service. At Corani near the dam between Cochabamba and Villa Tunari, look for the bizarre Casa de los Brujos (House of the Warlocks), an exceptional dwelling constructed by a local eccentric.

PUERTO VILLARROEL

The muddy tropical settlement of Puerto Villarroel lies several hours north-east of Villa Tunari and serves as one of northern Bolivia's major river ports. Although it consists of nothing but a collection of tumbledown wooden hovels, a military installation, a YPFB plant and an area that could be loosely described as a port, this town serves as both a vital transportation terminal and a gateway to the Amazon lowlands. If you just want a quick look at the rainforests, the trip to Puerto Villarroel is an easy two-day round trip from Cochabamba.

The best advice that can be offered is to

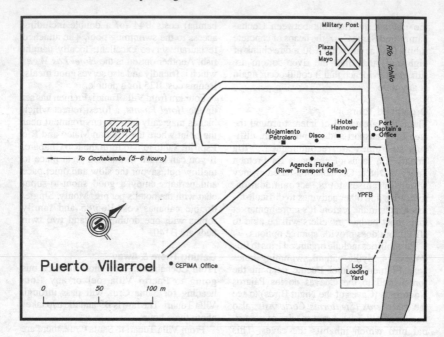

Puerto Villarroel

bring lots of good insect repellent. The second most important advice is to wear strong old shoes with lots of tread. Even in the dry season, the muddy streets of Puerto Villarroel will crawl up past your ankles and threaten to devour your footwear, so anything not well-secured to your feet may fall prey and be lost forever!

Places to Stay

There are only two hotels in Puerto Villarroel and both can be described as very marginal accommodation. If you've arranged river transport to Trinidad, however, you'll normally be permitted to sleep on the boat.

At the *Alojamiento Petrolero* the rooms are constructed of raw boards and scraps of wood pieced haphazardly together – the roof leaks and the beds get wet. Doors don't lock and people walk in and out of your room at will. When I was there, one such visitor was a local drunk who staggered in and decided to spend the rest of the night there singing,

yelling and slobbering on the floor. There aren't any showers but there is a toilet in the middle of a banana grove. For these conditions you'll pay B6 per person.

The *Hotel Hannover* is quite a bit nicer. It's got a pleasant shady courtyard, lawn furniture, a restaurant and a disco/bar. The latter, however, causes problems. Unless you want to stay up dancing, you'll stay awake fuming all hours of the night with your head stuffed under your pillow in an attempt to muffle some of the mega-decibel noise.

Places to Eat

There are half a dozen acceptable restaurants housed in the shacks along the main street. They're expensive when compared to similar standards in Cochabamba and they offer little variety, but if you don't mind fish or chicken, you'll be able to find nourishment. For good empanadas, snacks, hot drinks and juice, try the market on the main street.

As mentioned before, there's a loud (and sometimes obnoxious) disco beside the Hotel Hannover which plays both Latin and European/US music. Those staying at the Hannover may ultimately decide that it's a case of 'if you can't beat them, join them'!

Getting There & Away
Bus & Camión Direct access to Puerto Villarroel is provided by the bus marked 'Chapare' which leaves from the corner of avenidas 9 de Abril and Oquendo near Laguna Alalay in Cochabamba. The first bus of the day sets out at 6.30 am and subsequent buses depart when full. The fare for the entire trip is B10. The return bus to Cochabamba leaves at 7 am sharp from the main street and there are also occasional camiones which leave from the same place at any hour of the day, especially when there are boats in port. The Santa Cruz bus that passes through Villa Tunari from Cochabamba does not run via Puerto Villarroel.

Boat There are two types of boat which do the run between Puerto Villarroel and Trinidad. The small family-run cargo boats that putter up and down the Río Ichilo normally only travel by day and reach Trinidad in six to eight days. The larger commercial craft travel day and night and can do the run in about four days.

The average fare to Trinidad on either of these types is about B80 with food included. The quality of food naturally varies from boat to boat, but overall the shipboard diet consist of fish, dried meat, masaco, fruit and turtle eggs. (As turtles are endangered in some parts of the Bolivian Amazon, you might consider declining this last item on the menu.) Even if you do buy a passage with food, it's wise to carry along some emergency rations in case it all proves too unexciting for your tastes. It's also possible to buy passage without food for a few dollars less. Hammocks are available in Cochabamba, but it may be better to purchase one from a river traveller headed in the opposite direction or pick one up in Santa Cruz where they're a bit cheaper. Few boats along the Ichilo make cabins available to passengers. For further information, see the discussion of travel by boat in the Getting Around chapter or under Getting There & Away in the Trinidad section later in this chapter.

There are three offices in Puerto Villarroel which must be visited by all cargo transporters – the port captain's office, the CEPIMA office and the Transportes Fluviales (River Transport Office). A stop at any or all of these should provide you with at least a sketchy idea of when you can expect a boat to leave. Under normal conditions, you shouldn't have more than a three or four-day wait, but sometimes, military exercises and labour strikes effectively shut down cargo transport and prospective travellers may face a long wait.

Although most travellers go in this direction, it's also possible (naturally) to travel by river from Trinidad to Puerto Villarroel.

PARQUE NACIONAL ISIBORO-SÉCURE
Created in 1965, the 1.2 million-hectare Isiboro-Sécure National Park occupies a large triangle between the Ríos Isiboro and Sécure and the Serranias Sejerruma, Mosetenes and Yanakaka. It contains mountains, rainforest and savanna and was once (and in remoter sections, still is) home to profuse wildlife. Thanks to an obscure 1905 Department of Cochabamba resolution that the park should be opened to colonisation and settlement, however, it has now been overrun by humans and the wildlife has been almost wiped out. The formerly large Indian population, which consisted primarily of Yuracarés, followed by Chimanes, Sirionós and Trinitários, has been either displaced or exterminated by the settlers. Although stringent protection measures have been proposed or planned on several occasions, nothing has come of them.

Furthermore, the park is unfortunately positioned along major cocaine-producing and drug-running routes, so extreme caution and awareness should be exercised by anyone attempting to visit independently. The area is inaccessible between November and March due to flooding of the roads, and due to recent DEA activity in the area, foreigners may be considered *anti-cocaleros* and hence fair game for anyone with differing opinions. It's very dangerous unless you have all the proper letters of recommendation from higher-ups in the coca-growers' association. (As this book was going to press, the Bolivian government voted to expel US troops engaged in anti-drug activities. Travellers should still, however, exercise extreme caution venturing into this area.)

Because of the park's problems, we realise that few people will be inclined to visit, but we've included discussion of Isiboro-Sécure in order to increase awareness of its existence. Since the Bolivian government has declared that they haven't yet given up on this park – at least officially – perhaps international interest will compel them to take some sort of protective action.

Getting There & Away

Cochabamba-based Fremen Tours runs seven-day boat trips to Laguna Bolivia, the most interesting destination in the Isiboro-Sécure National Park. At present, this is the only truly safe way to visit the park, and is probably the easiest and most pleasant way to promote its preservation.

To get there on your own, take a bus from the end of Avenida Oquendo in Cochabamba to the village of Eterezama, where there's an alojamiento. Then hitch a lift on a camión to Isinuta, where you'll also find very basic alojamiento accommodation. From there, board yet another camión to the Trinitários Moxos community of Santísima Trinidad (not to be confused with the city of Trinidad further north!). If you keep following the road north of there, which, unless you're very lucky, will probably require travelling on foot, you'll go deeper and deeper into the park and its vast forests and savannas, passing the settlements of Aroma, Ycoya and Río Moleto.

Western Bolivian Amazon

RURRENABAQUE

Rurrenabaque, a bustling little frontier settlement on the Río Beni, is the loveliest village in the Bolivian lowlands. The original people of the area, the Tacana, were one of the few lowland tribes that resisted Christianity and Western-style civilisation. It was the Tacana who were responsible for the name *Beni*, which means 'wind'. The name Rurrenabaque (locally shortened to just 'Rurre') is derived from *Arroyo Inambaque*, the Spanish-ised version of the Tacana word *Suse-Inambaque*, which means the 'Ravine of Ducks'.

Rurrenabaque residents will be pleased to tell you that their town will be the setting for an upcoming feature film entitled *Return from Tuichi*, starring Emilio Estevez. The film is based on the true story of local guide Tico Tudela's 1981 rescue of Israeli Yossi Ginsberg who was lost in the wilderness after an ill-fated expedition. Filming began on location in April 1992.

The main draw for tourists to Rurrenabaque is the surrounding rainforest which still supports Amazonian wildlife in relatively large numbers. The aforementioned Tico Tudela organises unforgettable excursions into Rurrenabaque's forest hinterlands.

Information

There's no bank in Rurrenabaque but cash US dollars may be changed with Tico Tudela at Agencia Fluvial.

Electricity is available only between 7 pm and midnight.

Things to See & Do

Most of Rurrenabaque's appeal is natural and it's worth spending a day or two here. Behind the town is a low but steep hill affording a view across the seemingly endless Beni lowlands. It may be climbed via a track which leaves town from near the *colegio* (secondary school).

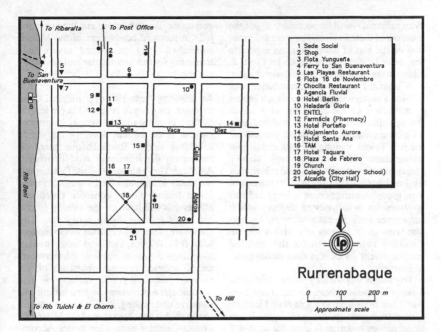

To Riberalta   To Post Office

To San
Buenaventura

Río Beni

To San
Buenaventura

Calle   Vaca   Diez

Celia

Abaroa

To Río Tuichi & El Chorro

To Hill

1 Sede Social
2 Shop
3 Flota Yungueña
4 Ferry to San Buenaventura
5 Las Playas Restaurant
6 Flota 16 de Noviembre
7 Chocita Restaurant
8 Agencia Fluvial
9 Hotel Berlín
10 Heladería Gloria
11 ENTEL
12 Farmácia (Pharmacy)
13 Hotel Porteño
14 Alojamiento Aurora
15 Hotel Santa Ana
16 TAM
17 Hotel Taquara
18 Plaza 2 de Febrero
19 Church
20 Colegio (Secondary School)
21 Alcaldía (City Hall)

Rurrenabaque

0   100   200 m

Approximate scale

Another option is to visit El Chorro, an idyllic pool and waterfall about one km up the Beni from town. A track leads up from the wet sand beach to this favourite swimming and picnicking spot. For transport, enquire at Agencia Fluvial. On the opposite side of the Beni not far from here is an ancient serpent engraving. It was intended as a warning to river travellers; when the water level reached serpent level, the Beni was considered unnavigable.

You may also enjoy watching the Beni's changing moods: the Amazonian sunsets are normally superb, and at night, a dense cloud of fog rolls down the river and creates a beautiful effect, especially during the full moon.

Jungle Trips

If you're interested in the wilder side of Bolivia, the jungle trips organised by Agencia Fluvial couldn't be improved upon. They're tailored to travellers' specific inter-

ests and no two trips are alike, so you can join several without revisiting the same camps, or doing or seeing the same things twice.

There are more interesting and unusual things to be seen and learned here than most people see in a year. The guides, most of whom have been reared in the area, are astonishingly knowledgeable about the fauna, flora and forest lore. They'll explain the animals' habits and habitats and demonstrate the uses of some of the forest's thousands of plant species, including the forest's natural medicine cabinet and its remedies for colds, fever, cuts, insect bites, diarrhoea and so on.

Whatever the duration of your tour, you can be sure it will be full of interesting activities; they'll take you exploring the forest floor, fishing, tracking tapirs and jaguars at night or making a show of catching (and releasing) an alligator with their bare hands. However, some knowledge of Spanish –

even minimal – will be necessary to get the most out of their services. For more information on the sort of things you can expect to see, refer to Amazon Notes under Flora & Fauna in the Facts about the Country chapter.

A standard trip from Rurrenabaque will include a motorised canoe trip which begins by travelling up the Río Beni as it winds through hills that could have been lifted from a Chinese painting. From there, you ascend the Río Tuichi, visiting various camps and taking shore walks along the way. There's plenty of time for swimming and relaxing as well as hiking and exploring. On the return trip, group construction of a large log raft provides for a hair-raising descent which sometimes ends in naval disaster. Groups that wish to do so may also visit a remote Chimane Indian village for the 'cultural enlightenment' of a smear-the-tourists game of football.

Trips aren't as touristy as the preceding description makes them sound. They normally last from three to six days and include canoe transport, guides and food. River camp accommodation is quite basic; you'll sleep on the river sand beneath a tarpaulin tent surrounded by a mosquito net at several of the more than 30 possible camps along the Tuichi.

Groups must more or less form themselves so you may want to organise four or five people before leaving La Paz or Coroico. For a four-day trip, expect to pay between B250 and B290 per person. Lots of good, strong mosquito repellent is absolutely essential. For other guidelines on what to take, see Amazon Basin Essentials under What to Bring in the Facts for the Visitor chapter.

Río Madidi The Río Madidi watershed, where oil exploration is scheduled to begin soon, still contains one of the most intact ecosystems in all of South America. The most ecologically sound section of the Madidi system lies further downstream and is all but inaccessible – which is precisely the reason it hasn't yet been hunted out. However, Tico can arrange guides to take

you up the Tuichi by river and then over the hills in the wild headwaters of the Madidi watershed. Plan on around seven days minimum for this spectacular and adventurous trip.

An Ecology Note However magical these trips are, they won't be possible for long if hunting continues in the area at its present pace or if the current development trends unfolding east of Rurrenabaque encroach further on the remaining wild rainforest. Although Tico's guides are quite flexible and are happy to hunt and feed tourists from the forest larder, please consider the direct effects this will have on the already fragile and rapidly destabilising ecosystem. The guides are great cooks and can work wonders with fish, veggies, rice and other market trimmings if you so request. Furthermore, they'll provide copious quantities of the sweetest grapefruit you'll ever taste!

Although ecotourism can be a lasting and lucrative undertaking, it must be approached sensitively. It may help to read the Minimum Impact Camping discussion under Accommodation in the Facts for the Visitor chapter. Encourage your guides to burn rubbish and carry out any plastic or metal items which can't be burned – or collect and carry them yourself; the example won't go unnoticed! If you can communicate in Spanish, you may also wish to vocally express concern that Agencia Fluvial continues to organise guided hunting trips in the region.

Places to Stay
Hotel owners in Rurrenabaque are subject to a fine if they don't advise foreign travellers to register with the police. It's basically just a police attempt to request charges for a stamp which does nothing but take up space in your passport. Just tell the hotel owners you'll be seeing the police soon...It's up to you whether you comply or not.

The favourite travellers' digs in Rurre is the *Hotel Santa Ana*, the most pleasant inexpensive accommodation in town. It has a nice courtyard with tables for enjoying the sun whilst sipping a cup of very nice Yungas coffee. Rooms with/without bath cost B15/10 per person.

The *Hotel Berlin* on the riverfront offers reasonable but rather unkempt accommodation with private bath and cold showers for a negotiable B15 per person. The wall facing the thatched restaurant is graced with a mural of a German warship being tossed about the waves before a Río Beni shoreline!

Alojamiento Aurora, further from the river, doesn't offer the warmest reception around, but at B6 per person, it's a cheap place to crash. The less-than-clean baths are communal and only cold showers are available.

Hotel Porteño, the standard accommodation for Bolivian travellers, costs B15 per person without private bath, while a room with bath and hot water will cost B25 per person. In our experience, the reception was rather surly. Especially during slow periods, prices are negotiable; beware of overcharging of foreigners.

Unbelievably, Rurrenabaque has a five-star option, the distinctly out-of-place *Hostal Taquara* on the main plaza, where relatively luxurious rooms with carpet and private baths go for B65/119 for a single/double. It's geared toward fly-in foreign tour groups, which are as yet rare, but it's apparent that the industry is anticipating upmarket eco-tourism interest in the area. Unfortunately, that's the only sort of tourism likely to save Rurrenabaque from large-scale logging and other development operations. Reservations should be made through the Hotel Plaza in La Paz.

For another option, see the following section on San Buenaventura.

Places to Eat

The nicest inexpensive food in town is found at Hotel Berlin's thatched restaurant. They serve great breakfasts, tropical specialties and Bolivian standards in a garden-like setting. The *Sede Social* on the main street serves drinks and palatable set meals for B3 per person. Another great place to eat is the homey unnamed restaurant in the post office

building; it's very friendly and even vegetarian food is available upon request!

On the river, the floating Agencia Fluvial serves fish and other dishes. Lunch is served daily, as are beer and refreshments. Dinner must be reserved in the afternoon.

Other fish restaurants occupy makeshift wooden shelters along the riverfront. *La Chocita* and *La Playa* are sporadically good, depending on the prevailing temperament and the catch of the day. They're recommended for anyone interested in sampling masaco, the staple food of Bolivian Amazonia. The latter establishment, however, is holding prisoner a very dejected spider monkey, who is the unfortunate victim of taunting by local children and prepubescent-mentality adults.

The most diverse menu in town is found at the hotel *La Taquara* on the plaza; the fare is excellent but pricey.

Everywhere in Rurre you can get excellent freshly brewed Yungas coffee; that in itself is reason enough to visit!

Getting There & Away

Air The flight to Rurrenabaque from La Paz is glorious on a clear day. The plane passes between 6000-metre peaks as it climbs over the spine of the Cordillera Real, then flies over the Yungas where the land dramatically drops away and opens onto the forested expanses of the Amazon Basin.

LAB flies from La Paz at sunrise on Monday morning and TAM has a flight on Thursday. For the return trip, LAB flies on Sunday and TAM on Thursday. Flights to elsewhere in Bolivia are all routed via La Paz.

Bus When the roads are dry and passable, Flota Yungueña runs Thursday and Saturday buses to Riberalta and Guayaramerín. Buses to La Paz depart on Monday, Wednesday, Thursday, Saturday and Sunday at 1 pm and cost B40. The Wednesday and Sunday buses originate in Guayaramerín.

In theory, there's a daily Flota 16 de Noviembre bus to Yucumo, the turnoff for San Borja and Trinidad, at 12.30 pm. The trip takes 2½ to three hours and costs B8. When it's not running for one reason or another, you'll have to crowd onto a La Paz-bound Flota Yungueña bus and pay B11.

Boat
Ferries between Rurrenabaque and San Buenaventura on the opposite shore of the Río Beni depart from the riverbank whenever there's sufficient interest. The fare is B.70 per person for the 10-minute trip.

Due to the opening of the road, river-cargo transport down the Río Beni to Riberalta is very limited and there's no traffic at all during periods of low water. If you do find something, plan on four or five days at around B20 per day for the 1000-km trip, including three meals daily. Going the opposite direction, the journey will require 10 to 12 days. Make enquiries at the restaurant located in the same building as the post office.

Again, due to the road, as well as low water levels in recent years, river-cargo transport between Guanay and Rurrenabaque has all but been curtailed and a new bridge has left Puerto Linares cut off from all but small canoe traffic. Travellers who prefer to go by river will have to endure some trying negotiations with canoe operators. For details, see Getting There & Away under Guanay in the Cordilleras & Yungas chapter.

SAN BUENAVENTURA
On the La Paz Department bank of the Río Beni opposite Rurrenabaque is the laid-back tropical town of San Buenaventura. Since residents mostly conduct their business across the river in Rurre, nothing much is going on in San Buenaventura and that's the way they seem to like it. Well, there is the Disco Musica Buena near the ferry landing which hums at weekends, and if you're looking for fine Beni leather wallets and bags, visit the well-known shop of leather artesan Manuel Pinto.

Places to Stay & Eat
The new *Hotel El Trapiche* (whose name means 'sugar-cane press') has recently opened as a quieter and gentler alternative to the pickings on the Rurre side. It boasts an opulent but affordable open-air restaurant with rustic furnishings. Fondues and other international – as well as traditional – dishes are served. Accommodation, which costs B20 per person including breakfast, is in comfortable cabañas with one bath and an electric shower for each two rooms. Book through Señor Ariel Fronck (☎ 358084 or 795649, La Paz).

Getting There & Away
There is no road link to San Buenaventura; you have to take the ferry across the Río Beni described under Rurrenabaque. For transport to the boat landing nearest the Hotel El Trapiche, contact Tico Tudela at Agencia Fluvial in Rurrenabaque.

REYES & SANTA ROSA
Both Reyes and Santa Rosa, as yet relatively undiscovered by tourists, have lovely lagoons with myriad birds, alligators and other local wildlife. Reyes is only a half hour from Rurrenabaque, and Santa Rosa, with its environmentally attractive Laguna Rogagua, is 1½ hours further on.

In Reyes, you can stay at the Residencial 6 de Enero and arrange horse rentals for trips around the lagoons with Señor Saúl Simons. At Santa Rosa there is a small alojamiento where the same Simons family organises horse rentals. Señor Pedro Sarmiento at Hotel El Trapiche in San Buenaventura is currently setting up two and three-day camping tours to both locations.

YUCUMO
The only Yucumo information of interest to travellers would be how to get there and away as quickly as possible. This frontier village, an eldorado for land-happy and development-crazed settlers, lies at the intersection of the La Paz-Guayaramerín road and the Trinidad turnoff.

The trip between Rurrenabaque and Yucumo passes through what was once thick rainforest. Since the roads came through just a couple of years ago, the rainforest has been falling fast and uncontrolled logging and development have all but consigned it to complete decimation. Every second building is a sawmill or chainsaw dealer; cattle already graze among the tree stumps on increasingly barren land; and logging trucks penetrate the deepest recesses of the forest on an expanding maze of rough-hewn tributary logging tracks bulldozed by donated Japanese machinery. Land is being cleared so rapidly that valuable resources are wasted; only the bottom five metres of superb mahogany trees are used for lumber while the remainder of the tree goes for firewood and charcoal! Less valuable tree species are simply burned on site.

Getting There & Away

You will need to reserve seats on the Flota 16 de Noviembre bus which leaves Rurrenabaque for Yucumo at 12.30 pm daily. The three-hour trip costs B8. When it isn't operating, which is frequently the case, the price for the alternative, Flota Yungueña, rises to B11 per person. This company, which goes to La Paz, doesn't reserve seats for Yucumo-bound passengers, so just hustle for any available seats or stand in the aisles. Alternatively, it's not too difficult to find a camión going in the right direction.

Once in Yucumo, connect with the white camionetas which will take you across the savanna to San Borja in less than an hour for B7. From San Borja, there are camiones and buses to the Reserva Biosférica del Beni (Beni Biosphere Reserve), San Ignacio de Moxos and Trinidad.

SAN BORJA

With a menacing undercurrent of illicit dealings, there's a sort of dark cast over San Borja and few travellers will want to tarry long. When a north wind blows and brings inclement weather, communications grind to a halt, and all vehicular traffic into, out of and around town is suspended to prevent the mud streets being churned into quagmires. For the benefit of the captive consumer audience which this creates, food and hotel prices are augmented and outsiders, both Bolivian and

foreign, may sense some of the clearly suspicious and unwelcoming vibes that permeate the place.

Things to See & Do

There's not a lot to keep you occupied in and around San Borja, but as evidence that there's money coming in from somewhere, you'll find a couple of suspiciously palatial homes a block behind the church.

A good return day walk along the road west of town will take you through an area of wetlands and small ponds frequented by numerous species of tropical birds. Although the road is little travelled, the dust from occasional vehicles may be annoying.

Places to Stay

The top of the hotel heap is *Hotel San Borja* on the plaza which charges B25/15 per person with/without bath. The *Hotel Trópico* is less elegant with constant noise and only screen windows to keep the mosquitoes at bay. They charge B10 per person, including hot water in the communal baths.

The *Hotel Victoria* opposite the Hotel Trópico costs B10 per person with attached bath but it's a bit of a dump. On the opposite side of the plaza is the *Hotel Copacabana* which is quite a flophouse. Rooms cost B10 per person without bath.

Places to Eat

One of the best meal options is the courtyard restaurant at the Hotel San Borja. Meals are fairly standard but there's ceaseless entertainment provided by caged parrots and other birds who've obviously spent a lot of time around small children. Their constant babble resembles the sound of a schoolyard at break time.

One block off the plaza is the popular *Restaurante Taurus* where it's lomo, lomo, lomo – as well as an assortment of lesser incarnations – all orchestrated by pounding rock music and slobbering drunks. It's not memorable but it's about the best you'll find in San Borja.

Smaller places just beyond the Taurus include *Snack Chinito* with a lovely painted

Jabirú Storks

Chinese face above the doorway and the oddly named *Snack Dos se Van, Tres Llegan*, which means 'Two Arrive, Three Leave'. Wierd!

Getting There & Away

Transport terminals in San Borja are lined up on the street heading south from the southeast corner of the plaza. They all belong to a syndicate so when one decides not to travel for one reason or another, they're all obligated to suspend service.

We had tickets to San Ignacio de Moxos; when it started to rain, however, the transport company decided not to travel. We found a private vehicle willing to brave the mud and the police gave the go-ahead but the transport company, indignant that their syndicate had been circumvented, refused to refund our tickets. If you're looking for an escape from San Borja, ascertain the correct prices before you choose a particular company, then reserve a place but don't purchase the ticket until departure is imminent. Alternatively, check with private vehicle owners who queue up to await passengers along the same street. They may charge a bit more than the syndicate, but will be considerably more comfortable.

Camionetas Trans-Moxos leaves daily for Trinidad and Santa Cruz; the fare is B10 to the Beni Biosphere Reserve, B20 to San Ignacio de Moxos, B35 to Trinidad and B75 to Santa Cruz for a seat in the back of a pickup. For a bit extra, you can ride in the cab.

Transportadora 10 de Febrero runs 'Mini-Jumbo' tourist buses to La Paz on Tuesday and Thursday and pickups to San Ignacio and Trinidad daily. Several other companies also do the trip to San Ignacio de Moxos and Trinidad and pickups frequently depart for the one-hour run to Yucumo, which costs B7 per person.

All along the road to or from San Ignacio de Moxos and Trinidad, watch in the forest and in roadside lagoons for wildlife and astonishing numbers and varieties of birds, including herons, jabiru storks, cormorants, birds of prey, egrets and myriad others. You may also spot capybaras and pink river dolphins at the several small river crossings along the way.

If you're setting off between San Borja and Trinidad, remember that the Mamoré balsa crossing closes at 6 pm and you'll require a minimum of five to six hours to reach it from San Borja. There's no place to stay on either side of the crossing.

RESERVA BIOSFÉRICA DEL BENI

Created by Conservation International in 1982 as a loosely protected natural area, the 334,200-hectare Beni Biological Reserve was recognised by UNESCO in 1986 as a 'Man & the Biosphere Reserve'. The following year, it received official Bolivian Congressional recognition through debt trade agreement with the Bolivian government (for details, see the Ecology & Environment section in the Facts about the Country chapter).

The abutting Reserva Forestal Chimane (Chimane Forest Reserve), a 1.15 million-hectare buffer zone and Indian reserve, has also been set aside for sustained subsistence use by the 1200 Chimane people living inside it. The combined areas are home to at least 500 species of tropical birds as well as more than 100 species of mammals including several species of monkey, jaguars, deer, two species of peccary, river otters, foxes, anteaters and bats.

In September 1990, the Chimane reserve was threatened when the government opened it up to logging interests. In response, 700 Chimanes and representatives of other tribes staged a 'March for Dignity and Territory' from Trinidad to La Paz to protest what would amount to the wholesale destruction of their land and its flora and fauna. The logging companies were faulted for not reforesting the logged land, as was required by law, and logging concessions were re-zoned but not altogether revoked.

Information

Admission to the reserve is B22 for foreigners and B18 for Bolivian citizens. Guides cost B15 per day if you provide their food or B22 if they must bring their own. Horse rentals are also available for B25 per eight-hour day.

Scientific personnel interested in carrying out research at the Beni Biosphere Reserve should address enquiries to Ms Carolina Zumarán, Outreach Program Coordinator, Beni Biological Station, Bolivian Academy of Natural Sciences (fax 591-2) 352071), PO Box 5829, La Paz, Bolivia. Casual visitors interested in the reserve should contact Conservation International at the address listed in the Ecology & Environment section of the Facts about the Country chapter.

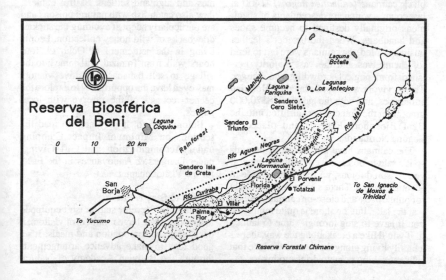

Exploring the Reserves

The best way to see the biosphere reserve and observe its wildlife is to secure the services of a guide and explore beyond the savannas in the first and second growth forests in the northern part of the reserve. Because El Porvenir lies on the savannas quite a distance from the true rainforest reserve, walks in the vicinity of the station will be of limited interest. If you wish to explore the inner reaches of the reserve, plan on a return trip of at least four days' walking from El Porvenir.

Climate & When to Go

The best time to visit the reserve is in June and July when there's little rain and days are clear; bring warm clothing to protect you against the occasional surazo, a cold wind from the Altiplano. During the rainy season, days are hot, rainy, muggy and miserable with mosquitoes. In August and September, the atmosphere becomes sombre with the smoke from rainforest-clearing in Brazil.

Laguna Normandia

The most popular destination, the savanna lake, Laguna Normandia, lies only two hours' walk from El Porvenir. It's chock-a-block with rare black caimans (caimanes negros) – 400 at last count – which are descendants of specimens originally destined to become shoes and handbags. When the breeder's leather business failed, the caimans were left to fend for themselves and the vast majority perished from neglect, crowding and hunger. The survivors were confiscated by Bolivian authorities, and with the aid of a US$20,000 grant from the French, were airlifted into the Beni Biosphere Reserve and placed in Laguna Normandia.

The caimans have no interest in humans so it's safe to observe them at close range; if you remain dubious, you can hire a guide to accompany you. There's a rowboat available for public use – and close-up caiman viewing – at the lake, but the shore is quite muddy so you'll have to slog through slime to launch it. If you'd like a break along the way, there's a family living along the route to the lake that sells refreshing pomelo drinks to hikers.

The Rainforest

To walk beyond the lake, a guide is required. A certified guide from El Porvenir will cost a mere B15 per day. From Laguna Normandia, it's a four-hour walk to the margin of the secondary growth rainforest. There, you'll find a small and bug-infested campamento beside a small stream where you can pitch a tent. The stream, which provides fresh, clean water, is ideal for swimming.

A further four hours' walking through the secondary forest will bring you to the primary forest. There's a river with lots of alligators and birds and a campsite with an established fire pit, but you'll need a tent. The river water is good to drink and you'll have a good chance of observing peccaries and various species of monkeys.

Totaizal & Reserva Forestal Chimane

Only a stone's throw from the road, 40 minutes' walk from El Porvenir, is Totaizal. The village, hidden in the forest of the Chimane reserve, is the friendly and well-organised home of 140 people. The Chimane are one of Bolivia's best known nomadic forest tribes and are currently being driven from their ancestral lands by lumber companies and highland settlers. Skilful hunters, they also catch fish with natural poisons and are particularly adept at avoiding the stickier drawbacks of wild honey collection. People living in the settlement of Ocho Ø, four hours' walk from Totaizal, will come into the village to sell bananas. Sensitive visitors may even have the opportunity to explore the deeper recesses of the reserve with local guides.

Before you go, it may help to read the sections on Minimum Impact Camping under Accommodation and Gift Giving, under Dangers & Annoyances in the Facts for the Visitor chapter.

Places to Stay & Eat

Although El Porvenir station isn't equipped to accommodate large numbers of visitors, it does offer accommodation and meals. It's a good idea to make advance arrangements through the Bolivian Academy of Natural

Sciences (for address and fax number, see the intro to this section). Foreigners pay B22 per person for a bed and an additional B22 for three meals. Don't expect anything opulent; often eggs and potatoes are the only items on hand. If you'd like to have a bit more control over your diet, carry food from elsewhere. With your own food and tent, it may be possible to negotiate the price down to around B10 per person daily.

Getting There & Away

Access to the Beni Biosphere Reserve is straightforward since El Porvenir lies just an easy hour's drive east of San Borja along the San Ignacio-Trinidad highway, and the station is only 200 metres from the highway. In addition to the several transport companies that operate camiones and camionetas between San Borja, San Ignacio de Moxos and Trinidad, the Beni Biosphere Reserve will also provide transport between San Borja and El Porvenir for B15 per person when your itinerary coincides with that of reserve personnel.

SAN IGNACIO DE MOXOS

This Moxos Indian village 89 km west of Trinidad was founded as San Ignacio de Loyola (after the founder of the Jesuit order) by the Jesuits on 1 November 1689. In 1760, the village suffered pestilence and had to be shifted to its present location on higher and healthier ground. Although the original Jesuit founders were expelled from South America shortly thereafter in 1768, priests of the Jesuit order are now returning not only to work among the Moxos but also to strike some sort of understanding between the Moxos, the dispossessed Chimane people and the rampaging settlers and loggers.

Despite the various factions vying for control of the Beni resources, San Ignacio de Moxos remains a friendly and tranquil agricultural village with an ambience quite distinct from any other in Bolivia. The people speak an indigenous dialect known locally as Ignaciano and their traditions, foods and demeanour are unique in the country.

Things to See

In the main plaza is a monument to Chirípieru, el Machetero Ignaciano, with his crown of feathers and formidable looking hatchet. The relatively recent church on the plaza is filled with local art and Ignaciano religious murals. At the museum in the Casa Belén near the north-west corner of the plaza, you can see things both Ignaciano and Moxos, including the bajones or immense zampoñas introduced by the Jesuits.

Laguna Isirere

North of town is the large Laguna Isirere, a great lake for swimming and fishing, but it's accessible only by hitching from town. There is also profuse birdlife and the possibility of seeing larger species, as well.

Fiesta del Santo Patrono de Moxos

Each 31 July, San Ignacio stages a huge fiesta known as the Fiesta del Santo Patrono de Moxos, in honour of the sacred protector of the Moxos. As in most Bolivian fiestas, the celebration sees a lot of games, music, dancing and drinking. The festivities culminate at 2 pm on the final day of the fiesta, when wildly clad dancers led by El Machetero himself proceed from the church, accompanied by fiddles and woodwind instruments.

Places to Stay

The friendly *Residencial 31 de Julio* normally charges B10 per person for clean and basic accommodation, but during the Fiesta del Santo Patrono, prices are raised according to demand. The owner justifies the price hike with the following explanation: 'During the fiesta, everyone gets drunk and sick. They smash up the place and when it's over, proprietors must repaint and clean up the mess'.

Residencial 22 de Abril on the plaza to the right of the church is known for its good breakfasts. It costs B10 per person and hot water is occasionally available.

Other similarly priced options include the *Residencial Tamarindo* and the *Residencial 14 de Septiembre*, both on the main street.

During the fiesta, visitors may set up tents at established sites in the environs of town.

Places to Eat

The recommended eating establishment is the clean and pleasant *Siriri Yarepá Vínica* on the corner of the plaza. They serve Ignaciano specialities and the dining room displays a wonderfully colourful hodge-podge décor. Sip some chicha de camote (sweet potato chicha) and sample the interesting and incredibly good *sopa de joco*, beet and pumpkin soup.

Getting There & Away

Access to San Ignacio from Trinidad is by camiones which leave in the morning from the east end of Calle La Paz near the river. All along the route there is good forest scenery. Be prepared for delays around the one-hour balsa traverse of the Río Mamoré between Puerto Barador and Puerto Ganadero. It costs B30 per vehicle and closes at 6 pm. There's no place to stay on either side so consider your timing before setting out to travel between San Ignacio and Trinidad.

Between March and October, the trip to or from Trinidad takes two to three hours, including the balsa crossing, but during the summer rainy season the road is impassable and the only way in is by air taxi.

Eastern Bolivian Amazon

TRINIDAD

At an altitude of 237 metres, Trinidad serves as the capital of the Beni Department and the nerve centre of just about everything that goes on in the Bolivian Amazon. Trinidad looks like Santa Cruz did 20 years ago; the population has already passed 40,000 and is likely to remain on the increase over the years to come. Only 14° latitude south of the equator, Trinidad experiences a humid tropical climate. The seasons are less pronounced than in the rest of Bolivia and tem-

peratures are uniformly hot year-round. Most of the rain falls during the summer in the form of more or less incessant downpours. Although winters are drier than summers, they also see a good measure of precipitation.

History

The city of La Santísima Trinidad, 'the Most Holy Trinity', was founded by Padre Cipriano Barace on 13 June 1686, as the second Jesuit mission in the flatlands of the Southern Beni. It was originally constructed on the banks of the Río Mamoré 14 km from its present location, but floods and pestilence along the riverbanks deemed it necessary to relocate the city. In 1769, it was moved to the Arroyo de San Juan, which now divides Trinidad in two.

Information

Tourist Office Trinidad's tourist office is found on Calle José de Sucre, 1½ blocks from the main plaza. It's open Monday to Friday in the morning and afternoon but don't expect miracles.

Beware of street names in Trinidad; that is, don't become flustered if you encounter discrepancies from map to map. A number of the city's street names were changed in 1987, but many never caught on and since then, some of the names have been changed back. Most maps and the local population still use the old names while some new maps use the revised names. Fortunately, the city isn't too big and the confusion caused by this will be only short-lived. Of note, Avenida Mariscal Santa Cruz is sometimes known as Avenida Pedro Ignacio Muiva, and Calle Junín is sometimes called Calle Pedro de la Rocha.

Money Street changers are found on Avenida 6 de Agosto between Calle Nicolás Suárez and Avenida 18 de Noviembre, but they only deal in cash US dollars.

The only place that will even consider changing travellers' cheques is the Hotel Ganadero. It helps if you're staying there, of course, but if they're in need of foreign exchange, you may be able to persuade them with a hard-luck story.

Post & Telecommunications Service at the main post office in Trinidad is slow and trying. If you're in a hurry and headed south, you may want to wait and post your items from La Paz, Cochabamba or Santa Cruz.

The public fax number in Trinidad is (591-46) 24100.

Dangers & Annoyances When we were researching this edition, Trinidad was the base for US anti-drug activities in Bolivia, and for us, it seemed reminiscent of a film about the Vietnam war – weapon fire at night and strings of low-flying helicopters buzzing the city at dawn. The DEA occupied two floors of the swank Hotel Ganadero and the commander of operations had set himself up in a US$1000/month home. Agents had confiscated all 42 light planes in Trinidad and taken over the airport, relegating commercial passengers to a hangar on a corner of the field. As mentioned earlier in this chapter, as this book was going to press, the DEA was expelled from Bolivia; however, given its recent residency in Trinidad, don't be surprised if locals react bemusedly – or even seem a bit resentful – toward foreigners.

Moto Rally
If you want to participate in the Trinidad social scene or you're in search of US-style nostalgia, spend an evening (particularly a Sunday evening) on the balcony of the Heladería Kivon ice-cream parlour and watch the motorbikes cruising around the plaza. It's all very 1950s, very high school and very North American.

When walking around the plaza, look for the several motionless sloths that are at home in the trees there.

Zoo
Trinidad has a small zoo at the university with specimens of indigenous animals.

Organised Tours
Although it's difficult to arrange a jungle trip

on your own, several tour agencies in Trinidad arrange low-key excursions into the surrounding area. The Turismo Moxos agency (☎ 21141) at Avenida 6 de Agosto 745 is probably the best known. They do tours to San Ignacio de Moxos and Loreto as well as canoe and horseback safaris into more remote areas.

The Flotel For a more upmarket option, try a cruise on the 'Flotel' *Reina de Enin*, a Dutch hotel boat based at Puerto Barador, which does excursions of one to four nights up and down the Mamoré with stops and tours in places of interest. For groups of fewer than 10 people, a one-night excursion will cost around B650 per person while a four-night tour will cost B1150 per person, including transport, sleeping quarters, tours and guide.

If you can arrange a larger group, the per person prices will be discounted slightly. For further information, contact Fremen Tours (☎ 47126, Cochabamba, fax (591-42) 48500), Casilla 1040, Calle Tumusla 0-245, Cochabamba, Bolivia. They also have offices in La Paz (☎ 327073) at Pedro Salazar 429 and in Sucre (☎ 30351) at Plaza 25 de Mayo 4.

Places to Stay – bottom end
The most pleasant budget hotel and the travellers' favourite is the clean and peaceful *Hotel Yacuma* (☎ 20690) at the corner of Calle La Paz and Avenida Santa Cruz. Singles/doubles cost B24/40 with bath and B12 per person without bath. Breakfast and lunch are served at their quiet patio restaurant.

Trinidad has a whole crop of medium to worse budget hotels strung mainly along Avenida 6 de Agosto. At the bottom of the barrel is the grotty *Residencial Brasilia* (☎ 21685). It smells of piss and some rooms lack windows. For B12 per person, you get a room without bath.

Residencial Palermo (☎ 20472), two blocks from the plaza, costs B17 per person with bath, and although it's a bit spartan, rooms are clean. *Hotel Beni* (☎ 20522) charges B15/30 for singles/doubles without

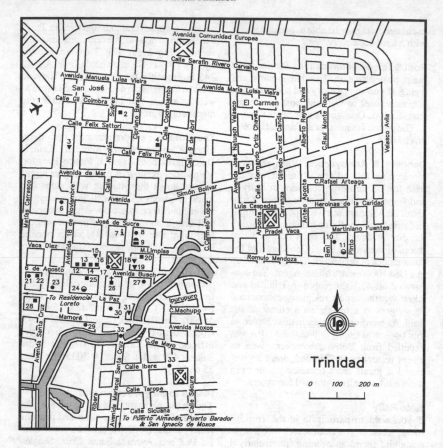

bath or B30/60 with private bath. The cheapest place in town is *Alojamiento Ortíz* which charges B10 per person.

Central, clean and newly renovated, *Residencial Paulista* (☎ 20018) charges B12 per person in singles or doubles or B20 for a double bed. It's set back from the street and new rooms with bath were being constructed at the time of writing.

A bit of a walk from the centre at the end of Calle La Paz is *Residencial Loreto* (☎ 22990) which charges B20 per person. It's far enough from the business district to be relatively free of motorbike noise.

Places to Stay – middle

Although it's on the expensive side, one of the cleanest and best middle-range options is the welcoming *Mi Residencia* (☎ 21529) at Calle Vaca Diez Manuel Limpias 76 half a block from the post office. They charge B99/123 for a single/double.

The three-star *Hotel Bajío* (☎ 21344) at Calle Nicolás Suárez 632 is good value at B54/87/119 for single/double/triple rooms with fan. With air-conditioning, you'll pay B79/108 for singles/doubles. All guests have access to the swimming pool and sauna.

The *Hotel Monte Verde* (☎ 22750) at

■ PLACES TO STAY

2	Hotel Bajío
4	Alojamiento Ortíz
12	Hotel Monte Verde
13	Hotel Beni
14	Residencial Brasilia & Snack Brasilia
16	Residencial Paulista
20	Mi Residencia
22	Residencial Palermo
25	Hotel Ganadero
28	Hotel Yacuma

▼ PLACES TO EAT

3	El Pacumutu
5	El Moro
15	Carlitos
18	La Casona
19	Heladería Kivon
31	El Dragón Chino

OTHER

1	Airport
6	TAM
7	Tourist Office (Fegabeni)
8	ENTEL
9	Post Office
10	Mercado Fátima
11	Bus Terminal
17	Motorbike Rentals
21	Distrito Naval
23	LAB
24	Bus to San Ignacio
26	Cathedral
27	Immigration
29	Transportes Fluviales (River Transport Office)
30	Mercado Central
32	Pompeya Bridge
33	Mercado Pompeya

Avenida 6 de Agosto 76 is a good upper middle-range option. All rooms have a fridge, TV, air-conditioning and good, non-electric hot showers. With a bit of friendly bargaining, you can get singles/doubles with bath for B60/85.

Places to Stay – top end

Trinidad's 'business' digs and a long-time favourite haunt of *narcotraficantes*, the four-star *Hotel Ganadero* (☎ 21644) is on Avenida 6 de Agosto appropriately just behind the BIG Beni (Banco Industrial y Ganadero del Beni!). Ironically, during US anti-drug activities in Trinidad, it held the distinction of being occupied by the DEA! Although it's not an altogether disagreeable place, the service is a bit surly and sour-faced, and rooms aren't great value. A single/double/triple room costs B145/175/211, and a suite (suitable for honeymoons, they say) goes for B235. Officially, foreigners are meant to pay an additional B18, but with a little coaxing you should have no trouble securing the Bolivian rate.

For your money, the Ganadero offers a dining room, wiskería/nightclub, rooftop

pool, air-conditioning(!), TV and piped music. Avoid the laundry service, however, or you'll need medical attention upon receiving the bill. Reservations may be secured by writing to Casilla 231, Trinidad, Bolivia.

Places to Eat

Snacks, light meals and English breakfasts are served at the bright and open *Heladería Kivon*, the local youth hangout on the plaza. You'll find ice cream, cakes, sweets, pastries, chicken, sandwiches, coffee and juice, as well as half a dozen types of masaco. Best of all, it remains open when everything else is closed, such as Saturday afternoon.

Another option for breakfast or snacks is the patio of the Hotel Yacuma. *Snack Brasilia* on Avenida 6 de Agosto does a standard menu of good inexpensive lunches.

Also on the plaza are *La Casona* pizzeria and *Carlitos* which specialises in parrillada, a Beni forte.

Since Trinidad is the heart of cattle country, there are a couple of places which specialise in beef. If you'd like to splurge on a meat and potatoes ensemble, try the over-priced dining room on the 5th floor of the

Hotel Ganadero. After dinner you can have a drink at the bar beside the rooftop pool and enjoy the commanding view over the bright lights of Trinidad. There's also a dining room at the Hotel Bajío.

An even better option with a great atmosphere is *El Pacumutu* which specialises in meat dishes and is highly popular with locals. *Pacumutus* are chopped chunks of an immense slab of beef that would otherwise bury a plate so get a *medio* (half) for two people. It'll still be too much, and combined with all the trimmings, it could possibly do you in.

For excellent local fish specialities, try *El Moro* on the corner of Avenida Simón Bolivar and Avenida José Natusch Velasco. It's just a short slog from the centre, but after dark, you may want to catch a taxi.

For something different, try *El Dragón Chino* on Calle Cipriano Barace opposite the Mercado Central. Although it's run by a Chinese woman from Beijing, the food is 'Bolivianised'. A filling meal will cost about B18 per person and after you've sloshed down a cool Tsingtao or two, the bill will double. Trinidad is not one of the easier places to be frugal.

If your budget is such that you're shocked by the prices at even the nondescript greasy spoon establishments scattered around town, there's always the Mercado Municipal. The fruits – especially grapefruit, oranges and bananas – are very good. For a pittance you can try the local speciality: *arroz con queso* (rice with cheese), kebab, yuca, plantain and salad.

Getting There & Away
Air On Monday, there's a LAB flight from La Paz that stops in Rurrenabaque and San Borja. LAB also has three nonstop flights per week between La Paz and Trinidad. Either LAB or TAM has at least one weekly connection to and from all major and some minor towns and settlements of the Beni and Pando, including Santa Ana del Yacuma, San Joaquín, Reyes, Magdalena, Guayaramerín, Riberalta and Cobija. LAB also flies nonstop to and from Santa Cruz and Cochabamba.

The LAB office (☎ 20595) is on Avenida Santa Cruz and TAM (☎ 20855) is on Avenida Simón Bolivar between 18 de Noviembre and Avenida Santa Cruz and has a notice board which keeps travellers up-to-date on flight changes and cancellations – particularly useful during the rainy season.

In addition to the B8 AASANA domestic air tax, there's an airport tax of B3 per person, which ostensibly goes to support old folks and finance public works.

Bus Flotas Pullman Oruro, Trans-Trópico, Expreso Unidos, Trans-Pullman Puñata, Pullman Urkupiña, Virgen de Cotoca and Trans-Princesa charge B30 for their daily run to Santa Cruz; they all depart between 5.30 and 6 pm. Slightly more luxurious is the Trans-Copacabana which has heating, air-conditioning, videos, onboard refreshments and a steward for B40. All these buses leave from the new central terminal at the corner of Pinto and Romulo Mendoza. During the dry season, expect a trip of at least 11 to 12 hours.

Trans-Copacabana leaves from the main terminal for San Ignacio and San Borja daily at around 9 am. Other buses and camionetas to San Ignacio and San Borja depart from the small terminals on Avenida Mariscal Santa Cruz, several blocks south of the Pompeya bridge. Camionetas to San Borja cost B40 in the cab or B35 in the back.

Boat River trips from Trinidad will carry you into the heart of Bolivia's greatest wilderness area, where you will experience the mystique and solitude for which the Amazon is renowned. For optimum enjoyment, go during the dry season which lasts roughly from May to September.

Although the scenery along the northern rivers changes little, few travellers are bored by it. The diversity of plant and animal species along the shore more than picks up any slack in the pace of the journey. The longer your trip, the deeper you'll gaze into the forest darkness and the more closely you'll scan the riverbanks for signs of movement. Free of the pressures and demands of active travel, you'll have time to relax and savour the passing scene.

Travellers seeking transport down the Río Mamoré to Guayaramerín or up the Ichilo to Puerto Villarroel in the Chapare region should first check the river transport office, Transportes Fluviales, on Calle Mamoré between Pedro de la Rocha and 18 de Noviembre, or the Distrito Naval (the navy sails comfortably to Puerto Villarroel three times monthly) on Avenida 6 de Agosto near Matías Carrasco. If nothing turns up, check departure schedules with the Capitanía del Puerto at Puerto Barador on the Río Mamoré 13 km from town. Alternatively, head for Puerto Barador and enquire around the riverboats themselves. For instructions on reaching the river ports from Trinidad, see under Puertos Almacén and Barador in the Around Trinidad section.

To travel down the Mamoré to Guayaramerín, you can expect to pay about B130 to B150 per person and about B80 to Puerto Villarroel, including food. Meals will consist mainly of masaco, charque, rice, noodles, thin soup and bananas in every conceivable form. In general, the food is pretty good – and it grows on you – but after a couple of days, you'd probably appreciate having brought some alternative or supplementary nourishment. If you're wisely wary of drinking pure river water, bring your own liquid or some form or water purification.

Be sure to discuss sleeping arrangements with the captain before setting out. Passengers will normally have to bring their own hammocks – they're available in Trinidad – but if you'd rather not purchase one, ask whether you can sleep on deck or on the roof of the boat. Don't forget to bring a sleeping bag or a blanket as well, especially in the winter when jungle nights can get surprisingly chilly. If you're fortunate enough to arrange passage on a boat that travels through the night, a mosquito net won't be necessary, but if you tie up along the shore at night and don't have one, sleep will be impossible and your night will range from miserable to unbearable.

Getting Around

To/From the Airport If you've got any nous at all, don't be lured into taking an automobile taxi from the airport to town; they're incredibly expensive at B30 to B35 for the very walkable distance of 1½ km. If you can't bear walking in the heat (or rain), however, you'll have to cough up the cash. Trinidad lacks a city bus system and it's not easy balancing a large pack while perched behind the driver of a motorbike taxi.

Taxi If you're looking for a taxi to outlying areas, phone Radio Taxi Progreso Beniano (☎ 22759). It's important to know the distances involved and to bargain on the fares or you'll be taken for a ride in more ways than one. Also, decide upon and factor into the negotiated price any waiting time required while you visit the sites. Plan on about B20 per hour for up to four people.

Motorbike Once you're settled in somewhere, consider hiring a motorbike to get out and see the area around town. The motorbike taxi drivers will all be happy to take the day off and hire out their bikes if the price is right. This normally hashes out to about B12 per hour or between B90 and B110 per 24-hour day. All you'll need to operate a motorbike is a driving licence from home.

AROUND TRINIDAD
Loma Suárez

Although it's of little real interest, Loma Suárez is a local landmark and a good motorbike destination. This artificial mound 12 km from Trinidad on the banks of the Ibare was first known as Loma Mocovi. When it was purchased by the Suárez brothers, it was renamed Loma Ayacucho. Later, it came to be known as Loma Suárez through common usage and the name stuck. There's a military post at the loma and you'll have to pass a checkpoint if you want to continue past it to Chuchini.

Transport in this direction from Trinidad leaves from the petrol station 15 minutes' walk from town beyond the Pompeya bridge. If you're trying to reach Chuchini, you'll

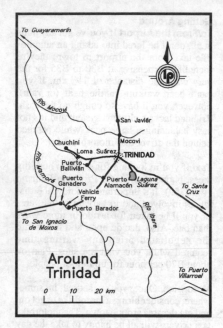

To Guayaramerín

Río Mocoví

San Javiér

Chuchini

Mocoví

Loma Suárez

TRINIDAD

Puerto
Ballivián

Río Mamoré

Puerto
Ganadero

Puerto
Alamacén

Laguna
Suárez

To Santa
Cruz

Vehicle
Ferry

Puerto Barador

Río Ibare

To San Ignacio
de Moxos

Around
Trinidad

To Puerto
Villarroel

0   10   20 km

probably have to walk the five km from Loma Suárez.

Chuchini

In the area between San Ignacio de Moxos and Loreto, well over 100 km of canals, hundreds of artificial mounds (*lomas*) and embankments, and more fanciful prehistoric earthworks depicting people and animals have been discovered. One anthropomorphic figure is over two km from head to toe: a rainforest version of Peru's famed Nazca Lines. According to archaeologists, the prehistoric structures of the Beni were constructed by the Paititi tribe 5500 years ago. Figurines, pottery, ceramic stamps, human remains and even tools made from stone imported to the region were buried inside the mounds. It's likely that the ancient civilisations of the Beni were the source of the legends of Gran Paititi.

Chuchini, 17 km from Trinidad, is one of the few easily accessible Paititi sites. The name means *madriguera del tigre* (the jaguar's lair). There's an idyllic and tranquil tourist camp beside the river which is run by Señor Efrem Hinojoso, and it's a perfect spot to escape the constant drone of Trinidad's thousands of buzzing motorbikes. The camp has shady covered picnic sites, trees, children's swings and a variety of native plants, birds and animals.

The camp itself sits on an artificial loma and there are numerous other lomas dotted throughout the surrounding forest. From camp, you can walk one km through the rainforest to a lagoon with profuse birdlife and caimans, as well as the chance of observing larger wild animals.

The real attraction is the onsite archaeological museum which displays articles excavated from the loma. Señor Hinojoso's daughter is knowledgeable and will guide you through the exhibits, explaining general thinking on the subject of Paititi. Items which have been uncovered in the area include bizarre statues with distinctly Mongol queues and slant eyes. One piece appears to be a female figure wearing a bikini bathing costume – it's presumed to be merely identification of specific body areas rather than an article of clothing. Admission to the museum is B2 per person.

If you'd like to spend more time, Chuchini has lovely and inexpensive campsites, as well as cabañas with room for six guests. The cabañas are rather steep at B110 per person, but that includes three meals per day. Exotic dishes are available in the restaurant; the food is great, but it's a bit pricey. If you'd prefer just a snack, ask them to prepare their tasty *chipilo*, fried green plantain chips.

For further information on Chuchini, write (in Spanish) to Efrem Hinojoso (☎ 22211), Calle 25 de Noviembre #199, Trinidad, Beni, Bolivia.

To reach Chuchini, follow the directions for Loma Suárez – hitching will be easiest on Sunday – and walk the final five km to the camp. It's also a good motorbike destination.

Laguna Suárez

This large, artificial lake five km from Trinidad reaches only 1½ metres in depth. Constructed by the Paititis, Laguna Suárez was originally known as Socoreno or 'lagoon of animals'. It's a relaxing spot, and like Chuchini, is very popular on Sundays when Trinidad families turn out in hordes to picnic, drink in the bar and eat lunch on the patio of the lakeside Restaurante Tapacaré. Children swim in the pool, canoe and play football and volleyball. Watch for the resort's pet tapacaré, a large bird similar to a secretary bird that hangs around the restaurant unfortunately suffering all sorts of abuse from children.

There's no public transport, so you'll have to walk, take a taxi, hire a motorbike or hitch. Follow the ring road toward Santa Cruz and turn right at a small white police post. From there, it's four km to the lake. Admission to the resort is B1 per person and pool use costs B5. For kayak rental, you'll pay B8 per hour double or B6 per hour single. Motorboats can be hired for B30 per hour.

Puertos Almacén & Barador

You may enjoy visiting one of the rickety fish restaurants in Puerto Almacén, eight km from Trinidad. This pointless little place is now the proud owner of a massive concrete bridge to nowhere, looming above the Ibare without approaches; the funding either ran out or went missing before the project was completed. You may prefer to cross the river by balsa and continue four km further to Puerto Barador. There you can observe pink river dolphins in small Mamoré tributaries or sample fresh fish at one of several pleasant portside restaurants.

Taxis from Trinidad to either port will cost in the vicinity of B48 each way, but camiones and camionetas leave frequently from Avenida Mariscal Santa Cruz, 1½ blocks south of Pompeya bridge in Trinidad. Any bus going to San Ignacio de Moxos will pass both Puerto Almacén and Puerto Barador en route. The fare to Puerto Almacén should be about B3, to Puerto Barador, B6.

LORETO

Loreto, the first Jesuit mission in the Beni lowlands, was founded on 29 June 1675 by Padres Cipriano Barace, Pedro Marbán and José de Castillo. From 4 to 7 October 1959, the statue image of Nuestra Señora de Loreto wept, as witnessed by the entire town, and Loreto, 54 km south of Trinidad, has become a pilgrimage site.

ASUNCIÓN DE GUARAYOS

This small Jesuit Indian settlement with a very nice old church lies on the Santa Cruz-Trinidad road, five to eight hours from Trinidad. The town is known for its *maricas*, little palm-leaf backpacks woven by the locals.

SANTA ANA DEL YACUMA

Originally known as San Lorenzo, Santa Ana del Yacuma, north-west of Trinidad, was founded by the Jesuits in 1693. This low-lying town is surrounded by a dyke to prevent flooding during the diluvian rainy seasons.

Traditionally a cattle town, it is now a booming cocaine processing and trafficking capital and one of the only towns to organise resistance against American DEA forces. In June 1991, an intensive DEA cleanup of Santa Ana netted 10 homes, 15 labs, 28 aeroplanes, assorted supplies and spare parts, and 110 kg of cocaine base, but no one was arrested; processors, traffickers and their Colombian accessories had all melted into the forest.

Although accessible by boat or air from Trinidad, it's scarcely worth a special trip and, as one might imagine, foreigners aren't particularly welcome anyway. If you find yourself landed here for one reason or another, check out the crop of blossoming palaces in the centre and the extravagant new terminal (like Dubai in miniature!) that graces the airstrip of this remote settlement. The Club Social on the plaza is now the town home of drug baron Roberto Suárez. The movers and shakers are here!

PERSEVERANCIA & RESERVA DE VIDA SALVAJE RÍOS BLANCO Y NEGRO

The 1.4 million-hectare Ríos Blanco y Negro Wildlife Reserve came into existence in 1990. It lies in the heart of Bolivia's largest wilderness area and still contains vast tracts of undisturbed rainforest with myriad species of plants and animals, including giant anteaters, peccaries, tapirs, jaguars, marmosets, capuchin monkeys, bush dogs, river otters, caimans, squirrel monkeys, deer and capybara. There are also curassows, six varieties of macaw and over 300 other bird species.

The area's only settlement, the privately owned estancia, Perseverancia, lies 350 km north of Santa Cruz. It started out as a centre of rubber production in the 1920s and continued until the last *seringueros* (rubber tappers) left in 1972. When the airstrip was completed, professional hunters went for river otters and large cats. By 1986, it was again abandoned and didn't receive any attention until the tourist resort was established in 1989.

Organised Tours

Amazonas Adventure Tours has established a wilderness lodge and a research and conservation centre at Perseverancia. It's open and accessible to visitors only during the dry season between March and October. They offer wilderness walks, horse trekking and dugout canoe trips, as well as plant identification, birdwatching and wildlife spotting activities, including a night at a *salitral* (salt lick) waiting for large animals.

Visits to Perseverancia are not cheap and are well out of range for budget travellers, but anyone who can manage the splurge will not regret it. Since a large portion of the total cost goes toward the plane ride from Santa Cruz, travellers in larger groups will pay less per person and similarly, those who factor their flight costs over a longer stay will pay less per day. For packages booked overseas, individuals in groups of four, for example, will pay US$963 from Santa Cruz for a seven-day stay including all meals, accommodation, transportation and guided activities at the reserve. For two people, the same trip will cost US$1275 per person.

For further information on tours, prices, access, accommodation or research possibil-

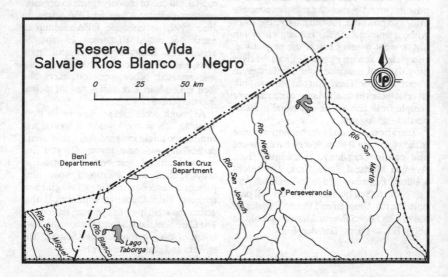

Jaguar

ities, contact Amazonas Adventure Tours (☎ 324099, fax (591-3) 337587), Casilla 2527, Santa Cruz, Bolivia or drop by their office at Calle Andrés Manso 342 in Santa Cruz. For places to stay and eat in Santa Cruz or information on getting there, refer to the Santa Cruz chapter.

Places to Stay & Eat
The lodge, chalets and kitchen at Perseverancia overlook the Río Negro. They're constructed of local materials – wood, mud bricks and *jatata* palm thatching. Only the chalets have private baths, but all rooms have access to solar hot showers. Accommodation and meals are included in package prices.

Getting There & Away
Perseverancia is a privately owned estancia, accessible only by prior arrangement. It's a 1½-hour flight in a light plane from El Trompillo Airport in Santa Cruz. As it currently stands, return flights to Perseverancia are included in the tour and lodging packages.

PARQUE NACIONAL NOEL KEMPFF MERCADO
Lying in the northernmost reaches of Santa Cruz Department, remote Noel Kempff Mercado between the Serrania de Caparuch and the banks of the Río Guaporé (called Río

Itenez on some maps) has the potential to become a favourite destination. Strongly reminiscent of Kakadu in Northern Australia, it enjoys the entire spectrum of Amazon flora and fauna and has the most dramatic scenery in northern Bolivia: rivers, rainforests, waterfalls, plateaux and rugged 500-metre escarpments.

Although it's commonly assumed that the classic literary work *The Lost World* was set among the *tepuis* (flat-topped mountains) of Amazonian Venezuela, it was actually inspired by these Bolivian plateaux and escarpments. British explorer, Colonel Fawcett, who was commissioned by the Bolivian government in the first decade of this century to survey the boundary between Bolivia and Brazil, spoke favourably of this area to his friend Sir Arthur Conan Doyle who was inspired by the description to write his book.

The 541,000-hectare park, originally called Huanchaca, was created in 1979 to protect the Serrania de Caparuch and its wildlife. In 1988, the name was officially changed to Noel Kempff Mercado in honour of the distinguished Bolivian biologist who was murdered by renegades at a remote park airstrip east of the Río Paucerna on 5 September 1986. Although the riverine section of the park is suffering from infiltration by drug-runners, Brazilian hunters and other opportunists, the vast interior remains relatively pristine.

Admission to the park is currently B75 per person.

Information
Responsibility for park conservation and infrastructure is currently in the hands of the Bolivian environmental organisation Fundación Amigos de la Naturaleza (FAN), which is working with the international organisation Nature Conservancy to develop Bolivian national parks. For further information, contact Executive Director Hermes Justiniano or Cristian Vallejos (☎ 333806), Casilla 1615, Avenida Irala 421, Santa Cruz, Bolivia.

Parque Nacional Noel Kempff Mercado

0   12.5   25 km

[] =Airstrip

Approximate scale

Campamento Paucerna

Flor de Oro

San Francisco

B R A Z I L

To Piso Firme
Projected road

← Río Guaporé

Campamento Las Torres

BOLIVIA

Ramoncito

Pimenteiras

Cataratas Arco Irís & Federico Alhfeld

Campamento Mangabalito

Mangabalito

Catamarca

Aserradero Caparuch []

To Vila Bela

Campamento Río Verde

Campamento Huanchaca

Laguna La Bahía

Catarata Huanchaca

To Piso Firme

Campamento Los Fierros

Mundo Perdido

La Florida []

B R A Z I L

Aserradero Moira

Puerto Pasto

Tarvo

Campamento Las Colmenas

To Santa Rosa de la Roca

Catarata Huanchaca

This amazing 150-metre waterfall, often known simply as 'Catarata', meaning 'waterfall', can be visited from Campamento Los Fierros. Access requires travelling 32 km east of the encampment by 4WD road. From road's end at the escarpment, continue 10 km along the footpath which will lead you up onto the *meseta* (tableland) to the falls. Further exploration of the vast meseta will require a guide, who may be hired at Campamento Los Fierros.

Río Paucerna

The two lovely 80-metre waterfalls, Arco Irís and Federico Alhfeld, on the Río Paucerna above Campamento Paucerna, are currently accessed by boat from the encampment. Road access from Flor de Oro is planned in the near future.

One legend describes a four-metre shark-like fish called a Paraíba whose existence in the Río Paucerna was supposedly confirmed by diving Brazilian *garimpeiros* (gold prospectors).

Places to Stay & Eat

Campamento Los Fierros, in the extreme south-west of the park and 10 km directly west of the escarpment, is an encampment which sleeps up to 100 people. Unless they're with an organised tour, guests are expected to provide petrol to fuel the generator which produces the camp's electricity. Visitors must also be self-sufficient in food and carry their own sleeping bags and cooking stove.

From Piso Firme, it's four hours up the Río Guaporé to Campamento Paucerna, near the confluence of the Río Paucerna and Río Guaporé, and 30 km upriver from there to Flor de Oro. New accommodation at Flor de Oro is more comfortable than Los Fierros and the new tourist and conservation centre currently being established charges visitors B220 per person per day, including three meals. FAN intends to construct a light road from Flor de Oro to the Río Paucerna waterfalls, but until that project is completed, visitors must travel to the falls by boat up the Río Paucerna.

Since interest in the park is very new and organisation of its infrastructure is ongoing, those interested in visiting either encampment should contact the FAN office in Santa Cruz for updated information on current travel conditions and requirements. Their address is included under Information earlier in this section.

Two other minor encampments, Las Torres and Mangabalito, up the Río Guaporé from Campamento Paucerna and Flor de Oro, are accessible by boat. They exist primarily to establish indisputable sovereignty over the park and protect it from unofficial Brazilian resource exploration. Three other encampments, Huanchaca, Río Verde and Las Colmenas, are currently planned in various areas of the park.

Getting There & Away
The park is accessible only during the dry season, roughly between the months of May and October.

Air To charter a five-seater aero taxi to Piso Firme from Santa Cruz costs US$200/hour for five hours flying time to and from the park *in each direction*. As soon as the Flor de Oro airstrip is cleared and upgraded, tour groups will have direct air access to that camp. If you're interested in joining an organised trip, enquire at Uimpex Travel in Santa Cruz or speak with FAN for recommendations.

Although other remote airstrips exist around the park, the only other recommended access field is at La Florida, 42 km west of Campamento Los Fierros.

Hitching The main overland access is from Santa Cruz via Santa Rosa de la Roca, but without a private 4WD vehicle, it's a long and complicated route. Basically, you must first get to either Concepción or San Ignacio de Velasco, north-east of Santa Cruz, then hitch to Santa Rosa de la Roca. From there, it's 80 km north to Aserradero Moira where the park road turns east toward Campamento Los Fierros, still 67 km away. The best hope of getting a lift will be with logging trucks, but you may also get lucky and ride in with park employees.

Piso Firme lies on the Río Paraguá 178 km north of Aserradero Moira. It's about 22 hours nonstop by road from Santa Cruz, and again, is only accessible by hitching with logging trucks.

Boat There's a fair amount of Brazilian cargo transport along the Ríos Mamoré and Guaporé between Guajará-Mirim and Costa Marques, in the Brazilian state of Rondônia,

and Vila Bela in the state of Mato Grosso. Although river transport passes Paucerna, Las Torres and Mangabalito, access to the Bolivian shore may be sticky; as yet, there's no immigration or police post in the park.

Northern Frontier

GUAYARAMERÍN
Guayaramerín, on the alligator-infested Río Mamoré opposite the Brazilian town of Guajará-Mirim, is a rail town where the railway never arrived. The line that would have connected the Río Beni town of Riberalta and the Brazilian city of Porto Velho was completed only as far as Guajará-Mirim just over the border – it never reached Bolivian territory!

Historically, the area was a centre of rubber production, and Nicolás Suárez, who made a fortune from the boom before the turn of the century, had his rubber exporting headquarters at Cachuela Esperanza, 60 km north-west of Guayaramerín. From there, he transported the cargo overland past the Mamoré rapids to the Río Madeira and shipped it downstream to the Amazon, the Atlantic and on to markets in Europe and North America. For more history, see the discussion of Guajará-Mirim, Brazil, later in this chapter.

Guayaramerín retains a strong frontier atmosphere and is a typically friendly Amazon town. It is actually the northern terminus for river transport along the Mamoré due to the same rapids that plagued the rubber boomers and render the river unnavigable just a few km north of the town.

Guayaramerín today has a population of just 14,000, and serves as a river port and an entry point to or from Brazil. It is also the terminus of the brand new road linking it and Riberalta, 90 km away, with Santa Ana, Rurrenabaque and La Paz. It is impassable when it's been raining.

Information
Money Cash US dollars may be exchanged

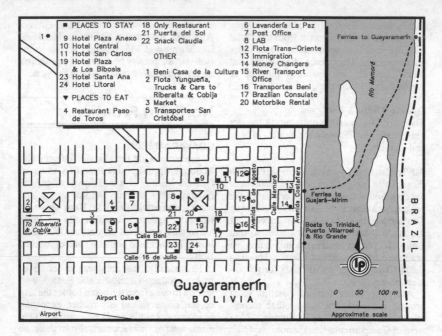

PLACES TO STAY	18	Only Restaurant	6	Lavandería La Paz
	21	Puerta del Sol	7	Post Office
9 Hotel Plaza Anexo	22	Snack Claudia	8	LAB
10 Hotel Central			12	Flota Trans—Oriente
11 Hotel San Carlos		OTHER	13	Immigration
19 Hotel Plaza			14	Money Changers
& Los Bibosis	1	Beni Casa de la Cultura	15	River Transport
23 Hotel Santa Ana	2	Flota Yungueña,		Office
24 Hotel Litoral		Trucks & Cars to	16	Transportes Beni
		Riberalta & Cobija	17	Brazilian Consulate
▼ PLACES TO EAT	3	Market	20	Motorbike Rental
	5	Transportes San		
4 Restaurant Paso		Cristóbal		
de Toros				

Guayaramerín
BOLIVIA

at the Hotel San Carlos for a good rate. Alternatively, exchange US dollars, bolivianos or Brazilian cruzeiros with the aggressive cambistas who hang around the port area.

Foreign Consulates There is a Brazilian Consulate in Guayaramerín, one block south of the main plaza. It's open from 9 am to 1 pm Monday to Friday and the friendly and efficient consul will issue visas on the same day. They are free for US citizens but other applicants must pay US$10.

Things to See

A particularly nice place to visit is the natural swimming hole near the tranca five km west of town along the Riberalta road. The water is clear and refreshing and it's a favourite local picnic spot. Dust from the road can sometimes be a problem, however.

You may also enjoy the interesting wall murals inside the church.

Places to Stay

The mellowest budget place to stay in Guayaramerín is undoubtedly the *Hotel Litoral* near the airport. Management offer private baths, refreshingly tepid showers and clean rooms for only B15 per person. In the courtyard there's a snack bar and a very popular TV set which plays Brazilian novelas to a full house. Watch for the Litoral's inedibly scrawny and independently minded pet chicken called Pinky; not just a dumb cluck, she spurns feathered company and fraternises instead with hotel staff and clientele, insistently making her demands known.

Across the street, the quiet and shady *Hotel Santa Ana* (☎ 2206) offers similar amenities for B15/12 per person with/ without private bath.

The *Hotel Central* (☎ 2042) costs B10 per person. It's a low-budget option with no double beds and only shared baths. *Hotel Plaza* (☎ 2085) charges B20/15 per person with/without private bath. It's a bit run down and not particularly good value, but it's worth having a look at their high security telephone box which looks more like a drying out cage for drunks!

Nicer is the *Hotel Plaza Anexo* (☎ 2086) with clean rooms, electric hot showers and a pleasant ambience for B20 per person.

The *Hotel San Carlos* (☎ 21152) is the upmarket place to stay in town with TV, sauna, air-conditioning, a billiard room and hot water at all times. A single room costs B56, a double goes for B90 and a gimmicky room called the Suite will cost B120. All rooms have private baths.

Places to Eat

Guayaramerín is fortunate enough to have the Beni's best restaurant which is, in fact, called the *Only Restaurant* (☎ 2397)! With an extensive international menu and a pleasant outdoor garden area, it's very popular with Brazilians and the staff even pass out key rings and stickers for your car! Out of town but also very good is *Sujal*; motorbike taxis will get you there for B1 each way.

On the corner of the plaza, *Pollo Pio Pio* isn't bad for cold drinks and snacks, but check your bill for spontaneous additions. *Los Bibosis*, also on the plaza, serves meals and snacks but its popularity lies primarily with those whose interests are limited to a few cold bottles of Paceña.

The *Puerto del Sol* is frequently recommended by locals but we reckon it's grossly overrated. The food is only average and serious overpricing of foreigners is in effect. The Hotel San Carlos dining room used to serve very nice breakfasts and dinners but it's temporarily closed and won't re-open until demand warrants it.

Things to Buy

Caritas, across the airfield from Guayaramerín, sells locally produced wooden carvings for reasonable prices.

Getting There & Away

Air Guayaramerín's airport, right at the edge of town, takes air safety seriously; just prior to our most recent visit, a bull had been mown down on the runway and the airport was closed down for two weeks!

The LAB office in Guayaramerín isn't yet on the computer line so book flights out of Guayaramerín from elsewhere or risk not getting a seat. LAB has flights from Trinidad daily except Tuesday, from Cochabamba and Santa Cruz on Wednesday and Sunday, and from La Paz on Friday. TAM has flights from La Paz to Guayaramerín on Monday and Wednesday and to La Paz on Tuesday and Thursday. You can fly to Cobija with TAM on Tuesday and with LAB on Friday for B165.

Bus Bus services to and from Guayaramerín operate only during the dry season – roughly from May to October. The two-hour journey to Riberalta on Flota Trans-Oriente costs B10. They depart at 8 am and 3 pm daily. Transportes Beni operates buses to La Paz and San Borja via Santa Rosa, Reyes and Rurrenabaque according to no particular schedule, and sporadic service to Cachuela Esperanza and Cobija is planned as soon as the road opens. Flota Yungueña departs for Riberalta, Rurrenabaque and La Paz on Tuesday and Sunday at 3 pm from the car and camión stop at the western end of town. The 36-hour trip to La Paz costs B140. Scheduled service to Cobija is planned for the near future.

Beware of bus services cancelling trips. If tickets aren't sold out, the run may be cancelled and irate would-be passengers are given a lame excuse. I was once told that a bridge along the route was damaged and the road would be closed until the following day. In the next breath, they suggested I try to find a camión to Riberalta – which would have had to use the same bridge. The 'damaged bridge' which had caused the closure of the road was not only not damaged, it was non-existent!

Boat From the port, cargo boats leave frequently for Trinidad, five to seven days up the Río Mamoré. For information regarding departures, the port captain's office has a notice board which lists any activity into or out of town. Further details about this route can be found in the section on Trinidad in this chapter.

Hitching Camiones to Riberalta leave from the main street 2½ blocks west of the market near the Flota Yungueña office. They charge the same as buses but make the trip in less time. If you'd like to travel a bit more comfortably, cars charge B24 and you're spared exposure to the choking red dust that seems to get into everything. To Cobija, YPFB petrol trucks and a white Volvo freight carrier depart occasionally from the same place.

Crossing the Border Even if you're not planning to travel further into Brazil, you can pop across the Río Mamoré and visit Guajará-Mirim. Between early morning and 6.30 pm, small motorised canoes and larger motor ferries cross the river from Guayaramerín every few minutes for B3.50. After hours, there are only express motorboats which cost B15 to B20 per boat. You may travel back and forth across the river at will, but those travelling beyond the frontier area will have to complete border formalities.

If you're leaving Bolivia from here, you must have your passport stamped at *migración* near the port in Guayaramerín and again at the Polícia Federal at Avenida Dr Antonio de Costa 842, five blocks from the port in Guajará-Mirim. The Polícia Federal is closed on Sundays.

Although officials don't always check, technically everyone needs a yellow fever vaccination certificate to enter Brazil here. If you don't have one, there is a convenient and relatively sanitary clinic at the port on the Brazilian side. The medical staff use an air gun rather than a hypodermic needle.

For information about onward travel into Brazil, see Getting There & Away in the following section on Guajará-Mirim.

Getting Around
You'll quickly discover that there are no automobile taxis in Guayaramerín, but then

the town is so small you can walk just about anywhere you'd like to go. Motorbike taxis cost B1 anywhere around town.

Those who want to do some exploring of the surrounding area can hire a motorbike from the main plaza for about B75 per 24-hour day. Don't be tempted to take a swig of the stuff sold in Coke bottles on the street; it's motorbike petrol!

GUAJARÁ-MIRIM (BRAZIL)
The contrast between Guajará-Mirim and Guayaramerín is striking. While the Brazilian town is a bustling metropolitan area with restaurants, shops, parks and traffic, the Bolivian town is still a small, dusty frontier settlement. The Portuguese words *onde fica* (AWN-gee FEE-ca), meaning 'where is', will go a long way in Guajará-Mirim. Furthermore, on this side of the river the ubiquitous Spanish *gracias* becomes *obrigado* (bree-GAH-doo) if you're a man, or *obrigada* (bree-GAH-dah) if you're a woman.

History
In 1907, the North American company Jeckyll & Randolph began work on a 364-km railway to link the village of Santo Antônio on the Río Madeira to the Bolivian town of Riberalta. The original intention of the railroad was to compensate Bolivia for the loss of the Acre territory – annexed by Brazil in 1903 – by providing a transport outlet to the Atlantic otherwise blocked by the Mamoré rapids beginning at Cachoeira das Bananeiras, 25 km north of Guayaramerín. German, Jamaican and Cuban workers and even Panama Canal hands were brought in to work on the project. The track was completed in 1912 after more than 6000 workers had perished from malaria, yellow fever, gunfights and accidents.

Since the railroad never arrived at Riberalta, its intended destination, and the world market price of rubber plummeted while it was still under construction, the railway became a white elephant before it was even put into operation. Still, both Guajará-Mirim and Porto Velho are the prod-

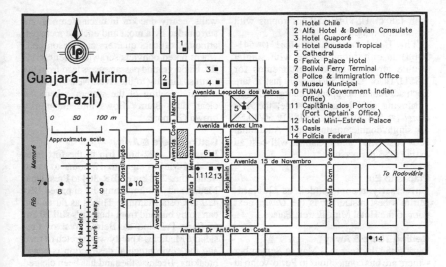

Guajará–Mirim
(Brazil)

0   50   100 m

Approximate scale

Rio Mamoré

Old Madeira – Mamoré Railway

Avenida Constituição

Avenida Presidente Dutra

Avenida Costa Marques

Avenida P Menezes

Avenida Leopoldo dos Matos

Avenida Mendez Lima

Avenida Benjamin Constant

Avenida 15 de Novembro

Avenida Dom Pedro

Avenida Dr Antônio de Costa

To Rodoviária

1 Hotel Chile
2 Alfa Hotel & Bolivian Consulate
3 Hotel Guaporé
4 Hotel Pousada Tropical
5 Cathedral
6 Fenix Palace Hotel
7 Bolivia Ferry Terminal
8 Police & Immigration Office
9 Museu Municipal
10 FUNAI (Government Indian Office)
11 Capitânia dos Portos (Port Captain's Office)
12 Hotel Mini-Estrela Palace
13 Oasis
14 Polícia Federal

ucts of the project. Today the road between Porto Velho and Guajará-Mirim uses the railway bridges, but the line itself is used only occasionally as a tourist novelty from the Porto Velho end.

Marcio Souza chronicles the whole brutal story in his book, *Mad Maria*, mandatory reading for anyone interested in how a small parcel of the Green Hell was briefly conquered. It is available in an English paperback edition by Avalon.

Information
Bolivian Consulate If you're entering Bolivia and require a visa, there is a Bolivian Consulate (☎ 541-2862) in Guajará-Mirim, open only on weekday mornings. It's a small, unassuming cubbyhole upstairs in the Alfa Hotel building at Avenida Leopoldo dos Matos 239; there's no sign. Have two photographs ready.

Museu Municipal
With a couple of old steam locomotives parked outside, the marginally interesting museum housed in the old railway station on Avenida 15 de Novembro focuses on the

history of the region and contains the remains of some of Rondônia's fiercely threatened wildlife. Particularly interesting are the huge anaconda which stretches the length of the main salon and a pathetically hideous turtle which inhabits the aquarium area. In a collection of photographs is an especially intriguing portrayal of an Indian attack – or defence, depending upon your reference – taken in the 1960s.

The museum is open weekdays from 7.30 am to noon and 2.30 to 5.30 pm. On weekends and holidays, it opens at 8 am. Admission is free.

Places to Stay
One popular place is the *Hotel Guaporé* on Avenida Benjamin Constant. It costs US$11/18 a single/double quarto including breakfast. Cheaper still is the *Fenix Palace Hotel* (☎ 541-2326), Avenida 15 de Novembre 459, which costs US$8.50/14 a single/double quarto and US$14/19 for a single/double apartamento, including electric fans. The popular *Hotel Mini-Estrela Palace* (☎ 541-2399) across the road charges US$11/18 for a single/double apartamento

with fan or US$14/19.50 for rooms with air-conditioning.

The *Hotel Pousada Tropical* (☎ 541-3308) is quite comfortable with single/double air-conditioned apartamentos for US$11/14 or US$8.50/11 with just a fan. Each additional occupant is charged US$3.

Moving slightly up the scale, the *Alfa Hotel* (☎ 541-3121) costs US$19.50/30.50 for single/double apartamentos. Additional beds cost US$7 and breakfast will cost an extra US$3 per person.

Places to Eat

Universally recommended as Guajará-Mirim's best restaurant is the *Oasis*, next door to the Hotel Mini-Estrela Palace.

Getting There & Away

During the dry season – May to September – there are bus connections to Porto Velho at 7 am, noon, 3 and 9 pm along the stretch of road commonly known – for what should be obvious reasons – as the 'Trans-Coca Highway'. The trip takes between eight and 12 hours.

Taba Airlines flies three times weekly to and from Porto Velho.

Crossing the Border Leaving Brazil, you may need to have your passport stamped at the Bolivian Consulate in Guajará-Mirim before getting a Brazilian exit stamp from the Polícia Federal at Avenida Dr Antonio da Costa 842 (closed Sunday). Once across the Río Mamoré, pick up an entrance stamp from Bolivian immigration at the ferry terminal. Motor ferries leave from the port every few minutes and cost US$1.25. For further information, refer to the section on Guayaramerín.

FORTE PRÍNCIPE DA BEIRA (BRAZIL)

Remote and little visited Forte Príncipe da Beira, 170 river km south of Guajará-Mirim, was constructed between 1776 and 1783 on the eastern bank of the Guaporé. The fort has 10-metre-high walls with four towers, each holding 14 cannons which took five years to carry from the state of Pará. The fortress walls, nearly one km in circumference, are surrounded by a moat and enclose a chapel, armoury, officers quarters and prison cells where bored convicts scrawled poetic graffiti. Underground passageways lead from the fortress directly to the river. Nearby, there's a mini 'meeting of the waters' where the clear, dark Baures flows into the murky brown Guaporé,

Getting There & Away

It's at least a 22-hour trip to the fort from Guajará-Mirim: eight to 12 hours to Porto Velho, then 278 km on BR-364 to Presidente Medici and 363 km along the unpaved BR-429 to Costa Marques. This is as far as you can go by bus and from there, it's still 20 km to Forte Príncipe da Beira. West of Presidente Medici is a pretty wild stretch of road and the environmental destruction is heartbreaking. Because the land has been cleared and settled only recently, there's a significant risk of malaria and other tropical diseases.

A preferable alternative is to travel by boat up the Ríos Mamoré and Guaporé. ENARO government boats ply this stretch of the river and reach the military post at Forte Príncipe da Beira from Guajará-Mirim in two to three days. They then continue to Costa Marques where food and accommodation are available. Enquire about schedules at the not-terribly-helpful Capitânia dos Portos in Guajará-Mirim.

CACHUELA ESPERANZA

Now all but abandoned, this tiny Río Beni settlement 60 km north-west of Guayaramerín was the capital of the economic empire built by Nicolás Suárez, the 'Rockefeller of Rubber'. Its location was dictated by the Beni and Mamoré rapids just downstream which halted all Atlantic-bound traffic.

In its heyday, Cachuela Esperanza was a self-contained marvel: homes and offices were clean and modern and the private hospital and doctors were the finest and best equipped in Bolivia. Suárez imported North American limousines for his personal use on roads he built himself, and a theatre was constructed so that an invitation could be extended to Theda Bara. Even after the rubber market collapsed, Suárez remained a wealthy man and was able to live in relative luxury until he died in 1940.

Getting There & Away
Transportes Beni connects Guayaramerín with Cachuela Esperanza, but runs according to no fixed schedule.

RIBERALTA
Riberalta seems to boast more private vehicles per capita than any other town in Bolivia, and the vast majority come in the form of tiny, buzzing Japanese motorbikes. Riberaltans' idea of a night out on the town is to pile the maximum possible number of people onto the bike, cruise down to the centre and spend a few hours doing laps around the main plaza.

If you sit in a footpath café beside the plaza, drink a few beers and stare at all this activity long enough, you'll begin to get the sensation that the needle playing your life's recording has somehow become stuck in one groove. The same faces, the same bikes, the same events are played out over and over!

Riberalta's rapidly increasing population is currently about 50,000. This is one of the few hot, sticky, dusty and bug-infested Amazonian towns that could nevertheless be accurately described as pleasant – if pouring rain isn't turning it all into a quagmire! It's a relatively modern town with a new church on the square, social clubs, a cinema and a generally mellower attitude than most other Bolivian places. It sits at an elevation of 175 metres on the banks of the Río Beni near its confluence with the Madre de Dios and on the highway linking La Paz to Guayaramerín, making it a hub of sorts.

Originally, Riberalta was a thriving centre of rubber production in northern Bolivia, but when that industry declined due to competition from Asian countries and the development of synthetics, the town resorted to its current mainstay industry: the growing, producing and exporting of oil from brazil nuts.

Above all else, Riberalta is one of those places that invites you to kick back and relax. During the heat of the day, all strenuous activity is suspended and the locals tend to search out the nearest hammock; visitors would probably be advised to follow their example – the heat can be paralysing. On a clear night, however, the place comes to life with the previously mentioned cruising motorbikes. Amid the buzz of activity, don't fail to notice the technicolour Amazonian sunsets; you can count on them to provide an impressive show.

Although it's becoming increasingly popular as a stopover for travellers, there's not a great deal laid on for visitors. You can hire a motorbike and explore the surrounding jungle tracks and trails or go for a swim in the river, but seek out a piranha-free area; locals will know where it's safe.

At Puerto Beni-Mamoré, within walking distance of the centre, you can watch the hand-carving and construction of small boats and dugouts by skilled artesans. In addition, two km east of the plaza along Ejército Nacional, you can visit an old rubber plantation, see coffee being roasted and visit a carpentry workshop. Riberalta carpenters specialise in high-quality rocking chairs and other furniture made from tropical hardwoods.

Information
Money As a service to travellers, Brother Casimiri at the vicarage changes cash US dollars, travellers' cheques and personal cheques. Although there are lots of compro dólares signs in shops around town, they change only cash and at a lower rate.

Post & Telecommunications The post office and ENTEL office are near the main plaza. Riberalta's public fax number is 472242.

Dangers & Annoyances Riberalta's municipal water supply is contaminated and the heat and open sewers make this town a pungent place. Drink only bottled or well-purified water.

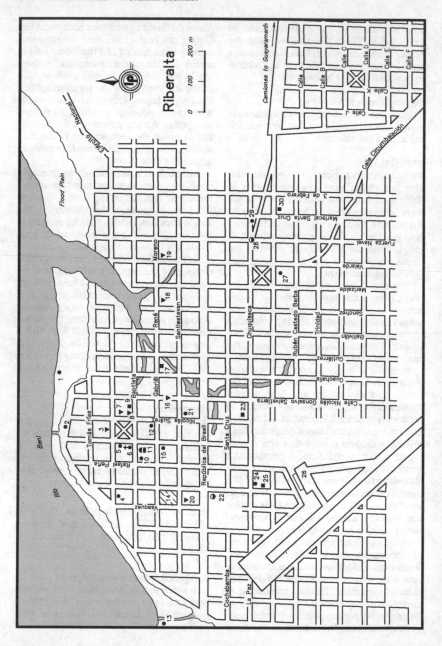

Riberalta

■ PLACES TO STAY

9	Hotel Colonial
17	Hotel Noroeste
23	Residencial Las Palmeras
25	Residencial Los Reyes
30	Alojamiento Navarro

▼ PLACES TO EAT

3	Cola
7	Club Social
8	Heladería Eslaba
16	Street Restaurants
18	Restaurant El Buchere
19	Restaurant El Padrino
20	Club Social Japonés
24	Discoteca Vereda Tropical

OTHER

1	Capitanía del Puerto
2	Parque Mirador La Costañera
4	Vicarage
5	Cinema
6	Church
10	ENTEL
11	Post Office
12	Motorbike Rental
13	Puerto Beni-Mamoré
14	Market
15	LAB
21	TAM
22	Flota Yungueña
26	Airport
27	Vargas Brazil Nuts
28	Camionetas to Tumichúcua
29	Plaza del Periodista

Parque Mirador la Costañera

This park on Riberalta's river bluff overlooks a broad, sweeping curve of the Río Beni affording the standard Amazonian view across water and rainforest. The African-style river steamer *Tahuamanu*, inaugurated in 1899 and used in the Acre War (1900 to 1904) and the Chaco War (1932 to 1935), stands planted in cement here 20 metres above the river. It was the first and last steamer used in the Bolivian Amazon.

Brazil Nut Factory

The Mario Vargas brazil nut factory, one of many in Riberalta, is happy to conduct tours of their operations. Here over 6000 Riberalta women enjoy a cracking career smashing brazil nuts. Once extracted, the nuts are dried for 24 hours prior to shipment to prevent them going rancid, and the shells are hauled away to massive dumps to be turned into road-building and patching material.

Tumichúcua

Tumichúcua once served as the Summer Institute of Linguistics of the Wycliffe Bible Society and headquarters for translation of the Bible into local indigenous languages. When the work was finished, most of the Indians left and the site and school were turned over to the Bolivian government. With a pleasant lake and picnic site, it's now Riberalta's get-away-from-it-all spot.

The lake lies 25 km from town along the road to Santa Rosa. To get there, it's easiest to catch a lift on weekends, particularly with camionetas which leave from the Plaza del Periodista. You should also have no problems catching a lift back to town.

Places to Stay

The nicest place to call home in Riberalta is the spotless and helpful *Residencial Los Reyes* (☎ 615) near the airport. It costs B20 per person for a room with fans and private baths. For the money, you also get a cool and shady area to while away the heat of the afternoon. Ice water and hot coffee are always available. Its only drawback is the disco just around the corner which rollicks with rocking adolescents until late on weekends.

If the Los Reyes is full, you can stay at the *Hotel Noroeste* (☎ 597) which, for B30 per person upstairs and B25 downstairs, is nothing special. All rooms have baths. The *Residencial Las Palmeras* (☎ 353) is a converted home near the airport. It's very friendly and clean, but is perhaps a bit expensive at B50/70 for a single/double.

A B1 motorbike taxi ride from the centre, *Alojamiento Navarro* is a quiet, friendly and low-key place from where it'll be easy to catch lifts to Guayaramerín. Male or female dormitory accommodation, popular with itinerant workers, costs B5 per person (don't leave your belongings in the rooms!). Singles/doubles with bath cost B15/20 while doubles with communal bath are only B10; with two people, this is better value than the dorms. This neighbourhood, which isn't on the municipal water system, has the only good tap water in Riberalta.

Though it has a nice façade, the quirky *Hotel Colonial* (☎ 212) has problems: showers are substandard, the rooms are sub-clean and the place, overall, is dumpy, dodgy and run down. For that you'll pay B20 per person. In addition, it's unfortunately screaming with tiny 747s and although the helpful owner will fumigate your room upon request, the chemical leaves a foul smell and a floor littered with corpses of the dead and dying. It can't be too healthy for humans, either.

Its redeeming feature is the breakfast served when the lady of the house is in. For a reasonable B10 or so, you can get steak, eggs, biscuits with jam and butter, fruit, coffee, and so on.

Places to Eat
The *Cola* on the main plaza is very popular with the locals but it's more of a sandwich/snack shop than a restaurant. Also on the plaza, the slightly high-strung *Club Social* serves inexpensive set lunches, superb filtered coffee, drinks and fine desserts. Determine prices in advance to avoid 'gringo pricing'. Not to be confused with this place, the *Club Social Japonés* near the market no longer serves Oriental meals, but it's still an option for standard Bolivian and Amazonian stand-bys.

Some things never change, especially the *Heladería Eslaba* beside the Club Social. It's still very good for coffee, breakfast, ice cream, juices, milkshakes, flan and sandwiches, as well as Beni beef-oriented meals. The footpath seating area also provides a front-row seat for the nightly Kawasaki derby on the plaza. Two blocks away are rows of outdoor street restaurants, or rather 'middle-of-the-street' restaurants, which

serve inexpensive dishes in a barbecue-style atmosphere.

On Gabriél René Moreno seven blocks from the centre is *Restaurant El Padrino* which would be a nice breezy place to eat were it not for the blaring music and loud drunks that render it too noisy for digestion!

If you want to sample Riberalta's famous brazil nuts, sugared or plain nuts are sold by children around town, especially around the airport. Another local favourite, which – for sentimental reasons – I'd rather not recommend, is *carne de jochi*. Jochi, or agouti, is a large and animated rodent which scurries around these rainforests.

Entertainment
The Discoteca Vereda Tropical is nothing special, but it's popular with Riberalta youth who migrate here when they've tired of video games and buzzing around the plaza on motorbikes.

Getting There & Away
Air Both LAB (☎ 239 or 294) and TAM serve Riberalta's grass airstrip and there are several weekly flights to La Paz, Santa Cruz, Trinidad, Guayaramerín and Cobija, but during the rainy season you may well be stuck here for some time. Riberaltans verify that during the summer, flights on both lines are often cancelled for weeks on end. Airport clocks will tell you how late you are in both local and Greenwich Mean Time!

There's a B3.50 municipal tax on all flights from Riberalta. In theory it goes toward municipality, forestry and engineering works, old folks and other various and sundry causes. The AASANA tax is only B6.

Bus Riberalta is probably best avoided in the soggy time between November and March. When the La Paz to Guayaramerín road is closed, Riberalta's only surface link is the Río Beni and even then, heavy rains or low water may create problems.

The trip to Guayaramerín passes through rapidly diminishing rainforest. At the balsa crossing en route, you may want to sample the unusual *pacay* beans hawked by local children there; peel the beans and eat only the softer insides. Transportes Beni buses run daily at 7.30 am and 6.30 pm and cost B10. Flota Trans-Oriente departs for Guayaramerín at noon and 6 pm daily. Alternatively, wait for a car or pickup just out of town along the road toward Guayaramerín. This dusty ride costs the same as the bus.

Flota Yungueña leaves for La Paz on Tuesday and Sunday at 6 pm. To La Paz, the fare is B130, to Rurrenabaque, B70.

A road to Cobija is scheduled to open sometime soon and YPFB tankers and freight trucks are already making the run. As soon as it's officially open to the public, Flota Yungueña plans to begin scheduled bus services.

Boat The Beni, formerly one of Bolivia's most important rivers, passes through countless twisting km of virgin rainforest and provides the longest single river trip available in Bolivia. Now that a highway is open all the way to La Paz, however, Río Beni transport traffic has declined significantly. The Capitanía del Puerto (Port Captain's office), where departure information is posted, is found at the northern end of Calle Guachalla. During times of high water or when the La Paz highway is closed, it may be possible to find transport up the Beni to Rurrenabaque and occasionally even further. Expect long waits, especially in the dry season.

Getting Around

Although everything in Riberalta is within reasonable walking distance of the centre, there are motorbike taxis which will take you anywhere in town for B1. Colectivos, which are rare, cost B.50 per person.

It's also possible to hire a motorbike from the *taxistas* who hang out on the corner of Nicolás Suárez and Gabriel René Moreno. With wheels, you can check out the surrounding river and rainforest country along plenty of tracks and trails cut across the landscape. The going rate is about B90 per 24-hour day.

Sloth

COBIJA

Cobija, with about 9000 people, is the capital of the Pando, Bolivia's youngest department. The Pando should have included Vaca Diéz province, with Riberalta as the capital of the new department and Cobija left out in the cold. When Riberalta decided to stay with the Beni, Cobija didn't protest.

Cobija was founded in 1906 under the name of Bahia. In the 1940s it grew into a booming rubber-producing centre, but when the rubber industry declined, Cobija's fortunes came crashing down heavily with it. The town was reduced to a forgotten hamlet of 5000 people, tucked away in the furthermost corner of the republic. With 1770 mm of precipitation falling annually, it is the rainiest spot in Bolivia.

The only available map of Cobija is about 10 years old and many of the streets marked thereon are now overgrown with vegetation. In fact, it once appeared that the town might someday be swallowed up entirely, but recently a spate of new projects has been launched. A new Japanese hospital has recently been completed but remains unopened; it's conjectured that 80% of the funding has somehow disappeared, and as a consequence, it is currently off line. Then there's the high-tech brazil nut processing plant just out of town; in contrast to the hospital, funding for this project mysteriously appeared – no one knows from where – and some doubts have been raised about its intended purpose. Cobija is also the site of a brand new international airport which will accommodate Boeing 727s; it hopes to attract planes flying the popular La Paz/Santa Cruz/Panama City/Miami flights. Huh?

Cobija serves as a port of entry with Brasiléia in the Brazilian state of Acre, across the International Bridge. At present, Cobija has no surface link with the rest of Bolivia but a highway to Riberalta and on to La Paz should be open by the time this book is published.

Information

Tourist Office There has been a Pando tourist office in Cobija on and off, but it wasn't operating at the time of writing. If you read Spanish, the best source of background information on this remote area will be the book *Pando es Bolivia* by Alberto Lavadenz Ribera, published in 1991. It's available at the LAB office in Cobija and outlines the history, development and official story of the entire Pando Department.

Money Casa de Cambio Horacio changes cruzeiros, bolivianos and US dollars at official rates. Travellers' cheques changed to US dollars or cruzeiros attract a 10% commission because they must be sent to La Paz.

If you're exchanging money over the border in Brasiléia, be sure to check official tourist and parallel rates before handing money over to a shopkeeper.

Post & Telecommunications The public fax number in Cobija is (591-842) 2292.

Foreign Consulate For US citizens and others who need a visa to enter Brazil, there is a consulate (☎ 2188) on the corner of Calle Beni and Avenida Fernandez Molina. It's open from 8.30 am to 12.30 pm Monday to Friday.

Immigration Bolivian immigration is located in the Prefectural building on the main plaza. The office opens at 9 am on weekdays but the immigration officer is often taken with wanderlust so you may have to hunt him up to get your entry or exit stamp.

Things to See

There are a few interesting things to see in the area, including rubber and brazil nut plantations, a number of lakes, and places to observe rainforest wildlife, but transportation is difficult and Cobija's hinterlands are not easily accessed. The very adventurous can hire a motorised dugout and head off upriver from nearby Porvenir to visit some of the very primitive Indian villages around the Peruvian border, but this is not recommended without a guide who has experience navigating overgrown and convoluted waterways.

A relatively new destination and a favourite with residents is Lago Bay, a fresh water lake, picnicking and fishing site near the Río Manuripi about 150 km south of Cobija along the Chivé road. There are basic cabañas to rent if you want to stay there. A return taxi from Cobija to Lago Bay will cost around B50.

If you're really bored, check out the

Cobija

1 Rowboat Ferry	11 Restaurant Nina
2 Snack Amazónico	12 Market
3 ENTEL	13 Casa de Cambio Horacio
4 Church	14 Hotel Prefectural
5 Immigration	15 Alojamiento 25 de Noviembre
6 LAB	16 TAM
7 Brazilian Consulate	17 International Bridge to Brazil
8 Confitería La Favorita	18 YPFB
9 Residencial Cocodrilo	19 Flota Yungueña
10 Residencial Frontera	20 Airport

0   100   200 m

bizarre painted portrait backdrop in the Foto Capri shop or take a look at the monument in front of the old hospital. It commemorates an apocryphal local youth who, during the Brazilian takeover of the Acre, shot a flaming arrow and set the fire that sent invading Brazilians packing back across the river.

Places to Stay

The very friendly Spanish-run *Hotel Prefectural* (☎ 2230), also known as the Hotel Pando, is under new management and has recently been upgraded considerably. Nice breezy rooms with fans and private baths cost B25 per person or B45 for a room with a double bed. Breakfast is included in the price. While you're there, say hello to their chatty parrot and take a look at the immense anaconda skin stretched across the reception area.

The *Residencial Frontera* is clean and relatively inexpensive at a negotiable B20 per person or B30 with a double bed. It's pleasant if you can get a room with a window onto the patio.

A third option is the *Residencial Cocodrilo* which charges B12 per person – also negotiable – for a pleasant but far from

Anaconda

opulent room in a nice tropical-style wooden building.

Rock-bottom accommodation is found for B6 per person at *Alojamiento 24 de Septiembre*; it's used mostly by locals.

Places To Eat

In the early morning, the market sells chicken empanadas but that's about all in the way of prepared food. Nothing stays fresh very long in this stifling and sticky climate, so most people wouldn't want to touch the meat available in the market. There is, however, a variety of fresh fruits and vegetables and lots of tinned Brazilian products, so with a stove, one can whip up something different.

During the day, try *Confitería La Favorita* for snacks, drinks and sandwiches or *Restaurant Nina* for basic inexpensive meals.

The *Churrasquería La Estancia* is Cobija's nicest restaurant, with outdoor tables beneath big sheltering trees. Try their excellent parrillada served with salad and yuca for B10. Local dogs seem to be impressed, anyway, and they patiently wait around for something to drop from tables. *Discoteca Restaurant Pachahuara* just opposite is Cobija's swinging night spot, serving snacks, standard meals and parrillada.

Getting There & Away

Air On Friday, TAM (☎ 2267) flies from La Paz to Cobija and return; it's a popular run

so book at least a week in advance. Every second week, it flies a circle route from La Paz on Monday, stopping at Cobija, Riberalta, Guayaramerín and Cochabamba, returning by the opposite route the following day. LAB (☎ 2170) flies to and from La Paz with intermediate stops in Riberalta, Guayaramerín and Trinidad. If you're on the LAB Fokker which flies this run, look for the golden plaque that hangs over the seat occupied by the Pope on his most recent Bolivian visit.

On arrival at the airport, you may claim baggage immediately or pick it up at the LAB office in town, a good idea if you're walking the two km to the centre in Cobija's sticky heat. Most taxis into town are motorbikes and it's not easy to find one that will accommodate much luggage.

Between November and March, Cobija runs are often cancelled; sometimes several weeks pass without a flight.

Bus At the time of writing, there was no surface transportation from Cobija to the rest of Bolivia without travelling literally thousands of km on a loop through Brazil, but that's due to change soon with the opening of the newly completed road to Riberalta. Freight and YPFB petrol trucks are already doing the trip and Flota Yungueña is on line to begin bus service at the earliest possible moment. Buses leave for Rio Branco from the rodoviária (bus terminal) in Brasiléia four times daily. From there it's easy to find connections to Porto Velho and the rest of Brazil.

Flota Cobija buses connect Cobija with the village of Porvenir 30 km away. They depart at 11.30 am daily from Confitería La Favorita and leave Porvenir for the return trip at 3 pm. The trip takes one hour each way and costs B3.

Crossing the Border Cobija is a recognised point of entry to the state of Acre, in Brazil. We have also heard that it is possible to enter Peru from north-western Bolivia.

To Brazil If you're going to or coming from Brazil, you'll have to get entry/exit stamps from immigration in Cobija and the Polícia Federal, just outside Brasiléia. A yellow fever vaccination certificate is required to enter Brazil from Cobija, but there is no vaccination clinic in Brasiléia so you'll have to track down a private physician if your health records aren't in order.

It's a rather long up-and-down slog from Cobija across the bridge to Brasiléia, so you may want to take a taxi. Negotiate the routing and the fare in advance. For about B12, the driver will take you to the Polícia Federal, wait while you complete immigration for-

malities and then take you to the centre or to the rodoviária (bus terminal).

Alternatively, take the rowboat ferry across the Río Acre for B1 per person. From the landing in the centre of Brasiléia, it's one km to the rodoviária and two km to the Polícia Federal.

To Peru Although we haven't tried either of the two routes, locals reckon that access to Peru from Cobija is possible for the adventurous traveller. Unfortunately, Peru's Madre de Dios Department has recently been a stage of operations for the Sendero Luminoso (Shining Path guerrillas), as well as the site of drug-running, lawless gold-digging and other renegade activities. We don't recommend trying this route, but if you do manage to get through, please write and let us know how it went!

The first option is to cross to Brasiléia and take a bus from there to Assis Brasil 90 km west; it will be necessary to complete Brazilian immigration procedures to do this transit route. Across the Río Acre from Assis Brasil is the muddy little Peruvian settlement of Iñapari where you must check into Peru with the police. There is a road of sorts from there to Puerto Maldonado which is accessible to

Capybaras

Cuzco on the Peruvian road system, but for practical purposes, it is impassable to all but pedestrian or motorbike traffic. You may be able to fly from Iñapari – there is an airport seven km from the village – to Puerto Maldonado on a Grupo Ocho cargo flight; just don't count on it.

Another possibility is to hitch from Cobija southward to road's end at Chivé on the Río Madre de Dios near Puerto Heath. There you'll have to hire a boat – neither easy nor cheap – to take you to Puerto Pardo on the Peruvian border. After securing a Bolivian exit stamp, arrange river transport further up the Madre de Dios to Puerto Maldonado – and Peruvian immigration – at the port. Expect to pay at least US$100 for the minimum two-day trip from the border to Puerto Maldonado and be prepared for long waits here, especially during periods of low water.

BRASILÉIA (BRAZIL)
Brasiléia, in the state of Acre, is the small Brazilian border town across the Ríos Abunã and Acre from Cobija. It has absolutely nothing of interest to travellers save an immigration stamp into or out of Brazil. The Polícia Federal is two km from the centre; dress neatly – no shorts allowed – or they may refuse to stamp your passport. For information on entering or leaving Brazil at this point, refer to the border crossing information under Cobija.

Information
There is a Bolivian Consulate in Brasiléia at Rua Major Salinas 114.

Places to Stay & Eat
If you're stuck in Brasiléia, try the *Carioca Charmé Hotel* (☎ 546-3045) near the church

Around Brasiléia

0   250   500 m

Approximate scale

in the centre. Double or *casal* (double bed) costs US$10 with bath. The *Restaurant Carioca* beside the hotel serves drinks, chicken and beef dishes and *prato feito*, a veritable feast of Brazilian carbohydrates!

Alternatively, there's the *Hotel Kador* near the turnoff to Brasiléia centre between the international bridge and the Polícia Federal.

Getting There & Away
From the rodoviária, there are four buses daily to Rio Branco and from there you'll find flights and bus connections to points all over Brazil.

contemporary craft design

Glossary

abra – opening; used to refer to a mountain pass

alcaldía – municipal hall

Altiplano – (High Plateau); the largest expanse of relatively level (and in places arable) land in the Andes; extends from Bolivia into Southern Peru, north-western Argentina and northern Chile

api – syrupy form of chicha made from maize, lemon, cinnamon and sugar

artesanía – local handicrafts

autocarril – bus which runs on rails

Aymará – indigenous Indian people of Bolivia; also known as Kollas. Aymará is also used to refer to the language of these people

barrio – district

bodega – boxcars, carried on some trains, in which 2nd-class passengers are permitted to travel

buna – giant ant, over one cm long

buñuelo – type of doughnut

cama matrimonial – double bed

camba – lowland Bolivia

cambista – street money changer

camino – road, path, way

camión – open-bed truck; a popular form of local transport

camioneta – pickup or other small truck; a form of local transport

cancha – plaza or open space in an urban area

cerro – hill; a laughably classic case of understatement given the altitudes of Bolivian peaks, but nevertheless used to refer to Bolivian mountains

cha'lla – offering or toast to an indigenous deity

charango – a traditional Bolivian ukelele-type instrument

charque kan – dried jerked meat served with mashed maize

chicha – popular beverage (often alcoholic)

made from such ingredients as yuca, sweet potato, and maize

Cholo(a) – Quechua or Aymará person who has migrated to the city but continues to wear ethnic dress

chullo – woollen hat

chullpa – Kolla funerary tower

colectivo – minibus or collective taxi

Colla – alternative spelling for Kolla

confitería – snack bar

cordillera – mountain range

DEA – Drug Enforcement Agency; US drug offensive body sent to Bolivia to assist in coca-crop substitution programmes and to assist in apprehension of drug magnates; expelled from Bolivia in mid-1992 by the Bolivian government

denuncio – affidavit

edificio – building

Ekeko – household god of abundance; name means 'dwarf' in Aymará

esquina – (abbrev. esq) corner

ferrobus – bus on bogies

flota – long-distance bus line

gaseosa – soft drink

guardaparque – national park ranger

iglesia – church

jochi – also called agouti; agile, long-legged rodent of the Amazon

Kallahuayas – itinerant medicine men of the remote Cordillera Apolobamba

Kolla – another name for Aymará

Kollasuyo – early indigenous name for Alto Peru; the area now known as Bolivia

La Diablada – the 'Dance of the Devils'; renowned Bolivian festival held annually in Oruro

lago – lake

laguna – lagoon; shallow lake

legía – alkaloid usually made of potato and quinoa ash which is used to draw the drug from coca leaves when chewed

llanos – plains

llareta – see yareta

loma – mound or hillock, sometimes artificial

Manco Capac – the first Inca emperor

masaco – charque served with mashed plantain and/or maize; a Bolivian Amazon staple

mercado – market

mestizo – people of Spanish American and American Indian parentage or descent

micro – small bus or minibus

milanesa – fairly greasy type of meat or chicken schnitzel

nevado – snow-covered mountain peak

oca – edible tuber

Pachamama – the earth mother

pahuichi – straw-thatched home, found primarily in Beni Department

parrillada – barbequed or grilled meat

peña – folk music show

pongaje – non-feudal system of peonage inflicted on the Bolivian peasantry; it was abolished following the April Revolution of 1952

quebrada – ravine or wash; normally dry

Quechua – highland (Altiplano) indigenous language of Ecuador, Peru and Bolivia; language of the Incas

quena – simple reed flute

queñua – dwarf tree that can survive at elevations over 5000 metres

quinoa – highly nutritious grain similar to sorghum, grown at high elevations, which is used to make flour and thicken stews

quirquincho – armadillo carapace used in the making of charangos

río – river

salar – saltpan

salteña – meat and vegetable pastie

soroche – simple altitude sickness; invariably suffered by newly arrived visitors to La Paz

surazo – cold wind blowing from Patagonia and the Argentine pampa

Tahuatinsuyo – the name of the Inca Empire

tambo – wayside market and meeting place selling staple domestic items; an inn

termas – hot springs

tinku – ritual fight which takes place primarily in northern Potosí Department during festivals

totora – type of reed; used as a building material in the Titicaca region

tranca – police post

trufi – colectivo taxi

wiskería – high-class bar

yareta (sometimes spelt llareta) – combustible salt-tolerant moss found on the salares of the southern altiplano that oozes a turpentine-like jelly used by locals as stove fuel

yatiri – witch doctor

yuca – manioc tuber

zampoña – pan flute which features in traditional music performances

Index

397

contemporary craft design

402

Thanks

Thanks to all the following travellers and others (apologies if we've misspelt your name) who took time to write to us about their experiences in Bolivia. If you can't find your name below, don't despair. You have probably been credited in Lonely Planet's *South America on a shoestring*.

Maria Christina Arroyo, Viki Banks (UK), K L Bell (UK), Kevin Bell, Hildegard Borgel (D), Rochelle Rhea Brand (USA), T B Burgess (UK), Deborah Craig (C), Greg Cumberford (UK), Jorge Raich Curco (Sp), Molly Curtin (USA), Martin Duchow (USA), Nancy Epanchin (USA), L E Fay (USA), John Feihl (C), B Feldballe (DK), Ferdinand Fellinger (A), Jonathan Fleisher (C), Richard Forty (UK), Gregory Frux (USA), G J Gagnon (C), Joan Giannecchini (USA), Dan Golopentia (USA), Hans Peter Graf (CH), Per Gregarsen (DK), Marlis Hagel (D), Tom Harriman (USA), Marc Hasson (F), Annalena Hedman (S), Virginia E Holl (USA), J Jacobs, Philippe Lamy (F), Aurolyn Luykx, David Lynch (UK), Jacqueline Marovac (USA), Brent Maupin (USA), Mario Morpurgo (I), Markus Muller (D), Stephen O'Dwyer (UK), Gilad Ostrousky (Isr), Tom Pfeffer, Paul Pichler (A), Ms Alex Rossi (UK), Michele Rouleau (C), Dawna Sawatzky (USA), Danny Schecter (USA), Herbert Schnurpfeil (A), Linda Slater, Mark Sletzer (C), Curtis D Smith (USA), Hanka Sokoko (NL), M J Spencer (AUS), Ann & Frank Spowart Taylor (UK), Mark Stambovsky (USA), Peter Thompson (C), Patrick Ward (UK), Trevor Wilson (AUS), Dan Wynne (USA), Paul L Younger

A – Austria, AUS – Australia, C – Canada, CH – Switzerland, D – Germany, DK – Denmark, F – France, I – Italy, Isr – Israel, NL – Netherlands, S – Sweden, Sp – Spain, UK – United Kingdom, USA – United States of America

contemporary craft design

Keep in touch!

We love hearing from you and think you'd like to hear from us.

The Lonely Planet Newsletter covers the when, where, how and what of travel. (AND it's free!)

When...is the right time to see reindeer in Finland?
Where...can you hear the best palm-wine music in Ghana?
How...do you get from Asunción to Areguá by steam train?
What...should you leave behind to avoid hassles with customs in Iran?

To join our mailing list just contact us at any of our offices. (details below)

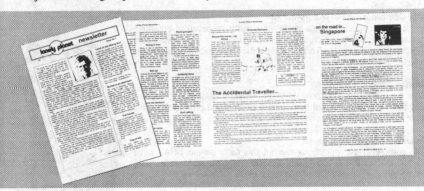

Every issue includes:

- *a letter from Lonely Planet founders Tony and Maureen Wheeler*
- *travel diary from a Lonely Planet author - find out what it's really like out on the road*
- *feature article on an important and topical travel issue*
- *a selection of recent letters from our readers*
- *the latest travel news from all over the world*
- *details on Lonely Planet's new and forthcoming releases*

Also available Lonely Planet T-shirts. 100% heavy weight cotton (S, M, L, XL)

LONELY PLANET PUBLICATIONS
Australia: PO Box 617, Hawthorn, 3122, Victoria (tel: 03-819 1877)
USA: Embarcadero West, 155 Filbert Street, Suite 251, Oakland, CA 94607 (tel: 510-893 8555)
UK: Devonshire House, 12 Barley Mow Passage, Chiswick, London W4 4PH (tel: 081-742 3161)

Guides to the Americas

Alaska – a travel survival kit
Travel through Alaska by foot, road, rail, barge and kayak: this guide has all the information you'll need to make the most of one of the world's great wilderness areas.

Argentina, Uruguay & Paraguay – a travel survival kit
This guide gives independent travellers all the essential information on three of South America's lesser-known countries. Discover some of South America's most spectacular natural attractions in Argentina; friendly people and beautiful handicrafts in Paraguay; and Uruguay's wonderful beaches.

Baja California – a travel survival kit
For centuries, Mexico's Baja peninsula – with its beautiful coastline, raucous border towns and crumbling Spanish missions – has been a land of escapes and escapades. This book describes how and where to escape in Baja.

Brazil – a travel survival kit
From the mad passion of Carnival to the Amazon – home of the richest ecosystem on earth – Brazil is a country of mythical proportions. This guide has all the essential travel information.

Canada – a travel survival kit
This comprehensive guidebook has all the facts on the USA's huge neighbour – the Rocky Mountains, Niagara Falls, ultramodern Toronto, remote villages in Nova Scotia, and much more.

Central America on a shoestring
Practical information on travel in Belize, Guatemala, Costa Rica, Honduras, El Salvador, Nicaragua and Panama. A team of experienced Lonely Planet authors reveals the secrets of this culturally rich, geographically diverse and breathtakingly beautiful region.

Chile & Easter Island – a travel survival kit
Travel in Chile is easy and safe, with possibilities as varied as the countryside. This guide also gives detailed coverage of Chile's Pacific outpost, mysterious Easter Island.

Colombia – a travel survival kit
Colombia is a land of myths – from the ancient legends of El Dorado to the modern tales of Gabriel Garcia Marquez. The reality is beauty and violence, wealth and poverty, tradition and change. This guide shows how to travel independently and safely in this exotic country.

Costa Rica – a travel survival kit
Sun-drenched beaches, steamy jungles, smoking volcanoes, rugged mountains and dazzling birds and animals – Costa Rica has it all.

Ecuador & the Galápagos Islands – a travel survival kit
Ecuador offers a wide variety of travel experiences, from the high cordilleras to the Amazon plains – and 600 miles west, the fascinating Galápagos Islands. Everything you need to know about travelling around this enchanting country.

Hawaii – a travel survival kit
Share in the delights of this island paradise – and avoid its high prices – both on and off the beaten track. Full details on Hawaii's best-known attractions, plus plenty of uncrowded sights and activities.

La Ruta Maya: Yucatán, Guatemala & Belize – a travel survival kit
Invaluable background information on the cultural and environmental riches of La Ruta Maya (The Mayan Route), plus practical advice on how best to minimise the impact of travellers on this sensitive region.

Mexico – a travel survival kit
A unique blend of Indian and Spanish culture, fascinating history, and hospitable people, make Mexico a travellers' paradise.

Peru – a travel survival kit
The lost city of Machu Picchu, the Andean altiplano and the magnificent Amazon rainforests are just some of Peru's many attractions. All the travel facts you'll need can be found in this comprehensive guide.

South America on a shoestring
This practical guide provides concise information for budget travellers and covers South America from the Darien Gap to Tierra del Fuego.

Trekking in the Patagonian Andes
The first detailed guide to this region gives complete information on 28 walks, and lists a number of other possibilities extending from the Araucanía and Lake District regions of Argentina and Chile to the remote icy tip of South America in Tierra del Fuego.

Also available:
Brazilian phrasebook, **Latin American Spanish** phrasebook and **Quechua** phrasebook.

Lonely Planet Guidebooks

Lonely Planet guidebooks cover every accessible part of Asia as well as Australia, the Pacific, South America, Africa, the Middle East, Europe and parts of North America. There are five series: *travel survival kits*, covering a country for a range of budgets; *shoestring guides* with compact information for low-budget travel in a major region; *walking guides*; *city guides* and *phrasebooks*.

Australia & the Pacific
Australia
Bushwalking in Australia
Islands of Australia's Great Barrier Reef
Fiji
Melbourne city guide
Micronesia
New Caledonia
New Zealand
Tramping in New Zealand
Papua New Guinea
Bushwalking in Papua New Guinea
Papua New Guinea phrasebook
Rarotonga & the Cook Islands
Samoa
Solomon Islands
Sydney city guide
Tahiti & French Polynesia
Tonga
Vanuatu
Victoria

South-East Asia
Bali & Lombok
Bangkok city guide
Cambodia
Indonesia
Indonesia phrasebook
Laos
Malaysia, Singapore & Brunei
Myanmar (Burma)
Burmese phrasebook
Philippines
Pilipino phrasebook
Singapore city guide
South-East Asia on a shoestring
Thailand
Thai phrasebook
Vietnam
Vietnamese phrasebook

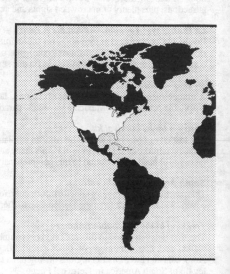

North-East Asia
China
Beijing city guide
Mandarin Chinese phrasebook
Hong Kong, Macau & Canton
Japan
Japanese phrasebook
Korea
Korean phrasebook
Mongolia
North-East Asia on a shoestring
Seoul city guide
Taiwan
Tibet
Tibet phrasebook
Tokyo city guide

Middle East
Arab Gulf States
Egypt & the Sudan
Arabic (Egyptian) phrasebook
Iran
Israel
Jordan & Syria
Middle East
Turkish phrasebook
Trekking in Turkey
Yemen

Indian Ocean
Madagascar & Comoros
Maldives & Islands of the East Indian Ocean
Mauritius, Réunion & Seychelles

Mail Order

Lonely Planet guidebooks are distributed worldwide. They are also available by mail order from Lonely Planet, so if you have difficulty finding a title please write to us. US and Canadian residents should write to Embarcadero West, 155 Filbert St, Suite 251, Oakland CA 94607, USA; European residents should write to 10 Barley Mow Passage, Chiswick, London W4 4PH; and residents of other countries to PO Box 617, Hawthorn, Victoria 3122, Australia.

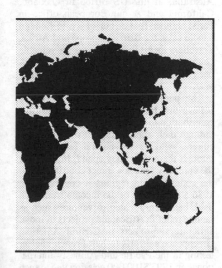

Indian Subcontinent
Bangladesh
India
Hindi/Urdu phrasebook
Trekking in the Indian Himalaya
Karakoram Highway
Kashmir, Ladakh & Zanskar
Nepal
Trekking in the Nepal Himalaya
Nepali phrasebook
Pakistan
Sri Lanka
Sri Lanka phrasebook

Africa
Africa on a shoestring
Central Africa
East Africa
Trekking in East Africa
Kenya
Swahili phrasebook
Morocco, Algeria & Tunisia
Arabic (Moroccan) phrasebook
South Africa, Lesotho & Swaziland
Zimbabwe, Botswana & Namibia
West Africa

Central America
Baja California
Central America on a shoestring
Costa Rica
La Ruta Maya
Mexico

North America
Alaska
Canada
Hawaii

Europe
Baltic States & Kaliningrad
Dublin city guide
Eastern Europe on a shoestring
Eastern Europe phrasebook
Finland
France
Greece
Hungary
Iceland, Greenland & the Faroe Islands
Ireland
Italy
Mediterranean Europe on a shoestring
Mediterranean Europe phrasebook
Poland
Scandinavian & Baltic Europe on a shoestring
Scandinavian Europe phrasebook
Switzerland
Trekking in Spain
Trekking in Greece
USSR
Russian phrasebook
Western Europe on a shoestring
Western Europe phrasebook

South America
Argentina, Uruguay & Paraguay
Bolivia
Brazil
Brazilian phrasebook
Chile & Easter Island
Colombia
Ecuador & the Galápagos Islands
Latin American Spanish phrasebook
Peru
Quechua phrasebook
South America on a shoestring
Trekking in the Patagonian Andes

The Lonely Planet Story

Lonely Planet published its first book in 1973 in response to the numerous 'How did you do it?' questions Maureen and Tony Wheeler were asked after driving, bussing, hitching, sailing and railing their way from England to Australia.

Written at a kitchen table and hand collated, trimmed and stapled, *Across Asia on the Cheap* became an instant local bestseller, inspiring thoughts of another book.

Eighteen months in South-East Asia resulted in their second guide, *South-East Asia on a shoestring*, which they put together in a backstreet Chinese hotel in Singapore in 1975. The 'yellow bible' as it quickly became known to backpackers around the world, soon became *the* guide to the region. It has sold well over half a million copies and is now in its 7th edition, still retaining its familiar yellow cover.

Today there are over 130 Lonely Planet titles in print – books that have that same adventurous approach to travel as those early guides; books that 'assume you know how to get your luggage off the carousel' as one reviewer put it.

Although Lonely Planet initially specialised in guides to Asia, they now cover most regions of the world, including the Pacific, South America, Africa, the Middle East and Europe. The list of *walking guides* and *phrasebooks* (for 'unusual' languages such as Quechua, Swahili, Nepali and Egyptian Arabic) is also growing rapidly.

The emphasis continues to be on travel for independent travellers. Tony and Maureen still travel for several months of each year and play an active part in the writing, updating and quality control of Lonely Planet's guides.

They have been joined by over 50 authors, 60 staff – mainly editors, cartographers & designers – at our office in Melbourne, Australia, at our US office in Oakland, California and at our European office in Paris; another five at our office in London handle sales for Britain, Europe and Africa. Travellers themselves also make a valuable contribution to the guides through the feedback we receive in thousands of letters each year.

The people at Lonely Planet strongly believe that travellers can make a positive contribution to the countries they visit, both through their appreciation of the countries' culture, wildlife and natural features, and through the money they spend. In addition, the company makes a direct contribution to the countries and regions it covers. Since 1986 a percentage of the income from each book has been donated to ventures such as famine relief in Africa; aid projects in India; agricultural projects in Central America; Greenpeace's efforts to halt French nuclear testing in the Pacific and Amnesty International. In 1993 $100,000 was donated to such causes.

Lonely Planet's basic travel philosophy is summed up in Tony Wheeler's comment, 'Don't worry about whether your trip will work out. Just go!'.

Contemporary Craft Design